Computer Communications and Networks

T0140540

For other titles published in this series, go to
www.springer.com/series/4198

The **Computer Communications and Networks** series is a range of textbooks, monographs and handbooks. It sets out to provide students, researchers and non-specialists alike with a sure grounding in current knowledge, together with comprehensible access to the latest developments in computer communications and networking.

Emphasis is placed on clear and explanatory styles that support a tutorial approach, so that even the most complex of topics is presented in a lucid and intelligible manner.

Charles R. Kalmanek · Sudip Misra
Y. Richard Yang
Editors

Guide to Reliable Internet Services and Applications

 Springer

Editors
Charles R. Kalmanek
AT&T Labs Research
180 Park Ave.
Florham Park NJ 07932
USA
crk@research.att.com

Y. Richard Yang
Yale University
Dept. of Computer Science
51 Prospect St.
New Haven CT 06511
USA
yry@cs.yale.edu

Sudip Misra
Indian Institute of Technology Kharagpur
School of Information Technology
Kharagpur-721302, India
smisra.editor@gmail.com

Series Editor
Professor A.J. Sammes, BSc, MPhil, PhD, FBCS, CEng
Centre for Forensic Computing
Cranfield University
DCMT, Shrivenham
Swindon SN6 8LA
UK

ISSN 1617-7975
ISBN 978-1-4471-2554-9   ISBN 978-1-84882-828-5(eBook)
DOI 10.1007/978-1-84882-828-5
Springer London Dordrecht Heidelberg New York

British Library Cataloguing in Publication Data
A catalogue record for this book is available from the British Library

Cover design: SPi Publisher Services

Printed on acid-free paper

Springer is part of Springer Science+Business Media (www.springer.com)

Foreword

An oft-repeated adage among telecommunication providers goes, "There are five things that matter: reliability, reliability, reliability, time to market, and cost. If you can't do all five, at least do the first three."

Yet, designing and operating reliable networks and services is a Herculean task. Building truly reliable components is unacceptably expensive, forcing us to construct reliable systems out of unreliable components. The resulting systems are inherently complex, consisting of many different kinds of components running a variety of different protocols that interact in subtle ways. Inter-networks such as the Internet span multiple regions of administrative control, from campus and corporate networks to Internet Service Providers, making good end-to-end performance a shared responsibility borne by sometimes uncooperative parties. Moreover, these networks consist not only of routers, but also lower-layer devices such as optical switches and higher-layer components such as firewalls and proxies. And, these components are highly configurable, leaving ample room for operator error and buggy software. As if that were not difficult enough, end users understandably care about the performance of their higher-level applications, which has a complicated relationship with the behavior of the underlying network.

Despite these challenges, researchers and practitioners alike have made tremendous strides in improving the reliability of modern networks and services. Their efforts have laid the groundwork for the Internet to evolve into a worldwide communications infrastructure – one of the most impressive engineering artifacts ever built. Yet, much of the amassed wisdom of how to design and run reliable networks has been spread across a variety of papers and presentations in a diverse array of venues, in tools and best-common practices for managing networks, and sometimes only in the minds of the many engineers who design networking equipment and operate large networks.

This brings us to this book, which captures the state-of-the-art for building reliable networks and services. Like the topic of reliability itself, the book is broad, ranging from reliability modeling and planning, to network monitoring and network configuration, to disaster preparedness and reliable applications. A diverse collection of experts, from both industry and the academe, have come together to distill the collective wisdom. The book is both grounded in practical challenges and forward looking to put the design and operation of reliable networks on a strong foundation. As such, the book can help us build more reliable networks and services today, and face the many challenges of achieving even greater reliability in the years ahead.

Jennifer Rexford
Princeton University

Preface

Overview

This book arose from a conversation at the Internet Network Management workshop (INM) in 2007. INM'07 was subtitled "The Five Nine's Workshop" because it focused on raising the availability of Internet services to "Five Nine's" or 99.999%, an availability metric traditionally associated with the telephone network. During our conversation, we talked about and vehemently agreed that there was a need for a comprehensive book on reliable Internet services and applications – a guide that would collect in one volume the accumulated wisdom of leading researchers and practitioners in the field.

Networks and networked application services using the Internet Protocol have become a critical part of society. Service disruptions can have significant impact on people's lives and business. In fact, as the Internet has grown, application requirements have become more demanding. In the early days of the Internet, the typical applications were nonreal-time applications, where packet retransmission and application layer retry would hide underlying transient network disruptions. Today, applications such as online stock trading, online gaming, Voice over IP (VoIP), and video are much more sensitive to small perturbations in the network. For example, following one undersea cable failure in the Pacific, AT&T restored the service on an alternate route, which introduced 5 ms of additional packet delay. This seemingly small additional delay was sufficient to cause problems for an enterprise customer that operated an application between a call center in India and a data center in Canada. This problem led to subsequent re-engineering of the customer's end-to-end connection.

In addition, networked application services have become an increasingly important part of people's lives. The Internet and virtual private networks support many mission critical business services. Ten years ago, it would have been just an inconvenience if someone lost their IP service. Today, people and businesses depend on Internet applications. Online stock trading companies are not in business if people cannot implement their trades. The Department of Defense cannot operate their information-based programs if their information infrastructure is not operating. Call centers with VoIP services cannot serve their customers without their IP network.

Although we started work on this book with a focus on network reliability, it should be obvious from the preceding description that it is important to consider both reliability and performance, and to consider both networks and networked application services. Examples of networked applications include email, VoIP, search engines, ecommerce sites, news sites, or content delivery networks.

Features

This book has a number of features that make it a unique and valuable guide to reliable Internet services and applications.

Systematic, interdisciplinary approach: Building and operating reliable network services and applications requires a systematic approach. This book provides comprehensive, systematic, and interdisciplinary coverage of the important technical topics, including areas such as networking; performance, and reliability modeling; network measurement; configuration, fault, and security management; and software systems. The book provides an introduction to all of the topics, while at the same time, going into enough depth for interested readers that already understand the basics.

Specifically, the book is divided into seven parts. Part I provides an introduction to the challenges of building reliable networks and applications, and presents an overview of the structure of a large Internet Service Provider (ISP) network. Part II introduces reliability modeling and network capacity planning. Part III extends the discussion beyond a single network administrative domain, covering interdomain reliability and overlay networks. Part IV provides an introduction to an important aspect of reliability: configuration management. Part V introduces network measurements, which provide the underpinning of network management. Part VI covers network and security management, and disaster preparedness. Part VII describes techniques for building application services, and provides a comprehensive overview of capacity and performance engineering for these services. Taken in total, the book provides a comprehensive introduction to an important topic.

Coverage of pragmatic problems arising in real, operational deployments: Building and operating reliable networks and applications require an understanding of the pragmatic challenges that arise in an operational setting. This book is written by leading practitioners and researchers, and provides a unique perspective on the subject matter arising from their experience. Several chapters provide valuable "best practices" to help readers translate ideas into practice.

Content and structure allows reference reading: Although the book can be read from cover to cover, each chapter is designed to be largely self-contained, allowing readers to jump to specific topics that they may be interested in. The necessary overlap across a few of the chapters is minimal.

Audience

The goal of this book is to present a comprehensive guide to reliable Internet services and applications in a form that will be of broad interest to educators and researchers. The material is covered in a level of detail that would be suitable for an advanced undergraduate or graduate course in computer science. It can be used as the basis or supplemental material for a one-or-two semester course, providing a solid grounding in both theory and practice. The book will also be valuable to researchers seeking to understand the challenges faced by service providers and to identify areas that are ripe for research.

The book is also intended to be useful to practitioners who want to broaden their understanding of the field, and/or to deepen their knowledge of the fundamentals. By focusing our attention on a large ISP network and associated application services, we consider a problem that is large enough to expose the real challenges and yet broad enough to expose guidelines and best practices that will be applicable in other domains. For example, though the book does not discuss access or wireless networks, we believe that the principles and approaches to reliability that are presented in this book apply to them and are in fact, broadly applicable to any large network or networked application. We hope that you will find the book to be informative and useful.

Florham Park, NJ
India
New Haven, CT

Charles R. Kalmanek
Sudip Misra
Y. Richard Yang

Acknowledgments

The credit for this book goes first and foremost to the authors of the individual chapters. It takes a great deal of effort to crystallize one's understanding of a topic into an overview that is self-contained, technically deep, and interesting. The authors of this volume have done an outstanding job.

The editors acknowledge the contributions of many reviewers, whose comments clearly improved the quality of the chapters. Simon Rees and Wayne Wheeler, our editors at Springer, have been helpful and supportive.

The editors also acknowledge the support that they have been given by their families and loved ones during the long evenings and weekends spent developing this book.

Contents

Part I
Introduction and Reliable Network Design

Chapter 1
The Challenges of Building Reliable Networks and Networked Application Services

Charles R. Kalmanek and Y. Richard Yang

1.1 Introduction

In the decades since the ARPANET interconnected four research labs in 1969 [1], computer networks have become a critical infrastructure supporting our information-based society. Our dependence on this infrastructure is similar to our dependence on other basic infrastructures such as the world's power grids and the global transportation systems. Failures of the network infrastructure or major applications running on top of it can have an enormous financial and social cost with serious consequences to the organizations and consumers that depend on these services.

Given the importance of this communications and applications infrastructure to the economy and society as a whole, reliability is a major concern of network and service providers. After a survey of major network carriers including AT&T, BT, and NTT, Telemark [7] concludes that, "The three elements which carriers are most concerned about when deploying communication services are network reliability, network usability, and network fault processing capabilities. The top three elements all belong to the reliability category." Unfortunately, the challenges associated with running reliable, large-scale networks are not well documented in the research literature. Moreover, while networking and software-educational curricula provide a good theoretical foundation, there is little training in the techniques used by experienced practitioners to address reliability challenges. Another issue is that while traditional telecommunications vendors gained extensive experience in building reliable software, the pace of change has accelerated as the Internet has grown and Internet system vendors do not meet the level of reliability traditionally associated with "carrier grade" systems. Newer vendors accustomed to building consumer software are

C.R. Kalmanek (✉)
AT&T Labs, 180 Park Ave., 07932, Florham Park, NJ, USA
e-mail: crk@research.att.com

Y.R. Yang
Yale University, 51 Prospect Street, New Haven, CT, USA
e-mail: yry@cs.yale.edu

C.R. Kalmanek et al. (eds.), *Guide to Reliable Internet Services and Applications*,
Computer Communications and Networks, DOI 10.1007/978-1-84882-828-5_1,
© Springer-Verlag London Limited 2010

entering the service provider market, but they do not have a culture that focuses on the higher level of required reliability. This places a greater burden on service providers who integrate their software to help these vendors "raise the bar" on reliability to offer reliable services.

Although we emphasize network reliability in the foregoing section, it is important to consider both reliability and performance and to consider both networks and networked application services. Users are interested in the performance of an end-to-end service. When a user is unable to access his e-mail, he does not particularly care whether the network or the application is at fault. Examples of network applications include e-mail, Voice over IP, search engines, e-commerce sites, news sites, or content delivery networks.

1.2 Why Is Reliability Hard?

Supporting reliable networks and networked application services involves some of the most complex engineering and operational challenges that are dealt with in any industry. Much of this complexity is intentionally transparent to the end users, who expect things to "just work." Moreover, the end users are typically not exposed to the root causes of network or service problems when their service is degraded or interrupted. As a result, it is natural for end users to assume that network and service reliability are not hard. In part, users get this impression because most service providers and Internet-facing web services operate at very high levels of reliability. Though it may look easy, this level of reliability is a result of solid engineering and "constant vigilance." The best service providers engage in a process of continuous improvement, similar to the Japanese "Kaizen" philosophy that was popularized by Deming [2]. In this book, we address the challenges faced by service providers and the approaches that they use to deliver reliable services to their users. Before delving into the solution, we ask ourselves, why is it so hard to build highly reliable networks and networked application services?

We can characterize the difficulty as resulting from three primary causes. The first challenge is scale and complexity; the second is that the services operate in the presence of constant change. These challenges are inherent to large-scale networks. The third challenge is less fundamental but still important. It relates to challenges with measurement and data.

1.2.1 Scale and Complexity Challenges

Scale and complexity challenges are fundamental to any large network or service infrastructure. As Steve Bellovin remarked, "Things break. Complex systems break in complex ways" [8]. In particular, large service provider networks contain hundreds of thousands of network elements distributed around the world, and tens of thousands of different models of equipment. These network elements are interconnected and must interoperate correctly to offer services to the network users. Failures in one part of the network can impact other parts of the network. Even if we consider only the infrastructure needed to provide basic IP connectivity services, it consists of a vast number of complex building blocks: routers, multiplexers, transmission equipment, servers, systems software, load balancers, storage, firewalls, application software, etc. At any given point in time, some network elements have failed, have been taken out of service, or will be operating at a degraded performance level.

The preceding description only hints at the challenges. Despite the careful engineering and modeling that is done through all stages of the service life cycle, if we look at the service infrastructure as a system, we note that *the system does not always behave as expected*. There are many reasons for this, including:

- Software defects in network elements;
- Inadequate modeling of dependencies;
- Complex software-support systems.

The vast majority of the elements involved in providing a network service contain software, which can be buggy, particularly when the software function is complex. If a bug is triggered, a piece of equipment can behave in unexpected ways. Even though the correct operation of router software is critical to service, we have seen design flaws in the way that the router-operating system handles resource management and scheduling, which manifest themselves as latent outages. The history of the telephone network contains examples of major network outages caused by software faults, such as the famous "crash" of the AT&T long-distance telephone network in 1990 [3]. Similarly, the network elements that make up the IP network infrastructure contain complex control-plane software implementing distributed protocols that must interoperate properly for the network to work. When compared to the telephone switching software, control plan software of IP networks changes more frequently and is far more likely to be subject to undetected software faults. These faults occasionally result in unexpected behaviors that can lead to outages or degraded performance.

In a large complex infrastructure, operators do not have a comprehensive model of all of the dependencies between systems supporting a given service: they rely on simplifying abstractions such as network layering and administrative separation of concerns. These abstractions can break down in unexpected ways. For example, there are complex interactions between network layers, such as the transport and IP layers, that affect reliability. Consider a link between two routers that is transported over a SONET ring. Networks are typically designed so that protection switching at the SONET layer is transparent to the IP layer. However, several years ago, AT&T experienced problems in the field, whereby a SONET "protection switching event" triggered a router-software bug that caused several minutes of unexpected customer downtime. Since the protection switch occurred correctly, the problem did not trigger an alarm and was only uncovered by correlating customer trouble tickets with network event data. This cross-layer interaction is an example of the kinds of dependency that can be difficult to anticipate and troubleshoot.

In addition to the scale of the network and the complexity of the network equipment, correct operation depends on the operation of complex software systems that manage the network and support customer care. Router-configuration files contain a large number of parameters that must be configured correctly. Incorrect configuration of an access control list can create security vulnerabilities, or alternatively, can cause traffic to be "blackholed" by blocking legitimate traffic. If there is a mismatch between the Quality of Service settings on a customer-edge router and those on the provider-edge router that it connects, some applications may experience performance problems under heavy load. An inconsistency between the network inventory database and the running network can lead to stranded network capacity, service degradations, network outages, etc. These problems sometimes manifest themselves weeks or months after the inconsistency appeared – for this reason, they are sometimes referred to as "time bombs."

1.2.2   Constant Change

The second challenge relates to the fact that any large-scale service infrastructure undergoes constant change. Maintenance and customer-provisioning activities in a large global network are ongoing, spanning multiple time zones. On a typical workday, new customers are being provisioned, service for departing customers is being turned down, and *change orders* to change some service characteristic are being processed for existing customers. Capacity augmentation and traffic grooming, whereby private-line connections are rearranged to use network resources more efficiently, take place daily. Routine maintenance activities such as software upgrades also take place during predefined maintenance "windows." More complex maintenance activities, such as network migrations, also occur periodically. Examples of network migration include moving a customer connection from one access router to another, replacing a backbone router, or consolidating all of a regional network's traffic onto a national backbone network in order to retire an older backbone. Replacing a backbone router in a service provider network requires careful planning and execution of a sequence of moves of the "uplinks" from access routers in order to minimize the amount of traffic that is dropped. Decision-support tools are used to model the traffic that impinges on all of the affected links at every step of the move to ensure that links are not congested.

In the midst of these day-to-day changes, network failures can occur at any time. The network is designed to automatically restore service after a failure. However, during planned maintenance activities, it is possible that some network capacity has been removed from service temporarily, potentially leaving the network more vulnerable to specific failures. Under normal conditions, maintenance to repair the failed network element is scheduled to occur later at a convenient time, after which the network traffic may revert back to its original path.

Finally, in addition to the day-to-day changes of new customers, or the occasional changes that come from major network migrations, there are also architectural changes. These changes might result from the introduction of new features and services, or new protocols. An example might be the addition of a new "class of service" in the backbone. Another example might be turning up support for multicast services in MPLS-based VPNs. The first example (class of service) involves configuration changes that may touch every router in the network. The second example involves introducing a new architectural element (i.e., a PIM rendezvous point), enabling a new protocol (i.e., PIM), validating the operation of multicast monitoring tools, etc. All of these changes would have been tested in the lab prior to the First Field Application (FFA), which is typically the first time that everything comes together in an operational network carrying live customer traffic. If there are problems during the FFA with the new feature that is being deployed, network operations will execute procedures to gracefully back out of the change until the root cause of the problem is analyzed and corrected.

1.2.3   Measurement and Data Challenges

The third challenge associated with building reliable networks is associated with measurement and data. Vendor products deployed by service providers often suffer from an inadequate implementation of basic telemetry functions that are necessary to monitor and manage the equipment. In addition, because of the complexity of the operating environment described earlier, there are many, diverse data sources, with highly variable data quality. We present two examples. Despite the maturity of SNMP [4], AT&T has seen an implementation of a commercial SNMP poller that did not correctly handle the data impacts of router reboots or loss of data in transit. Ideally, problems like this are discovered in the lab, but occasionally they are not discovered until the equipment is deployed and supporting live service. Data problems are not limited to network layer equipment: vendor-developed software components running on servers may not support monitoring agents that export the data necessary to implement a comprehensive performance-monitoring infrastructure. When these software components are combined in a complex, multitiered application, the workflow and dependencies among the components may not be fully understood even by the vendor. When such a system is deployed, even with a well-designed server instrumentation, it may be difficult to determine exactly which component is the bottleneck with limited system throughput.

Another issue is that data are often "locked up" in management system "silos." This can result from selecting a vendor's proprietary element-management system. Typically, proprietary systems are not designed to make data export easy, since the vendor seeks to lock the service provider into a complete "solution." Data silos can also result from internal implementations. These often result from organizational silos: a management system is specified and built to address a specific set of functions, without the involvement of subject matter experts from other domains.

Whatever the cause, the end result is that the data necessary to monitor and manage the infrastructure may not exist or may be difficult to access by analysts who are trying to understand the system.

1.3   Toward Network and Service Reliability

The examples in Section 1.2 give only a glimpse into the complex challenges faced by service providers who seek to provide reliable services. Despite these complexities, the vast majority of users receive good service. How is this achieved? At the highest level, network and service reliability involve both good engineering design and good operational practices. These practices are inextricably linked: no matter how good the operations team is, good operation practices cannot make up for a poorly thought out design. Likewise, a good design that is implemented or operated poorly will not result in reliable service.

It should be obvious that reliable services start with good design and engineering. The service design process relies on extensive domain knowledge and a good understanding of the business and service-level objectives. Network engineers develop detailed requirements for each network element in light of the end-to-end objectives for reliability, availability, and operability. Network elements are selected carefully. After a detailed paper and lab evaluation, an engineering team selects a specific product to meet a particular need. Once the product is selected, it enters a change control process where differences between the requirements and the product's capabilities are managed by the service provider in conjunction with the vendor. The service designers, working closely with test engineers, develop comprehensive engineering rules for each of the network elements, including safe operating limits for resources such as bandwidth or CPU utilization. Detailed engineering documents are developed that describe how the network element is to be used, its engineering limits, etc. Network management requirements for the new network element are developed in conjunction with operations personnel and delivered to the IT team responsible for the operations-support systems (OSSs). Before the FFA of the new element, the element, and OSSs undergo an Operations Readiness Test (ORT), which verifies that the element and the associated OSSs work as expected, and can be managed by network operations.

The preceding paragraph gives a brief overview of some of the engineering "best practices" involved in building a reliable network. In addition, reliability and capacity modeling must be done for the network as a whole. The network architecture includes the appropriate recovery mechanisms to address potential failures. Reliability modeling tools are used to model the impact on the network of failures in light of both current and forecast demands. Where possible, the tools model cross-layer dependencies between IP layer links and the underlying transport or physical layer network, such as the existence of "shared risk groups" – links or elements that may be subject to simultaneous failure. By simulating all possible failure scenarios, these tools allow the network designers to trade off network cost against survivability. The network design also includes a comprehensive security design that considers the important threats to the network and its customers, and implements appropriate access controls and other security detection and mitigation strategies.

An operations organization is typically responsible for managing the network or service on a day-to-day basis. The operations team is supported by the operations-support systems mentioned earlier. These include configuration-management systems responsible for maintaining network inventory data and configuring the network elements, and service assurance systems that collect telemetry data from the network to support fault and performance management functions. The fault and performance management systems are the "eyes" of the operations team into the service infrastructure to figure out, in the case of problems, what needs to be repaired. We can consider fault and performance management systems as involving the following areas:

- Instrumentation layer;
- Data management layer;
- Management application layer.

We start thinking about the instrumentation layer by asking what telemetry or measurement data need to be collected to validate that the service is meeting its service-level objectives (or to troubleshoot problems if it is not). Standardized router MIB data provide a base level of information, but additional instrumentation is needed to manage large networks supporting complex applications. Passive monitoring techniques support collection of data directly from network elements and dedicated passive monitoring devices, but active monitoring, involving the injection and monitoring of synthetic traffic, is also required and is commonly used. Since the correct operation of the IP forwarding layer (data plane) critically depends on the correct operation of the IP control plane, both data plane and the control-plane monitoring are important. In software-based application services, the telemetry frequently does not adequately capture "soft" failure modes, such as transaction timeouts between devices or errors in software settings and parameters. Both the servers supporting application software and the applications themselves need to be instrumented and monitored for both faults and key performance parameters.

Large service providers typically have a significant number of data sources that are relevant to service management, and the data management layer needs to be able to handle large volumes of telemetry and alarm data. As a result, the data-collection and data-management infrastructure presents challenging systems design problems. A good design allows data-source-specific collectors to be easily integrated. It also provides a framework for data normalization, so that common fields such as timestamps, router names, etc., can be normalized to a common key during data ingest so that application developers are spared some of the complexity of understanding details of the raw data streams. Ideally, the design of the data management layer supports a common real-time and archival data store that is accessed by a range of applications.

The management applications supported on top of the data management layer support routine operations functions such as fault and performance management, in addition to supporting more complex analyses. Given the vast quantity of event data that is generated by the network, the event management system must appropriately filter the information that must be acted upon by the operations team to avoid flooding them with spurious information. The impact of alarm storms (and the importance of alarm filtering) can be illustrated by the story of Three Mile Island, in which the computer system noted 700 distinct error conditions within the first minute of the problem, followed by thousands of error reports and updates [5]. The operators were drowning in a sea of information at a time when they needed a small number of actionable items to work on.

Management applications also enable operations personnel to control the network, including performing routine tasks such as resetting a line card on a router as well as more complex tasks. Standard tasks are handled through an operations interface to an operations-support system. Ad hoc tasks that involve a complex workflow may require operations staff to use a scripting language that accesses the network inventory database and sends commands to network elements or element-management systems. Ideally, the operations-support systems automate most of the routine tasks to a large extent, audit the results of these tasks, and back them out if there are problems.

It is useful to note that operations personnel are typically organized in multiple response tiers. The lower tiers of operations staff work on immediate problems, following established procedures. The tools that they use have constrained functionality, targeted at the functions that they are expected to perform. The highest tier of operations personnel consists of senior operations staff charged with diagnosing complex problems in real-time or performing postmortem analysis of complex, unresolved problems that occurred in the past. These investigations may take more time than lower-tier operations staff can afford to spend on a specific problem. When there are serious problems affecting major customers or the network as a whole, engineers from the network engineering team are also called upon to assist. In these cases, one or more analysts do exploratory data mining (EDM) using data exploration tools [6] that support data drill down, statistical data analysis, and data visualization. Well-designed data exploration tools can make a huge difference when analysts are faced with the "needle in the haystack" problem – trying to sort through huge quantities of telemetry data to draw meaningful conclusions. When analysts uncover the root cause of a particular problem, this information can be used to eliminate the problem, e.g., by pressing a vendor to fix a software bug, by repairing a configuration error, etc.

As we mentioned in Section 1.2, a broad goal of both the network designers and network operations is to maintain and continuously improve network reliability, availability, and performance, despite the challenges. "Holding the gains" or staying flat on network performance is insufficient to meet increasingly tight customer and application requirements. There is evidence that the principles and best practices presented in this book have results. Figure 1.1 shows measured Defects-per-Million

UNPLANNED DPM

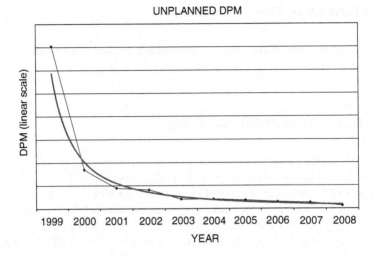

Fig. 1.1 Unplanned DPM for AT&T IP Backbone

(DPM) on the AT&T IP Backbone since the AT&T Managed Internet Service was first offered in 1999. This chart plots the total number of minutes of port outages during a year (i.e., the number of minutes each customer port was out of service), divided by the number of port minutes in that year (i.e., the number of ports times the number of minutes each was in service), times a normalization factor of 1,000,000. The points are measured data; the smooth curve resembles a classic improvement curve. Over the first 2 years of the service, DPM was reduced significantly as vendor problems were addressed, architectural improvements were put in place, and operations processes were matured. Further improvements continue to be achieved. While DPM is only one of the many fault and performance metrics that must be tracked and managed, this chart illustrates how good design and good operations pay off.

The principles that underlie design and operation of reliable networks are also critical to the design and operation of reliable application services. However, there are also many differences between these two domains, including wide differences in the domain knowledge of the typical network engineer and the typical software developers. The life cycle of reliable software starts with understanding the requirements, and involves every step of the development process, including field support and application monitoring. As in networks, capacity and performance engineering of application services rely on both modeling and data collection.

This section has described some of the design and network management practices that are performed by large service providers that run reliable networks and services. In Section 1.4, we provide an overview of the material that is covered in the book.

1.4   A Bird's Eye View of the Book

The book consists of six parts, covering both reliable networks and reliable network application services.

1.4.1   Part I: Reliable Network Design

Part I introduces the challenges of building reliable networks and services, and provides background for the rest of the book. Following this chapter, Chapter 2 presents an overview of the structure of a large ISP backbone network. Since IP network reliability is tied intimately to the underlying transport network layers, this chapter presents an overview of these technologies. Section 2.4 provides an overview of the IP control plane, and introduces Multi-Protocol Label Switching (MPLS), a routing and forwarding technology that is used by most large ISPs to support Internet and Virtual Private Network (VPN) services on a shared backbone network. Section 2.5 introduces network restoration, which allows the network to rapidly recover from failures. This section provides a performance analysis of the limitations of OSPF failure detection and recovery to motivate the deployment of MPLS Fast Reroute. The chapter concludes with a case study of an IP network supporting IPTV services that links together many of the concepts.

1.4.2   Part II: Reliability Modeling and Network Planning

Part II of the book covers network reliability modeling, and its close cousin, network planning. Chapter 3 starts with an overview of the main router elements (e.g., routing processors, line cards, switching fabric, power supply, and cooling system), and their failure modes. Section 3.2 introduces redundancy mechanisms for router elements, as they are important for availability modeling. Section 3.3 shows how to compute the reliability metrics of a single router with and without redundancy mechanisms. Section 3.4 extends the reliability model from a single router to a large network of edge routers and presents reliability metrics that consider device heterogeneity. The chapter also provides an overview of the challenges in measuring end-to-end availability, which is the focus of Chapter 4.

Chapter 4 provides a theoretical grounding in performance and reliability (performability) modeling in the context of a large-scale network. A fundamental challenge is that the size of the state space is exponential in the number of network elements. Section 4.2 presents a hierarchical network model used for performability modeling. Section 4.3 discusses the performability evaluation problem in general and presents the state-generation approach. The chapter also introduces the *nperf* network performability analyzer, a software package developed at AT&T Labs

Research. Section 4.4 concludes by presenting two case studies that illustrate the material of this chapter, the first involving an IPTV distribution network, and the second dealing with architecture choices for network access.

Chapter 5 focuses on network planning. Since capacity planning depends on utilization and traffic data, the chapter takes a systems view: since network measurements are of varying quality, the modeling process must be robust to data-quality problems while giving useful estimates that can be used for planning: "Essentially, all models are wrong, but some are useful." This chapter is organized around the key steps in network planning. Sections 5.2 and 5.3 cover measurements, analysis, and modeling of network traffic. Section 5.4 covers prediction, including both incremental planning and green-field planning. Section 5.5 presents optimal network planning. Section 5.6 covers robust planning.

1.4.3   Part III: Interdomain Reliability and Overlay Networks

Part III extends beyond the design of a large backbone network to interdomain and overlay networks. Chapter 6 provides an overview of interdomain routing. Section 6.3 highlights the limitations of the BGP routing protocol. For example, the protocol design does not guarantee that routing will converge to a stable route. Section 6.4 presents measurement results that quantify the impact of interdomain routing impairments on end-to-end path performance. Section 6.5 presents a detailed overview of the existing solutions to achieve reliable interdomain routing, and Section 6.6 points out possible future research directions.

Overlay networks are discussed in Chapter 7 as a way of providing end-to-end reliability at the application or service layer. The overlay topology can be tailored to application requirements; overlay routing may choose application-specific policies; and overlay networks can emulate functionality not supported by the underlying network. This chapter surveys overlay applications with a focus on how they are used to increase network resilience. The chapter considers how overlay networks can make a distributed application more resilient to flash crowds, to component failures and churn, network failures and congestion, and to denial-of-service attacks.

1.4.4   Part IV: Configuration Management

Network design is just one part of building a reliable network or service infrastructure; configuration management is another critical function. Part IV discusses this topic.

Chapter 8 discusses network configuration management, presenting a high-level view of the software system involved in managing a large network of routers in support of carrier class services. Section 8.2 reviews key concepts to structure the types of data items that the system must deal with. Section 8.3 describes the subcomponents of the system and the requirements of each subcomponent. This section also discusses two approaches that are commonly used for router configuration – policy-based and template-based, and highlights the different requirements associated with provisioning consumer and enterprise services. Section 8.4 gives an overview of one of the key challenges in designing a configuration-management system, which is handling changes. Finally, the chapter presents a step-by-step overview of the subscriber provisioning process.

While a well-designed configuration-management system does configuration auditing, Chapter 9 looks at auditing from a different perspective, describing the need for bottom-up, network-wide configuration validation. Section 9.2 provides a case study of the challenges of configuring a multi-organization "collaboration network," the types of vulnerabilities caused by configuration errors, the reasons these arise, and the benefits derived from using a configuration validation system. Section 9.3 abstracts from experience and proposes a reference design of a validation system. Section 9.4 discusses the IPAssure system and the design choices it has made to realize this design. Section 9.5 surveys related technologies for realizing this design. Section 9.6 discusses the experience with using IPAssure to assist a US government agency with compliance with FISMA requirements.

1.4.5 *Part V: Network Measurement*

While measurement was not a priority in the original design of the Internet, the complexity of networks, traffic, and the protocols that mediate them now require detailed measurements to manage the network, to verify that performance meets the required goals, and to diagnose performance degradations when they occur. Part V covers network measurement, with a focus on reliability and performance monitoring.

Chapter 10 covers data plane measurements. Sections 10.2–10.5 describe a spectrum of passive traffic measurement methods that are currently employed in provider networks, and also describe some newer approaches that have been proposed or may even be deployed in the medium term. Section 10.6 covers active measurement tools. Sections 10.7–10.8 review IP performance metrics and their usage in service-level agreements. Section 10.9 presents multiple approaches to deploy active measurement systems.

The control plane in an IP network controls the overall flow of traffic in the network, and is critical to its operation. Chapter 11 covers control-plane measurements. Section 11.2 gives an overview of the key protocols that make up the "unicast" control plane (OSPF and BGP) describes how they are monitored, and surveys key applications of the measurement data. Section 11.3 presents the additional challenges that arise in performing multicast monitoring.

1.4.6   Part VI: Network and Security Management, and Disaster Preparedness

Chapter 12 focuses on the network management systems and the tasks involved in supporting the day-to-day operations of an IP network. The goal of network operations is to keep the network up and running, and performing at or above designed levels of service performance. Section 12.2 covers fault and performance management – detecting, troubleshooting, and repairing network faults and performance impairments. Section 12.3 examines how process automation is incorporated in fault and performance management to automate many of the tasks that were originally executed by humans. Process automation is the key ingredient that enables a relatively small Operations group to manage a rapidly expanding number of network elements, customer ports, and complexity. Section 12.4 discusses tracking and managing network availability and performance over time, looking across larger numbers of network events to identify opportunities for performance improvements. Section 12.5 then focuses on planned maintenance. The chapter also presents areas for innovation and a set of best practices.

Chapter 13 presents a service provider's view of network security. Section 13.2 provides an exposition of the network security threats and their causes. A fundamental concern is that in the area of network security, the economic balance is heavily skewed in favor of bad actors. Section 13.3 presents a framework for network security, including the means of detecting security incidents. Section 13.4 deals with the importance of developing good network security intelligence. Section 13.5 presents a number of operational network security systems used for the detection and mitigation of security threats. Finally, Section 13.6 summarizes important insights and then briefly considers important new and developing directions and concerns in network security as an indication of where resources should be focused both tactically and strategically.

Chapter 14 discusses disaster preparedness as the critical factor that determines an operator's ability to recover from a network disaster. For network operators to effectively recover from a disaster, a significant investment must be made to prepare *before* the disaster occurs, so that network operations are prepared to act quickly and efficiently. This chapter describes the creation, exercise, and management of disaster recovery plans. With good disaster preparedness, disaster recovery becomes the disciplined management of the execution of disaster recovery plans.

1.4.7   Part VII: Reliable Application Services

Large-scale networks exist to connect users to applications. Part VII expands the scope of the book to the software and servers that support network applications.

Chapter 15 presents an approach to the design and development of reliable network application software. This chapter presents the entire life cycle of what it takes to build reliable network applications, including software development process, requirements development, architecture, design and implementation, testing methodology, support, and reporting. This chapter also discusses techniques that aid in troubleshooting failed systems as well as techniques that tend to minimize the duration of a failure. The chapter presents best practices for building reliable network applications.

Chapter 16 provides a comprehensive overview of capacity and performance engineering (C/PE), which is especially critical to the successful deployment of a networked service platform. At the highest level, the goal is to ensure that the service meets all performance and reliability requirements in the most cost-effective manner, where "cost" encompasses such areas as hardware/software resources, delivery schedule, and scalability. The chapter uses e-mail as an illustrating example. Section 16.4 covers the architecture assessment phase of the C/PE process, including the flow of critical transactions. Section 16.5 covers the workload/metric assessment phase, including the workload placed on platform elements and the service-level performance/reliability metrics that the platform must meet. Sections 16.6 and 16.7 develop analytic models to predict how a proposed platform will handle the workload while meeting the requirements (reliability/ availability assessment and capacity/performance assessment). Sections 16.8 and 16.9 develop engineering guidelines to size the platform initially (scalability assessment) and to maintain service capacity, performance, and reliability post deployment (capacity/performance management). Best practices of C/PE are given at the end of the chapter.

1.5 Conclusion

With our society's increasing dependence on networks and networked application services, the importance of reliability and performance engineering has never been greater. Unfortunately, large-scale networks and services present significant challenges: scale and complexity, the need for correct operation in the presence of constant change, as well as measurement and data challenges. Addressing these challenges requires good design and sound operational practices. Network and service engineers start with a firm understanding of the design objectives, the technology, and the operational environment for the service; follow a comprehensive service design process; and develop capacity and performance engineering models. Network and service management rely on a well-thought out measurement design, a data collection and storage infrastructure, and a suite of management tools and applications. When done right, the end result is a network or service that works well. As customers and applications become more demanding, this "raises the bar" for reliability and performance, ensuring that this field will continue to provide opportunities for research and improvements in practice.

References

1. *A History of the ARPANET*. Bolt, Beranek, and Newman, 1981.
2. Deming, W. E. (2000). *The new economics for government, industry and education* (2nd ed.). Cambridge, MA: MIT Press. ISBN 0–262–54116–5.
3. AT&T statement (1990). The Risks Digest, 9(63).
4. Wilson, A. M. (1998). *Alarm management and its importance in ensuring safety, Best practices in alarm management*, Digest 1998/279.
5. Stallings, W. (1999). *SNMP, SNMPv2, SNMPv3, and RMON 1 and 2 (3rd ed.)*. Reading, MA: Addison-Wesley.
6. Mahimkar, A., Yates, J., Zhang, Y., Shaikh, A., Wang, J., Ge, Z., et al. (December 2008). Troubleshooting chronic conditions in large IP networks. Proceedings of the 4th ACM international conference on emerging Networking Experiments and Technologies (CoNEXT).
7. Telemark Survey. http://www.telemarkservices.com/
8. Schwartz, J. (2007). Who needs hackers? *New York Times*, September 12, 2007.

Chapter 2
Structural Overview of ISP Networks

Robert D. Doverspike, K.K. Ramakrishnan, and Chris Chase

2.1 Introduction

An *Internet Service Provider (ISP)* is a telecommunications company that offers its customers access to the Internet. This chapter specifically covers the design of a large Tier 1 ISP that provides services to both residential and enterprise customers. Our primary focus is on a large *IP backbone* network in the continental USA, though similarities arise in smaller networks operated by telecommunication providers in other parts of the world. This chapter is principally motivated by the observation that in large carrier networks, the IP backbone is not a self-contained entity; it co-exists with numerous access and transport networks operated by the same or other service providers. In fact, how the IP backbone interacts with its neighboring networks and the transport layers is fundamental to understanding its structure, operation, and planning. This chapter is a hands-on description of the practical structure and implementation of IP backbone networks. Our goal is complicated by the complexity of the different network layers, each of which has its own nomenclature and concepts. Therefore, one of our first tasks is to define the nomenclature we will use, classifying the network into *layers* and *segments*. Once this partitioning is accomplished, we identify where the IP backbone fits and describe its key surrounding layers and networks.

This chapter is motivated by three aspects of the design of large IP networks. The first aspect is that the design of an IP backbone is strongly influenced by the details of the underlying network layers. We will illustrate how the evolution

R.D. Doverspike (✉)
Executive Director, Network Evolution Research, AT&T Labs Research,
200 S. Laurel Ave, Middletown, NJ 07748, USA
e-mail: rdd@research.att.com

K.K. Ramakrishnan
Distinguished Member of Technical Staff, Networking Research, AT&T Labs Research,
Shannon Labs, 180 Park Avenue, Florham Park, NJ 07932, USA

C. Chase
AT&T Labs, 9505 Arboretum Blvd, Austin, TX 78759, USA
e-mail: chase@labs.att.com

C.R. Kalmanek et al. (eds.), *Guide to Reliable Internet Services and Applications*,
Computer Communications and Networks, DOI 10.1007/978-1-84882-828-5_2,
© Springer-Verlag London Limited 2010

of customer access through the metro network has influenced the design of the backbone. We also show how the evolution of the *Dense Wavelength-Division Multiplexing* (DWDM) layer has influenced core backbone design.

The second aspect presents the use of *Multiprotocol Label Switching (MPLS)* in large ISP networks. The separation of routing and forwarding provided by MPLS allows carriers to support *Virtual Private Networks (VPNs)* and *Traffic Engineering* (TE) on their backbones much more simply than with traditional IP forwarding.

The third aspect is how network outages manifest in multiple network layers and how the network layers are designed to respond to such disruptions, usually through a set of processes called *network restoration*. This is of prime importance because a major objective of large ISPs is to provide a known level of quality of service to its customers through *Service Level Agreements (SLAs)*. Network disruptions occur from two major sources: failure of network components and maintenance activity. Network restoration is accomplished through preplanned network design processes and real-time network control processes, as provided by an *Interior Gateway Protocol* (IGP) such as *Open Shortest Path First* (OSPF). We present an overview of OSPF reconvergence and the factors that affect its performance. As customers and applications place more stringent requirements on restoration performance in large ISPs, the assessment of OSPF reconvergence motivates the use of MPLS Fast Reroute (FRR).

Beyond the motivations described above, the concepts defined in this chapter lay useful groundwork for the succeeding chapters. Section 2.2 provides a structural basis by providing a high-level picture of the network layers and segments of a typical, large nationwide terrestrial carrier. It also provides nomenclature and technical background about the equipment and network structure of some of the layers that have the largest impact on the IP backbone. Section 2.3 provides more details about the architecture, network topology, and operation of the IP backbone (the IP layer) and how it interacts with the key network layers identified in Section 2.2. Section 2.4 discusses routing and control protocols and their application in the IP backbone, such as MPLS. The background and concepts introduced in Sections 2.2–2.4 are utilized in Section 2.5, where we describe network restoration and planning. Finally, Section 2.6 describes a "case study" of an IPTV backbone. This section unifies many of the concepts presented in the earlier sections and how they come together to allow network operators to meet their network performance objectives. Section 2.7 provides a summary, followed by a reference list, and a glossary of acronyms and key terms.

2.2   The IP Backbone Network in Its Broader Network Context

2.2.1   Background and Nomenclature

From the standpoint of large telecommunication carriers, the USA and most large countries are organized into metropolitan areas, which are colloquially referred to as *metros*. Large intrametro carriers place their transmission and switching equipment in buildings called *Central Offices (COs)*. Business and residential customers typically obtain telecommunication services by connecting to a designated first CO called a *serving* central office. This connection occurs over a *feeder network* that extends from the CO toward the customer plus a *local loop* (or *last mile*) segment that connects from the last equipment node of the feeder network to the customer premise. Equipment in the feeder network is usually housed in above-ground huts, on poles, or in vaults. The feeder and last-mile segments usually consist of copper, optical fiber, coaxial cable, or some combination thereof. Coaxial cable is typical to a cable company, also called a *Multiple System Operator (MSO)*. While we will not discuss metro networks in detail in this chapter, it is important to discuss their aspects that affect the IP backbone. However, the metro networks we describe coincide mostly with those carriers whose origins are from large telephone companies (sometimes called "Telcos").

Almost all central offices today are interconnected by optical fiber. Once a customer's data or voice enters the serving central office, if it is destined outside that serving central office, it is routed to other central offices in the same metro area. If the service is bound for another metro, it is routed to one or more gateway COs. If it is bound for another country, it eventually routes to an international gateway. A metro gateway CO is often called a *Point of Presence (POP)*. While POPs were originally defined for telephone service, they have evolved to serve as intermetro gateways for almost all telecommunication services. Large intermetro carriers have one or more POPs in every large city.

Given this background, we now employ some visualization aids. Networks are organized into *network layers*, which we depict vertically with two network graphs vertically stacked on top of one another in Fig. 2.1. Each of the network layers can be considered to be an *overlay network* with respect to the network below.

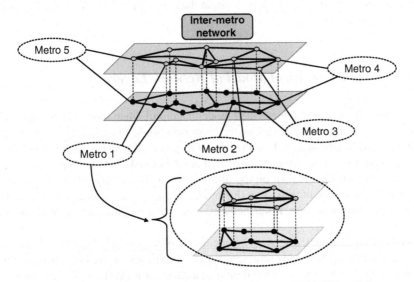

Fig. 2.1 Conceptual network layers and segmentation

We can further organize these layers into *access, metro,* and *core* network segments. Figure 2.1 shows the core segment connected to multiple metro segments. Each metro segment represents the network layers of the equipment located in the central offices of a given metropolitan area. The access segment represents the feeder network and loop network associated with a given metro segment. The core segment represents the equipment in the POPs and network structures that connect them for intermetro transport and switching.

In this chapter, we focus on the ISP backbone network, which is primarily associated with the core segment. We refer only briefly to access architectures and will discuss portions of the metro segment to the extent to which they interact and connect to the core segment. Also, in this chapter we will not discuss broader telecommunication contexts, such as international networks (including undersea links), satellite, and wireless networks. More detail on the various network segments and their network layers and a historical description of how they arose can be found in [11].

Unfortunately, there is a wide variety of terminology used in the industry, which presents a challenge for this chapter because of our broad scope. Some of the terminology is local to an organization, application, or network layer and, thus, when used in a broader context can be confused with other applications or layers. Within the context of network-layering descriptions, we will use the term *IP layer*. However, we use the term "IP backbone" interchangeably with "IP layer" in the context of the core network segment. The terms *Local Area Network (LAN)*, *Metropolitan Area Network (MAN)*, and *Wide Area Network (WAN)* are also sometimes used and correlate roughly with the access, metro, and core segments defined earlier; however, LAN, MAN, and WAN are usually applied only in the context of packet-based networks. Therefore, in this chapter, we will use the terms access, metro, and core, since they apply to a broader context of different network technologies and layers. Other common terms for the various layers within the core segment are *long-distance* and *long-haul* networks.

2.2.2 Simple Graphical Model of Network Layers

The following simple graph-oriented model is helpful when modeling routing and network design algorithms, to understand how network layers interact and, in particular, how to classify and analyze the impact of potential network disruptions. This model applies to most *connection-oriented* networks and, thus, will apply to some higher-layer protocols that sit on top of the IP layer. The IP layer itself is *connectionless* and does not fit exactly in this model. However, this model is particularly helpful to understand how lower network layers and neighboring network layers interact.

In the layered model, a network layer consists of *nodes, links* (also called *edges*), and *connections*. The nodes represent types of switches or cross-connect equipment that exchange data in either digital or analog form via the links that connect them. Note that at the lowest layer (such as fiber) nodes represent equipment, such as fiber-optic patch panels, in which connections are switched manually by cross-connecting fiber patch cords from one interface to another. Links can be modeled as *directed* (unidirectional) or *undirected* (bidirectional). Connections are cross-connected (or switched) by the nodes onto the links, and thus form paths over the nodes and links of the graph. Note that the term *connection* often has different names at different layers and segments. For example, in most telecommunication carriers, a connection (or portions thereof) is called a *circuit* in many of the lower network layers, often referred to as *transport* layers. Connections can be *point-to-point* (unidirectional or bidirectional), *point-to-multipoint* or, more rarely, *multipoint-to-multipoint*. Generally, connections arise from two sources. First, telecommunication services can arise "horizontally" (relative to our conceptual picture of Fig. 2.1) from a neighboring network segment. Second, connections in a given layer can originate from edges of a higher-layer network layer. In this way, each layer provides a connection "service" for the layer immediately above it to provide connectivity. Sometimes, a "client/server" model is referenced, such as the *User-Network Interface (UNI)* model [29] of the *Optical Internetworking Forum (OIF)*, wherein the links of higher-layer networks are "clients" and the connections of lower-layer networks are "servers". For example, see G.7713.2 [19] for more discussion of connection management in lower-layer transport networks.

Recall that the technology layers we define are differentiated by the nodes, which represent actual switching or cross-connect equipment, rather than more abstract entities, such as protocols within each of these technology layers that can create multiple protocol *sublayers*. An early manifestation of protocol layering is the OSI model developed by the ISO standards organization [37] and the resulting classification of packet layering, such as *Layer 1*, *Layer 2*, *Layer 3*, which subsequently emerged in the industry. Although these layering definitions can be somewhat strained in usage, the industry generally associates IP with Layer 3 and MPLS or Ethernet VLANS with Layer 2 (which will be described later in the chapter). Layer 1, or the Physical Layer (PHY layer) of the OSI stack, covers multiple technology layers that we will cover in the next section.

We illustrate this graphical network-layering model in Fig. 2.2, which depicts two layers. Note that for simplicity, we depict the edges in Fig. 2.2 as undirected. The cross-connect equipment represented by the nodes of Layer U ("upper layer") connect to their counterpart nodes in Layer L ("lower layer") by interlayer links, depicted as lightly dashed vertical lines. While this model has no specific geographical correlation, we note that the switching or cross-connect equipment represented in Layer U usually are colocated in the same buildings/locations (central offices in carrier networks) as their lower-layer counterparts in Layer L. In such representations, the interlayer links are called *intra-office* links. The links of Layer U are transported as connections in lower Layer L. For example, Fig. 2.2 highlights a link between nodes 1 and 6 of layer U. This link is transported via a connection between nodes 1 and 6 of Layer L. The path of this connection is shown through nodes (1, 2, 3, 4, 5, 6) at Layer L.

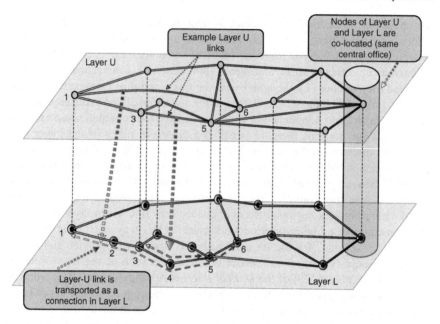

Fig. 2.2 Example of network layering

Another example is given by the link between nodes 3 and 5 of Layer U. This routes over nodes $(3, 4, 5)$ in Layer L. As this layered model illustrates, the concept of a "link" is a logical construct, even in lower "physical layer(s)". Along these lines, we identify some interesting observations in Fig. 2.2:

1. There are more nodes in Layer L than in Layer U.
2. When viewed as separate abstract graphs, the degree of logical connectivity in Layer L is less than that for Layer U. For example, there are at the most three edge-diverse paths between nodes 1 and 6 in layer U. However, there are at the most, only two edge-diverse paths between the corresponding pair of nodes in Layer L.
3. When we project the links of Layer U onto their connection paths in Layer L, we see some overlap. For example, the two logical links highlighted in Layer U overlap on links $(3, 4)$ and $(4, 5)$ of Layer L.

These observations generalize to the network layers associated with the IP backbone and affect how network layers are designed and how network failures at various layers affect higher-layer networks. The second observation says that while the logical topology of an upper-layer network, such as the IP layer, looks like it has many alternate paths to accommodate network disruptions, this can be deceiving unless one incorporates the lower-layer dependencies. For example, if link 3–4 of Layer L fails, then both links 1–6 and 3–5 of Layer U fail. Put more generally, failures of links of lower-layer networks usually cause multiple link failures in higher-layer networks. Specific examples will be described in Section 2.3.2.

2.2.3   Snapshot of Today's Core Network Layers

Figure 2.3 provides a representation of the set of services that might be provided by a large US-based carrier, and how these services map onto different network layers in the core segment. This figure is borrowed from [11] and depicts a mixture of legacy network layers (i.e., older technologies slowly being phased out) and current or emerging network layers. For a connection-oriented network layer (call it layer L), demand for connections comes from two sources: (1) links of higher network layers that route over layer L and (2) demand for telecommunications services provided by layer L but which originate outside layer L's network segment. The second source of demand is depicted by rounded rectangles in Fig. 2.3. Note that Fig. 2.3 is a significant simplification of reality; however, it does capture most predominant layers and principal interlayer relationships relevant to our objectives. Note that an important observation in Fig. 2.3 is that links of a given layer can be spread over multiple lower layers including "skipping" over intermediate lower layers.

Before we describe these layers, we provide some preliminary background on Time Division Multiplexing (TDM), whose signals are often used to transport links of the IP layer. Table 2.1 summarizes the most common TDM transmission rates. The Synchronous Optical Network (SONET) digital-signal standard [35], pioneered

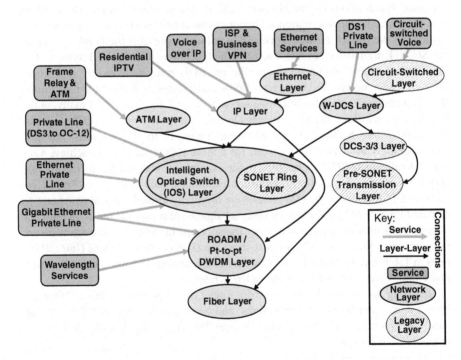

Fig. 2.3 Example of core-segment network layers

Table 2.1 Time division multiplexing (TDM) digital hierarchy (partial list)

Approximate rate	DS-n	Plesiosynchronous	SONET	SDH	OTN wrapper
64 Kb/s	DS-0	E0			
1.5 Mb/s	DS-1				
2.0 Mb/s		E-1			
34 Mb/s		E-3			
45 Mb/s	DS-3				
51.84 Mb/s			STS-1	VC-3	
155.5 Mb/s			OC-3	STM-1	
622 Mb/s			OC-12	STM-3	
2.5 Gb/s			OC-48	STM-16	ODU-1
10 Gb/s			OC-192	STM-48	ODU-2
40 Gb/s			OC-768	STM-192	ODU-3
100 Gb/s					ODU-4

Kb/s = kilobits per second; Mb/s = megabits per second; Gb/s = gigabits per second.
OTN line rates are higher than payload. ODU-2 includes 10 GigE and ODU-3 includes 40 GigE (under development). ODU-4 only includes 100 GigE

by Bellcore (now Telcordia) in the early 1990s, is shown in the fourth column of Table 2.1. SONET is the existing higher-rate digital-signal hierarchy of North America. Synchronous Digital Hierarchy (SDH) is a similar digital-signal standard later pioneered by the International Telecommunication Union (ITU-T) and adopted by most of the rest of the world. The DS-n column represents the North American pre-SONET digital-signal rates, most of which originated in the Bell System. The Plesiosynchronous column represents the pre-SDH rates used mostly in Europe. However, after nearly 30 years, both DS-n and Plesiosynchronous are still quite abundant and their related private-line services are still sold actively. Finally, in the last column, we show the more recent *Optical Transport Network (OTN)* signals, also standardized by the ITU-T [18]. Development of the OTN signal standards were originally motivated by the need for a more robust standard to achieve very high bit rates in *DWDM* technologies; for example, it was needed to incorporate and standardize various bit-error recovery techniques, such as *Forward Error Correction (FEC)*. As such, the OTN rates were originally termed "digital wrappers" to contain high rate SONET, SDH, or Ethernet signals, plus provide the extra fault notification information needed to reliably transport the high rates. Although there are many protocol layers in OTN, we just show the *Optical channel Data Unit (ODU)* rates in Table 2.1. To minimize confusion, in the rest of this chapter, we will mostly give examples in terms of DS-n and SONET rates.

Referring back to the layered network model of the previous section, Table 2.2 gives some examples of the nodes, links, and connections in Fig. 2.3. We only list those layers that have relevance to the IP layer. We will briefly describe these layers in the following sections.

Table 2.2   Examples of nodes, links, and connections for network layers of Fig. 2.3

Core layer	Typical node	Typical link	Typical connection
IP	Router	SONET OC-n, 1/10 gigabit Ethernet, ODU-n	IP is connection-less
Ethernet	Ethernet switch or router with Ethernet functionality	1/10 Gigabit Ethernet or rate-limited Ethernet private line	Ethernet can refer to both connection-less and connection-oriented services
Asynchronous transfer mode (ATM)	ATM switch	SONET OC-12/48	Permanent virtual circuit (PVC), Switched virtual circuit (SVC)
W-DCS	Wideband digital cross-connect system (DCS)	SONET STS-1 (channelized)	DS1
SONET Ring	SONET add-drop multiplexer (ADM)	SONET OC-48/192	SONET STS-n, DS-3
IOS	Intelligent optical switch (IOS) or broadband digital cross-connect system (DCS)	SONET OC-48/192	SONET STS-n
DWDM	Point-to-point DWDM terminal or reconfigurable optical add-drop multiplexer (ROADM)	DWDM signal	SONET, SDN, or 1/10/100 gigabit Ethernet
Fiber	Fiber patch panel or cross-connect	Fiber optic strand	DWDM signal or SONET, SDH, or Ethernet signal

2.2.4   Fiber Layer

The commercial intercity fiber layer of the USA is privately owned by multiple carriers. In addition to owning fiber, carriers lease bundles of fiber from one another using various long-term *Indefeasible Right of Use (IROU)* contracts to cover needed connectivity in their networks. Fiber networks differ significantly between metro and rural areas. In particular, in carrier metro networks, optical fiber cables are usually placed inside PVC pipes, which are in turn placed inside concrete conduits. Additionally, fiber for core networks is often corouted in conduit or along rights-of-way with metro fiber. Generally, in metro areas, optical cables are routed and spliced between central offices. In the central office, most carriers prefer to connect the fibers to a fiber patch panel. Equipment that use (or will eventually use) the interoffice fibers are also cross-connected into the patch panels. This gives the carrier flexibility to connect equipment by simply connecting fiber patch cords on the patch panels. Rural areas differ in that there are often long distances between central offices and, as such, intermediate huts are used to splice fibers and place equipment, such as optical amplifiers.

2.2.5 DWDM Layer

Although many varieties of DWDM systems exist, we show a simplified view of a (one-way) point-to-point DWDM system in Fig. 2.4. Here, *Optical Transponders (OTs)* are *Optical-Electrical-to-Optical (O-E-O)* converters that input optical digital signals from routers, switches, or other transmission equipment using a receive device, such as a photodiode, on the *add/drop* side of the OT. The input signal has a standard intra-office wavelength, denoted by λ_0. The OT converts the signal to electrical form. Various other physical layer protocols may be applied at this point, such as incorporating various handshaking called *Link Management Protocols (LMPs)* between the transmitting equipment and the receiving OT. A transponder is in *clear channel* mode if it does not change the transport protocols of the signal that it receives and essentially remains invisible to the equipment connecting to it. For example, *Gigabit Ethernet (GigE)* protocols from some routers or switches sometimes incorporate signaling messages to the far-end switch in the interframe gaps. If clear channel transmission is employed by the OT, such messages will be preserved as they are routed over the DWDM layer.

After conversion to electrical form, the signal is retransmitted using a laser on the *network* or *line-side* of the OT. However, typical of traditional point-to-point systems, the wavelength of the laser is fixed to correspond to the wavelength assigned to a specific channel of the DWDM system, λ_k. The output light pulses from multiple OTs at different wavelengths are then multiplexed into a single fiber by sending them through an optical multiplexer, such as an *Arrayed Waveguide Grating*

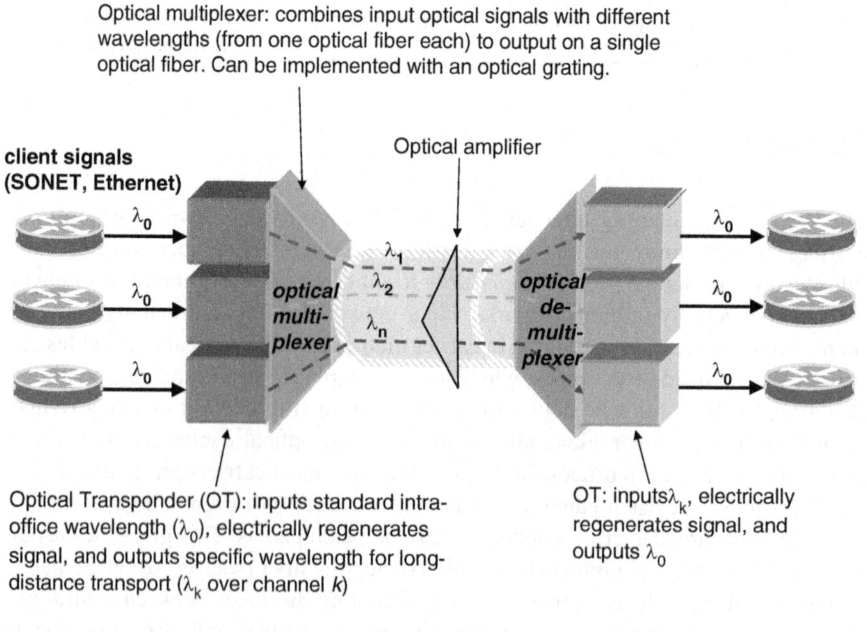

Optical multiplexer: combines input optical signals with different wavelengths (from one optical fiber each) to output on a single optical fiber. Can be implemented with an optical grating.

client signals
(SONET, Ethernet)

Optical amplifier

Optical Transponder (OT): inputs standard intra-office wavelength (λ_0), electrically regenerates signal, and outputs specific wavelength for long-distance transport (λ_k over channel k)

OT: inputs $\lambda_{k'}$, electrically regenerates signal, and outputs λ_0

Fig. 2.4 Simplified view of point-to-point DWDM system

(AWG) or similar device. If the distance between the DWDM terminals is sufficiently long, optical amplifiers are used to boost the power of the signal. However, power balancing among the DWDM channels is a major concern of the design of the DWDM system, as are other potential optical impairments. These topics are beyond the scope of this chapter. On the right side of Fig. 2.4, typically, the same (or similar) optical multiplexer is used in reverse, in which case, it becomes an optical *demultiplexer*. The OTs on the right side (the receive direction of the DWDM system) basically work in reverse to the transmit direction described above, by receiving the specific interoffice wavelength, λ_k, converting to electrical, and then using a laser to generate the intra-office wavelength, λ_0.

Carrier-based DWDM systems are usually deployed in bidirectional configurations. To see this, the reader can visually reproduce the entire system in Fig. 2.4 and then flip it (mirror it) right to left. The multiplexed DWDM signal in the opposite direction is transmitted over a separate fiber. Therefore, even though the electronics and lasers of the one-way DWDM system in the reverse direction operate separately from the shown direction, they are coupled operationally. For example, the two fiber ports (receive and transmit) of the OT are usually deployed on the same line card and arranged next to one another.

Optical amplification is used to extend the distance between terminals of a DWDM system. However, multiple systems are required to traverse the continental USA. Connections can be established between different point-to-point DWDM systems in an intermediate CO via an *intermediate-regenerator* OT (not pictured in Fig. 2.4). An intermediate-regenerator OT has the same effect on a signal as back-to-back OTs. Since the signal does not have to be cross-connected elsewhere in the intermediate central office, cost savings can be achieved by omitting the intermediate lasers and receivers of back-to-back OTs. However, we note that most core DWDM networks have many vintages of point-to-point systems from different equipment suppliers. Typically, an intermediate-regenerator OT can only be used to connect between DWDM systems of the same equipment supplier.

A difficulty with deploying point-to-point DWDM systems is that in central offices that interface multiple fiber spans (i.e., the node in the fiber layer has degree >2), all connections demultiplex in that office and pass through OTs. OTs are typically expensive and it is advantageous to avoid their deployment where possible. A better solution is the Reconfigurable Optical Add-Drop Multiplexer (ROADM). We show a simplified diagram of a ROADM in Fig. 2.5. The ROADM allows for multiple interoffice fibers to connect to the DWDM system. Appropriately, it is often called a *multidegree ROADM* or *n-degree ROADM*. As Fig. 2.5 illustrates, the ROADM is able to optically (i.e., without use of OTs) cross-connect channel k (transmitting at wavelength λ_k) arriving on one fiber to channel k (wavelength λ_k) outgoing on another fiber. Note that the same wavelength must be used on the two fibers. This is called the *wavelength continuity* constraint. The ROADM can also be configured to terminate (or "drop") a connection at that location, in which case it is cross-connected to an OT to connect to routers, switches, or transmission equipment. A "dropped" connection is illustrated by λ_2 on the second fiber from the top on the left in Fig. 2.5 and an "added" connection is illustrated by λ_n on the bottom

Optical Transponders (OT) also provided in bidirectional
mode for regeneration at intermediate nodes

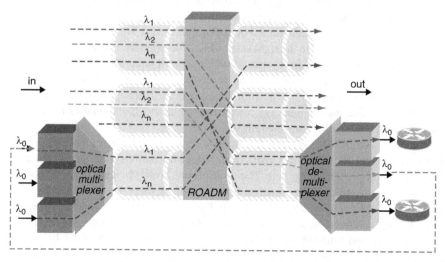

Fig. 2.5 Simplified view of Reconfigurable Optical Add-Drop Multiplexer (ROADM)

fiber on the left. As with the point-to-point DWDM system, optical properties of the system impose distance (also called *reach*) constraints.

Many transmission technologies, including optical amplification, are used to extend the distance between the optical add/drop points of a DWDM system. Today, this separation is designed to be about 1,500 km for a long-distance DWDM system, as a trade-off between cost and the all-optical distance for a US-wide network. Longer connections have to regenerate their signals, usually with an intermediate-regenerator OT. As with point-to-point DWDM systems, connections crossing ROADMS from different equipment suppliers usually must add/drop and connect through OTs.

We illustrate a representative ROADM layer for the continental USA in Fig. 2.6. The links represent fiber spans between ROADMS. As described above, to route a connection over the network of Fig. 2.6 may require points of regeneration. We also note, though, that today's core transport carriers usually have many vintages of DWDM technology and, thus, there may be several ROADM networks from different equipment suppliers, plus several point-to-point DWDM networks. All this complexity must be managed when routing higher-layer links, such as those of the IP backbone, over the DWDM layer.

We finish this introduction of the DWDM layer with a few observations. While most large carriers have DWDM technology covering their core networks, this is not generally true in the metro segment. The metro segment typically consists of a mixture of DWDM spans and fiber spans (i.e., spans with no DWDM). If fact, in metro areas usually only a fraction of central office fiber spans have DWDM technology routed over them. This affects how customers interface to the IP backbone network for higher-rate interfaces. Finally, we note that while most

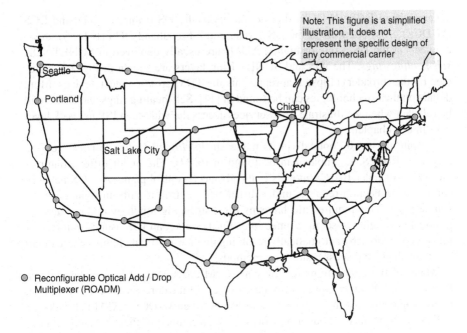

Note: This figure is a simplified illustration. It does not represent the specific design of any commercial carrier

○ Reconfigurable Optical Add / Drop
   Multiplexer (ROADM)

Fig. 2.6 Example of ROADM Layer topology

of the connections for the core DWDM layer arise from links of the IP layer, many of the connections come from what many colloquially call "wavelength services" (denoted by the rounded rectangle in Fig. 2.3). These come from high-rate private-line connections emanating from outside the core DWDM layer. Examples are links between switches of large enterprise customers that are connected by leased-line services.

2.2.6 TDM Cross-Connect Layers

In this section, we will briefly describe the TDM cross-connect layers. TDM cross-connect equipment can be basically categorized into two common types: a SONET/SDH *Add-Drop Multiplexer (ADM)* or a *Digital Cross-Connect System (DCS)*. Consistent with our earlier remark about the use of terminology, the latter often goes by a variety of colloquial or outmoded model names of equipment suppliers, such as DCS-3/1, DCS-3/3, DACS, and DSX. A TDM cross-connect device interfaces multiple high-rate digital signals, each of which uses time division multiplexing to break the signal into lower-rate channels. These channels carry lower-rate TDM connections and the TDM cross-connect device cross-connects the lower-rate signals among the channels of the different high-rate signals. Typically, an ADM only interfaces two high-rate signals, while a DCS interfaces many. However, over time these distinctions have blurred. Telcordia classified DCSs into three layers:

a narrowband DCS (N-DCS) cross-connects at the DS-0 rate, a wideband-DCS (W-DCS) cross-connects at the DS-1 rate, and a broadband-DCS (B-DCS) cross-connects at the DS-3 rate or higher. ADMs are usually deployed in SONET/SDH *self-healing rings*. The IOS and SONET Ring layers are shown in Fig. 2.3, encircled by the (broader) ellipse that represents the TDM cross-connect devices. More details on these technologies can be found in [11]. Self-healing rings and DCSs will be relevant when we illustrate how services access the wide-area ISP network layer later in this chapter.

Despite the word "optical" in its name, an *Intelligent Optical Switch (IOS)* is a type of B-DCS. Examples can be found in [6, 34]. The major differentiator of the IOS over older B-DCS models is its advanced control plane. An IOS network can route connection requests under distributed control, usually instigated by the source node. This requires mechanisms for distributing topology updates and internodal messaging to set up connections. Furthermore, an IOS usually can restore failed connections by automatically rerouting them around failed links. More detail is given when we discuss restoration methods.

Many of the connections for the core TDM-cross-connect layers (ring layers, DCS layers, IOS layer) come from higher layers of the core network. For example, many connections of the IOS layer are links between W-DCSs, ATM networks, or lower-rate portions of IP layer networks. However, much of their demand for connections comes from subwavelength private-line services, shown by the rounded rectangle in Fig. 2.3. A portion of this private-line demand is in the form of *Ethernet Private Line (EPL)* services. These services usually represent links between Ethernet switches or routers of large enterprise customers. For example, the Gigabit Ethernet signal from an enterprise customer's switch is transported over the metro network and then interfaces an Ethernet card either residing on the IOS itself or on an ADM that interfaces directly onto the IOS. The Ethernet card encapsulates the Ethernet frames inside concatenated $n \times$ STS-1 signals that are transported over the IOS layer. The customer can choose the rate of transport, and hence the value of n he/she wishes to purchase. The ADM Ethernet card polices the incoming Ethernet frames to the transport rate of $n \times$ STS-1.

2.2.7 IP Layer

The nodes of the IP layer shown in Fig. 2.3 represent routers that transport packets among metro area segments. IP generally define pairwise *adjacencies* between ports of the routers. In the IP backbone, these adjacencies are typically configured over SONET, SDH, or Ethernet, or OTN interfaces on the routers. As described above, these links are then transported as connections over the interoffice lower-layer networks shown in Fig. 2.3. Note that different links can be carried in different lower-layer networks. For example, lower-rate links may be carried over the TDM cross-connect layers (IOS or SONET Ring), while higher-rate links may be carried directly over the DWDM layer, thus "skipping" the TDM cross-connect layers. We will describe the IP layer in more detail in subsequent sections.

2.2.8 Ethernet Layer

The *Ethernet layer* in Fig. 2.3 refers to several applications of Ethernet technology. For example, Ethernet supports a number of physical layer standards that can be used for Layer 1 transport. Ethernet also refers to connection-oriented Layer 2 *pseudowire* services [16] and connection-less *transparent LAN* services. For example, intra-office links between routers often use an Ethernet physical layer riding on optical fiber.

An important application of Ethernet today is providing wide-area Layer 2 Virtual Private Network (VPN) services for enterprise customers. Although many variations exist, these services generally support enterprise customers that have Ethernet LANs at multiple locations and need to interconnect their LANs within a metro area or across the wide area. Most large carriers provide these services as an overlay on their IP layer, and hence, why we show the layered design in Fig. 2.3. Prior to the ability to provide such services over the IP layer, Ethernet private lines were supported by TDM cross-connect layers (i.e., Ethernet frames encapsulated over Layer 1 TDM private lines as described in Section 2.2.6). However, analogous to why wide-area Frame Relay displaced wide-area DS-0 private lines in the 1990s, wide-area packet networks are often more efficient than private lines to connect LANs of enterprise customers.

The principal approach that intermetro carriers use to provide wide-area Ethernet private network services is *Virtual Private LAN Service (VPLS)* [24, 25]. In this approach, carriers provide such Ethernet services with routers augmented with appropriate Ethernet capabilities. The reason for this approach is to provide the robust carrier-grade network capabilities provided by routers. With wide-area VPLS, the enterprise customer is connected via the metro network to the edge routers on the edge of the core IP layer. We describe how the metro network connects to the core IP layer network in the next section. The VPLS architecture is described in more detail in Section 2.4.2 when we describe MPLS.

We conclude this section with the comment that standards organizations and industry forums (e.g., IEEE, IETF, and Metro Ethernet Forum) have explored the use of Ethernet switches with upgraded carrier-grade network control protocols rather than using routers as nodes in the IP layer. For example, see *Provider Backbone Transport (PBT)* [27] and *Provider Backbone Bridge – Traffic Engineering (PBB-TE)* [15]. However, most large ISPs are deploying MPLS-based solutions. Therefore, we concentrate on the layering architecture shown in Fig. 2.3 in the remainder of this chapter.

2.2.9 Miscellaneous/Legacy Layers

For completeness, we depict other "legacy" network layers with dashed ovals in Fig. 2.3. These technologies have been around for decades in most carrier-based core networks. They include network layers whose nodes represent ATM switches, Frame-Relay switches, DCS-3/3s (a B-DCS that cross-connects DS3s), Voice-switches (DS-0 circuit switches), and pre-SONET ADMs. Most of these layers are not material to the spirit of this chapter and we do not discuss them here.

2.3 Structure of Today's Core IP Layer

2.3.1 Hierarchical Structure and Topology

In this chapter, we further break the IP layer into *Access Routers (ARs)* and *Backbone Routers (BRs)*. Customer equipment homes to access routers, which in turn home onto backbone routers. An AR is either colocated with its backbone routers or not; the latter is called a *Remote Access Router (RAR)*. Of course, there are alternate terminologies. For example, the IETF defines similar concepts to customer equipment, access routers, and backbone routers with its definitions, respectively, of *Customer-Edge (CE)* equipment, *Provider-Edge (PE)* routers, and *Provider (P)* routers. A simplified picture of a typical central office containing both ARs and BRs is shown in Fig. 2.7. Access routers are *dual-homed* to two backbone routers to enable higher levels of service availability. The links between routers in the same office are typically Ethernet links over intra-office fiber. While we show only two ARs in

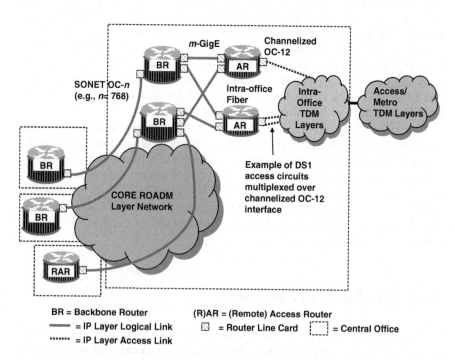

Fig. 2.7 Legacy central office interconnection diagram (Layer 3)

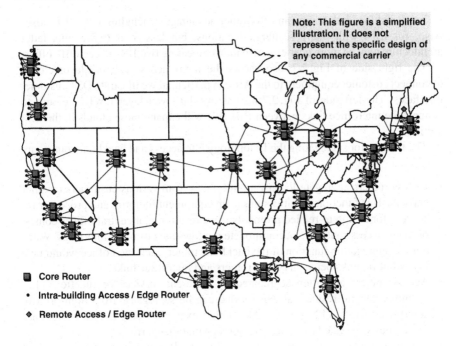

Note: This figure is a simplified illustration. It does not represent the specific design of any commercial carrier

■ Core Router

• Intra-building Access / Edge Router

◆ Remote Access / Edge Router

Fig. 2.8 Example of IP layer switching hierarchy

Fig. 2.7, note that typically there are many ARs in large offices. Also, due to scaling and sizing limitations, there may be more than two backbone routers or switches per central office used to further aggregate AR traffic before it enters the BRs.

Moreover, we show a remote access router that homes to one of the BRs. Figure 2.8 illustrates this homing arrangement in a broader network example, where small circles represent ARs, diamonds represent RARs, and large squares represent BRs. Note that remote ARs are homed to BRs in different offices. Homing remote ARs to BRs in different central offices raises network availability. However, a stronger motivation for doing this is that RAR–BR links are usually routed over the DWDM layer, which generally does not offer automatic restoration, and so the dual-homing serves two purposes: (1) protect against BR failure or maintenance activity and (2) protect against failure or maintenance of a RAR–BR link.

While the homing scheme described here is typical of large ISPs, other variations exist. For example, there are dual-homing architectures where (nonremote) ARs are homed to a BR colocated in the same central office and then a second BR in a different central office. While this latter architecture provides a slightly higher level of network availability against broader central office failure, it can be more costly owing to the need to transport the second AR–BR link. However, the latter architecture allows more load balancing across BRs because of the extra flexibility in homing ARs.

Improved load balancing can offer other advantages, including lower BR costs. Also, for ISPs with many scattered locations, but less total traffic, this latter architecture may be more cost-effective than colocating two BRs in each BR-office. The right side of Fig. 2.7 also shows the metro/access network-layer clouds to connect customer equipment to the ARs. In particular, we illustrate DS1 customer interfaces. The left side of Fig. 2.7 also shows the lower-layer DWDM clouds to connect the interoffice links between BRs. We will expand these clouds in the next sections.

The reasons for segregating the IP topology into access and backbone routers are manifold:

- Access routers aggregate lower-rate interfaces from various customers or other carriers. This function requires significant equipment footprint and processor resources for customer-related protocols. As a result, major central offices consist of many access routers to accommodate the low-rate customer interfaces. Without the aggregation function of the backbone router, each such office would be a myriad of tie links between access routers and interoffice links.
- Access routers are often segregated by different services or functions. For example, general residential ISP service can be segregated from high-priority enterprise private VPN service. As another example, some access routers are sometimes segregated to be peering points with other carriers.
- Backbone routers are primarily designed to be IP-transport switches equipped only with the highest speed interfaces. This segregation allows the backbone routers to be optimally configured for interoffice IP forwarding and transport.

2.3.2 Interoffice Topology

Figure 2.9 expands the core lower ROADM Layer cloud of Fig. 2.7. It shows ports of interoffice links between BRs connecting to ports on ROADMs. These links are transported as connections in the ROADM network. For example, today these links go up to 40 gigabits per second (Gb/s) or SONET OC-768. These connections are routed optically through intermediate ROADMs and regenerated where needed, as described in Section 2.2.5. Also, we note that the link between the remote ARs and BRs route over the same ROADM network, although the rate of this RAR–BR link may be at lower rate, such as 10 Gb/s. Figure 2.10 shows a network-wide example of the IP layer interoffice topology. There are some network-layering principles illustrated in Fig. 2.10 that we will describe. First, if we compare the IP layer topology of Fig. 2.8 with that of the DWDM layer (ROADM layer) of Fig. 2.10, we note that there is more connectivity in the IP layer graph than the DWDM layer. The reason for this is the existence of what many IP layer planners call *express* links. If we examine the link labeled "direct link" between Seattle and Portland, we find that when we route this link over the DWDM layer topology, there are no intermediate ROADMs. In fact, there are two types of direct links. The first type connects through

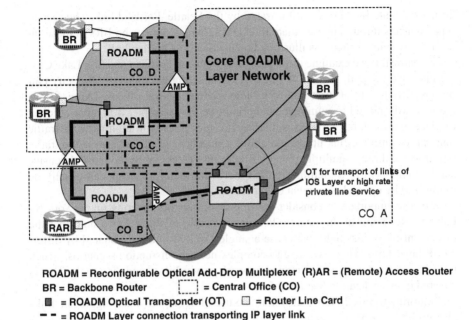

ROADM = Reconfigurable Optical Add-Drop Multiplexer (R)AR = (Remote) Access Router
BR = Backbone Router   [ⵊ⵿⵿] = Central Office (CO)
▣ = ROADM Optical Transponder (OT)   ▢ = Router Line Card
▬ ▬ = ROADM Layer connection transporting IP layer link

Fig. 2.9 Core ROADM Layer diagram

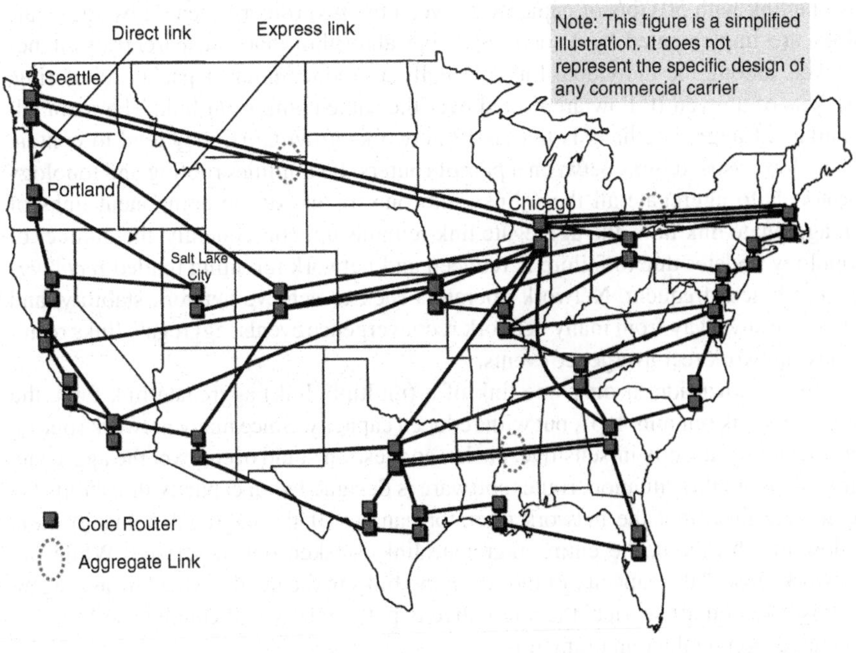

Direct link   Express link

Note: This figure is a simplified
illustration. It does not
represent the specific design of
any commercial carrier

Seattle

Portland

Chicago

Salt Lake
City

▣ Core Router

⊙ Aggregate Link

Fig. 2.10 Example of IP layer interbackbone topology

no intermediate ROADMs, as illustrated by the Seattle–Portland link. The second type connects through intermediate ROADMS, but encounters no BRs in those intermediate central offices, as illustrated by the Seattle–Chicago link.

In contrast, if we examine the express link between Portland and Salt Lake City, we find that any path in the DWDM layer connecting the routers in that city pair bypasses routers in at least one of its intermediate central offices. Express links are primarily placed to minimize network costs. For example, it is more efficient to place express links between well-chosen router pairs with high network traffic (enough to raise the link utilization above a threshold level); otherwise the traffic will traverse through multiple routers. Router interfaces can be the most-expensive single component in a multilayered ISP network; therefore, costs can usually be minimized by optimal placement of express links.

It is also important to consider the impact of network layering on network reliability. Referring to the generic layering example of Fig. 2.2, we note that the placement of express links can cause a single DWDM link to be shared by different IP layer links. This gives rise to complex network disruption scenarios, which must be modeled using sophisticated network survivability modeling tools. This is covered in more detail in Section 2.5.3.

Returning to Fig. 2.10, we also note the use of *aggregate links*. Aggregate links also go by other names, such as *bundled links* and *composite links*. An aggregate link bundles multiple physical links between a pair of routers into a single virtual link from the point of view of the routers. For example, an aggregate link could be composed of five OC-192 (or 10 GigE) links. Such an aggregate link would appear as one link with 50 Gb/s of capacity between the two routers. Generally, aggregate links are implemented by a load-balancing algorithm that transparently switches packets among the individual links. Usually, to reduce jitter or packet reordering, packets of a given IP flow are routed over the same component link. The main advantage of aggregate links is that as IP networks grow large, they tend to contain many lower-speed links between a pair of routers. It simplifies routing and topology protocols to aggregate all these links into one. If one of the component links of an aggregate link fails, the aggregate link remains up; consequently, the number of topology updates due to failure is reduced and network rerouting (called *reconvergence*) is less frequent. Network operators seek to achieve network stability, and therefore shy away from many network reconvergence events; aggregate links result in less network reconvergence events.

On the downside, if only one link of a (multiple link) aggregate link fails, the aggregate link remains "up", but with reduced capacity. Since many network routing protocols are capacity in-sensitive, packet congestion could occur over the aggregate link. To avoid this situation, router software is designed with capacity thresholds for aggregate links that the network operator can set. If the aggregate capacity falls below the threshold, the entire aggregate link is taken out of service. While the network "loses" the capacity of the surviving links in the bundle when the aggregate link is taken out of service, the alternative is potentially significant packet loss due to congestion on the remaining links.

2.3.3   Interface with Metro Network Segment

Figure 2.11 is a blowup of the clouds on the right side of Fig. 2.7. It provides a simplified example of how three business ISP customers gain access to the IP backbone. These could be enterprise customers with multiple branches who subscribe to a VPN service. Each access method consists of a DS1 link encapsulating IP packets that is transported across the metro segment. In carrier vernacular, using packet/TDM links to access the IP backbone is often called *TDM backhaul*. We do not show the inner details of the metro network here. Detailed examples can be found in [11]. Even suppressing the details of the complex metro network, the TDM backhaul is clearly a complicated architecture. To aid his/her understanding, we suggest the reader to refer back to the TDM hierarchy shown in Table 2.1.

The customer's DS-1 (which carries encapsulated IP packets) interfaces to a low-speed multiplexer located in the customer building, such as a small SONET ADM. This ADM typically serves as one node of a SONET ring (usually a 2-node ring). Each link of the ring is routed over diverse fiber, usually at OC-3 or OC-12 rate. Eventually, the DS-1 is routed to a SONET OC-48 or OC-192 ring that has one of its ADMs in the POP. The DS-1 is transported inside an STS-1 signal that is divided into 28 time slots called *channels* (a *channelized* STS-1), as specified by the SONET standard. The ADM routes all the SONET STS-1s carrying DS-1 traffic bound for the core carrier to a metro W-DCS. Note that there are often multiple

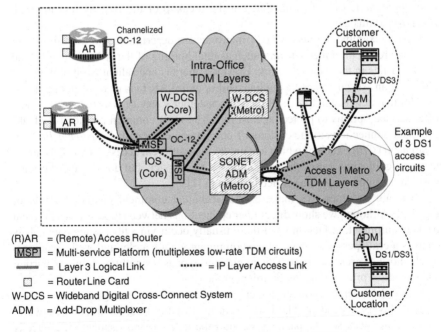

Fig. 2.11 Legacy central office interconnection diagram (intra-office TDM layers)

core carriers in a POP, and hence, the metro W-DCS cross-connects all the DS-1s destined for a given core carrier into channelized STS-1s and hands them off to the core W-DCS(s) of that core carrier. However, note that this handoff does not occur directly between the two W-DCSs, but rather passes through a higher-rate B-DCS, in this case the Intelligent Optical Switch (IOS) introduced in Section 2.2.6. The IOS cross-connects most of the STS-1s (multiplexed into OC-n interfaces) in a central office. Also, notice that the IOS is fronted with *Multi-Service Platforms (MSPs)*. An MSP is basically an advanced form of SONET ADM that gathers many types of lower-speed TDM interfaces and multiplexes them up to OC-48 or OC-192 for the IOS. It usually also has Ethernet interfaces that encapsulate IP packets into TDM signals (e.g., for Ethernet private line discussed earlier). The purpose of such a configuration is to minimize the cost and scale of the IOS by avoiding using its interface bay capacity for low-speed interfaces.

Finally, the core W-DCS cross-connects the DS1s destined for the access routers in the central office onto channelized STS-1s. Again, these STS-1s are routed to the AR via the IOS and its MSPs. The DS-1s finally reach a channelized SONET card on the AR (typically OC-12). This card on the AR de-multiplexes the DS-1s from the STS-1, de-encapsulates the packets, and creates a virtual interface for each of our three example customer access links in Fig. 2.11. The channelized SONET card is colloquially called a *CHOC* card (CHannelized OC-n).

Note that the core and metro carriers depicted in Fig. 2.11 may be parts of the same corporation. However, this complex architecture arose from the decomposition of long-distance and local carriers that was dictated by US courts and the *Federal Communications Commission (FCC)* at the breakup of the Bell System in 1984. It persists to this day.

If we reexamine the above TDM metro access descriptions, we find that there are many restoration mechanisms, such as dual homing of the ARs to the BRs and SONET rings in the metro network. However, there is one salient point of potential failure. If an AR customer-facing line card or entire AR fails or is taken out of service for maintenance in Fig. 2.11, then the customer's service is also down. Carriers offer service options to protect against this. The most common provide two TDM backhaul connections to the customer's equipment, often called *Customer Premise Equipment (CPE)*, each of which terminates on a different access router. This architecture significantly raises the availability of the service, but does incur additional cost. An example of such a service is given in [1].

To retain accuracy, we make a final technical comment on the example of Fig. 2.11. Although we show direct fiber connections between the various TDM and packet equipment, in fact, most of these usually occur via a fiber patch panel. This enables a craftsperson to connect the equipment via a simple (and well-organized) patch chord or cross-connect. This minimizes expense, simplifies complex wiring, and expedites provisioning work orders in the CO.

Figure 2.12 depicts how customers access the AR via emerging metro packet network layers instead of TDM. Here, instead of the traditional TDM network, the customer accesses the packet core via Ethernet. The most salient difference is the substantially simplified architecture. Although many different types of services

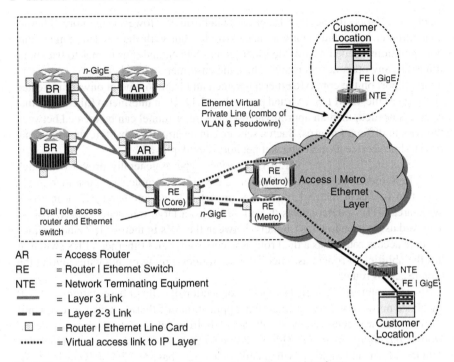

Fig. 2.12 Central office interconnection diagram (metro Ethernet interface)

are possible, we describe two fundamental types of Ethernet service: Ethernet virtual circuits and Ethernet VPLS. Most enterprise customers will use both types of services.

There are three basic types of connectivity for Ethernet virtual circuits: (1) intrametro, (2) ISP access via establishment of Ethernet virtual circuits between the customer location and IP backbone, and (3) intermetro. Since our main focus is the core IP backbone, we discuss the latter two varieties. For ISP access, in the example of Fig. 2.12, the customer's CPE interfaces the metro network via *Fast Ethernet (FE)* or GigE into a small Ethernet switch placed by the metro carrier called *Network Terminating Equipment (NTE)*. The NTE is the packet analog of the small ADM in the TDM access model in Fig. 2.11. For most metro Ethernet services, the customer can usually choose which policed access rate he/she wishes to purchase in increments of 1 Mb/s or similar. For example, he/she may wish 100 Mb/s for his/her *Committed Information Rate (CIR)* and various options for his/her *Excess Information Rate (EIR)*. The EIR options control how his bandwidth bursts are handled/shared when they exceed his CIR. The metro packet networks uses *Virtual Local Area Network (VLAN)* identifiers [14] and pseudowires or MPLS LSPs to route the customer's Ethernet virtual circuit to the metro Ethernet switch/router in the POP, as shown in Fig. 2.12. VLANs can also be used to segregate a particular customer's services, such as the two fundamental services (VPLS vs Internet access) described here. The *metro* Ethernet switch/router has high-speed links (such as 10 Gb/s) to the *core* Ethernet switch/router. However, the core Ethernet switch/router is fundamentally an access router, but with the needed features and configurations needed to provide Ethernet and VPLS, and thus homes to backbone routers as any other access router. Thus, the customer's virtual circuit is mapped to a virtual port on the core AR/Ethernet-Switch and from that point onward is treated similarly as the TDM DS-1 virtual port in Fig. 2.11. If an intermetro Ethernet virtual circuit is needed, then an appropriate pseudowire or tunnel can be created between the ARs in different metros. Such a service can eventually substitute for traditional private-line service as metro packet networks are deployed.

The second basic type of Ethernet service type is generally provided through the VPLS model described in Section 2.2.8. For example, the customer might have two LANs in metro-1, one LAN in metro-2 and another LAN in metro-3. Wide-area VPLS interconnects these LANs into a large transparent LAN. This is achieved using pseudowires (tunnels) between the ARs in metros-1, 2, and 3. Since the core access router has a dual role as access router and Ethernet VPLS switch, it has the abilities to route customer Ethernet frames among pseudowires among the remote access routers.

Besides enterprise Ethernet services, connection of cellular base stations to the IP backbone network is another important application of Ethernet metro access. Until recently, this was achieved by installing DS-1s from cell sites to circuit switches in *Mobile Telephone Switching Offices (MTSOs)* to provide voice service. However, with the advent and rapid growth of cellular services based on 3G or 4G technology, there is a growing need for high-speed packet-based transport from cell sites to the IP backbone. The metro Ethernet structure for this is similar to that of the enterprise customer access shown in Fig. 2.12. The major differences occur in the equipment at the cell site, the equipment at the MTSO, and then how this equipment connects to the access router/Ethernet switch of the IP backbone.

2.4 Routing and Control in ISP Networks

2.4.1 IP Network Routing

The IP/MPLS routing protocols are an essential part of the architecture of the IP backbone, and are key to achieving network reliability. This section introduces these control protocols.

An Interior Gateway Protocol (IGP) disseminates routing and topology information within an *Autonomous System (AS)*. A large ISP will typically segment its IP network into multiple autonomous systems. In addition, an ISP's network interconnects with its customers and with other ISPs. The *Border Gateway Protocol (BGP)* is used to exchange global reachability information with ASs operated by the same ISP, by different ISPs, and by customers. In addition, IP multicast is becoming more widely deployed in ISP networks, using one of several variants of the *Protocol-Independent Multicast (PIM)* routing protocol.

2.4.1.1   Routing with Interior Gateway Protocols

As described earlier, Interior Gateway Protocols are used to disseminate routing and topology information within an AS. Since IGPs disseminate information about topology changes, they play a critical role in network restoration after a link or node failure. Because of the importance of restoration to the theme of this chapter, we discuss this further in Section 2.5.2.

The two types of IGPs are distance vector and link-state protocols. In link-state routing [32], each router in the AS maintains a view of the entire AS topology using a *Shortest Path First (SPF)* algorithm. Since link-state routing protocols such as *Open Shortest Path First (OSPF)* [26] and *Intermediate System–Intermediate System (IS–IS)* [30] are the most commonly used IGPs among large ISPs, we will not discuss distance vector protocols further. For the purposes of this chapter, which focuses on network restoration, the functionality of OSPF and IS–IS are similar. We will use OSPF to illustrate how IGPs handle failure detection and recovery.

The view of network topology maintained by OSPF is conceptually a directed graph. Each router represents a vertex in the topology graph and each link between neighboring routers represents a unidirectional edge. Each link also has an associated weight (also called *cost*) that is administratively assigned in the configuration file of the router. Using the weighted topology graph, each router computes a shortest path tree (SPT) with itself as the root, and applies the results to build its forwarding table. This assures that packets are forwarded along the shortest paths in terms of link weights to their destinations [26]. We will refer to the computation of the shortest path tree as an *SPF computation*, and the resultant tree as an *SPF tree*.

As illustrated in Fig. 2.13, the OSPF topology may be divided into areas, typically resulting in a two-level hierarchy. Area 0, known as the "backbone area", resides at the top level of the hierarchy and provides connectivity to the nonbackbone areas (numbered 1, 2, etc.). OSPF typically assigns a link to exactly one area. Links may be in multiple areas, and multi-area links are addressed in more detail in Chapter 11 (Measurements of Control Plane Reliability and Performance by Aman Shaikh and Lee Breslau). Routers that have links to multiple areas are called *border routers*. For example, routers E, F and I are border routers in Fig. 2.13. Every router maintains its own copy of the topology graph for each area to which it is connected. The router performs an SPF computation on the topology graph for each area and thereby knows how to reach nodes in all the areas to which it connects. To improve scalability, OSPF was designed so that routers do not need to learn the entire topology of remote areas. Instead, routers only need to learn the total weight of the path from one or more area border routers to each node in the remote area. Thus, after computing the SPF tree for the area it is in, the router knows which border router to use as an intermediate node for reaching each remote node.

Every router running OSPF is responsible for describing its local connectivity in a *Link-State Advertisement (LSA)*. These LSAs are flooded reliably to other routers in the network, which allows them to build their local view of the topology. The flooding is made reliable by each router acknowledging the receipt of every LSA it receives from its neighbors. The flooding is hop-by-hop and hence does not depend

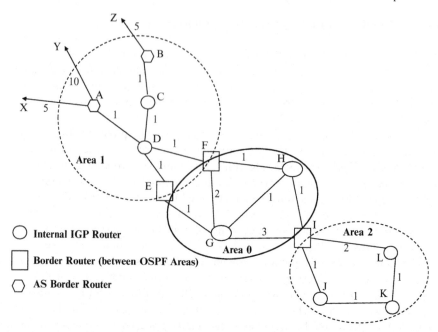

Fig. 2.13 OSPF topology: areas and hierarchy

on routing. The set of LSAs in a router's memory is called a *Link-State Database (LSDB)* and conceptually forms the topology graph for the router.

OSPF uses several types of LSAs for describing different parts of topology. Every router describes links to all its neighbor routers in a given area in a *Router LSA*. Router LSAs are flooded only within an area and thus are said to have an area-level flooding scope. Thus, a border router originates a separate Router LSA for every area to which it is connected. Border routers summarize information about one area and distribute this information to adjacent areas by originating *Summary LSAs*. It is through Summary LSAs that other routers learn about nodes in the remote areas. Summary LSAs have an area-level flooding scope like Router LSAs. OSPF also allows routing information to be imported from other routing protocols, such as BGP. The router that imports routing information from other protocols into OSPF is called an *AS Border Router (ASBR)*. Routers A and B are ASBRs in Fig. 2.13. An ASBR originates External LSAs to describe the external routing information. The External LSAs are flooded in the entire AS irrespective of area boundaries, and hence have an AS-level flooding scope. While the capability exists to import external routing information from protocols such as BGP, the number of such routes that may be imported may be very large. As a result, this can lead to overheads both in communication (flooding the external LSAs) as well as computation (SPF computation scales with the number of routes). As a consequence of the scalability problems they pose, the importing of external routes is rarely utilized.

Two routers that are neighbor routers have link-level connectivity between each other. Neighbor routers form an *adjacency* so that they can exchange routing information with each other. OSPF allows a link between the neighbor routers to be used for forwarding only if these routers have the same view of the topology, i.e., the same link-state database. This ensures that forwarding data packets over the link does not create loops. Thus, two neighbors have to make sure that their link-state databases are synchronized, and they do so by exchanging parts of their link-state databases when they establish an adjacency. The adjacency between a pair of routers is said to be "full" once they have synchronized their link-state databases. While sending LSAs to a neighbor, a router bundles them together into a *Link-State Update* packet. We will re-examine the OSPF reconvergence process in more detail when we discuss network disruptions in Section 2.5.2.1.

Although elegant and simple, basic OSPF is insensitive to network capacity and routes packets hop-by-hop along the SPF tree. As mentioned in Section 2.3.2, this has some potential shortcomings when applied to aggregate links. While aggregate-link capacity thresholds can be tuned to minimize this potentially negative effect, a better approach may be to use capacity-sensitive routing protocols, often called *Traffic Engineering (TE)* protocols, such as *OSPF-TE* [21]. Alternatively, one may use routing protocols with a greater degree of routing control, such as MPLS-based protocols. Traffic Engineering and MPLS are discussed later in this chapter.

2.4.1.2 Border Gateway Protocol

The Border Gateway Protocol is used to exchange routing information between autonomous systems, for example, between ISPs or between an ISP and its large enterprise customers. When BGP is used between ASs, it is referred to as *Exterior BGP (eBGP)*. When BGP is used within an AS to distribute external reachability information, it is referred to as *Interior BGP (iBGP)*. This section provides a brief summary of BGP. It is covered in much greater detail in Chapters 6 and 11.

BGP is a connection-oriented protocol that uses TCP for reliable delivery. A router advertises *Network Layer Reachability Information (NLRI)* consisting of an IP address prefix, a prefix length, a BGP next hop, along with path attributes, to its BGP peer. Packets matching the route will be forwarded toward the BGP next hop. Each route announcement can also have various attributes that can affect how the peer will prioritize its selection of the best route to use in its routing table. One example is the AS_PATH attribute which is a list of ASes through which the route has been relayed.

Withdrawal messages are sent to remove NLRI that are no longer valid. For example in Fig. 2.14, A|z denotes an advertisement of NLRI for IP prefix z, and W|s, r denotes that routes s and r are being withdrawn and should be removed from the routing table. If an attribute of the route changes, the originating router announces it again, replacing the previous announcement. Because BGP is connection-oriented, there are no refreshes or reflooding of routes during the lifetime of the BGP connection, which makes BGP simpler than a protocol like OSPF. However, like OPSF, BGP has various timers affecting behavior like hold-offs on route installation and route advertisement.

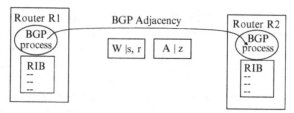

Fig. 2.14 BGP message exchange

BGP maintains tables referred to as *Routing Information Bases* (RIBs) containing BGP routes and their attributes. The Loc-RIB table contains the router's definitive view of external routing information. Besides routes that enter the RIB from BGP itself, routes enter the RIB via distribution from other sources, such as static or directly connected routes or routing protocols such as OSPF. While the notion of a "route" in BGP originally meant an IPv4 prefix, with the standardization of Multiprotocol BGP (MP-BGP) it can represent other kinds of reachability information, referred to as address families. For example, a BGP route can be an IPv6 prefix or an IPv4 prefix within a VPN.

External routes advertised in BGP must be distributed to every router in an AS. The hop-by-hop forwarding nature of IP requires that a packet address be looked up and matched against a route at each router hop. Because the address information may match external networks that are only known in BGP, every router must have the BGP information. However, we describe later how MPLS removes the need for every interior router to have external BGP route state.

Within an AS, the BGP next hop will be the IP address of the exit router or exit link from the AS through which the packet must route and BGP is used by the exit router to distribute the routes throughout the AS. To avoid creating a full mesh of iBGP sessions among the edge and interior routers, BGP can use a hierarchy of *Route Reflectors (RR)*. Figure 2.15 illustrates how BGP connections are constructed using a Route Reflector.

BGP routes may have their attributes manipulated when received and before sending to peers, according to policy design decisions of the operator. Of the BGP routes received by a BGP router, BGP first determines the validity of a route (e.g., is the BGP next hop reachable) and then chooses the best route among valid duplicates with different paths. The best route is decided by a hierarchy of tiebreakers among route attributes such as IGP metric to the next hop and BGP path attributes such as AS_PATH length. The best route is then relayed to all peers except the originating one. One variation of this relay behavior is that any route received from an iBGP peer on a nonroute reflector is not relayed to any other iBGP peer.

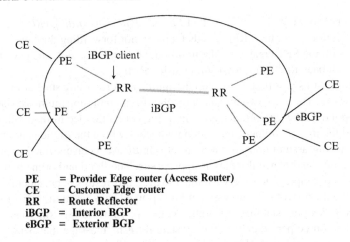

PE   = Provider Edge router (Access Router)
CE   = Customer Edge router
RR   = Route Reflector
iBGP = Interior BGP
eBGP = Exterior BGP

Fig. 2.15 BGP connections in an ISP with Route Reflectors (RR)

2.4.1.3 Protocol-Independent Multicast

IP Multicast is very efficient when a source sends data to multiple receivers. By using multicast at the network layer, a packet traverses a link only once, and therefore the network bandwidth is utilized optimally. In addition, the processing at routers (forwarding load) as well as at the end-hosts (discarding unwanted packets) is reduced. Multicast applications generally use UDP as the underlying transport protocol, since there is no unique context for the feedback received from the various receivers for congestion control purposes. We provide a brief overview of IP Multicast in this section. It is covered in greater detail in Chapter 11.

IP Multicast uses group addresses from the Class "D" address space (in the context of IPv4). The range of IP addresses that are used for IP Multicast group addresses is 224.0.0.0 to 239.255.255.255. When a source sends a packet to an IP Multicast group, all the receivers that have joined that group receive it. The typical protocol used between the end-hosts and routers is *Internet Group Management Protocol (IGMP)*. Receivers (end-hosts) announce their presence (join a multicast group) by sending an IGMP report to join a group. From the first router, the indication of the intent of an end-host to join the multicast group is forwarded through routers upwards along the shortest path to the root of the multicast tree. The root for an IP Multicast tree can be a source in a source-based distribution tree, or it may be a "rendezvous point" when the tree is a shared distribution tree. The routing protocol used in conjunction with IP multicast is called *Protocol-Independent Multicast (PIM)*. PIM has variants of the routing protocol used to form the multicast tree to forward traffic from a source (or sources) to the receivers. A router forwards a multicast packet only if it was received on the upstream interface to the source or to a rendezvous point (in a shared tree). Thus, a packet sent by a source follows the distribution tree. To avoid loops, if a packet arrives on an interface that is not on the shortest path toward the source of rendezvous point, the packet is discarded (and thus not forwarded). This is called *Reverse Path Forwarding (RPF)*, a critical aspect of multicast routing. RPF avoids loops by not forwarding duplicate packets. PIM relies on the SPT created by the traditional routing protocols such as OSPF to find the path back to the multicast source using RPF.

IP Multicast uses soft-state to keep the multicast forwarding state at the routers in the network. There are two broad approaches for maintaining multicast state. The first is termed *PIM-Dense Mode*, wherein traffic is first flooded throughout the network, and the tree is "pruned" back along branches where the traffic is not wanted. The underlying assumption is that there are multicast receivers for this group at most locations, and hence flooding is appropriate. The flood and prune behavior is repeated, in principle, once every 3 min. However, this results in considerable overhead (as the traffic would be flooded until it is pruned back) each time. Every router also ends up keeping state for the multicast group. To avoid this, the router downstream of a source periodically sends a "state refresh" message that is propagated hop-by-hop down the tree. When a router receives the state refresh message on the RPF interface, it refreshes the prune state, so that it does not forward traffic received subsequently, until a receiver joins downstream on an interface.

While PIM-Dense Mode is desirable in certain situations (e.g., when receivers are likely to exist downstream of each of the routers – densely populated groups – hence the name), *PIM-Sparse Mode (PIM-SM)* is more appropriate for wide-scale deployment of IP multicast for both densely and sparsely populated groups. With PIM-SM, traffic is sent only where it is requested, and receivers are required to explicitly join a multicast group to receive traffic. While PIM-SM uses both a shared tree (with a rendezvous point, to allow for multiple senders) as well as a per-source tree, we describe a particular mode, *PIM-Source Specific Multicast (PIM-SSM)*, which is more commonly used for IPTV distribution. More details regarding PIM-SM, including PIM using a shared tree, is described in Chapter 11. PIM-SSM is adopted when the end-hosts know exactly which source and group, typically denoted (S,G), to join to receive the multicast transmissions from that source. In fact, by requiring that receivers signal the combination of source and group to join, different sources could share the same group address and not interfere with each other. Using PIM-SSM, a receiver transmits an IGMP join message for the (S,G) and the first hop router sends a (S,G) join message directly along the shortest path toward the source. The shortest path tree is rooted at the source.

One of the key properties of IP Multicast is that the multicast routing operates somewhat independently of the IGP routing. Changes to the network topology are reflected in the unicast routing using updates that operate on short-time scales (e.g., transmission of LSAs in OSPF reflect a link or node failure immediately). However, IP Multicast routing reflects the changed topology only when the multicast state is refreshed. For example, with PIM-SSM, the updated topology is reflected only when the join is issued periodically (which can be up to a minute or more) by the receiver to refresh the state. We will examine the consequence of this for wide-area IPTV distribution later in this chapter.

2.4.2   *Multiprotocol Label Switching*

2.4.2.1   Overview of MPLS

Multiprotocol Label Switching (MPLS) is a technology developed in the late 1990s that added new capabilities and services to IP networks. It was the culmination of various IP switching technology efforts such as multiprotocol over ATM, Ipsilon's IP Switching, and Cisco's tag switching [7,20]. The key benefits provided by MPLS to an ISP network are:

1. Separation of routing (the selection of paths through the network) from forwarding/switching via IP address header lookup
2. An abstract hierarchy of aggregation

To understand these concepts, we first consider how normal IP routing in an ISP network functions. In an IP network without MPLS, there is a topology hierarchy with edge and backbone routers. There is also a routing hierarchy with BGP carrying external reachability information and an IGP like OSPF carrying internal reachability information. BGP carries the information about which exit router (BGP next hop) is used to reach external address space. OSPF picks the paths across the network between the edges (see Fig. 2.16). It is important to note that every OSPF router knows the complete path to reach all the edges. The internal paths that OSPF picks and the exit routers from BGP are determined before the first packet is forwarded. The connection-less and hop-by-hop forwarding behavior of IP routing requires that every router have this internal and external routing information present.

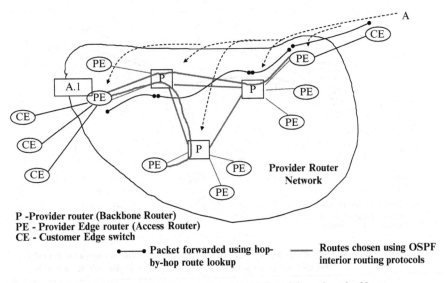

P -Provider router (Backbone Router)
PE - Provider Edge router (Access Router)
CE - Customer Edge switch

●———● Packet forwarded using hop-   ——— Routes chosen using OSPF
by-hop route lookup   interior routing protocols

Fig. 2.16 Traditional IP routing with external routes distributed throughout backbone

Consider the example in Fig. 2.16, where a packet enters on the left with address A.1 destined to the external network A on the upper right. When the first packet arrives, the receiving provider edge router (PE) looks up the destination IP address. From BGP, it learns that the exit router for that address is the upper right PE. From OSPF, the path to reach that exit PE is determined. Even though the ingress PE knows the complete path to reach the exit PE, it simply forwards the packet to the next-hop backbone router, labeled as a P-router (P) in the figure. The backbone router then repeats the process: using the packet IP address, it determines the exit from BGP and the path to the exit from OSPF to forward the packet to the next-hop BR. The process repeats again until the packet reaches the exit PE.

The repeated lookup of the packet destination to find the external exit and internal path appears to be unnecessary. The lookup operation itself is not expensive, but the issue is the unnecessary state and binding information that must be carried inside the network. The ingress router knows the path to reach the exit. If the packet could somehow be bound to the path itself, then the successive next-hop routers would only need to know the path for the packet and not its actual destination. This is what MPLS accomplishes.

Consider Fig. 2.17 where MPLS sets up an end-to-end *Label Switched Path (LSP)* by assigning labels to the interior paths to reach exits in the network. The LSP might look like the one shown in Fig. 2.18. The backbone routers are now called *Label Switch Routers (LSR)*. Via MPLS signaling protocols, the LSR knows how to forward a packet carrying an incoming label for an LSP to an outgoing interface and outgoing label; this is called a "swap" operation. The PE router also acts as an LSR, but is usually at the head (start) or end (tail) of the LSP where, respectively, the initial label is "pushed" onto the data or "popped" (removed) from the data.

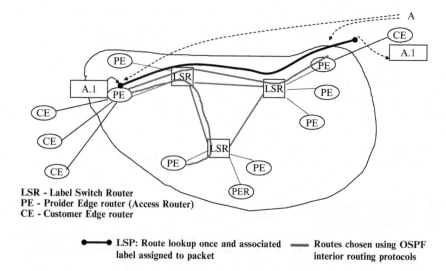

LSR - Label Switch Router
PE - Proider Edge router (Access Router)
CE - Customer Edge router

●————● LSP: Route lookup once and associated   ▬▬ Routes chosen using OSPF
label assigned to packet   interior routing protocols

Fig. 2.17 Routing with MPLS creates Label Switched Paths (LSP) for routes across the network

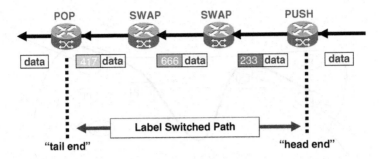

Fig. 2.18 Within an LSP, labels are assigned at each hop by the downstream router

In the example of Fig. 2.17, external BGP routing information such as routes to network A is only needed in the edges of the network. The interior LSRs only need to know the interior path among the edges as determined by OSPF. When the packet with address A.1 arrives at the ingress PE, the same lookup operation is done as previously: the egress PE is determined from BGP and the interior path to reach the egress is found from OSPF. But this time the packet is given a label for the LSP matching the OSPF path to the egress. The internal LSRs now forward the packet hop-by-hop based on the labels alone. At the exit PE, the label is removed and the packet is forwarded toward its external destination.

In this example, the binding of a packet to paths through the network is only done once – at the entrance to the network. The assignment of a packet to a path through the network is separated from the actual forwarding of the packet through the network (this is the first benefit that was identified above). Further, a hierarchy of forwarding information is created: the external routes are only kept at the edge of the network while the interior routers only know about interior paths. At the ingress router all received packets needing to exit the same point of the network receive the same label and follow the same LSP.

MPLS takes these concepts and generalizes them further. For example, the LSP to the exit router could be chosen differently from the IGP shortest path. IPv4 provides a method for explicit path forwarding in the IP header, but it is very inefficient. With MPLS, explicit routing becomes very efficient and is the primary tool for traffic engineering in IP backbones. In the previous example, if an interior link was heavily utilized, the operator may desire to divert some traffic around that link by taking a longer path as shown in Fig. 2.19. Normal IP shortest path forwarding does not allow for this kind of traffic placement.

The forwarding hierarchy can be used to create *provider-based VPNs*. This is illustrated in Fig. 2.20. Virtual private routing contexts are created at the PEs, one per customer VPN. The core of the network does not need to maintain state information about individual VPN routes. The same LSPs for reaching the exits of the network are used, but there are additional labels assigned for separating the different VPN states.

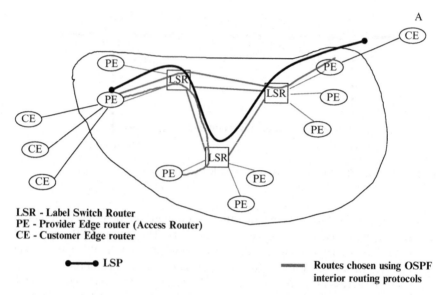

Fig. 2.19 MPLS with Traffic Engineering can use alternative to the IGP shortest path

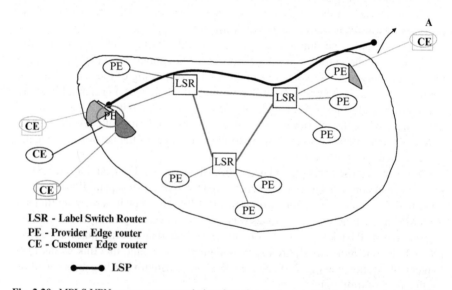

Fig. 2.20 MPLS VPNs support separated virtual routing contexts in PEs interconnected via LSPs

In summary, the advantages to the IP backbone of decoupling of routing and forwarding are:

- It achieves efficient explicit routing.
- Interior routers do not need any external reachability information.

- Packet header information is only processed at head of LSP (e.g., edges of the network).
- It is easy to implement nested or hierarchical identification (such as with VPNs).

2.4.2.2   Internet Route Free Core

The ability of MPLS to remove the external BGP information plus Layer 3 address lookup from the interior of the IP backbone is sometimes referred to as an *Internet Route Free Core*. The "interior" of the IP backbone starts at the left-side (BR-side) port of the access routers in Fig. 2.7. Some of the advantages of Internet Route Free Core include:

- Traffic engineering using BGP is much easier.
- Route reflectors no longer need to be in the forwarding plane, and thus can be dedicated to IP layer control plane functions or even placed on a server separate from the routers.
- *Denial of Service (DoS)* attacks and security holes are better controlled because BGP routing decisions only occur at the edges of the IP backbone.
- Enterprise VPN and other priority services can be better isolated from the "Public Internet".

We provide more clarification for the last advantage. Many enterprise customers, such as financial companies or government agencies, are concerned about mixing their priority traffic with that of the public Internet. Of course, all packets are mixed on links between backbone routers; however, VPN traffic can be functionally segregated via LSPs. In particular, since denial of service attacks from the compromised hosts on the public Internet rely on reachability from the Internet, the private MPLS VPN address space isolates VPN customers from this threat. Further, enterprise premium VPN customers are sometimes clustered onto access routers dedicated to the VPN service. Furthermore, higher performance (such as packet loss or latency) for premium VPN services can be provided by implementing priority queueing or providing them bandwidth-sensitive LSPs (discussed later). A similar approach can be used to provide other performance-sensitive services, such as Voice-over-IP (VoIP).

2.4.2.3   Protocol Basics

MPLS encapsulates IP packets in an MPLS header consisting of one or more MPLS labels, known as a label stack. Figure 2.21 shows the most commonly used MPLS encapsulation type. The first 20 bits are the actual numerical label. There are three bits for inband signaling of class of service type, followed by and End-of-Stack bit (described later) and a time-to-live field, which serves the same function as an IP packet time-to-live field.

MPLS encapsulation does not define a framing mechanism to determine the beginning and end of packets; it relies on existing underlying link-layer technologies.

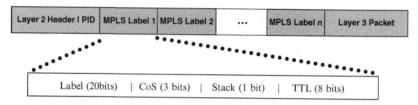

Fig. 2.21 Generic MPLS encapsulation and header fields

Existing protocols such as Ethernet, *Point-to-Point Protocol (PPP)*, ATM, and Frame Relay have been given new protocol IDs or new link-layer control fields to allow them to directly encapsulate MPLS-labeled packets.

Also, MPLS does not have a protocol ID field to indicate the type of packet encapsulated, such as IPv4, IPv6, Ethernet, etc. Instead, the protocol type of the encapsulated packet is implied by the label and communicated by the signaling protocol when the label is allocated.

MPLS defines the notion of a *Forwarding Equivalence Class (FEC)* (not to be confused with Forward Error Correction (FEC) in lower network layers defined earlier). All packets with the same forwarding requirements, such as path and priority queuing treatment, can belong to the same FEC. Each FEC is assigned a label. Many FEC types have been defined by the MPLS standards: IPv4 unicast route, VPN IPv4 unicast route, IPv6 unicast route, Frame Relay permanent virtual circuit, ATM virtual circuit, Ethernet VLAN, etc.

Labels can be stacked, with the number of stacked labels indicated by the end-of-stack bit. This allows hierarchical nesting of FECs, which permits VPNs, traffic engineering, and hierarchical routing to be created simultaneously in the same network. Consider the previous VPN example where a label may represent the interior path to reach an exit and an inner label may represent a VPN context.

MPLS is entitled "multiprotocol" because it can be carried over almost any transport as mentioned above, ironically even IP itself, and because it can carry the payload for many different packet types – all the FEC types mentioned above.

Signaling of MPLS FECs and their associated label among routers and switches can be done using many different protocols. A new protocol, the *Label Distribution Protocol (LDP)*, was defined specifically for MPLS signaling. However, existing protocols have also been extended to signal FECs and labels: *Resource Reservation Protocol (RSVP)* [3] and BGP, for example.

2.4.2.4 IP Traffic Engineering and MPLS

The purpose of IP traffic engineering is to enable efficient use of backbone capacity. That is, both to ensure that links and routers in the network are not congested and that they are not underutilized. Traffic engineering may also mean ensuring that certain performance parameters such as latency or minimum bandwidth are met.

To understand how MPLS traffic engineering plays a role in ISP networks, we first explain the generic problem to be solved – the multicommodity flow problem – and how it was traditionally solved in IP networks versus how MPLS can solve the problem.

Consider an abstract network topology with traffic demands among nodes. There are:

Demands $d(i, j)$ from node i to j
Constraints – link capacity $b(i, j)$ between nodes
Link costs $C(i, j)$
Path $p(k)$ or route for each demand

The traffic engineering problem is to find paths for the demands that fit the link constraints. The problem can be specified at different levels of difficulty:

1. Find any feasible solution, regardless of the path costs.
2. Find a solution that minimizes the costs for the paths.
3. Find a feasible or a minimum cost solution after deleting one or more nodes and/or links.

Traffic Engineering an IP Network

In an IP network, the capacities represent link bandwidths between routers and the costs might represent delay across the links. Sometimes, we only want to find a feasible solution, such as in a multicast IPTV service. Sometimes, we want to minimize the maximum path delay, such as in a Voice-over-IP service. And sometimes, we want to ensure a design that is survivable (meaning it is still feasible to carry the traffic) for any single- or dual-link failure.

Consider how a normal ISP without traffic engineering might try to solve the problem. The tools available on a normal IP network are:

- Metric manipulation, i.e., pick OSPF weights to create a feasible solution.
- Simple topology or link augmentation: this tends to overengineer the network and restrict the possible topology.
- Source or policy route using the IPv4 header option or router-based source routes. Source routes are very inefficient resulting in tremendously lower router capacity and they are not robust, making the network very difficult to operate.

Figure 2.22 illustrates a network with a set of demands and an example of the way that particular demands might be routed using OSPF. Although the network has sufficient total capacity to carry the demands, it is not possible to find a feasible solution (with no congested links) by only setting OSPF weights. A small ISP facing this situation without technology like MPLS would probably resort to installing more link capacity on the A-D-C node path.

The generic solution to an arbitrary traffic engineering problem requires specifying the explicit route (path) for each demand. This is a complex problem that can take an indeterminate time to solve. But there are other approaches that can solve a large subset of problems. One suboptimal approach is *Constraint-based Shortest*

Fig. 2.22 IP routing
is limited in its ability to meet
resource demands. It cannot
successfully route
the demands within the link
bandwidths in this example

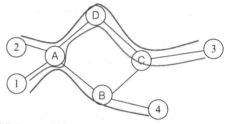

All link capacities = 1 unit, except C-3 = 2 units
Demand (2,3) = 0.75 units
Demand (1,3) = 0.4 units
Demand (1,4) = 0.4 units

Path First (CSPF). CSPF has been implemented in networks with ATM *Private Network-to-Network Interface (P-NNI)* and IP MPLS. For currently defined MPLS protocols, the constraints can be bandwidths per class of service for each link. Also, links can be assigned a set of binary values, which can be used to include or exclude the links from routing a given demand.

CSPF is implemented in a distributed fashion where all nodes have a full knowledge of network resource allocation. Then, each node routes its demands independently by:

1. Pruning the network to only feasible paths
2. Pick the shortest of the feasible paths on the pruned network

Although CSPF routing is suboptimal when compared with a theoretical multi-commodity flow solution, it is a reasonable compromise to solving many traffic engineering problems in which the nodes route their demands independently of each other. For more complex situations where CSPF is inadequate, network planners must use explicit paths computed by an offline system. The next section discusses explicit routing in more detail.

Traffic Engineering Using MPLS

The main problems with traffic engineering an IP backbone with only a Layer 3 IGP routing protocol (such as OSPF) are (1) lack of knowledge of resource allocation and (2) no efficient explicit routing. The previous example of Fig. 2.22 shows how OPSF would route all demands onto a link that does not have the necessary capacity. Another example problem is when a direct link is needed for a small demand between nodes to meet certain delay requirements. But OSPF cannot prevent other traffic demands from routing over this smaller link and causing congestion. MPLS solves this with extensions to OSPF (OSPF-TE) [21] to provide resource allocation knowledge and RSVP-TE [2] for efficient signaling of explicit routes to use those resources.

See Fig. 2.23 for a simple example of how an explicit path is created. RSVP-TE can create an explicit hop-by-hop path in the PATH message downstream. The PATH

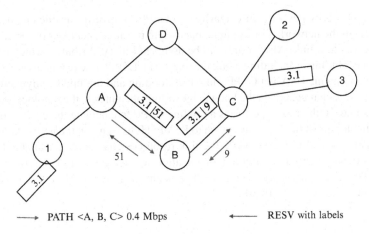

⟶ PATH <A, B, C> 0.4 Mbps   ⟵ RESV with labels

Fig. 2.23 RSVP messaging to set up explicit paths

Fig. 2.24 MPLS-TE enables
efficient capacity usage
through traffic engineering
to solve the example
in Fig. 2.22

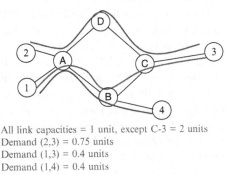

All link capacities = 1 unit, except C-3 = 2 units
Demand (2,3) = 0.75 units
Demand (1,3) = 0.4 units
Demand (1,4) = 0.4 units

message can request resources such as bandwidth. The return message is an RESV, which contains the label that the upstream node should use at each link hop. In this example, a traffic-engineered LSP is created along path A-B-C for 0.4 Mb/s. These LSPs are referred to as traffic engineering tunnels. Tunnels can be created and differentiated for many purposes (including restoration to be defined in later sections). But in general, primary (service route) tunnels can be considered as a routing mechanism for all packets of a given FEC between a given pair of routers or router interfaces. Using this machinery, Fig. 2.24 illustrates how MPLS-TE can be used to solve the capacity overload problem in the network shown in Fig. 2.22.

The explicit path used in RSVP-TE signaling can be computed by an offline system and automatically configured in the edge routers or the routers themselves can compute the path. In the latter case, the edge routers must be configured with the IP prefixes and their associated bandwidth reservations that are to be traffic-engineered to other edges of the network. Because the routers do this without knowledge of other demands being routed in the network, the routers must receive periodic updates about bandwidth allocations in the network.

OSPF-TE provides a set of extensions to OSPF to advertise traffic engineering resources in the network. For example, bandwidth resources per class of service can be allocated to a link. Also, a link can be assigned binary attributes, which can be used for excluding or including a link for routing an LSP. These resources are advertised in an opaque LSA via OSPF link-state flooding and are updated dynamically as allocations change. Given the knowledge of link attributes in the topology and the set of demands, the router performs an online CSPF to calculate the explicit paths. The path outputs of the CSPF are given to RSVP-TE to signal in the network. As TE tunnels are created in the network, the link resources change, i.e., available bandwidth is reduced on a link after a tunnel is allocated using RSVP-TE. Periodically, OSPF-TE will advertise the changes to the link attributes so that all routers can have an updated view of the network.

2.4.2.5 VPNs with MPLS

Figure 2.20 illustrates the key concept in how MPLS is used to create VPN services. VPN services here refer to carrier-based VPN services, specifically the ability of the service provider to create private network services on top of a shared infrastructure. For the purposes of this text, VPNs are of two basic types: a Layer 3 IP routed VPN or a Layer 2 switched VPN. *Generalized MPLS (GMPLS)* [19] can also be used for creating Layer 1 VPNs, which will not be discussed here.

A Layer 3 IP VPN service looks to customers of the VPN as if the provider built a router backbone for their own use – like having their own private ISP. VPN standards define the PE routers, CE routers, and backbone P-routers interconnecting the PEs. Although the packets share (are mixed over) the ISP's IP layer links, routing information and packets from different VPNs are virtually isolated from each other.

A Layer 2 VPN provides either point-to-point connection services or multipoint Ethernet switching services. Point-to-point connections can be used to support end-to-end services such as Frame Relay permanent virtual circuits, ATM virtual circuits, point-to-point Ethernet circuits (i.e., with no *Media Access Control (MAC)* learning or broadcasting) and even a circuit emulation over packet service. Interworking between connection-oriented services, such as Frame Relay to ATM interworking, is also defined. This kind of service is sometimes called a Virtual Private Wire Service (VPWS).

Layer 2 VPN multipoint Ethernet switching services support a traditional Transparent LAN over a wide-area network called Virtual Private LAN Service (VPLS) [24, 25].

Layer 3 VPNs over MPLS

As mentioned previously, Layer 3 VPNs maintain a separate virtual routing context for each VPN on the PE routers at the edge of the network. External CEs connect to the virtual routing context on a PE that belongs to a customer's VPN.

Layer 3 VPNs implemented using MPLS are often referred to as BGP MPLS VPNs because of the important role BGP has in the implementation. BGP is used to carry VPN routes between the edges of the network. BGP keeps the potentially overlapping VPN address spaces unique by prepending onto the routes a *route distinguisher (RD)* that is unique to each VPN. The RD + VPN IPv4 prefix combination creates a new unique address space carried by BGP, sometimes called the VPNv4 address space.

VPN routes flow from one virtual routing instance into other virtual routing instances on PEs in the network using a BGP attribute called a *Route Target (RT)*. An RT is an address configured by the ISP to identify all virtual routing instances that belong to a VPN. RTs constrain the distribution of VPN routes among the edges of the network so that the VPN routes are only received by the virtual routing instances belonging to the intended (targeted) VPN.

We note that RDs and RTs are only used in the BGP control plane – they are not values that are somehow applied to user packets themselves. Rather, for every advertised VPNv4 route, BGP also carries a label assignment that is unique to a particular virtual router on the advertising PE.

Every VPN packet that is forwarded across the network receives two labels at the ingress PE: an inner label associated with the advertised VPNv4 route and an outer label associated with the LSP to reach the egress advertising PE (dictated by the BGP next-hop address). See Fig. 2.25 for a simplified example. In this example,

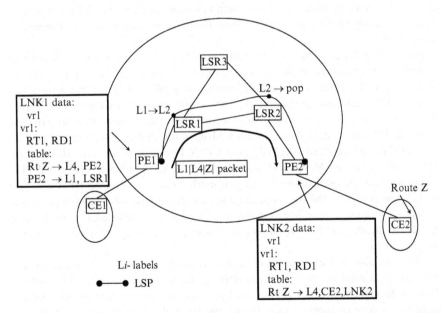

Fig. 2.25 In this VPN example, a virtual routing context (vr1) in the PEs contains the VPN label and routing information such as route target (RT1) and route distinguisher (RD1), attached CE interfaces, and next-hop lookup and label binding. VPN traffic is transported using a label stack of VPN label and interior route label

there is a VPN advertising a route Z, which enters the receiving virtual router (vr1) and is distributed by BGP to other PE virtual routers using RTs. A packet entering the VPN destined toward Z is looked up in the virtual routing instance, where the two labels are found – the outer label to reach the egress PE and the inner label for the egress virtual routing instance.

Layer 2 VPNs over MPLS

The implementation of Layer 2 VPNs over MPLS is similar to Layer 3 VPNs. Because there is no IP routing in the VPN service, there is instead a virtual switching context created on the edge PEs to isolate different VPNs. These virtual switching contexts keep the address spaces of the edge services from conflicting with each other across different VPNs.

Layer 2 VPNs use a two-label stack approach that is similar to Layer 3 VPNs. Reaching an egress PE from an ingress PE is done using the same network interior LSPs that the Layer 3 VPN service would use. And then, there is an inner label associated with either the VPWS or VPLS context at the egress PE. This inner label can be signaled using either LDP or BGP. The inner label and the packet encapsulation comprise a pseudowire, as defined in the PWE3 standards [16]. The pseudowire connects an ingress PE to an egress PE switching context and is identified by the inner label. The VPWS service represents a single point-to-point connection, so there will only be a single pseudowire setup in each direction. For VPLS however, carriers typically set up a full mesh of pseudowires/LSPs among all PEs belonging to that VPLS.

Forwarding for a VPWS is straightforward: the CE connection is associated with the appropriate pseudowires in each direction when provisioned. For VPLS, forwarding is determined by the VPLS forwarding table entry for the destination Ethernet MAC address. Populating the forwarding table is based on source MAC address learning. The forwarding table records the inbound interface on which a source MAC was seen. If the destination MAC is not in the table, then the packet is flooded to all interfaces attached to the VPLS. Flooding of unknown destination MACs and broadcast MACs follows some special rules within a VPLS. All PEs within a backbone are assumed to be full mesh connected with pseudowires. So, packets received from the backbone are not flooded again into the backbone, but are only flooded onto CE interfaces. On the other hand, packets from a CE to be flooded are sent to all attached CE interfaces and all pseudowire interfaces toward the other backbone PEs.

There is also a VPLS variation called Hierarchical VPLS to constrain the potential explosion of mesh point-to-point LSPs needed among the PE routers. This might happen with a PE that acts like a spoke with a single pseudowire attached to a core of meshed PEs. In this model, a flooding packet received at a mesh connected PE from a spoke PE pseudowire is sent to all attached CEs and pseudowires. In such a model, the PE interconnectivity must be guaranteed to be loop-free or a spanning tree protocol may be run among the PEs for that VPLS.

2.5   Network Restoration and Planning

The design of an IP backbone is driven by the traffic demands that need to be supported, and network availability objectives. The network design tools model the traffic carried over the backbone links not only in a normal "sunny day" scenario, but also in the presence of network disruptions.

Many carriers offer *Service Level Agreements (SLAs)*. SLAs will vary across different types of services. For example, SLAs for private-line services are quite different from those for packet services. SLAs also usually differ among different types of packet services. The SLAs for general Internet, VPN, and IPTV services will generally differ. A packet-based SLA might be expressed in terms of *Quality of Service (QoS)* metrics.for example, the SLA for a premium IP service may cover up to three QoS metrics: latency, jitter, and packet loss. An example of the latter is "averaged over time period Y, the customer will receive at least $X\%$ of his/her packets transmitted." Some of these packet services may be further differentiated by offering different levels of service, also called *Class of Service (CoS)*.

To provide its needed SLAs, an ISP establishes internal network objectives. Network availability is a key internal metric used to control packet loss. Furthermore, network availability is also sometimes used as the key QoS metric for private-line services. Network availability is often stated colloquially in "9s". For example, "four nines" of availability means the service is available at least 0.9999 of the time. Stated in the contra-positive, the service should not be down more than 0.0001 of the time (approximately 50 min per year). Given its prime importance, we will concentrate on network availability in the remainder of this section.

The single largest factors in designing and operating the IP backbone such that it achieves its target network availability are modeling its potential network disruptions and the response of the network to those disruptions. Network disruptions most typically are caused by network failures and maintenance activities. Maintenance activities include upgrading of equipment software, replacement of equipment, and reconfiguration of network topologies or line cards. Because of the complex layering and segmentation of networks surrounding the IP backbone and because of the variety and vintage of equipment that accumulates over the years, network planners, architects, network operators, and engineers spend considerable effort to maintain network availability. In this section, we will briefly describe the types of restoration methods we find at the various network layers. Then, we will describe how network disruptions affect the IP backbone, the types of restoration methods used to handle them, and finally how the network is designed to meet the needed availability.

Table 2.3 summarizes typical restoration methods used in some of today's network core layers that are most relevant to the IP backbone. See [11] for descriptions of restoration methods used in other layers shown in Fig. 2.3. In the next sections, we will describe the rows of this table. Note that the table is approximate and does not apply universally to all telecommunication carriers.

Table 2.3 Example of core-segment restoration methods

Network layer	Restoration method(s) against network failures that originate at that layer or lower layers	Exemplary restoration time scale
Fiber	No automatic rerouting	Hours (manual)
DWDM	1) Manual	1) Hours (manual)
	2) 1 + 1 restoration (also called *dedicated protection*)	2) 3–20 ms
SONET Ring	Bidirectional Line-Switched Rings (BLSR)	50–100 ms
IOS (DCS)	Distributed path-based mesh restoration	Sub-second to seconds
W-DCS	No automatic rerouting	Hours
IP backbone	1) IGP reconfiguration	1) 10–60 s
	2) MPLS Fast Reroute (FRR)	2) 50–100 ms

2.5.1 Restoration in Non-IP Layers

2.5.1.1 Fiber Layer

As we described earlier, in most central offices today, optical interfaces on switching or transport equipment connect to fiber patch panels. Some carriers have installed an automated fiber patch panel, also called a *Fiber Cross-Connect (FXC)*, which has the ability for an operator to remotely control the cross-connects. Some of the enabling technologies include physical crossbars using optical collometers and *Micro-Electro-Mechanical Systems (MEMS)*. A good overview of these technologies can be found in [12]. When disruptions occur to the fiber layer, most commonly from construction activity, network operators can reroute around the failed fiber by using a patch panel to cross-connect the equipment onto undamaged fibers. This may require coordination of cross-connects at intermediate central offices to patch a path through alternate COs if an entire cable is damaged. Of course, this typically is a slow manual process, as reflected in Table 2.3 and so higher-layer restoration is usually utilized for disruptions to the fiber layer.

2.5.1.2 DWDM Layer

Some readers may be surprised to learn that carriers have deployed few (if any) automatic restoration methods in their DWDM layers (neither metro nor core segment). The one type of restoration occasionally deployed is *one-by-one (1:1)* or *one-plus-one (1 + 1)* tail-end protection switching, which switches at the end-points of the DWDM layer connection. With 1 + 1 switching, the signal is duplicated and transmitted across two (usually) diversely routed connections. The path of the connection during the nonfailure state is usually called the *working path* (also called the *primary* or *service path*); the path of the connection during the failure state is called the *restoration path* (also called *protection path* or *backup path*). The receiver consists of a simple detector and switch that detects failure of the signal on the working path (more technically, detects performance errors such as average BER threshold crossings) and switches to the restoration path upon alarm. Once adequate signal performance is again achieved on the signal along the working path (including a time-out threshold to avoid link "flapping"), it switches back to the working path. In 1:1 protection switching, there is no duplication of signal, and thus the restoration connection can be used for other transport in nonfailure states. The transmitted signal is switched to the restoration path upon detection of failure of the service path and/or notification from the far end.

Technically speaking, in ROADM or Point-to-point DWDM systems, $1 + 1$ or 1:1 protection switching is usually implemented electronically via the optical transponders. Consequently, these methods can be implemented at other transport layers, such as DCS, IOS, and SONET. The major advantage of $1 + 1$ or 1:1 methods is that they can trigger in as little as 3–20 ms. However, because these methods require restoration paths that are dedicated (one-for-one) for each working connection, the resulting restoration capacity cannot be shared among other working connections for potential failures. Furthermore, the restoration paths are diversely routed and are often much longer than their working paths. Consequently, $1 + 1$ and 1:1 protection switching tend to be the costliest forms of restoration.

2.5.1.3 SONET Ring Layer

The two most common types of deployed SONET or SDH self-healing ring technology are *Unidirectional Path Switched Ring (UPSR-2F)* and *Bidirectional Line-Switched Ring (BLSR-2F)*. The "2F" stands for "2-Fibers". For simplicity, we will limit our discussion to SONET rings, but there is a very direct analogy for SDH rings. However, note that ADM-ADM ring links are sometimes transported over a lower DWDM layer, thus forming a "connection" that is routed over channels of DWDM systems, instead of direct fiber. Although there is no inherent topographical orientation in a ring, many people conceptually visualize each node of a SONET self-healing ring as an ADM with an *east* bidirectional OC-n interface (i.e., a transmit port and a receive port) and a *west* OC-n interface. Typically, $n = 48$ or 192. An STS-k SONET-Layer connection enters at an add/drop port of an ADM, routes around the ring on k STS-1 channels of the ADM–ADM links and exits the ring at an add/drop port of another ADM. The UPSR is the simplest of the devices and works similarly to the $1 + 1$ tail-end switch described in Section 2.5.1.2, except that each direction of transmission of a connection routes counterclockwise on the "outer" fiber around the ring (west direction) and therefore an STS-k connection used the same k STS-1 channels on all links around the ring. At each add/drop transmit port, the signal is duplicated in the opposite direction on the "inner" fiber. The selector responds to a failure as described above.

The BLSR-2F partitions the bidirectional channels of its East and West high-speed links in half. The first half is used for working (nonfailure) state, and the second half is reserved for restoration. When a failure to a link occurs, the surrounding ADMs loop back that portion of the connection paths onto the restoration channels around the opposite direction of the ring. The UPSR has very rapid restoration, but suffers the dedicated-capacity condition described in Section 2.5.1.2; as a consequence, today UPSRs are now confined mostly to the metro network, in particular to the portion closest to the customer, often extending into the feeder network. Because BLSR signaling is used to advertise failures among ADMs and real-time intermediate cross-connections have to be made, a BLSR restores more slowly than a UPSR. However, the BLSR is capable of having multiple connections share restoration channels over nonsimultaneous potential network failures, and is thus almost always deployed in the middle of the metro network or parts of the core network. Rings are described in more detail in [11].

2.5.1.4 IOS Layer

The typical equipment that comprise today's IOS layer use distributed control to provision (set-up) connections. Here, links of the IOS network (SONET bidirectional OC-n interfaces) are assigned routing weights. When a connection is provisioned over the STS-1 channels of an IOS network, its source node (IOS) computes its working path (usually along a minimum-weight path) plus also computes its restoration path that is diversely routed from the working path. After the connection is set up along its working path, the restoration path is stored for future use. The nodes communicate the state of the network connectivity via topology update messages transmitted over the SONET overhead on the links between the nodes. When a failure occurs, the nodes flood advertisement messages to all nodes indicating the topology change. The source node for each affected connection then instigates the restoration process for its failed connections by sending connection request messages along the links of the (precalculated) restoration path, seeking spare STS-1 channels to reroute its connections. Various handshaking among nodes of the restoration paths are implemented to complete the rerouting of the connections. Note that in contrast to the dedicated and ring methods, the restoration channels are not prededicated to specific connections and, therefore, connections from a varied set of source/destination pairs can potentially use them. Such a method is called *shared* restoration because a given spare channel can be used by different connections across nonsimultaneous failures. Shared mesh restoration is generally more capacity-efficient than SONET rings in mesh networks (i.e., networks with average connectivity greater than 2).

We now delve a little more into IOS restoration to make a key point that will become relevant to the IP backbone, as well. The example in Fig. 2.2 shows two higher-layer connections routing over the same lower-layer link. In light of the discussion above about the restoration path being diverse from the working path in the IOS layer, the astute reader may ask "diverse relative to what?" The answer is that, in general, the path should be diverse all the way down through the DWDM and Fiber Layers. This requires that the IOS links contain information about how they share these lower-layer links. Often, this is accomplished via a mechanism called "bundle groups". That is, a bundle group is created for each lower-layer link, but is expressed as a group of IOS links that share (i.e., route over) that link. Diverse restoration paths can be discovered by avoiding IOS links that belong to the same bundle group of a link on the working path. Of course, the equipment in the IOS-Layer cannot "see" its lower layers, and consequently has no idea how to define and create the bundle groups. Therefore, bundle groups are provisioned in the IOSs using an *Operations Support System (OSS)* that contains a database describing the mapping of IOS links to lower-layer networks. This particular example illustrates the importance of understanding network layering; else we will not have a reliable method to plan and engineer the network to meet the availability objective. This point will be equally important to the IP backbone. A set of bundled links is also referred to as a *Shared Risk Link Group (SRLG)* in the telecommunications industry, since it refers to a group of links that are subject to a shared risk of disruption.

2.5.1.5   W-DCS Layer and Ethernet Layer

There are few restoration methods provided at the W-DCS layer itself. This is because most disruptions to a W-DCS link occurs from a disruption of (1) a W-DCS line card or (2) a component in a lower layer of which the link routes. Disruptions of type (1) are usually handled by providing 1:1 restorable intra-office links between the W-DCS and TDM node (IOS or ADM). Disruptions of type (2) are restored by the lower TDM layers. This only leaves failure or maintenance of the W-DCS itself as an unrestorable network disruption. However, a W-DCS is much less sophisticated than a router and less subject to failure.

Restoration of Layer 2 VPNs in an IP/MPLS backbone is discussed in Section 2.5.2. We note here that restoration in enterprise Ethernet networks is typically based on the Rapid Spanning Tree Protocol (RSTP). When enterprise Ethernet VPNs are connected over the IP backbone (such as VPLS), an enterprise customer who employs routing methods such as RSTP expects it to work in the extended network. By encapsulating the customer's Ethernet frames inside pseudowires ensures that the client's RTSP control packets are transported transparently across the wide area. For example, a client VPN may choose to restore local link disruptions by routing across other central offices or even distant metros. Since all this appears as one virtual network to the customer, such applications may be useful.

2.5.2   IP Backbone

There are two main restoration methods we describe for the IP layer: IGP reconfiguration and MPLS *Fast Reroute (FRR)*.

2.5.2.1 OSPF Failure Detection and Reconvergence

In a formal sense, the IGP reconvergence process responds to topology changes. Such topology changes are usually caused by four types of events:

1. Maintenance of an IP layer component
2. Maintenance of a lower-layer network component
3. Failure of an IP layer component (such as a router line card or common component)
4. Failure of a lower-layer network component (such as a link)

When network operations staff perform planned maintenance on an IP layer link, it is typical to raise the OSPF administrative weight of the link to ensure that all traffic is diverted from the link (this is often referred to as "costing out" the link). In the second case, most carriers have a maintenance procedure where organizations that manage the lower-layer networks schedule their daily maintenance events and inform the IP layer operations organization. The IP layer operations organization responds by costing out all the affected links before the lower-layer maintenance event is started.

In the first two cases (planned maintenance activity), the speed of the reconvergence process is usually not an issue. This is because the act of changing an IGP routing weight on a link causes LSAs to be issued. During the process of updating the link status and recomputation of the SPF tree, the affected links remain in service (i.e., "up"). Therefore, once the IGP reconfiguration process has settled, the routers can redirect packets to their new paths. While there may be a transient impact during the "costing out" period, in terms of transient loops and packet loss, the service impact is kept to a minimum by using this costing out technique to remove a link from the topology for performing maintenance.

In the last two cases (failures), once the affected links go down, packets may be lost or delayed until the reconvergence process completes. Such a disruption may be unacceptable to delay or loss-sensitive applications. This motivates us to examine how to reduce the time required for OSPF to converge from unexpected outages. This is the focus of the remainder of this section.

While most large IP backbones route over lower layers, such as DWDM, those do not provide restoration. Layer 1 failure detection is a key component of the IP layer restoration process. A key component of the overall failure recovery time in OSPF-based networks is the failure detection time. However, lower-layer failure detection mechanisms sometimes do not coordinate well with higher-layer mechanisms and do not detect disruptions that originate in the IP layer control plane. As a result, OSPF routers periodically exchange `Hello` messages to detect the loss of a link adjacency with a neighbor.

If a router does not receive a `Hello` message from its neighbor within a `RouterDeadInterval`, it assumes that the link to its neighbor has failed, or the neighbor router itself is down, and generates a new LSA to reflect the changed topology. All such LSAs generated by the routers affected by the failure are flooded throughout the network. This causes the routers in the network to redo the SPF calculation and update the next-hop information in their respective forwarding tables. Thus, the time required to recover from a failure consists of: (1) the failure detection time, (2) LSA flooding time, (3) the time to complete the new SPF calculations and update the forwarding tables.

To avoid a false indication that an adjacency is down because of congestion related loss of Hello messages, the RouterDeadInterval is usually set to be four times the HelloInterval – the interval between successive Hello messages sent by a router to its neighbor. With the RFC suggested default values for these timers (HelloInterval value of 10 s and RouterDeadInterval value of 40 s), the failure detection time can take anywhere between 30 and 40 s. LSA flooding times consist of propagation delay and additional pacing delays inserted by the router. These pacing delays serve to rate-limit the frequency with which LSUpdate packets are sent on an interface. Once a router receives a new LSA, it schedules an SPF calculation. Since the SPF calculation using Dijkstra's algorithm (see e.g., [8]) constitutes a significant processing load, a router typically waits for additional LSAs to arrive for a time interval corresponding to spfDelay (typically 5 s) before doing the SPF calculation on a batch of LSAs. Moreover, routers place a limit on the frequency of SPF calculations (governed by a spfHoldTime, typically 10 s, between successive SPF calculations), which can introduce further delays.

From the description above, it is clear that reducing the HelloInterval can substantially reduce the Hello protocol's failure detection time. However, there is a limit to which the HelloInterval can be safely reduced. As the HelloInterval becomes smaller, there is an increased chance that network congestion will lead to loss of several consecutive Hello messages and thereby cause a false alarm that an adjacency between routers is lost, even though the routers and the link between them are functioning. The LSAs generated because of a false alarm will lead to new SPF calculations by all the routers in the network. This false alarm would soon be corrected by a successful Hello exchange between the affected routers, which then causes a new set of LSAs to be generated and possibly new path calculations by the routers in the network. Thus, false alarms cause an unnecessary processing load on routers and sometimes lead to temporary changes in the path taken by network traffic. If false alarms are frequent, routers have to spend considerable time doing unnecessary LSA processing and SPF calculations, which may significantly delay important tasks such as Hello processing, thereby leading to more false alarms.

False alarms can also be generated if a Hello message gets queued behind a burst of LSAs and thus cannot be processed in time. The possibility of such an event increases with the reduction of the RouterDeadInterval. Large LSA bursts can be caused by a number of factors such as simultaneous refresh of a large number of LSAs or several routers going down/coming up simultaneously. Choudhury [5] studies this issue and observes that reducing the HelloInterval lowers the threshold (in terms of number of LSAs) at which an LSA burst will lead to generation of false alarms. However, the probability of LSA bursts leading to false alarms is shown to be quite low.

Since the loss and/or delayed processing of `Hello` messages can result in false alarms, there have been proposals to give such packets prioritized treatment at the router interface as well as in the CPU processing queue [5]. An additional option is to consider the receipt of any OSPF packet (e.g., an LSA) from a neighbor as an indication of the good health of the router's adjacency with the neighbor. This provision can help avoid false loss of adjacency in the scenarios where `Hello` packets get dropped because of congestion, caused by a large LSA burst, on the link between two routers. Such mechanisms may help mitigate the false alarm problem significantly. However, it will take some time before these mechanisms are standardized and widely deployed.

It is useful to make a realistic assessment regarding how small the `HelloInterval` can be, to achieve faster detection and recovery from network failures while limiting the occurrence of false alarms. We summarize below the key results from [13]. This assessment was done via simulations on the network topologies of commercial ISPs using a detailed implementation of the OSPF protocol in the NS2 simulator. The work models all the important OSPF protocol features as well as various standard and vendor-introduced delays in the functioning of the protocol. These are shown in Table 2.4.

Goyal [13] observes that with the current default settings of the OSPF parameters, the network takes several tens of seconds before recovering from a failure. Since the main component in this delay is the time required to detect a failure using the `Hello` protocol, Goyal [13] examines the impact of lower `HelloInterval` values on failure detection and recovery times.

Table 2.5 shows typical results for failure detection and recovery times after a router failure. As expected, the failure detection time is within the range of three to four times the value of `HelloInterval`. Once a neighbor detects the router failure, it generates a new LSA about 0.5 s after the failure detection. The new LSA is flooded throughout the network and will lead to scheduling of an SPF calculation 5 s (`spfDelay`) after the LSA receipt. This is done to allow one SPF calculation to take care of several new LSAs. Once the SPF calculation is done, the router takes about 200 ms more to update the forwarding table. After including the LSA propagation and pacing delays, one can expect the failure recovery to take place about 6 s after the 'earliest' failure detection by a neighbor router.

Notice that many entries in Table 2.5 show the recovery to take place much sooner than 6 s after failure detection. This is partly an artifact of the simulation because the failure detection times reported by the simulator are the "latest" ones rather than the "earliest". In one interesting case (seed 2, `HelloInterval` 0.75 s), the failure recovery takes place about 2 s after the 'latest' failure detection. This happens because the SPF calculation scheduled by an earlier false alarm takes care of the LSAs generated because of router failure. There are also many cases in which failure recovery takes place more than 6 s after failure detection (notice entries for `HelloInterval` 0.25 s, seeds 1 and 3). Failure recovery can be delayed because of several factors. The SPF calculation frequency of the routers is limited by `spfHoldTime` (typically 10 s), which can delay the new SPF calculation in response to the router failure. The delay caused by spfDelay is also a contribution.

Table 2.4   Various delays affecting the operation of OSPF protocol

Standard configurable delays	
RxmtInterval	The time delay before an un-acked LSA is retransmitted. Usually 5 s.
HelloInterval	The time delay between successive Hello packets. Usually 10 s.
RouterDeadInterval	The time delay since the last Hello before a neighbor is declared to be down. Usually four times the HelloInterval.
Vendor-introduced configurable delays	
Pacing delay	The minimum delay enforced between two successive Link-State Update packets sent down an interface. Observed to be 33 ms. Not always configurable.
spfDelay	The delay between the shortest path calculation and the first topology change that triggered the calculation. Used to avoid frequent shortest path calculations. Usually 5 s.
spfHoldTime	The minimum delay between successive shortest path calculations. Usually 10 s.
Standard fixed delays	
LSRefreshTime	The maximum time interval before an LSA needs to be reflooded. Set to 30 min.
MinLSInterval	The minimum time interval before an LSA can be reflooded. Set to 5 s.
MinLSArrival	The minimum time interval that should elapse before a new instance of an LSA can be accepted. Set to 1 s.
Router-specific delays	
Route install delay	The delay between the shortest path calculation and update of forwarding table. Observed to be 0.2 s.
LSA generation delay	The delay before the generation of an LSA after all the conditions for the LSA generation have been met. Observed to be around 0.5 s.
LSA processing delay	The time required to process an LSA including the time required to process the Link-State Update packet before forwarding the LSA to the OSPF process. Observed to be less than 1 ms.
SPF calculation delay	The time required to do shortest path calculation. Observed to be $0.00000247x^2 + 0.000978$ s on Cisco 3600 series routers; x being the number of nodes in the topology.

Finally, the routers with a low degree of connectivity may not get the LSAs in the first try because of loss due to congestion. Such routers may have to wait for 5 s (RxmtInterval) for the LSAs to be retransmitted.

The results in Table 2.5 show that a smaller value of HelloInterval speeds up the failure detection but is not effective in reducing the failure recovery times beyond a limit because of other delays like spfDelay, spfHoldTime, and RxmtInterval. Failure recovery times improve as the HelloInterval reduces down to about 0.5 s. Beyond that, as a result of more false alarms, we find that the recovery times actually go up. While it may be possible to further speed up

Table 2.5 Failure detection time and failure recovery time for a router failure with different `HelloInterval` values

Hello interval (s)	Seed 1		Seed 2		Seed 3	
	FDT (s)	FRT (s)	FDT (s)	FRT (s)	FDT (s)	FRT (s)
10	32.08	36.60	39.84	46.37	33.02	38.07
2	7.82	11.68	7.63	12.18	7.79	12.02
1	3.81	9.02	3.80	8.31	3.84	10.11
0.75	2.63	7.84	2.97	5.08	2.81	7.82
0.5	1.88	6.98	1.82	6.89	1.79	6.85
0.25	0.95	10.24	0.84	6.08	0.99	13.41

the failure recovery by reducing the values of these delays, eliminating such delays altogether is not prudent. Eliminating `spfDelay` and `spfHoldTime` will result in potentially additional SPF calculations in a router in response to a single failure (or false alarm) as the different LSAs generated because of the failure arrive one after the other at the router. The resulting overload on the router CPUs may have serious consequences for routing stability, especially when there are several simultaneous changes in the network topology. Failure recovery below the range of 1–5 s is difficult with OSPF.

In summary, OSPF recovery time can be lowered by reducing the value of `HelloInterval`. However, too small a value of `HelloInterval` will lead to many false alarms in the network, which cause unnecessary routing changes and may lead to routing instability. The optimal value for the `HelloInterval` that will lead to fast failure recovery in the network, while keeping the false alarm occurrence within acceptable limits for a network, is strongly influenced by the expected congestion levels and the number of links in the topology. While the `HelloInterval` can be much lower than current default value of tens of seconds, it is not advisable to reduce it to the millisecond range because of potential false alarms. Further, it is difficult to prescribe a single `HelloInterval` value that will perform optimally in all cases. The network operator needs to set the `HelloInterval` conservatively taking into account both the expected congestion as well as the number of links in the network topology.

2.5.2.2 MPLS Fast Reroute

MPLS Fast Reroute (FRR) was designed to improve restoration performance using the additional protocol layer provided by MPLS LSPs [17]. Primary and alternate (backup) LSPs are established. Fast rerouting over the alternate paths after a network disruption is achieved using preestablished router forwarding table entries. Equipment suppliers have developed many flavors of FRR, some of which are not totally compliant with standardized MPLS FRR. This section provides an overview of the basic concept.

There are two basic varieties of backup path restoration in MPLS FRR, called *next-hop* and *next-next-hop*. The next-hop approach identifies a unidirectional link to be protected and a *backup* (or *bypass*) unidirectional LSP that routes around the

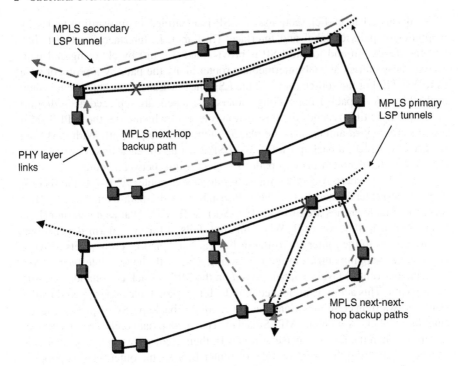

Fig. 2.26 Example of Fast Reroute backup paths

link if it fails. The protected link can be a router–router link adjacency or even another layer of LSP tunnel itself. The backup LSP routes over alternate links. The top graph in Fig. 2.26 illustrates a next-hop backup path for the potential failure of a given link (designated with an "X"). For now ignore the top path labeled "MPLS secondary LSP tunnel", which will be discussed later. With the *next-next-hop* approach, the primary entities to protect are two-link working paths. The backup path is an alternate path over different links and routers than the protected entity. In general, a next-hop path is constructed to restore against individual link failures while next-next-hop paths are constructed to restore against both individual link failures and node failures. The trade-off is that next-hop paths are simpler to implement because all flows routing over the link can be rerouted similarly, whereas next-next-hop requires more LSPs and routing combinations. This is illustrated in the lower example of Fig. 2.26, wherein the first router along the path carries flows that terminate on different second hop routers, and therefore must create multiple backup LSPs that originate at that node.

We will briefly describe an implementation of the next-hop approach to FRR. A primary end-to-end path is chosen by RSVP. This path is characterized by the Forwarding Equivalence Class (FEC) discussed earlier and reflects packets that are to be corouted and have similar CoS queuing treatment and ability to be restored with FRR. Often, a mesh of fully connected end-to-end LSPs between the backbone routers (BRs) is created.

As discussed in earlier sections, an LSP is identified in forwarding tables by mappings of pairs of label and interface: (In-Label, In-Interface)→ (Out-Label, Out-Interface). An end-to-end LSP is provisioned (set up) by choosing and populating these entries at each intermediate router along the path by a protocol such as RSVP-TE. For the source router of the LSP, the "In-Label" variable is equivalent to the FEC. As a packet hops along routers, the labels are replaced according to the mapping until it reaches the destination router, in which case, the MPLS shim headers are *popped* and packets are placed on the final output port. With next-hop, *facility-based* FRR, a backup (or bypass) LSP is set up for each link. For example, consider a precalculated backup path to protect a link between routers A and B, say (A-1, B-1), where A-1 is the transmit interface at router A, B-1 is the receive interface at router B, and L-1 is the MPLS label for the path over this link. The forwarding table entries are of form (L-i, A-k) → (L-1, A-1) at router A and (L-1, B-1) → (L-j, B-s) at router B. When this link fails, a Layer 1 alarm is generated and forwarded to the router controller or line card at A and B. For packets arriving at router A, mapping entries in the forwarding table with the Out-Interface = A-1 have another (outer) layer of label *pushed* on the MPLS stack to coincide with the backup path. This action is preloaded into the forwarding table and triggered by the alarm. Forwarding continues along the routers of this backup LSP by processing the outer layer labels as with any MPLS packet. The backup path ends at router B and, therefore, when the packets arrive at router B, their highest (exterior) layer label is popped. Then, from the point of view of router B, after the outer label is popped, the MPLS header is left with (In-Label, In-Interface) = (L-1, B-1) and therefore the packets continue their journey beyond router B just as they would if link (A-1, B-1) were up. In this way, all LSPs that route over the particular link are rerouted (hence the term "facility based"). Various other specifications can be made to segregate the backup path to be pushed on given classes of LSPs, for example to provide restoration for some IP CoSs rather than others.

Another common implementation of next-hop FRR defines 1-hop pseudowires for each key link. Each pseudowire has defined a primary LSP and backup LSP (a capability found in most routers). If the link fails, a similar alarm mechanism causes the pseudowire to reroute over the backup LSP. When the primary LSP is again declared up, the pseudowire switches back to the primary path. An advantage of this method is that the pseudowire appears as a link to the IGP routing algorithm. Weights can be used to control how packets route over it or the underlying Layer 1 link. Section 2.6 illustrates this method for an IPTV backbone network.

MPLS FRR has been demonstrated to work very rapidly (less than 100 ms) in response to single-link (IP layer PHY link) failures by many vendors and carriers. Most FRR implementations behave similarly during the small interval immediately after the failure and before IGP reconvergence. However, implementations differ in what happens after IGP reconvergence. We describe two main approaches in the context of next-hop FRR here. In the first approach, the backup LSP stays in place until the link goes back into service and IGP reconverges back to its non-failure state. This is most common when a separate LSP or pseudowire is associated with each link in next-hop FRR. In this case, the link-LSP is rerouted onto its backup LSP and stays that way until the primary LSP is repaired.

In the second approach, FRR provides rapid restoration and then, after a short settling period, the network recomputes its paths [4]. Here, each primary end-to-end LSP is recomputed during the first IGP reconfiguration process after the failure. Since the IGP knows about the failed link(s), it reroutes the primary end-to-end LSPs around them and the backup LSPs become moot. This is illustrated in the three potential paths in the topmost diagram of Fig. 2.26. The IP flow routes along the primary LSP during the nonfailure state. Then, the given link fails and the path of the flow over the failed link deviates along the backup LSP, as shown by the lower dashed line. After the first IGP reconfiguration process, the end-to-end LSP path is recomputed, illustrated by the topmost dashed line.

When a failed component is repaired or a maintenance procedure is completed, the disrupted links are put back into service. The process to return the network to its nonfailure state is often called *normalization*. During the normalization process, LSAs are broadcast by the IGP and the forwarding tables are recalculated. The normalization process is often controlled by an MPLS route mechanism/timer. A similar procedure would occur for next-next hop.

The reason for the second approach is that while FRR enables rapid restoration, because these paths are segmental "patches" to the primary paths, the alternate route is often long and capacity-inefficient. With the first approach, IP flows continue routing over the backup paths until the repair is completed and alarms clear, which may span hours or days. Another reason is that if multiple link failures occur, then some of the backup FRR paths may fail; some response is needed to address this situation. These limitations of the first approach were early key inhibitors to implementation of FRR in large ISPs.

The key to implementing this second FRR strategy is that the switch from FRR backup paths to new end-to-end paths is *hitless* (i.e., negligible packet loss), else we may suffer three hits from each single failure (the failure itself, the process to reroute the end-to-end paths immediately after the failure, and then the process to revert to the original paths after repair). If the alternate end-to-end LSPs are presetup and the forwarding table changes implemented efficiently for most routers (often using pointers), this process is essentially hitless for most IP *unicast* (point-to-point) applications. However, we note that today's *multicast* does not typically enjoy hitless switchover to the new forwarding table because most multicast trees are usually built via join and prune request messages issued backwards (upstream) from the destination nodes. However, it is expected that different implementations of multicast will fix this problem in the future. We discuss this again in Section 2.6 and refer the reader to [36] for more discussion of hitless multicast.

For the network design phase of implementing FRR, for next-hop FRR, each link (say L) along the primary path needs a predefined a backup path whose routing is diverse in lower layers. That is, the paths of all lower-layer connections that support the links of the backup path are disjoint from the path of the lower-layer connection for link L. The key is in predefining the backup tunnels. While next-next-hop paths can be also used to restore against single-link failures, the network becomes more complex to design if there is a high degree of lower-layer link overlap. More generally, the major difficulty for the FRR approach is defining the backup LSPs so that the service paths can be rerouted, given a predefined set of lower-layer failures. Furthermore, when multiple lower-layer failures occur and MPLS backup paths fail, FRR does not work and the network must revert to the slower primary path recalculation approach (described in method 2 above).

2.5.3 Failures Across Multiple Layers

Now that the reader is armed with background on network layering and restoration methods, we are poised to delve deeper into the factors and carrier decision variables that shape the availability of the IP backbone.

Let us briefly revisit Fig. 2.9, which gives a simple example of the core ROADM Layer Diagram. Consider a backbone router (BR) in central office B with a link to one of the backbone routers in central office A. Furthermore, consider the remote access router (RAR) that is homed to the backbone router in office A. However, let us add a twist wherein the link between the RAR and BR routes over the IOS layer instead of directly onto the ROADM (DWDM layer) as pictured in Fig. 2.9. This can occur for RAR–BR links with lower bandwidth. This modification will illustrate more of the potential failure modes. In particular, we have constructed this simple example to illustrate several key points:

- Computing an estimate of the availability of the IP backbone involves analysis of many network layers.
- Network disruptions can originate from many different sources within each layer.
- Some lower layers may provide restoration and others do not; how does this affect the IP backbone?

Figure 2.27 gives examples of the types of individual component disruptions ("down events") that might cause links to fail in this network example, but still only shows a few of the many disruptions that can originate at these layers. As one can see, this is a four-layer example; and, some of the layers are skipped. Note that for simplicity, we illustrate point-to-point DWDM systems at the DWDM layer; however, the concepts apply equally well for ROADMs. Some readers perhaps may think that the main source of network failures is fiber cuts and, therefore, the entire area of multilayer restoration can be reduced to analyzing fiber cuts. However, this oversimplifies the problem. For example, an amplifier failure can often be as disruptive as a fiber cable cut and will likely result in the failure of multiple IP layer links. Furthermore, amplifier failures are more frequent. Let us examine the effect of some of the failures illustrated in Fig. 2.27.

IOS interface failure: The IOS network has restoration capability, as described in earlier sections. Consequently, the IOS layer reroutes its failed SONET STS-n connection that supports the RAR–BR link onto its restoration path. In this case, once the SONET alarms are detected by the two routers (the RAR and BR), they take the link out of service and generate appropriate LSAs to the correct IGP

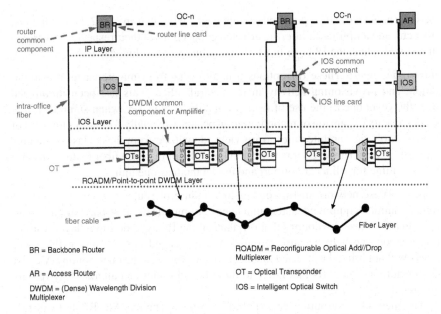

Fig. 2.27 Example of components disruptions (failure or maintenance activity) at multiple layers

administrative areas or control domains to announce the topology change. Assuming that the IOS-layer restoration is successful, the AR–BR link comes back after a short time (as specified in the IOS layer of Table 2.3) and the SONET alarm clears. After perhaps, an appropriate time-out on the routers to avoid link flapping, the link is brought back up by the router and the topology change is announced via LSAs. We note that in a typical AR/BR homing architecture, the LSAs from an AR–BR link are only announced in subareas and so do not affect unaffected ARs or BRs.

Fiber cut: In the core network, the probability of a fiber cut is roughly proportional to its length. They are less frequent than many of the other failures, but highly disruptive, where usually many simultaneous IP layer links fail because of the concentration of capacity enabled by DWDM.

Optical Transponder: OT failure is the most common of the failures shown in Fig. 2.27. However, a single OT failure only affects individual IP backbone links. Some of the more significant problems with OT failures are (1) performance degradation, where bit errors occasionally trip BER threshold crossing alerts and (2) there is a nonnegligible probability of multiple failures in the network, in which an OT fails while another major failure is in progress or vice versa.

DWDM terminal or amplifier: Amplifier failure is usually the most disruptive of failures because of its impact (multiple wavelengths) and sheer quantity, often placed every 50–100 miles, depending on the vintage and bit rate of the wavelengths of the DWDM equipment. Failure of the DWDM terminal equipment not associated with amplifiers and OTs is less probable because of the increased use of passive (nonelectrical or powered) components. Note that in Fig. 2.27, for the OT, fiber cut, and amplifier failure, the affected connections at their respective layers are unrestored. Thus, the IP layer must reroute around its lost link capacity.

Intra-office fiber: These disruptions usually occur from maintenance, reconfiguration, and provisioning activity in the central office. This has been minimized over the years due to the use of fiber patch panels; however, when significant network capacity expansion or reconfiguration occurs, especially for the deployment of new technologies, architectures, or services, downtime from these class of failures typically spikes. However, it is typical to lump the intra-office fiber disruptions into the downtime for a linecard or port and model them as one unit.

Router: These network disruptions include failure of router line cards, failure of router common equipment, and maintenance or upgrade of all or parts of the router. Note that for these disruptions that originate at the IP layer, no lower-layer restoration method can help because rerouting the associated connections at the lower layers will not bring the affected link back up. However, in the dual-homing AR–BR architecture, all the ARs that home to the affected router can alternatively reroute through the mate BR.

The method of rerouting the AR traffic to the surviving AR–BR links differs per carrier. Usually, IGP reconfiguration is used. However, this can be unacceptably slow for some high-priority services, as evidenced by Table 2.3. Therefore, other faster techniques are sometimes used, such as Ethernet link load balancing or MPLS FRR.

We generalize some simple observations on multilayer restoration illustrated by Fig. 2.27 and its subsequent discussion:

1. Because of the use of express links, a single network failure or disruption at a lower layer usually results in multiple link failures at higher layers.
2. Failures that originate at an upper layer cannot be restored at a lower layer.
3. To meet most ISP network availability objectives, some form of restoration (even if rudimentary) must be provided in upper layers.

2.5.4 IP Backbone Network Design

Network design is covered in more detail in Chapter 5. However, to tie together the concepts of network layering, network failure modeling, and restoration, we provide a brief description of IP network design here to illustrate its importance in meeting network availability targets. In this section, we give a brief description about how these factors are accommodated in the network design. To illustrate this, we describe a very simplified network design (or network planning) process as follows. This process would occur every planning period or whenever major changes to the network occur:

1. Derive a traffic matrix.
2. Input the existing IP backbone topology and compute any needed changes. That is, determine the homing of AR locations to the BR locations and determine which BR pairs are allowed to have links placed between them.
3. Determine the routing of BR–BR links over the lower-layer networks (e.g., DWDM, IOS, fiber).
4. Route the traffic matrix over the topology and size the links. This results in an estimate of network cost across all the needed layers.
5. Resize the links by finding their maximum needed capacity over all possible events in the *Failure Set*, which models potential network disruptions (both component failures and maintenance activity). This step simulates each failure event, determining which IP layer link or nodes fail after lower-layer restoration, if it exists, is applied and determining the capacity needed after traffic is rerouted using IP layer restoration.
6. Re-optimize the topology by going back to step 2 and iterating with the objective of lowering network cost.

Note in steps 2 and 3 that most carriers are reluctant to make large changes to the existing IP backbone topology, since these can be very disruptive and costly events. Therefore, steps 2 and 3 usually incur small topology changes from one planning period to another planning period. We will not describe detailed algorithms for the above in detail here. Approaches to the above problem can be found in [22, 23].

The traffic matrix can come in a variety of forms, such as the peak 5-min average loads between AR-pairs or average loads, etc. Unfortunately, many organizations responsible for IP network design either have little or no data about their current or future traffic matrices. In fact, many engineers who manage IP networks expand their network by simply observing link loads. When a link load exceeds some threshold, they add more capacity. Given no knowledge or high uncertainty of the true, stochastic traffic matrix, this may be a reasonable approach. However, network failures and their subsequent restorations are the phenomena that cause the greatest challenges with such a simple approach. Because of the extensive rerouting that can occur after a network failure, there is no simple or intuitive parameter to determine the utilization threshold for each link. Traffic matrix estimation is discussed in detail in Chapter 5.

A missing ingredient in the above network design algorithm is we did not describe how to model the needed network availability for an ISP to achieve its SLAs. Theoretically, even if we assume the traffic matrix (present and/or future) is completely accurate, to achieve the network design availability objective, all the component failure modes and all the network layering must be modeled to design the IP backbone. The decision variables are the layers where we provide restoration (including what type of restoration should be used) and how much capacity should be deployed at each layer to meet the QoS objectives for the IP layer. This is further complicated by the fact that while network availability objectives for transport layers are often expressed in worst-case or average-case connection uptimes, IP backbone QoS objective often use packet-loss metrics.

However, we can approximate the packet loss constraints in large IP layer networks by establishing maximum link utilization targets. For example, through separate analysis it might be determined that every flow can achieve the objective maximum packet loss target by not exceeding 90% utilization on any 40 Gb/s link, with perhaps lower utilization maxima needed on lower-rate links. Then, one can model when this utilization condition is met over the set of possible failures, including subsequent restoration procedures. By modeling the probabilities of the failure set, one can compute a network availability metric appropriate for packet networks. The probabilities of events in the failure set can be computed using Markov models and the *Mean Time Between Failures (MTBF)* and the *Mean Time to Repair (MTTR)* of the component disruptions. These parameters are usually obtained from a combination of equipment-supplier specifications, network observation/data, and carrier policies and procedures.

A major stumbling block with this theoretical approach is that the failure event space is exponential in size. Even for very small networks and a few layers, it is intractable to compute all potential failures, let alone the subsequent restoration and network loss. An approach to probabilistic modeling to solve this problem is presented in more detail in Chapter 4 and in [28].

Armed with this background, we conclude this section by revisiting the issue of why we show the IP backbone routing over an unrestorable DWDM layer in the network layering of Fig. 2.3. This at first may seem counterintuitive because it is generally true that, per unit of capacity, the cost of links at lower layers is less than that of higher layers. Some of the reasons for this planning decision, which is consistent with most large ISPs, were hinted at in Section 2.5.3. We summarize them here.

1. Backbone router disruptions (failures or maintenance events) originate within the IP layer and cannot be restored at lower layers. Extra link capacity must be provided at the IP layer for such disruptions. Once placed, this extra capacity can then also be used for IP layer link failures that originate at lower layers. This obviates most of the cost advantages of lower-layer restoration.

2. Under nonfailure conditions, there is spare capacity available in the IP layer to handle uncertain demand. For example, restoration requirements aside, to handle normal service demand, IP layer links could be engineered to run below 80% utilization during peak intervals of the traffic matrix and well below that at off-peak intervals. If we allow higher utilization levels during network disruption events, then this provides an existing extra buffer during those events. Furthermore, there may be little appreciable loss during network disruptions during off-peak periods.

As QoS and CoS features are deployed in the IP backbone, there is yet another advantage to IP layer restoration. Namely, the IP layer can assign different QoS objectives to different service classes. For example, one such distinction might be to plan network restoration so that premium services receive better performance than best-effort services during network disruptions. In contrast, the DWDM layer cannot make such fine-grain distinctions; it either restores or does not restore the entire IP layer link, which carries a mixture of different classes of services.

2.6   IPTV Backbone Example

Some major carriers now offer nationwide digital television, high-speed Internet, and Voice-over-IP services over an IP network. These services typically include hundreds of digital television channels. Video content providers deliver their content to the service provider in digital format at select locations called *super hub offices (SHOs)*. This in turn requires that the carrier have the ability to deliver high-bandwidth IP streaming to its residential customers on a nationwide basis. If such content is delivered all the way to residential set-top boxes over IP, it is commonly called *IPTV*. There are two options to providing such an IPTV backbone. The first option is to create a virtual network on top of the IP backbone. Since video service consists mostly of streaming channels that are broadcast to all customers, IP multicast is usually the most cost-effective protocol to transport the content. However, users have high expectations for video service and even small packet losses negatively impact video quality. This requires the IP backbone to be able to transport multicast traffic at a very high level of network availability and efficiency. The first option results in a mixture of best-effort traffic and traffic with very high quality of service on the same IP backbone, which in turn requires comprehensive mechanisms for restoration and priority queuing.

Consequently, some carriers have followed the second option, wherein they create a separate overlay network on top of the lower-layer DWDM or TDM layers. In reality, this is another (smaller) IP layer network, with specialized traffic, network structure, and restoration mechanisms. We describe such an example in this section. Because of the high QoS objectives needed for broadcast TV services, the reader will find that this section builds on most of the previous material in this chapter.

2.6.1   Multicast-Based IPTV Distribution

Meeting the stringent QoS required to deliver a high-quality video service (such as low latency and loss) requires careful consideration of the underlying IP-transport network, network restoration, and video and packet recovery methods.

Figure 2.28 (borrowed from [9]) illustrates a simplified architecture for a network providing IPTV service. The SHO gathers content from the national video content providers, such as TV networks (mostly via satellite today) and distributes it to a large set of receiving locations, called *video hub offices (VHOs)*. Each VHO in turn feeds a metropolitan area. IP routers are used to transport the IPTV content in the SHO and VHOs. The combination of SHO and VHO routers plus the links that connect them comprise the IPTV backbone. The VHO combines the national feeds with local content and other services and then distributes the content to each metro area. The long-distance backbone network between the SHO and the VHO includes a pair of redundant routers that are associated with each VHO. This allows for protection against router component failures, router hardware maintenance, or software

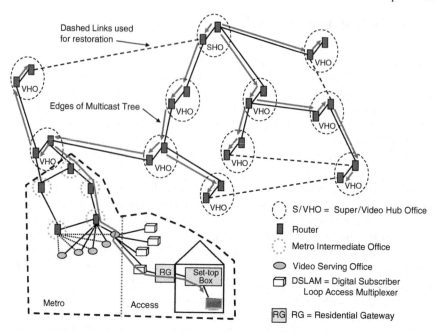

Fig. 2.28 Example nationwide IPTV network

upgrades. IP multicast is used for delivery as it provides economic advantages for the IPTV service to distribute video. With multicast, packets traverse each link at most once.

The video content is encoded using an encoding standard such as *H.264*. Video frames are packetized and are encapsulated in the *Real-Time Transport Protocol (RTP)* and UDP. In this example, PIM-SSM is used to support IP multicast over the video content. Each channel from the national live feed at the SHO is assigned a unique multicast group. There are typically hundreds of channels assigned to standard-definition (SD) (1.5 to 3 Mb/s) and high-definition (HD) (6 to 10 Mb/s) video signals plus other multimedia signals, such as "picture-in-picture" channels and music. So, the live feed can be multiple gigabits per second in aggregate bandwidth.

2.6.2 Restoration Mechanisms

The IPTV network can use various restoration methods to deliver the needed video QoS to end-users. For example, it can recover from relatively infrequent and short bursts of loss using a combination of video and packet recovery mechanisms and protocols, including the Society of Motion Picture and Television Engineers (SMPTE; www.smpte.org/standards) 2022–1 Forward Error Correction (FEC) standard, retransmission approaches based on RTP/RTCP [33] and Reliable UDP (R-UDP) [31], and video player loss-concealment algorithms in conjunction with set-top box buffering. R-UDP supports retransmission-based packet-loss recovery. In addition to protecting against video impairments due to last-mile (loop) transmission problems in the access segment, a combination of these methods can recover from a network failure (e.g., fiber link or router line card) of 50 ms or less. Repairing network failures usually takes far more than 50 ms (potentially several hours), but when combined with link-based FRR, this restoration methodology could meet the stringent requirements needed for video against single-link failures.

Figure 2.29 (borrowed from [9]) illustrates how we might implement link-based FRR in an IPTV backbone by depicting a network segment with four node pairs that have defined virtual links (or pseudowires). This method is the pseudowire, next-hop FRR approach described in Section 2.5.2.2. For example, node pair E-C has a lower-layer link (such as SONET OC-*n* or Gigabit Ethernet) in each direction and a pseudowire in each direction (a total of four unidirectional logical links) used for FRR restoration. The medium dashed line shows the FRR backup path for the pseudowire E→C. Note that links such as E-A are for restoration and, hence, have no pseudowires defined. Pseudowire E→C routes over a primary path that consists of the single lower-layer link E→C (see the solid line in Fig. 2.29). If a failure occurs to a lower-layer link in the primary path such as C-E, then the router at node E attempts to switch to the backup path using FRR. The path from the root to node A will switch to the backup path at node E (E-A-B-C). Once it reaches node C, it will

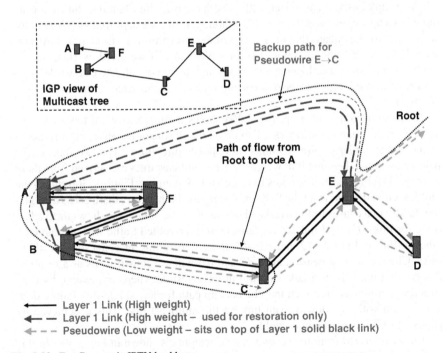

Fig. 2.29 Fast Reroute in IPTV backbone

continue on its previous (primary) path to node A (C-B-F-A). The entire path from E to A during the failure is shown by the outside dotted line. Although the path retraces itself between the routers B and C, the multicast traffic does not overlap because of the links' unidirectionality. Also, although the IGP view of the topology realizes that the lower-layer links between E and C have gone "down," because the pseudowire from E→C is still "up" and has the least weight, the shortest path tree remains unchanged. Consequently, the multicast tree remains unchanged. The IGP is unaware of the actual routing over the backup path. Note that these backup paths are precomputed, by analyzing all possible link failures in a comprehensive manner, a priori.

If we route the pseudowire FRR backup path on a lower-layer path that is diverse from its primary path, FRR operates rapidly (suppose around 50 ms), and we set the hold-down timers appropriately, IGP will not detect the effect of any single fiber or DWDM layer link failure. Therefore, the multicast tree will remain unaffected, reducing the outage time of any single-link failure from tens of seconds to approximately 50 ms. This order of restoration time is needed to achieve the stringent IPTV network availability objectives.

2.6.3 Avoiding Congestion from Traffic Overlap

A drawback of restoration using next-hop FRR is that since it reroutes traffic on a link-by-link basis, it can suffer traffic overlap during link failures, thus requiring more link capacity to meet the target availability. Links are deployed bidirectionally, and traffic overlap means that the packets of the same multicast flows travel over the same link (in the same direction) two or more times. If we avoid overlap, we can run the links at higher utilization and thus design more cost-effective networks. This requires that the multicast tree and backup paths be constructed so that traffic does not overlap.

To illustrate traffic overlap, Fig. 2.30a shows a simple network topology with node S as the source and nodes $d1$ to $d8$ as the destinations. Here, each router is connected by a pair of directed links (in opposite directions). The two links of the pair are assigned the same IGP weight and the multicast trees are derived from these weights. The Fig. 2.30a illustrates two sets of link weights. Figure 2.30b shows the multicast tree derived from the first set of weights. In this case, there exists a single-link failure that causes traffic overlap. For example, the dotted line shows the backup route for link $d1$–$d4$. If link $d1$–$d4$ fails, then the rerouted traffic will overlap with other traffic on links S-$d2$ and $d2$–$d6$, thereby resulting in congestion on those links. Client routers downstream of $d2$ and $d6$ will see impairments as a result of this congestion. It is desirable to avoid this congestion wherever possible by constructing a multicast tree such that the backup path for any single-link failure does not overlap with any downstream link on the multicast tree. This is achieved by choosing OSPF link weights suitably.

The tree derived from the second pair of weights is shown in Fig. 2.30c. In this case, the backup paths do not cause traffic overlap in response to any single-link

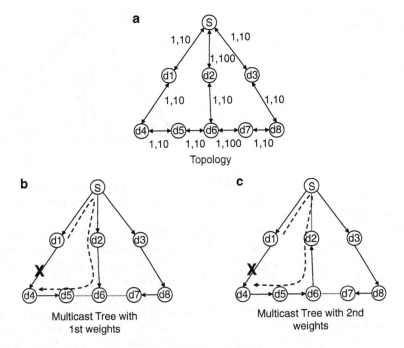

Fig. 2.30 Example of traffic overlap from single-link failure

failure. The multicast tree link is now from $d6$ to $d2$. The backup path for link $d1$–$d4$ is the same as in Fig. 2.30b. Observe that traffic on this backup path does not travel in the same direction as any link of the multicast tree. An algorithm to define FRR backup paths and IGP weights so that the multicast tree does not overlap from any single failure can be found in [10].

2.6.4 Combating Multiple Concurrent Failures

The algorithm and protocol in [10] helps in avoiding traffic overlap of the multicast tree during single-link failures. However, multiple link failures can still cause overlap. An example is shown in Fig. 2.31. Assume that links $d1$–$d4$ and $d3$–$d8$ are both down. If the backup path for edge $d1$–$d4$ is $d1$-S-$d2$-$d6$-$d5$-$d4$ (as shown in Fig. 2.30b and in Fig. 2.31) and the backup path for edge $d3$–$d8$ is $d3$-S-$d2$-$d6$-$d7$-$d8$, traffic will overlap paths on edges S-$d2$ and $d2$-$d6$. There would be significant traffic loss due to congestion if the links of the network are sized to only handle a single stream of multicast traffic.

This situation essentially occurs because MPLS FRR occurs at Layer 2 and therefore the IGP is unaware of the FRR backup paths. Furthermore, the FRR backup paths are precalculated and there is no real-time (dynamic) accommodation for

Fig. 2.31 Example of traffic
overlap from multiple link
failures

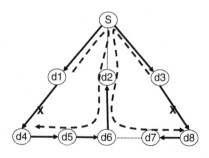

different combinations of *multiple*-link failures. In reality, multiple (double and even triple) failures can happen. When they occur, they can have a large impact on the performance of the network.

Yuksel [36] describes an approach that builds on the FRR mechanism but limits its use to a short period. When a single link fails and a pseudowire's primary path fails, the traffic is rapidly switched over to the backup path as described above. However, soon afterwards, the router sets the virtual link weight to a high value and thus triggers the IGP reconvergence process – this is colloquially called "costing out" the link. Once IGP routing converges, a new PIM tree is rebuilt automatically. This avoids long periods where routing occurs over the FRR backup paths, which are unknown to the IGP. This ensures rapid restoration from single-link failures while allowing the multicast tree to dynamically adapt to any additional failures that might occur during a link outage. It is only during this short, transient period when FRR starts and IGP reconvergence finishes that another failure could expose the network to a path overlapping on the same link. The potential downside of this approach is that it incurs two more network reconvergence processes – that is, the period right after FRR has occurred and then again when the failure is repaired. If it is not carefully executed, this alternative approach can cause many new video interruptions due to small "hits" after single failures.

Yuksel [36] proposes a careful multicast recovery methodology to accomplish this approach, yet avoid such drawbacks. A key component of the method is the *make-before-break change* of the multicast tree – that is, the requirement to hitlessly switch traffic from the old multicast tree to the new multicast tree. When the failure is repaired, the method normalizes the multicast tree to its original shortest path tree again in a hitless manner. The key modification to the multicast tree-building process (pruning and joining nodes) is that the prune message to remove the branch to the previous parent is not sent until the router receives PIM–SSM data packets from its new parent for the corresponding (S,G) group. Another motivation for this modification is because current PIM–SSM multicast does not have an explicit acknowledgement to a join request. It is only through the receipt of a data packet on that interface that the node knows that the join request was successfully received and processed at the upstream node. The *soft-state* approach of IP Multicast (refresh the state by periodically sending join requests) is also used to ensure consistency. This principle is used to guide the tree reconfiguration process at a node in reaction to a failure. In this way, routers do not lose data packets during the switchover period. Of course, this primarily works in the PIM-SSM case, where there is a single source.

As we can observe from the description above, building an IPTV backbone with high network availability builds on most of the protocols, multilayer failure models, and restoration machinery we have described in the previous sections of the chapter. In particular, given the underlying probabilities of network failures plus these complex failure and restoration mechanisms, such an approach must include the network design methodology to evaluate and estimate the theoretical network availability of the IPTV backbone. If such a methodology was not utilized, a carrier would run the risk of having its video customers dissatisfied with their video service because of inadequate network availability.

2.7 Summary

This chapter presents an overview of the layered network design that is typical in a large ISP backbone. We emphasized three aspects that influence the design of an IP backbone. The first aspect is that the IP network design is strongly influenced by its relationship with the underlying network layers (such as DWDM and TDM layers) and the network segments (core, metro, and access). ISP networks use a hierarchy of specialized routers, generally called access and backbone routers. At the edge of the network, the location of access routers, and the types of interfaces that they need to support are strongly influenced by the way the customers connect to the backbone through the metro network. In the core of a large carrier network, backbone routers are interconnected using DWDM transmission technology. As IP traffic is the dominant source of demand for the DWDM layer, the backbone demands drive requirements for the DWDM layer. The need for multiple DWDM links has driven the evolution of aggregate links in the core.

The second aspect is that ISP networks have evolved from traditional IP forwarding to support MPLS. The separation of routing and forwarding and the ability to support a routing hierarchy allow ISPs to support new functionality including Layer 2 and Layer 3 VPNs and flexible traffic engineering that could not be as easily supported in a traditional IP network.

Finally, this chapter provided an overview of the issues that affect IP network reliability, including the impact of network disruptions at multiple network layers and, conversely, how different network layers respond to disruptions through network restoration. We described how failures and maintenance events originate at various network layers and how they impact the IP backbone. We presented an overview of the performance of OSPF failure recovery to motivate the need for MPLS Fast Reroute. We summarized the interplay between network restoration and the network design process.

To tie these concepts together, we presented a "case study" of an IPTV backbone. An IPTV network can be thought of as an IP layer with a requirement for very high performance, essentially high network availability and low packet loss. This requires the interlacing of multiple protocols, such as R-UDP, MPLS Fast Reroute, IP Multicast, and Forward Error Control. We described how lower-layer failures (including multiple failures) affect the IP layer and how these IP layer routing and control protocols respond. Understanding the performance of network restoration protocols and the overall availability of the given network design requires careful modeling of the types and likelihood of network failures, as well as the behavior of the restoration protocols. This chapter endeavored to lay a good foundation for reading the remaining chapters of this book.

We conclude by alerting the reader to an important observation about IP network design. Telecommunications and its technologies undergo constant change. Therefore, this chapter describes a point in time. The contents of this chapter are different from what they would have been 5 years ago. There will be further changes over the next 5 years and, consequently, the chapter written 5 years from now may look quite different.

References

1. AT&T (2003). Managed Internet Service Access Redundancy Options, from http://www. pnetcom.com/AB-0027.pdf. Accessed 15 April 2009.
2. Awduche, D., Berger, L., Gan, D., Li. T., Srinivasan, V., & Swallow, G. (2001). RSVP-TE: Extensions to RSVP for LSP Tunnels. IETF RFC 3209, Dec. http://tools.ietf.org/html/rfc3209. Accessed 29 January 2010.
3. Braden, R., Zhang, L., Berson, S., Herzog, S., & Jamin, S. (1997). Resource ReSer-Vation Protocol (RSVP) – Version 1 Functional Specification. IETF RFC 2205, Sept. http://tools.ietf.org/html/rfc2205. Accessed 29 January 2010.
4. Chiu, A., Choudhury, G., Doverspike, R., & Li, G. (2007). Restoration design in IP over re-configurable all-optical networks. NPC 2007, Dalian, P.R. China, September 2007.
5. Choudhury, G. (Ed.) (2005). Prioritized Treatment of Specific OSPF Version 2 Packets and Congestion Avoidance. IETF RFC 4222, Oct.
6. Ciena Core Director. http://www.ciena.com/products/products_coredirector_product_overview. htm. Accessed 13 April 2009.
7. Cisco (1999). Tag Switching in *Internetworking Technology Handbook*, Chapter 23, http://www.cisco.com/en/US/docs/internetworking/technology/handbook/Tag-Switching.pdf, accessed 12/26/09.
8. Cormen, T. H., Leiserson, C. E., Rivest, R. L., & Stein, C. (2001). Introduction to algorithms, second edition (pp. 595–601). Cambridge: MIT Press, New York: McGraw-Hill. ISBN 0–262–03293–7. Section 24.3: Dijkstra's algorithm.
9. Doverspike R., Li, G., Oikonomou, K. N., Ramakrishnan, K. K., Sinha, R. K., Wang, D., et al. (2009). Designing a reliable IPTV network. *IEEE Internet Computing Magazine* May/June, pp. 15–22.
10. Doverspike, R., Li, G., Oikonomou, K., Ramakrishnan, K. K., & Wang, D. (2007). IP back-bone design for multimedia distribution: architecture and performance. INFOCOM-2007, Anchorage Alaska April 2007.
11. Doverspike, R., & Magill, P. (2008). Commercial optical networks, overlay networks and services. In I. Kaminow, T. Li, & A. Willner, (Eds), Chapter 13 in *Optical fiber telecommunications VB*. San Diego, CA: Academic.
12. Feuer, M., Kilper, D., & Woodward, S. (2008). ROADMs and their system applications. In I. Kaminow, T. Li, & A. Willner, (Eds), Chapter 8 in *Optical fiber telecommunications VB*. San Diego, CA: Academic.

13. Goyal, M., Ramakrishnan K. K., & Feng W. (2003) "Achieving Faster Failure Detection in OSPF Networks," IEEE International Conference on Communications (ICC 2003), Alaska, May 2003.
14. IEEE 802.1Q-2005 (2005) Virtual Bridged Local Area Networks; ISBN 0–7381–3662-X.
15. IEEE: 802.1Qay – Provider Backbone Bridge Traffic Engineering. http://www.ieee802. org/1/pages/802.1ay.html. Accessed October 7, 2008.
16. IETF PWE3: Pseudo Wire Emulation Edge to Edge (PWE3) Working Group. http://www. ietf.org/html.charters/pwe3-charter.html. Accessed 7 Nov 2008.
17. IETF RFC 4090 (2005) Fast Reroute Extensions to RSVP-TE for LSP Tunnels. http:// www.ietf.org/rfc/rfc4090.txt. May 2005. Accessed 7 Nov 2008.
18. ITU-T G.709, "Interfaces for the Optical Transport Network," March 2003.
19. ITU-T G.7713.2. Distributed Call and Connection Management: Signalling mechanism using GMPLS RSVP-TE.
20. Kalmanek, C. (2002). A Retrospective View of ATM. ACM Sigcomm CCR, Vol. 32, Issue 5, Nov, ISSN: 0146–4833.
21. Katz, D., Kompella, K., & Yeung, D. (2003). IETF RFC 3630: Traffic Engineering (TE) Extensions to OSPF Version 2. http://tools.ietf.org/html/rfc3630. Accessed 4 May 2009.
22. Klincewicz, J. G. (2005). Issues in link topology design for IP networks. SPIE Conference on performance, quality of service and control of next-generation communication networks III, SPIE Vol. 6011, Boston, MA.
23. Klincewicz, J. G. (2006). Why is IP network design so difficult? Eighth INFORMS telecommunications conference, Dallas, TX, March 30–April 1, 2006.
24. Kompella, K., & Rekhter, Y. (2007). IETF RFC 4761: Virtual private LAN service (VPLS) using BGP for auto-discovery and signaling. http://tools.ietf.org/html/rfc4761, accessed 12/26/09.
25. Lasserre, M., & Kompella, V. (2007). IETF RFC 4762: Virtual private LAN service (VPLS) using label distribution protocol (LDP) signaling. http://tools.ietf.org/html/rfc4762, accessed 12/26/09.
26. Moy, J. (1998). IETF RFC 2328: OSPF Version 2. http://tools.ietf.org/html/rfc2328, accessed 12/26/09.
27. Nortel. (2007). Adding scale, QoS and operational simplicity to Ethernet. http://www.nortel. com/solutions/collateral/nn115500.pdf, accessed 12/26/09.
28. Oikonomou, K., Sinha, R., & Doverspike, R. (2009). Multi-Layer Network Performance and Reliability Analysis. The International Journal of Interdisciplinary Telecommunications and Networking (IJITN), Vol. 1 (3), pp. 1–29, Sept.
29. Optical Internetworking Forum (OIF) (2008). OIF-UNI-02.0-Common–User Network Interface (UNI) 2.0 Signaling Specification: Common Part. http://www.oiforum.com/public/ documents/OIF-UNI-02.0-Common.pdf.
30. Oran, D. (1990). IETF RFC 1142: OSI IS-IS intra-domain routing protocol. http://tools. ietf.org/html/rfc1142.
31. Partridge, C., & Hinden, R. (1990). Version 2 of the Reliable Data Protocol (RDP), IETF RFC 1151. April.
32. Perlman, R. (1999). Interconnections: Bridges, Routers, Switches, and Internetworking Protocols, 2e. Addison-Wesley Professional Computing Series.
33. Schulzrinne, H., Casner, S., Frederick, R., & Jacobson, V. (2003). RTP: A Transport Protocol for Real-Time Application, IETF RFC 3550. http://www.ietf.org/rfc/rfc3550.txt, accessed 12/26/09.
34. Sycamore Intelligent Optical Switch. (2009). http://www.sycamorenet.com/products/sn16000. asp. Accessed 13 April 2009.
35. Telcordia GR-253-CORE (2000) Synchronous Optical Network (SONET) Transport Systems: Common Generic Criteria.
36. Yuksel, M., Ramakrishnan, K. K., & Doverspike, R. (2008). Cross-layer failure restoration for a robust IPTV service. LANMAN-2008, Cluj-Napoca, Romania September.
37. Zimmermann, H. (1980). OSI reference model – the ISO model of architecture for open systems interconnection. *IEEE Transactions on Communications*, 28(Suppl. 4), 425–432.

Glossary of Acronyms and Key Terms

1:1	One-by-one (signal switched to restoration path on detection of failure)
1 + 1	One-plus-one (signal duplicated across both service path and restoration path; receiver chooses surviving signal upon detection of failure)
Access Network Segment	The feeder network and loop segments associated with a given metro segment
ADM	Add/Drop Multiplexer
Administrative Domain	Routing area in IGP
Aggregate Link	Bundles multiple physical links between a pair of routers into a single virtual link from the point of view of the routers. Also called bundled or composite link
AR	Access Router
AS	Autonomous System
ASBR	Autonomous System Border Router
ATM	Asynchronous Transfer Mode
AWG	Arrayed Waveguide Grating
B-DCS	Broadband Digital Cross-connect System (cross-connects at DS-3 or higher rate)
Backhaul	Using TDM connections that encapsulate packets to connect customers to packet networks
BER	Bit Error Rate
BGP	Border Gateway Protocol
BLSR	Bidirectional Line-Switched Ring
BR	Backbone Router
Bundled Link	See Aggregate Link
CE switch	Customer-Edge switch
Channelized	A TDM link/connection that multiplexes lower-rate signals into its time slots
CHOC Card	CHannelized OC-n card
CIR	Committed Information Rate
CO	Central Office
Composite Link	See Aggregate Link
Core Network Segment	Equipment in the POPs and network structures that connect them for intermetro transport and switching
CoS	Class of Service
CPE	Customer Premises Equipment

CSPF	Constraint-based Shortest Path First
DCS	Digital Cross-connect System
DDoS	Distributed Denial of Service (security attack on router)
DoS	Denial of Service (security attack on router)
DS-0	Digital Signal – level 0 a pre-SONET signal carrying one voice-frequency channel at 64 kb/s)
DS-1	Digital Signal – level 1 (a 1.544 Mb/s signal). A channelized DS-1 carries 24 DS0s
DS-3	Digital Signal – level 3 (a 44.736 Mb/s signal). A channelized DS-3 carries 28 DS1s
DWDM	Dense Wavelength-Division Multiplexing
E-1	European plesiosynchronous (pre-SDH) rate of 2.0 Mb/s
eBGP	External Border Gateway Protocol
EGP	Exterior Gateway Protocol
EIGRP	Enhanced Interior Gateway Routing Protocol
EIR	Excess Information Rate
EPL	Ethernet Private Line
FCC	Federal Communications Commission
FE	Fast Ethernet (100 Mb/s)
FEC	Forward Error Correction – bit-error recovery technique in TDM transmission and some IPs
FEC	Forwarding Equivalence Class – classification of flows defined in MPLS
Feeder Network	The portion of the access network between the loop and first metro central office
FRR	Fast Re-Route
FXC	Fiber Cross-Connect
Gb/s	Gigabits per second (1 billion bits per second)
GigE	Gigabit Ethernet (nominally 1 Gb/s)
GMPLS	Generalized MPLS
HD	High definition (short for HDTV)
HDTV	High-definition TV (television with resolution exceeding 720×1280)
Hitless	Method of changing network connections or routes that incur negligible loss
iBGP	Interior Border Gateway Protocol
IETF	Internet Engineering Task Force
IGP	Interior Gateway Protocol
Internet Route Free Core	Where MPLS removes external BGP information plus Layer 3 address lookup from the interior of the IP backbone
IGMP	Internet Group Management Protocol
Inter-office Links	Links whose endpoints are contained in different central offices

Intra-office Links	Links that are totally contained within the same central office
IOS	Intelligent Optical Switch
IP	Internet Protocol
IPTV	Internet Protocol television (i.e., entertainment-quality video delivered over IP)
IROU	Indefeasible Right of Use
IS-IS	Intermediate-System-to-Intermediate-System (IP routing and control plane protocol)
ISO	International Organization for Standardization (not an acronym)
ISP	Internet Service Provider
ITU	International Telecommunication Union
Kb/s	Kilobits per second (1,000 bits per second)
LAN	Local Area Network
LATA	Local Access and Transport Area
Layer n	A colloquial packet protocol layering model, with origins to the OSI reference model. Today, roughly Layer 3 corresponds to IP packets, Layer 2 to MPLS LSPs, pseudowires, or Ethernet-based VLANs, and Layer 1 to all lower-layer transport protocols
LDP	Label Distribution Protocol
LMP	Link Management Protocol
Local Loop	The portion of the access segment between the customer and feeder network. Also called "last mile"
LSA	Link-State Advertisement
LSDB	Link-State Database
LSP	Label Switched Path
LSR	Label Switch Router
MAC	Media Access Control
MAN	Metropolitan Area Network
Mb/s	Megabits per second (1 Million bits per second)
MEMS	Micro-Electro-Mechanical Systems
Metro Network Segment	The network layers of the equipment located in the central offices of a given metropolitan area
MPEG	Moving Picture Experts Group
MPLS	Multiprotocol Label Switching
MSO	Multiple System Operator (typically coaxial cable companies)
MSP	Multi-Service Platform – A type of ADM enhanced with many forms of interfaces
MTBF	Mean Time Between Failure

MTSO	Mobile Telephone Switching Office
MTTR	Mean Time to Repair
Multicast	Point-to-multipoint flows in packet networks
N-DCS	Narrowband Digital Cross-connect System (cross-connects at DS0 rate)
n-degree ROADM	A ROADM that can fiber to more than three different ROADMS (also called multidegree ROADM)
Next-hop	Method in MPLS FRR that routes around a down link
Next-next-hop	Method in MPLS FRR that routes around a down node
Normalization	Step in network restoration after all failures are repaired to bring the network back to its normal state
NTE	Network Terminating Equipment
OC-n	Optical Carrier – level n (designation of optical transport of a SONET STS-n)
ODU	Optical channel Data Unit – protocol data unit in ITU OTN
O-E-O	Optical-to-Electrical-to-Optical
OIF	Optical Internetworking Forum
OL	Optical Layer
OSPF	Open Shortest Path First
OSPF-TE	Open Shortest Path First – Traffic Engineering
OSS	Operations Support System
OT	Optical Transponder
OTN	Optical Transport Network – ITU optical protocol
P Router	Provider Router
PBB-TE	Provider Backbone Bridge – Traffic Engineering
PBT	Provider Backbone Transport
PE Router	Provider-Edge Router
PIM	Protocol-Independent Multicast
PL	Private Line
P-NNI	Private Network-to-Network Interface (ATM routing protocol)
POP	Point Of Presence
PPP	Point-to-Point Protocol
PPPoE	Point-to-Point Protocol over Ethernet
Pseudowire	A virtual connection defined in the IETF PWE3 that encapsulates higher-layer protocols
PVC	Permanent Virtual Circuit
PWE3	Pseudo-Wire Emulation Edge-to-Edge
QoS	Quality of Service
RAR	Remote Access Router
RD	Route Distinguisher
Reconvergence	IGP process to update network topology and adjust routing tables

RIB	Router Information Base
ROADM	Reconfigurable Optical Add/Drop Multiplexer
RR	Route Reflector
RSTP	Rapid Spanning Tree Protocol
RSVP	Resource Reservation Protocol
RT	Route Target (also Remote Terminal in metro TDM networks)
RD	Route Distinguisher
RTP	Real-Time Protocol
SD	Standard Definition (television with resolution of about 640×480)
SDH	Synchronous Digital Hierarchy (a synchronous optical networking standard used outside North America, documented by the ITU in G.707 and G.708)
Serving CO	The first metro central office to which a given customer homes
SHO	Super Hub Office
SLA	Service Level Agreement
SRLG	Shared Risk Link Group
SONET	Synchronous Optical Network (a synchronous optical networking standard used in North America, documented in GR-253-CORE from Telcordia)
SONET/SDH self-healing rings	Typically UPSR or BLSR rings
SPF	Shortest Path First
STS-n	Synchronous Transport Signal – level n (a signal level of the SONET hierarchy with a data rate of $n \times 51.84$ Mb/s)
SVC	Switched Virtual Circuit
TCP	Transmission Control Protocol
TDM	Time Division Multiplexing
UDP	User Data Protocol
UNI	User-Network Interface
Unicast	Point-to-point flows in packet networks
UPSR	Unidirectional Path-Switched Ring
VHO	Video Hub Office
VLAN	Virtual Local Area Network
VoD	Video on Demand
VoIP	Voice-over-Internet Protocol
VPLS	Virtual Private LAN Service (i.e., Transparent LAN Service)
VPN	Virtual Private Network

WAN	Wide Area Network
Wavelength continuity	A restriction in DWDM equipment that a through connection must be optically cross-connected to the same wavelength on both fibers
W-DCS	Wideband Digital Cross-connect System (cross-connects at DS-1, SONET VT-n or higher rate)
DWDM	Wavelength-Division Multiplexing

Part II
Reliability Modeling and Network Planning

Chapter 3
Reliability Metrics for Routers in IP Networks

Yaakov Kogan

3.1 Introduction

As the Internet has become an increasingly critical communication infrastructure for business, education, and society in general, the need to understand and systematically analyze its reliability has become more important. Internet Service Providers (ISPs) face the challenge of needing to continuously upgrade the network and grow network capacity, while providing a service that meets stringent customer-reliability expectations. While telecommunication companies have long experience providing reliable telephone service, the challenge for an ISP is more difficult because changes in Internet technology, particularly router software, are significantly more frequent and less rigorously tested than was the case in circuit-switched telephone networks. ISPs cannot wait until router technology matures – a large ISP has to meet high reliability requirements for critical applications like financial transactions, Voice over IP, and IPTV using commercially available technology. The need to use less mature technology has resulted in a variety of redundancy solutions at the edge of the network, and in well-thought-out designs for a resilient core network that is shared by traffic from all applications.

The reliability objective for circuit-switched telephone service of "no more than 2 hours downtime in 40 years" has been applied to voice communication since 1964 [1]. It has been achieved using expensive redundancy solutions for both switches and transmission facilities. Though routers are less reliable than circuit switches, commercial IP networks have three main advantages when designing for reliability, in comparison with legacy telephone networks. First, packet switching is a far more economically efficient mechanism for multiplexing network resources than circuit switching, given the bursty nature of data traffic. Second, protocols like Multi-Protocol Label Switching (MPLS) support a range of network restoration options that are more economically efficient in restoration from failures of transmission facilities than traditional 1:1 redundancy. Third, commercial

Y. Kogan (✉)
AT&T Labs, 200 S. Laurel Ave, Middletown, NJ 07748, USA
e-mail: yaakovkogan@att.com

C.R. Kalmanek et al. (eds.), *Guide to Reliable Internet Services and Applications*,
Computer Communications and Networks, DOI 10.1007/978-1-84882-828-5_3,
© Springer-Verlag London Limited 2010

IP networks can provide different levels of redundancy to different commercial customers, for example, by offering access diversity or multihoming options, pricing the service depending on its reliability. This allows Internet service providers to satisfy customers who are price-sensitive [2] while recovering the high cost of redundancy from customers who require increased reliability to support mission critical applications.

The reliability of modern provider edge routers, which have a large variety of interface cards, cannot be accurately characterized by a single downtime or reliability metric because it requires averaging the contributions of the various line cards that may hide the poor reliability of some components. We address this challenge by introducing granular metrics for quantifying the reliability of IP routers. Section 3.2 provides an overview of the main router elements and redundancy mechanisms. In Section 3.3, we use a simplified router reliability model to demonstrate the application of different reliability metrics. In Section 3.4, we define metrics for measuring the reliability of IP routers in production networks. Section 3.5 provides an overview of challenges with measuring end-to-end availability.

3.2   Redundancy Solutions in IP Routers

This section provides an overview of the primary elements of a modern router and associated redundancy mechanisms, which are important for availability modeling of services in IP networks. A high-speed IP router is a special multiprocessor system with two types of processors, each with its own memory and CPU: Route Processors (RPs) and Line–Cards (LCs). Each line–card receives packets from other routers via one or more logical interfaces, and performs forwarding operations by sending them to outbound logical interfaces using information in its local Forwarding Information Base (FIB). The route processor controls the operation of the entire router, runs the routing protocols, maintains the necessary databases for route processing, and updates the FIB on each line–card. This separation implies that each LC can continue forwarding packets based on its copy of the FIB when the RP fails. Figure 3.1 provides a simplified illustration of router hardware architecture, where two route processors (active and backup) and multiple line-cards are interconnected through a switch fabric. The Monitor bus is used exclusively for transmission of error and management messages that help one to isolate the fault when a component is faulty and to restore the normal operation of the router, if the failed component is backed up by a redundant unit. Data traffic never goes through Monitor bus but across the switch fabric. These hardware (HW) components operate under the control of an Operating System (OS). Additional details for Cisco and Juniper routers can be found in [3, 4] and [5], respectively.

A typical Mean Time Between Failures (MTBF) for both RPs and LCs is about 100,000 h (see, e.g., Table 9.3 in [6]). This MTBF accounts only for hard failures requiring replacement of the failed component, in contrast with soft failures, from which the router can recover, for example, by card reset. A typical example of a soft

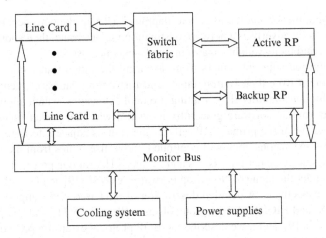

Fig. 3.1 Generic router hardware architecture

hardware failure is parity error. Router vendors do not usually provide an MTBF for the OS, as it varies over a wide range. According to our experience, a new OS version may have an MTBF well below 100,000 h as a result of undetected software errors that are first encountered after the OS is deployed to the field. According to our experience, the MTBF for a stable OS is typically above 100,000 h, though even with a stable OS, changes in the operating environment can trigger latent software errors.

Without redundancy solutions at the edge of the network, component failures interrupt customer traffic until the failed component is recovered by reset, which may take about a minute, or until it is replaced, which can take hours. To reduce failure impacts, shared HW components whose failure would impact the entire router (e.g., RP, switch fabric, power supply, and cooling system) are typically redundant. In this case, the restoration time (assuming a successful failover to the redundant component) is defined by the failover time. For example, in Cisco 12000 series routers [3] and Juniper T640 router [7], the switch fabric consists of five cards, four of which are active and one provides redundancy with a subsecond restoration time when an active card fails. Failure of one power supply or cooling element does not have any impact on service.

RP redundancy is provided by a configuration with two RP cards: primary and backup. A first attempt at reducing the failover time has been made by running the backup RP in standby mode with partial synchronization between the active and standby RPs that enables the standby RP to maintain all Layer 1 and Layer 2 sessions and recover the routing database from adjacent nodes when the primary RP fails. However, when a primary RP fails, BGP adjacencies with adjacent routers go down. The loss of BGP adjacency has the same effect on network routing as failure of the entire router until the standby RP comes on-line and re-establishes BGP adjacencies with its neighbors. During this time, the routing protocols will reconverge to another route and then back again that will cause transient packet loss – a phenomenon known as "route flapping." (Route flapping occurs when a router alternately advertises a network destination via one route, then another (or as unavailable, and then available again) in quick sequence [8].)

To prevent the adjacent routers from declaring the failed router out of service and removing it from their routing tables and forwarding databases, vendors have developed high availability (HA) routing protocol extensions, which allow a router to restart its routing software gracefully in such a way that packet forwarding is not disrupted when the primary RP fails. If the routers adjacent to a given router support these extensions, they will continue to advertise routes from the restarting router during the grace period. Cisco's and Juniper's HA routing protocol extensions are known under the name of Non-Stop Forwarding (NSF) [9] and Graceful Restart (GR) [10], respectively. A detailed description of the Cisco NSF support for BGP, OSPF, IS-IS, and EIGRP routing protocols as well as for MPLS-related protocols can be found in [9]. Here, we describe the BGP protocol extension procedures that follow the implementation specification provided in the IETF proposed standard "Graceful Restart Mechanism for BGP" [11]. Let R1 be the restarting router and R2 be a peer. The goal is to restart a BGP session between R1 and peering routers without redirecting traffic around R1.

1. R1 and R2 signal each other that they understand Graceful Restart in their initial exchange of BGP OPEN messages when the initial BGP connection is established between R1 and R2.
2. An RP failover occurs, and the router R1 BGP process starts on the newly active RP. R1 does not have a routing information base and must reacquire it from its peer routers. R1 will continue to forward IP packets destined for (or through) peer routers (R2) using the last updated FIB.
3. When R2 detects that the TCP session with R1 is cleared, it marks routes, learned from R1, as STALE, but continues to use them to forward packets. R2 also initializes a Restart-timer for R1. Router R2 will remove all STALE routes unless it receives an OPEN message from R1 within the specified Restart-time.
4. R1 establishes a new TCP session with R2 and sends an OPEN message to R2, indicating that its BGP software has restarted. When R2 receives this OPEN message, it resets its own Restart-timer and starts a Stalepath-timer.
5. Both routers re-established their session. R2 begins to send UPDATE messages to R1. R1 starts an Update-delay timer and waits until up to 120 s to receive End-of-RIB (EOR) from all its peers.
6. When R1 receives EOR from all its peers, it will begin the BGP Route Selection Process.
7. When this process is complete, it will begin to send UPDATE messages to R2. R1 indicates completion of updates by EOR and R2 starts its Route Selection Process.
8. While R2 waits for an EOR, it also monitors Stalepath time. If the timer expires, all STALE routes will be removed and "normal" BGP process will be in effect. When R2 has completed its Route Selection Process, then any STALE entries will be refreshed with newer information or removed from the BGP RIB and FIB. The network is now converged.

One drawback of NSF/GR is that there is a potential for transient routing loops or packet loss if a restarting router loses its forwarding state (e.g., owing to a power failure). A second drawback of NSF/GR is that it can prolong delays of network-layer re-routing in cases where the service is NOT restored by RP failover. In addition, to be effective in a large ISP backbone, NSF/GR extensions would need to be deployed on all of the peering routers. However, the OSPF NSF extension is Cisco proprietary. The respective drafts were submitted to the IETF but not approved as standards. Since most large ISP networks use routers from multiple vendors, the lack of standardization and universal adoption by vendors limits the usefulness of the NSF and GR extensions.

Another approach to router reliability, called Non-Stop Routing (NSR), is free from the drawbacks of graceful restart. It is a self-contained solution that does not require protocol extensions and has a faster failover time. With NSR, the standby RP runs its own version of each protocol and there is continuous synchronization between the active and standby RPs to the extent that it enables the standby RP to take over when the active RP fails without any disruption in the existing peering sessions. The first implementation of NSR was done by Avici Systems [12] in 2003 in the Terabit Switch Router (TSR) router that was used in the AT&T core network. Later, other router vendors implemented their versions of NSR (see, e.g., [13]).

It is important to note that router outages can be divided into two categories: planned and unplanned outages. Much of the preceding discussion focused on RP failures or unplanned outages. Planned outages are caused by scheduled maintenance activities, which include software and hardware upgrades as well as card replacement and installation of additional line-cards. Router vendors are developing a software solution on top of NSR to support in-service software upgrade, or ISSU (see, e.g., [13–15]). The goal of ISSU is a significant reduction in downtime due to software upgrades, potentially eliminating this category of downtime if both the old and new SW versions support ISSU.

We now turn our attention to line-card failures. Line-card failures are distinct from link failures – while link failures can often be recovered by the underlying transport technology, e.g., SONET ring (see Chapter 2), line-card failures require traffic to be handled by a redundant line-card provisioned on the same or a different router. Line-card redundancy is particularly important for reducing the outage duration of PE (provider-edge) routers that terminate thousands of low-speed customer ports. The first candidate for redundancy is an uplink LC that is used for connection to a P (core) router. Without redundancy, any uplink LC downtime will cause PE router isolation. In addition, a redundant uplink LC allows us to connect a PE router to two P routers using physically diverse transport links. This configuration results in the near elimination of PE router downtime caused by periodic maintenance activities on P routers, under the assumption that maintenance is not performed on these two P routers simultaneously. PE router downtime is nearly eliminated in this case because the probability of PE isolation caused by the failure of the second uplink or the other P router is negligibly small if the maintenance window is short. Restoration from an uplink LC failure is provided at the IP-Layer with restoration time of the order of 10 s as described in Chapter 2.

SONET interfaces on IP routers may support the ability to automatically switch traffic from a failed line-card to a redundant line-card, using a technique called Automatic Protection Switching (APS) [16]. Implementation of APS requires installation of two identical line-cards; one card is designated as primary, the other as secondary. A port on the primary LC is configured as the working interface and the port with the same port number on the secondary LC as the protection interface. The ports form a single virtual interface. Ports on the secondary LC cannot be configured with services; they can only be configured as protection ports for the corresponding ports on the primary LC. The protection and working interfaces are connected to a SONET ADM (Add-Drop Multiplexer), which sends the same signal payload to the working and protection interfaces. When the working interface fails, its traffic is switched to the protection interface. According to our experience, the switchover time is of the order of 1 min. Hitless switchover requires protocol synchronization between the line–cards, which was not available at the time of writing of this chapter. APS is only available in a 1:1 configuration. As a result, it is considered to be expensive. An alternative line-card redundancy approach developed at AT&T [17] is based on a new ISP edge architecture called *RouterFarm*. RouterFarm utilizes 1:N redundancy, in which a single PE backup router can support multiple active routers. The RouterFarm architecture supports customer access links that connect to PE routers over a dynamically reconfigurable access network. When a PE router fails or is taken out of service for planned maintenance, control software rehomes the customer access links from the affected router to a selected backup router and copies the appropriate router configuration data to the backup router. Service is provided by the backup router once the rehoming is complete. After the primary router is repaired or required maintenance is performed, customers can be rehomed back to the primary router.

3.3 Router Reliability Modeling

As described in Section 3.2, router outages can be divided into two categories: planned and unplanned. Planned outages are caused by scheduled maintenance activities. Customers with a single connection to an ISP edge router are notified in advance about planned maintenance. Outages outside of the maintenance window are referred to as unplanned. The common practice is to evaluate router reliability metrics for planned and unplanned outages separately. Table 3.1 provides an example[1] of downtime calculation for software (SW) and hardware (HW) upgrades that require the entire router to be taken out of service. The downtime is calculated based on upgrade frequency per year in the second column and mean upgrade duration in the third column. The total mean downtime per year for planned outages is 42 min.

---

[1] All examples are for illustrative purposes only and are not meant to model or describe any network or vendor's product.

Table 3.1 Planned downtime for SW and HW upgrades

Activity	Freq/year	Duration (min)	Downtime (min)
SW upgrade	2	15	30
HW upgrade	0.2	60	12

The router downtime is close to 0 for unplanned outages if the router supports RP and LC redundancy. If LC redundancy is not supported, unplanned router downtime depends on the ratio r_{LC}/m_{LC} where r_{LC} and m_{LC} denote LC MTTR (Mean Time To Repair) and MTBF, respectively. Using the fact that $r_{LC} \ll m_{LC}$, one can approximate the downtime probability by r_{LC}/m_{LC} and calculate the average unplanned router downtime per year as

$$d_{LC} = (r_{LC}/m_{LC}) \times 525,600 \ (\text{min}/\text{year}).$$

The factor $525,600 = 365 \times 24 \times 60$ is the number of minutes in a 365-day year. With stable hardware and software, $r_{LC}/m_{LC} \approx 4 \times 10^{-5}$ and unplanned downtime d_{LC} is around 21 min, which is less than the planned downtime due to upgrades by a factor of 2.

The reliability improvement due to RP and LC redundancy for unplanned outages can be evaluated using the following simplified router reliability model described by a system consisting of two independent components representing the LC and RP. Component 1 corresponds to the LC and component 2 corresponds to the RP. Each component alternates between periods when it is up and periods when it is down. The system is working if both components are up. For nonredundant component $i, i = 1, 2$, denote MTBF and MTTR by m_i and r_i, respectively. For a component consisting of primary and backup units, we assume that once a primary unit fails, the backup unit starts to function with probability p_i after a random delay with mean $\tau_i \ll r_i$. With probability $1 - p_i$, the switchover to the backup unit fails, in which case the mean downtime is r_i. Thus, the MTTR for a redundant component is

$$b_i = p_i \tau_i + (1 - p_i) r_i. \tag{3.1}$$

Two important particular cases correspond to $p_i = 0$ (no redundancy) and $\tau_i = 0$ (instantaneous switchover). The MTBF for a redundant component is

$$c_i = m_i \text{ if } \tau_i > 0$$
$$c_i = m_i/(1 - p_i) \text{ if } \tau_i = 0. \tag{3.2}$$

The steady state probability that the system (component) is working is referred to as availability. The complementary probability is referred to as unavailability. Based on our assumptions, the availability of component i is

$$A_i = \frac{c_i}{c_i + b_i} \tag{3.3}$$

and the system availability is

$$A = A_1 A_2. \qquad (3.4)$$

In our case, $r_i \ll m_i$ that allows us to obtain the following simple approximation for the system unavailability:

$$U = 1 - A_1 A_2 = 1 - (1 - U_1)(1 - U_2) \approx U_1 + U_2 \qquad (3.5)$$

where $U_i = b_i / (c_i + b_i)$ is unavailability of component i. Another important reliability metric is the rate f_s at which the system fails. In our case (see, e.g., 7c in [18])

$$f_s \approx 1/c_1 + 1/c_2. \qquad (3.6)$$

Redundancy without instantaneous switchover decreases the mean component downtime b_i and the component and the system unavailability. However, the system failure rate does not decrease because the component uptime $c_i = m_i$ remains unchanged if $\tau_i > 0$. Instantaneous switchover decreases both the unavailability and the system failure rate.

The availability of LCs and RPs with no redundancy is typically better than 0.9999 (four nines) but worse than 0.99999 (five nines). We can compute an estimate of the improvement due to redundancy using Eq. (3.1). If the redundancy of component i is characterized by a probability of successful switchover $p_i = 0.95$ and $\tau_i / r_i = 0.05$, then the mean component downtime b_i and therefore its unavailability would decrease by about a factor of 10, resulting in a component availability exceeding five nines. The system availability would be limited by the availability of any nonredundant component.

3.4 Reliability Metrics for Routers in Access Networks

Figure 3.2 depicts a typical Layer 3 access topology for enterprise customers. It includes n provider-edge routers PE1, ..., PEn and two core or backbone routers P1 and P2, which are responsible for delivering traffic from customer edge (CE)

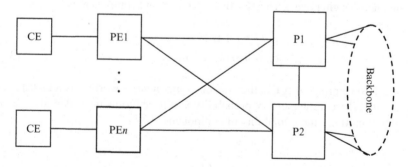

Fig. 3.2 Access network elements

routers at a customer location into the commercial IP network backbone. The service provided by an ISP to an enterprise customer is typically associated with a customer "access port." An access port is a logical interface on the line-card in a PE, where the link from a customer's CE router terminates. In general, a PE has a variety of line-cards with different port densities depending on the port speed. For example, a channelized OC-12 card provides up to 336 T1/E1 ports, while a channelized OC-48 card can provide up to either 48 T3 ports, or 16 OC3 ports, or 4 OC12 ports. In Fig. 3.2, each PE is dual-homed to two different P (core) routers using two physically diverse transport links terminating on different line-cards at the PE router. (These transport links are referred to as uplinks.) The links that connect P routers at different nodes are generally provided by an underlying transport network. Dual-homing is used to reduce the impact on the customer due to outages – from a potentially long repair interval to short-duration packet loss caused by protocol reconvergence. Dual-homing is used to address the following outage scenarios:

- Outage of uplink transport equipment
- Outage of an uplink line-card at PE routers
- Outage of an uplink line-card at P routers
- Outage of one P router or its associated backbone links

Customer downtime can be caused by a failure in a PE component, such as a failed interface or line-card, or from a total PE outage.

Our goal in this section is to provide a practical way of applying the traditional reliability metrics like availability and MTBF to a large network of edge routers. The calculation of these metrics is straightforward in the case of K identical systems $s_1, \ldots, s_K$, where each system alternates between periods when it is up and periods when it is down. Assume that $k \leq K$ different systems $s_{i_1}, \ldots, s_{i_k}$ failed during time interval of length T, and let t_j be the total outage duration of system j. The unavailability U_j of system j can be estimated as

$$U_j = t_j/T \text{ for } j = i_1, \ldots, i_k \tag{3.7}$$

and $U_j = 0$ otherwise. Then, the average unavailability is

$$\overline{U} = \frac{\sum_{j=1}^{K} U_j}{K} = \frac{\sum_{j=1}^{k} t_{i_j}}{KT} \tag{3.8}$$

and the average availability is

$$\overline{A} = 1 - \overline{U}. \tag{3.9}$$

Finally, the average time between failures is estimated as KT/L, where $L \geq k$ is the total number of failures during time interval T.

There are two main difficulties with extending these estimates to routers. First, routers experience failures of a single line-card in addition to entire router failures. Second, routers may not be identical. The initial approach to overcome these difficulties was to assign to each failure a weight that represents the fraction of the access network impacted by the failure. Such an approach is adequate for access networks consisting of the same type routers and line-cards with port speeds in a sufficiently narrow range, which was the case of early access networks with Cisco's 7500 routers. Modern access networks may consist of several router platforms and high-speed routers may have line-cards with port speed varying in a wide range. For these networks, averaging failures over various router platforms and line-cards with different port speeds is not sufficient. We start with presenting the existing averaging techniques and demonstrating their deficiencies and then describe a granular approach where availability is described by a vector with components representing the availability for each type of access line-cards.

Two frequently used expressions for calculating the fraction of the impacted access network are based on different parameterizations of impacted access ports in service and have the following forms [19]:

$$f = \frac{\text{Number of impacted access ports in service}}{\text{Total number of all access ports in service}} \tag{3.10}$$

and

$$f = \frac{\text{Total bandwidth of impacted access ports in service}}{\text{Total bandwidth of all access ports in service}} \tag{3.11}$$

Having the fraction f_i of access port impacted and failure duration D_i for each failure $i, i = 1, \ldots, L$ during time interval of length T, we can estimate the average access unavailability and availability as

$$\overline{U}_{\text{access}} = \sum_{i=1}^{L} f_i \frac{D_i}{T} \quad \text{and} \quad \overline{A}_{\text{access}} = 1 - \overline{U}_{\text{access}} \tag{3.12}$$

respectively. Formally, one can use Eq. (3.12) with port-weighting or bandwidth-weighting fractions f_i for estimating the average unavailability (availability) of any access network with different router platforms. However, there are several problems with these averaging techniques that limit their usefulness:

- Port-weighted fraction (3.10) emphasizes line-card failures with low-speed ports while failures of high-speed ports are heavily discounted because the port density on a line-card is inversely proportional to the port speed.
- Bandwidth-weighted fraction (3.11) assigns lower weight to failures of line-cards with low-speed ports because they do not utilize the entire bandwidth of the line-card.
- Any averaging over different router platforms or even for one router platform with a variety of line-cards that have different quality of hardware and software may hide defects.

These issues are illustrated by the following example. Consider an access network consisting of 100 Cisco gigabit switch routers (GSRs) and assume that each router has two access line-cards of each of the following three types:

- Channelized OC12 with up to 336 T1 ports
- Channelized OC48: one card is with up to 48 T3 ports while another card is either with up to 16 OC3 ports (50 routers) or with up to 4 OC12 ports (50 routers)
- 1-port OC48.

The total number of ports in service and their respective bandwidth (BW) are shown in Table 3.2. The number of ports in the third column of Table 3.2 is obtained by multiplying the number of ports in service given in the second column of Table 3.3 by the total number of cards with the respective port speed. For T1 and OC48, the total number of cards of each type is $200 = 2 \times 100$. For T3, OC3, and OC12, the total number of cards is 100, 50, and 50, respectively. In Table 3.3, we use Eqs. (3.10) and (3.11) to calculate port-weight and bandwidth-weight for failure of one line-card depending on the number of ports in service given in the second column. The bandwidth of a line-card is obtained as a product of the number of ports in service, given in the second column of Table 3.3, and the respective speed given in the second column of Table 3.2. One can see that port-weighting practically disregards failures of line-cards with OC48 and OC12 ports, while contribution of failures of line-cards with T3 and OC3 ports is discounted relative to T1 ports by a factor of 6.7 and 20, respectively. As a result, the availability of the access network is dominated by the availability of channelized OC12 card with T1 ports. As one could expect, bandwidth-weighting is biased toward failures of line-cards with an OC48 port. However, failures of other line-cards, except for a channelized OC12 card with T1 ports, become more visible in comparison with port-weighting.

As a result of these problems with port and bandwidth-weighting techniques, a more useful approach is to evaluate average availability for each router platform and for each type of access LC separately. The increasing variety of edge routers and access line-cards justifies such an approach, since it allows the ISP to track

Table 3.2 Total number of ports in service and their bandwidth

Port	Speed (Mbps)	Number of ports	BW (Gbps)
T1	1.5	40,000	60.0
T3	45	3,000	135.0
OC3	155	500	77.5
OC12	622	150	93.3
OC48	2,400	200	480.0
Total		43,850	845.8

Table 3.3 Port-weight and bandwidth-weight per line-card

Port	In service	P-weight	BW-weight
T1	200	0.00456	0.00035
T3	30	0.00068	0.00160
OC3	10	0.00023	0.00183
OC12	3	6.8E-05	0.00221
OC48	1	2.3E-05	0.00284

the reliability with finer granularity. Consider a set of edge routers of the same type with J types of access line–cards, which are monitored for failures during time interval of length T. For each customer impacting failure $i, i = 1, \ldots, L$, we record the number n_{ij} of type j cards affected and the respective failure duration t_{ij}. In the case of access line-card redundancy, only failures of active (primary) line-card are counted and then only if the failover to the backup line-card was not hitless. The average unavailability of type j access line-card is calculated as

$$U_j = \frac{\sum_{i=1}^{L} n_{ij} t_{ij}}{N_j T} \tag{3.13}$$

where N_j is the total number of type j active cards. The average unavailability can be expressed as

$$U_j = \frac{R_j}{M_j} \tag{3.14}$$

where

$$R_j = \frac{\sum_{i=1}^{L} n_{ij} t_{ij}}{\sum_{i=1}^{L} n_{ij}} \tag{3.15}$$

is the average repair time for an LC of type j, and

$$M_j = \frac{N_j T}{\sum_{i=1}^{L} n_{ij}} \tag{3.16}$$

can be interpreted as the average time between router failures impacting customers on access line-cards of type j. Metric M_j can be considered as an extension of the traditional field hardware MTBF. For the field MTBF, only individual line-card failures, which require card replacement, are counted in the denominator. In M_j, we count all failures of type j cards outside the maintenance window, including those caused by reset, software bugs, and all impacted cards of type j in case of entire router failure. This distinction is important since we want a metric that accurately captures customer impact caused by all HW and SW failures. For example, each reset of an active (primary) line-card can cause a protocol reconvergence event resulting in short-duration packet loss. Metrics R, M, and U can also be defined for the entire population of access line-cards without differentiating failure by LC type. Denote

$$N = \sum_{j=1}^{J} N_j, \quad n = \sum_{j=1}^{J} \sum_{i=1}^{L} n_{ij}, \quad t = \sum_{j=1}^{J} \sum_{i=1}^{L} t_{ij}. \tag{3.17}$$

Then

$$R = \frac{t}{n}, \ M = \frac{NT}{n} \tag{3.18}$$

and the average unavailability

$$U = \frac{R}{M}. \tag{3.19}$$

The value of using M_j in addition to the average unavailability is demonstrated by the following example.

Example 3.1. Consider a set of 400 routers and let $T = 1,000$ h. Each router has two cards of Type 1, three cards of Type 2, and five cards of Type 3. The number of failures for the entire router and each card type with their duration is given in Table 3.4. In case of single card failures, $n_{ij} = 1$ if LC of type j failed and $n_{ij} = 0$ otherwise. In the case of entire router failure, $(n_{i1}, n_{i2}, n_{i3}) = (2, 3, 5)$. In this example, we assume constant failure duration $t_{ij} = t_j$ of type j cards and a constant duration of the entire router failure. The failure duration is measured in hours. The failure parameters in Table 3.4 are referred to as Scenario 1. We also consider a Scenario 2, in which the only difference with Scenario 1 is that the number of failures of entire routers is increased from 1 to 5.

The reliability metrics for two scenarios are given in Table 3.5. The results in columns R and M for LC Type $j, j = 1, 2, 3$, and for All Cards are calculated using Eqs. (3.15), (3.16), and (3.18), respectively. The unavailability for LC Type $j, j = 1, 2, 3$, and for All Cards is calculated using Eqs. (3.14) and (3.19), respectively. The defects per million (DPM) is a commonly used metric that is obtained by multiplying the respective unavailability by 1,000,000.

Note that for All Cards, defects per million (DPM) are below 10 in both scenarios, implying a high availability exceeding 99.999% (five nines), while the average time between customer impacting failures M in Scenario 2 is almost half of that in Scenario 1. Therefore, DPM, in contrast with average time between customer impacting failures, is not sensitive to the frequency of short failures of the entire router.

Table 3.4 Failures and their duration: Scenario 1

Failure	# Failures	Duration
Router	1	0.1
LC type 1	30	0.8
LC type 2	6	1.5
LC type 3	2	0.5

Table 3.5 Reliability metrics

LC type	Scenario 1			Scenario 2		
	R	M	DPM	R	M	DPM
1	0.76	25,000	30.25	0.63	20,000	31.25
2	1.03	133,333	7.75	0.50	57,143	8.75
3	0.21	285,714	0.75	0.13	74,074	1.75
All Cards	0.73	83,333	8.75	0.44	45,455	9.75

If an ISP were only tracking DPM and router outages increased from one outage per 1,000 h to five outages per 1,000 h, it might miss the significant decrease in reliability as seen from the customer's perspective.

The metrics in the All Cards row hide a low average time between failures and high DPM for LC Type 1 in both scenarios. The average time between customer impacting failures by LC type amplifies the difference between the two scenarios. For example, for LC Type 3, the average time between failures M_3 decreased almost by a factor of 4 in Scenario 2, in comparison with Scenario 1. This example illustrates the importance of measuring reliability metrics by the type of access linecards. It also illustrates the significant impact that even short-duration outages of an entire router have on reliability. Furthermore, it shows why nonstop routing and in-service software-upgrade capabilities described in Section 3.2 are considered to be so important by ISPs.

3.5 End-to-End Availability

Evaluation of the end-to-end availability requires evaluation of the backbone availability in addition to the access availability discussed in Section 3.4. Given the scale and complexity of a large ISP backbone, there is no generally agreed upon approach for measuring and modeling end-to-end availability. Chapter 4 provides a fairly general approach for performance and reliability (performability) evaluation of networks consisting of independent components with finite number of failure modes. Its application involves the steady state probability distribution that is used for calculation of the expected value of the measure F defined on the set of network states. This section presents a brief overview of some results related to state aggregation and the selection of function F for evaluating the backbone availability.

Large ISP backbones are typically designed to ensure that the network stays connected under all single-failure scenarios. Furthermore, the links are designed with enough capacity to carry the peak traffic load under all single-failure scenarios. Therefore, the majority of failures do not cause loss of backbone connectivity. Typically, when a failure happens, P routers detect the failure and trigger a failover to a backup path. If the failover were hitless and the backup path did not increase the end-to-end delay and also had enough capacity to carry all traffic, then the failure would not have any customer impact. Failures impacting customer traffic include the following events:

1. Loss of connectivity
2. Increased end-to-end delay on the backup path
3. Packet loss due to insufficient capacity of the backup path
4. Routing reconvergence triggered by the original failure. Such a reconvergence may cause packet loss during several seconds.

Assume that the duration of each event can be measured. Two approaches to measuring the backbone availability are based on knowing the actual point-to-point traffic demand matrix that allows us to calculate the amount of impacted traffic for each event. In the first approach [20], only events 3 and 4 are included. The backbone unavailability is defined as the fraction of traffic lost over a given time period. In the second approach [21], all four events are included. Availability is measured for each origin–destination pair as the percentage of time that the network can satisfy a service-level agreement including 100% connectivity and thresholds on packet loss and delay. The main complexity in the implementation of either approach is in measuring event durations. The determination of event durations requires specially designed network instrumentation involving synthetic (active) measurements. Reference [22] describes a standardized point-to-point approach to path-level measurements and reference [23] describes a novel approach that uses a single measurement host to collect network-wide one-way performance data. These approaches also require a well-thought-out data management infrastructure and computationally intensive processing of their output [24]. Application of edge-to-edge availability distribution to evaluation of VoIP (Voice over IP) reliability [25] is addressed in [26].

References

1. Malec, H., (1998). Communications reliability: A historical perspective. *IEEE Transactions on Reliability, 47*, 333–345.
2. Claffy, kc., Meinrath, S., & Bradner, S. (2007). The (un)economic Internet? *IEEE Internet Computing, 11*, 53–58.
3. Bollapragada, V., Murphy, C., & White, R. (2000). *Inside Cisco IOS software architecture*. Indianapolis, IN: Cisco Press.
4. Schudel, G., & Smith, D. (2008). *Internet protocol operations fundamentals. In Router security strategies*. Indianapolis, IN: Cisco Press.
5. Garrett, A., Drenan, G., & Morris, C. (2002). *Juniper networks field guide and reference*. Reading, MA: Addison-Wesley.
6. Oggerino, C. (2001). *High availability network fundamentals: A practical guide to predicting network availability*. *Indianapolis*, IN: Cisco Press.
7. T640 *Internet router node overview*, from http://www.juniper.net/techpubs/software/nog/nog-hardware/download/t640-router.pdf.
8. *Route flapping*, from http://en.wikipedia.org/wiki/Route_flapping.
9. Cisco nonstop forwarding with stateful switchover (2006). *Deployment guide*. Cisco Systems, from http://www.cisco.com/en/US/technologies/tk869/tk769/technologies_white_paper0900aecd801dc5e2.html.
10. *Graceful restart concepts*, from http://www.juniper.net/techpubs/software/junos/junos93/swconfig-high-availability/graceful-restart-concepts.html#section-graceful-restart-concepts.
11. Sangli, S., Chen, E., Fernando, R., & Rekhter, Y. (2007). *Graceful restart mechanism for BGP. RFC 4724. Internet Official Protocol Standards*, from http://www.ietf.org/rfc/rfc4724.txt.
12. Kaplan, H. (2002). *NSR Non-stop routing technology. White paper*. Avici Systems Inc., from http://www.avici.com/technology/whitepapers/reliability_series/NSRTechnology.pdf.
13. Router high availability for IP networks (2005). White paper. *Alcatel*, from http://www.telecomreview.ca/eic/site/tprp-gecrt.nsf/vwapj/Router_HA_for_IP.pdf/$FILE/Router_HA_for_IP.pdf.
14. ISSU: A planned upgrade tool (2009). *White paper. Juniper Networks*, from http://www.juniper.net/us/en/local/pdf/whitepapers/2000280-en.pdf.

15. Cisco IOS XE In Service Software Upgrade process (2009). *Cisco Systems*, from http://www.cisco.com/en/US/docs/ios/ios_xe/ha/configuration/guide/ha-inserv_updg_xe.pdf.
16. Single-router APS for the Cisco 12000 series router, from http://www.cisco.com/en/US/docs/ios/12_0s/feature/guide/12ssraps.pdf.
17. Agraval, M., Bailey, S., Greenberg, A., et al. (2006). RouterFarm: Towards a dynamic manageable network edge. *In: SIGCOMM'06 Workshops, Pisa, Italy.*
18. Ross, S. (1989). Introduction to probability models. San Diego, CA: Academic.
19. Access availability of routers in IP-based networks (2003) Committee T1 tech rep T1.TR.78–2003.
20. Kogan, Y., Choudhury, G., & Tarapore, P. (2004). Evaluation of impact of backbone outages in IP networks. *In ITCOM 2004, Philadelphia, PA.*
21. Wang, H., Gerber, A., Greenberg, A., et al. (2007). *Towards quantification of IP network reliability*, from http://www.research.att.com/~jiawang/rmodel-poster.pdf.
22. Ciavattone, L., Morton, A., & Ramachandran, G. (2003). Standardized active measurements on a Tier 1 IP backbone. *IEEE Communications Magazine, 41*, 90–97.
23. Burch, L., & Chase, C. (2005). Monitoring link delays with one measurement host. *ACM SIGMETRICS Performance Evaluation Review 33*, 10–17.
24. Choudhury, G., Eisenberg, M., Hoeflin, D., et al. (2007). New reliability metrics and measurement techniques for IP networks. *Proceedings of Distributed computer and communication networks, RAS, Moscow*, 126–130.
25. Johnson, C., Kogan, Y., Levy, Y., et al. (2004). VoIP Reliability: A service provider perspective. *IEEE Comunications Magazine, 42*, 48–54.
26. Lai, W., Levy, Y., & Saheban, F. (2007). Characterizing IP network availability and VoIP service reliability. *Proceedings of Distributed computer and communication networks, RAS, Moscow*, 126–130.

Chapter 4
Network Performability Evaluation

Kostas N. Oikonomou

4.1 Introduction

This chapter is an introduction to the area of performability evaluation of networks. The term *performability*, which stands for performance plus reliability, was introduced in the 1980s in connection with the performance evaluation of fault-tolerant, degradable computer systems [23].[1] In network performability evaluation, we are interested in investigating a network's performance not only in the "perfect" state, where all network elements are operating properly, but also in states where some elements have failed or are operating in a degraded mode (see, e.g., [8]). The following example will introduce the main ideas.

Consider the network (graph) of Fig. 4.1. On the left, the network is in its perfect state, and on the right one node and one edge have failed.[2] Node and edge failures occur independently, according to certain probabilities, which we assume to be known. An assignment of "working" or "failed" states to the network elements defines a state of the network. By the independence assumption, the probability of that state is the product of the state probabilities of the elements.

There are two traffic flows in this network: one from node 1 to node 5, and the other from 7 to 3. The flows are deterministic, of constant size, and there is no queuing at the nodes. Our interest is in the *latency* of each flow, defined as the minimum number of hops (edges) that the flow must traverse to get to its destination when it is routed on the shortest path. In each state of the network, a flow has a given latency: in the perfect state, both flows have latency 2 (hops), but in the example failure state the first flow has latency 3 and the second ∞. The simplest characterization of the latency metric would be to find its expected value over the possible network states,

K.N. Oikonomou (✉)
200 Laurel Ave, Middletown, NJ, 07748
e-mail: ko@research.att.com

[1] Unfortunately, the terminology is not completely standard and some authors still use the term "reliability" for what we call performability; see, e.g., [1]. One may also encounter other terms such as "availability" or "dependability".

[2] When a node fails, we consider that all edges incident to it also fail.

C.R. Kalmanek et al. (eds.), *Guide to Reliable Internet Services and Applications*,
Computer Communications and Networks, DOI 10.1007/978-1-84882-828-5_4,
© Springer-Verlag London Limited 2010

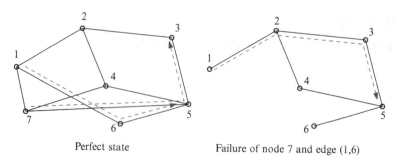

Perfect state   Failure of node 7 and edge (1,6)

Fig. 4.1 A 7-node, 10-edge network with 2^{17} possible states. The performance metric is traffic latency, measured in hops

of which there are $2^{17} \approx 130{,}000$. A more complete characterization would be to find its entire probability distribution. This would allow one to answer questions such as "what is the probability that the latency of flow 1 does not exceed 3?", and "what upper bound on the latency of flow 2 can be guaranteed with probability 0.999?". The answers to these questions (*performability guarantees*) are useful in setting performance targets for the network, or SLAs.

This basic example illustrates several points, all of which will be covered in more detail in later sections.

Reliability/Performance Trade-Off in the Analysis

A fundamental fact is that the size of the state space is exponential in the number of network elements. In the above example, if the number of network elements is doubled, the number of network states becomes about $17 \cdot 10^9$, and this is still a small network, with only 34 elements; a network model with several hundred elements would be much more typical. This means that for any realistic network model the state space is practically infinite, so the amount of work that can be done in each state to compute the performance metrics is limited. In other words, in performability, analysis there is a fundamental trade-off between the reliability (state space) and performance aspects. A consequence of this trade-off is that the performance model cannot be as detailed as it would be in a pure performance analysis: in the example, we assumed constant traffic flows and no queuing at nodes. Another aspect of the trade-off is that only the investigation of the *steady-state* behavior of the model is, in general, feasible: in the example, we treated the network elements as two-valued random variables, not as two-state random processes. However, a mitigating factor is that the network states generally have very different probabilities, so that we may be able to calculate *bounds* on the performance metrics by computing their values only on a reasonable number of states, those with high probability. With this fundamental trade-off in mind, we now discuss ways in which the simple performability model of the example can be extended.

Enhancements to the Simple Model

To make the model presented in the example more useful for a realistic analysis, we could add capacities to the graph's edges. We could also add sizes to the traffic flows, and have more sophisticated routing that allows only shortest paths that have enough capacity for a flow. Further, for a better latency measure, we could add lengths to the graph edges. Another category of enhancements would be aimed at representing failures more realistically. To begin with, the network elements could be allowed to have more than one failure mode, e.g., an edge could operate at full capacity, half capacity, or zero capacity (fail). We could separate the network elements from the entities that fail by introducing "components" that have failure modes and affect the graph elements in certain ways. For example, such a component could represent an optical fiber over which two graph edges are carried, and whose failure (cut) would fail both of these edges at the same time. In Section 4.2 we describe a *hierarchical* network model that has all the features mentioned above, among others. Finally, we could allow different types of routing for traffic flows, and also introduce the notion of network *restoration* into the model. These additions are described in Section 4.3.

Network Performability in the Literature

A number of network performability studies have appeared in the literature. Levy and Wirth [21] investigate the *call completion rate* in a communications network. Alvarez et al. [4] study performability guarantees for the *time* required to satisfy a web request in a network with up to 50 nodes, where only nodes can fail, but without restoration. Levendovszky et al. [19] study the expected lost *traffic* in the Hungarian backbone SDH network with 52 nodes and 59 links, and no restoration. Carlier et al. [7] use a three-level network model, and study expected lost *traffic* in a 111-node, 180-link network using k-shortest path restoration. Gomes and Craveirinha [12] study a 46-node, 693-link representation of the Lisbon urban network with a three-level performability model, and compute *blocking probabilities* for a Poisson model of the network traffic, with no restoration. Finally, layered specification of a network for the purposes of performability evaluation has been used in [7,12], which separate the network into a "physical" and a "functional" layer, and in [22], which uses a special-purpose separation into "node cluster" and "call-processing path" layers.
   Some further references are given in Section 4.4.3.

Chapter Outline

In Section 4.2 we describe a four-level, hierarchical network model, suited for performability analysis, and illustrate it with an IP-over-optical network example. In Section 4.3 we discuss the performability evaluation problem in general, give a mathematical formulation, present the state-generation approach to the performability evaluation of networks, and discuss basic performance measures and related issues. We also introduce the `nperf` network performability analyzer, a software package developed in AT&T Labs Research. In Section 4.4 we conclude by presenting two case studies that illustrate the material of this chapter, the first involving an IPTV distribution network, and the second dealing with architecture choices for network access.

4.2 Hierarchical Network Model

For the purpose of our performability modeling, we will think of a "real" network as consisting of three layers[3]: a *traffic* layer, a *transport* layer, and a *physical* layer. On the other hand, as shown in Fig. 4.2, our performability model is divided into four levels: *traffic*, *graph*, *component*, and *reliability*. (In terms of the ISO OSI reference model, both models address layers 1 through 3.) To illustrate the correspondence between the three network layers and the four model levels, we use the case of an IP-over-optical "real" network. The four-level performability model applies to many other types of real networks as well: for example, Oikonomou et al. [25] describe its application to a set of satellites that communicate among themselves and a set of ground stations via microwave links, whereas the ground stations are interconnected by a terrestrial network.

4.2.1 *IP-Over-Optical Network Example*

A modern commercial packet network typically consists of IP routers connected by links, which are transported by an underlying optical network. We describe how we model the traffic, transport, and physical layers of such a network, and how we map them to the levels of the performability model in Fig. 4.2. (For more on this topic, see Chapter 2.)

Traffic Layer

Based on an estimate of the peak or average traffic pattern, we create a matrix giving the demand or "flow" between each pair of routers. (Methods for creating such a traffic matrix from measurements are described in Chapter 5.) A demand has a rate, a unit, and possibly a type or class associated with it.

---

[3] We say "real" because any description is itself at some level of abstraction and omits aspects which may be important if one adopts a different viewpoint.

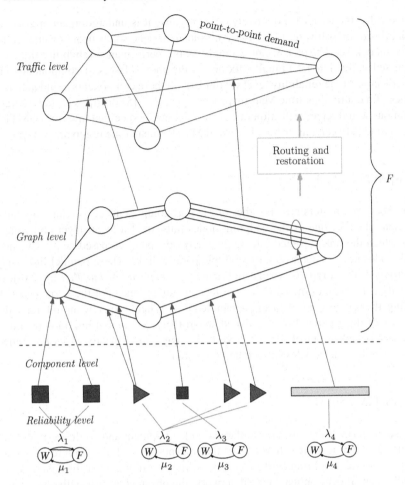

Fig. 4.2 The four-level network performability model used by the `nperf` performability analyzer. F is the performance measure, discussed in Section 4.3.3

Transport Layer Nodes

A network node represents an IP router. At the component level this node expands into a data plane, a control plane, a hardware and software upgrade component, and a number of networking interfaces (line cards/ports). The data plane, or switching fabric, is responsible for routing packets, while the control plane computes routing tables and processes other network signaling protocols, such as OSPF or BGP. When a data plane component fails, all the links incident to its router fail. When a control plane component fails, the router continues to switch packets, but cannot participate in rerouting, including restoration. Failure of a port component fails the corresponding link(s). The "upgrade" component represents the fact that, periodically, the router is effectively down because it is undergoing an upgrade of its hardware or software. (This is by no means a very sophisticated router reliability model, see Chapter 3, but exemplifies the performance-reliability trade-off discussed in Section 4.1.) Finally, fix one of the above classes of components, say router cards. At the reliability level we think of all these components as independent copies of a continuous-time Markov process (see, e.g., [5] or [6]) with failure transition rate λ and repair transition rate μ, which may be specified in terms of MTBF (mean time between failures, $= 1/\lambda$), and MTTR (mean time to repair, $= 1/\mu$).

Transport Layer Links

A link between routers fails if either of the port components at its endpoints fails, if a data plane of one of the endpoint nodes fails, or if a lower-layer component over which the link is routed fails (e.g., a network span, discussed next). Two network nodes may be connected by multiple parallel links. These parallel links may be grouped into a type of virtual link called a *composite* or *bundled* link, whose capacity is the sum of the capacities of its constituent links. For the purposes of IP routing, the routers see only a single bundled link. When a constituent link fails, the capacity of the bundled link is reduced accordingly. A bundled link fails (or more precisely is "taken out of service") when the aggregate capacity of its non-failed constituent links falls below a specified threshold.

Physical Layer Spans

We use the term "span" to refer to the network equipment and media (e.g., optical fiber) at the physical layer that carries the transport-layer links. Failure of a span component affects all transport-layer links which are routed over this span. When modeling an IP-over-optical layered network, the physical layer usually uses dense wavelength division multiplexing (DWDM), and a span consists of a concatenation of point-to-point DWDM systems called optical transport systems (OTS).[4] In turn, an OTS is composed of many elements, such as optical multiplexers/demultiplexers, optical amplifiers, and optical transponders. Also, a basic constraint in commercial transport networks is that a span is considered to be working only if *both* of its directions are working. With this assumption, it is not difficult to compute the failure probability of a span based on the failure probabilities of its individual elements in both directions. Thus, for simplicity, we generally represent a network span by a single "lumped" component whose MTBF and MTTR are calculated as explained in [28].

---

[4] There are more complex DWDM systems with various optically-transparent "add/drop" capabilities, which, for simplicity, we do not discuss here.

Other Types of Components

A set of fibers that is likely to fail together because they are contained in a single conduit/bundle can be represented by a *fiber cut* component that brings down all network spans (hence all the higher IP-layer links) that include this fiber bundle. Other types of catastrophic failures of sets of graph nodes and edges may be similarly represented.

So far we have mentioned only binary components, i.e., with just two modes of operation, "working" or "failed". We discuss components with more than two modes in Section 4.2.2.2.

4.2.2   More on the Graph and Component Levels

4.2.2.1   Graph Element Attributes

The graph is the level of the performability model at which the network routing and restoration algorithms operate. Graph edges have associated *capacities* and (routing) *costs*. In general, an edge's capacity can be a vector, and this vector has a capacity *threshold* associated with it, such that the edge is considered failed if the sum of the capacities of its non-failed elements falls below the threshold. An edge with vector capacity can directly represent a bundled link. The nperf performability analyzer presented in Section 4.3 also allows many other attributes for edges, such as lengths, latencies, etc., as well as operations on these attributes. These operations are covered in Section 4.2.2.3.

4.2.2.2   Multi-Mode Components

Each component, representing an independent failure or degradation mechanism, has a single working mode and an arbitrary number of failure modes. If it has a single failure mode it is referred to as a "binary" component, otherwise it is called "multi-mode". In the nperf analyzer a component is represented by a *star* Markov process, as shown in Fig. 4.3.

At the reliability level, the ith failure mode of a particular component is defined by its mean time between failures and its mean time to repair by setting $\lambda_i = 1/\mathrm{MTBF}_i$ and $\mu_i = 1/\mathrm{MTTR}_i$.

We now give some examples of using multi-mode components in network modeling.

Router Upgrades We mentioned in Section 4.2.1 (binary) software and hardware upgrade components for routers. Now suppose that there is an intelligent network maintenance policy in place, by which router upgrades are scheduled so that only one router in the network undergoes a software or hardware upgrade at any time.

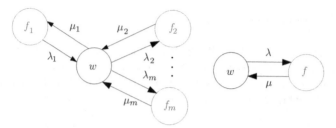

Fig. 4.3 A multi-mode component with m failure modes $f_1, \ldots, f_m$ (*left*), and the special case of a binary component (*right*). The components are continuous-time Markov processes of the "star" form. The ith mode is entered with (failure) rate λ_i and exited with (repair) rate μ_i

This policy cannot be modeled by using binary upgrade components associated with the routers, because (independence) there is nothing to prevent more than one of them failing at a time. However, for an n-router network, the mutually exclusive upgrade events can be represented by defining an $(n + 1)$-mode component whose mode 1 corresponds to no upgrades occurring anywhere in the network, and each of the remaining n modes corresponds to the upgrade of a single router.

Traffic Matrix Suppose we want to take into account daily variations in traffic patterns/levels, e.g., for 60% of a typical day the traffic is represented by matrix T_1, for 20% by matrix T_2, and for another 20% by matrix T_3. This can be done by letting the traffic matrix be controlled by a multi-mode component whose modes w, f_1, f_2 have probabilities $0.6, 0.2, 0.2$, respectively, and they set the traffic matrix to T_1, T_2, T_3, respectively.

Restoration Figure 4.2 implicitly assumes that network restoration happens at only one level. However, multi-mode components afford the capability to model restoration occurring at more than one network layer. The details of how this is done, using the example of IP over SONET, can be found in [25].

4.2.2.3 Failure Mapping

Recall that failure of a binary component may affect a whole *set* of graph-level elements: the spans of Section 4.2.1 are an example. More generally, when a multi-mode component enters one of its failure modes, the effect on a graph element is to *change some of the element's attributes*. For example, the capacity of an edge may decrease, or a node may become unable to perform routing. Depending on the final values of the attributes, e.g., total edge capacity $\leq$ some threshold, the graph element may be considered "failed". We refer to the effects of the components on the graph as the component-to-graph- level *failure mapping*. Some of the ways that a component can affect a graph element attribute are to add a constant to it, subtract a constant from it, multiply it by a constant, or set its value to a constant.

4.3   The nperf Network Performability Analyzer

In this section, we begin by discussing how the general, i.e., not specific to networks, performability evaluation problem can be defined mathematically, and then discuss various aspects of this definition. We then review the so-called state generation approach to performability evaluation, and some basic ingredients of the performance measures used when evaluating the performability of networks. We finally present an outline of the nperf network performability analyzer, a tool developed in AT&T Labs Research.

Useful background on performability in general is in [16] and in [32]. A more extensive reference on the nperf analyzer itself and the material of this section is [28].

4.3.1   The Performability Evaluation Problem

It is useful to understand the mathematical formulation of the network performability evaluation problem. Let $C = \{c_1, \ldots, c_n\}$ be a set of "components", each of which is either working or failed. (As already mentioned in Section 4.2.2, components can be in more than two states, called "modes" to distinguish them from network states, but to simplify the exposition here we restrict ourselves to two mode, or "binary" components.) Abstractly, a component represents a failure or degradation mechanism; examples were given in Section 4.2.1.

Component c_i is in its working mode with probability p_i and in its failed mode with probability $q_i = 1 - p_i$, both assumed known. Our basic assumption is that all components are *independent* of one another, so that, e.g., the probability that c_i is down, c_j is up, and c_k is down is $q_i p_j q_k$. A network *state* is an assignment of a mode to every component in C and can be represented by a binary n-vector. The set of all network states $S(C)$ has size 2^n, and the probability of a particular state is the product of the mode probabilities of the n components. Let F be a vector-valued *performance measure* (a function) defined on $S(C)$, mapping each state to an m-tuple of real numbers; examples are given in Section 4.3.3.

The *performability evaluation* problem consists in computing the expected value of the measure F over the set $S(C)$ of network states:

$$\bar{F} = \sum_{s \in S(C)} F(s) \Pr(s). \tag{4.1}$$

There are various points to note here.

Complexity   It is well known that the exact evaluation of (4.1) is difficult, even if F is very simple. Intuitively this is because the size of the state space $S(C)$ is exponential in the size of the set of components C. For a more precise demonstration of the complexity, suppose that each component corresponds to an edge of a graph, the graph's nodes do not fail, and we want to know the probability that there is a path between two specific nodes a and b of the graph. This is known as the TWO TERMINAL NETWORK RELIABILITY evaluation problem, and in this case F takes only two values: $F(s)$ is 1 if there is a path from a to b in the graph state s, and 0 otherwise. Despite the very simple F, this problem is known to be #P-complete (see e.g., [15, 32], or [8]). A consequence of this computational complexity is that, in general, only *approximate* performability evaluation is feasible. We will return to this in Sect. 4.3.2.

Performability Guarantees In practice, we are interested in computing more sophisticated characteristics of F than its expectation $\bar{F}$, such as the probability, over the set of network states, that F is less than some number x, or greater than some number y. For example, we may want to claim that "with probability at least 99.9%, at most 2% of the total traffic is down, and with probability at least 90% at most 10% of it is down". Formally, such claims are statements of the type

$$\begin{aligned} &\Pr(F < x_1) \geqslant P_1, \quad \Pr(F < x_2) \geqslant P_2, \quad \ldots, \quad \text{or} \\ &\Pr(F > y_1) \leqslant Q_1, \quad \Pr(F > y_2) \leqslant Q_2, \quad \ldots \end{aligned} \qquad (4.2)$$

that hold over the entire network state space; they are known as *performability guarantees*, and they can, for example, be used to set SLAs. The important point is that the computation of (4.2) reduces easily to just the computation of expectations of the type (4.1); see, e.g., [28].

Network When we are using the formalism leading to (4.1) to evaluate the performability of a network, all the complexity is in the measure F. As Fig. 4.2 shows, F then includes the failure mapping from the component to the graph level, the routing and restoration algorithms, and the traffic level.

Time Recalling the reliability level of Fig. 4.2, each c_i is in reality a two-state Markov process, whose state fluctuates in time. If so, what is the meaning of the expectation $\bar{F}$ of the measure F? It can be shown that if we average F over a *long time* as the network moves through its states, this average will approach $\bar{F}$, if we take the probabilities p_i and q_i associated with c_i to be the *steady-state* probabilities of the working and failed states of the Markov process representing c_i.

Steady State The reader familiar with the performance analysis of Markov reward models (see, e.g., [5, 11]) will recognize that the definition (4.1) of the performability evaluation problem is based on *steady state* expectations of measures. In many cases it is *transient*, also known as *finite-time*, measures that may be of interest. The evaluation of such measures on very large state spaces is much more difficult than that of steady state measures, and outside the scope of the treatment in this chapter, but it is currently an area of further development of the nperf tool.

4.3.2   State Generation and Bounds

A number of approaches to computing the expectation $\bar{F}$ in (4.1) approximately have been developed. Without attempting to be comprehensive, they can be classified into (a) upper and lower bounds for certain F such as connectivity (using the notions of cut and path sets), or special network/graph structures (see [16, 32]), (b) "most probable states" methods ([13, 14, 16, 17, 31–33]), (c) Monte Carlo sampling approaches ([7, 16]), and (d) probabilistic approximation algorithms for simple F, e.g., [18]. Methods of types (a) and (b) produce *algebraic* bounds on $\bar{F}$ (i.e., not involving any random sampling), while (c) and (d) yield *statistical* bounds.

Here we will discuss the "most probable states" methods, which are algorithms for generating network states in order of decreasing probability. The rationale is that if the component failure probabilities are small, most of the probability mass is concentrated on a relatively small fraction of the state space. Thus, as these methods generate states one by one and evaluate F on them, they are attempting to update $\bar{F}$ with terms of highest value first. The most probable states methods are particularly well suited to evaluating the performability of complex networks because they make no assumptions (at least to first order) about what the performance measure F might be or what properties it might have, which is especially important in view of the fact that the complexity of network routing and restoration schemes is included in F. The classical algorithms of [13, 33] apply to systems of only binary components, whereas the algorithms of [14, 17, 30] can handle arbitrary multi-mode components. nperf uses a *hybrid* state-generation algorithm described in [28], which handles arbitrary multi-mode components and is suited especially to "mostly binary" systems, that is systems where the proportion of components with more than two modes is small. We find that such systems dominate performability models for practical networks.

To explain what we mean by "at least to first order", let ω and α be the smallest and largest values of F over $S(\mathcal{C})$, and suppose we generate the k highest-probability elements of $S(\mathcal{C})$. If these states have total probability P, we have the algebraic lower and upper bounds on $\bar{F}$

$$\bar{F}_l = \sum_{i=1}^{k} F(s_i) \Pr(s_i) + (1 - P)\omega, \quad \bar{F}_u = \sum_{i=1}^{k} F(s_i) \Pr(s_i) + (1 - P)\alpha, \quad (4.3)$$

first pointed out in [20]. The bounds (4.3) are valid for arbitrary F, but may sometimes require the generation of a large number of states to achieve a small enough $\bar{F}_u - \bar{F}_l = (1 - P)(\alpha - \omega)$. Tighter bounds are possible, but only by requiring F to have some special property, such as monotonicity, limited growth, etc. See [27] for further details.

4.3.3 Performance Measures

There are two measures of fundamental importance in network performability analysis, both having to do with lost traffic. These are

$$t_{\text{lnr}}(s) = \text{total traffic lost because of no route in } s$$
$$t_{\text{lcg}}(s) = \text{total traffic lost because of congestion in } s \qquad (4.4)$$

(We do not mean to imply that these are the only measures of importance. Depending on the application, the focus may shift to considerations other than lost traffic, e.g., to latency, or to many others.) To define terms, we refer to the IP-over-optical example of Section 4.2.1. A *demand* corresponds to a source-destination pair of routers; we use *traffic* to mean the size (volume) of a demand, or of a set of demands.

The definition of t_{lnr} is straightforward: a demand fails if a link (multi-edge) on its route fails, and a failed demand is *lost* because of no route if no path for it can be found after the network restoration process completes. $t_{\text{lnr}}(s)$ is the sum of the volumes of all lost demands in state s.

Our definition of t_{lcg} is more involved.[5] If the network routing allows congestion, a demand is *congested* if its route includes an edge with utilization that exceeds a threshold U_c. t_{lcg} is a certain function (not the sum) of all congested demands. Suppose we fix a routing R in state s; then we define t_{lcg} to be the total traffic offered to the network minus the maximum possible total flow $\mathcal{F}$ that can be carried in state s using routing R without congestion. Here "there is congestion under R" means "there is a (working) edge with utilization above the threshold U_c". Equation (4.5) formalizes this definition. Note that if the network uses flow control, such as TCP in an IP network, the flow control will "throttle" traffic as soon as it detects congestion, so that few packets will be really lost; in that case it is more accurate to call our measure *loss in network bandwidth*. Now using the "link-path" formulation [29], let D be the set of all subdemands (path flows) and $D(e, R)$ be the set of subdemands using the non-failed edge e under the routing R. Also let f_d be the flow corresponding to subdemand d. Then $\mathcal{F}$ is the solution of the linear program

$$\mathcal{F} = \max \sum_{d \in D} f_d \qquad (4.5)$$

subject to

$$\forall e, \quad \sum_{d \in D(e,R)} f_d \leq U_c c_e, \qquad f_d \leq v_d,$$

where c_e is the capacity of edge e and v_d the volume of demand d.

---

[5] This definition is by no means unique, we claim only that it is useful in a wide variety of contexts.

Consistent with what we noted in Section 4.3.1, the above discussion centered around steady-state expectations of measures as the quantities of interest. In the context of the case study in Section 4.4.2 we will touch on one interesting sub-class of finite-time measures, event counts.

4.3.4   Network Routing and Restoration

The presence of network routing and restoration in the performance measure makes the performability analysis of networks different from other such analyses. The nperf analyzer incorporates three main kinds of network routing methods:

Uncapacitated Minimum-Cost This is meant to represent routing by, e.g., the OSPF (Open Shortest Path First) protocol [24]. Link costs correspond to OSPF administrative weights. OSPF path computation does *not* take into account the capacities or utilizations of the links. Another main IP-layer routing protocol, IS-IS (Intermediate System–Intermediate System) behaves similarly for our purposes.

"Optimal" Routing This routing is based on multi-commodity flows ([2, 29]). nperf incorporates both integral and non-integral ("real") multi-commodity flow methods. These methods could be regarded as representing variants of OSPF-TE. Details are in [28].

Multicast Routing This type of routing sends the traffic originating from a source node on a shortest-path tree rooted at this node and spanning a set of destination nodes. The shortest paths to the destinations are determined by so-called reverse-path forwarding.

These routing methods are not meant to be emulations of real network protocols; they include only the features of these protocols that are important for the kind of analysis that nperf is aimed at. In particular, a lot of details associated with timing and signaling are absent (another instance of the reliability/performance trade-off noted in Section 4.1).

4.3.5   Outline of the nperf Analyzer

With the above material in mind, Fig. 4.4 depicts the structure of the core of the nperf tool. At the top we have the most probable state generation algorithms of [13, 28, 33], mentioned in Section 4.3.2. The "routers" at the bottom of the figure are the routing methods discussed in Section 4.3.4: "iMCF" corresponds to integral multi-commodity flow, "rMCF" to non-integral ("real" or "fractional") multi-commodity flow, and "USP" to uncapacitated shortest paths.

The four-level network model is specified by a set of plain text files, listed in Table 4.1.

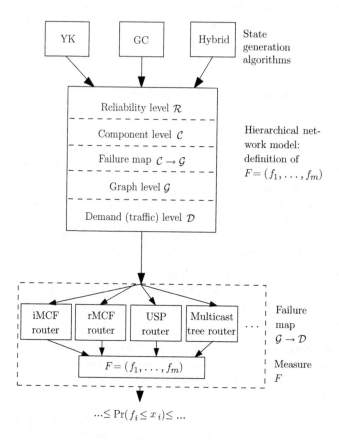

Fig. 4.4 Structure of the core nperf software

Table 4.1 Network model specification files

net.graph	Specifies the network graph (nodes and edges)
net.dmd, net.units	Specify the traffic demands, if the network has a traffic layer
net.comp	Specifies the network components and the $\mathcal{C} \to \mathcal{G}$ failure mapping
net.rel	Lists (MTBF, MTTR) pairs for the modes of the components
net.perf	Parameters for the performance measure(s)

The MTBFs for the components are typically obtained from a combination of manufacturer data and in-house testing. The MTTRs are usually determined by network maintanance policies, except for some special types of repairs, such as a software reboot. (Of course, one always has the freedom to use hypothetical values when performing a "what-if" analysis.) Uncertainties in the MTBFs and MTTRs may be dealt with by repeating an analysis with different values of MTBFS and/or MTTRs, and nperf has some facilities to ease this task. A more sophisticated

Table 4.2 Publicly-available tools that have some relation to `nperf`. Web sites valid as of 2009

PTOLEMY	Modeling and design of concurrent, real-time, embedded systems
	`http://ptolemy.eecs.berkeley.edu/`
TANGRAM II	Computer and communication system modeling
	`http://www.land.ufrj.br/tools/tangram2/tangram2.html`
MOBIUS	Model-based environment for validation of system reliability, availability
	security, and performance
	`http://www.mobius.uiuc.edu/`
PRISM	Probabilistic model checker
	`http://www.prismmodelchecker.org/`
TOTEM	Toolbox for Traffic Engineering Methods
	`http://totem.run.montefiore.ulg.ac.be/`

alternative is to assign uncertainties (prior probability distributions) to the MTBFs and MTTRs and propagate them to posterior distributions on $\bar{F}$ via a Bayesian analysis. However, this is outside the scope of this chapter.

4.3.6 Related Tools

Performance and reliability analyses of systems are vast areas with many ramifications. At this point there exist a number of tools that are, in one way or another, related to some of what `nperf` does. Table 4.2 mentions some of the author's favorites, all in the public domain; the interested reader may pursue them further.

Vis-a-vis these tools, the main distinguishing features of `nperf` are that it is geared toward networks (hierarchical model, routing, restoration), and represents them by large numbers of relatively simple independent (noninteracting) components.

4.4 Case Studies

We conclude by presenting two case studies that, among other things, illustrate the application of the `nperf` tool. The first study is on a multicast network for IPTV distribution, and the second involves choosing among a set of topologies for network access.

4.4.1 An IPTV Distribution Network

In this study we analyzed a design for an IPTV distribution network similar to the one discussed in [9], but with 65 nodes distributed across the continental US.

These nodes are called VHOs (Video Head Offices), and there is an additional node called an SHO (Super Hub Office), which is the source of all the traffic. The traffic stream from the SHO is sent to the VHOs by multicast[6]: when a node receives a packet, it puts a copy of it on each of its outgoing links. Thus traffic flows on the edges of a *multicast tree* rooted at the SHO, and each VHO is a node on this tree. The tree forms a sub-network of the provider's overall network. The multicast sub-network uses two mechanisms to deal with failures:

- *fast re-route*: each edge of the tree has a pre-defind *backup* path for it, which uses edges of the encompassing network that are not on the tree.
- *tree re-computation*: if a tree edge fails, and fast-reroute is unable to protect it because the backup path itself has also failed, a new tree is computed. This computation is done by so-called *reverse path forwarding*: each VHO computes a shortest path from it to the SHO, and the SHO then sends packets along each such path in the reverse direction.

The advantage of fast re-route (FRR) is that it takes much less time, milliseconds instead of seconds, than tree re-computation. Given a properly designed FRR capability, an interesting feature of the multicast network from the viewpoint of performability analysis is that it essentially tolerates any single link failure.[7] Therefore, interesting behavior appears only under failures of higher multiplicity. Indeed, it turns out that multiple failures can result in *congestion*: the backup paths for different links are not necessarily disjoint and so when FRR is used to bypass a whole set of failed links, a particular network link belonging to more than one backup path may receive traffic belonging to more than one flow. If the link capacity is such that this causes congestion, the congestion will last until the failure is repaired, which may take time of the order of hours. One way to deal with this problem is to compute a new multicast tree after FRR is done, and to begin using this new tree as soon as the computation is complete, as suggested in [9]. This retains the speed advantage of FRR and limits the duration of any congestion to the tree re-computation time.

For this network, performance must be guaranteed for every VHO (worst case), not just overall. So, in the terms of Section 4.3.3, the multicast performability measures are two 65-element vectors, one for loss due to no path and one for loss due to congestion, whose elements are computed on each network state.

We now summarize some of the results of this study. An initial network design, known as design A, was carried out by experienced network designers. Its performance, after normalizing the expectations of the measures by the total traffic and converting the result to time per year,[8] is shown in Fig. 4.5, top. Since this was a well-designed network to begin with, its levels of traffic loss were quite low, better than "five 9s". Within these low levels, Fig. 4.5 shows that the loss due to no path, the t_{lnr} of (4.4), is dominant for most VHOs, but some of them also exhibit

---

[6] Specifically by Protocol Independent Multicast (PIM).

[7] By "link" here we mean an edge at the graph level of the model of Fig. 4.2.

[8] For example, a traffic loss of 0.01% of the total translates to $1/10,000$ of a year, i.e., about 52 min/year.

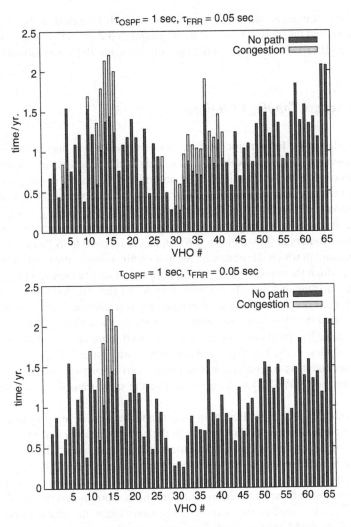

Fig. 4.5 Expected lost traffic, expressed in time per year, because of no path and congestion in design A (*top*), and in design C (*bottom*). These are the t_{lnr} and t_{lcg} defined in (4.4). Design C is A with tuned OSPF weights. For the purposes of comparing the two designs, the time unit of the y-axis is irrelevant

significant loss because of congestion (t_{lcg}). Even though the performability of this network was entirely acceptable, we decided to see if the loss due to congestion could be reduced. A detailed study of the network states generated by `nperf` that led to congestion in Fig. 4.5 top, revealed that they were double and triple failures. Further, we found that for VHOs 30 to 41 congestion could be practically eliminated by tuning a certain set of OSPF link weights. The result, known as design C, performed as shown in Fig. 4.5 bottom. It can be seen that a lot of congestion-induced losses were eliminated while the loss due to no path remained at the same level throughout, and this was achieved without adding to the cost of the network design at all. See [10] for more details on the subject of reliable IPTV network design.

4.4.2 Access Topology Choices

An issue that arose for a major Internet service provider was that traffic in its network was increasing, but the backbone routers had limited expansion capability (numbers of slots in the chassis). To get around this limitation it was proposed to introduce intermediate *aggregation routers* in the access part of the network, and the question was how this would affect the reliability of the access.

The configuration of the provider's backbone offices before the introduction of aggregation routers is shown in Fig. 4.6 top, and is referred to as "base"; there is a "local" variant in which all routers are located within a single office, and a "remote" variant in which the routers are in different offices. In reality there are many access routers connecting to a pair of backbone routers, but showing just one in Fig. 4.6 is enough for our purposes. There were two proposals for introducing the aggregation routers, called the "box" and the "butterfly" designs, shown in Fig. 4.6 middle and bottom. These had local and remote variants as well. Further, there was a premium "diverse" option in the butterfly remote design in which the links between a backbone router and its two aggregation routers were carried on two separate underlying optical transport (DWDM) systems, instead of the same transport (the "common" option).

It was clear that the box alternative was cheaper because of fewer links, but what was the reduction in availability relative to the costlier butterfly design? Also, how did either of these options compare with the existing base design? The failure modes of interest in all these designs were network spans, router ports, and software failures or procedural errors; these failure modes are depicted as components in Fig. 4.7. The metric chosen to compare the availabilities of the various designs was the *mean time between access disconnections*, i.e., situations where the access router A had no path to any backbone router BB. Note that network restoration is immaterial for such events.

nperf models for the designs of Fig. 4.6 were constructed; given the metric of interest, the models did not include a traffic layer. Typical values for the reliability attributes of the components were selected as in Chapter 3. At a high level, note that the longer links between the aggregation and backbone routers in the remote designs are less reliable than the corresponding links in the local designs. The results of the study are summarized in Table 4.3.

The mean access disconnection times are separated into two categories, of which "hardware" includes the first three types of components listed in Fig. 4.7. The most notable result in Table 4.3 is that *irrespective of the architecture*, software and procedural errors are by far the dominant cause for access router isolations. These events are the ones that cannot be helped by redundancy. The second most important

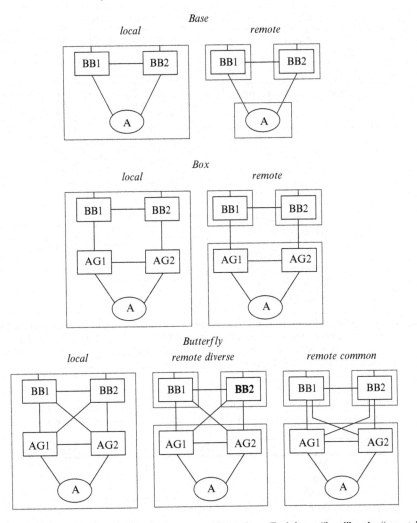

Fig. 4.6 "Base", "box", and "butterfly" access configurations. Each has a "local" and a "remote" version. The remote versions have routers spread among different offices (*the enclosing blue boxes*). *BB* are backbone routers, *AG* are aggregation routers, and *A* is an access router

feature is that compared to the base case, the introduction of aggregators *doubles* the risk of access router isolation due to software and procedural errors, again irrespective of the design. With respect to hardware failures in the local case, the box design increases the risk of isolation by a factor of 3 compared to the base case, but the butterfly design is just as good as the base. In the remote case, the box design is about twice as bad as the base, but the butterfly is in fact better, by at least a factor of 2.75.

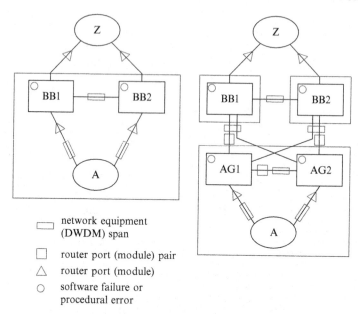

Fig. 4.7 Components for the simplest "base" and most complex "butterfly remote common" topologies. A component affects the edges or nodes which it overlaps in the diagram (the connection to the Z router is fictitious, representing the part of the network beyond the backbone routers, which is common to all alternatives)

Table 4.3 Mean access disconnection time (years), i.e., time between disconnections of access router A from both backbone routers BB, for the access topologies of Fig. 4.6

		Hardware	Software & procedural error
Local	Base	700	10
	Box	232	5
	Butterfly	699	5
Remote	Base	120	10
	Box	61	5
	Butterfly diverse	676	5
	Butterfly common	329	5

Summarizing availability by reporting only means makes comparisons easy, but hides information that is important in assessing the risk. By making the reasonable assumption that the isolation events occur according to a Poisson distribution with means as specified in Table 4.3, we see that the 5-year mean implies that in a single year one isolation event occurs with probability $\approx 16\%$ and two events with probability $\approx 2\%$.

4.4.3   Other Studies

Besides what was presented above, nperf has been used in a variety of other studies: the performability of a backbone network under two different types of routing was analyzed in [3], the performability of a multimedia distribution network that tolerates any single link failure was studied in [9, 10], two-layer IP-over-SONET restoration in a satellite network was investigated in [25], and techniques for setting thresholds for bundled links in an IP backbone network were studied in [26].

4.5   Conclusion

This chapter presents an overview of analyzing the combined performance and reliability, known as performability, of networks. Performability analysis may be thought of as repeating a performance analysis in many different states (failures or degradations) of the network, and is thus much more difficult than either reliability or performance analysis on its own. Successful analysis rests on finding a point on the reliability–performance spectrum appropriate to the problem at hand. Our particular approach to network performability analysis is based on a four-level hierarchical network model, and on the nperf software tool, which embodies a number of methods known in the literature, some new techniques developed by us, and is under active development in AT&T Labs Research (finite-time measures, quality-of-service additions to the traffic layer, etc.). We illustrated the ideas of analysing performability by two case studies carried out with nperf and gave references to other studies in the literature.

References

1. Aven, T., & Jensen, U. (1999). *Stochastic models in reliability*. New York: Springer.
2. Ahuja, R., Magnanti, T., & Orlin, J. (1998). *Network flows*. Englewood Cliffs, NJ: Prentice-Hall.
3. Agrawal, G. Oikonomou, K. N., & Sinha, R. K. (2007). Network performability evaluation for different routing schemes. *Proceedings of the OFC*. Anaheim, CA.
4. Alvarez, G., Uysal, M., & Merchant, A. (2001). Efficient verification of performability guarantees. In *PMCCS-5: The fifth international workshop on performability modelling of computer and communication systems*. Erlangen, Germany.
5. Bolch, G., Greiner, S., de Meer, H., & Trivedi, K. S.(2006). *Queueing networks and Markov chains*. Wiley, New Jersey.
6. Bremaud, P. (2008). *Markov chains, Gibbs fields, Monte Carlo simulation, and queues*. New York: Springer.
7. Carlier, J., Li, Y., & Lutton, J. (1997). Reliability evaluation of large telecommunication networks. *Discrete Applied Mathematics, 76*(1–3), 61–80.
8. Colbourn, C. J. (1999). Reliability issues in telecommunications network planning. In B. Sansó (Ed.), *Telecommunications network planning*. Boston: Kluwer.

9. Doverspike, R. D., Li, G., Oikonomou, K. N., Ramakrishnan, K. K., & Wang, D. (2007). IP backbone design for multimedia distribution: architecture and performance. In *Proceedings of the IEEE INFOCOM*, Alaska.

10. Doverspike, R. D., Li, G., Oikonomou, K. N., Ramakrishnan, K. K., Sinha, R. K., Wang, D., & Chase, C. (2009). Designing a reliable IPTV network. *IEEE internet computing, 13*(3), 15–22.

11. de Souza e Silva, E., & Gail, R. (2000). Transient solutions for Markov chains. In W. K. Grassmann (Ed.), *Computational probability*. Kluwer, Boston.

12. Gomes, T. M. S., & Craveirinha, J. M. F. (1997). A case ctudy of reliability analysis of a multiexchange telecommunication network. In C. G. Soares (Ed.), *Advances in safety and reliability*. Elsevier Science.

13. Gomes, T. M. S., & Craveirinha J. M. F. (April 1998). Algorithm for sequential generation of states in failure-prone communication network. *IEE proceedings-communications, 145*(2).

14. Gomes, T., Craveirinha, J., & Martins, L. (2002). An efficient algorithm for sequential generation of failures in a network with multi-mode components. *Reliability Engineering & System Safety, 77*, 111–119.

15. Garey, M., & Johnson, D. (1978). *Computers and intractability: a guide to the theory of NP-completeness*. San Francisco, CA: Freeman.

16. Harms, D. D., Kraetzl, M., Colbourn, C. C., & Devitt, J. S. (1995). *Network reliability: experiments with a symbolic algebra environment*. Boca Raton, FL: CRC Press.

17. Jarvis, J. P., & Shier, D. R. (1996). An improved algorithm for approximating the performance of stochastic flow networks. *INFORMS Journal on Computing, 8*(4).

18. Karger, D. (1995). A randomized fully polynomial time approximation scheme for the all-terminal network reliability problem. In *Proceedings of the 27th ACM STOC*.

19. Levendovszky, J., Jereb, L., Elek, Zs., & Vesztergombi, Gy. (2002). Adaptive statistical algorithms in network reliability analysis. *Performance Evaluation, 48*(1–4), 225–236.

20. Li, V. K., & Silvester, J. A. (1984). Performance analysis of networks with unreliable components. *IEEE Transactions on Communications, 32*, 1105–1110.

21. Levy, Y. & Wirth, P. E. (1989). A unifying approach to performance and reliability objectives. In *Teletraffic science for new cost-effective systems, networks and services, ITC-12*. Elsevier Science.

22. Menditta, V. B. (2001). A hierarchical modelling approach for analyzing the performability of a telecommunications system. In *PMCCS-5: the fifth international workshop on performability modelling of computer and communication systems*.

23. Meyer, J. F. (1995). Performability evaluation: where it is and what lies ahead. In *First IEEE computer performance and dependability symposium (IPDS)*, pp 334–343. Erlangen, Germany.

24. Moy, J. T. (1998). *OSPF: anatomy of an internet routing protocol*. Reading, MA: Addison Wesley.

25. Oikonomou, K. N. Ramakrishnan, K. K., Doverspike, R. D., Chiu, A., Martinez Heath, M., & Sinha, R. K. (2007). Performability analysis of multi-layer restoration in a satellite network. Managing traffic performance in converged networks, ITC 20 (LNCS 4516). Springer.

26. Oikonomou, K. N., & Sinha, R. K. (2008). Techniques for probabilistic multi-layer network analysis. In *Proceedings of the IEEE Globecomm*, New Orleans.

27. Oikonomou, K. N., & Sinha, R. K. (February 2009). Improved bounds for performability evaluation algorithms using state generation. *Performance Evaluation, 66*(2).

28. Oikonomou, K. N., Sinha, R. K., & Doverspike, R. D. (2009). Multi-layer network performance and reliability analysis. *The International Journal of Interdisciplinary Telecommunications & Networking (IJITN), 1*(3).

29. Pióro, M., & Medhi, J. (2004). *Routing, flow, and capacity design in communication and computer networks*. Morgan-Kaufmann.

30. Rauzy, A. (2005). An $m \log m$ algorithm to compute the most probable configurations of a system with multi-mode independent components. *IEEE Transactions on Reliability, 54*(1), 156–158.

31. Shier, D. R., Bibelnieks, E., Jarvis, J. P., & Lakin, R. J. (1990). Algorithms for approximating the performance of multimode systems. In *Proceedings of IEEE Infocom*.
32. Shier, D. R. (1991). *Network reliability and algebraic structures*. Oxford: Clarendon.
33. Yang, C. L., & Kubat, P. (1990). An algorithm for network reliability bounds. *ORSA Journal on Computing, 2*(4), 336–345.

Chapter 5
Robust Network Planning

Matthew Roughan

5.1 Introduction

Building a network encompasses many tasks: from network planning to hardware installation and configuration, to ongoing maintenance. In this chapter, we focus on the process of *network planning*. It is possible (though not always wise) to design a small network by eye, but automated techniques are needed for the design of large networks. The complexity of such networks means that any "ad hoc" design will suffer from unacceptable performance, reliability, and/or cost penalties.

Network planning involves a series of quantitative tasks: measuring the current network traffic and the network itself; predicting future network demands; determining the optimal allocation of resources to meet a set of goals; and validating the implementation. A simple example is capacity planning: deciding the future capacities of links in order to carry forecast traffic loads, while minimizing the network cost. Other examples include traffic engineering (balancing loads across our existing network) and choosing the locations of Points-of-Presence (PoPs) though we do not consider this latter problem in detail in this chapter because of its dependence on economic and demographic concerns rather than those of networking.

Many academic papers about these topics focus on individual components of network planning: for instance, how to make appropriate measurements, or on particular optimization algorithms. In contrast, in this chapter we will take a system view. We will present each part as a component of a larger system of network planning. In the process of describing how the various components of network planning interrelate, we observe several recurring themes:

1. *Internet measurements are of varying quality.* They are often imperfect or incomplete and can contain errors or ambiguities. Measurements should not be taken at face value, but need to be continually recalibrated [48], so that we have

M. Roughan (✉)
School of Mathematical Sciences, University of Adelaide, Adelaide, SA 5005, Australia
e-mail: matthew.roughan@adelaide.edu.au

C.R. Kalmanek et al. (eds.), *Guide to Reliable Internet Services and Applications*,
Computer Communications and Networks, DOI 10.1007/978-1-84882-828-5_5,
© Springer-Verlag London Limited 2010

some understanding of the errors, and can take them into account in subsequent processing. We will describe common measurement strategies in Section 5.2.

2. *Analysis and modeling* of data can allow us to estimate and predict otherwise unmeasurable quantities. However, in the words of Box and Draper, "Essentially, all models are wrong, but some are useful" [9]. We must be continually concerned with the quality of model-based predictions. In particular, we must consider where they apply, and the consequences of using an inaccurate model. A number of key traffic models are described in Section 5.3, and their use in prediction is described in Section 5.4.

3. *Decisions based on quantitative data are at best as good as their input data, but can be worse.* The quality of input data and resulting predictions are variable, and this can have consequences for the type of planning processes we can apply. Numerical techniques that are sensitive to such errors are not suitable for network engineering. Discussion of robust, quantitative network engineering is the main consideration of Sections 5.5 and 5.6.

Noting all of the above, it should not be surprising that a robust design process requires validation. The strategy of "set and forget" is not viable in today's rapidly changing networking environment. The errors in initial measurements, predictions, and the possibility for mistakes in deployment mean that we need to test whether the implementation of our plan has achieved our goals.

Moreover, actions taken at one level of operations may impact others. For example, Qiu et al. [51] noted that attempts to balance network loads by changing routing can cause higher-layer adaptive mechanisms such as overlay networks to change their decisions. These higher-level changes alter traffic, leading to a change of the circumstances that originally lead us to reroute traffic.

Thus, the process of **measure→analyze/predict→control→validate** should not stop. Once we complete this process, the cycle begins again, with our validation measurements feeding back into the process as the input for the next round of network planning, as illustrated in Fig. 5.1. This cycle allows our planning process to correct problems, leading to a robust process.

In many ways this resembles the more formal feedback used in control systems, though robust planning involves a range of tasks not typically modeled in formal control theory. For instance, the lead times for deploying network components such as new routers are still quite long. It can take months to install, configure, and test new equipment when done methodically. Even customers ordering access facilities

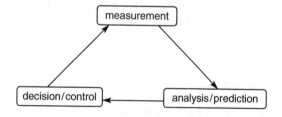

Fig. 5.1 Robust network planning is cyclic

can experience relatively long intervals from order to delivery, despite the obvious benefits to both parties of a quick startup. So if our network plan is incorrect, we cannot wait for the planning cycle to complete to redress the problem.

We need processes where the cycle time is shorter. It is relatively simple to reroute traffic across a network. It usually requires only small changes to router configurations, and so can be done from day to day (or even faster if automated). Rebalancing traffic load in the short term – in the interim before the network capacities can be physically changed – can alleviate congestion caused by failures of traffic predictions. This process is called *traffic engineering*.

Another aspect of robust planning is incorporation of reliability analysis. Internet switches and routers fail from time to time, and must sometimes be removed from service for maintenance. The links connecting routers are also susceptible to failures, given their vulnerability to natural or man-made accident (the canonical example is the careless back-hoe driver). Most network managers plan for the possibility of node or link failures by including redundant routers and links in their network. A network failure typically results in traffic being rerouted using these redundant pathways. Often, however, network engineers do not plan for overloads that might occur as a result of the rerouted traffic. Again, we need a robust planning process that takes into account the potential failure loads. We call this approach *network reliability analysis*.

We organize this chapter around the key steps in network planning. We first consider the standard network measurements that are available today. Their characteristics determine much of what we can accomplish in network planning. We then consider models and predictions, and then finally the processes used in making decisions, and controlling our network. As noted, robust planning does not stop there, we must continue to monitor our network, but there are a number of additional steps we can perform in order to achieve a robust network plan and we consider them in the final section of this chapter.

The focus of this chapter is backbone networks. Though many of the techniques described here remain applicable to access networks, there are a number of critical differences. For instance, access network traffic is often *very* bursty, and this affects the approaches we should adopt for prediction and capacity planning. Nevertheless, the fundamental ideas of robust planning that we discuss here remain valid.

5.2   Standard Network Measurements

Internet measurements are considered in more detail in Chapters 10 and 11, but a significant factor in network planning is the type of measurements available, and so we need some planning-specific discussions. In principle, it is possible to collect extremely good data, but in practice the measurements are often flawed, and the nature of the flaws are important when considering how to use the data.

The traffic data we might like to collect is a packet trace, consisting of a record of all packets on a subsection of a network along with timestamps. There are various mechanisms for collecting such a trace, for instance, placing a splitter into an optical fiber, using a monitor port on a router, or simply running tcpdump on one of the hosts on a shared network segment. A packet trace gives us all of the information we could possibly need but is prohibitively expensive at the scale we require for planning. The problem with a packet trace (apart from the cost of installing dedicated devices) is that the amount of data involved can be enormous, for example, on an OC48 (2.5 Gbps) link, one might collect more than a terabyte of data per hour. More importantly, a packet trace is overkill. For planning we do not need such detail, but we do need good coverage of the whole network. Packet traces are only used on lower speed networks, or for specific studies of larger networks.

There are several approaches we can use to reduce data to a more manageable amount. Filtering, so that we view only a segment of the traffic (say the HTTP traffic) is useful for some tasks, but not planning. A more useful approach is aggregation, where we only store records for some aggregated version of the traffic, thereby reducing the number of such records needed. A common form of aggregation is at the flow-level where we aggregate the traffic through some common characteristics. The definition of "flow" depends on the keys used for aggregation, but we mean here flows aggregated by the five-tuple formed from IP source and destination address, TCP port numbers, and protocol number. Flow data is typically collected within some time frame, for instance, 15 min periods. What is more, flow-level collection is often a feature of a router, and so does not require additional measurement infrastructure other than the Network Management Station (NMS) at which the data is stored. However, the volume of data can still be large (one network under study collected 500 GB of data per day), and the collection process may impact the performance of the router.

As a result, flow-level data is often collected in conjunction with a third method for data reduction: sampling. Sampling can be used both before the flows are created, and afterward. Prior to flow aggregation, sampling is used at rates of around 1:100–1:500 packets. That is, less than 1% of packets are sampled. This has the advantage that less processing is required to construct flow records (reducing the load on the router collecting the flows) and typically fewer flow records will be created (reducing memory and data transmission requirements). However, sampling prior to flow aggregation does have flaws, most obviously, it biases the data collection toward long flows. These flows (involving many packets) are much more likely to be sampled than short flows. However, this has rarely been seen as a problem in network planning where we are not typically concerned with the flow length distribution.

Sampling can also be used after flow aggregation to reduce the transmission and storage requirements for such data. The degree of sampling depends on the desired trade-off between accuracy of measurements, and storage requirements for the data. Good statistical approaches for this sampling, and for estimating the resulting accuracy of the samples are available [16, 17], though, as noted above, these are predominantly aimed at preserving details such as flow-length distributions, which are largely inconsequential for the type of planning discussed here, so sampling prior to flow construction is often sufficient for planning.

Of more importance here is the fact that any type of sampling introduces errors into measurements. Any large-scale flow archives must involve significant sampling, and so will contain errors.

An alternative to flow-level data is data collected via the Simple Network Management Protocol (SNMP) [39]. Its advantage over flow-level data collection is that it is more widely supported, and less vendor specific. However, the data provided is less detailed. SNMP allows an NMS to poll MIBs (Management Information Bases) at routers. Routers maintain a number of counters in these MIBs. The widely supported MIB-II contains counters of the number of packets and bytes transmitted and received at each interface of a router. In effect, we can see the traffic on each link of a network. In contrast to flow-level data, SNMP can only see link volumes, not where the traffic is going.

SNMP has a number of other issues with regard to data collection. The polling mechanism typically uses UDP (the User Datagram Protocol), and SNMP agents are given low priority at routers. Hence SNMP measurements are not reliable, and it is difficult to ensure that we obtain uniformly sampled time series. The result is missing and error-prone data.

Flow-level data contains only flow start and stop times, not details of packet arrivals, and typically SNMP is collected at 5-min intervals. The limit on timescale of both data sets is important in network planning. We can only see average traffic rates over these periods, not the variations inside these interval. However, congestion and subsequent packet loss often occur on much shorter timescales. The result is that such average measurements must always be used with care. Typically some overbuild of capacity is required to account for the sub-interval variations in traffic. The exact overbuild will depend on the network in question, and has typically been derived empirically through ongoing performance and traffic measurements. Values are usually fairly conservative in major backbones resulting in apparent underutilization (though this term is unfair as it concerns average utilizations not peak loads), and more aggressive in smaller networks.

In addition to traffic data, network planning requires a detailed view of any existing network. We need to know

- The (layer 3) topology (the locations of, and the links between routers)
- The network routing policies (for instance, link weights in a shortest-path protocol, areas in protocols such as OSPF, and BGP policies where multiple interdomain links exist)
- The mapping between current layer 3 links and physical facilities (WDM equipment and optical fibers), and the details of the available physical network facilities and their associated costs

The topology and routing data is principally needed to allow us to map traffic to links. The mapping is usually expressed through the *routing matrix*. Formally, $A = \{A_{ir}\}$ is the matrix defined by

$$
A_{ir} = \begin{cases} F_{ir}, & \text{if traffic for } r \text{ traverses link } i \\ 0, & \text{otherwise,} \end{cases}
\tag{5.1}
$$

where F_{ir} is the fraction of traffic from source/destination pair $r = (s, d)$ that traverses link i. A network with N nodes, and L links will have an $L \times N(N - 1)$ routing matrix.

Network data is also used to assess how changes in one component will affect the network (e.g., how changes in OSPF link weights will impact link loads); determine shared risk-of-failure between links; and determine how to improve our network incrementally without completely rebuilding it in each planning cycle. The latter is an important point because although it might be preferable to rebuild a network from scratch, the capital value of legacy equipment usually prevents this option, except at rare intervals.

For a small, static network, the network data may be maintained in a database, however, best practice for large, complex, or dynamic networks is to use tools to extract the network structure directly from the network. There are several methods available for discovering this information. SNMP can provide this information through the use of various vendor tools (HP Openview, or Cisco NCM, e.g.), but it is not the most efficient approach. A preferable approach for finding layer 3 information is to parse the configuration files of routers directly, for instance, as described in [22, 24]. The technique has been applied in a number of networks [5, 38]. The advantages of using configuration files are manifold. The detail of information available is unparalleled in other data sources. For instance, we can see details of the links (such as their composition should a single logical link be composed of more than one physical link).

The other major approach for garnering topology and routing information is to use a route monitor. Internet routing is built on top of distributed computations supported by routing protocols. The distribution of these protocols is often considered a critical component in ensuring reliability of the protocols in the face of network failures. The distribution also introduces a hook for topology discovery. If any router must be able to build its routing table from the routing information distributed through these protocols, then it must have considerable information about the network topology. Hence, we can place a dummy router into the network to collect such information. Such routing monitors have been deployed widely over the last few years. Their advantage is that they can provide an up-to-date dynamic view. Examples of such monitors exist for OSPF [61, 62], and IS-IS [1, 30], as well as for BGP (the Border Gateway Protocol) [2, 3].

5.3   Analysis and Modeling of Internet Traffic

5.3.1   Traffic Matrices

We will now consider the analysis and modeling of Internet data, in particular, traffic data. When considering inputs to network planning, we frequently return to the topic of *traffic matrices*. These are the measurements needed for many network planning tasks, and thus the natural structure around which we shall frame our analysis.

A Traffic Matrix (TM) describes the amount of traffic (the number of packets or more commonly bytes) transmitted from one point in a network to another during some time interval, and they are naturally represented by a three-dimensional data structure $T_t(i, j)$, which represents the traffic volume (in bytes or packets) from i to j during a time interval $[t, t + \Delta t)$. The locations i and j are generally considered to be physical geographic locations making i and j spatial variables. However, in the Internet, it is common to associate i and j with logical structures related to the address structure of the Internet, i.e., IP addresses, or natural groupings of such by common prefix corresponding to a subnet.

Origin/Destination Matrices One natural approach to describe traffic matrices is with respect to traffic volumes between IP addresses or prefixes. We refer to this as an origin/destination TM because the IP addresses represent the closest approximation we have for the end points of the network (though HTTP-proxies, firewalls, and NAT and other middle-boxes may be obscuring the true end-to-end semantics). IPv4 admits nearly 2^{32} potential addresses, so we cannot describe the full matrix at this level of granularity. Typically, such a traffic matrix would be aggregated into blocks of IP addresses (often using routing prefixes to form the blocks as these are natural units for the control of traffic). The origin/destination matrix is our ideal input for many network planning tasks, but the Internet is made up of many connected networks. Any one network operator only sees the traffic carried by its own network. This reduced visibility means that our observed traffic matrix is only a segment of the real network traffic. So we can't really observe the origin/destination TM. Instead we typically observe the ingress/egress traffic matrix.

Ingress/Egress versus Origin/Destination A more practical TM, the ingress/egress TM provides traffic volumes from ingress link to egress link across a single network. Note that networks often interconnect at multiple points. The choice of which route to use for egress from a network can profoundly change the nature of ingress/egress TMs, so these may have quite different properties to the origin/destination matrix. Forming an ingress/egress TM from an origin/destination TM involves a simple mapping of prefixes to ingress/egress locations in a network, but in practice this mapping can be difficult unless we monitor traffic as it enters the network. We can infer egress points of traffic using the routing data described above, but inferring ingress is more difficult [22, 23], so it is better to measure this directly.

Spatial Granularity of Traffic Matrices As we have started to see with origin/destination traffic matrices, we can measure them at various levels of granularity (or resolution). The same is true of ingress/egress TMs. At the finest level, we measure traffic per ingress/egress link (or interface). However, it is common to aggregate this data to the ingress/egress router. We can often group routers into larger sub-groups. A common such group is a Point-of-Presence (PoP), though there are other sub- and super-groupings (e.g., topologically equivalent edge routers are sometimes grouped, or we may form a regional group). Given subsets S and D of locations, may simply aggregate a TM across these by taking

$$T_t(S, D) = \sum_{i \in S} \sum_{j \in D} T_t(i, j). \qquad (5.2)$$

Typical large networks might have 10s of PoPs, and 100s of routers, and so such TMs are of a more workable size. In addition, as we aggregate traffic into larger groupings, statistical multiplexing reduces the relative variance of the traffic and allows us to perform better estimates of traffic properties such as the mean and variance.

Temporal Granularity of Traffic Matrices We cannot make instantaneous measurements of a traffic matrix. All such observations occur over some time interval $[t, t + \Delta t)$. It would be useful to make the interval Δt smaller (for instance, for detecting anomalies), but typically we face a trade-off against the errors and uncertainties in our measurements. A longer time interval allows more "averaging-out" of errors, and minimizes the impact of missing data. The best choice of time interval for TMs is typically determined by the task at hand, and the network under study, but a common choice is a 1 hour interval. In addition to being easily understood by human operators, this interval integrates enough SNMP or flow-level data to reduce the impact of (typical) missing data and errors, while allowing us to still observe important diurnal patterns in the traffic.

5.3.2 Patterns in Traffic

It is useful to have some understanding of the typical patterns we see in network traffic. Such patterns are only visible at a reasonable level of aggregation (otherwise random temporal variation dominates our view of the traffic), but for high degrees of aggregation (such as router-to-router traffic matrices on a large backbone network) the pattern can be very regular. There are two main types of patterns that have been observed: patterns across time, and patterns in the spatial structure. Each is discussed below.

Temporal Patterns Internet traffic has been observed to follow both daily (diurnal) and weekly cycles [33–35,57,64]. The origin of these cycles is quite intuitive. They arise because most Internet traffic is currently generated by humans whose activities follow such cycles. Typical examples are shown in Figs. 5.2 and 5.3. Figure 5.2 shows a RRD Tool graph[1] of the traffic on a link of the Australian Academic Research Network (AARNet). Figure 5.3 shows the total traffic entering AT&T's North American backbone network at a Point of Presence (PoP) over two consecutive

---

[1] RRDTool (the Round Robin Database tool) [47] and its predecessor MRTG (the Multi-Router Traffic Grapher [46]) are perhaps the most common tools for collecting and displaying SNMP traffic data.

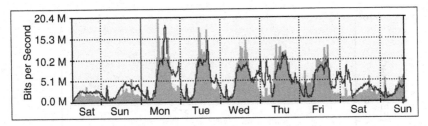

Fig. 5.2 Traffic on one link in the Australian Academic Research Network (AARNet) for just over 1 week. The two curves show traffic in either direction along the link

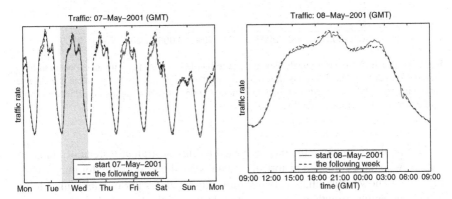

Fig. 5.3 Total traffic into a region over 2 consecutive weeks. The solid line is the first week's data (starting on May 7), and the dashed line shows the second week's data. The second figure zooms in on the shaded region of the first

weeks in May 2001. The figure illustrates the daily and weekly variations in the traffic by overlaying the traffic from the 2 weeks. The striking similarity between traffic patterns from week to week is a reflection of the high level of aggregation that we see in a major backbone network.

The observation of cycles in traffic is not new. For many years they have been seen in telephony [13]. Typically telephone service capacity planning has been based on a "busy hour", i.e., the hour of the day that has the highest traffic. The time of the busy hour depends on the application and customer base. Access networks typically have many domestic consumers, and consequently their busy hour is in the evening when people are at home. On the other hand, the busy hour of business customers is typically during the day. Obviously, time-zones have an effect on the structure of the diurnal cycle in traffic, and so networks with a wide geographic dispersion may experience different busy hours on different parts of their network.

In addition to cyclical patterns, Internet traffic has shown strong growth over many years [45]. This long-term trend has often been approximated by exponential growth, although care must be taken because sometimes such estimates have been based on poor (short or erratic) data [45]. Long-term trends should be estimated from multiple years of carefully collected data.

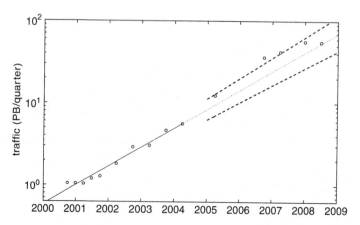

Fig. 5.4 ABS traffic measurements showing Australian Internet traffic, with an exponential fit to the data from 2000 to 2005. Data is shown by 'o', and the fit by the straight line. Note that the line continuing past 2005 is a prediction based on the pre-2005 data, showing also the 95th percentile confidence bounds for the predictions

One public example is the data collected by the Australian Bureau of Statistics (ABS)[2] who have collected historical data on Australian ISP traffic for many years. Figure 5.4 shows Australia's network traffic in petabytes per quarter with a log-y axis. Exponential growth appears as a straight line on the log-graph, so we can obtain simple predictions of traffic growth through linear regression. The figure shows such a prediction based on pre-2005 data. It is interesting to note that the most recent data point does not, as one might assume without analysis, represent a significant drop in traffic growth. Relative to the long-term data the last point simply represents a reversion to the long-term growth from rather exceptional traffic volumes over 2007. We will discuss such prediction in more detail in the following sections.

Standard time-series analysis [10] can be used to build a model of traffic containing long-term trends, cyclical components (often called *seasonal* components in other contexts), and random fluctuations. We will use the following notation here:

$$S(t) = \text{seasonal (cyclical) component,} \tag{5.3}$$

$$L(t) = \text{long-term trend,} \tag{5.4}$$

$$W(t) = \text{random fluctuations.} \tag{5.5}$$

The seasonal component is periodic, i.e., $S(t + kT_S) = S(t)$, for all integers k, where T_S is the period (which is either 24 hour or 1 week). Before we can consider how to estimate the seasonal (and trend) components of the traffic, we must

---

[2] www.abs.gov.au

model these components.[3] At the most basic level, consider the traffic to consist of two components, a time varying (but deterministic) mean $m(t)$ and a stochastic component $W(t)$. At this level we could construct the traffic by addition or multiplication of these components (both methods are used in econometric and census data). However, in traffic data, a more appropriate model [43, 56] is

$$x(t) = m(t) + \sqrt{am(t)}\, W(t), \qquad (5.6)$$

where a is called the *peakedness* of the traffic, $W(t)$ is a stochastic process with zero mean, and unit variance, and $x(t)$ represents the average rate of some traffic (say a particular traffic matrix element) at time t. More highly aggregated traffic is smoother, and consequently would have a smaller value for a. The reason for this choice of model lies in the way network traffic behaves when aggregated. When multiple flows are aggregated onto a non-congested link, we should expect them to obey the same model (though perhaps with different parameters). Our model has this property: for instance, take N traffic streams x_i with mean m_i, peakedness a_i, and stochastic components, which are independent realizations of a (zero mean, unit variance) Gaussian process. The multiplexed traffic stream is

$$x = \sum_{i=1}^{N} m_i + \sum_{i=1}^{N} \sqrt{a_i m_i}\, W_i. \qquad (5.7)$$

The mean of the new process is $m = \sum_{i=1}^{N} m_i$, and the peakedness (derived from the variance) is $a = \frac{1}{m} \sum_{i=1}^{N} a_i m_i$, which is a weighted average of the component peakednesses. The relative variance becomes

$$V_x = Var\{x\}/E\{x\} = \frac{1}{m^2} \sum_{i=1}^{N} a_i m_i. \qquad (5.8)$$

If we take identical streams, then the relative variance decreases as we multiplex more together, which is to be expected. The result is that in network traffic the level of aggregation is important in determining the relative variance: more highly aggregated traffic exhibits less random behavior. The data in Fig. 5.3 from AT&T shows an aggregate of a very large number of customers (an entire PoP of one of North America's largest networks). The consequence is that we can see the traffic is very smooth. In contrast the traffic shown in Fig. 5.2 is much less aggregated, and shows more random fluctuations.

The model described above is not perfect (none are), but it is useful because it (i) allows us to calculate variances for aggregated traffic streams in a consistent way and to use these when planning our network, and (ii) its parameters are relatively

---

[3] The reader should beware of methods, which do not explicitly model the data, because in these methods there is often an implicit model.

easy to measure, and therefore to use in traffic analysis. To do so, however, we find it useful to spilt the mean $m(t)$ into the cyclic component (which we denote $S(t)$) and the long-term trend $L(t)$ by taking the product

$$m(t) = L(t)S(t). \tag{5.9}$$

We combine the two components through a product because as the overall load increases the range of variation in the size of cycles also increases. When estimating parameters of our models, it is important to allow for unusual or anomalous events, for instance, a Denial of Service (DoS) attack. These events are rare (we hope), but it is important to separate them from the normal traffic. Such terms can sometimes be very large, but we do not plan network capacity to carry DoS attacks! The network is planned around the paying customers. We separate them by including an impulsive term, $I(t)$, in the model, so that the complete model is

$$x(t) = L(t)S(t) + \sqrt{aL(t)S(t)}\, W(t) + I(t). \tag{5.10}$$

We will further discuss this model in Section 5.4, where we will consider how to estimate its parameters, and to use it in prediction.

Spatial Patterns Temporal models are adequate for many applications: for instance, where we consider dimensioning of a single bottleneck link (perhaps in the design of an access network). However, spatial patterns in traffic provide us with addition planning capabilities. For instance, if two traffic sources are active at different times, then clearly we can carry them both with less capacity than if they activate simultaneously.

Spatial patterns refer to the structure of a Traffic Matrix (TM) at a single time interval. It is common that TM elements are strongly correlated because they show similar diurnal (and weekly) patterns. For example, in a typical network (without wide geographic distribution) one will find that the busy hour is almost the same for all elements of the TM, but there is additional structure.

For a start, TMs often come from skewed distributions. A common example is where the distribution follows a rough 80–20 law (80% of traffic is generated by the largest 20% of TM elements). Similar distributions have often been observed, though often even more skewed: for instance 90–10 laws are not uncommon. However, the distribution is not "heavy-tailed". Observed distributions have shown a lighter tail than the log-normal distribution [55]. Consequently, traffic matrix work often concentrates on these larger flows, but traditional (rather than heavy-tailed) statistical techniques are still applicable.

Another simple feature one might naively expect of TMs – symmetry – is not present. Internet routing is naturally asymmetric, as is application traffic (a large amount of traffic still follows a client–server model, which results in strongly asymmetric traffic). Hence, the matrix will not (generally) be symmetric [21], i.e., $T(i, j) \neq T(j, i)$.

We observe some additional structure in these matrices. The simplest model that describes some of the observed structure is the *gravity model*. In network applications, gravity models have been used to model the volume of telephone calls in a network [31]. Gravity models take their name from Newton's law of gravitation, and are commonly used by social scientists to model the movement of people, goods or information between geographic areas [49,50,63]. In Newton's law of gravitation the force is proportional to the product of the masses of the two objects divided by the distance squared. Similarly, in gravity models for interactions between cities, the relative strength of the interaction might be modeled as proportional to the product of the cities' populations, so a general formulation of a gravity model is given by

$$T(i, j) = \frac{R_i \cdot A_j}{f_{ij}}, \tag{5.11}$$

where R_i represents the *repulsive* factors that are associated with leaving from i; A_j represents the *attractive* factors that are associated with going to j; and f_{ij} is a friction factor from i to j. The gravity model was first used in the context of Internet traffic matrices in [67] where we can naturally interpret the repulsion factor R_i as the volume of incoming traffic at location i, and the attractivity factor A_j as the outgoing traffic volume at location j. The friction matrix (f_{ij}) encodes the locality information specific to different source–destination pairs, however, as locality is not as large a factor in Internet traffic as in the transport of physical goods, it is common to assume $f_{ij} = const$. The resulting gravity model simply states that the traffic exchanged between locations is proportional to the volumes entering and exiting at those locations.

Formally, let $T^{in}(i)$ and $T^{out}(j)$ denote the total traffic that enters the network via i, and exits via j, respectively. The gravity model can then be computed by

$$T(i, j) = \frac{T^{in}(i)T^{out}(j)}{T^{tot}}, \tag{5.12}$$

where T^{tot} is the total traffic across the network. Implicitly, this model relies on a conservation assumption, i.e., traffic is neither created nor destroyed in the network so that $T^{tot} = \sum_k T^{in}(k) = \sum_k T^{out}(k)$. The assumption may be violated, for instance, when congestion causes packet loss. However, in most backbones congestion is kept low, and so the assumption is reasonable.

In the form just described, the gravity model has distinct limitations. For instance, real traffic matrices may have non-constant f_{ij} (perhaps as a result of different time zones). Moreover, even if an origin destination traffic matrix matches the gravity model well, the ingress/egress TM may be systematically distorted [7]. Typically, networks use hot-potato routing, i.e., they choose the egress point closest to the ingress point, and this results in a systematic distortion of ingress/egress traffic matrices away from the simple gravity model. These distortions and others related to the asymmetry of traffic and distance sensitivity may be incorporated in generalizations of the gravity model where sufficient data exists to measure such deviations [13,21,67].

The use of temporal patterns in planning is relatively obvious. The use of spatial patterns such as the gravity model is more subtle. The spatial structure gives us the capability to fill in missing values of the traffic matrix when our data is not perfect. Hence we can still plan our network, even in the extreme case where we have no data at all.

5.3.3 Application Profile

We have so far discussed network traffic along two dimensions: the temporal and spatial. There is a third aspect of traffic to consider: its application breakdown, or profile. Common applications on the Internet are email, web browsing (and other server-based interactions), peer-to-peer file transfers, video, and voice. Each may have a different traffic matrix, and as some networks move toward differentiated Quality of Service (QoS) for different classes of traffic, we may have to plan networks based on these different traffic matrices.

Even where differentiated service is not going to be provided, a knowledge of the application classes in our network can be very useful. For instance

- Voice traffic is less variable than data, and so can require less overhead for sub-measurement interval variations.
- Peer-to-peer applications typically generate more symmetric traffic than web traffic, and so downstream capacity (toward customer eyeballs) is likely to be more balanced when peer-to-peer applications dominate.
- We may be planning to eliminate some types of traffic in future networks (e.g., peer-to-peer traffic has often been considered to violate service agreements that prohibit running servers).

The breakdown of traffic on a network is not trivial to measure. As noted, typical flow-level data collection includes TCP/UDP port numbers, and these are often associated with applications using the IANA (Internet Assigned Numbers Authority) list of registered ports.[4] However, the port numbers used today are often associated with incorrect applications because:

- Ports are not defined with IANA for all applications, e.g., some peer-to-peer applications.
- An application may use ports other than its well-known ports to circumvent access control restrictions, e.g., nonprivileged users often run WWW servers on ports other than port 80, which is restricted to privileged users on most operating systems, while port 80 is often used for other applications (than HTTP) in order to work around firewalls.
- In some cases server ports are dynamically allocated as needed. For example, FTP allows the dynamic negotiation of the server port used for the data transfer.

---

[4] http://www.iana.org/assignments/port-numbers

This server port is negotiated on an initial TCP, connection which is established using the well-known FTP control port, but which would appear as a separate flow.

- Malicious traffic (e.g., DoS attacks) can generate a large volume of bogus traffic that should not be associated with the applications that normally use the affected ports.

In addition, there are some incorrect implementations of protocols, and ambiguous port assignments that complicate the problem. Better approaches to classification of traffic exist (e.g., [58]), but are not always implemented on commercial measurement systems.

Application profiles can be quite complex. Typical Internet providers will see some hundreds of different applications. However, there are two major simplifications we can often perform. The first is a clustering of applications into classes. QoS sometimes forms natural classes (e.g., real-time vs bulk-transfer classes), but regardless we can often group many applications into similarly structured classes, e.g., we can group a number of protocols (IMAP, POP, SMTP, etc.) into one class "email". Common groupings are shown in Table 5.1, along with exemplar applications.

There may be a larger number of application classes, and often there is a significant group of unknown applications, but a typical application profile is highly skewed. Again, it is common to see 80–20 or 90–10 rules. In these cases, it is common to focus attention on those applications that generate the most traffic, reducing the complexity of the profile.

However, care must be taken because some applications that generate relatively little traffic on average may be considered very important, and/or may generate high volumes of traffic for short bursts. There are several such examples in enterprise networks, for instance, consider a CEO's once-a-week company-wide broadcast, or nightly backups. Both generate a large amount of traffic, but in a relative short-time interval, so their proportion of the overall network traffic may be small. More generally, much of the control-plane traffic (e.g., routing protocol traffic) in networks is relatively low volume, but of critical importance.

Table 5.1 Typical application classes grouped by typical use

Class	Example applications
Bulk-data	FTP, FTP-Data
Database access	Oracle, MySQL
Email	IMAP, POP, SMTP
Information	finger, CDDBP, NTP
Interactive	SSH, Telnet
Measurement	SNMP, ICMP, Netflow
Network control	BGP, OSPF, DHCP, RSVP, DNS
News	NNTP
Online gaming	Quake, Everquest
Peer-to-peer	Kazaa, Bit-torrent
Voice over IP	SIP, Skype
www	HTTP, HTTPS

5.4 Prediction

There are two common scenarios for network planning:

1. Incremental planning for network evolution
2. Green-fields planning

In the first case, we have an existing network. We can measure its current traffic, and extrapolate trends to predict future growth. In combination with business data, quite accurate assessments of future traffic are possible. Typically, temporal models are sufficient for incremental network planning, though better results might be possible with recently developed full spatio-temporal models [52].

In green-fields planning, we have the advantage that we are not constrained in our network design. We may start with a clean slate, without concerning ourselves with a legacy network. However, in such planning we have no measurements on which to base predictions. All is not lost, however, as we may exploit the spatial properties of traffic matrices in order to obtain predictions. We discuss each of these cases below.

There are other scenarios of concern to the network planner. For example

- Network mergers, for instance when two companies merge and subsequently combine their networks.
- Network migrations, for instance, as significant services such as voice or frame-relay are migrated to operate on a shared backbone.
- Addition (or loss) of a large customer (say a broadband access provider, a major content provider, or a hosting center).
- A change in interdomain routing relationships. For instance, the conversion of a customer to a peer would mean that traffic no longer transits from that peer, altering traffic patterns.

The impact of these types of event is obviously dependent on the relative volume of the traffic affected. Such events can be particularly significant for smaller networks, but it is not unheard of for them to cause unexpected demands on the largest networks (for instance, the migration of an estimated half-million customers from Excite@home to AT&T in 2002[5]). However, the majority of such cases can be covered by one or both of the techniques below.

5.4.1 Prediction for Incremental Planning

Incremental planning involves extending, or evolving a current network to meet changing patterns of demands, or changing goals. The problem involves prediction of future network demands, based on extrapolation of past and present network

---

[5] http://news.cnet.com/ExciteHome-to-shut-down-ATT-drops-bid/2100-1033_3-276550.html

measurements. The planning problems we encounter are often constrained by the fact that we can make only incremental changes to our network, i.e., we cannot throw away the existing network and start from a clean slate, but let us first consider the problem of making successful traffic predictions.

Obviously, our *planning horizon* (the delay between our planning decisions and their implementation) is critical. The shorter this horizon, the more accurate our predictions are likely to be, but the horizon is usually determined by external factors such as delays between ordering and delivery of equipment, test and verification of equipment, planned maintenance windows, availability of technical staff, and capital budgeting cycles. These are outside the control of the network planner, so we treat the planning horizon as a constant.

The planning horizon also suggests how much historical data is needed. It is a good idea to start with historical data extending several planning horizons into the past. Such a record allows not only better determination of trends, but also an assessment of the quality of our prediction process through analysis of past planning periods. If such data is unavailable, then we must consider green-fields planning (see Section 5.4.2), though informed by what measurements are available.

Given such a historical record, our primary means for prediction is temporal analysis of traffic data. That is, we consider the traffic measurements of interest (often a traffic matrix) as a set of time-series.

However, as noted earlier the more highly we aggregate traffic, the smaller its relative variance, and the easier it is to work with. As a result, it can be a good idea to predict traffic at a high level of aggregation, and then use a spatial model to break it into components. For instance, we might perform predictions for the total traffic in each region of our network, and then break it into components using the current traffic matrix percentages, rather than predicting each element of the traffic matrix separately.

There are many techniques for prediction, but we concentrate here on just one, which works reasonably for a wide range of traffic, but we should note that as in all of the work presented here, the key is not the individual algorithms but their robust application through a process of measurement, planning, and validation.

5.4.1.1 Extracting the Long-Term Trend

We will exploit the previously presented temporal model for traffic, and note that the key to providing predictions for use in planning is to estimate the long-term trend in the data. We could form such an estimate simply by aggregating our time-series over periods of 1 week (to average away the diurnal and weekly cycles) and then performing standard trend analysis. However, knowledge of the cycles in traffic data is often useful. Sometimes we design networks to satisfy the demand during a "busy hour." More generally though, the busiest hours for different components of the traffic may not match (particularly in international networks distributed over several time-zones), and so we need to plan our network to have sufficient capacity at all hours of the day or night.

Hence, the approach we present provides the capability to estimate both the long-term trend, and the seasonal components of the traffic. It also allows an estimate of the peakedness, providing the ability to estimate the statistical variations around the expected traffic behavior. The method is hardly the only applicable time-series algorithm for this type of analysis (for another example see [44]), but it has the advantage of being relatively simple. The method is based on a simple signal processing tool, the *Moving Average* (MA) filter, which we discuss in detail below.

The moving average can be thought of as a simple low-pass filter as it "passes" low-frequencies, or long-term behavior, but removes short-term variations. As such it is ideally suited to extracting the trend in our traffic data. Although there are many forms of moving average, we shall restrict our attention to the simplest: a rectangular moving average

$$MA_x(t;n) = \frac{1}{2n+1} \sum_{s=t-n}^{s=t+n} x(s), \tag{5.13}$$

where n is the width of the filter, and $2n+1$ is its length. The length of the filter must be longer than the period of the cyclic component in order to filter out that component. Longer filters are often used to allow for averaging out of the stochastic variation as well. The shortest filter we should consider for extracting the trend is three times the period, which in Internet traffic data is typically 1 week. For example, given traffic data $x(t)$, measured in 1 hour intervals, we could form our estimate $\hat{L}(t)$ of the trend by taking a filter of length 3 weeks (e.g., $2n + 1 = 504 = 24 \times 7 \times 3$), i.e., we might take $\hat{L}(t) = MA_x(t; 252)$ where MA_x is defined in (5.13).

Care must always be taken around the start and end of the data. Within n data points of the edges the MA filter will be working with incomplete data, and so these estimates should be discounted in further analysis.

Once we have obtained estimates for the long-term trend, we can model its behavior. Over the past decade, the Internet has primarily experienced exponential growth (for instance, see Fig. 5.4 or [45]) i.e.,

$$L(t) = L(0)e^{\beta t}, \tag{5.14}$$

where $L(0)$ is the starting value, and β is the growth rate. If exponential growth is suspected the standard approach is to transform the data using the log function so that we see

$$\log L(t) = \log L(0) + \beta t, \tag{5.15}$$

where we can now estimate $L(0)$ and β from linear regression of the observed data. Care should obviously be taken that this model is reasonable. Regression provides diagnostic statistics to this end, but comparisons to other models (such as a simple linear model) can also be helpful.

Such a model can be easily extrapolated to provide long-term predictions of traffic volumes. Standard diagnostics from the regression can also be used to provide confidence bounds for the predictions, allowing us to predict "best" and "worst" case scenarios for traffic growth, and an example of such predictions is given in Fig. 5.4 using the data from 2000 to 2004 to estimate the trend, and then extrapolating this until 2009. The figure shows the extrapolated optimistic and pessimistic trend estimates. We can see that actual traffic growth from 2005 to 2007 was on the optimistic side of growth, but that in 2008 the measured traffic was again close to the long-term trend estimate.

This example clearly illustrates that understanding the potential variations in our trend estimate is almost as important as obtaining the estimate in the first place. It also illustrates how instructive historical data can be in assessing appropriate models and prediction accuracy.

Often, in traffic studies, managers are keen to know the *doubling time*, the time it takes traffic to double. This can be easily calculated by estimating the value of t such that $L(t) = 2L(0)$, or $e^{\beta t} = 2$. Again, taking logs we get the doubling time

$$t^* = \frac{1}{\beta} \ln 2. \qquad (5.16)$$

The Australian data shown in Fig. 5.4 has a doubling time of 477 days.

The trend by itself can inform us of growth rate but modeling the cyclic variations in traffic is also useful. We do this by extending the concept of moving average to the *seasonal moving average*, but before doing so we broadly remove the long-term trend from the data (by dividing our measurements $x(t)$ by $\hat{L}(t)$).

5.4.1.2   Extracting the Cyclical Component

The goal of a Seasonal Moving Average (SMA) is to extract the cyclic component of our traffic. We know, a priori, the period (typically 7 days) and so the design of a filter to extract this component is simple. It resembles the MA used previously in that it is an average, but in this case it is an average of measurements separated in time by the period. More precisely we form the SMA of the traffic with the estimated trend removed, e.g.,

$$\hat{S}(t) = \frac{1}{N} \sum_{n=0}^{N-1} x(t + nT_S)/\hat{L}(t + nT_S), \qquad (5.17)$$

where T_S is the period, and NT_S is the length of the filter. In effect the SMA estimates the traffic volume for each time of day and week as if they were separate time series. It can be combined with a short MA filter to provide some additional smoothing of the results if needed.

The advantage of using an SMA as opposed to a straightforward seasonal average is that the cyclical component of network traffic can change over time. Using the SMA allows us to see such variability, while still providing a reasonably stable model for extrapolation. There is a natural trade-off between the length of the SMA, and the amount of change we allow over time (longer filters naturally smooth out transient changes). Typically, the length of filter desired depends on the planning horizon under which we are operating. We extrapolate the SMA in various ways, but the simplest is to repeat the last cycle measured in our data into the future, as if the cyclical component remained constant into the future. Hence, when operating with a short planning horizon (say a week), we can allow noticeable week-to-week variations, and still obtain reasonable predictions, and so a filter length of three to four cycles is often sufficient. Where our planning horizon is longer (say a year) we must naturally assume that the week-to-week variations in the cyclical behavior are smaller in order to extrapolate, and so we use a much longer SMA, preferably at least of the order of the length of the planning horizon.

5.4.1.3 Estimating the Magnitude of Random Variations

Once we understand the periodic and trend components of the traffic, the next thing to capture is the random variation around the mean. Most metrics of variation used in capacity planning do not account for the time-varying component, and so are limited to busy-hour analysis. In comparison, we now have an estimate of $\hat{m}(t) = \hat{L}(t)\hat{S}(t)$ and so can use (5.6) to estimate the stochastic or random component of our traffic by $z(t) = (x(t) - \hat{m}(t))/\sqrt{\hat{m}(t)}$. We can now measure the variability of the random component of the traffic using the variance of $z(t)$, which forms an estimate $\hat{a}$ for the traffic's peakedness. The estimator for $\hat{a}$ including the correction for bias is given in [57]. Note that it is also important to separate the impulsive, anomaly terms from the more typical variations. There are many anomaly detection techniques available (see [66] for a review of a large group of such algorithms). These algorithms can be used to select anomalous data points that can then be excluded from the above analysis.

5.4.1.4 From Traffic Matrix to Link Loads

Once we have predictions of a TM, we often need to use these to compute the link loads that would result. The standard approach is to write the TM in vectorized form $\mathbf{x}$, where the vector $\mathbf{x}$ consists of the columns of the TM (at a particular time) stacked one on top of another. The link loads $\mathbf{y}$ can then be estimated through the equation

$$\mathbf{y} = \mathbf{Ax}, \tag{5.18}$$

where A is the routing matrix. The equation above can also be extended to project observations or predictions of a TM over time into equivalent link loads.

Although there are multiple time-series approaches that can be used to predict future behavior (e.g., Holt-Winters [11]), our approach has the advantage that it naturally incorporates multiplexing. As a result, Eq. 5.18 can be extended to other aspects of the traffic model. For instance, the variances of independent flows are additive (the variance of the multiplexed traffic is the sum of the variances of the components), and so the variance of link traffic follows the same relationship, i.e.,

$$\mathbf{v}_y = A\mathbf{v}_x, \tag{5.19}$$

where $\mathbf{v}_y$ and $\mathbf{v}_x$ are the variances of the link loads and TM, respectively. We can use $\mathbf{v}_y$ to deduce peakedness parameters for the link traffic using (5.7).

So far, we have assumed that the network (at least the location of links, and the routing) is static. In reality, part of network planning involves changing the network, and so the matrix A is really a potential variable. When we consider network planning, A appears implicitly as one of our optimization variables. Likewise, A may change in response to link or router failures.

The reason-traffic matrices are so important is that they are, in principle, *invariant* under changes to A. Hence predictions of link loads under the changes in A can be easily made. For example, imagine a traffic engineering problem where we wish to balance the load on a network's internal links more effectively. We will change routing in the network in order to balance the traffic on links more effectively. In doing so, the link loads are not invariant (the whole point of traffic engineering is to change these). However, the ingress/egress TM is invariant, and projecting this onto the links (via the routing matrix) will predict the link loads under proposed routing changes.

In reality, invariance is an approximation. Real TMs are not invariant under all network changes, for instance, if network capacities are chosen to be too small, congestion will result. However, the Transmission Control Protocol (TCP) will act to alleviate this congestion by reducing the actual traffic carried on the network, thereby changing the traffic matrix. In general, different sets of measurements will have different degrees of invariance. For instance, an origin/destination TM is invariant to changes in egress points (due to routing changes), whereas an ingress/egress TM is not. It is clearly better to use the right data set for each planning problem, but the desired data is not always available.

The lack of true invariance is one of the key reasons for the cyclic approach to network planning. We seek to correct any problems caused by variations in our inputs in response to our new network design.

5.4.2 Prediction for Green-Fields Planning

The above section assumes that we have considerable historical data to which we apply time-series techniques to extrapolate trends, and hence predict the future traffic demands on our network. This has two major limitations:

1. IP traffic is constrained by the pipe through which it passes. TCP congestion control ensures that such traffic does not overflow by limiting the source transmission rate. In most networks our measurements only provide the *carried load*, not the *offered load*. If the network capacities change, the traffic may increase in response. This is a concern if our current network is loaded to near its capacity, and in this case we must discount our measurements, or at least treat them with caution.
2. When we design a new network there is nothing in place for us to measure.

We will start by considering available strategies for the latter case. We can draw inspiration from the spatial models previously presented. The fact that the simple gravity model describes, to some extent, the spatial structure of Internet traffic matrices presents us with a simple approach to estimate an initial traffic matrix.

The first step is to estimate the total expected traffic for the network, based on demographics and market projections. Let us take a simple example: in Australia the ABS measures Internet usage. Across a wide customer base the average usage per customer was roughly 3 GB/month (since 2006). The total traffic for our network is the usage per customer multiplied by the projected number of customers. We can derive traffic estimates per marketing region in the same fashion. Note that the figure used above is for the broad Australian market and is unlikely to be correct elsewhere (typical Australian ISPs have an tiered pricing structure). Where more detailed figures exist in particular markets these should be used.

The second step is to estimate the "busy-hour" traffic. As we have seen previously the traffic is not uniformly distributed over time. In the absence of better data, we might look at existing public measurements (such as presented in Figs. 5.2 and 5.3, or as appears in [44]) where the peak to mean ratio is of the order of 3 to 2. Increasing our traffic estimates by this factor gives us an estimate of the peak traffic loads on the network.

The third step is to estimate a traffic matrix. The best approach, in the absence of other information, to derive the traffic matrix is to apply the gravity model (5.12). In the simple case, the gravity model would be applied directly using the local regional traffic estimates. However, where additional information about the expected application profile exists, we might use this to refine the results using the "independent flow model" of [21]. Additional structural information about the network might allow use of the "generalized gravity model" of [68]. Each of these approaches allows us to use additional information, but in the absence of such information the simple gravity model gives us our initial estimate of the network traffic matrix.

What about the case where we have historical network traffic measurements, but suspect that the network is congested so that the carried load is significantly below the offered load? In this case, our first step is to determine what parts of the traffic matrix are affected. If a large percentage of the traffic matrix is affected, then the only approach we have available is to go back through the historical record until we reach a point (hopefully) where the traffic is not capacity constrained. This has limitations: for one thing, we may not find a sufficient set of data where capacity constraints have left the measurements uncorrupted. Even where we do obtain sufficient data, the missing (suspect) measurements increase the window over which we must make predictions, and therefore the potential errors in these predictions.

However, if only a small part of the traffic matrix is affected we may exploit techniques developed for traffic matrix inference to fill in the suspect values with more accurate estimates. These methods originated due to the difficulties in collecting flow-level data to measure traffic matrices directly. Routers (particularly older routers) may not support an adequate mechanism for such measurements (or suffer a performance hit when the measurements are used), and installation of stand-alone measurement devices can be costly. On the other hand, the Simple Network Management Protocol (SNMP) is almost ubiquitously available, and has little overhead.

Unfortunately, it provides only link-load measurements, not traffic matrices. However, the two are simply related by (5.18). Inferring $\mathbf{x}$ from $\mathbf{y}$ is a so-called "network tomography" problem. For a typical network the number of link measurements is $O(N)$ (for a network of N nodes), whereas the number of traffic matrix elements is $O(N^2)$ leading to a massively underconstrained linear inverse problem. Some type of side information is needed to solve such problems, usually in the form of a model that roughly describes a typical traffic matrix. We then estimate the parameters of this crude model (which we shall call $\mathbf{m}$), and perform a regularization with respect to the model and the measurements by solving the minimization problem

$$\underset{\mathbf{x}}{\operatorname{argmin}} \, \|\mathbf{y} - \mathbf{A}\mathbf{x}\|_2^2 + \lambda^2 d(\mathbf{x}, \mathbf{m}), \qquad (5.20)$$

where $\| \cdot \|_2$ denotes the l^2 norm, $\lambda > 0$ is a regularization parameter, and $d(\mathbf{x}, \mathbf{m})$ is a distance between the model $\mathbf{m}$ and our estimated traffic matrix $\mathbf{x}$. Examples of suitable distance metrics are standard or weighted Euclidean distance and the Kullback–Leibler divergence. Approaches of this type, generally called *strategies for regularization of ill-posed problems* are more generally described in [29], but have been used in various forms in many works on traffic matrix inference. The method works because the measurements leave the problem underconstrained, thereby allowing many possible traffic matrices that fit the measurements, but the model allows us to choose one of these as best. Furthermore, through λ the method allows us to tradeoff our belief about the accuracy of the model against the expected errors in the measurements.

We can utilize TM structure to interpolate missing values by solving a similar optimization problem

$$\underset{\mathbf{x}}{\operatorname{argmin}} \, \|\mathscr{A}(\mathbf{x}) - \mathbf{M}\|_2^2 + \lambda^2 d(\mathbf{x}, \mathbf{m}_g), \qquad (5.21)$$

where $\mathscr{A}(\mathbf{x}) = \mathbf{M}$ expresses the available measurements as a function of the traffic matrix (whether these be link measurements or direct measurements of a subset of the TM elements we do not care), and $\mathbf{m}_g$ is the gravity model. This regularizes our model with respect to the measurements that are considered valid. Note that the gravity model in this approach will be skewed by missing elements, so this approach is only suitable for interpolation of a few elements of the traffic matrix. If larger numbers of elements are missing, we can use more complicated techniques such as those proposed in [52] to interpolate the missing data.

5.5   Optimal Network Plans

Once we have obtained predictions of the traffic on our network we can commence the actual process of making decisions about where links and routers will be placed, their capacities, and the routing policies that will be used. In this section we discuss how we may optimize these quantities against a set of goals and constraints.

The first problem we consider concerns capacity planning. If this component of our network planning worked as well as desired, we could stop there. However, errors in predictions, coupled with the long planning horizon for making changes to a network mean that we need also to consider a short-term way of correcting such problems. The solution is typically called *traffic engineering* or simply load balancing, and is considered in Section 5.5.2.

5.5.1 Network Capacity Planning

There are many good optimization packages available today. Commercial tools such as CPLEX are designed specifically for solving optimization problems, while more general purpose tools such as Matlab often include optimization toolkits that can be used for such problems. Even Excel includes some quite sophisticated optimization tools, and so we shall not consider optimization algorithms in detail here. Instead we will formulate the problem, and provide insight into the practical issues. There are three main components to any optimization problem: the variables, the objective, and the constraints.

The variables here are obviously the locations of links, and their capacities.

The objective function – the function which we aim to minimize – varies depending on business objectives. For instance, it is common to minimize the cost of a network (either its capital or ongoing cost), or packet delays (or some other network performance metric). The many possible objectives in network design result in different problem formulations, but we concentrate here on the most common objective of cost minimization.

The cost of a network is a complex function of the number and type of routers used, and the capacities of the links. It is common, however, to break up the problem hierarchically into inter-PoP, and intra-PoP design, and we consider the two separately here.

The constraints in the problem fall into several categories:

1. Capacity constraints require that we have "sufficient" link capacity. These are the key constraints for this problem so we consider these in more detail below.
2. Other technological constraints, such as limited port numbers per router.
3. Constraints arising as a result of the difficulties in multiobjective optimization. For example, we may wish to have a network with good performance and low cost. However, multiobjective optimization is difficult, so instead we minimize cost subjected to a constraint on network performance.
4. Reliability constraints require that the network functions even under network failures. This issue is so important that other chapters of this book have been devoted to this issue, but we shall consider some aspects of this problem here as well.

5.5.1.1 Capacity Constraints and Safe-Operating Points

Unsurprisingly, the primary constraints in capacity planning are the capacity constraints. We must have a network with sufficient capacity to carry the offered traffic. The key issue is our definition of "sufficient." There are several factors that go into this decision:

1. Traffic is not constant over the day, so we must design our network to carry loads at all times of day. Often this is encapsulated in "busy hour" traffic measurements, but busy hours may vary across a large network, and between customers, and so it is better to design for the complete cycle.
2. Traffic has observable fluctuations around its average behavior. Capacity planning can explicitly allow for these variations.
3. Traffic also has unobservable fluctuations on shorter times than our measurement interval. Capacity planning must attempt to allow for these variations.
4. There will be measurement and prediction errors in any set of inputs.

Ideally, we would use queueing models to derive an exact relationship between measured traffic loads, variations, and so determine the required capacities. However, despite many recent advances in data traffic modeling, we are yet to agree on sufficiently precise and general queueing models to determine sufficient capacity from numerical formulae. There is no "Erlang-B" formulae for data networks. As a result, most network operators use some kind of engineering rule of thumb, which comes down to an "over-engineering factor" to allow for the above sources of variability.

We adopt the same approach here, but the term "over-engineering factor" is misleading. The factor allows for *known* variations in the traffic. The network is not over-engineered, it only appears so if capacity is directly compared to the available but flawed measurements. In fact, if we follow a well-founded process, the network can be quite precisely engineered.[6]

We therefore prefer to use the term *Safe Operating Point* (SOP). A SOP is defined statistically with respect to the available traffic measurements on a network. For instance, with 5-min SNMP traffic measurements, we might define our SOP by requiring that the load on the links (as measured by 5-min averages) should not exceed 80% of link capacity more than five times per month. The predicted traffic model could then be used to derive how much capacity is needed to achieve this bound.

Traffic variance depends on the application profile and the scale of aggregation. Moreover, the desired trade-off between cost and performance is a business choice for network operators. So there is no single SOP that will satisfy all operators. Given the lack of precision in current queueing models and measurements, the SOP needs to be determined by each network operator experimentally, preferably starting from conservative estimates. Natural variations in network conditions often allow enough

---

[6] It is a common complaint that backbone networks are underutilized. This complaint typically ignores the issues described above. In reality, many of these networks may be quite precisely engineered, but crude average utilization numbers are used to defer required capacity increases.

scope to see the impact of variable levels of traffic, and from these determine more accurate SOP specifications, but to do this we need to couple traffic and performance measurements (a topic we consider later).

A secondary set of capacity constraints arises because there is a finite set of available link types, and capacity must be bought in multiples of these links. For instance, many high-speed networks use either SONET/SDH links (typically giving 155 Mbps times powers of 4) and/or Ethernet link capacities (powers of 10 from 10 Mbps to 10 Gbps). We will denote the set of available link capacities (including zero) by C.

Finally, most high-speed link technologies are duplex, and so we need to allocate capacity in each direction, but we typically do so symmetrically (i.e., a link has the same capacity from $i \rightarrow j$ as from $j \rightarrow i$ even when the traffic loads in each direction are different).

5.5.1.2 Intra-PoP Design

We divide the network design or capacity planning problem into two components and first consider the design of the network inside a PoP. Typically this involves designing a tree-like network to aggregate traffic up to regional hubs, which then transit the traffic onto a backbone.[7] The exact design of a PoP is considered in more detail in Chapter 4, but note that in each of the cases considered there we end up with a very similar optimization problems at this level.

There are two prime considerations in such planning. Firstly, it is typical that the majority of traffic is nonlocal, i.e., that it will transit to or from the backbone. Local traffic between routers within the PoP in the Internet is often less than 1% of the total. There are exceptions to this rule, but these must be dealt with on an individual basis. Secondly, limitations on the number of ports on most high-speed routers mean that we need at least one layer of aggregation routers to bring traffic onto the backbone: for instance, see Fig. 5.5. For clarity, we show a very simple design (see Chapter 4 for more examples). In our example, Backbone Routers (BRs)

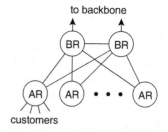

Fig. 5.5 A typical PoP design. Aggregation Routers (AR) are used to increase the port density in the PoP and bring traffic up to the Backbone Routers (BR)

---

[7] In small PoPs, a single router (or redundant pair) may be sufficient for all needs. Little planning is needed in this case beyond selecting the model of router, and so we do not include this simple case in the following discussions.

and the corresponding links to Aggregation Routers (ARs) are assigned in pairs in order to provide redundancy, but otherwise the topology is a simple tree.

There are many variations on this design, for instance, additional BRs may be needed, or multiple layers. However, in our simple model, the design is determined primarily by the limitations on port density. The routers lie within a single PoP, so links are short and their cost has no distance dependence (and they are relatively cheap compared to wide-area links). The number of ARs that can be accommodated depends on the number of ports that can be supported by the BRs, so we shall assume that ARs have a single high-capacity uplink to each BR to allow for a maximum expansion factor in a one-level tree. As a result, the job of planning a PoP is primarily one of deciding how many ARs are needed.

As noted earlier we do not need a TM for this task. The routing in such a network is predetermined, and so current port allocations and the uplink load history are sufficiently invariant for this planning task. We use these to form predictions of future uplink requirements and the loads on each router. When predictions show that a router is reaching capacity (either in terms of uplink capacity, traffic volume, or port usage) we can install additional routers based on our predictions over the planning horizon for router installation.

There is an additional improvement we can make in this type of problem. It is rare for customers to use the entire capacity of their link to our network, and so the uplink capacity between AR and BR in our network need not be the sum of the customers' link capacities. We can take advantage of this fact through simple measurement-based planning, but with the additional detail that we may allocate customers with different traffic patterns to routers in such a way as to leverage different peak hours and traffic asymmetries (between input and output traffic), so as to further reduce capacity requirements.

The problem resembles the bin packing problem. Given a fixed link capacity C for the uplinks between ARs and BRs, and K customers with peak traffic demands $\{T_i\}_{i=1}^{K}$, the bin packing problem would be as follows: determine the smallest integer B, such that we can find a B-partition $\{S_k\}_{k=1}^{B}$ of the customers[8] such that

$$\sum_{i \in S_k} T_i \leq C \quad \text{for all } k = 1, \ldots, B. \tag{5.22}$$

The number of subsets B gives the number of required ARs, and although the problem is NP-hard, there are reasonable approximation algorithms for its solution [18], some of which are online, i.e., they can be implemented without reorganization of existing allocations.

The real problem is more complicated. There are constraints on the number of ports that can be supported by ARs dependent on the model of ARs being

---

[8] A B-partition of our customers is a group of B non-empty subsets $S_k \subset \{1, 2, \ldots, K\}$ that are disjoint, i.e., $S_i \cap S_j = \phi$ for all $i \neq j$, and which include all customers, i.e., $\cup_{k=1}^{B} S_k = \{1, 2, \ldots, K\}$.

deployed, constraints on router capacity, and in addition, we can take advantage of the temporal, and directional characteristics of traffic. Customer demands take the form $[I_i(t), O_i(t)]$, where $I_i(t)$ and $O_i(t)$ are incoming and outgoing traffic demands for customer i at time t. So the appropriate condition for our problem is to find the minimal number B of ARs such that

$$\sum_{i \in S_k} I_i(t) \leq C \quad \text{and} \quad \sum_{i \in S_k} O_i(t) \leq C \text{ for all } k, t. \tag{5.23}$$

This is the so-called *vector bin packing* problem, which has been used to model resource constrained processor scheduling problems, and good approximations have been known for some time [15, 28].

The major advantage of this type of approach is that customers with different peak traffic periods can be combined onto one AR so that their joint traffic is more evenly distributed over each 24-hour period. Likewise, careful distribution of customers whose primary traffic flows *into* our network (for instance, hosting centers) together with customers whose traffic flows *out of* the network (e.g., broadband access companies) can lead to more symmetric traffic on the uplinks, and hence better overall utilization. In practice, multiplexing gains may improve the situation, so that less capacity is needed when multiple customers' traffic is combined, but this effect only plays a dominant role when large numbers (say hundreds) of small customers are being combined.

5.5.1.3 Inter-PoP Backbone Planning

The inter-PoP backbone design problem is somewhat more complicated. We start by assuming, we know the locations at which we wish to have PoPs. The question of how to optimize these locations does come up, but it is common that these locations are predetermined by other aspects of business planning. In inter-PoP planning, distance-based costs are important. The cost of a link is usually considered to be proportional to its length, though this is approximate. The real cost of a link has a fixed component (in the equipment used to terminate a line) in addition to distance-dependent terms derived from the cost to install a physical line, e.g., costs of cables, excavation and right of ways. Even where leased lines are used (so there are minimal installation costs) the original capital costs of the lines are usually passed on through some type of distance sensitive pricing.

In addition, higher speed links generally cost more. The exact model for such costs can vary, but a large component of the bandwidth-dependent costs is in the end equipment (router interface cards, WDM mux/demux equipment, etc.). In actuality-real costs are often very complicated: vendors may have discounts for bulk purchases, whereas cutting-edge technology may come at a premium cost. However, link costs are often approximated as linear with respect to bandwidth because we could, in principle, obtain a link with capacity $4c$ by combining four links of capacity c.

In the simple case then, cost per link has the form

$$f(d_e, c_e) = \alpha + \beta d_e + \gamma c_e, \tag{5.24}$$

where α is the fixed cost of link installation, β is the link cost per unit distance, and γ is the cost per unit bandwidth. As the distance of a link is typically a fixed property of the link, we often rewrite the above cost in the form

$$f_e(c_e) = \alpha_e + \gamma c_e, \tag{5.25}$$

where now the cost function depends on the link index e.

We further simplify the problem by assuming that BRs are capable of dealing with all traffic demands so that only two (allowing for redundancy) are needed in each PoP, thus removing the costs of the router from the problem.

Finally, we simplify our approach by assuming that routes are chosen to follow the shortest possible geographic path in our network. There are reasons (which we shall discuss in the following section) why this might not be the case, however, *a priori*, it makes sense to use the shortest geographic path. There are costs that arise from distance. Most obviously, if packets traverse longer paths, they will experience longer delays, and this is rarely desirable. In addition, packets that traverse longer paths use more resources. For instance, a packet that traverses two hops rather than one uses up capacity on two links rather than one.

As noted earlier, we need to specify the problem constraints, the basic set of which are intended to ensure that there is sufficient capacity in the network. When congestion is avoided, queueing delays will be minimal, and hence delays across the network will be dominated by propagation delays (the speed of light cannot be increased). So ensuring sufficient capacity implicitly serves the purpose of reducing networking delays. As noted, we adopt the approach of specifying an SOP, which we do in the form of a factor $\lambda \in (0, 1)$, which specifies the traffic limit with respect to capacity. That is, we shall require that the link capacity c_e be sufficient that traffic takes up only λ of the capacity, leaving $1 - \lambda$ of the capacity to allow for unexpected variations in the traffic.

The possible variables are now the link locations and their capacities. So, given the (vectorized) traffic matrix $\mathbf{x}$, our job is to determine link locations and capacities c_e, which implicitly defined the network routes (and hence the routing matrix A), such that we solve

$$\begin{aligned} \text{minimize} \quad & \sum_{e \in E} \alpha_e I(c_e > 0) + \gamma c_e \\ \text{such that} \quad & A\mathbf{x} \le \lambda \mathbf{c}, \\ & c_e \in C, \end{aligned} \tag{5.26}$$

where $A\mathbf{x} = \mathbf{y}$, the link loads, $\mathbf{c}$ is the vector of links capacities, E is the set of possible links, $I(c_e > 0)$ is an indicator function (which is 1 where we build a link, and 0 otherwise), and C is the set of available link capacities (which includes 0).

Implicit in the above formulation is the routing matrix A, which results from the particular choice of links in the network design, so A is in fact a function of the network design. Its construction imposes constraints requiring that all traffic on the network can be routed. The problem can be rewritten in a more explicit form using flow-based constraints, but the above formulation is convenient for explaining the differences and similarities between the range of problems we consider here.

There may be additional constraints in the above-mentioned problem resulting from router limitations, or due to network performance requirements. For instance, if we have a maximum throughput on each router, we introduce a set of constraints of the form $B\mathbf{x} \leq \eta\mathbf{r}$, where $\mathbf{r}$ are router capacities, and B is similar to a routing matrix in that it maps end-to-end demands to the routers along the chosen path. Port constraints on a router might be expressed by taking constraints of the form $\sum_j I(c_{i,j} > 0) \leq p_i$, where p_i is the port limit on router i. Port constraints are complicated by the many choices of line cards available for high-speed routers, and so have sometimes been ignored, but they are a key limitation in many networks. The issue is sometimes avoided by separation of inter- and intra-PoP design, so that a high port density on BRs is not needed.

The other complication is that we should aim to optimize the network for 24×7 operations. We can do so simply by including one set of capacity constraints for each time of day and week, i.e., $A\mathbf{x}_t \leq \lambda\mathbf{c}$. The resulting constraints are in exactly the same form as in (5.26) but their number increases. However, it is common that many of these constraints are redundant, and so can be removed from the optimization (without effect) by a pre-filtering phase.

The full optimization problem is a linear integer program, and there are many tools available for solution of such programs. However, it is not uncommon to relax the integer constraints to allow any $c_e \geq 0$. In this case, there is no point in having excess capacity, and so we can replace the link capacity constraint by $A\mathbf{x} = \lambda\mathbf{c}$. We then obtain the actual design by rounding up the capacities. This approach reduces the numerical complexity of the problem, but results in a potentially suboptimal design. Note though, that integer programming problems are often NP hard, and consequently solved using heuristics, which likewise can lead to suboptimal designs. Relaxation to a linear program is but one of a suite of techniques that can be used to solve problems in this context, often in combination with other methods.

Moreover, it is common, the mathematical community to focus on finding provably optimal designs, but this is not a real issue. In practical network design we know that the input data contains errors, and our cost models are only approximate. Hence, the mathematically optimal solution may not have the lowest cost of all realizable networks. The mathematical program only needs to provide us with a very good network design.

The components of real network suffer outages on a regular basis: planned maintenance and accidental fiber cuts are simple examples (for more details see Chapters 3 and 4). The final component of network planning that we discuss here is reliability planning: analyzing the reliability of a network. There are many algorithms aimed at maintaining network connectivity, ranging from simple designs such as rings or meshes, to formal optimization problems including connectivity constraints. Commonly, networks are designed to survive all single link or node outages, though more careful planning would concern all Shared Risk Groups (SRG), i.e., groups of links and/or nodes who share fates under common failures. For instance, IP links that use wavelengths on the same fiber will all fail simultaneously if the fiber is cut.

However, when a link (or SRG) fails, maintaining connectivity is not the only concern. Rerouted traffic creates new demands on links. If this demand exceeds capacity, then the resulting congestion will negatively impact network performance. Ideally, we would design our network to accommodate such failures, i.e., we would modify our earlier optimization problem (5.26) as follows:

$$
\begin{aligned}
\text{minimize} \quad & \sum_{e \in E} \alpha_e I(c_e > 0) + \gamma c_e \\
\text{such that} \quad & A\mathbf{x} \le \lambda \mathbf{c}, \\
\text{and} \quad & A_i \mathbf{x} \le \zeta \mathbf{c}, \quad \forall i \in \mathscr{F},
\end{aligned}
\tag{5.27}
$$

where $\mathscr{F}$ is the set of all failure scenarios considered likely enough to include, and A_i is the routing matrix under failure scenario i. Naively implemented with $\lambda = \zeta$, this approach has the limitation that the capacity constraints under failures can come to dominate the design of the network so that most links will be heavily underutilized under normal conditions. Hence, we allow that the SOPs with respect to normal loads, and failure loads to be different, $\lambda < \zeta < 1$, so that the mismatch is somewhat balanced, i.e., under normal conditions links are not completely underutilized, but there is likely to be enough capacity under common failures. For example, we might require that under normal loads, peak utilizations remain at 60%, while under failures, we allow loads of 85%.

Additionally, the number of possible failure scenarios can be quite large, and as each introduces constraints, it may not be practical to consider all failures. We may need to focus on the likely failures, or those that are considered to be most potentially damaging. However, it is noteworthy that only constraints that involve rerouting need be considered. In most failures, a large number of links will be unaffected, and hence the constraints corresponding to those links will be redundant, and may be easily removed from the problem.

The above formulation presumes that we design our network from scratch, but this is the exception. We typically have to grow our network incrementally. This introduces challenges – for instance, it is easy to envisage a series of incremental steps that are each optimal in themselves, but which result in a highly suboptimal network over time. So it is sometimes better to design an optimal network from scratch, particularly when the network is growing very quickly. In the mean time we can include the existing network through a set of constraints in the form $c_e \ge l_e + c_e'$, where l_e is the legacy link capacity on link e, and c_e' is the additional link capacity. The real situation is complicated by some additional issues: (i) typical IP router load balancing is not well suited for multiple parallel links of different capacities so we must choose between increasing capacity through additional links (with capacity equal to the legacy links) or paying to replace the old links with a single higher capacity link; and (ii) the costs for putting additional capacity between two routers may be substantially different from the costs for creating an entirely new link. Some work [40] has considered the problem of evolvability of networks, but without all of the addition complexities of IP network management, so determining long-term solutions for optimal network evolution is still an open problem.

5.5.2 Traffic Engineering

In practice, it takes substantial time to build or change a network, despite modern innovations in reconfigurable networks. Typical changes to a link involve physically changing interface cards, wiring, and router configurations. Today these changes are often made manually. They also need to be performed carefully, through a process where the change is documented, carefully considered, acted upon, and then tested. The time to perform these steps can vary wildly between companies, but can easily be 6 months once budget cycles are taken into account.

In the mean time we might find that our traffic predictions are in error. The best predictions in the world cannot cope with the convulsive changes that seem to occur on a regular basis in the Internet. For instance, the introduction of peer-to-peer networking both increased traffic volumes dramatically in a very short time frame, and changed the structure of this traffic (peer-to-peer traffic is more symmetric that the previously dominant client–server model). YouTube again reset providers' expectations for traffic. The result will be a suboptimal network, in some cases leading to congestion.

As noted, we cannot simply redesign the network, but we can often alleviate congestion by better balancing loads. This process, called *traffic engineering* (or just load balancing) allows us to adapt the network on shorter time scales than capacity planning. It is quite possible to manually intervene in a network's traffic engineering on a daily basis. Even finer time scales are possible in principle if traffic engineering is automated, but this is uncommon at present because there is doubt about the desirability of frequent changes in routing. Each change to routing protocols can require a reconvergence, and can lead to dropped packets. More importantly, if such automation is not very carefully controlled it can become unstable, leading to oscillations and very poor performance.

The Traffic Engineering (TE) problem is very similar to the network design problem. The goal or optimization objective is often closely related to that in design. The constraints are usually similar. The major difference is in the planning horizon (typically days to weeks), and as a result the variables over which we have control. The restriction imposed by the planning horizon for TE is that we cannot change the network hardware: the routers and links between them are fixed. However, we can change the way packets are routed through the network, and we can use this to rebalance the traffic across the existing network links.

There are two methods of TE that are most commonly talked about. The most often mentioned uses MultiProtocol Label Switching (MPLS) [54], by which we can arbitrarily tunnel traffic across almost any set of paths in our network. Finding a general routing minimizing max-utilization is an instance of the classical multi-commodity flow problem, which can be formulated as a linear program

[6, Chapter 17], and is hence solvable using commonly available tools. We shall not spend much time on MPLS TE, because there is sufficient literature already (for instance, see [19, 36]). We shall instead concentrate on a simpler, less well known, and yet almost as powerful method for TE.

Remember that we earlier argued that shortest-geographic paths made sense for network routing. In fact, shortest-path routing does not need to be based on geographic distances. Most modern Interior Gateway Protocols allow administratively defined distances (for instance, Open Shortest Path First (OSPF) [42] and Intermediate System-Intermediate System (IS-IS) [14]). By tweaking these distances we can improve network performance. By making a link distance smaller, you can make a link more "attractive", and so route more traffic on this link. Making the distance longer can remove traffic. Configurable link weights can be used, for example, to direct traffic away from expensive (e.g., satellite) links.

However, we can formulate the TE problem more systematically. Let us consider a shortest-path protocol with administratively configured link *weights* (the link distances) w_e on each link e. We assume that the network is given (i.e., we know its link locations and capacities), and that the variables that we can control are the link weights. Our objective is to minimize the congestion on our network. Several metrics can be used to describe congestion. Network-wide metrics such as that proposed in [25, 26] can have advantages, but we use the common metric of maximum utilization here for its simplicity.

In many cases, there are additional "human" constraints on the weights we can use in the above optimization. For instance, we may wish that the resulting weights do not change "too much" from our existing weights. Each change requires reconfiguration of a router, and so reducing the number of changes with respect to the existing routing may be important. Likewise, the existing weights are often chosen not just for the sake of distance, but also to make the network conceptually simpler. For instance, we might choose smaller weights inside a "region" and large weights between regions, where the regions have some administrative (rather than purely geographical) significance. In this case, we may wish to preserve the general features of the routing, while still fine-tuning the routes. We can express these constraints in various ways, but we do so below by setting minimum and maximum values for the weights. Then the optimization problem can be written: choose the weights $\mathbf{w}$, such that we

$$\text{minimize } \max_{e \in E} y_e / c_e$$
$$\text{such that } Ax = y, \tag{5.28}$$
$$\text{and } w_e^{\min} \leq w_e \leq w_e^{\max}, \quad \forall e \in E$$

where A is the routing matrix generated by shortest-path routing given by link weights w_e, and the link utilizations are given by y_e / c_e (the link load divided by its capacity). The $w_e^{\min}$ and $w_e^{\max}$ constrain the weights for each link into a range determined by existing network policies (perhaps within some bound of the existing weights). Additional constraints might specify the maximum number of weights we are allowed to change, or require that links weights be symmetric, i.e., $w_{(i,j)} = w_{(j,i)}$.

The problem is in general NP-hard, so it is nontrivial to find a solution. Over the years, many heuristic methods [12,20,25,26,37,41,53] have been developed for the solution of this problem.

The exciting feature of this approach is that it is very simple. It uses standard IP routing protocols, with no enhancements other than the clever choice of weights. One might believe that the catch was that it cannot achieve the same performance as full MPLS TE. However, the performance of the above shortest-path optimization has been shown on real networks to suffer only by a few percent [59,60], and importantly, it has been shown to be more robust to errors in the input traffic matrices than MPLS optimization [60]. This type of robustness is critical to real implementations.

Moreover, the approach can be used to generate a set of weights that work well over the whole day (despite variations in the TM over the day) [60], or that can help alleviate congestion in the event of a link failure [44], a problem that we shall consider in more detail in the following section.

5.6 Robust Planning

A common concern in network planning is the consequence of mistakes. Traffic matrices used in our optimizations may contain errors due to measurement artifacts, sampling, inference, or predictions. Furthermore, there may be inconsistencies between our planned network design, and the actual implementation through misconfiguration or last minute changes in constraints. There may be additional inconsistencies introduced through the failure of invariance in TMs used as inputs, for example, caused by congestion alleviation in the new network.

Robust planning is the process of acknowledging these flaws, and still designing good networks. The key to robustness is the cyclic approach described in Section 5.1: measure → predict → plan → and then measure again. However, with some thought, this process can be made tighter. We have already seen one example of this through TE, where a short-term alteration in routing is used to counter errors in predicted traffic. In this section we shall also consider some useful additions to our kitbag of robust planning tools.

5.6.1 Verification Measurements

One of the most common sources of network problems is misconfiguration. Extreme cases of misconfigurations that cause actual outages are relatively obvious (though still time-consuming to fix). However, misconfigurations can also result in more subtle problems. For instance, a misconfigured link weight can mean that traffic takes unexpected paths, leading to delays or even congestion.

One of the key steps to network planning is to ensure that the network we planned is the one we observe. Various approaches have been used for router configuration validation: these are considered in more detail in Chapter 9. In addition, we recommend that direct measurements of the network routing, link loads, and performance can be made at all times. Routing can be measured through mechanisms such as those discussed in Section 5.2 and in more detail in Chapter 11. When performed from edge node to edge node, we can use such measurements to confirm that traffic is taking the routes we intended it to take in our design.

By themselves, routing measurements only confirm the direction of traffic flows. Our second requirement is to measure link traffic to ensure that it remains within the bounds we set in our network design. Unexpected traffic loads can often be dealt with by TE, but only once we realize that there is a problem.

Finally, we must always measure performance across our network. In principle, the above measurements are sufficient, i.e., we might anticipate that a link is congested only if traffic exceeds the capacity. However, in reality, the typical SNMP measurements used to measure traffic on links are 5-min averages. Congestion can occur on smaller time scales, leading to brief, but nonnegligible packet losses that may not be observable from traffic measurements alone. We aim to reduce these through choice of SOP, but note that this choice is empirical in itself, and an accurate choice relies on feedback from performance measurements. Moreover, other components of a network have been known to cause performance problems even on a lightly loaded network. For instance, such measurements allowed us to discover and understand delays in routing convergence times [32, 61], and that during these periods bursts of packet loss would occur, from which improvements to Interior Gateway Protocols have been made [27]. The importance of the problem would never have been understood without performance measurements. Such measurements are discussed in more detail in Chapter 10.

5.6.2   Reliability Analysis

IP networks and the underlying SONET/WDM strata on which they run are often managed by different divisions of a company, or by completely different companies. In our planning stages, we would typically hope for joint design between these components, but the reality is that the underlying physical/optical networks are often multiuse, with IP as one of several customers (either externally or internally) that use the same infrastructure. It is often hard to prescribe exactly which circuits will carry a logical IP link. Therefore, it is hard in some cases to determine, prior to implementation, exactly what SRG exist.

We may insist, in some cases, that links are carried over separate fibers, or even purchase leased lines from separate companies, but even in these cases great care should be taken. For instance, it was only during the Baltimore train tunnel fire (2001) [4] it was discovered that several providers ran fiber through the same tunnel.

Our earlier network plan can only accommodate planned network failure scenarios. In robust planning, we must somehow accommodate the SRGs that have arisen in the implementation of our planned network. The first step, obviously, is to determine the SRGs. The required data mapping IP links to physical infrastructure is often stored in multiple databases, but with care it is possible to combine the two to obtain a list of SRGs. Once we have a complete list of failure scenarios we could go through the planning cycle again, but as noted, the time horizon for this process would leave our network vulnerable for some time.

The first step therefore is to perform a network reliability analysis. This is a simple process of simulating each failure scenario, and assessing whether the network has sufficient capacity, i.e., whether $A_i \mathbf{x} \leq \zeta \mathbf{c}$. If this condition is already satisfied, then no action need to be taken. However, where the condition is violated, we must take one of two actions. The most obvious approach to deal with a specific vulnerability is to expedite an increase in capacity. It is often possible to reduce the planning horizon for network changes at an increased cost. Where small changes are needed, this may be viable, but it is clearly not satisfactory to try to build the whole network in this way.

The second alternative is to once again use traffic engineering. MPLS provides mechanisms to create failover paths, however, it does not tell you where to route these to ensure that congestion does not occur. Some additional optimization and control is needed. However, we cannot do this after the failure, or recovery will take an unacceptable amount of time. Likewise, it is impractical in today's networks to change link weights in response failures. However, previous studies have shown that shortest-path link weight optimization can be used to provide a set of weights that will alleviate congestive effects under failures [44], and such techniques have (anecdotally) been used in large networks with success.

5.6.3 Robust Optimization

The fundamental issue we deal with is "Given that I have errors in my data, how should I perform optimization?" Not all the news are bad. For instance, once we acknowledge that our data is not perfect, we realize that finding the mathematically optimal solution for our problem is not needed. Instead, heuristic solutions that find a near optimal solution will be just as effective. This chapter is not principally concerned with optimization, and so we will not spend a great deal of time on specific algorithms, but note that once we decide that heuristic solutions will be sufficient, several meta-heuristics such as genetic algorithms and simulated annealing become attractive. They are generally easy to program, and very flexible, and so allow us to use more complex constraints and optimization objective functions than we might otherwise have chosen. For instance, it becomes easy to incorporate the true link costs, and technological constraints on available capacities.

The other key aspect to optimization in network planning directly concerns robustness. We know there are errors in our measurements and predictions. We can save much time and effort in planning if we accommodate some notion of these errors in our optimization. A number of techniques for such optimization have been proposed: oblivious routing [8], and Valiant network design [69, 70]. These papers present methods to design a network and/or its routing so that it will work well for any arbitrary traffic matrix. However, this is perhaps going too far. In most cases we do have some information about possible traffic whose use is bound to improve our network design.

A simple approach is to generate a series of possible traffic matrices by adding random noise to our predicted matrix, i.e., by taking $\mathbf{x}_i = \mathbf{x} + \mathbf{e}_i$, for $i = 1, 2, \ldots, M$. Where sufficient historical data exist, the noise terms $\mathbf{e}_i$ should be generated in such a way as to model the prediction errors. We can then optimize against the set of TMs, i.e.,

$$\text{minimize} \sum_{e \in E} \alpha_e I(c_e > 0) + \gamma c_e$$
$$\text{such that } A\mathbf{x}_i \leq \lambda\mathbf{c}, \ \forall i = 1, 2, \ldots, M. \tag{5.29}$$

Once again this can increase the number of constraints dramatically, particularly in combination with reliability constraints, unless we realize that again many of these constraints will be redundant, and can be pruned by preprocessing.

The above approach is somewhat naive. The size of the set of TMs to use is not obvious. Also we lack guidance about the choice we should make for λ. In principle, we already accommodate variations explicitly in the above optimization and so we might expect $\lambda = 1$. However, as before we need $\lambda < 1$ to accommodate inter-measurement time interval variations in traffic, though the choice should be different than in past problems.

Moreover, there may be better robust optimization strategies that can be applied in the future. For instance, robust optimization has been applied to the traffic engineering problem in [65], where the authors introduce the idea of COPE (Common-case Optimization with a Penalty Envelope) where the goal is to find the optimal routing for a predicted TM, and to ensure that the routing will not be "too bad" if there are errors in the prediction.

5.6.4 Sensitivity Analysis

Even where we believe that our optimization approach is robust, we must test this hypothesis. We can do so by performing a sensitivity analysis. The standard approach in such an analysis is to vary the inputs and examine the impact on the outputs. We can vary each possible input to detect robustness to errors in this input, though the most obvious to test is sensitivity to variations in the underlying traffic matrix. We can test such sensitivity by considering the link loads under a set of TMs generated, as before, by adding prediction errors, i.e., $\mathbf{x}_i = \mathbf{x} + \mathbf{e}_i$, for $i = 1, 2, \ldots, M$, and then simply calculating the link loads $\mathbf{y}_i = A\mathbf{x}_i$. There is an obvious relationship to robust optimization, in that we should not be testing against the same set of matrices against which we optimized. Moreover, in sensitivity analysis it is common to vary the size of the errors. However, simple linear algebra allows us to reduce the problem to a fixed load component $\mathbf{y} = A\mathbf{x}$ and a variable component $\mathbf{w}_i = A\mathbf{e}_i$, which scales linearly with the size of the errors, and which can be used to see the impact of errors in the TM directly.

5.7 Summary

"Reliability, reliability, reliability" is the mantra of good network operators. Attaining reliability costs money, but few companies can afford to waste millions of dollars on an inefficient network. This chapter is aimed at demonstrating how we can use robust network planning to attain efficient but reliable networks, despite the imprecision of measurements, uncertainties of predictions, and general vagaries of the Internet.

Reliability should mean more than connectivity. Network performance measured in packet delay or loss rates is becoming an important metric for customers deciding between operators. Network design for reliability has to account for possible congestion caused by link failures. In this chapter we consider methods for designing networks where performance is treated as part of reliability.

The methodology proposed here is built around a cyclic approach to network design exemplified in Fig. 5.1. The process of **measure → analyze/predict → control → validate** should not end, but rather, validation measurements are fed back into the process so that we can start again. In this way, we attain some measure of robustness to the potential errors in the process. However, the planning horizon for network design is still quite long (typically several months) and so a combination of techniques such as traffic engineering are used at different time scales to ensure robustness to failures in predicted behavior. It is the combination of this range of techniques that provides a truly robust network design methodology.

Acknowledgment This work was informed by the period M. Roughan was employed at AT&T research, and the author owes his thanks to researchers there for many valuable discussions on these topics. M. Roughan would also like to thank the Australian Research Council from whom he receives support, in particular through grant DP0665427.

References

1. Python routing toolkit ('pyrt'). Retrieved from http://ipmon.sprintlabs.com/pyrt/.
2. Ripe NCC: routing information service. Retrieved from http://www.ripe.net/projects/ris/.
3. University of Oregon Route Views Archive Project. Retrieved from www.routeviews.org.
4. CSX train derailment. Nanog mailing list. Retrieved July 18, 2001 from http://www.merit.edu/mail.archives/nanog/2001-07/msg00351.html.
5. Abilene/Internet2. Retrieved from http://www.internet2.edu/observatory/archive/data-collections.html#netflow.
6. Ahuja, R. K., Magnanti, T. L., & Orlin, J. B. (1993). *Network flows: Theory, algorithms, and applications*. Upper Saddle River, NJ: Prentice Hall.

7. Alderson, D., Chang, H., Roughan, M., Uhlig, S., & Willinger, W. (2006). The many facets of Internet topology and traffic. *Networks and Heterogeneous Media*, *1*(4), 569–600.

8. Applegate, D., & Cohen, E. (2003) Making intra-domain routing robust to changing and uncertain traffic demands: Understanding fundamental tradeoffs. In *ACM SIGCOMM* (pp. 313–324). Germany: Karlsruhe. 2003.

9. Box, G. E. P., & Draper, N. R. (2007). *Response surfaces, mixtures and ridge analysis* (2nd ed.). New York: Wiley.

10. Brockwell, P., & Davis, R. (1987). *Time series: Theory and methods*. New York: Springer.

11. Brutag, J. D. (2000). Aberrant behavior detection and control in time series for network monitoring. In *Proceedings of the 14th Systems Administration Conference (LISA 2000)*, New Orleans, LA, USA, USENIX.

12. Buriol, L. S., Resende, M. G. C., Ribeiro, C. C., & Thorup, M. (2002) A memetic algorithm for OSPF routing. In *Proceedings of the 6th INFORMS Telecom* (pp. 187–188).

13. Cahn, R. S. (1998). *Wide area network design*. Los Altos, CA: Morgan Kaufman.

14. Callon, R. (1990). Use of OSI IS-IS for routing in TCP/IP and dual environments. Network Working Group, Request for Comments: 1195.

15. Chekuri, C., & Khanna, S. (2004) On multidimensional packing problems. *SIAM Journal of Computing*, *33*(4), 837–851.

16. Duffield, N., & Lund, C. (2003). Predicting resource usage and estimation accuracy in an IP flow measurement collection infrastructure. In *ACM SIGCOMM Internet Measurement Conference*, Miami Beach, Florida, October 2003.

17. Duffield, N., Lund, C., & Thorup, M. (2004). Flow sampling under hard resource constraints. *SIGMETRICS Performance Evaluation Review*, *32*(1), 85–96.

18. Coffman, J. E. G., Garey, M. R., & Johnson, D. S. (1997). Approximation algorithms for bin packing: A survey. In D. Hochbaum (Ed.), *Approximation algorithms for NP-hard problems*. Boston: PWS Publishing.

19. Elwalid, A., Jin, C., Low, S. H., & Widjaja, I. (2001). MATE: MPLS adaptive traffic engineering. In *INFOCOM* (pp. 1300–1309).

20. Ericsson, M., Resende, M., & Pardalos P. (2002). A genetic algorithm for the weight setting problem in OSPF routing. *Journal of Combinatorial Optimization*, *6*(3), 299–333.

21. Erramilli, V., Crovella, M., & Taft, N. (2006). An independent-connection model for traffic matrices. In *ACM SIGCOMM Internet Measurement Conference (IMC06)*, New York, NY, USA, ACM (pp. 251–256).

22. Feldmann, A., Greenberg, A., Lund, C., Reingold, N., & Rexford, J. (2000). Netscope: Traffic engineering for IP networks. *IEEE Network Magazine*, *14*(2), 11–19.

23. Feldmann, A., Greenberg, A., Lund, C., Reingold, N., Rexford, J., & True, F. (2001). Deriving traffic demands for operational IP networks: Methodology and experience. *IEEE/ACM Transactions on Networking*, *9*, 265–279.

24. Feldmann, A., & Rexford, J. (2001). IP network configuration for intradomain traffic engineering. *IEEE Network Magazine*, *15*(5), 46–57.

25. Fortz, B., & Thorup, M. (2000). Internet traffic engineering by optimizing OSPF weights. In *Proceedings of the 19th IEEE Conference on Computer Communications (INFOCOM)* (pp. 519–528).

26. Fortz, B., & Thorup, M. (2002). Optimizing OSPF/IS-IS weights in a changing world. *IEEE Journal on Selected Areas in Communications*, *20*(4), 756–767.

27. Francois, P., Filsfils, C., Evans, J., & Bonaventure, O. (2005). Achieving sub-second IGP convergence in large IP networks. *SIGCOMM Computer Communication Review*, *35*(3), 35–44.

28. Garey, M., Graham, R., Johnson, D., & Yao, A. (1976). Resource constrained scheduling as generalized bin packing. *Journal of Combinatorial Theory A*, *21*, 257–298.

29. Hansen, P. C. (1997). *Rank-deficient and discrete ill-posed problems: Numerical aspects of linear inversion*. Philadelphia, PA: SIAM.

30. Iannaccone, G., Chuah, C.-N., Mortier, R., Bhattacharyya, S., & Diot, C. (2002). Analysis of link failures over an IP backbone. In *ACM SIGCOMM Internet Measurement Workshop*, Marseilles, France, November 2002.

31. Kowalski, J., & Warfield, B. (1995). Modeling traffic demand between nodes in a telecommunications network. In *ATNAC'95*.
32. Labovitz, C., Ahuja, A., Bose, A., & Jahanian, F. (2000). Delayed Internet routing convergence. In *Proceedings of ACM SIGCOMM*.
33. Lakhina, A., Crovella, M., & Diot, C. (2004). Characterization of network-wide anomalies in traffic flows. In *ACM SIGCOMM Internet Measurement Conference*, Taormina, Sicily, Italy.
34. Lakhina, A., Crovella, M., & Diot, C. (2004). Diagnosing network-wide traffic anomalies. In *ACM SIGCOMM*.
35. Lakhina, A., Papagiannaki, K., Crovella, M., Diot, C., Kolaczyk, E. D., & Taft, N. (2004). Structural analysis of network traffic flows. In *ACM SIGMETRICS/Performance*.
36. Lakshman, U., & Lobo, L. (2006). *MPLS traffic engineering*. Cisco Press. Available from http://www.ciscopress.com/articles/article.asp?p=426640, 2006.
37. Lin, F., & Wang, J. (1993). Minimax open shortest path first routing algorithms in networks supporting the SMDS services. In *Proceedings of the IEEE International Conference on Communications (ICC)*, 2, 666–670.
38. Maltz, D., Xie, G., Zhan, J., Zhang, H., Hjalmtysson, G., & Greenberg, A. (2004). Routing design in operational networks: A look from the inside. In *ACM SIGCOMM*, Portland, OR, USA.
39. Mauro, D. R., & Schmidt, K. J. (2001) *Essential SNMP*. Sabastopol, CA: O'Reilly.
40. Maxemchuk, N. F., Ouveysi, I., & Zukerman, M. (2000). A quantitative measure for comparison between topologies of modern telecommunications networks. In *IEEE Globecom*.
41. Mitra, D., & Ramakrishnan, K. G. (1999). A case study of multiservice, multipriority traffic engineering design for data networks. In *Proceedings of the IEEE GLOBECOM* (pp. 1077–1083).
42. Moy, J. T. (1998). OSPF version 2. Network Working Group, Request for comments: 2328, April 1998.
43. Norros, I. (1994). A storage model with self-similar input. *Queueing Systems, 16*, 387–396.
44. Nucci, A., & Papagiannaki, K. (2009) *Design, measurement and management of large-scale IP networks*. New York: Cambrigde University Press.
45. Odlyzko, A. M. (2003). Internet traffic growth: Sources and implications. In B. B. Dingel, W. Weiershausen, A. K. Dutta, & K.-I. Sato (Eds.), *Optical transmission systems and equipment for WDM networking II* (Vol. 5247, pp. 1–15). Proceedings of SPIE.
46. Oetiker, T. MRTG: The multi-router traffic grapher. Available from http://oss.oetiker.ch/mrtg//.
47. Oetiker, T. RRDtool. Available from http://oss.oetiker.ch/rrdtool/.
48. Paxson, V. (2004). Strategies for sound Internet measurement. In *ACM Sigcomm Internet Measurement Conference (IMC)*, Taormina, Sicily, Italy.
49. Potts, R. B., & Oliver, R. M. (1972). *Flows in transportation networks*. New York: Academic Press.
50. Pyhnen, P. (1963). A tentative model for the volume of trade between countries. *Weltwirtschaftliches Archive, 90*, 93–100.
51. Qiu, L., Yang, Y. R., Zhang, Y., & Shenker, S. (2003). On selfish routing in internet-like environments. In *ACM SIGCOMM* (pp. 151–162).
52. Qui, L., Zhang, Y., Roughan, M., & Willinger, W. (2009). Spatio-Temporal Compressive Sensing and Internet Traffic Matrices", Yin Zhang, Matthew Roughan, Walter Willinger, and Lili Qui, ACM Sigcomm, pp. 267–278, Barcellona, August 2009.
53. Ramakrishnan, K., & Rodrigues, M. (2001). Optimal routing in shortest-path data networks. *Lucent Bell Labs Technical Journal, 6*(1), 117–138.
54. Rosen, E. C., Viswanathan, A., & Callon, R. (2001). Multiprotocol label switching architecture. Network Working Group, Request for Comments: 3031, 2001.
55. Roughan, M. (2005). Simplifying the synthesis of Internet traffic matrices. *ACM SIGCOMM Computer Communications Review, 35*(5), 93–96.
56. Roughan, M., & Gottlieb, J. (2002). Large-scale measurement and modeling of backbone Internet traffic. In *SPIE ITCOM*, Boston, MA.
57. Roughan, M., Greenberg, A., Kalmanek, C., Rumsewicz, M., Yates, J., & Zhang, Y. (2003). Experience in measuring Internet backbone traffic variability: Models, metrics, measurements and meaning. In *Proceedings of the International Teletraffic Congress (ITC-18)* (pp. 221–230).

58. Roughan, M., Sen, S., Spatscheck, O., & Duffield, N. (2004). Class-of-service mapping for QoS: A statistical signature-based approach to IP traffic classification. In *ACM SIGCOMM Internet Measurement Workshop* (pp. 135–148). Taormina, Sicily, Italy.

59. Roughan, M., Thorup, M., & Zhang, Y. (2003). Performance of estimated traffic matrices in traffic engineering. In *ACM SIGMETRICS* (pp. 326–327). San Diego, CA.

60. Roughan, M., Thorup, M., & Zhang, Y. (2003). Traffic engineering with estimated traffic matrices. In *ACM SIGCOMM Internet Measurement Conference (IMC)* (pp. 248–258). Miami Beach, FL.

61. Shaikh, A., & Greenberg, A. (2001). Experience in black-box OSPF measurement. In *Proceedings of the ACM SIGCOMM Internet Measurement Workshop* (pp. 113–125).

62. Shaikh, A., & Greenberg, A. (2004). OSPF monitoring: Architecture, design and deployment experience. In *Proceedings of the USENIX Symposium on Networked System Design and Implementation (NSDI)*.

63. Tinbergen, J. (1962). Shaping the world economy: Suggestions for an international economic policy. The Twentieth Century Fund.

64. Uhlig, S., Quoitin, B., Balon, S., & Lepropre, J. (2006). Providing public intradomain traffic matrices to the research community. *ACM SIGCOMM Computer Communication Review, 36*(1), 83–86.

65. Wang, H., Xie, H., Qiu, L., Yang, Y. R., Zhang, Y., & Greenberg, A. (2006). COPE: Traffic engineering in dynamic networks. In *ACM SIGCOMM* (pp. 99–110).

66. Zhang, Y., Ge, Z., Roughan, M., & Greenberg, A. (2005). Network anomography. In *Proceedings of the Internet Measurement Conference (IMC '05)*, Berkeley, CA.

67. Zhang, Y., Roughan, M., Duffield, N., & Greenberg, A. (2003). Fast accurate computation of large-scale IP traffic matrices from link loads. In *ACM SIGMETRICS* (pp. 206–217). San Diego, CA.

68. Zhang, Y., Roughan, M., Lund, C., & Donoho, D. (2003). An information-theoretic approach to traffic matrix estimation. In *ACM SIGCOMM* (pp. 301–312). Karlsruhe, Germany.

69. Zhang-Shen, R., & McKeown, N. (2004). Designing a predictable Internet backbone. In *HotNets III*, San Diego, CA, November 2004.

70. Zhang-Shen, R., & McKeown, N. (2005). Designing a predictable Internet backbone with Valiant load-balancing. In *Thirteenth International Workshop on Quality of Service (IWQoS)*, Passau, Germany, June 2005.

Part III
Interdomain Reliability and Overlay Networks

Chapter 6
Interdomain Routing and Reliability

Feng Wang and Lixin Gao

6.1 Introduction

Routing as the "control plane" of the Internet plays a crucial role on the performance of data plane in the Internet. That is, routing aims to ensure that there are forwarding paths for delivering packets to their intended destinations. Routing protocols are the languages that individual routers speak in order to cooperatively achieve the goal in a distributed manner. The Internet routing architecture is structured in a hierarchical fashion. At the bottom level, an Autonomous System (AS) consists of a network of routers under a single administrative entity. Routing within an AS is achieved via an Interior Gateway Protocol (IGP) such as OSPF or IS-IS. At the top level, an interdomain routing protocol glues thousands of ASes together and plays a crucial role in the delivery of traffic across the global Internet. In this chapter, we provide an overview of the interdomain routing architecture and its reliability in maintaining global reachability.

Border Gateway Protocol (BGP) is the current de-facto standard for interdomain routing. As a path vector routing protocol, BGP requires each router to advertise only its best route for a destination to its neighbors. Each route includes attributes such as AS path (the sequence of ASes to traverse to reach the destination), and local preference (indicating the preference order in selecting the best route). Rather than simply selecting the route with the shortest AS path, routers can apply complex routing policies (such as setting a higher local preference value for a route through a particular AS) to influence the best route selection, and to decide whether to propagate the selected route to their neighbors. Although BGP is a simple path vector protocol, configuring BGP routing policies is quite complex. Each AS typically

F. Wang
School of Engineering and Computational Sciences, Liberty University
e-mail: fwang@liberty.edu

L. Gao (✉)
Department of Electrical and Computer Engineering, University of Massachusetts, Amherst, Amherst, MA01002, USA
e-mail: lgao@ecs.umass.edu

C.R. Kalmanek et al. (eds.), *Guide to Reliable Internet Services and Applications*,
Computer Communications and Networks, DOI 10.1007/978-1-84882-828-5_6,
© Springer-Verlag London Limited 2010

configures its routing policy according to its own goals, such as load-balancing traffic among its links, without coordinating with other networks. However, arbitrary policy configurations might lead to route divergence or persistent oscillation of the routing protocol. That is, although BGP allows flexibility in routing policy configuration, BGP itself does not guarantee routing convergence. Arbitrary policy configurations, such as unintentional mistakes or intentional malicious configuration, can lead to persistent route oscillation [9, 11].

Besides being a policy-based routing protocol, BGP has many features that aim to scale a large network such as the global Internet. One feature is that BGP sends incremental updates upon routing changes rather than sending complete routing information. BGP speaking routers send new routes only when there are changes. Related with the incremental update feature, BGP uses a timer, referred to as the *Minimum Route Advertisement Interval* (MRAI) timer, to determine the minimum amount of time that must elapse between routing updates in order to limit the number of updates for each prefix. Therefore, BGP does not react to changes in topology or routing policy configuration immediately. Rather, it controls the frequency in which route changes can be made in order to avoid overloading router CPU cycles or reduce route flap. While MRAI timers can be effective in reducing routing update frequency, the slow reaction to changes can delay route convergence. More importantly, during the delayed route convergence process, routes among neighboring routers might be inconsistent. This can lead to transient routing loops or transient routing outages (referred to as *transient routing failures*) caused by the delay in discovering alternate routes.

The goal of this chapter is to provide an overview of BGP, to give practical guidelines for configuring BGP routing policy and offer a framework for understanding how undesirable routing states such as persistent routing oscillation and transient routing failures or loops can arise. We also present a methodology for measuring the extent to which these undesirable routing states can affect the quality of end-to-end packet delivery. We will further describe proposed solutions for reliable interdomain routing. Toward this end, we outline this chapter as follows.

We begin with an introduction to BGP in Section 6.2. We first describe interdomain routing architecture, and then illustrate the details of how BGP enables ASes to exchange global reachability information and various BGP route attributes. We further present routing policy configurations that enable each individual AS to meet its goal of traffic engineering or commercial agreement.

In Section 6.3, we introduce multihoming technology. Multihoming allows an AS to have multiple connections to upstream providers in order to survive a single point of failure. We present various multihoming approaches, such as multihoming to multip le upstream providers or single upstream provider to show the redundancy and load-balancing benefits associated with being multihomed.

In Section 6.4, we highlight the limitations of BGP. For example, the protocol design does not guarantee that routing will converge to a stable route. We further show how incentive compatible routing policies can prevent routing oscillation, and how transient routing failures or loops can occur even under incentive compatible routing configuration or redundant underlying infrastructure.

Having understood the potential transient routing failures and routing loops, we describe a measurement methodology, and measurement results that quantify the impact of transient routing failures and routing loops on end-to-end path performance in Section 6.5. This illustrates the severity that routing outages can affect the quality of packet delivery.

In Section 6.6, we present a detailed overview of the existing solutions to achieve reliable interdomain routing. We show that both protocol extensions and routing policies can enhance the reliability of interdomain routing. Finally, we conclude the chapter by pointing out possible future research directions in Section 6.7.

6.2   Interdomain Routing

This section introduces the interdomain routing architecture, the interdomain routing protocol, BGP, and BGP routing policy configuration.

6.2.1   Interdomain Routing Architecture

The Internet consists of a large collection of hosts interconnected by networks of links and routers. The Internet is divided into thousands of ASes. Examples range from college campuses and corporate networks to global Internet Service Providers (ISPs). An AS has its own routers and routing policies, and connects to other ASes to exchange traffic with remote hosts. A router typically has very detailed knowledge of the topology within its AS, and limited reachability information about other ASes. Figure 6.1 shows an example of the Internet topology, where there are large transit ISPs such as MCI or AT&T, and stub ASes, such as the University of Massachusetts' network, which does not provide transit service to other ASes.

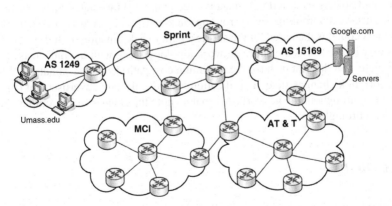

Fig. 6.1 An example topology of interconnection among Internet service providers and stub networks

Note that the topologies of the transit ISPs and stub ASes shown in this example are much simpler than those in reality. Typically, a large transit ISP consists of hundreds or thousands of routers.

ASes interconnect at public Internet exchange points (IXPs) such as MAE-EAST or MAE-WEST, or dedicated point-to-point links. Public exchange points typically consist of a shared medium such as a Gigabit Ethernet, or an ATM switch, that interconnects routers from several different ASes. Physical connectivity at the IXP does not necessarily imply that every pair of ASes exchanges traffic with each other. AS pairs negotiate contractual agreements that control the exchange of traffic. These relationships include provider-to-customer, peer-to-peer, and backup, and are discussed in more detail in Section 6.4.1.

Each AS has responsibility for carrying traffic to and from a set of customer IP addresses. The scalability of the Internet routing infrastructure depends on the aggregation of IP addresses in contiguous blocks, called *prefixes*, each consisting of a 32-bit IP address and a mask length (e.g., 1.2.3.0/24). An IP address is generally shown as four octets of numbers from 0 to 255 represented in decimal form. The mask length is used to indicate the number of significant bits in the IP address. That is, a prefix aggregates all IP addresses that match the IP address in the significant bits. For example, prefix 1.2.3.0/24 represents all addresses between 1.2.3.0 and 1.2.3.255.

An AS employs an *intradomain* routing protocol (IGP) such as OSPF or IS-IS to determine how to reach routers and networks within itself, and employs an *interdomain* routing protocol, i.e., Border Gateway Protocol (BGP) in the current Internet, to advertise the reachability of networks (represented as prefixes) to neighboring ASes.

6.2.2 IGP

Each AS uses an intradomain routing protocol or IGP for routing within the AS. There are two classes of IGP: (1) distance vector and (2) link state routing protocol. In distance-vector routing, every routing message propagated by a router to its neighbors contains the length of the shortest path to a destination. In link-state routing, every router learns the entire network topology along with the link costs. Then it computes the shortest path (or the minimum cost path) to each destination. When a network link changes state, a notification, called link state advertisement (LSA), is flooded throughout the network. All routers note the change and recompute their routes accordingly.

6.2.3 BGP

The interdomain routing protocol, BGP, is the glue that pieces together the various diverse networks or ASes that comprise the global Internet today. It is used among

ASes to exchange network reachability information. Each AS has one or more border routers that connect to routers in neighboring ASes, and possibly a number of internal BGP speaking routers.

BGP is a path-vector routing protocol that facilitates routers to exchange the path used for reaching a destination. By including the path in the route update information, one can avoid loops by eliminating any path that traverses the same node twice. Using a path vector protocol, routers running BGP distribute reachability information about destinations (network prefixes) by sending route updates – containing route announcements or withdrawals – to their neighbors in an incremental manner. BGP constructs paths by successively propagating advertisements between pairs of routers that are configured as *BGP peers*. Each advertisement concerns a particular prefix and includes the list of ASes along the path (the *AS path*) to the network containing the prefix. By representing the path to be traversed by the ASes, BGP hides the details of the topology and routing information inside each AS. Before accepting an advertisement, the receiving router checks for the presence of its own AS number in the AS path to discard routes with loops. Upon receiving an advertisement, a BGP speaking router must decide whether or not to use this path and, if the path is chosen, whether or not to propagate the advertisement to neighboring ASes (after adding its own AS number of the AS path). BGP requires that a router simply advertise its best route for each destination to its neighbors. A BGP speaking router withdraws an advertisement when the prefix is no longer reachable with this route, which may lead to a sequence of withdrawals by upstream ASes that are using this path.

When there is an event affecting a router's best route to a destination, that router will compute a new best route and advertise the routing change to its neighbors. If the router no longer has any route to the destination, it will send a withdrawal message to neighbors for that destination. When an event causes a set of routers to lose their current routing information, the routing change will be propagated to other routers. To limit the number of updates that a router has to process within a short time period, a rate-limiting timer, called the Minimum Route Advertisement Interval (MRAI) timer, determines the minimum amount of time that must elapse between routing updates to a neighbor [26]. This has the potential to reduce the number of routing updates, as a single routing change might trigger multiple transient routes during the *path exploration* or route convergence process before the final stable route is determined. If new routes are selected multiple times while waiting for the expiration of the MRAI timer, the latest selected route shall be advertised at the end of MRAI. To avoid long time loss of connectivity, RFC 4271 [26] specifies that the MRAI timer is applied to only BGP announcements, not to explicit withdrawals. However, some router implementations might apply the MRAI timer to both announcements and withdrawals.

BGP sessions can be established between router pairs in the same AS (we refer the BGP session as iBGP session) or different ASes (we refer the BGP session as eBGP session). Figure 6.2 illustrates examples of iBGP and eBGP sessions. Each BGP speaking router originates updates for one or more prefixes, and can send the updates to the immediate neighbors via an iBGP or eBGP session. iBGP sessions

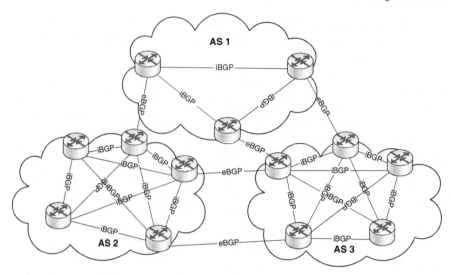

Fig. 6.2 Internal BGP (iBGP) versus external BGP (eBGP)

are established between routers in the same AS in order for the routers to exchange routes learned from other ASes. In the simplest case, each router has an iBGP session with every other router (i.e., *fully meshed* iBGP configuration). In the fully-meshed iBGP configuration, a route received from an iBGP router cannot be sent to another iBGP speaking router, since a route via an iBGP peer should be directly received from the iBGP peer.

In practice, an AS with hundreds or thousands of routers may need to improve scalability using route reflectors to avoid a fully-meshed iBGP configure. These optimizations are intended to reduce iBGP traffic without affecting the routing decision. Each *route reflector* and its clients (i.e., iBGP neighbors that are not route reflectors themselves) form a cluster. Figure 6.3 shows an example of route reflector cluster, where cluster 1 contains route reflector RR1 and its three clients. Typically, route reflectors and their clients are located in the same facility, e.g., in the same *Point of Presence (PoP)*. Route reflectors themselves are fully meshed. For example, in Fig. 6.3, the three route reflectors RR1, RR2 and, RR3 are fully meshed. A route reflector selects the best route among the routes learned via clients in the cluster, and sends the best route to all other clients in the cluster except the one from which the best route is learned, as well as to all other route reflectors. Similarly, it also reflects routes learned from other route reflectors to all of its own clients.

6.2.4 Routing Policy and Route Selection Process

The simplest routing policy is the shortest AS path routing, where each AS selects a route with the shortest AS path. BGP, however, allows much more flexible routing

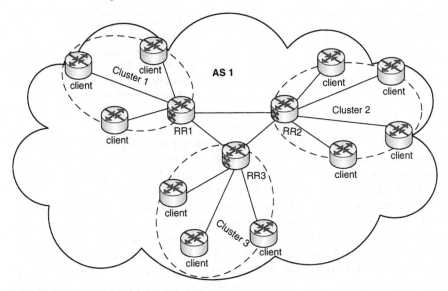

Fig. 6.3   An example of route reflector configuration for scaling iBGP

Fig. 6.4   Import policies, route selection, and export policies

policies than the shortest AS path routing. An AS can favor a path with a longer AS path length by assigning a higher *local preference* value. BGP also allows an AS to send a hint to a neighbor on the preference that should be given to a route by using the *community* attribute. BGP also enables an AS to control how traffic enters its network by assigning a different *multiple exit discriminator* (MED) value to the advertisements it sends on each link to a neighboring AS. Otherwise, the neighboring AS would select the link based on the link cost within its own intradomain routing protocol. An AS can also discourage traffic from entering its network by performing *AS prepending*, which inflates the length of the AS path by listing an AS number multiple times.

Processing an incoming BGP update involves three steps as shown in Fig. 6.4:

1. *Import policies* that decide which routes to consider
2. *Path selection* that decides which route to use
3. *Export policies* to decide whether (and what) to advertise a neighboring AS

An AS can apply both implicit and explicit import policies. Every eBGP peering session has an implicit import policy that discards a routing update when the receiving BGP speaker's AS already appears in the AS path; this is essential to avoid

Table 6.1 Steps in the BGP
path selection process

1. Highest local preference
2. Shortest AS path
3. Lowest origin type
4. Smallest MED
5. Smallest IGP path cost to egress router
6. Smallest next-hop router id

introducing a cycle in the AS path. The explicit import policy includes denying or permitting an update, and assigning a local-preference value. For example, an explicit import policy could assign local preference to be 100 if a particular AS appears in the AS path or deny any update that includes AS 2 in the path.

After applying the import policies for a route update from an eBGP session, each BGP speaking router then follows a route selection process that picks the best route for each prefix, which is shown in Table 6.1. The BGP speaking router picks the route with the highest local preference, breaking ties by selecting the route with the shortest AS path. Note that local preference overrides the AS-path length. Among the remaining routes, the BGP speaking router picks the one with the smallest MED, breaking ties by selecting the route with the smallest cost to the BGP speaking router that passes the route via an iBGP session. Note that, since the tie-breaking process draws on intradomain cost information, two BGP speaking routers in the same AS may select different best routes for the same prefix. If a tie still exists, the BGP speaking router picks the route with the smallest next hop router ID.

Each BGP speaking router sends only its best route (one best route for each prefix) via BGP sessions, including eBGP and iBGP sessions. The BGP speaking router applies implicit and explicit export policies on each eBGP session to a neighboring BGP speaker. Each BGP speaking router applies an implicit policy that sets MED to default values, assigns next hop to interface that connects the BGP session, and prepends the AS number of the BGP speaking router to the AS path. Explicit export policies include permitting or denying the route, assigning MED, assigning community set, and prepending the AS number one or more times to the AS path. For example, an AS could prepend its AS number several times to the AS path for a prefix.

Although the BGP route selection process aims to select routes based mostly on BGP attributes, it is not totally independent from IGP. In fact, IGP cost can influence route selection when the best path is based on the comparison of the IGP cost to the egress routers. We refer to this tie-break BGP route selection as *hot-potato routing*, since with all other BGP attributes being equal, each AS selects the route with the shortest path to exit its network. For example, in Fig. 6.5, AS 3 learns BGP routes to destination, originated by AS 0 at egress routers C1 and C2 from AS 1 and AS 2, respectively. The value on each link within AS 3 represents the corresponding IGP cost. Suppose that the two learned routes to the destination have identical local preferences. We see that the AS path lengths of the two routes are equal. Router C3 learned two routes from C1 and C2, respectively, and selects the one learned from C1 as the best route because the IGP cost of path (C3 C1) is smaller

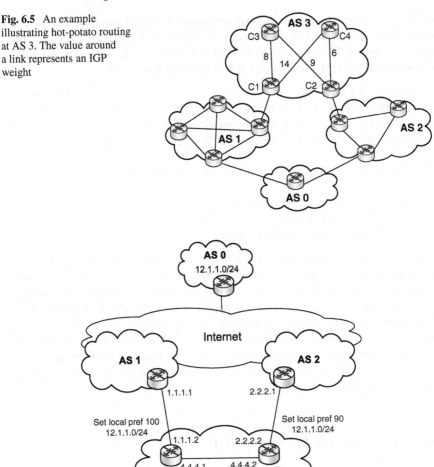

Fig. 6.5 An example illustrating hot-potato routing at AS 3. The value around a link represents an IGP weight

Fig. 6.6 Local preference configuration

than that of path (C3 C2). Similarly, router C4 will select the route learned from C2 as the best route because the path has smaller IGP cost than path (C4 C2). However, hot-potato routing means that changing IGP weight can cause BGP speaking routers to select a different best rout and therefore, shift egress routers. For instance, by changing the IGP link cost between router C1 and C3 from 8 to 10, router C3 will change its egress router from C1 to C2.

BGP routing policy configuration is typically indicated by a router configuration file. A BGP routing policy can be assigned based on the destination prefix or the next hop AS. For example, in Fig. 6.6, AS 0 advertises a prefix "10.1.1.0/24" to the Internet. AS 3 connects to AS 1 and AS 2, and will get routing updates about the destination "10.1.1.0/24" from the two ASes. AS 3 decides what path its outbound traffic to the destination is going to take. Suppose that AS 3 prefers to use the connection via AS 1 to reach the destination. As shown in the following configuration based on Cisco IOS commands, Router RTA at AS 3 sets an explicit import policy that assigns a local preference value 100 to the route from AS 1:

```
router bgp 3
neighbor 1.1.1.1 remote-as 1
neighbor 1.1.1.1 route-map AS1-IN in
neighbor 4.4.4.2 remote-as 3

access-list 1 permit 0.0.0.0 255.255.255.255

route-map AS1-IN permit
  match ip address 1
  set local-preference 100
```

We describe the commands in the above configuration as follows. The first command starts a BGP process with an AS number of 3 at router RTA. The second command sets up an eBGP session with router at AS 1. The route-map command associated with the neighbor statement applies route map AS1-IN to inbound updates from AS 1. Just like the first neighbor command, the fourth command sets up an iBGP session with router RTB. The access-list command creates an access list named 1 to permit all advertisements. The route-map command creates a route map named AS1-IN that uses the access list 1 to identify routes to be assigned local preference of 100.

6.2.5 Convergence Process of BGP

In this section, we illustrate how BGP routing processes converge to stable routes. Figure 6.7 shows an example of a routing policy configuration of a simple topology. In this chapter, we simplify the representation of the network using graph theoretical notations of nodes and edges, where a node represents either an AS or a BGP speaking router, and an edge represents the link between two nodes. In this example, we use a node to represent an AS. Furthermore, throughout this chapter, we focus on one destination prefix, d, which is always originated from AS 0. The figure indicates the export policy by showing all AS paths that an AS can receive from the adjacent

Fig. 6.7 An example of policy configuration that converges. The paths around a node represents its permissible AS paths and the paths are ordered in the descending order of preference

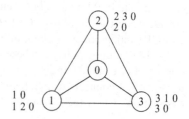

router on the associated interface (referred to as *permissible AS paths*). The figure also indicates the import policy by ordering the paths in the descending order of local preference. The BGP routing process converges as follows.

1. Destination prefix d is announced to ASes 1, 2, 3 via direct links.
2. ASes 1, 2, and 3 all choose its direct path as their best route since those are the only route they received, and announce these direct paths to neighbors.
3. AS 1 now has two paths, (1 0) and (1 2 0), since these are only permissible paths. AS 2 now has two paths, (2 0) and (2 3 0). AS3 now has two paths, (3 0) and (3 1 0). According to the local preference of each AS, AS 1 ends up choosing (1 0) as its best route, AS 3 chooses (3 1 0) as its best route, and AS 2 chooses (2 3 0) as its best route.
4. AS 3 announces its best path (3 1 0), and therefore, implicitly withdraws its route announcement of (3 0) from AS 2. Now, with (2 0) as its only path, AS 2 chooses (2 0) as its best path.
5. AS 2 announces its best path to both AS 1 and AS 3. However, such an announcement does not change the route that AS 1 or AS 3 chooses.

Therefore, all ASes choose a stable route where no routers need to send new update messages, and hence the BGP process converges. Note that during the convergence process, each AS selects and/or announces its best route in an asynchronous manner that is determined by the expiration of MRAI timers. We simplify the process by assuming that route announcements are performed in "a lock step". Nevertheless, it can be proved that in this example, no matter what the exact steps of the convergence process are, the stable route reached by each AS is the same.

6.3 Multihoming Technology

In this section, we provide an overview of the current multihoming technology, which is widely used to provide redundant connection. Multihoming refers to the technology where an AS connects to the Internet through multiple connections via one or more upstream providers. It is intended to enhance the reliability of the Internet connectivity. When one of the connections fails or is in maintenance, the AS can still connect to the Internet via other connections. Multihoming configuration can be achieved using BGP configuration, static routes, Network Address Translation (NAT), or a combination of the above. In this section, we focus on describing multihoming with BGP configuration.

The redundancy provided by multihoming can bring additional complexity to the network configuration. First of all, it is imperative to designate primary and backup connections in such a manner so that when the primary connection fails, it can automatically fall back to the backup connection. Second, it is desirable to distribute traffic across multiple connections. Traffic can be classified into inbound and outbound traffic. *Outbound traffic* is the traffic originating within the multihomed AS or its customers destined to other ASes; *inbound traffic* is the traffic destined to the AS or its customers coming from other ASes.

A multihomed AS can be multihomed to a single provider, or to multiple providers. We will describe how multihoming to a single provider and multiple providers can be configured in the next two Sections 6.3.1 and 6.3.2.

6.3.1 Multihoming to a Single Provider

The simplest way for an AS to connect to the Internet is by setting up a single connection with a provider. However, the AS has only one connection to send and receive data. This single-homed configuration cannot be resilient to a single point of failure such as link or router failure or maintenance. To address this issue, the AS can set up multiple connections to the provider. Four types of connections can be established between an AS and its provider. We describe each type of the connections as follows:

- *Multiple Connections Between a Single Customer Router and Single Provider Access Router (SSA)* An AS has a single border router connected to its provider's access router with multiple links. As illustrated in Fig. 6.8a, AS 0 has a single

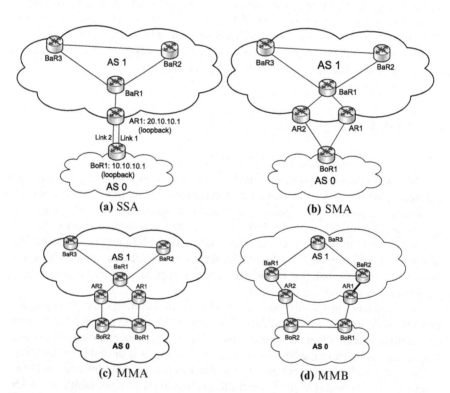

Fig. 6.8 Four types of multihoming connections

border router BoR1, which connects to AS 1's access router, AR1, via two links. If one of the links fails, the other link can be used.

- *Multiple Connections Between a Single Customer Router and Multiple Provider Access Routers (SMA)* An AS has a single router connected to its provider's multiple access routers. For example, in Fig. 6.8b, BoR1 connects to AS 1 at both AR1 and AR2. This configuration can maintain connectivity with a single point of failure of links or the access routers, but cannot do so with a failures of the customer router.

- *Multiple Connections Between Multiple Customer Routers and Multiple Provider Access Routers (MMA)* An AS has multiple routers connected to its provider's multiple access routers. Note that those multiple access routers at the provider are connected to the same backbone router. For example, in Fig. 6.8c, AS 0 has two routers: BoR1 and BoR2. Each border router connects to an access router (AR) in AS 1. This configurations can maintain connectivity with a single point of failure of access routers or border routers. However, the two access routers connect to the same backbone router, BaR1. A failure at BaR1 can cause both the connections to become unavailable.

- *Multiple Connections Between Multiple Customer Routers and Multiple Provider Backbone Routers (MMB)* An AS has multiple connections between its multiple border routers and multiple backbone routers as its provider. This configuration can achieve higher reliability than that of MMA. For example, in Fig. 6.8d, AS 0 has two border routers, BoR1 and BoR2, which are connected to geographically separate backbone routers at AS 1. AS 0's BoR1 connects to AS 1's access router AR 1, and they are at the same geographical location, while the border router BoR2 is connected to another backbone router BaR1. A private physical connection connects the customer AS's border router BoR2 and the backbone router BaR1. This method can maintain connectivity even under a failure of the backbone router.

Next, we describe how an AS can control traffic over the primary and backup link. First, we discuss the control of outbound traffic. A multihomed AS can assign different local preference values to the routes learned from its provider to control its outgoing traffic. For example, in Fig. 6.8b, BoR1 will receive two identical routes for each destination prefix. AS 0 can assign higher local preference values to prefer the routes received through one particular connection over other routes for the same destination received through the other connection. Multihomed configurations of SSA, MMA or MMB can apply the same method to control outbound traffic over the primary link. In addition, an AS multihomed to a single provider with SSA, can use another method – setting the next hop to a virtual address to control outbound traffic. For example, in Fig. 6.8a, AR1 can be assigned a virtual address – a loopback interface. BoR1 will set up a connection with the loopback address. As a result, all routes that BoR1 receives from AR1 will have the same next hop 20.10.10.1. Since next hop 20.10.10.1 can be reached via two connections, outbound traffic can be distributed over the two links.

Second, we discuss how an AS multihomed to a single provider can control its inbound traffic. In this case, the multihomed AS can tweak the BGP attribute values, such as AS path length or MED, to influence route selection at the providers' router. For example, an AS can prepend its AS number on the AS path of the route update announced via the backup link, or send the route update via the backup link with a higher MED value than that via the primary link. As a result, the primary link is used in normal situations since it has a shorter AS path or lower MED value. When the primary link is down, the backup link will be used.

6.3.2 Multihoming to Multiple Providers

The availability of the Internet connectivity provided by upstream providers is very important for an AS. Multihoming to more than one provider can ensure that the AS maintains the global Internet connectivity even if the connection to one of its providers fails [1]. For example, in Fig. 6.9. AS 0 is multihomed to two upstream providers: AS 1 and AS 2. AS 0 may use one of its providers as its primary provider, and the other as a backup provider. When connectivity through the primary provider fails, AS 0 still has its connectivity to the Internet through the backup provider.

A multihomed AS can be configured to direct its outbound traffic through the primary provider. Only when the connection through the primary provider fails, its outbound traffic can use the connection through the backup provider. To achieve this goal, a multihomed AS can use the same approach described for the AS multihomed to a single provider. That is, an AS may assign a higher local preference for the route through the primary provider than that through the backup. For its outbound

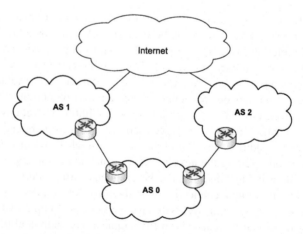

Fig. 6.9 An example of an AS multihomed to two upstream providers

traffic, an AS multihomed to multiple providers can use the same approach as those described for an AS multihomed to a single provider.

A multihomed AS might control which provider its inbound traffic can use. There are several approaches to control the route used for inbound traffic. The simplest approach is to advertise its prefixes only to the primary provider so that inbound traffic can use the primary provider. For example, in Fig. 6.9, AS 0 can advertise its prefix to its primary provider, say, AS 1. However, such selective advertisement cannot provide the redundancy afforded by multihoming. In the above example, if the link between AS 1 and AS 0 fails, AS 0 becomes unreachable until AS 0 notices the failure and advertises its prefixes to the backup provider, AS 2. In this case, the time it takes to fail over to the backup provider depends on how fast the multihomed AS detects the failure and determines to announce its profixes to the backup provider, and how fast the announcement propagates to the global Internet.

Alternatively, an AS can control the route taken by the inbound traffic by splitting its prefix into several specific prefixes, and advertise the more specific prefixes to the primary providers. For example, in Fig. 6.10, AS 0 has a prefix, "12.0.0.0/19". AS 0 splits the prefix into two more specific prefixes: "12.0.0.0/20" and "12.0.16.0/20". AS 0 can announce "12.0.0.0/20" to AS 1, and "12.0.16.0/20" to AS 2. At the same time, AS 0 can advertise its prefix, "12.0.0.0/19" to both providers. As a result, inbound traffic to "12.0.0.0/20" comes from AS 1, while inbound traffic to "12.0.16.0/20" comes from AS 2. This approach can balance the traffic load between the two providers by designating each one as the primary provider for a specific prefix. At the same time, the approach can tolerant failure of links to providers. For example, if the link between AS 0 and AS 1 fails, destinations within prefix "12.0.0.0/20" can still be reached via AS 2 since prefix "12.0.0.0/19" is announced via AS 2. Despite the advantage of load balancing and fault tolerance, this approach has the drawback of potentially increasing the number of prefixes announced to the global Internet.

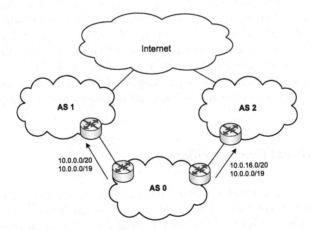

Fig. 6.10   An example of splitting prefixes

Another approach to control the route of inbound traffic is via AS prepend. An AS can prepend its AS number, one or several times when announcing to the backup provider. This can "discourage" other AS to select the route via the backup provider. Note that this approach cannot ensure that all inbound traffic will go through the primary provider. It is possible for an AS to use the longer backup path rather than the shorter primary path if the backup path has a higher local preference. In fact, most providers prefer customers over providers. Consider the example network in Fig. 6.9, AS 2 learns paths to reach prefixes in AS 0 from both the direct and its upstream connections, but AS 2 will prefer the direct connection, although AS 0 intends it to be a backup path.

In summary, multihoming techniques aim to provide redundant connectivity. Nevertheless, the extent that these multihoming techniques can ensure continuous connectivity is hinged on how long it takes for the routing protocol, BGP, to failover to backup routes. In Section 6.4.2, we will discuss how BGP can recover from a failure and how long it takes BGP to discover alternate routes.

6.4 Challenges in Interdomain Routing

Failures and changes in topology or routing policy are fairly common in the Internet due to various causes such as maintenance, router crash, fiber cuts, and misconfiguration [4, 17, 18]. Ideally, when such changes occur, routing protocols should be able to quickly react to those failures to find alternate paths. However, BGP is a policy-based routing protocol, and is not guaranteed to converge to a stable state, in which all routers agree on a stable set of routes. Persistent route oscillation can significantly degrade the end-to-end performance of the Internet. Furthermore, even if BGP converges, it has been known to be slow to react and recover from network changes. During routing convergence, there are three potential routing states from the perspective of any given router: *path exploration* during which an alternate route instead of the final stable route is used, *transient failures* during which there is no route to a destination but a route will be eventually discovered, and *transient forwarding loops* in which routes to a destination form a forwarding loop and the forwarding loop will eventually disappear. Path exploration does not lead to packet drops, while transient failures or transient loops do. In this chapter, we describe how persistent route oscillation, routing failures, and routing loops can occur.

6.4.1 Persistent Route Oscillation

BGP routing protocol provides great flexibility in routing policies that can be set by each AS. However, arbitrary setting of routing policies can lead to persistent route oscillation. For example, Fig. 6.11 shows the "bad gadget" example used in [9]. In this example and all of the following examples, we focus on a single destination

Fig. 6.11 An example of
BGP routing policy that leads
to persistent route oscillation.
The AS paths around a node
represent a set of permissible
paths, which are ordered in
the descending order of local
preference

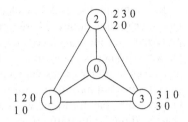

prefix that originates from AS 0, without losing generality. In this example, ASes 1, 2, and 3 receive only the direct path to AS 0 and indirect path via their clockwise neighbor, and prefer to route via their clockwise neighbor over the direct path to AS 0. For example, AS 2 receives only paths (2 1 0) and (2 0) and prefers route (2 1 0) over route (2 0). This routing policy configuration will lead to persistent route oscillation. In fact, it can be proved that no matter what route an AS chooses initially [9], it will keep changing its route and never reach a stable route. For example, the following sequence of route changes shows how a persistent route oscillation can occur.

1. Initially, ASes 1, 2, and 3 choose paths (1 2 0), (2 0), and (3 0), respectively.
2. After AS 2 receives path (3 0) from AS 3, it changes from its current path (2 0) to the higher preference path (2 3 0), which in turn forces AS 1 to change its path from (1 2 0) to (1 0) because path (1 2 0) is no longer available.
3. When AS 3 notices that AS 1 uses path (1 0), it changes its path (3 0) to (3 1 0). This in turn forces AS 2 to change its path to (2 0).
4. After AS 2 sends path (2 0) to AS 1, AS 1 changes its path (1 0) to (1 2 0), which in turn forces AS 3 to change its path (3 1 0) to (3 0), and the oscillation begins again.

In practice, however, routing policies are typically set according to commercial contractual agreements between ASes. Typically, there are two types of AS relationship: *provider-to-customer* and *peer-to-peer*. In the first case, a customer pays the provider to be connected to the Internet. In the second case, two ASes agree to exchange traffic on behalf of their respective customers free of charge. Note that contractual agreement between peering ASes typically requires that traffic via both directions of the peering link has to be within a ratio negotiated between peering ASes. In addition to these two common types of relationship, an AS may have a *backup* relationship with a neighboring AS. Having a backup relationship with a neighbor is important when an AS has limited connectivity to the rest of the Internet. For example, two ASes could establish a bilateral backup agreement for providing the connection to the Internet in the case that one AS' link to its primary provider fails. Typically, provider-to-customer relationships among ASes are hierarchical. The hierarchical structure arises because an AS typically selects a provider with a network of larger size and scope than its own. An AS serving a metropolitan area is likely to have a regional provider, and a regional AS is likely to have a national provider as its provider. It is very unlikely that a nationwide AS would be a customer of a metropolitan-area AS.

It is common for an AS to adopt an import routing policy, referred to as *prefer customer* routing policy, where routes received from an AS' customers are always preferred over those received from its peers or providers. Such a partial order on the set of routes is compatible with economic incentives. Each AS has economic incentives to prefer routes via a customer link to those via peer or provider links, since it does not have to pay for the traffic via customer links. On the other hand, the AS has to pay for traffic via provider links, and traffic sent to its peer has to be "balanced out" with traffic from its peer. It is also common for an AS to adopt an export routing policy, referred to as *no-valley* routing policy, where an AS does not announce a route from a provider or peer to another provider or peer. For example, in Fig. 6.12, and the following examples, an arrowed line between two nodes represents a provider-to-customer relationship, with the arrow ending at the customer. A dashed line represents a peer-to-peer relationship. We visualize a sequence of customer-to-provider links as an uphill path, for example, path (1 3 5) is an uphill path. We define a sequence of provider-to-customer links as a down hill path, for example, path (5 4 1) is a down hill path. A peer-to-peer link is defined as a horizontal path. The no-valley routing policy ensures that no path contains a valley where a downhill path is followed by either a peer-to-peer link or uphill path, or a peer-to-peer link is follower by an uphill path or a peer-to-peer link. That is, an AS path may take one of the following forms: (1) an uphill path followed by one or no peer-to-peer link, (2) a downhill path, (3) a peer-to-peer link followed by a downhill path, (4) an uphill path followed by a downhill path, or (5) a uphill path followed by a peering link, followed by a downhill path. For example, in Fig. 6.12, paths (3 5 4) and (1 3 5 6 4 2) are no-valley paths while AS paths (3 1 4) and (3 1 2 6) are not no-valley paths.

ASes adopt these rules since there is no economic incentive for an AS to transit traffic between its providers and peers. Note that we name it no-valley routing policy since such an export policy ensures that no route traverses a provider-to-customer link and then a customer-to-provider link, or a provider-to-customer link and then a

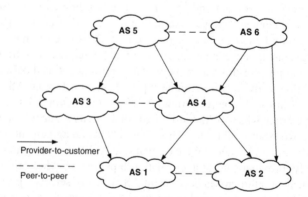

Fig. 6.12 Paths (3 5 4) and (1 3 5 6 4 2) are no-valley paths while AS paths (3 1 4) and (3 1 2 6) are not no-valley paths

peer-to-peer link, or a peer-to-peer link and then another peer-to-peer link, or peer-to-peer link and then customer-to-provider link, all of which are valley paths if there is a hierarchical structure in provider-to-customer relationships.

It has been proved that under the hierarchical provider-to-customer relationships, these common routing policies can indeed ensure route convergence [8]. Furthermore, these policies ensure route convergence under router or link failures, and changes in routing policy. Note that each AS can configure its routers with the prefer customer routing policy without knowing the policies applied in other ASes. Therefore, each AS has an economic incentive to follow the preferred customer routing policy. In addition, it is practical to implement the policy since ASes can set their routing policies without coordinating with other ASes.

In addition to local preference setting, it has been observed that certain iBGP configuration may result in persistent route oscillation [2, 10]. Figure 6.13 shows an example of route reflector and policy configuration that can lead to persistent route oscillation. AS 1 consists of two route reflectors, A and B. A has two clients, C1 and C2, while B has one client, C3. The IGP cost of the link between two nodes is indicated beside the link, and the MED value of the routes is indicated in parentheses. It can be proved that no matter what the initial route is for each router, it is not possible for the routers to reach a stable route. As an example, we show below a possible sequence of route changes that lead to persistent oscillation.

1. Route reflector A selects path p_2 and route reflector B selects path p_3.
2. Route reflector A receives p_3 and selects p_1 because p_3 has a lower MED than p_2 and p_1 has lower IGP metric than p_3.
3. Route reflector B receives p_1 and selects p_1 as the best path (due to a lower IGP cost) and withdraws p_3.
4. Route reflector A selects p_2 over p_1 (due to a lower IGP cost) and withdraws p_1.
5. Route reflector B selects p_3 over p_2 (due to lower MED). Now both A and B return back to their initial routes.

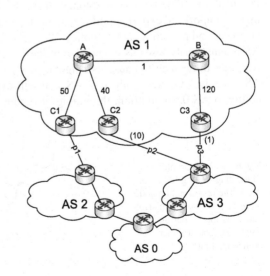

Fig. 6.13 An example route reflector configuration that leads to persistent oscillation

One of the reasons that this route reflector configuration can lead to persistent route oscillation is that MED is compared only among links in the same AS. It is possible to enforce a rule that MED is always compared even when they come from links to different ASes. Other guidelines have also been proposed to prevent route reflector configuration from persistent oscillation. These guidelines include exploiting the hierarchical structure of route reflector configuration [10] similar to that proposed in [8]. That is, if a route reflector configuration ensures that a route reflector chooses a route from its client over that from another route reflector (e.g. with IGP cost setting), then it can ensure route convergence.

6.4.2 Transient Routing Failures

Even when BGP eventually converges to a set of stable routes, network failures, maintenance events, and router configuration changes can cause BGP to reconverge. Ideally, when such an event occurs, routing protocols should be able to react quickly to those failures to find alternate paths. However, BGP is known to be slow in reacting and recovering from network events. Previous measurement studies have shown that BGP may take tens of minutes to reach a consistent view of the network topology after a failure [17–19].

During the convergence period, a router might contain routing information that lags behind the state of the network. For example, it is possible for a router to eventually discover an alternate path when one of the links in its original path fails. However, during the discovery process, the router might lose all of its paths before an alternate path is discovered. Such a transient loss of reachability is referred to as a *transient routing failure*.

Figure 6.14 shows an example of policy configuration and link failure scenario that can lead to a transient routing failure. In this example, AS 1 and AS 2 are providers of AS 3, AS 0 is a customer of AS 1, and AS 1 is a peer of AS 2. Note that the import and export policies are realistic in the sense that it follows the prefer-customer and no-valley routing policy. When the link between AS 3 and AS 0 fails, AS 3 temporarily loses its connection to the destination AS 0. AS 3 has to send a withdrawal message to cause its neighbor AS 1 to select a new best path. Before AS 3 receives the new path from AS 1, it will experience transient loss of reachability to AS 0. In addition, the timing of sending withdrawal and announcement

Fig. 6.14 An example illustrating routing failure at AS 3. The text around a node represents a set of permissible paths and their ordering in local preference (higher preference first)

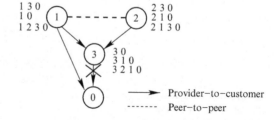

Fig. 6.15 Transient routing failures take place in a typical eBGP system. The AS paths around a node represent a set of permissible paths, which are ordered in the descending order of local preference

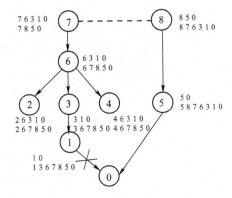

messages are determined by the expiration of MRAI timers, which can take several seconds to tens of seconds. During this period, all packets destined to AS 0 at AS 3 will be dropped.

In a typical AS where the prefer-customer and no-valley routing policies are followed, it is quite likely to have ASes experience transient failures. In fact, when an event causes an AS to change from a customer route to a provider route and all of its providers use it to reach a destination, the AS will definitely experience a transient failure. This is because the AS has to withdraw the customer route first before its provider can discover an alternate path and send the path to it. Please refer to [30] for a proof. Figure 6.15 shows an example to illustrate this point. Suppose that before the link between AS 1 and AS 0 fails, AS 1, AS 3, and AS 6 all have only one path via their customers to reach the destination. When the link failure occurs, the ASes will experience transient failure before they can learn the route via their providers. AS 2 may experience the failure (depending on whether the withdrawal from AS 6 is suppressed the MRAI timer), but AS 7 does not experience any transient routing failure.

In previous section, we have shown that multihoming technology can provide redundant underlying connections. Here, we use several examples to discuss whether BGP can fully exploit the redundancy to quickly recover from failures. In fact, BGP fails to take advantage of this redundancy to provide high degree of path diversity. The reason is due to the iBGP configuration. A *typical hierarchical iBGP system* consists of a core with fully meshed core routers, i.e., route reflectors, and the edge routers which are the clients of the relevant route reflectors. Transient routing failures can occur within a hierarchical iBGP system. Figure 6.16 shows an example that illustrates how routing failures can occur due to iBGP configuration. A multihoming AS AS 0 has two providers: AS 1 and AS 2. AS 1 can reach a destination originated at AS 0 via one of two access routers, AR1 or AR2. According to the prefer-customer routing policy, the path via AR1 is assigned higher local preference value than those via AR2. As a result, all routers inside AS 1 will use the path via AR1 to reach the destination except the access router AR2. Once the link between AR1 and AS 2 fails, all routers except AR2 might experience transient routing failures, before failover to the path via AR2.

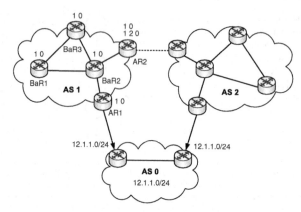

Fig. 6.16 An AS with a hierarchical iBGP configuration can experience transient failures

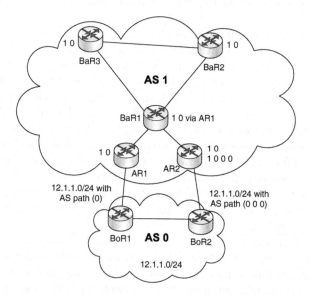

Fig. 6.17 An AS with multiple connections to a destination prefix can experience transient failures

Our second example, shown in Fig. 6.17, is used to show the reliability issue for an AS with multiple connections to a single provider. In this example, AS 0 has two connections to AS 1. Suppose that AS 0 considers the connection via AS 1's AR1 as the primary link, and the other connection via AR2 as the backup link. Suppose that AS 0 uses AS path prepending to implement this configuration. AS 0's BoR2 advertises its prefix with AS path (0 0 0). As a result, all routers inside AS 1 except router AR2 have only one single route to reach the destination. If the link between AS 0's BoR1 and AS 1's AR1 fails, all routers within AS 1 except AR2 will experience transient failures.

Our third example, shown in Fig. 6.18, is used to show the reliability issue for an
AS with multiple geographical connections to a single provider. In this example, we
assume that AS 0 considers the connection via AS 1's AR2 as the primary link,
and the connection via AR1 as the backup link. Just like the previous example,
suppose that AS 0 uses AS path prepending to implement this configuration. As a
result, all routers inside AS 1 except router AR2 has only one single route to reach
the destination. If the link between AS 0's BoR2 and AS 1's AR2 fails, all routers
within AS 1 except AR2 will experience transient failures.

Our last example used to show load balancing can avoid transient routing failures. In Fig. 6.19, AS 0 distributes its inbound traffic among the two connections
by applying hot-potato routing policy. That is, the backbone routers within AS 1
select the best route according to IGP costs to the egress routers, AR1 and AR2.

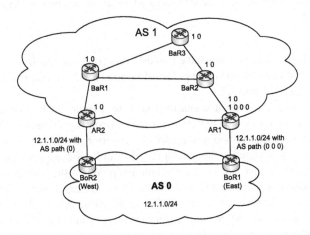

Fig. 6.18 An AS with geographical connections to a destination prefix can experience transient
failures

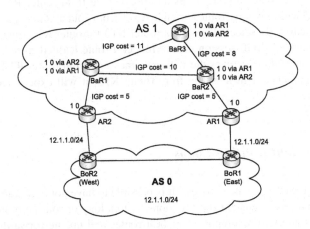

Fig. 6.19 Load balancing configuration can avoid transient failures

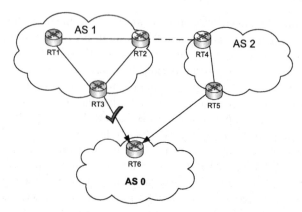

Fig. 6.20 A transient failure experienced by router RT1 when the link between AS 0 and AS 1 is added or recovered

As a result, all backbone routers have two different routes to reach the destination. This configuration can avoid single points of failures for backbone routers and link failures between AS 1 and AS 0.

So far we have focused on scenarios that lose a route. In fact, when gaining a route, it is still possible to experience transient routing failures. For example, Fig. 6.20 shows a scenario where a router can experience transient routing failure due to iBGP configuration. In this example, AS 1 and AS 2 are providers of AS 0, and AS 1 and AS 2 have peer-to-peer relationship. When the link between AS 1 and AS 0 is added or recovered from a failure, AS 1 prefers direct path to destination AS 0. Before the link is recovered, all routers within AS 1 select the path via AS 2 as their best paths. After the recovery event, all routers within AS 1 use the path through the recovered link. During the route convergence process, router RT3 first selects the direct path to AS 0 and then sends the new route to router RT2 and router RT1. Once router RT2 receives the direct route from router RT3, it selects the route and withdraws its route through AS 2 from router RT1, since it cannot announce its currently selected route via router RT3 to router RT2 (due to the fact that a fully meshed iBGP session cannot reflect a route learned from one peer to another). If router RT1 receives the withdraw message from router RT2 before receiving the announcement message from router RT3, it will experience transient routing failures.

6.4.3 Transient Routing Loops

During the route convergence process, it is possible to have not only transient routing failures, but also transient routing loops. A topology or routing policy change can lead the routers to recompute their best routes and update forwarding tables. During this process, the routers can be in an inconsistent forwarding state, causing

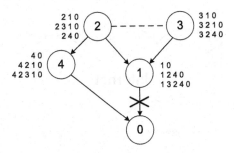

Fig. 6.21 An example of transient routing loop between AS 2 and AS 3. The list of AS paths shown beside each node is the set of permissible paths for the node, and the permissible paths are ordered in the descending order of local preference

transient routing loops. Measurement studies have shown that the transient loops can last for more than several seconds [13, 29, 31]. Figure 6.21 shows a scenario where a transient routing loop can occur. In this example, when the link between AS 1 and AS 0 fails, AS 2 and AS 3 receive a withdrawal message from AS 1. These two ASes will each select the path via the other to reach the destination because the local preference value of a path via a peer is higher than that of a path via a provider. As a result, there is a routing loop. After AS 2 and AS 3 exchange their new routes, AS 2 will remove the path from AS 3 and select the path from AS 4 as the best path. Finally, all ASes will use the path via AS 4.

6.5   Impact of Transient Routing Failures and Loops on End-to-End Performance

In this section, we aim to understand the impact that transient routing failures and loops have on end-to-end path performance. We describe an extensive measurement study that involves both controlled routing updates of a prefix and active probes from a diverse set of end hosts to the prefix.

6.5.1   Controlled Experiments

The infrastructure for the controlled experiments is shown in Fig. 6.22. The infrastructure includes a BGP Beacon prefix from the Beacon routing experiment infrastructure [21]. The BGP Beacon is multihomed to two tier-1 providers to which we refer to as $ISP1$ and $ISP2$. We control routing events by injecting well-designed routing updates from BGP Beacon at scheduled times to emulate link failures and recoveries. To understand the impact of routing events on the data plane performance, we select geographic and topologically diverse probing locations from the PlanetLab experiment testbed [25] to conduct active probing while routing changes are in effect.

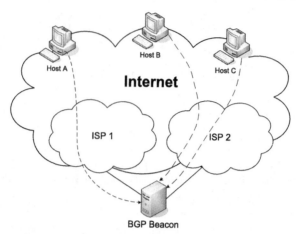

Fig. 6.22 Measurement infrastructure

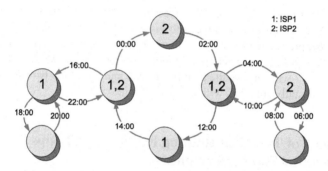

Fig. 6.23 Time schedule (GMT) for injecting routing events from BGP beacon

Every 2 hours, the BGP Beacon sends a route withdrawal or announcement to one or both providers according to the time schedule shown in Fig. 6.23. Each circle denotes a state, indicating the providers offering transit service to the Beacon. Each arrow represents a routing event and state transition, marked by the time that the routing event (either a route announcement or a route withdrawal) occurs. For example, at midnight Beacon withdraws the route through ISP 1, and at 2:00 a.m., Beacon announces the route through ISP 1. There are 12 routing events every day. Only eight routing events keep the Beacon connected to the Internet; the other four serve the purpose of resetting the Beacon connectivity. These eight beacon events are classified into two categories: failover beacon event and recovery beacon event. In a *failover beacon event*, the Beacon changes from the state of using both providers to the state of using only a single provider. In a *recovery beacon event*, the Beacon changes from the state of using a single provider for connectivity to the state of using both providers. These two classes of routing changes emulate the control plane changes that a multihomed site may experience in terms of losing and restoring a link to one or more of its providers. For example, between midnight and 2:00 a.m., the BGP Beacon is in a state that is only connected to ISP 2; at 2:00 a.m., it announces the Beacon prefix to ISP 1, leading to connectivity to both ISPs. This event emulates a link recovery event. At 4:00 a.m., the Beacon sends a withdrawal to ISP 1 so that the Beacon is in a state that is only connected to ISP2. This event emulates a failover event.

A set of geographically diverse sites in the PlanetLab infrastructure probe a host within the Beacon prefix by using three probing methods: UDP packet probing, ping, and traceroute. Probing is performed every hour during injected routing events and when there are no routing events, so as to calibrate the results. At every hour, every probing source sends a UDP packet stream marked by sequence numbers to the BGP Beacon host at 50 ms interval. The probe starts 10 min before each hour and ends 10 min after that hour (i.e., the probing duration is 20 min for each hour). Upon the arrival of each UDP packet, the Beacon host records the timestamp and sequence number of the UDP packet. In addition, ping and traceroute are sent from the probe hosts toward the Beacon host, for measuring round-trip time (RTT) and IP-level path information during the same 20 min time period. Both ping and traceroute are run as soon as the previous ping or traceroute probe completes. Thus, their probing frequency is limited by the round-trip delay and the probe response time from routers.

6.5.2   Overall Packet Loss

In this section, we present data plane performance during failover and recovery beacon events. Packet loss and loss burst length are used to measure the impact of routing events on end-to-end path performance. We refer to a series of consecutively lost packets during a routing event as a loss burst. Loss burst length is the maximum number of consecutive lost packets during a routing event. Since several lost bursts can be observed during a routing event, we consider the one with the maximum number of consecutive lost packets, which represents the worst-case scenario during the event.

Figure 6.24a shows the number of loss bursts over all probing hosts during failover beacon events for the entire duration of measurement. The x-axis represents the start time of a loss burst, which is measured (in second) relative to the injection of withdrawal messages. We observe that the majority of loss bursts occur right after time 0, i.e., the time when a withdrawal message is advertised. Figure 6.24b shows the number of loss bursts during recovery beacon events across all probe hosts undergoing path changes. We observe that loss bursts occur right after time 0, and can last for 10 s.

Figure 6.25a shows the distributions of loss burst length before, during, and after a path change for failover beacon events. The x-axis is shown in log scale. We find that the packet loss burst length during path change can have as many as 480 consecutive packets. Compared with the loss burst length during a path change, the packet loss burst size before and after a path change are quite short. Figure 6.25b

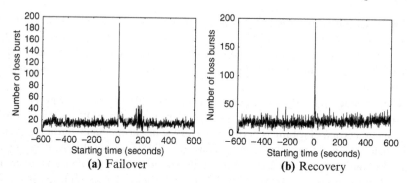

Fig. 6.24 Number of loss bursts starting at each second [31] (Copyright 2006 Association for Computing Machinery, Inc. Reprinted by permission)

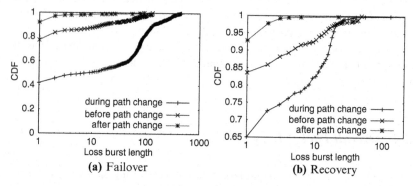

Fig. 6.25 The cumulative distribution of loss burst length [31] (Copyright 2006 Association for Computing Machinery, Inc. Reprinted by permission)

shows the loss burst length during recovery beacon events. We observe that the loss burst length during routing change does not show a significant difference compared with those before or after routing change. In addition, loss burst length can be as long as 140 packets for recovery beacon events. Such loss is most likely caused by routing failures.

6.5.3 Packet Loss Due to Transient Routing Failures or Loops

From the measurement results, we see that during both events, many packet loss bursts occur. Packet loss can be attributed to network congestion or routing failures. In order to identify routing failures, ICMP response messages, as measured by traceroutes and pings, are used. After deriving loss burst, unreachable responses from traceroutes and pings are correlated with the loss bursts. Since hosts in PlanetLab are NTP time synchronized, the loss bursts are correlated with ICMP messages using the time window $[-1$ s, 1s]. When a router does not have a route entry for an incoming packet, it will send an ICMP network unreachable error message back to the source to indicate that the destination is unreachable if it is allowed to do so. Based on the ICMP response message, we can determine when and which router does not have a route entry to the Beacon host. Loss bursts that have corresponding unreachable ICMP messages are attributed to routing failures. In addition, if a packet is trapped in forwarding loops, its TTL value will decrease until the value reaches 0 at some router. The router will send a "TTL exceeded" message back to the source. Thus, from traceroute data, we can observe forwarding loops.

Table 6.2 shows the number of failover beacon events, the number of loss bursts, and the number of lost packets that can be verified as caused by routing failures or loops. We verify that 23% of the loss bursts, corresponding to 76% of lost packets, are caused by routing failures or loops. We are unable to verify the remaining 77% of loss bursts, which correspond to only 24% of packet loss. These loss bursts may be caused by either congestion or routing failures for which traceroute or ping is not sufficient (due to either insufficient probe frequency or lack of ICMP messages) for the verification.

Similar to our analysis on failover events, we correlate ICMP unreachable messages with loss bursts occurring during recovery events. Table 6.3 shows that 26% of packet loss is verified to be caused by routing failures.

Since routers in the Internet may filter out ICMP packets, it is possible that some loss packets do not have corresponding ICMP messages even if those loss bursts might be caused by routing failures or routing loops. As a result, we may underestimate the number of loss bursts due to routing failures or routing loops. Therefore, the number of loss bursts caused by routing failures or routing loops might be more than what can be identified by our methodology.

Table 6.2 Overall packet loss caused by routing failures or loops during failover events

Causes	Failover beacon events	Loss bursts	Lost packets
Routing failures	451 (38%)	607 (16%)	37,751 (42%)
Routing loops	208 (18%)	239 (7%)	30,592 (34%)
Unknown	539 (44%)	2,875 (77%)	21,948 (24%)

Table 6.3 Packet loss caused by routing changes during recovery events

Causes	Recovery beacon events	Loss bursts	Loss packets
Routing failures	17 (5%)	39 (2%)	480 (11%)
Routing loops	24 (7%)	37 (2%)	640 (15%)
Unknown	290 (88%)	1,714 (96%)	3,266 (74%)

We measure the duration of a loss burst as the time interval between the latest received packets before the loss and the earliest one after the loss. Figure 6.26a shows the duration of loss bursts that can and cannot be verified as caused by routing failures or routing loops during failover events. Again, we observe that the loss bursts that are verified as caused by routing failures or routing loops last longer than those unverified loss bursts. Figure 6.26b further shows that loss bursts caused by routing loops last longer than those caused by routing failures.

Figure 6.27a shows the cumulative distribution of the duration of loss bursts that are verified and unverified as caused by routing failures or routing loops during recovery events. We observe that verified loss bursts on average are longer than those unverified. In addition, during recovery events, more than 98% of routing failures or routing loops last less than 5 seconds, while during failover events, about 80% of routing failures or routing loops last less than 5 seconds as shown in Fig. 6.26. This means that loss bursts caused by routing failures during recovery events last much shorter than those during failover events. We also observe that unverified loss bursts

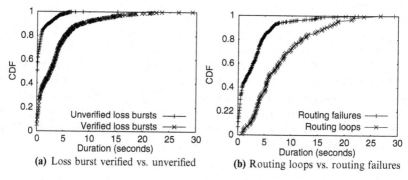

(a) Loss burst verified vs. unverified   **(b)** Routing loops vs. routing failures

Fig. 6.26 Duration for verified vs. unverified loss bursts during failover events [31] (Copyright 2006 Association for Computing Machinery, Inc. Reprinted by permission.)

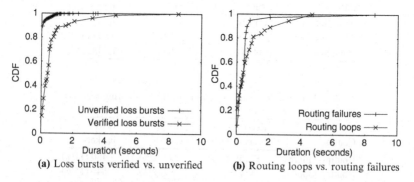

(a) Loss bursts verified vs. unverified   **(b)** Routing loops vs. routing failures

Fig. 6.27 Duration of verified loss bursts during recovery events [31] (Copyright 2006 Association for Computing Machinery, Inc. Reprinted by permission.)

last less than 4 seconds. Figure 6.27b shows the duration of verified loss bursts that are caused by routing failures and loops during recovery events. We observe that 57% of packet loss is due to forwarding loops, which is slightly higher than that for failover events (47%). This implies that forwarding loops are also quite common during recovery events.

6.6   Research Approaches

We have seen from the measurement study in the previous section that routing failures and routing loops contribute to degraded end-to-end path performance significantly. Several approaches have been proposed to address the problem of routing failures and routing loops. These approaches can be broadly classified into three categories: convergence-based solution, path protection-based solution, and multiple path-based solution.

- *Convergence-Based Solutions*   These approaches focus on reducing BGP convergence delay. In particular, they aim to reduce convergence delay by eliminating invalid routes quickly. Reducing convergence delay may indirectly shrink the periods of routing failures or routing loops since it takes less time to converge to a stable route.
- *Path Protection-Based Solutions*   These approaches focus on preestablishing recovery paths before potential network events. These preestablished paths supplement the best path selected by BGP. When there is a routing outage, the recovery path is used to route traffic. The recovery path could be a preestablished protection tunnel, or an alternate AS path.
- *Multipath-Based Solutions*   The goal of these approaches is to exploit path diversity to provide fault tolerance. To increase path diversity, multipath routes are discovered. For example, multiple routing trees can be created on the same underlying topology. When one of the routes fails, other routes can be probed and then used if valid to route traffic.

6.6.1   Convergence Based Solutions

BGP is a path vector protocol. Each BGP speaking router has to rely on its neighbors' announcements to select its best route. Since each BGP speaking router does not have the topology information, it is possible that an AS explores many AS paths before eventually reaching the final stable path. Figure 6.28 shows an example of the path exploration process during BGP convergence. Suppose the link between AS 1 and AS 0 fails. This failure event makes the destination unreachable at each AS. We refer to this type of events as *fail-down events*. The following potential sequence of route changes shows how path exploration can occur.

Fig. 6.28 An example of path exploration during BGP convergence. The list of AS paths shown beside each node is the set of permissible paths for the node, and the permissible paths are ordered in the descending order of local preference

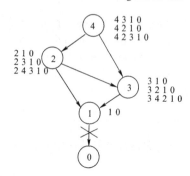

1. AS 1 sends a withdrawal message to AS 2 and AS 3, respectively.
2. As AS 2 receives the withdrawal, it removes path (2 1 0) from its routing table, selects path (2 3 1 0) as its new best path, and advertises the new path to all neighbors.
3. After AS 3 receives the withdrawal from AS 1, it will use path (3 2 1 0), and advertise it to its neighbors.
4. When AS 2 and AS 3 learn the new paths (2 3 1 0) and (3 2 1 0) from each other, they will remove their best paths, and use path (2 4 3 1 0) and path (3 4 2 1 0), respectively.
5. Since both AS 2 and AS 3 use the paths from AS 4, they will send AS 4 withdrawal messages to withdraw their previously advertised paths. As a result, AS 4 loses its all paths, and sends a withdrawal message to AS 2 and AS 3, respectively.
6. After AS 2 and AS 3 receive the withdrawals from AS 4, their routing tables do not have any route to the destination.

This example shows that each node literally has to try several AS paths that traverse the failed link/node before it finally chooses the best valid path or determines that there is no best path. For instance, AS 2 might explore the sequence AS paths (2 1 0) → (2 3 1 0) → (2 4 3 1 0) before it removes all paths from its routing table. Previous measurement studies have shown that BGP may take tens of minutes to reach a consistent view of the network topology after a failure [17–19]. Note that although this example shows a fail-down scenario, we can indeed extend it to show a fail-over scenario in which an AS has to explore many invalid paths before finalizing to a stable valid path.

Several solutions have been proposed to rapidly indicate and remove invalid routes to suppress the exploration of obsoleted paths [5, 7, 23, 24]. Consistency Assertions (CA) [24] tries to achieve this goal by examining path consistency based solely on the AS path information carried in BGP announcements. Suppose that an AS has learned two paths to a destination from neighbor N_1 and neighbor N_2, respectively. N_1 advertises path (N_1 A B C 0) and neighbor N_2 advertises (N_2 B X Y 0). CA assumes that each AS can only use one path. Thus, by comparing these two paths, it can detect that the two paths advertised by AS B ((B C 0) and (B X Y 0)) are not consistent. We use an example shown in Fig. 6.28 to show how an AS can take advantage of consistency checking to accelerate route convergence. A router can use a withdrawal received directly from a neighbor to check path consistency. When the link between AS 1 and AS 0 fails, AS 1 sends withdrawals to AS 2 and AS 3. Once AS 2 and AS 3 notice that their neighbor AS 1 withdraws its path to the destination, they check whether AS 1 appears in any existing path. Since the two path (2 3 1 0) and (2 4 3 1 0) contains path (1 0), neither can be selected and AS 2 removes them from its routing table. Similarly, AS 3 removes path (3 2 1 0) and (3 4 2 1 0). Eventually, AS 2 and AS 3 will withdraw their paths to the destination. As a result, CA eliminates the paths to be explored.

However, the AS path consistency might not contain sufficient information about invalid paths. It is hard to accurately detect invalid routes based solely on the AS path information. For example, in Fig. 6.28, after AS 2 and AS 3 receive the withdrawals sent by AS 1 due to link (1 0) failure, AS 2 and AS 3 send withdrawals to AS 4 since all of their paths go through AS 1. Now suppose that AS 2's withdrawal reaches AS 4 before AS 3 does. In this case, AS 4 cannot consider path (4 3 1 0) as an invalid path since the path does not contain the withdrawn path (2 1 0). AS 4 cannot determine if the withdrawal of path (2 1 0) is due to the failure of link (2 1) or link (1 0).

To accurately identify invalid paths, Ghost Flushing [5] reduces convergence delay by aggressively sending explicit withdrawals to quickly remove invalid paths. Whenever an AS's current best path is replaced by a less preferred route, Ghost Flushing allows the AS to immediately generate and send explicit withdrawal messages to all its neighbors before sending the new path. The withdrawal messages is to flush out the path previously advertised by the AS. For example, in Fig. 6.28, after AS 2 receives the withdrawal sent by AS 1 due to link (1 0) failure, AS 2 will use less preferred path (2 3 1 0). Before sending the path (2 3 1 0) to its neighbors, AS 2 sends extra withdrawal messages to its neighbors AS 3 and AS 4. Because BGP withdrawal messages are not subjected to the MRAI timer, invalid paths can potentially be quickly deleted from the AS's neighbors. For example, the withdrawal sent by AS 2 will help AS 3 to remove the invalid path (3 2 1 0). From this example, we know that Ghost Flushing does not really prevent path exploration, but instead attempts to speed up the process.

To further identify invalid routes quickly, additional information can be incorporated into BGP route updates. BGP-RCN and EPIC [7, 23] propose to use with location information about failures, or root cause information, to identify invalid routes. When a link failure occurs, the nodes adjacent to the link will detect the change. The node, referred to as the root cause node (RCN), will attach its name to the routing update it sends out. The RCN is propagated to other ASes along each impacted path. Thus, an AS can use the RCN to remove all the invalid paths at once. For example, Fig. 6.28 illustrates the basic idea of BGP-RCN. When the link between AS 1 and AS 0 fails, root cause notification is sent with a withdrawal by AS 1. When AS 2 receiving the withdrawal, it uses the root cause notification to find invalid paths that contain AS 1. Thus, path (2 3 1 0) is considered as an invalid path and will be removed. Similarly, at AS 3, path (3 2 1 0) is detected as an invalid route. AS 2 and AS 3 send withdrawals to AS 4, and piggyback the root cause in the

Table 6.4 Properties of convergence-based solutions. M is the MRAI timer value. n is the number of ASes in the network. D is the diameter of the network. $|E|$ is the number of AS level links. h is the processing delay for a BGP update message to traverse an AS hop

Protocols	Convergence delay (fail-down)	Messages (fail-down)	Modification to BGPs messages	Modification to BGP route selection	eBGP	iBGP
Standard BGP	$M \cdot n$	$|E| \cdot n$	N/A	N/A	N/A	N/A
CA	$M \cdot n$	$|E|$	No	Yes	Yes	No
Ghost Flushing	$h \cdot n$	$2|E|n\frac{h}{M}$	No	Yes	Yes	Yes
BGP-RCN	$h \cdot D$	$|E| - n + 1$	Yes	Yes	Yes	No
EPIC	$h \cdot D$	$|E| - 1$	Yes	Yes	Yes	Yes

withdrawals. After receives the withdrawal messages with root cause, AS 4 removes all its routes because all paths contain the root cause node AS 1.

EPIC [7] further extends the idea of root cause notification so that it can be applied to a router rather than an AS. In general, a failure can occur to a router or a link between a pair of routers. A failure on a link between two ASes does not necessarily mean that all links between the two ASes fail. The root cause notification in BGP-RCN can only indicate failures on an AS or links between a pair of ASes. EPIC further allows routing information that contains failure information about router or link between a pair of routers.

We summarize important properties of the four approaches in Table 6.4. We consider the upper bound of convergence time and the number of messages during a fail-down event. We also compare those approaches in term of the modifications need from the standard BGP. For example, we consider if an approach needs to modify to BGP's messages format or BGP route selection, and if those approaches can be applied to eBGP or iBGP.

6.6.2 Path Protection-Based Solutions

The convergence based-approaches focus on rapidly removing invalid routes to accelerate BGP convergence process. They are efficient in reducing convergence delay. However, simply applying those methods might not necessarily lead to reliable routing. In fact, accelerating the process of identifying invalid routes might sometimes exacerbate routing outages. Figure 6.29 shows such an example. We first consider the case of running the standard BGP. When the link between AS 1 and AS 0 fails, AS 1 sends a withdrawal to AS 2 and AS 3 immediately, and AS 2 sends a withdrawal to AS 3 right after. Upon receiving the withdrawal, AS 3 will quickly switch to the path (3 4 0). At the same time, when AS 2 receives the withdrawal message, it selects path (2 3 1 0). Even though this path is invalid, AS 2 still reroutes traffic to a valid next hop AS, which has a valid path. Therefore, in this case, AS 2 can reroute traffic to the destination before it receives the valid path (3 4 0).

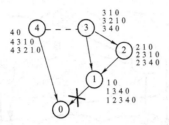

Fig. 6.29   An example showing transient routing failures at AS 2 when RCN is used. The list of AS paths shown beside each node is the set of permissible paths for the node, and the permissible paths are ordered in the descending order of local preference

On the contrary, if the root cause information is sent with the withdrawal by AS 1. AS 2 will remove path (2 3 1 0), and temporarily lose its reachability to AS 0 until receiving the new path from AS 3. The duration of temporary loss of reachability could last longer than that in the case of the standard BGP. The duration that AS 2 loses its reachability depends on the delay to get the alternate path from AS 3, which is determined by the time it takes to receive the announcement of path (3 4 0) from AS 3, which is subjected to MRAI timer. Without using the root cause information, the duration that AS 2 loses its reachability depends on the propagation delay of the withdrawal from AS 1 to AS 2, which is not subjected to MRAI timer [26].

The path protection-based solutions are designed specifically for improving the reliability of interdomain routing. The major idea is that local protection paths are identified before failures. When the primary path fails, local protection paths are temporarily used. Many approaches have been proposed for link-state intradomain routing protocols to protect intradomain link failures [6, 14, 16, 27, 33]. However, the BGP speaking routers do not have the knowledge of the global network topology. They have routing information from neighbors only. Therefore, there are two challenges in implementing path protection in BGP; first, one needs to find local preplanned protection paths; second, one needs to decide how and when to use the protection paths. Next, we present several path protection-based approaches. We first focus on how they address the first challenge. We then discuss how they address the second challenge.

Bonaventure et al. [3] have proposed a fast reroute technique, referred to as *R-Plink*, to protect direct interdomain links. The basic idea is that each router pre-computes recovery path for each of its BGP peering links, which is used to reroute traffic when the protected BGP link fails. In order to discover an appropriate recovery path, each edge router inside an AS advertises its currently active eBGP sessions by using a new type of iBGP update message. After having other routers' routing information, an edge router chooses a path to protect its current active eBGP session from all recovery routes. Figure 6.30 shows an example to illustrate this approach. In this example, AS 2 advertises the same destination to AS 1's two routers A and C. Suppose that the routing policies on AS 1 are configured to select the path via router A as the best path. However, router A cannot learn any route via router C through BGP because of the local-preference settings on this router.

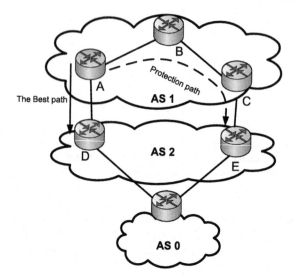

Fig. 6.30 A precomputed protection path is used to protect the interdomain link between AS 1 and AS 2

To automatically discover the alternate path, routers A and C advertise their active eBGP sessions. Thus, router A will know an alternate path via routers C and E, and choose the path to protect its current path to the destination. Once the link (A D) fails, router A can forward the packets affected by the failure through the alternate path via (C E) link.

In contrast of R-Plink, R-BGP aims to solve the transient routing failures problem for any interdomain link failure, not just for the failure of a direct neighboring interdomain link [15]. R-BGP precomputes an alternate path for each AS to protect interdomain links. In particular, an AS first checks all paths it knows, and then selects the one most disjoint from its current best path, which is defined as the *failover path*. Finally, the AS advertises the failover path only to the next-hop AS along its best path. Note that in the standard BGP, an AS should not advertise its best path to the neighbor currently used to reach that destination, since this path would generate a loop. Advertising a failover path guarantees that, whenever a link goes down, the AS immediately upstream of the down link knows a failover path and can avoid unnecessary packet drops. One limitation of this approach is that it guarantees to avoid routing failures only under the hierarchical provider-customer relationships and the common routing policy, i.e., the no-valley and prefer-customer routing policy. Further, it does not address the routing failures caused by iBGP configuration.

Backup Route Aware Routing Protocol (BRAP) is to achieve fast transient failure recovery considering both eBGP routing policy and iBGP configurations [28]. To achieve this, BRAP requires that a router should be enabled to advertise an alternate path if its best path is not allowed to be advertised due to loop prevention or routing policies. The general idea for BRAP is as follows: a router should advertise following policy compliant paths in addition to the best path: (1) a failover

Table 6.5 Comparing path protection-based solutions. $|E|$ is the number of AS level links, $|E_r|$ is the number of router level links

Protocols	Messages (failover)	Modification to BGPs messages	Modification to other part of BGP	eBGP	iBGP
R-Plink	N/A	Yes	Yes	Yes	Yes
R-BGP	$|E|$	Yes	Yes	Yes	No
BRAP	$|E_r|$	Yes	Yes	Yes	Yes

path to the nexthop router along the best path; and (2) a loop-free alternate path, defined as a temporary backup path, to its upstream neighbors. BRAP extends BGP to distribute the alternate routes along eBGP and iBGP sessions.

Now, we describe how to use a protection path. When a router needs to use a protection path, the router needs to inform the other routers along the path of the change. Otherwise, redirecting traffic to the protection path could cause forwarding loops. For example, in Fig. 6.30, when router A sends traffic along the alternate path via routers B and C, their routing tables still consider router A as the next hop. Protection tunnels on the data plane is proposed to avoid such forwarding loops [3]. Protection tunnels can be implemented by using encapsulation schemes such as MPLS over IP. With MPLS over IP, only the ingress border router consults its BGP routing table to forward a packet, and encapsulates IP header with the destination set to the IP address of the egress border router. All the other routers inside the AS will rely on their IGP routing tables or their label forwarding table to forward the packet. R-BGP utilizes "virtual" connections to avoid forwarding loops. There are two "virtual" connections between each pair of BGP-speaking routers, one for the primary path traffic, and the other for the failover traffic. The virtual connection can be implemented by using virtual interfaces when the two routers are physically connected, or MPLS or IP tunnels if they are not. Similarly, BRAP uses a protection path through MPLS or IP tunnels.

We summarize the features of the three path protection-based solutions in Table 6.5. We consider the upper bound of the number of messages during a failover event, modification to BGP, and whether those approaches can be applied to eBGP or iBGP.

6.6.3 Multiple Path-Based Solution

A straightforward solution to improve the route reliability is to discover multiple paths. There are two proposals for multiple path interdomain routing. The first one is MIRO [32] that allows routers to inform their neighbors multiple routes instead of only the best one. Thus, MIRO can allow ASes to have more control over the flow of traffic in their networks, as well as enable quick reaction to path failures. The second one is Path Splicing [22], which aims to take advantage of alternate paths in BGP routing table to discover multiple paths. Instead of using only the best path in the BGP routing table, a packet can select any path in the BGP routing table by indicating which one to use in its header. Clearly, probing has to be deployed before multiple paths can be discovered since arbitrary selection of alternate paths can lead to routing loops.

6.7 Conclusion and Future Directions

Interdomain routing is the glue that binds thousands of networks in the Internet together. Its reliability plays determinable role on the end-to-end path performance. In this chapter, we have presented the challenges in designing and implementing a reliable interdomain routing protocol. Specifically, through measurement studies, we present a clear overview of the impact of transient routing failures and transient routing loops on the end-to-end path performance. Finally, we have critically reviewed the existing proposals in this field, highlighting pros and cons of those approaches.

While certain efforts have been made to enhance interdomain routing reliability, this issue remains open. We believe that the development of new routing infrastructure, for example, multipath routing is one promising direction of future research. Reliability enhancement through multiple path advertisement is not a new idea. Many efforts have been been made to extend BGP to allow the advertisement of multiple paths [12, 20]. However, designing scalable interdomain routing through multiple path advertisement is challenging. One of those challenges is to understand the degree of path diversity provided by multiple path advertisement is sufficient to overcome network failures. At the same time, this challenge highlights the need for designing new path diversity metrics. Path diversity metrics such as the number of node-disjoint and link-disjoint links can be used to compute the inter-AS path diversity. However, new path diversity metrics needs to be devised to take into account the performance, reliability, and stability.

Acknowledgments The authors would like to thank the editors, Chuck Kalmanek and Richard Yang, for their comments and encouragement. This work is partially supported by NSF grants CNS-0626617 and CNS-0626618.

References

1. Akella, A., Maggs, B., Seshan, S., Shaikh, A., & Sitaraman, R. (2003). A measurement-based analysis of multihoming. In *Proceedings of ACM SIGCOMM*, August 2003.
2. Basu, A., Ong, L., Shepherd, B., Rasala, A., & Wilfong, G. (2002). Route oscillations in I-BGP with route reflection. In *Proceedings of the ACM SIGCOMM*.
3. Bonaventure, O., Filsfils, C., & Francois, P. (2007). Achieving sub-50 milliseconds recovery upon BGP peering link failures. *IEEE/ACM Transactions on Networking (TON), 15*(5), 1123–1135.
4. Boutremans, C., Iannaccone, G., Bhattacharyya, S. C., Chuah, C., & Diot, C. (2002). Characterization of failures in an IP backbone. In *Proceedings of ACM SIGCOMM Internet Measurement Workshop*, November, 2002.

5. Bremler-Barr, A., Afek, Y., & Schwarz, S. (2003). Improved BGP convergence via ghost flushing. In *Proceedings of IEEE INFOCOM* 2003, vol. 2, San Francisco, CA, Mar. 30-Apr. 3, 2003, pp. 927–937.

6. Bryant, S., Shand, M., Previdi, S. (2009). IP fast reroute using not-via addresses. Draft-ietf-rtgwg-ipfrr-notvia-addresses-04.

7. Chandrashekar, J., Duan, Z., Zhang, Z. L., & Krasky, J. (2005). Limiting path exploration in BGP. In *Proceedings of IEEE INFOCOM* 2005, Miami, Florida, March 13–17 2005, Volume: 4, 2337–2348.

8. Gao, L., & Rexford, J. (2001). A stable internet routing without global coordination. *IEEE/ACM Transactions on Networking, 9*(6), 681–692.

9. Griffin, T. G., & Willfong, G. (1999). An analysis of BGP convergence properties. In *Proceedings of ACM SIGCOMM*, pp. 277–288, Boston, MA, September 1999.

10. Griffin, T. G., & Willfong, G. (2002). On the correctness of IBGP configuration. In *Proceedings of ACM SIGCOMM*, pp. 17–29, Pittsburgh, PA, August 2002.

11. Griffin, T. G., Shepherd, B. F., & Wilfong, G. (2002). The stable paths problem and interdomain routing. *IEEE/ACM Transactions on Networking (TON), 10*(2) pp. 232–243.

12. Halpern, J. M., Bhatia, M., & Jakma, P. (2006). Advertising Equal Cost Multipath routes in BGP. Draft-bhatia-ecmp-routes-in-bgp-02.txt

13. Hengartner, U., Moon, S., Mortier, R., & Diot, C. (2002). Detection and analysis of routing loops in packet traces. In *Proceedings of the 2nd ACM SIGCOMM Workshop on Internet measurement*, Marseille, France, pp. 107–112.

14. Iselt, A., Kirstdter, A., Pardigon, A., Schwabe, T. (2004). Resilient routing using ECMP and MPLS. In *Proceedings of HPSR 2004*, Phoenix, Arizona, USA April 2004, pp. 345–349.

15. Kushman, N., Kandula, S., Katabi, D.,& Maggs, B. (2007). R-BGP: staying connected in a connected world. In *4th USENIX Symposium on. Networked Systems Design & Implementation*, Cambridge, MA, April 2007, pp. 341–354.

16. Kvalbein, A., Hansen, A. F., Cicic, T., Gjessing, S., & Lysne, O. (2006). Fast IP network recovery using multiple outing configurations. In *Proceedings IEEE INFOCOM*, pp. 23–26, Barcelona, Spain, Mar. 2006.

17. Labovitz, C., Malan, G. R., & Jahanian, F. (1998). Internet routing instability. *IEEE/ACM Transactions on Networking 6*(5): 515–528 (1998).

18. Labovitz, C., Ahuja, A., Bose, A., et al. (2001). Delayed internet routing convergence. *IEEE/ACM Transactions on Networking, Publication Date: June 2001, 9*(3), pp. 293–306.

19. Labovitz, C., Ahuja, A., Wattenhofer, R., et al. (2001). The impact of internet policy and topology on delayed routing convergence. In *Proceedings of IEEE INFOCOM'01*, Anchorage, AK, USA, April 2001, pp. 537–546.

20. Mohapatra, P., Fernando, R., Filsfils, C., & Raszuk, R. (2008). Fast connectivity restoration using BGP add-path. Draft-pmohapat-idr-fast-conn-restore-00.

21. Morley Mao, Z., Bush, R., Griffin, T., & Roughan, M. (2003). BGP Beacons. In *Proceedings of IMC*, October 27–29, 2003, Miami Beach, Florida, USA, pp. 1–14.

22. Motiwala, M., Feamster, N., & Vempala, S. (2008). Path splicing. SIGCOMM 2008. Seattle, WA: August.

23. Pei, D., Azuma, M., Massey, D., & Zhang, L. (2005). BGP-RCN: improving BGP convergence through root cause notification. *Computer Networks, 48*(2), 175–194.

24. Pei, D., Zhao, X., Wang, L., Massey, D., Mankin, A., Wu, S. F., & Zhang, L. (2002). Improving BGP convergence through consistency assertions. In *Proceedings of the IEEE INFOCOM 2002, vol. 2*, New York, NY, June 23–27, 2002, pp. 902–911.

25. PlanetLab, http://www.planet-lab.org

26. Rekhter, Y., Li, T., Hares, S. (2006). A border gateway protocol 4 (BGP-4). RFC 4271.

27. Stamatelakis, D., & Grover, W. D. (2000). IP layer restoration and network planning based on virtual protection cycles. *IEEE Journal on Selected Areas in Communications, 18*(10), Oct 2000, pp. 1938–1949.

28. Wang, F., & Gao, L. (2008). A backup route aware routing protocol – fast recovery from transient routing failures. *Proceedings of IEEE INFOCOM Mini-Conference*, April 2008. Arizona: Phoenix.

29. Wang, F., Gao, L., Spatscheck, O., & Wang, J. (2008). STRID: Scalable trigger-based route incidence diagnosis. *Proceedings of IEEE ICCCN 2008*, St. Thomas, U.S. Virgin Islands, August 3–7, 2008, pp. 1–6.

30. Wang, F., Gao, L., Wang, J., & Qiu, J. (2009). On understanding of transient interdomain routing failures. *IEEE/ACM Transactions on Networking, 17*(3), June 2009, pp. 740–751.

31. Wang, F., Mao, Z. M., Gao, L., Wang, J., & Bush, R. (2006). A measurement study on the impact of routing events on end-to-end internet path performance. *Proceedings of ACM SIGCOMM 2006*, September 11–15. Pisa, Italy, pp. 375–386.

32. Xu, W., & Rexford, J. (2006). MIRO: multi-path interdomain routing. In *Proceedings of ACM-SIGCOMM 2006*, pp. 171–182, Pisa, Italy.

33. Zhong, Z., Nelakuditi, S., Yu, Y., Lee, S., Wang, J., & Chuah, C.-N. (2005). Failure inferencing based fast rerouting for handling transient link and node failures. In *Proceedings of IEEE Global Internet*, Miami, Fl, USA, Mar. 2005, pp. 2859–2863.

Chapter 7
Overlay Networking and Resiliency

Bobby Bhattacharjee and Michael Rabinovich

7.1 Introduction

An "overlay" is a coordinated collection of processes that use the Internet for communication. The overlay uses the connectivity provided by the network to form any overlay topologies and information flows fitting its applications, irrespective of the topology of the underlying network infrastructure. In a broad sense, every distributed system and application forms an overlay. Certainly, routing protocols form overlays as does the interconnection of NNTP servers that form the Usenet. We use the term "overlay networks" in a narrower sense: an application uses an overlay only if processes on end-hosts are used for routing and relaying messages. The overlay network is layered atop the physical network, which enables additional flexibility. In particular, the overlay topology can be tailored to application requirements (e.g., overlay topologies can be set up to provide low-latency lookup on flat names spaces), overlay routing may choose application-specific policies (e.g., overlay routing meshes can find paths in contradiction of policies exported by BGP), and overlay networks can emulate functionality not supported by the underlying network (e.g., overlays can implement application-layer multicast over an unicast network).

The flexibility enabled by overlay networks can be both a blessing and a curse. On the one hand, it gives application developers the control they need to implement sophisticated measures to improve the resilience of their application. On the other hand, overlay networks are built over end-hosts, which are inherently less stable, reliable, and secure than lower-layer network components comprising the Internet fabric. This presents significant challenges in overlay network design.

B. Bhattacharjee
Department of Computer Science, University of Maryland, College Park, MD 20742, USA
e-mail: bobby@cs.umd.edu

M. Rabinovich
Electrical Engineering and Computer Science, Case Western Reserve University,
10900 Euclid Avenue, Cleveland, Ohio 44106–7071, USA
e-mail: misha@eecs.case.edu

C.R. Kalmanek et al. (eds.), *Guide to Reliable Internet Services and Applications*,
Computer Communications and Networks, DOI 10.1007/978-1-84882-828-5_7,
© Springer-Verlag London Limited 2010

In this chapter, we concentrate on the former aspect of overlay networks and present a survey of overlay applications with a focus on how they are used to increase network resilience. We begin with a high-level overview of some issues that can hamper the network operation and how overlay networks can help address these issues. In particular, we consider how overlay networks can make a distributed application more resilient to flash crowds and overload, to component failures and churn, network failures and congestion, and to denial of service attacks.

7.1.1 Resilience to Flash Crowds and Overload

The emergence of the Web has led to a new phenomenon where Internet resources are exposed to potentially unlimited demand. It is difficult (and indeed inefficient) for content providers to provision sufficient capacity for the worst-case load (which is often hard to predict). Inability to predict worst-case load leaves content providers susceptible to *flash crowds*: rapid surges of demand that exceed the provisioned capacity.

Approaches to address flash crowds differ by resource type. It is useful to distinguish the following types of Internet resources:

- Large files, exemplified by software packages and media files, with file sizes on the order of megabytes for audio tracks, going up to tens or even hundreds of megabytes for software packages and gigabytes for full-length movies.
- Web objects, consisting of typical text and pictures on Web pages, with sizes ranging from one to hundreds of kilobytes.
- Streaming media, where the download (often at bounded bit rates) continues over the duration of content consumption.
- Internet applications, where a significant part of service demand to process a client request is due to the computation at the server rather than delivering content from the server to the client.

IP multicast is a mechanism at the IP level that could potentially address the flash crowd problem in the first three of these resource types. At a high level, IP multicast creates a tree with the content source as the root, and the content consumers as the leaves. The source sends only one copy of a packet, and routers inside the network forward and *duplicate* packets as necessary to implement forwarding to all receivers. IP multicast decouples the resources requirements at the source from the number of simultaneous receivers of identical data. However, IP multicast cannot help when different contents need to be sent to different clients, or when the same content needs to be sent at different times, or when one needs to scale up an Internet application. Furthermore, although IP multicast is widely implemented, access to the IP multicast service is enabled only in the confine of individual ISPs to selected applications.

Overlay networks can help overcome these limitations. Content delivery networks are an overlay-based approach widely used for streaming, large file, and Web content delivery. A content delivery network (CDN) is a third-party infrastructure that content providers employ to deliver their data. In a sense, it emulates multicast at the application level, with content providers' sites acting as roots of the multicast trees and servers within the CDN infrastructure as internal multicast tree nodes. What distinguishes a CDN from IP multicast is that, as with any overlays, its deployment does not rely on additional IP services beyond the universal IP unicast service, and that CDN nodes have long-term storage capability, allowing the distribution trees to encompass clients consuming content at different times.

A CDN derives economy of scale from the fact that its infrastructure is shared among multiple content providers who subscribe to the CDN's service. Indeed, because flash crowds are unlikely to occur at the same time for multiple content providers, a CDN needs much less overprovisioning of its infrastructure than an individual content provider: a CDN can reuse the same capacity slack to satisfy peak demands for different content at different times.

Another overlay approach, called peer-to-peer (P2P) delivery, provides resilience to flash crowds by utilizing client bandwidth in delivering content. By integrating clients into the delivery infrastructure, P2P approaches promise the ability to organically scale with the demand surge: the more clients want to obtain certain content, the more resources are added to the delivery infrastructure. The P2P paradigm has been explored in various contexts, but most widely used are P2P approaches to large-file downloads and streaming content.

Peer-to-peer or peer-assisted delivery of streaming content is particularly compelling because streaming taxes the capacity of the network and at the same time imposes stringent timing requirements. Consider, for example, a vision for a future Internet TV service (IPTV), where viewers can seamlessly switch between tens of thousands of live broadcast channels from around the world, millions of video-on-demand titles, and tens of millions of videos uploaded by individual users using capabilities similar to those provided by today's YouTube-type applications. Consider a global carrier providing this service in high-definition to 500 million subscribers, with 200 million simultaneous viewers at peak demand watching different streams – either distinct titles or the same titles shifted in time. Assume conservatively that a high-definition stream requires a streaming rate of 6 Mbps (it is currently close to 10 Mbps but is projected to reduce with improvements in coding). The aggregate throughput to deliver these streams to all the viewers is 1.2 Petabits per second. Even if a video server could deliver 10 Gbps of content, the carrier would need to deploy 120,000 video servers to satisfy this demand through naive unicast. Given these demands on the network and server capacities, overlay networks – in particular peer-to-peer networks – are important technologies to enable IPTV on a massive scale.

7.1.2   Resilience to Component Failures and Churn

A distributed application needs to be able to operate when some of its components
fail. For example, we discussed how P2P networks promise resiliency to flash
crowds. However, because they integrate users' computers into the content delivery infrastructure, they are especially prone to component failures (e.g., when a user
kills a process or terminates a program) and to peer churn (as users join and leave
the P2P networks). The flexibility afforded by overlay networks can be exploited
to incorporate a range of redundancy mechanisms. These mechanisms allow system designers to utilize many failure prone components (often user processes on
end-hosts) to craft highly resilient applications.

Existing P2P networks have proven this resiliency by functioning successfully
despite constant peer churn. Besides traditional file-sharing P2P networks, other
examples of churn-resistant overlay network designs include a peer-to-peer Web
caching system [36] and a churn-resistant distributed hash table [52].

7.1.3   Resilience to Network Failures and Congestion

Overlay networks can mitigate the effects of network outages and hotspots. Two
end-hosts communicating over an IP network have little control over path selection
or quality. The end-to-end path is a product of the IGP routing metrics used within
the involved domains, and the BGP policies (set by administrators of these domains)
across the domains. These metrics and policies are often entirely nonresponsive to
transient congestion; in some case, two nodes may fail to find a path (due to BGP
policies) even when a path exists.

Overlay networks allow end-users finer-grained control over routing and thus
can be agile in reacting to the underlying network conditions. Consider a hypothetical voice-over-IP communication between hosts at the University of Maryland
(in College Park, Maryland) and Case Western Reserve University (in Cleveland,
Ohio). The default path may traverse an Internet2 router in Pennsylvania. However,
if this router is congested, an overlay-based routing system that is sensitive to path
latency could try to route around the congestion. For instance, the routing overlay
could tunnel the packets through overlay nodes at the University of Virginia and the
University of Illinois, which might bypass the temporary congestion on the default
path.

Systems such as RON [4], Detour [55, 56], and Peerwise [38] create such routing overlays that route around adverse conditions in the underlying IP network.
These systems build meshes for overlay routing and make autonomous routing decisions. RON builds a fully connected mesh and continually monitors all edges.
When the direct path between two nodes fails or has shown degraded performance,
communication is rerouted through the other overlay nodes. Not all systems build a
fully connected mesh: Nakao et al. [44] use topology information and geography-
based distance prediction to build a mesh that is representative of the underlying

physical network. Peerwise creates overlay links only between nodes that can provide shortcuts to each other. Experiments with all of these systems show that it is indeed possible to reduce end-to-end latency and improve connectivity using routing overlays.

7.1.4   Resilience to DoS Attacks

Overlay networks can be used to protect content providers from Distributed Denial-of-Service (DDoS) attacks. During a DDoS attack, an attacker directs a set of compromised machines to flood the victim's incoming links. DDoS attacks are effective because (1) the content provider often cannot distinguish an attacking connection from a legitimate client connection, (2) the number of attacking hosts can be large enough that it is difficult for the victim's network provider to set up static address filters, and (3) the attackers may spoof their source IP addresses. Over the last decade, DDoS attacks have interrupted service to many major Internet destinations, and in some cases, have been the root cause for the termination of service [31]. Networking researchers have developed many elegant approaches to mitigating the effect of and tracing the root of DDoS attacks; unfortunately, almost all of them require changes to the core Internet protocols.

Overlay services can be used to provide resiliency without changing protocols or infrastructure. SOS [28] and Mayday [3] are overlay services that "hide" the address of the content-providing server. Instead the server is "protected" by an overlay, and access to the server may require strong authentication or captchas (that can distinguish attackers from legitimate clients). The protective overlay is large enough that it is not feasible or profitable to attack the entire overlay. The content provider's ISP blocks all access to the server except by a small set of (periodically changing) trusted nodes who relay legitimate requests to the server.

7.1.5   Chapter Organization

We have discussed various ways in which overlay networks can improve resiliency of networked applications. In the rest of this chapter we discuss some of these applications in more detail. We begin by introducing a foundational concept used in many overlay applications – a distributed hash table – in Section 7.2. We then discuss representative overlay applications including streaming media systems in Section 7.3 and Web content delivery networks in Section 7.4. Section 7.5 describes an overlay approach to improving the resiliency of Web services against DDoS attacks. We discuss swarming protocols for bulk transfer in Section 7.6, and conclude in Section 7.7.

7.2 A Common Building Block: DHTs

Distributed applications often maintain large sets of identifiers or *keys*, such as names of files, IDs of game players, or addresses of chat rooms. For scalability, resilience, and load-balance, the task of maintaining these keys is divided amongst the nodes participating in the system. This approach scales since each node only deals with a limited subset of keys, it is resilient since a single key can be replicated onto more than one node, and finally it balances load since lookups and storage overhead are distributed (relatively) evenly over all the participants.

A node responsible for a key may perform various application-specific actions related to this key: store the corresponding data, act as a control server for a named group, and so forth. A fundamental capability such a system must support is to allow each participating node to identify the node(s) responsible for a given key. Once a seeking node locates the node(s) that store a key, it may initiate corresponding actions.

Distributed Hash Tables (DHTs) are a technique for efficiently distributing keys among nodes. DHTs provide this capability while limiting the knowledge each node must maintain about the other nodes in the system: instead of directly determining a responsible node (as would be the case with regular hashing), a node can only determine some nodes that are "closer" (by some metric) to the responsible node. The node then sends its request to one of the closer nodes, which in turn would forward the request toward a responsible node until the request reaches its target. Good DHTs ensure that requests must traverse only a small number of overlay hops en route to a responsible node. In a system with n nodes, many DHT protocols limit this hop count to $O(\log n)$ while storing only $O(\log n)$ routing state at each node for forwarding requests. Newer designs reduce some of the overheads to constants [23, 41, 50].

DHTs are a common building block for many types of distributed services, including distributed file systems [18], publish–subscribe systems [14, 58], cooperative Web caching [25], and name service [6]. They have even been proposed as a foundation for general Internet infrastructures [58]. DHTs can be built using a *structured network*, in which the DHT protocol chooses which nodes in the network are linked (and uses the structure inherent in these connections to reduce lookup time) or an *unstructured network*, in which the node interconnection is either random or an external agent specifies which nodes may be connected (as can be the case if links are constrained as in a wireless network or have specific semantics such as trust). We next describe prototypical DHT systems that are designed for cooperative environments.

7.2.1 Chord: Lookup in Structured Networks

Chord [59] was one of the first DHTs that routed requests in $O(\log n)$ overlay hops while requiring each node to store only $O(\log n)$ routing state. The routing state at each node contains pointers to some other nodes and is called a node's *finger table*. Nodes responsible for a key store a data item associated with this key; the DHT can be used to lookup data items by key.

Chord assigns an identifier (uniformly at random) to each node from a large ID space (2^N IDs, N is usually set at 64 or 128). Each item to be stored in the DHT is also assigned an ID from the same space. Chord orders IDs onto a ring modulo 2^N. An item is mapped to the node with the smallest ID larger than the item's ID modulo 2^N. Using this definition, we say that each item is mapped onto the node "closest" to the item in the ID space.

A node with ID x stores a "finger table", which consists of references to nodes closest to IDs $x + 2^i, i \in \{0, N-1\}$. The successor of i, denoted as $s(i)$, is the node whose ID is immediately greater than i's ID modulo 2^N. Likewise, the predecessor of i, $p(i)$, is the node whose ID is immediately less than n's (Fig. 7.1). Each Chord node is responsible for the half-open interval consisting of its predecessor's ID (non-inclusive) and its own ID (inclusive).

When a new node joins, it finds its "place" on the ring by routing to its own ID (say x), and can populate its own routing table by successively querying for nodes with the appropriate IDs ($x + 1, x + 2, x + 4, \ldots$). In the worst case, this incurs $O(\log^2 n)$ overhead.

A node returns the data (if any) upon receiving a lookup for a key in the range of IDs it stores. For other lookups, it "routes" (forwards) the query to the node in its finger table with the highest ID (modulo 2^N) smaller than the key. This process iterates until the item is found or it is determined that there is no item corresponding to the lookup. Figure 7.2 shows two examples of lookups in Chord. In the first case, the data corresponding to key value 3 is looked up (starting from node 52); in the

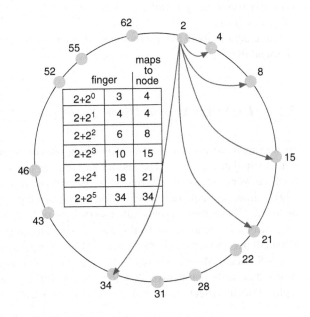

Fig. 7.1 Finger table state for Node 2

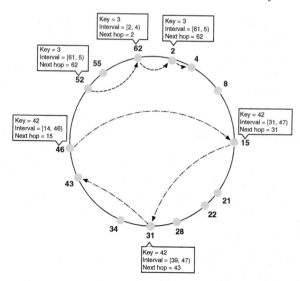

Fig. 7.2 Two lookups on the Chord ring

second, 42 is looked up starting from node 46. The figure shows the nodes visited by the queries in each case, and also the interval (part of the Chord space) each node is responsible for.

In practice, Chord nodes inherit most of their routing table from their neighbors (and avoid the $O(\log^2 n)$ work to populate tables). Nodes periodically search the ring for "better" finger table entries. As nodes leave and rejoin, the Chord ring is kept consistent using a *stabilize* protocol, which ensures eventual consistency of successor pointers.

More details about Chord, including the details of the stabilization protocol, can be found in [60].

7.2.2 LMS: Lookup on Given Topologies

As we saw in the previous section, Chord imposes the overlay topology on its nodes that is stipulated by node IDs, and lookup queries traverse routes in this topology. Such networks are often referred to as *structured*. In contrast, some overlay networks allow participating nodes to form arbitrary topologies, irrespective of their node IDs. These networks are called *unstructured*. The simplest form of lookup on an unstructured topology is to flood the query. Flooding searches, while adequate for small networks, quickly become infeasible as networks grow larger.

LMS (Local Minima Search [43]) is a protocol designed for unstructured networks that scale better than flooding. In LMS, the owner of each object places replicas of the object on several nodes. Like in a DHT, LMS places replicas onto nodes which have IDs "close" to the object. Unlike in a DHT, however, in an unstructured topology there is no deterministic mechanism to route to the node, which is the closest to an item. Instead, LMS introduces the notion of a *local minimum*: a node u is a local minimum for an object if and only if the ID of u is the closest to the item's ID in u's *neighborhood* (those nodes within h hops of u in the network, where h is a parameter of the protocol, typically 1 or 2).

In general, for any object there are many local minima in a graph, and replicas are placed onto a subset of these. During a search, random walks are used to locate minima for a given object, and a search succeeds when a local minimum holding a replica is located. While DHTs typically provide a worst-case bound of $O(\log n)$ steps for lookups in a network of size n, LMS provides a worst-case bound of $O(T(G) + \log n)$, where $T(G)$ is the *mixing time* of G (the time by which a random walk on the topology G approaches its stationary distribution). $T(G)$ is $O(\log n)$ or polylogarithmic in n for a wide range of randomly-grown topologies. This "$O(T(G) + \log n)$" is typically in the 6–15 range in networks of size up to $100,000$. Let d_h be the minimum size of the h-hop neighborhood of any node in G. LMS achieves its performance by storing $O(\sqrt{n/d_h})$ replicas, and with a message complexity (in its lookups) of $O(\sqrt{n/d_h} \cdot (T(G) + \log n))$. This is notably worse than DHTs, but is a considerable improvement over other (essentially linear-time) lookup techniques in networks that cannot support a structured protocol, and a vast improvement over flooding-based searches [43].

The use of local minima in LMS provides a high assurance that object replicas are distributed randomly throughout the network. This means that even if the lookup part of the LMS protocol is not used (such as for searches on object attributes that consequently cannot use the virtualized object identifier), flooding searches will succeed with high probability even with relatively small bounded propagation distances. Finally, LMS also provides a high degree of fault-tolerance.

7.2.3 Case Study: OpenDHT

Since many distributed applications can benefit from a lookup facility, a logical step is to develop a DHT substrate. OpenDHT is an example of such a substrate[53].

An application using a DHT may need to execute application-specific actions at each node along DHT routing paths or at the node responsible for a given key. However, to satisfy a range of applications, OpenDHT takes a minimalist approach: it only allows applications to associate a data item with a given key and store it in the substrate (at a node or nodes that OpenDHT selects to be responsible for this key) as well as retrieve it from the substrate. The DHT routing is done "under covers" within the substrate and is not exposed to the application.

In other words, OpenDHT is an external storage platform for third-party applications. While OpenDHT in itself is a peer-to-peer overlay network, application end-hosts do not participate in it directly. Instead, it runs on PlanetLab [16] nodes; applications that use OpenDHT may or may not use PlanetLab.

OpenDHT provides two simple primitives to applications: *put(key, data)* which is used to store a data item and an associated key, and *get(key)* which retrieves previously stored data given its key.[1] Multiple puts with the same key append their data items to the already existing ones, so a subsequent get would retrieve all these data. OpenDHT, therefore, implements an application-agnostic shared storage facility. Due to its open nature, OpenDHT includes special mechanisms to prevent resource hoarding by any given user. It also limits the size of data items to 1 KB and times out deposited data items that are not explicitly renewed by the application. Renewal is done by issuing an identical "put" before the original data item expires.

The shared storage provided by OpenDHT allows end-hosts in a distributed application to conveniently share state, without any administrative overhead. This capability turned out to be powerful enough to support a growing number of applications. In fact, OpenDHT primitives can be used to implement an application that employs its own DHT routing among the application's end-hosts [53].

While a great deal of engineering ingenuity ensures that OpenDHT nodes' resources are shared fairly among competing applications, OpenDHT's resiliency and scalability come from its overlay network architecture. Besides demonstrating these benefits of overlays, OpenDHT has shown the generality of the DHT concept by using it as a foundation of a substrate that has proved useful for a number of diverse applications.

7.2.4 Securing DHTs

Chord and LMS are only two of many different contemporary lookup protocols. These two protocols assume that nodes are cooperative and altruistic. While these protocols are highly resilient to random component failures, it is more difficult to protect them against malicious attacks. This is especially a concern since DHTs may be built using public, non-centrally administered nodes, some of which may be corrupt or compromised. There are several ways in which adversarial nodes may attempt to subvert a DHT. Malicious nodes may return incorrect results, may attempt to route requests to other incorrect nodes, provide incorrect routing updates, prevent new nodes from joining the system, and refuse to store or return items. There are several DHT design that provide resilience to these types of attacks. We describe one in detail next.

7.2.5 Case Study: NeighborhoodWatch

The NeighborhoodWatch DHT [11] provides security against malicious users that attempt to subvert a DHT instance by misrouting or dropping queries,

---

[1] The actual API includes additional primitives and parameters, which are beyond the scope of our discussion.

refusing to store items, preventing new nodes from joining, and similar attacks. NeighborhoodWatch employs the same circular ID space as Chord [59], and also maps its nodes into neighborhoods as in [20]. However, in NeighborhoodWatch, each node has its own neighborhood that consists of itself, it's k successors, and k predecessors, where k is a system parameter. NeighborhoodWatch's security guarantees hold if and only if for every sequence of $k + 1$ consecutive DHT nodes, at least one is alive and honest.

NeighborhoodWatch employs an on-line trusted authority, the Neighborhood Certification Authority (NCA) to attest to the constituents of neighborhoods. The NCA has a globally known public key. The NCA may be replicated, and the state shared between NCA replicas is limited to the NCA private key, a list of malicious nodes, and a list of complaints of non-responsive nodes.

The NCA creates, signs, and distributes neighborhood certificates, or nCerts, to each node. Nodes need a current and valid nCert in order to participate in the system. Upon joining, nodes receive an initial nCert from the NCA. nCerts are not revoked; instead nodes must renew their nCerts on a regular basis by contacting the NCA. nCerts list the current membership of a neighborhood, accounting for any recent changes in membership that may have occurred. Using signed nCerts, any node can identify the set of nodes that are responsible for storing an item with a given ID. NeighborhoodWatch employs several mechanisms that detect and prove misbehavior (described in detail in [11]). The NCA removes malicious nodes from the DHT by refusing to sign a fresh nCert for that node.

Nodes maintain and update their finger tables as in Chord. The join procedure is shown in Fig. 7.3. For each of node n's successors, predecessors, and finger table

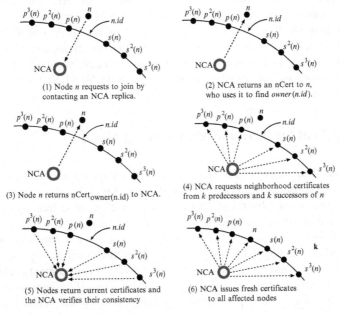

(1) Node n requests to join by contacting an NCA replica.

(2) NCA returns an nCert to n, who uses it to find $owner(n.id)$.

(3) Node n returns $nCert_{owner(n.id)}$ to NCA.

(4) NCA requests neighborhood certificates from k predecessors and k successors of n

(5) Nodes return current certificates and the NCA verifies their consistency

(6) NCA issues fresh certificates to all affected nodes

Fig. 7.3 The join process in the NeighborhoodWatch DHT [11]. Here $k = 3$

entries, n stores a full nCert (instead of only the node ID and IP address as in Chord). When queried as part of a lookup operation, nodes return nCerts rather than information about a single node. Routing is iterative: if a node on the path fails (or does not answer), the querier can contact another node in the most recently obtained nCert.

Recall that NeighborhoodWatch assumes that every sequence of $k + 1$ consecutive nodes in the DHT contains at least one node that is alive and honest. The insight is that if nodes cannot choose where they are placed in the DHT, malicious nodes would have to corrupt a large fraction of the nodes in the DHT in order to obtain a long sequence of consecutive, corrupt nodes. By making routing depend on long sequences of nodes (neighborhoods), nodes are guaranteed to know of at least one other honest node that is "near" a given point in the DHT. In order to protect against a given fraction f of malicious nodes, the system operator chooses a value of k such that this assumption holds with high probability.

Items published to the DHT are self-certifying. In addition, when a node stores an item, it returns a signed receipt to the publisher. This receipt is then stored back in the DHT. This prevents nodes from lying about whether they are storing a given item: if a querier suspects that a node is refusing to return an item, it can look for a receipt. If it finds a receipt, it can petition the NCA to remove the misbehaving node from the DHT.

7.2.6 Summary and Further Reading

In this section, we have described the basic functionality provided by DHTs, and provided case studies that demonstrate different flavors of DHTs and lookup protocols. We have described how DHTs attain their lookup performance, and also described how DHT protocols can be subverted by attackers. Finally, we have presented a DHT design that is more resilient to noncooperative and malicious behavior. Our review is not comprehensive; there are many other interesting DHT designs. We point the interested reader to [12, 20, 23, 41, 50, 51, 54, 66].

7.3 Resilient Overlay-Based Streaming Media

Overlay-based streaming media systems can be decomposed into three broad categories depending on their data delivery mechanism (Fig. 7.4).

Participants in a **single-tree** system arrange themselves into a tree. By definition, this implies that there is a single, loop-free, path between any two tree nodes. The capacity of each tree link must be at least the streaming rate. Content is forwarded (i.e., pushed) along the established tree paths. The source periodically issues a content packet to its children in the tree. Upon receiving a new content packet, each node immediately forwards a copy to its children. The uplink bandwidth of leaf nodes remains unused (except by recovery protocols) in a single tree system.

Fig. 7.4 Decomposition
of Streaming Media Protocols

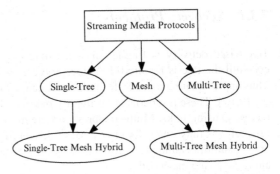

Examples of single-tree systems include ESM [15], Overcast [26], ZIGZAG [61], and NICE [8].

In a **multi-tree** system, each participating node joins k different trees and the content is partitioned into k *stripes*. Each stripe is then disseminated in one of the trees, just as in a single-tree system. In a multi-tree protocol, each member node can be an interior node in some tree(s) and a leaf node in other trees. Further, each stripe requires only $1/k$th the full stream bandwidth, enabling multi-trees to utilize forwarding bandwidths that are a fraction of the stream rate. These two properties enable multi-tree systems to utilize available bandwidth better than a single-tree. SplitStream [13], CoopNet [45], and Chunkyspread [62] are examples of multi-tree systems.

In **mesh-based** or **swarming** overlays, the group members construct a random graph. Often, a node's degree in the mesh is proportional to the node's forwarding bandwidth, with a minimum node degree (typically five [69]) sufficient to ensure that the mesh remains connected in the presence of churn.

The source periodically makes a new content block available, and each node advertises its available blocks to all its neighbors. A missing block can then be requested from any neighbor that advertises the block. Examples of mesh-based systems are CoolStreaming [69], Chainsaw [46], PRIME [39], and PULSE [47].

As Fig. 7.4 shows, the base dataplanes can be combined to form **hybrid** dataplanes. Hybrid dataplanes combine tree- and mesh-based systems by employing a tree backbone and an auxiliary mesh structure. Typically, blocks are "pushed" along the tree edges (as in a regular tree protocol) and missing blocks are "pulled" from mesh neighbors (as in a regular mesh protocol).

Prototypical examples of single-tree-mesh systems are mTreeBone [65] and Pulsar [37]. Bullet [29] is also a single-tree mesh but instead of relying on the primary tree backbone to deliver the majority of blocks, random subsets of blocks are pushed along a given tree edge and nodes recover the missing blocks via swarming. PRM [9] is a probabilistic single-tree mesh system. Chunkyspread [62], GridMedia [68], and Coolstreaming+ [33, 34] are multi-tree-mesh systems. CPM [22] is a server-based system that combines server multicast and peer-uploads.

7.3.1 Recovery Protocols

Tree-based delivery is fragile, since a single failure disconnects the data delivery until the tree is repaired. Existing protocols have added extra edges to a tree (thus approximating a mesh) for reducing latency [40] and for better failure recovery [9, 67]. These protocols are primarily tree-based, but augment tree delivery (or recovery) using links. Multi-tree protocols are more resilient, since a single failure often affects only one (of k) trees. Mesh delivery is robust by design; single node or even multiple failures are not of high consequence since the data is simply pulled along surviving mesh paths.

We next describe in detail different delivery protocols with a focus on their recovery behavior.

7.3.2 Case Study: Recovery in Trees Using Probabilistic Resilient Multicast (PRM)

PRM [10] introduces three new mechanisms – randomized forwarding, triggered NAKs and ephemeral guaranteed forwarding – to tree delivery. We discuss randomized forwarding in detail.

In *randomized forwarding*, each overlay node, with a small probability, proactively sends a few extra transmissions along randomly chosen overlay edges. Such a construction interconnects the data delivery tree with some cross edges and is responsible for fast data recovery in PRM under high failure rates of overlay nodes. We explain the details of proactive randomized forwarding [10] using the example shown in Fig. 7.5. In the original data delivery tree (Panel 0), each overlay node forwards data to its children along its tree edges. However, due to network losses on overlay links (e.g., $\langle A, D \rangle$ and $\langle B, F \rangle$) or failure of overlay nodes (e.g., C, L, and Q), a subset of existing overlay nodes do not receive the packet (e.g., D, F, G, H, J, K and M). We remedy this as follows. When any overlay node receives the first copy of a data packet, it forwards the data along all other tree edges (Panel 1). It also chooses a small number (r) of other overlay nodes and forwards

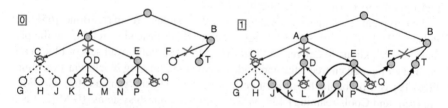

Fig. 7.5 The basic idea behind PRM. The *circles* represent the overlay nodes. The *crosses* indicate link and node failures. The arrows indicate the direction of data flow. The curved edges indicate the chosen cross overlay links for randomized forwarding of data. [10]

data to each of them with a small probability, β. For example, node E chooses to forward data to two other nodes using cross edges F and M. Note that as a consequence of these additional edges some nodes may receive multiple copies of the same packet (e.g., node T in Panel 1 receives the data along the tree edge $\langle B, T \rangle$ and cross edge $\langle P, T \rangle$). Therefore, each overlay node needs to detect and suppress such duplicate packets. Each overlay node maintains a small duplicate suppression cache, which temporarily stores the set of data packets received over a small time window. Data packets that miss the latency deadline are dropped. Hence the size of the cache is limited by the latency deadline desired by the application. In practice, the duplicate suppression cache can be implemented using the playback buffer already maintained by streaming media applications. It is easy to see that each node on average sends or receives up to $1 + \beta r$ copies of the same packet. The overhead of this scheme is βr, where we choose β to be a small value (e.g., 0.01) and r to be between 1 and 3. In PRM, nodes discover other random nodes by employing periodic random walks.

It is instructive to understand why such a simple, low-overhead randomized forwarding technique is able to increase packet delivery ratios with high probability, especially when many overlay nodes fail. Consider the example shown in Fig. 7.6, where a large fraction of the nodes have failed in the shaded region. In particular, the root of the subtree, node A, has also failed. So if no forwarding is performed along cross edges, the entire shaded subtree is partitioned from the data delivery tree. No overlay node in this entire subtree would receive data packets until the partition is repaired. However, using randomized forwarding along cross edges a number of nodes from the unshaded region will have random edges into the shaded region as shown ($\langle M, X \rangle, \langle N, Y \rangle$ and $\langle P, Z \rangle$). The overlay nodes that receive data along such randomly chosen cross edges will subsequently forward data along regular tree edges and any chosen random edges. Since the cross edges are chosen uniformly at random, a large subtree will have a higher probability of cross edges being incident on it. Thus as the size of a partition increases, so does its chance of repair using cross edges.

Triggered NAKs are the reactive components of PRM. An overlay node can detect missing data using gaps in received sequence numbers. This information is used to trigger NAK-based retransmissions. PRM further includes a *Ephemeral Guaranteed Forwarding* technique, which is useful for providing uninterrupted data service

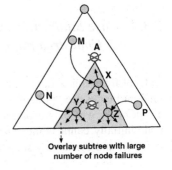

Fig. 7.6 PRM provides successful delivery with high probability because large subtrees affected by a node failure get randomized recovery packets with high probability. [10]

Overlay subtree with large
number of node failures

when the overlay construction protocol is detecting and repairing a partition in the data delivery tree. Here, when the tree is being repaired, the root of an affected subtree receives a stream of data from a "random" peer. More details about PRM are available in [10].

7.3.3 Case Study: Multi-Tree Delivery Using Splitstream

In Splitstream, the media is divided into k stripes, using a coding techniques such as multi-descriptive coding (MDC). All of the stripes in aggregate provides perfect quality, but each stripe can be used independent of the others and each received stripe progressively improves the stream quality. Splitstream forms k trees, such that, ideally, each node is an interior node in only one tree. The source multicasts stripes onto different trees, and each node receives all stripes and forwards only one stripe.

When a node departs, at most one tree is affected since every node is a leaf in all but one tree. Therefore, node departures do not affect delivery quite as much as a single tree system. Further, the forwarding bandwidth of every node is now used, since each node is an interior node in at least one stripe tree. Finally, since each stripe is approximately $1/k$th the bandwidth of the original stream, each node can serve more children, which results in a shorter tree (higher average outdegree) and lower latency.

Splitstream is built atop Scribe, which itself is an overlay multicast protocol built using the Pastry DHT. Due to bandwidth constrains on individual nodes, it is not always feasible to form the ideal interior-disjoint trees such that each node is an interior node in only one tree. In particular, a stripe tree may run out of forwarding bandwidth (because all of its leaf nodes are interior nodes in some other tree). To solve this problem, Splitstream maintains a "Spare Capacity Group (SCG)," which contains nodes with extra capacity that can forward onto more than one stripe. In bandwidth-scare deployments, nodes may have to use the SGC to locate a parent. In extreme cases, it may be impossible to form a proper Splitstream forest; however, this condition is rare and analysed in detail in [13].

7.3.4 Case Study: Recovery Using a Mesh in CoolStreaming/DONet

In Coolstreaming, a random mesh connects the members of the data overlay, and random blocks are "pulled" from different mesh neighbors. Each node maintains an *mCache*, which is a partial list of other active nodes in the overlay. A new node initially contacts the source; the source selects a random "deputy" from its *mCache*, and the deputy supplies the new node with currently active nodes. Each node periodically percolates a message (announcing itself) onto the overlay using a gossip protocol.

The media stream is divided into fixed sized segments; each segment has a sequence number and each node maintains a bitmap, called the buffer map, to represent the availability of segments. In CoolStreaming, the default buffer map contains 120 bits. Each node maintains neighbors (called partners) proportional to its forwarding bandwidth, while still maintaining a minimum number of partners (typically 5).

Nodes periodically (usually every second) exchange their buffer maps with their partners, and use a scheduling heuristic to exchange blocks. The scheduling algorithm must select a block to request, and an eligible node to request the block from. The block requested is the scarcest block (supplied by least number of nodes). The node from which this block is requested is the eligible node (which has advertised the scarce block) with the most bandwidth. The origin node serves only as a supplier and publishes a new content block every second.

Partners can be updated from the node's *mCache* as needed, and the *mCache* is updated using the periodic gossip. Individual node failures have very little effect on the delivery since a node can simply select a different partner to receive a block. However, the trade-off is control overhead (bitmap exchange) and latency (which is now proportional to the *product* of buffer map size and overlay diameter).

7.4 Web Content Delivery Networks

Resource provisioning is a fundamental challenge for Internet content providers. Too much provision and the infrastructure will simply depreciate without generating return on investment; too little provision and the web site may lose business and potentially steer users to competitors.

A *content delivery network* (CDN) offers a service to content providers that helps address this challenge. A typical CDN provider deploys a number of CDN servers around the globe and uses them as a shared resource to deliver content from multiple content providers that subscribe to the CDN's service. The CDN servers are also known as *edge servers* because they are often located at the edges of the networks in which they are deployed. Content delivery networks represent a type of overlay network because they route content between the origin sites and the clients through edge servers.

A CDN improves resiliency and performance of subscribing web sites in several ways.

- As already mentioned in Section 7.1.1, a CDN can reuse capacity slack to absorb demand peaks for different content providers at different times. By sharing a large slack across a diverse pool of content providers, CDNs improve resiliency of the subscribing web sites to flash crowds.

- A CDN promises a degree of protection against denial of service attacks because the enormous capacity the attacker would need to saturate to exert any noticeable performance degradation.
- A CDN improves the performance of content delivery under normal load because it can process client requests from a nearby edge server.

CDNs are used to deliver a variety of content, including static web objects, software packages, multimedia files, and streaming content – both video-on-demand and live. For video-on-demand, edge servers deliver streams to viewers from their cached files; typically, these files are pre-loaded to the edge server caches from origin sites as they become available. However, if a requested file is not cached, the edge server will typically obtain the stream from the origin and forward it to the viewer, while also storing the content locally for future requests. In the case of live streaming ("Webcasts"), content flows form a distribution tree, with viewers as leaves, edge servers as intermediate nodes, and the origin as the root. Often, however, CDN servers form deeper trees. In either case, Webcast delivery through a CDN can benefit from various tree-based approaches to streaming media systems such as those discussed in Section 7.3. In the rest of this section, we will limit our discussion to how CDNs deliver static files, including static web objects, software packages, multimedia files, etc.

7.4.1 CDN Basics

A CDN must interpose its infrastructure transparently between the content provider and the user. Furthermore, unlike P2P networks where users run specialized peer software, a CDN must serve clients using standard web browsers. Thus, a fundamental building block in a CDN is a mechanism to transparently reroute user requests from the content provider's site (known as the "origin size" in the CDN parlance) to the CDN platform. The two main techniques that have been used for this purpose are *DNS outsourcing* and *URL rewriting*. Both techniques rely on the domain name system (DNS), which maps human-readable names, such as www.firm-x.com, to numeric Internet protocol (IP) addresses. A browser's HTTP request is preceded by a DNS query to resolve the host name from the URL. The DNS queries are sent by browsers' *local DNS servers* (LDNS) and processed by the web sites' authoritative DNS servers (ADNS).

In URL rewriting, a content provider rewrites its web pages so that embedded links use host names belonging to the CDN domain. For example, if a page www.firm-x.com contains an image picture.jpg that should be delivered by the CDN, the image URL would be rewritten to a form such as http://images.firm-x.com.cdn-foo.net/real.firm-x.com/picture.jpg. In this case, the DNS query for images.firm-x.com.cdn-foo.net would arrive to CDN's DNS server in a normal way, without redirection from firm-x.com's ADNS. Note that URL rewriting only works for embedded and hyperlinked content. The container pages (i.e., the entry points to the web sites) would have to be delivered from the origin site directly.

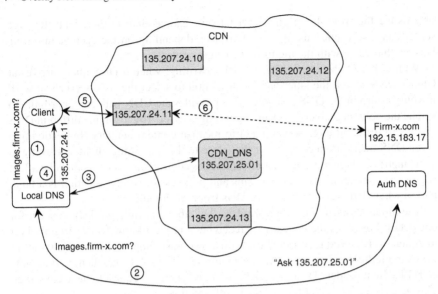

Fig. 7.7 A high-level view of a CDN architecture

DNS outsourcing refers to techniques that exploit mechanisms in the DNS protocol that allow a query to be redirected from one DNS server to another. Beside responses containing IP addresses, the DNS protocol allows two response types that can be used for redirection. An *NS-type* response specifies a different DNS server that should be contacted to resolve the query. A *CNAME-type* response specifies a *canonical name*, a different host name that should be used instead of the name contained in the original query. Either response type can be used to implement DNS outsourcing.

Figure 7.7 depicts a high-level architecture of a CDN utilizing DNS outsourcing. Consider a content provider – firm-x.com in the example – that subscribes to CDN services to deliver its content from the images.firm-x.com subdomain. (Content from other subdomains, such as www.firm-x.com might be delivered independently, perhaps by the provider's origin server itself.)

When a client wants to access a URL with this hostname, it first needs to resolve this hostname into the IP address of the server. To this end, it sends a DNS query to its LDNS (step 1), which ultimately sends it to the ADNS server for firm-x.com (step 2). ADNS now engages the CDN by redirecting LDNS's query to the DNS server operated by the CDN provider (CDN_DNS in the figure). ADNS does it by returning, in the exchange of step 2, an NS record specifying CDN_DNS. LDNS now sends the query for images.firm-x.com to CDN_DNS, which can now choose an appropriate edge server and return its IP address to LDNS (step 3). The LDNS server forwards the response to the client (step 4), which now downloads the file from the specified server (step 5). When the request arrives at the edge server, the server may or may not have the requested file in its local cache. If it does not, it obtains the file from the origin server (step 6) and sends it to the client; the edge server can also cache this file for future use, depending on the cache-controlling headers that came with the file from the origin server.

With either DNS outsourcing or URL rewriting, when a DNS query arrives at CDN's DNS server, the latter has the discretion to select the edge server whose IP it would return in the DNS response. This provides the CDN with an opportunity to spread the content delivery load among its edge servers (by resolving different DNS queries to different edge servers) and to localize content delivery (by resolving a given DNS query to an edge server that close to the requesting client, according to some metric). There are a number of sometimes contradicting factors that can affect edge server selection. The mechanisms and policies for server selection is a large part of what distinguishes different CDNs from one another.

The much-simplified architecture described above is fully workable except for one detail: how does the edge server receiving a request know which origin server to contact for the requested file? CDNs use two basic approaches to this issue. In the example of Fig. 7.7, assuming the client uses HTTP 1.1, the client will include an HTTP Host header "Host:images.firm-x.com" with its request to the edge server. This gives the edge server the necessary information.

Another approach, which does not rely on the host header, involves embedding provider identity into the path portion of the URL. This technique is used in particular with URL rewriting. For example, with the above URL http://images.firm-x.com.cdn-foo.net/real.firm-x.com/picture.jpg, the client's request to the edge serve will be for file "real.firm-x.com/picture.jpg", providing edge server with the information about the origin server.

7.4.2 Bag of DNS Tricks

Looking at Fig. 7.7, an immediate concern with this architecture is the CDN_DNS server. First, it is a centralized component that can become the bottleneck in the system. Second, it undermines localized data delivery to some degree because all DNS queries must travel to this centralized component no matter where they come from. These issues are exacerbated by the fact that, in order to retain fine-grained control over edge server selection, CDN_DNS must limit the amount of time its responses can be cached and reused by clients. It does so by assigning a low *time-to-live* (TTL) value to its responses, a standard DNS protocol feature for controlling response caching. This increases the volume of DNS queries that CDN_DNS must handle.

Moderate-sized CDNs sometimes disregard these concerns because DNS queries usually take little processing, with a single server capable of handling several thousand queries per second. With additional consideration that DNS server load is easily distributed in a server cluster, the centralized DNS resolution can handle large amounts of load before becoming the bottleneck in practice. Furthermore, the overhead of nonlocalized DNS processing only becomes noticeable in practice for delivering small files. For large file downloads, such as software packages or multimedia files, a few hundred millisecond of initial delay will be negligible compared to several minutes of the download itself.

Large CDNs, however, deal with extraordinary total loads and provide content delivery services for all file sizes. Thus, they implement their DNS service as a distributed system in its own right.

One approach to implement a distributed DNS service again utilizes DNS redirection mechanisms. For example, the Akamai CDN [1] implements a two-level DNS system. The top-level DNS server is a centralized component and is registered as the authoritative DNS server for the accelerated content. Thus, initial DNS queries arrive at this server. The top-level DNS server responds to queries with an NS-type response, redirecting the requester to a nearby low-level DNS server. Moreover, these redirecting responses are given a long TTL, in effect pinning the requester to the selected low-level DNS server. The actual name resolution occurs at the low-level DNS servers. Because most DNS interactions occur between clients and low-level CDN-DNS servers, the DNS load is distributed and the interactions are localized in the network.

Another approach uses a flat DNS system, and utilizes *IP anycast* to spread the load among them. A CDN using this approach deploys a number of CDN-DNS servers in different Internet locations but assigns them the same IP address. Then, it relies on the underlying IP routing infrastructure to deliver clients' DNS queries destined to this IP address to the closest CDN-DNS server. In this way, DNS processing load is both distributed and localized among the flat collection of DNS servers. The Limelight CDN [35] utilizes this technique.

Beside DNS service scalability, Limelight further leverages the above technique to sidestep the decision about which of the data centers would be the closest to the client. In particular, Limelight deploys a DNS server in every data center; then each given request will be delivered by the anycast mechanism to its closest data center. The DNS server receiving a request then simply picks one of the edge servers co-located in the same data center for the subsequent download. This approach, however, is not without drawbacks. One limitation is that it relies exclusively on the proximity notion reflected in Internet routing; there are other considerations, such as network congestion and costs. Another limitation is due to the originator problem discussed in the next subsection.

7.4.3 Issues

The basic idea behind CDNs might seem simple, but many technical challenges lurk. An obvious challenge is server selection, which is an open-ended issue. There are a number of factors that may affect the selection.

A basic factor is proximity: one of the key promises of CDN technology is that they can deliver content from a nearby network location. But what does "nearby" mean? To start with, there are a number of proximity metrics one could use, which differ in how closely they correlate with end-to-end performance and how hard they are to obtain. Geographical distance, autonomous system hops, and router hops, could be used as relatively static proximity metrics. Static metrics may incorporate domain knowledge, such as maps of private peering points among network providers, since private peering points can be more reliable than public network access points. Then, one could consider dynamic path characteristics, such as packet loss, network packet travel delay (one-way or round-trip), and available path bandwidth. Obtaining these dynamic metrics and keeping them fresh is much more challenging. Further, a CDN may account for economic factors, such as the preference of utilizing certain network carriers even at the expense of a slight performance degradation.

Once the proximity metrics are figured out, the next question is how to combine them with server load metrics, since in the end we need to pick a certain edge server for a given request. Server loads are inherently dynamic. They raise a number of questions of their own, with their own research literature. How long a history of past data to consider, and which load characteristics to measure? One can consider a variety of characteristics, including CPU usage, network utilization, memory, and disk IO. How frequently to collect load measurements, and how frequently to recompute load metrics? How to avoid a "herd effect" [19], where a CDN sends too much the demand to an underloaded server, only to overload it in the next cycle?

The next set of questions is architectural in nature. As we discussed earlier, the prevalent mechanism in CDNs for routing requests to a selected edge server is based on DNS. DNS-based routing raises so-called originator and hidden load problems [49].

The originator problem is due to the fact that CDN proximity-based server selection can only be done relative to the originator of the DNS query, which is the client's DNS server, and not the actual host that will be downloading the content. Thus, the quality of any proximity-based server selection is limited by how close the actual client is to the LDNS it is using. While there has been some work on determining the distance between clients and their LDNSs [42, 57], the end-to-end effect of this issue on user-perceived performance is not yet fully known.

One way to sidestep the originator problem is to utilize IP anycast for the HTTP interaction [2]. Similar to anycast-based DNS interactions considered previously, different edge servers in this case would advertise the same IP address. This address would be returned to the clients by CDN_DNS, and packets from a given browser machine would be delivered to the closest edge server naturally thanks to IP routing. Anycast was previously considered unsuitable for HTTP downloads for two reasons. First, unlike DNS that uses the UDP transport protocol by default, HTTP runs on top of TCP. TCP is a stateful connection-oriented protocol, and if a routing path changes in the middle of the ongoing download, the edge server browser may attempt to continue the download from a different edge server, leading to a broken TCP connection. Second, IP anycast selects among end-points for packet delivery without consideration for the routing path quality or end-point load. However, recent insights into the anycast behavior [7] and network traffic engineering [63] alleviate these concerns, especially when a CDN is deployed within one autonomous system. ICDS – a CDN service by AT&T [5] – is currently pursuing a variant of this approach.

The hidden load problem arises because of drastically different number of clients behind different LDNS servers. A large ISP likely has thousands of clients sharing the same LDNS. Then, a single DNS query from this LDNS can result in a large amount of demand for the selected edge server. At the same time, a single query from the LDNS of a small academic department will impose much smaller load. Because a CDN distributes load at the granularity of DNS queries, potentially drastic and unknown imbalances of load resulting from single queries complicate proper load balancing.

Another architectural issue relates to the large number of edge servers a CDN maintains. When new popular content appears and generates a large number of requests, these requests will initially miss in the edge server caches and will be forwarded to the origin server. These missed requests may overload the origin server in the beginning of a flash crowd, until edge servers populate their caches [27]. CDNs often pre-load new content to the edge servers when the content is known to be popular. However, unpredictable flash crowds present a danger. Consequently, CDNs sometimes deploy peer-to-peer cooperation among their edge servers, with edge servers forwarding missed requests to each other rather than directly to the origin server. This gives rise to more complex overlay network topologies than the one-hop overlay routing in the basic CDN architecture described here. In fact, the underlying mechanisms can be even more complex: the complex overlay topologies add overhead due to application-level processing at each hop. Thus, one could try to use simple one-hop topology under normal load and add more complex request routing dynamically once the danger of a "miss storm" is detected. This in turn opens a range of interesting algorithmic questions involved in deciding when to start forming a complex topology and how to form it.

This overview is necessarily brief. Its goal is only to convey the fact that content delivery networks represent an important aspect of Internet infrastructure and a rich environment for research and innovation. We refer the reader to more targeted literature, such as [24, 49, 64]

7.5 Attack-Resilient Services

We have seen that overlay systems provide resilience by design: the lack of centralized entities naturally provides a measure of resilience against component failures. Overlay systems can also form the building block for systems that are resilient to malicious attack. SOS [28] and a subsequent derivative, Mayday [3], are the two overlay systems that provide denial-of-service protection for Internet services. We discuss SOS next.

7.5.1 Case Study: Secure Overlay Service (SOS)

Secure Overlay Services (SOS) is an overlay network designed to protect a server (the target) from distributed denial of service attacks.

SOS enables a "confirmed" user to communicate with the protected service. Conceptually, the service is protected by a "ring" of SOS overlay nodes, which are able to confirm incoming requests as valid. Once a request is validated, it is forwarded on to the service. Users, by themselves, are not able to directly communicate with the service (initially); in fact, the protected server's address may be hidden or changing.

SOS forms a distributed firewall around the target server. The server advertises the SOS overlay nodes (called Service Overlay Access Points [SOAPs])) as its initial point of contact. Users initiate contact to the server by connecting to one of the SOS overlay nodes. Malicious users may attack overlay nodes, but by assumption are not able to bring down the entire overlay.

The server's ISP filters all packets to the server's address, except for a chosen few (who are allowed to traverse this firewall). These privileged nodes are called "secret servlets". Secret servlets designate a few SOAP nodes (called Beacons) as the rendezvous point between themselves and incoming connections. Regular SOAP nodes use an overlay routing protocol (such as Chord) to route authenticated requests to the Beacons.

Beacons know of and forward requests to the secret servlets. Only secret servlets are allowed through the ISP firewall around the target, and the servlets finally forward the authenticated request to the protected server.

7.6 File-Sharing Peer-to-Peer Networks

Consider the task of distributing a large file (e.g., in the order of hundreds of MB) to a large number of users. We already discussed one overlay approach – CDNs – targeting such an application. However, the CDN approach requires the source of the file to subscribe to CDN services (and pay the resultant service fees). Furthermore, this approach requires a CDN company to be vigilant in provisioning enough resources to keep up with the potential scale of downloads involved.

Peer-to-peer networks provide an appealing alternative, which organizes users themselves into an overlay distribution platform. This approach is appealing to content providers because it does not require a CDN subscription. It also scales naturally with the popularity of a download: the more users are downloading a file, the more resources take part in the overlay distribution network adding the capacity to the delivery platform. Some peer-to-peer networks also provide administrative resiliency, as they have no special centralized administrative component. In fact, the utilization of the client upload bandwidth and CPU capacity in content delivery can also make P2P techniques interesting as an adjunct (rather than an alternative) to a CDN service.

In this section, we will concentrate on unique challenges that arise when the P2P system downloads a large (e.g., on the order of 100s of MB) file. In particular, we will consider the following two challenges:

- *Block Distribution*   Imagine a flash crowd downloading a 100 MB software package. A naive approach (pursued by early P2P networks) would let each peer download the entire file and then make itself available as a source of this file for other peers. This approach, however, would not be able to sustain a flash crowd. Indeed, each peer would take a long time – tens of minutes over a typical residential broadband connection – to download this file and in the meantime the initial file source would have no help in coping with the demand. The solution is to chop the file into blocks and distribute different blocks to different peers, so that they can start using each other faster for block distribution. But this creates an interesting challenge. Obviously, the system needs to make a diverse set of blocks available as quickly as possible, so that each peer has a better chance of finding another peer from which to obtain missing blocks. But achieving this diversity is difficult when no peer possesses global knowledge about block distribution at any point in time.
- *Free Riders*   A particularly widespread phenomenon is that of selfish peers: peers that attempt to make use of the peer content delivery without contributing their own resources. These peers are called "free riders". More generally, a peer may try to bypass fairness mechanisms in the P2P network and obtain more than its share of resources, thus getting better service at the expense of other users.

We will consider these two challenges in the context of the mesh model of content distribution. Using the terminology of BitTorrent – a popular P2P network – the key components of a mesh P2P network are seeds, trackers, and peers (or leechers). Originally the file exists at the source server (or servers) called *seeds*. There is a special *tracker* node that keeps track of at least some subset of the peers who are in the process of downloading the file. A new peer joins the download (a *swarm*) by contacting the tracker, obtaining a random subset of existing peers, and establishing P2P connections (i.e., overlay network links) with them. The download makes collective progress by peers exchanging missing blocks along the overlay edges. Having completed the download, a peer may stay in the swarm as a seed, uploading without downloading anything more in return.

7.6.1 Block Distribution Problem

BitTorrent attempts to achieve a uniform distribution of blocks (or "pieces": a set of blocks in BitTorrent) among the peers through localized decisions. Neighboring peers exchange lists of blocks that they already have. A peer determines which of the blocks it is missing are the rarest in its local neighborhood and requests these blocks first. Because the neighborhoods in the BitTorrent protocol evolve over time, the rarest-first block distribution leads to more uniform distribution of blocks in the network and to better chance of a peer finding a useful block without contacting the source.

Recently, an ingenious alternative to the BitTorrent protocol has been proposed, which *removes* the issue of choosing the blocks completely [21]. This new approach, called Avalanche, follows the same mesh model with seeds, trackers, and peers, as BitTorrent. However, Avalanche makes virtually every block useful to any peer through *network coding* as follows.

Peers no longer choose a single, original block to download from their neighbors at a time. Instead, every time a peer uploads a block to a neighbor, it simply computes a linear combination of all the blocks it currently has from a given file using random coefficients, and uploads the result along with auxiliary information, derived from the coefficients it used and those previously received with its own downloaded blocks. Once a peer collects enough encoded blocks (usually the same number as the number of blocks in the file), it can reconstruct the original file by solving a system of linear equations. A system implementing these ideas has been publicly available as Microsoft Secure Content Downloader since 2007, although the original author of BitTorrent raised questions about the importance of the removal of the block distribution problem in practice and the possible performance overhead involved [17]. These concerns have been reflected in recent empirical studies demonstrating that BitTorrent's rarest-first piece selection strategy effectively provides block uniformity [30].

7.6.2 Free Riders Problem: Upload Incentives

To improve its resiliency to free riding, BitTorrent utilizes an incentives mechanism. The goal of this mechanism is to ensure that peers who contribute more to content upload receive better download service. Just like its approach to block distribution problem, BitTorrent implements its incentives mechanism largely through localized decisions by each peer using a round-based *unchoking* algorithm to decide how much to send to its neighbors.

When a peer learns a set of other peers from the file's tracker (usually around 30–50), the peer starts by establishing connections to these peers, some of which will agree to send blocks to the peer. At the end of every unchoking round (10 s in most BitTorrent clients), the peer decides which of the peers it should upload blocks to in the next round. To this end, the peer considers the throughput of its download from the peers in the previous round and selects a small number (four in Azureus, a popular BitTorrent client implementation) of peers to which it will upload blocks in the next round. Selecting a peer for uploading is called "unchoking" a peer. In addition to unchoking the top four peers who have given in the past, a peer also unchokes another peer at random in each round. This helps the peer to bootstrap new peers, to discover potentially higher-performing peers, and to ensure that every peer, even with poor connectivity, makes some progress; without this "optimistic unchoking," these impoverished peers would end up choked by everybody. Except for optimistic unchoking, a peer only uploads to other peers if they have blocks that it does not. If two peers have blocks that the other lacks, the peers are said to be *interested* in one another.

This protocol works because a free rider will end up being choked by most of its neighbors, only relying on random unchokes to make any progress. However, recent work [48] has found that the BitTorrent protocol penalizes high-capacity peers: as the upload performance of a peer increases, its download performance grows but less than proportionally to the upload contribution. In other words, the protocol is not entirely tit-for-tat in a usual sense of the word.

Consequently, a new BitTorrent client called BitTyrant has been implemented that improves the download performance of high-capacity peers [48]. BitTyrant achieves this goal by exploiting the following observation. Regular BitTorrent peers allocate their upload capacity equally among their unchoked neighbors. Because of this, a strategic peer does not need to upload to regular peers at its maximum capacity: it only needs to upload faster than most of its peers' other neighbors, so that its peers would keep it unchoked.

Thus, the key idea behind the BitTyrant client is to keep an estimate of the individual upload rates to its neighbors that is sufficient to stay in the neighbors' unchoked set most of the time, and to upload to each neighbor at just that rate. Then, BitTyrant uses the spared upload capacity to unchoke more peers and hence to increase its download performance. Furthermore, the BitTyrant client selects only the peers with the highest return-on-investment: those peers whose data capacity can be obtained "cheaply." The authors of BitTyrant observed significant reduction in file download times by their modified client. However, if *all* clients adopted selfish BitTyrant behavior with cut-off of expensive peers as mentioned above, the overall performance for all clients would decrease, especially for low-capacity clients. Thus, while discouraging free riding, BitTorrent still relies on altruistic contribution of high-capacity peers to achieve its performance.

Although BitTorrent's unchoking algorithm of giving to the top-four contributors has been broadly described as being tit-for-tat, recent work has shown that it is more accurately represented as an auction [32]. Each unchoking round can be viewed as an auction, where the "bids" are other peers' uploads in previous rounds, and the "good" being auctioned is the peer's upload bandwidth. Viewed this way, BitTyrant's strategy of "coming in the last (winning) place" is easily seen as the clear winning strategy. Also by reframing BitTorrent as an auction, a solution to strategic attempts like BitTyrant arises: change the way peers "clear" their auction.

A new client has been introduced that replaces BitTorrent's top-four strategy with a *proportional share* response. Proportional share is a simple strategy: if a peer has given some fraction, say 10%, of all of the blocks you received in the previous round, then allot to that peer the same fraction, 10%, of your upload bandwidth. Note that this does not necessarily result in peers providing the same *number* of blocks in return, rather the same *fraction* of bandwidth. This results in what turns out to be a very robust form of fairness: the more a peer gives, the more that peer gets. Even highly provisioned peers therefore have incentive to contribute as much of their bandwidth as possible. The authors of this PropShare client have demonstrated that proportional share is resilient to a wide array of strategic manipulation. Further, PropShare outperforms BitTorrent and BitTyrant, and as more users adopt the PropShare client, the overall performance of the system improves. This work demonstrates the importance of an accurate model of incentives in a complex system such as BitTorrent.

A strategic peer can achieve higher download performance by manipulating the list of blocks it announces to its neighbor [32]. Suppose node p in a BitTorrent swarm possesses some rare blocks. Since p has rare blocks, it is going to be *interesting* to many of its neighbors, who will all want to upload blocks to p in exchange for these rare blocks. However, once p announces these blocks, p's neighbors will download these blocks from p and exchange them amongst themselves. Node p can sustain interest amongst its neighbors longer by *under-reporting* its block map, in particular, by strategically revealing the rare blocks one by one. This strategy guarantees p remains interested for longer since p's neighbors, who all get the same rare block from p, cannot benefit by exchanging amongst themselves.

This observation suggests a general under-reporting strategy. A node can remain interesting to its neighbors longest by announcing only the blocks *necessary* to maintain interest but no more. Similar to an all-BitTyrant strategy, when all peers strategically under-report their blocks in this manner [32], the overall performance of the system degrades.

In general, BitTorrent's incentives mechanisms have come under intense scrutiny. Through rich empirical studies and analyses that incorporate various economic principles, BitTorrent continues to grow more robust to cheating clients. Whether a system as complex as BitTorrent can be made fully robust to such users remains open.

7.7 Conclusion

This chapter considers ways by which overlays-based techniques improve application resiliency. We have described how applications can utilize overlay networks to better cope with challenges such as flash crowds, the need to scale to often unpredictable loads, network failures and congestion, and denial of service attacks. We have considered a representative sample of these applications, focusing on their use of overlay network concepts. This sample included distributed hash tables, network storage, large file distribution by peer-to-peer networks, streaming content delivery, content delivery networks, and web services. It is simply not feasible to comprehensively cover overlay applications and research within one chapter. Instead, we hope that this chapter conveys sufficient information to give the reader a sampling of the various application domains where overlays are useful, and a sense for the flexibility that overlay networks provide to an application designer.

Acknowledgments The authors thank Katrina LaCurts, Dave Levin, and Adam Bender for their comments on this chapter. The authors are grateful to the editors, Chuck Kalmanek and Richard Yang, for their comments and encouragement.

References

1. Akamai Technologies. Retrieved from http://www.akamai.com/html/technology/index.html
2. Alzoubi, H. A., Lee, S., Rabinovich, M., Spatscheck, O., & Van der Merwe, J. (2008). Anycast cdns revisited. In *Proceedings of WWW '08* (pp. 277–286). New York, NY: ACM. DOI http://doi.acm.org/10.1145/1367497.1367536
3. Andersen, D. G. (2003). Mayday: Distributed filtering for Internet services. In *USITS*.
4. Andersen, D. G., Balakrishnan, H., Kaashoek, M. F., & Morris, R. (2001). Resilient overlay networks. In *Proceedings of 18th ACM SOSP*, Banff, Canada.
5. ATT ICDS: Retrieved from http://www.business.att.com/service_fam_overview.j-sp?serv_fam=eb_intelligent_content_distribution
6. Balakrishnan, H., Lakshminarayanan, K., Ratnasamy, S., Shenker, S., Stoica, I., & Walfish, M. (2004). A layered naming architecture for the Internet. In *Proceedings of the ACM SIGCOMM*, Portland, OR.
7. Ballani, H., Francis, P., & Ratnasamy, S. (2006). A measurement-based deployment proposal for IP anycast. In *Proceedings of the ACM IMC*, Rio de Janeiro, Brazil.
8. Banerjee, S., Bhattacharjee, B., & Kommareddy, C. (2002). Scalable application layer multicast. In *Proceedings of ACM SIGCOMM*, Pittsburg, PA.
9. Banerjee, S., Lee, S., Bhattacharjee, B., & Srinivasan, A. (2003). Resilient multicast using overlays. In *Proceedings of the Sigmetrics 2003*, Karlsruhe, Germany.
10. Banerjee, S., Lee, S., Bhattacharjee, B., & Srinivasan, A. (2006). Resilient overlays using multicast. *IEEE/ACM Transactions of Networking, 14*(2), 237–248.
11. Bender, A., Sherwood, R., Monner, D., Goergen, N., Spring, N., & Bhattacharjee, B. (2009). Fighting spam with the NeighborhoodWatch DHT. In *INFOCOM*.
12. Castro, M., Druschel, P., Ganesh, A. J., Rowstron, A. I. T., & Wallach, D. S. (2002). Secure routing for structured peer-to-peer overlay networks. In *OSDI*.
13. Castro, M., Druschel, P., Kermarrec, A., Nandi, A., Rowstron, A., & Singh, A. (2003). Splitstream: High-bandwidth multicast in a cooperative environment. In *Proceedings of the 19th ACM Symposium on Operating Systems Principles (SOSP 2003)*, Lake Bolton, NY.
14. Castro, M., Druschel, P., Kermarrec, A. M., & Rowstron, A. (2002). Scribe: A large-scale and decentralized application-level multicast infrastructure. *IEEE Journal on Selected Areas in Communication, 20*(8), 1489–1499. DOI 10.1109/JSAC.2002.803069
15. Chu, Y., Ganjam, A., Ng, T., Rao, S., Sripanidkulchai, K., Zhan, J., & Zhang, H. (2004). Early experience with an Internet broadcast system based on overlay multicast. In *Proceedings of USENIX Annual Technical Conference*, Boston, MA.
16. Chun, B., Culler, D., Roscoe, T., Bavier, A., Peterson, L., Wawrzoniak, M., & Bowman, M. (2003). Planetlab: An overlay testbed for broad-coverage services. *SIGCOMM Computer Communication Review, 33*(3), 3–12.
17. Cohen, B. Avalanche. Retrieved from http://bramcohen.livejournal.com/20140.html
18. Dabek, F., Kaashoek, M. F., Karger, D. R., Morris, R., & Stoica, I. (2001). Wide-area cooperative storage with cfs. In *SOSP* (pp. 202–215).
19. Dahlin, M. (2000). Interpreting stale load information. *IEEE Transactions on Parallel and Distributed Systems, 11*(10), 1033–1047.
20. Fiat, A., Saia, J., & Young, M. (2005). Making chord robust to Byzantine attacks. In *ESA*.
21. Gkantsidis, C., & Rodriguez, P. (2005). Network coding for large scale content distribution. In *INFOCOM* (pp. 2235–2245).

22. Gopalakrishnan, V., Bhattacharjee, B., Ramakrishnan, K. K., Jana, R., & Srivastava, D. (2009). Cpm: Adaptive video-on-demand with cooperative peer assists and multicast. In *Proceedings of INFOCOM*, Rio De Janeiro, Brazil.

23. Gupta, I., Birman, K. P., Linga, P., Demers, A. J., & van Renesse, R. (2003). Kelips: Building an efficient and stable p2p dht through increased memory and background overhead. In *IPTPS* (pp. 160–169).

24. Hofmann, M., & Beaumont, L. R. (2005). *Content networking: Architecture, protocols, and practice.* San Francisco, CA: Morgan Kaufmann.

25. Iyer, S., Rowstron, A. I. T., & Druschel, P. (2002). Squirrel: A decentralized peer-to-peer web cache. In *PODC* (pp. 213–222).

26. Jannotti, J., Gifford, D., Johnson, K. L., Kaashoek, M. F., & Jr., J. W. O. (2000). Overcast: reliable multicasting with an overlay network. In *Proceedings of the Fourth Symposium on Operating System Design and Implementation (OSDI)*, San Diego, CA.

27. Jung, J., Krishnamurthy, B., & Rabinovich, M. (2002). Flash crowds and denial of service attacks: Characterization and implications for cdns and web sites. In *WWW* (pp. 293–304).

28. Keromytis, A. D., Misra, V., & Rubenstein, D. (2002). SOS: Secure overlay services. In *SIGCOMM*.

29. Kostic, D., Rodriguez, A., Albrecht, J., & Vahdat, A. (2003). Bullet: High bandwidth data dissemination using an overlay mesh. In *Proceedings of SOSP* (pp. 282-297), Lake George, NY.

30. Legout, A., Urvoy-Keller, G., & Michiardi, P. (2006). Rarest first and choke algorithms are enough. In *IMC*.

31. Lemos, R.: Blue security folds under spammer's wrath. http://www.securityfocus.com/news/11392

32. Levin, D., LaCurts, K., Spring, N., & Bhattacharjee, B. (2008). Bittorrent is an auction: Analyzing and improving bittorrent's incentives. In *SIGCOMM* (pp. 243–254).

33. Li, B., Xie, S., Qu, Y., Keung, G., Lin, C., Liu, J., & Zhang, X. (2008). Inside the new coolstreaming: Principles, measurements and performance implications. In *Proceedings of the INFOCOM 2008*, Phoenix, AZ (pp. 1031–1039).

34. Li, B., Yik, K., Xie, S., Liu, J., Stoica, I., Zhang, H., & Zhang, X. (2007). Empirical study of the coolstreaming system. *Proceedings of the IEEE Journal on Selected Areas in Communication* (Special Issues on Advance in Peer-to-Peer Streaming Systems), 25(9), 1627-1639.

35. http://www.limelightnetworks.com/network.htm

36. Linga, P., Gupta, I., & Birman, K. (2003). A churn-resistant peer-to-peer web caching system. In *2003 ACM Workshop on Survivable and Self-Regenerative Systems* (pp. 1–10).

37. Locher, T., Meier, R., Schmid, S., & Wattenhofer, R. (2007). Push-to-pull peer-to-peer live streaming. In *Proceedings of the International Symposium of Distributed Computing*, Lemesos, Cyprus.

38. Lumezanu, C., Baden, R., Levin, D., Spring, N., & Bhattacharjee, B. (2009). Symbiotic relationships in internet routing overlays. In *Proceedings of NSDI*, Boston, MA.

39. Magharei, N., & Rejaie, R. (2007). PRIME: Peer-to-peer receiver-drIven MEsh-based streaming. In *Proceedings of the INFOCOM 2007*, Anchorage, Alaska (pp. 1424–1432).

40. Magharei, N., Rejaie, R., & Guo, Y. (2007). Mesh or multiple-tree: A comparative study of live p2p streaming approaches. In *Proceedings of the INFOCOM 2007*, Anchorage, Alaska.

41. Malkhi, D., Naor, M., & Ratajczak, D. (2002). Viceroy: A scalable and dynamic emulation of the butterfly. In *PODC* (pp. 183–192).

42. Mao, Z. M., Cranor, C. D., Douglis, F., Rabinovich, M., Spatscheck, O., & Wang, J. (2002). A precise and efficient evaluation of the proximity between web clients and their local dns servers. In *USENIX Annual Technical Conference* (pp. 229–242).

43. Morselli, R., Bhattacharjee, B., Marsh, M. A., & Srinivasan, A. (2007). Efficient Lookup on Unstructured Topologies. *IEEE Journal on Selected Areas in Communications*, 25(1), 62–72.

44. Nakao, A., Peterson, L., & Bavier, A. (2006). Scalable routing overlay networks. *SIGOPS Operating Systems Review*, 40(1), 49–61.

45. Padmanabhan, V., Wang, H., Chou, P., & Sripanidkulchai, K. (2002). Distributing streaming media content using cooperative networking. In *NOSSDAV*, Miami Beach, FL, USA.

46. Pai, V., Kumar, K., Tamilmani, K., Sambamurthy, V., & Mohr, A. (2005). Chainsaw: Eliminating trees from overlay multicast. In *IPTPS 2005*, Ithaca, NY, USA.

47. Painese, F., Perino, D., Keller, J., & Biersack, E. (2007). PULSE: An adaptive, incentive-based, unstructured p2p live streaming system. IEEE Trans. on Multimedia 9(8), 1645–1660.

48. Piatek, M., Isdal, T., Anderson, T. E., Krishnamurthy, A., & Venkataramani, A. (2007). Do incentives build robustness in bittorrent? (awarded best student paper). In *NSDI*.

49. Rabinovich, M., & Spatscheck, O. (2001). Web caching and replication. Reading, MA: Addison-Wesley, Longman Publishing Co., Inc. Boston, MA, USA.

50. Ramasubramanian, V., & Sirer, E. G. (2004). Beehive: O(1) lookup performance for power-law query distributions in peer-to-peer overlays. In *NSDI* (pp. 99–112).

51. Ratnasamy, S., Francis, P., Handley, M., Karp, R., & Shenker, S. (2001). A scalable content-addressable network. In *SIGCOMM*.

52. Rhea, S., Geels, D., Roscoe, T., & Kubiatowicz, J. (2004). Handling churn in a dht. In *USENIX Annual Technical Conference*.

53. Rhea, S. C., Godfrey, B., Karp, B., Kubiatowicz, J., Ratnasamy, S., Shenker, S., Stoica, I., & Yu, H. (2005). Opendht: A public dht service and its uses. In *SIGCOMM* (pp. 73–84).

54. Rowstron, A., & Druschel, P. (2001). Pastry: Scalable, distributed object location and routing for large-scale peer-to-peer systems. In *IFIP/ACM Middleware 2001*, Heidelberg, Germany.

55. Savage, S., Anderson, T., Aggarwal, A., Becker, D., Cardwell, N., Collins, A., Hoffman, E., Snell, J., Vahdat, A., Voelker, G., & Zahorjan, J. (1999). Detour: A case for informed internet routing and transport *IEEE Micro*, *19*(1), 50–59.

56. Savage, S., Collins, A., Hoffman, E., Snell, J., & Anderson, T. (1999). The end-to-end effects of Internet path selection. In *SIGCOMM*.

57. Shaikh, A., Tewari, R., & Agrawal, M. (2001). On the effectiveness of DNS-based server selection. In *Proceedings of IEEE Infocom*, Anchorage, Alaska.

58. Stoica, I., Adkins, D., Zhuang, S., Shenker, S., & Surana, S. (2002). Internet indirection infrastructure. In *SIGCOMM* (pp. 73–86).

59. Stoica, I., Morris, R., Karger, D. R., Kaashoek, M. F., & Balakrishnan, H. (2001). Chord: A scalable peer-to-peer lookup service for internet applications. In *SIGCOMM* (pp. 149–160).

60. Stoica, I., Morris, R., Liben-Nowell, D., Karger, D. R., Kaashoek, M. F., Dabek, F., & Balakrishnan, H. (2003). Chord: A scalable peer-to-peer lookup protocol for internet applications. IEEE/ACM Transactions on Networking, **11**(1), 17–32.

61. Tran, D., Hua, K., & Do, T. (2003). ZIGZAG: An efficient peer-to-peer scheme for media streaming. In *Proceedings of the INFOCOM 2003*, San Francisco, CA.

62. Venkataraman, V., Francis, P., & Calandrino, J. (2006). Chunkyspread: Multi-tree unstructured peer-to-peer multicast. In *Proceedings of the 1st International Workshop on Peer-to-Peer Systems (IPTPS '06)*, Santa Barbara, CA.

63. Verkaik, P., Pei, D., Scholl, T., Shaikh, A., Snoeren, A., & Van der Merwe, J. (2007). Wresting control from BGP: Scalable fine-grained route control. In *2007 USENIX Annual Technical Conference*.

64. Verma, D. C. (2001). *Content distribution networks: An engineering approach*. New York: Wiley.

65. Wang, F., Xiong, Y., & Liu, J. (2007). mTreebone: A hybrid tree/mesh overlay for application-layer live video multicast. In *Proceedings of the ICDCS 2007*, Toronto, Canada.

66. Wang, P., Hopper, N., Osipkov, I., & Kim, Y. (2006). Myrmic: Secure and robust DHT routing. Technical Report, University of Minnesota.

67. Yang, M., & Fei, Z. (2004). A proactive approach to reconstructing overlay multicast trees. In *Proceedings of the IEEE Infocom 2004*, Hong Kong.

68. Zhang, M., Luo, J., Zhao, L., & Yang, S. (2005). A peer-to-peer network for live media streaming – Using a push-pull approach. In *Proceedings of the ACM Multimedia*, Singapore.

69. Zhang, X., Liu, J., Li, B., & Yum, T. (2005). Donet: A data-driven overlay network for efficient live media streaming. In *Proceedings of the INFOCOM 2005*. Miami, FL.

Part IV
Configuration Management

Chapter 8
Network Configuration Management

Brian D. Freeman

8.1 Introduction

This chapter will discuss network configuration management by presenting a high-level view of the software systems that are involved in managing a large network of routers in support of carrier class services. It is meant to be an overview, highlighting the major areas that a network operator should assess while designing or buying a configuration management system, and not the final source of all information needed to build such a system.

When a service and its network are small, network configuration management is typically done manually by a knowledgeable technician with some form of workflow to get the data needed to perform their configuration tasks from the sales group. Inventory tracking may be handled by simply inserting comments into the interface description fields on the router and perhaps by maintaining some spreadsheets on a file server. The technician might or might not use an element management system (EMS) to do the configuration changes. If the network is new, for example, supporting the needs of a small company or the network needs of an "Internet startup," most of the configuration tasks represent a "new order." Configuration requests occur at low volume and the technician probably has a great deal of flexibility in how he or she goes about meeting the needs of the new network service.

As the number of users of the service grows, the expectations placed on the network operator to meet a certain level of reliability and performance grows accordingly. In time, because of growth in the sheer volume of orders, the single knowledgeable worker becomes a department, and "change orders" that modify the configuration associated with an existing customer of the network start becoming a larger and larger share of the effort. At this point, the network may contain multiple types of routers purchased from different vendors, each of which has different features and resource limits. Changes made to a router configuration to support one customer can now affect another customer. For example if one customer's

B.D. Freeman (✉)
AT&T Labs, Middletown, NJ, USA
e-mail: bdfreeman@att.com

C.R. Kalmanek et al. (eds.), *Guide to Reliable Internet Services and Applications*,
Computer Communications and Networks, DOI 10.1007/978-1-84882-828-5_8,
© Springer-Verlag London Limited 2010

configuration change causes a router resource such as table size to be exceeded, multiple customers might be affected. In addition, other departments or areas within the business now need data on the installed inventory to drive customer reporting, usage-based billing or ticketing, etc. Finally, as the volume grows, there is a need for automation or "flow through provisioning" to both reduce cost/time and protect against mistakes. The simple, manual approaches no longer work: an end-to-end view is needed for network configuration management so that all the pieces required to support the business can be integrated.

This chapter provides an overview of the elements of a robust network configuration management system. There are many goals for such a system, but the primary goal of any network configuration management system is to protect the network while providing the ordered service for the customers. Since changing the network configuration can cause outages if not done correctly, a key requirement of a network configuration management system is to ensure that the configuration changes do not destabilize the network. The system must provide the ordered service for the customer without affecting other customers, other ports associated with the customer being provisioned or the network at large.

The network configuration management system is also typically the primary source of data – the source of truth – used by many business systems and processes that surround the network. The functions that depend on configuration data are as mundane as trouble ticketing and spare part tracking, to more sophisticated capabilities like traffic reporting, for which the association of ports to customers must be obtained so that traffic reports can be properly displayed on the customer service portal.

Finally, the network configuration management system is the enforcer of the engineering rules that specify the maximum safe resources to be consumed on the routers for various features. As such, in addition to protecting the network, the system also impacts profitability, since inventory is either used efficiently or inefficiently. This depends on how good the configuration management system is at implementing the engineering rules as well as how good it is at processing service cancellation or disconnect requests in a timely fashion. If the configuration management system does not properly return a port that is no longer in service to the inventory available for new requests, expensive router hardware can be stranded indefinitely.

In summary, the primary goal of a network configuration management system is to manage router configurations to support customer service, subject to three key secondary goals:

- Protect the network
- Be the source of truth about the network
- Enforce the business and engineering rules

To explore this topic further, we will first review some key concepts to help structure the types of data items the system must deal with in Section 8.2. Section 8.3 describes the subcomponents of the system and the unique requirements of each subcomponent. This section also discusses the two approaches that are commonly used for router configuration – policy-based and template-based approaches – since this is a key aspect of the problem to be solved. Section 8.3 also touches on the differences between provider-edge (PE) and customer-edge (CE) router configuration tasks and the differences between consumer and enterprise IP router services in their typical approaches to configuration management. We present a brief overview of provisioning audits, which is discussed in more detail in Chapter 9. Provisioning audits are important to ensure that the network configuration management system stays as a good source of truth for the other systems and business processes that need data about the network. Finally, one of the key challenges in a large network is handling changes, ranging from an isolated change to a setting on an individual customer's interface, to more complex changes such as bulk changes to a large number of routers and interfaces. To illustrate these issues, Section 8.4 discusses the data model and process issues associated with moving a working connection from one configuration to the next. This section also touches on some typical network maintenance activities that impact a system in different ways than a customer provisioning focus. Section 8.5 shows a complete step by step example of provisioning a port order.

8.2   Key Concepts

There are two important types of data that a network configuration management system must handle: physical inventory data and logical inventory data. In addition to these data types, the system has to be designed to appropriately handle and resolve data discords between the state of the network ("What it is") and the view of the network that is contained in the network inventory database ("What it should be"). This section introduces these concepts.

8.2.1   Physical Inventory

The physical inventory database, as the name implies, contains the network hardware that is deployed in the field. The basic unit is usually a chassis with a set of components, including common elements like route processor cards or power supplies, and line cards with transport interfaces that support one or more customer "ports." These ports are what carry the customer-facing and backbone-facing traffic. Line cards that support multiple customer ports are often referred to as channelized interfaces (e.g. channelized T3 cards or channelized OC48 cards). The physical inventory database keeps track of whether the subchannels on these line cards are assigned to a customer with a state for each channel of "assigned" or "unassigned." The data model for physical inventory often reflects the physical world in which cards are contained in a chassis and a chassis is contained in a cabinet. Each customer port is associated with a subchannel on a physical interface.

8.2.2 Logical Inventory

The logical inventory database includes the inventory data that are not physical. This is a broad and less rigid category of information, since it includes multiple database entities with ephemeral ties to the physical inventory. An IP address is a good example of a database entity with an ephemeral tie. IP addresses exist on an interface, but we can move addresses to ports on another router; hence, an address is not permanently tied to a single piece of physical equipment. Many logical components are inventoried as database entities and assigned as needed by the carrier. IP addresses, VLAN tags, BGP community strings [1], and Autonomous System Numbers (ASNs) [2] are all examples of logical data that need to be tracked and managed. Generally, logical inventory assigned to a customer is associated with a particular piece of physical inventory. However, the association can change over time. A good example of a change in the association between physical and logical inventory occurs when a customer's connection is upgraded from a T1 to a T3. The physical inventory will change drastically but the logical inventory in terms of the IP address, BGP routing, and QoS settings may not change. It is also useful to understand that some logical inventory is associated with a single piece of equipment like an IP address while other logical inventory is "network wide" and is associated with multiple pieces of equipment like MPLS Route Distinguishers and Route Targets.

8.2.3 Discords: What It Is Versus What It Should Be?

Data discords are a fact of life in production systems. Through a variety of means, the data in the network and the data in the inventory system get out of synch. In plain language, a situation is created where the inventory view of the world, "what it should be," does not match with truth or the network view of the world, "what it is."

Both physical and logical inventory can contain discords. Generally, the physical inventory discords occur because of card replacements and initial installation errors that occur without a corresponding update of the database. For example, a discord would occur if a 4-port Ethernet card was replaced with an 8-port Ethernet card, but the database was not updated. Autodiscovery of hardware components can greatly assist in reducing the data discords in the physical inventory. Many production systems back up the router configuration daily and use commands from the vendor to collect detailed firmware and hardware data from the equipment. The command "show diag" dumps this kind of detailed information and the output can be saved to a file. Very accurate physical inventory information can be obtained by parsing the output of commands run on the router to obtain hardware information like the "show diag" command or various SNMP MIB queries. Automatic discovery of physical inventory can reduce the physical discords to zero. Many spare part tracking processes are dependent on the ability to automatically discover changes in serial numbers on components so that failure rates on cards can be tracked and replacement parts restocked as needed. Maintaining control on "What it is" is part of the physical inventory audit process.

Logical inventory discords also happen frequently but are harder to resolve. As an example, if a customer port that is running in the network has static routing and the inventory database indicates that it should be BGP routing, which is correct? Another example of logical inventory discord is the mismatch between the service that the customer currently has and the ordered service. In general, it is easier to detect logical inventory discords than to resolve them. Given their impacts on the external support processes and billing, detection, reporting, and correcting these situations is important.

Another key concept that the industry uses is that "the network is the database." This concept results from a desire by network operators to use the network configuration as ground truth to drive processes. Most equipment has some mechanism for querying for configuration data. However, practical matters require externally accessible views of those data. Fault management, for example, cannot query the network in real time on every SNMP trap that gets generated (this can be thousands per second); so a copy of the configuration data has to reside in a database and consequently a process/program to audit and synchronize that data with the network has to be part of the overall network configuration management system.

With these key concepts in mind, we will discuss the elements of a network configuration management system.

8.3   Elements of a Network Configuration Management System

Figure 8.1 provides a high-level view of the elements that make up a Network Configuration Management System. The external interfaces are to technicians and Operating Support Systems/Business Support Systems (OSS/BSS) on the top and the Network Elements at the bottom. Each of the major elements inside the system will be addressed in subsequent sections.

8.3.1   Inventory Database

A database of the physical and logical inventory is the core of the system. This database will consist of both the real assets purchased and deployed by the corporation (the physical inventory discussed in Section 8.2.1) and the logical assets that need to be tracked (e.g., WAN and LAN IP address assignments, number of QoS connections per router, max assigned Virtual Route Forwarding (VRF) tables [3] on the router, etc.).

The database entities have parent/child relationships that form a tree as you place items in the schema. For example, a complex is a site with a set of cabinets. A cabinet within a site may have multiple chassis or routers. A router has multiple cards,

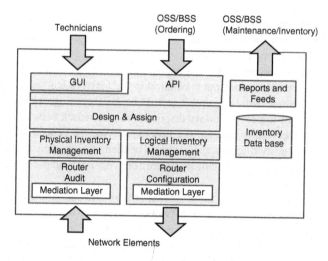

Fig. 8.1 High-level view of network configuration management system

each in a slot on the chassis. A card can have multiple ports. When viewed graphically, this parent/child relationship is a tree with the single item complex at the top and the ports at the "leaves" of the tree. A robust inventory database will have a schema with multiple "regions" of data with linkages between them as needed. One major ISP has an inventory database with over 1,000 tables to handle the inventory and the various applications that deal with the inventory.

The two main regions are the physical equipment tree of data (e.g., complex/cabinet/router/slot/port) and logical inventory tree of data (e.g., customer, premise, service, and connection). The service database entity (one node up from the connection entity in the tree) typically contains the linkage to other logical assignments like Serial IP address, VRF labels, Route Distinguishers [3], Route Targets [3], etc. The reason the data are separated into these regions is to permit the movement of logical assets to different ports (i.e., connections) and to support changes in the physical assets associated with a customer as a result of changes in technology or network-grooming activities. Changes in technology, such as a new router with lower port costs, and network grooming, moving connections from one router/circuit to another to improve efficiency, are examples of carrier changes that may also affect the data model. These carrier decisions are sometimes even more complex than the customer-initiated changes to deal with correctly in the inventory database.

Without separation of the regions, the ongoing life-cycle management of the service is difficult. For example, at points in time, we need to have multiple assets available for testing and move the "active" connection to the new assets only after satisfactory testing has completed. This means that we maintain multiple "services" for the same physical port, both the old service and the future service.

The inventory database stores the "What should be" for the corporation and the current and future state of the equipment and connections for a customer.

Many subsystems of a configuration management system are dependent on the inventory database. One of the major dependencies is the audit subsystem. The audit subsystem must store information for the physical "What it is" form of the network in a schema. Typically, since audit or discovery starts with the physical assets, the physical inventory model at the router/component level is reused for the "What it is" model. It is interesting to note that cabinet and location of equipment data are typically not discoverable, so those are usually inferred through naming conventions like the encoding of the router hostname. For example, a router might have a hostname like "n54ny01zz1" where the "n54" indicates a particular office in New York City and "ny" is for New York State. The "01" indicates that it is the first router in the office and the "zz1" would indicate the type or model of the router. The encoding is not an industry standard, but most carriers use something similar.

The logical "What it is" model is also based on the rich "What it should be" model. It is again interesting to note that the logical discovery does not have the non-network data items like street address of the customer or other business information. A prudent network operation puts processes in place to encode pertinent information in the interface description line so that linkages to business support systems can be maintained and audited.

For example, large carriers tend to automatically encode a customer name and pointers to location records to make it easier to manage events pertinent to the interface in customer care and ticketing systems. The example below shows an active port in maintenance (MNX), for a customer, ACME MARKETING that is located in ANYTOWN, NJ, on circuit DHEC.123456..ATI. Various database keys are also encoded.

interface Serial4/0.11/8:0
description MNX | ACME TECHNICAL MARKETING | ANYTOWN | NJ | DHEC.123456..ATI | 19547 | 3933470 | 4151940 | USA | MIS | |

The two main inputs to the inventory database are the physical and logical inventory on the router and the customer order data. The physical and logical router data are typically inserted through the GUI during network setup by the capacity management organization as assets are installed, tested, and made ready for service. Another practice in use is to install the equipment and then use the autodiscovery tools to "learn" the equipment's physical inventory. Logical assets are entered into the system as appropriate since they are not necessarily tied to the equipment in all cases.

The customer order data are created usually through an API from the OSS/BSS during the ordering phase of a customer's request for service and updated as the order progresses through the business processes to move from an order to an installed and tested connection.

A note of caution, the amount of customer order data that are replicated into the network configuration management system should be minimized. A good design incorporates just enough to make it easier for people to deal with problems encountered in provisioning and activities that the upstream OSS/BSS may not have the capability to manage like custom features. The more customer order data stored in the network configuration management system, the more the management of that data alone becomes a problem. Customer contact data are an example of data that should not be in the network configuration management system, since they are volatile and in fact may pertain to broader applications than the network service.

8.3.2 Router Configuration Subsystem

The second subsystem we will discuss is the Router configuration management system. This subsystem takes the information from the inventory database and creates configuration changes for the installed router. The inventory database typically provides data needed to drive configuration details like the types and versions of commands to use for configuration (these can vary by make and model), the IP addresses/hostnames and passwords for access to the routers, and the customer order data for the specific configuration. The generation of the specific router configuration commands is the more difficult aspect. There are numerous approaches to the creation of the configuration changes, but the two main ones large carriers use today are policy management and templates.

8.3.2.1 Policy Management Approach

The policy management approach attempts to break down the router configuration into a set of conditions and actions (e.g., policies) and generates the combined configuration on the router by evaluating the conditions and action in a set of policies. For example, QoS settings fit nicely into the policy management approach, since the router typically has a configuration statement to define the condition and action for applying QoS. The configuration statement can be shared by multiple ports and any interface can be assigned to that policy. Creating a QoS policy that assigns 20% of the bandwidth to high-priority class (e.g., voice traffic) and the remainder to a best-effort class could be reused by many ports on a router. One condition/action definition (e.g., policy) reused multiple times is easy to implement and maintain. Some configurations are more difficult to implement in a policy management system since they do not adhere nicely to a condition/action policy format. An example of this is IP addressing (or address management), which typically uses fairly complex rules to determine which address to assign to an interface.

Large policy management systems do exist, but the linkage between different policies can be subject to scaling issues when dealing with the application of a large number of network and customer policies as in a VPN with a large number (e.g., thousands) of end points. Configuration auditing (described later) in particular becomes difficult to manage in a policy management system because the policy view of the data sometimes is not readily apparent to the knowledgeable network engineer when looking at the more detailed CLI commands in the backup configuration file used for audits. Finally, testing of policy-based systems is complicated, since it is not always clear what the resulting policy-based configuration will be in the CLI.

The number of test cases increases to make sure the policy engine generates all the configuration change options that the network certification process has confirmed as working correctly.

8.3.2.2   Template Management Approach

Template management uses a more simplistic approach. The details of tested sets of configurations are documented in a template and the data to drive a particular template is pulled from the inventory database. The benefit of a template approach is that only the configurations that are known to be valid are put into the network. This approach is a more reliable method of ensuring that the network is always configured to operate in a configuration supported by the testing and certification program. Policy-management systems have a more difficult time ensuring that they are always configuring the router into a condition that matches the certified configurations.

The challenge is building the template from the set of features ordered by the customer. Generally, the template languages have a nesting structure so that the range of templates can be kept under control. As the set of templates grows, there is some complication in applying the correct template, but the resulting router configuration tends to be cleaner and more optimized (since each template is a test case) than the policy-based configurations.

Both approaches have merit and a growing set of functions can be handled more readily with policies; so the likely system for a large carrier is a mixture of these techniques with templates for the basic configurations like basic IP conditions and routing and policies for the more advanced functions like QoS configuration on CPE routers. Large ISPs will have hybrid approaches to provide the best fit tool for each problem.

An important aspect of the router configuration subsystem is the interaction between the users of current inventory (processes like ticketing and fault management) and the need to deal with future changes. Growing from a 512 kb/s link to a full T1 or growing from a single T1 to Multilink PPP (MLPPP) [4] are examples with very different degrees of complexity but both have the need to track both the current connection data and the future connection data. The router configuration system has to be able to handle modifying the current configuration to move an active connection to the new connection configuration. To handle failure conditions properly, this subsystem has to deal with roll forward and roll back of the configuration. Sometimes, the template approach is cleaner, since the "before" configuration can be captured directly from the router and re-applied even if the original data for it are not readily available.

There are some key differences in managing provider-edge and customer-edge configurations that influence the choice of template-based or policy-based configuration management that we discuss here.

Provider-edge (PE) routers tend to have a large number of interfaces (100 or more) with many interfaces of the same basic type. Generally, the configurations are relatively simple since the router's primary role is stability, reliability, and fast packet forwarding. Since large carrier router configurations tend to be less variable, we tend to see template-based configuration management systems on the PE. However, since MPLS VPNs have the added complexity of multiple router configurations being involved to correctly implement the VPN, usage of policy-based configuration management is growing.

Customer-edge (CE) routers tend to have a much smaller number of interfaces (less than 10) with a wide variation in configurations depending on the business/industry of the customer. For example, the CE router may need advanced traffic-shaping rules to ensure that performance-sensitive traffic has a priority on their internal network over the access to the internet proxy/firewall. Other customers might need to do video streaming for training and thus need QoS setting for video priority over other data traffic. Some customer may even be running internet applications that require prioritization of the http/ftp traffic to/from their router to provide service to their customers. The CE router is closer to the customer and thus gets the burden of handling more customer-specific applications like firewalls, packet shaping, and complicated internal routing policies. Policy-based router configuration management systems are commonly used on CE routers because that is a better fit to the disparate customer needs for the edge environment.

Finally, for the network carrier it is important to understand the different challenges that a mass-market consumer broadband internet access service places on the configuration management system. Mass-market configuration tends to have a very small set of routing configuration options. The most obvious variable in the configurations is the access speed. While you might think setting up QoS and ACLs would tend to increase the configuration options, it really only adds complexity and not much variation, since the configurations tend to be similar across large sets of connections. Although the number of different configurations is small, the rate of change is large. Initial provisioning rates are not only much larger than the enterprise space but the volumes of change orders are large as well. An Enterprise Internet access service might typically need to process several thousand orders a week with a similar magnitude of change orders. A mass-market service might need to process thousands of orders per day and tens of thousands of change orders per day. Mass-market router configuration systems tend toward template-based approaches because of the simplicity of the configuration, the smaller range of features, and the performance advantages of the template approach for large-scale processing.

8.3.2.3 Mediation Layer

Most service providers have multiple vendor platforms in their network, but even single vendor network will have multiple models and versions of the router operating system. The router configuration subsystem that writes data to the routers usually has a mediation layer to deal with the router-specific commands. The mediation layer also exists when reading data for the audit layer to turn the vendor-specific commands/output into a common syntax for use by the audit application. The mediation layer will also handle nuances of the security model for accessing the routers that may vary based on vendor and region of the globe.

8.3.3   GUI/API

The GUI/API subsystem deals with the typical functions of retrieval, display, and data input for the system. The technology of this subsystem is typical of large-scale systems. This subsystem uses HTTP Web server technology with an html-based GUI and a SOAP/XML-based API. A critical aspect for large carrier is that the API becomes the predominant flow into the system. At scale, the API is used to handle the large volume order flow from the business support systems (BSS), both to electronically transfer the data and trigger the various automated functions in the router configuration management system. The GUI is used infrequently for customer provisioning and is used primarily for correcting any fallout that might have occurred. Having a robust set of APIs is critical to business success. Obviously, the APIs must also keep pace, as new features are added to the router so that the automated processes can trigger them. The GUI comes into play for manual interaction and maintenance activities and various other tasks that are not economic to automate through APIs. The other important aspect of the GUI is the implementation of a robust authentication/authorization layer, since some user groups should not have access to the router configuration change functions to prevent unintended changes that could cause a service outage.

One aspect of the GUI that is also worth mentioning is read access to the "What it is" state of the router. Typically, there are sets of read-only CLI commands that the customer care organization depends on for responding to customer-reported problems. Most router platforms have a limited set of connections, so it is problematic to give a large customer care team direct access to the router CLI. The solution large carriers typically use is to put a web-based GUI in place with a limited set of functions that can be selected by the customer care agents. The GUI then acts as a proxy through the router configuration subsystem to execute these commands on the router. These commands include the various "show" commands as well as options to run limited repair functions like "clear counters" and/or "shutdown"/"no shutdown" on the interface. Exposing these functions through the GUI reduces the impact on the router and provides a mechanism for the throttling and audit rules to be applied to prevent a negative impact. The edit checks that occur before commands are executed on the router also help one to prevent unintended effects.

8.3.4   Design and Assign

This subsystem applies the engineering rules to select a port for a customer's service and can accept or reject a request for service based on available inventory. The subsystem has an API that takes the service request parameters and other customer network information and generates an assignment to a particular port on a router. That assignment is typically called a Tie Down and the data set is Tie Down Information (TDI). The API can be called either through the GUI or directly by the BSS. Assignment is nontrivial, since the function must ensure that all engineering rules that help protect the network are satisfied like finding a port on a card with sufficient resources while also satisfying the business rules, which seek to limit transport costs and latency by picking a router closer to the customer. For example, the engineering rules may limit the number of QoS configured ports on certain card types. As an example of router assignment, a poor assignment would be to pick a router in California for a customer in New York.

The assignment function calculates both an optimal assignment and the current assignment. The optimal assignment is the first choice router location that minimizes backhaul cost (e.g., ideally a customer in Ohio will be homed to a router in Ohio). However, it could be that the Ohio router complex does not have a router with sufficient capacity (bandwidth, QoS ports, etc.). The design and assign function system needs to be designed to implement the appropriate business rules in this case. For example, the business rule in this case is to "home" the customer on an alternate router in a different location. Alternatively, the business rule could be to reject the order. Typically, the "reject the order" business rule applies in mass-market situations. Business rules for enterprise markets usually choose to have longer backhaul costs rather than reject the order. In the enterprise market, the business rule might select a router in an alternate location like Indiana if no routers in Ohio had sufficient resources.

The business would like the flexibility to be able to move the port from the Indiana router to an Ohio router in the future without impacting the customer. Consequently, the "assign" function will allocate a Serial IP address from a logical inventory pool associated with Ohio's router complex, assign it to the interface on the router in Illinois, and "exception route" that address to Indiana. This assignment permits the CE/PE connection to be re-homed from Ohio to Indiana without affecting the customer's router configuration, since their WAN IP address would not change and then the exception route for Indiana can be removed to get to a more optimum network routing configuration as well as a reduced backhaul configuration. The tracking of the optimal and current assignment data adds complexity to this subsystem, the inventory database, and the router configuration system (for the exception routes), but it is a good example of the types of business decisions that can ripple back into the router configuration management system requirements.

8.3.5 Physical Inventory Management

Physical inventory management deals with the entering and tracking of data about the router equipment. It deals not only with equipment configuration details like what cards are installed in the routers but also where those routers are located for maintenance dispatch. The physical database also contains the parameters for the engineering rules that vary by equipment make and model. These parameters come either from the router vendor documentation or from certification testing. The parameters and the associated rules can range from simple rules like maximum bandwidth per line card to complex rules like the maximum number of VPN routes with QoS on all line cards on the router with version 3 of the line card firmware. As new routers or cards are added to the network, this subsystem tracks all the associated data for these assets including tracking whether a router or port is "in service" and available for assignment. As ports are assigned to customers, the physical inventory removes those ports from the assets that are available for assignment. The physical inventory also deals with the tracking of serial numbers of cards so that as cards are replaced or upgraded, the new parameters can be used for the engineering rules. For example, a card with 256 MB of memory could be upgraded to 512 MB and thus be able to support more QoS connections. The physical inventory subsystem keeps track of these engineering parameters (sometimes called reference data) about vendor equipment for use by other subsystems. Here are a few of the typical parameters tracked:

Maximum logical ports
Maximum aggregate bandwidth
Maximum card assignment
Maximum PVCs
Logical channel limits
IDB limit
VRF limit
BGP limit
COS limit
Routes limit

8.3.6 Logical Inventory Management

Logical inventory management deals with the entering and tracking of data about the logical assets (IP addresses, ACLs, Route Distinguishers, Route Targets, etc.). This can be a large subsystem depending on the different features available, but the hardest item in the category is the IP address management. IP address management deals with the assignment of efficient blocks to the various intended uses. Typically, the engineering rules require different blocks of addresses to be used for infrastructure connections, WAN IP address blocks, and customer LAN address blocks. This requires not only higher-level IP address block management functions so that access control lists can be managed efficiently but also functions to deal with external systems like the ARIN registry. Service Providers typically update the ARIN "Who Is" database through an API so that LAN IP blocks assigned to enterprise customers appear as being assigned to those customers. This aids the service provider in obtaining additional IP address blocks from the registrar if needed. The tracking of per router elements like ACL numbers is simpler but has its own nuances and complexity, since the goal is to reuse ACL numbers where it is possible to reduce the load on the router. Typically, memory is consumed for every ACL on a router. The ACLs for different ports for the same customer tend to be identical so that memory utilization (and processing time on the ACL) can be reduced by compressing the disparate ACLs into a single ACL that can be shared among a custom's ports. Numerous other items have to be tracked in logical inventory and assigned during the assignment function depending on the feature or service being provided and the logical inventory management system grows in complexity as more logical features are added to the service.

8.3.7 Reports and Feeds

The reports and feeds subsystem is responsible for distributing inventory data to users and systems required to run the business. The main users of this subsystem are the fault/service assurance system and the ticketing system. The fault/service assurance system needs data about the in-service assets so that alarms can be processed correctly. Its source of truth is usually the "What it is" data from the inventory database. The ticketing system is more concerned with the data about the customer, since they get notification of an event from the fault/service assurance system and have need to understand for a given port/card/router problem which customer or customers are affected. Fault and ticketing systems tend to get feeds of the inventory data, since their query volume can be quite high and the load can best be managed with a local cache of the data rather than directly querying the inventory database. Generally, the inventory data does not change rapidly; so a local cache is sufficient and alarms/tickets do not need these data until after test and turn up of the interface.

Other users need various reports and feeds from the inventory database, and generally these are pulled either as a report from the GUI or APIs. A GUI-based reporting application can easily be deployed on the inventory database for items like port utilization reports for capacity management. APIs can be created as needed for generating bulk files or responding to simple queries.

8.3.8 Router Audit

The router audit subsystem is responsible for doing both the discovery of the "What it is" state of the router and comparing the "What it is" with the "What it should be" in the inventory database. The audit function described in this section is designed to detect differences with the inventory data. There are other mechanisms that can be applied to look at the larger set of configuration rules. Some of these are covered in Chapter 9.

Discovery is typically done with an engine that parses the router configurations into database attributes. As described before, the parsed router configuration data are stored in the inventory database but in a separate set of tables from the physical and logical inventory. The schemas of the audit tables are similar to the physical and logical inventory tables, but they lack some attributes that do not exist in the router configuration; the major attributes are the same so that they can be compared with the "what it should be" tables. After storage, the compare or audit function does an item-by-item comparison, tracking any discords. The audit is CPU- and disk-intensive and typically is only done across the entire network data set on a daily basis. The discovery/audit process is also used to pick up changes like card replacements. It is typical for this audit function to take 4–6 hours to complete across a large network even when high-end servers are employed. The good news is that the process can typically be run using the backup copies of the router configuration files so that there is no impact on the network and limited impact on the users of the system. Incremental audits can also be done on a port or card basis on demand as part of the router configuration process.

It is worth noting that the tracking of discords requires a historical view: when a discord was first detected and when was the last time it was detected. New discords could correlate with an alarm or customer-reported problem. Old discords might be indicative of data integrity error from a manual correction that was implemented to repair a customer problem but not appropriately reflected back into the inventory database.

While perhaps less visible to the overall router configuration management process than other aspects of the configuration workflow, audit is a key step. Real-time validations must be implemented for a change order so that if there is a discord, the process will stop the change order from being applied to prevent a problem. It is important to subsequently find and fix these discords so that future change orders are not affected.

8.4   Dealing with Change

An important aspect of a configuration management system is to deal with changes to an existing service. For example, the initial configuration of an interface can be done in various phases and with little concern for timing until the interface is moved from the shutdown state to the active state. However, an active interface has a different set of rules. Generally, the timing associated with configuration changes is more critical and the set of checks on the data and the configuration are more involved.

First, a robust network configuration management system will validate the current configuration of the interface ("What it is") against the "What it should be" data and if there is a mismatch it should stop the change. The reasons are probably obvious that unless the "What it is" and "What it should be" data sets are in agreement, we are running the risk of changing to a configuration that will not work for the customer because of a previous data inconsistency. For instance, if there have been problems with a previous re-home and the ACLs are not the same between the old configuration and the new configuration, it could prevent the customer from accessing their network services.

Second, for the intended change, the configuration management system should validate the data set against the interface data, the global configuration of the router, and to the extent possible the larger network for the customer to ensure that the change is consistent with other "What it is" data. This usually consists of a set of rules applied by the configuration management subsystem to ensure that a successful change will be applied. A good example is again a re-home. If the old port is still advertising its WAN IP address, you cannot bring up the same WAN IP address on a different router or instabilities can be introduced (duplicate IP address detection is an important validation rule).

8.4.1 Test and Turn Up

Bringing up a new connection involves testing that the connection works correctly as ordered and then turning up the port for full service. Turning up a large connection like a 10 Gb Ethernet connection is something done carefully because if mis-configured it could either drive large amounts of traffic into a customer's network before they are prepared for it or remove traffic from a customer's network by mistake. For most changes against a running configuration, the process of applying the change has to be coordinated with a maintenance window[1] since service could be impacted. Some changes may also require changes on the customer's side of the connection; so proper scheduling with the customer's staff is required. For changes that involve the physical connection (speed changes and re-homes), typically two ports are in assignment at the same time and operations would like to test all or parts of the new port before swinging the customer's connection over. This "testing phase" creates database complexity, since the new port has to be reserved for the customer but it is not the "in-service" port from an alarming/ticketing standpoint. Both the old and new have to be tracked until the port is fully migrated to the new configuration. This requires the concept of "Pending" port assignments/connections and database transactions to move a port from "Pending" to "Active," from "Active" to "Disconnected," and finally the old record is deleted from the database.

The router configuration system has to maintain the ability to generate router configurations for each of the interim steps in moving an active connection from one port to another. There are configurations to bring up the new interface on temporary information (e.g., temporary serial IP addresses and/or RD/RT/VRF information for testing), steps to "shutdown" the old interface, steps to "no shutdown" the new interface, and steps to reverse the entire process to roll back to the old interface. All these need to be able to be driven through the API for relatively straightforward changes with automated PE side re-homes that do not affect the customer premise router and via the GUI for those more complicated changes that require coordination with the customer. It is with dealing with change that the entire system is stressed the most to meet the needs of not only ensuring that the network is protected but also that the entire system responds fast enough to meet the human- or machine-driven process requirements.

---

[1] The Maintenance Window is a time period when there is expected to be low traffic and is used by an operator for planned activities that could impact service. Usually it is in the late night/ early morning of the time zone of the router like 3–6 a.m.

Another attribute of change that is worth mentioning is changes to active interfaces that are infrastructure connections (e.g., two or more backbone links that connect network routers). A routine task is to change the OSPF metric on one link to "cost it out"[2] of use so that maintenance on the connection can be done. A problem exists if the state of this link is left in the "costed out" state. Failure of the now single primary link causes isolation, since one link could be hard failed and the other link is out of service by being "costed out." A robust configuration management system also has maintenance functions to permit the operations staff to cost out a link, to record that the link is "costed out," and to generate an alarm condition if the link stays "costed out" for a period of time.

Finally, a type of change that is of growing importance in large networks is the ability to apply changes in bulk. The complexity of modern routers leads to situations where a latent bug or security vulnerability is found in a router that can only be repaired by changing the configuration on a large number of ports in the network. This requires special update processes to handle the updates in a bulk fashion. Typically, this is a customized application on the router configuration subsystem that is targeted at dealing with the bulk processing. The reason why this gets complicated is not only because of tracking that all the changes are applied (routers sometimes tend to refuse administrative requests under heavy load) but also throttling the updates to specific routers so as not to overload them.

8.5 Example of Service Provisioning

This section will tie all the pieces together in an example of service provisioning for a simple Internet access service.

Once all the order data are collected and optionally entered into an automated order management, the provisioning steps can occur including downloading the configurations to the router. The individual configurations are called configlets, since they are usually incremental changes to an interface or pieces of the global configuration, and not an entire router configuration. They are outlined below.

1. Create customer
2. Create premise/site
3. Create service instance
4. Create connection and reserve inventory
5. Download initial configuration
6. Download loopback test configlet
7. Download shutdown configlet
8. Download final configlet with "no shutdown"
9. Run daily audit

---

[2] When OSPF costs on a set of links are adjusted to shift traffic off of one link and onto another link, the process is informally called "costing out" the link.

1. **Create customer**

   This task is simply to group all the customer data into one high-level account by creating (or using a previously created) customer entity in the database. Sometimes, it relates to an enterprise but oftentimes because of mergers and acquisitions or even departmental billing arrangement the "customer" at this level does not uniquely identify a corporation. There can even be complicated arrangements with wholesalers that must be reflected in various customer attributes.

2. **Create premise/site**

   This task creates a database entity corresponding to the physical site that the access circuit terminates in at the customer's site. Street address, city, state/province, country etc. are typical parameters. Corporations can have multiple services at an address so that we track the address partly not only to make it easier to work with the customer but also because these data will impact the selection of the optimum router to reduce backhaul costs.

3. **Create service instance**

   This task collects the parameters about the intended service on this connection. It will define the speed, any service options like quality of service, and all the other logical connection parameters. These data directly affect the set of engineering rules that will be applied to actually find an available port on an optimum router.

4. **Create connection and reserve inventory**

   This task combines the above data into an assignment. The selection of a router complex is done first using the parameters of address to look for a complex with a short backhaul. This is called "Homing." After a preliminary complex is assigned, the routers in the complex are checked for available port capacity and if there is port capacity, the engineering rules for this connection on that router are tested. For example, a router may have available ports, but there may be insufficient resources for additional QoS or MPLS VPN routes on the cards. The system will recursively examine all routers in the complex to look for an available port that matches the engineering rules. If no router is found, the system will examine a next best optimum complex and repeat the search. This assignment function can take a substantial amount of system resources to complete and is not guaranteed to find a solution due to resource or other business rule constraints.

   Once a complex, router, and port has been selected, the logical inventory will be tied to the physical inventory and this Tie Down Information (TDI) will be returned to the ordering system so that it can order the layer 1 connection from the router to the customer premise. It is important to note that at this point the Inventory database must set a state of the port so that no other customer can use that router port. If the customer's order is cancelled, the business process must ensure that the port assignment is deleted as well to avoid stranded inventory.

   At this point, the inventory database would show the port as "PENDING," since the inventory has been assigned but it is not in service. All the logical data needed to configure the interface are in the database and any provider inventory items have been assigned (serial IP addresses, ACL numbers, etc.).

5. **Download initial configuration**

   After the inventory has been assigned, an initial configuration of the port is downloaded to the router to define the basic interface. This configlet typically only includes the serial IP address and default routing and defines the interface in a shutdown state. This is also the first real-time audit step. This audit will confirm that the assigned port is not used by some other connection. While rare, data discords of this type do occur. This download need not occur in real time, since it will typically be some amount of time before the Layer 1 connection is ready.

6. **Download the loopback test configlet**

   This step depends on the layer 1 connection to be installed so that it can occur days, weeks, or months after step 5. In addition, after Layer 1 is installed, this step typically occurs 24 h before the scheduled turn up date for a customer. This configlet contains all the routing and configuration data for the connection. Downloading a configlet to do loopback testing on the network side of the connection provides a final check of the provider's part of the work. Just before the configlet is downloaded, a series of real-time audits are again conducted, since the initial configlet audits could have been months ago. These audits check both the static order data against the running router and attributes on other ports on the router. For example, there is a verification that any new ACL number is not already in use on another port for another customer. This check makes sure that a manually configured port was not done in error. There is a verification that any new VRF does not already exist on the router to check and see if another order has been processed in parallel. There are numerous other validations as well. This real-time audit is more detailed than the audit done for the initial configlet, since it contains all the routing, QoS, and VPN data. If all validations are successful, the configuration is downloaded and activated for testing with Layer 1 in loopback.

7. **Download shutdown configlet**

   After successful pretesting, the router port is left in a shutdown state. It can remain in this configuration for some period of time but because routing instances may have been defined even though the port is shutdown typically operators do not leave a shutdown interface in the router configuration for more than 48 hours or so. A shutdown interface is still discoverable from an SNMP network management perspective so that a large number of admin down interfaces simply adds load to the fault management system without adding value. If it is not successfully turned up, the configuration will be rolled back to the initial configuration. While the Layer 1 circuit is being ordered/installed, there will likely be many daily audits that run. These audits will find the port in the router in shutdown state. The discord analysis will compare the "What it is" configuration and state with the "What it should be" configuration and state and report any problems. For our example, there is no problem but the audit might find that the port is in a "no shutdown" state in the network indicating that perhaps a test and turn up occurred but was not completed in the inventory database. The daily audit would also find if the router card had been replaced for some reason and update tracking data like serial numbers, etc.

8. **Download final configlet with "no shutdown"**

At activation, the system will download the final router configuration with "no shutdown" of the interface. Final testing may occur with the customer. The testing for single-link static routed interfaces is usually automated but for advanced configurations with multiple links or BGP routing, manual testing procedures are typical. It is at this point that the inventory database will update its status on the port to active and mark the port "In service" for downstream systems like the Fault Management and Ticketing systems.

9. **Run daily audit**

The daily audit will find the new state of the port to be active and the "What it should be" state of "ACTIVE" matches the "What it is" state in the network.

8.6 Conclusion

Hopefully, we have provided a useful overview of a robust router configuration management system and helped to tie the key functions and subsystems back to the business needs that drive complexity. From inventory management to provisioning the customer's service to handling changes to dealing with bulk security updates, a large carrier cannot provide reliable service without a robust router configuration management system.

Here is a summary of some "best practice" principles that will be helpful when designing a Network Configuration Management system.

- Recognize data discords as a fact of life. Separate "What it is" and "What it should be" data in the inventory database
- Configuration management is the source of truth for the business about the current network using the "What it is" data
- Protect the network through real-time validation and auditing of the running network
- Design for change so that logical data are not permanently tied to physical data
- Separate the schema for physical inventory and logical inventory
- Use templates to make configuration, discord detection, and testing easier
- Track port history, and not just the current state
- Design for multiple configurations of a port to handle the current port configuration and the pending port configuration
- Design the system to support testing a port before it is turned up and roll-back to an earlier configuration when tests fail
- Limit the amount of business data in the network-facing system so that you do not create a problem of maintaining consistency

References

1. Chandra, R., Traina, R., & Li, T. IETF Request for Comments 1997, *BGP Communities Attribute*, August 1996.
2. Hawkinson, J., & Bates, T. IETF Request for Comments 1930, *Guidelines for creation, selection, and registration*, March 1996.
3. Rosen, E., & Rekhter, Y. IETF Request for Comments 4364, BGP/MPLS *Virtual Private Networks*, April 2006.
4. Sklower, K., Lloyd, B., McGregor, G., Carr, D., & Coradetti, T. IETF Request for Comments 1990, *The PPP Multilink Protocol*, August 1996.

Chapter 9
Network Configuration Validation[1]

Sanjai Narain, Rajesh Talpade, and Gary Levin

9.1 Introduction

To set up network infrastructure satisfying end-to-end requirements, it is not only necessary to run appropriate protocols on components but also to correctly configure these components. Configuration is the "glue" for logically integrating components at and across multiple protocol layers. Each component has configuration parameters, each of which can be set to a definite value. However, today, the large conceptual gap between end-to-end requirements and configurations is manually bridged. This causes large numbers of configuration errors whose adverse effects on security, reliability, and high cost of deployment of network infrastructure are well documented. For example:

- "Setting it [security] up is so complicated that it's hardly ever done right. While we await a catastrophe, simpler setup is the most important step toward better security." – Turing Award winner Butler Lampson [42].
- "... human error is blamed for 50 to 80 percent of network outages." – Juniper Networks [40].
- "The biggest threat to increasingly complex systems may be systems themselves." – John Schwartz [61].
- "Things break and complex things break in complex ways." – Steve Bellovin [61].
- "We don't need hackers to break systems because they're falling apart by themselves." – Peter Neumann [61].

S. Narain (✉), R. Talpade, and G. Levin
Telcordia Technologies, Inc., 1 Telcordia Drive, Piscataway, NJ 08854, USA
e-mail: narain@research.telcordia.com; rrt@research.telcordia.com;
glevin@research.telcordia.com

[1] This material is based upon work supported by Telcordia Technologies, and Air Force Research Laboratories under contract FA8750-07-C-0030. Any opinions, findings and conclusions or recommendations expressed in this material are those of the authors and do not necessarily reflect the views of Telcordia Technologies or of Air Force Research Laboratories. Approved for Public Release; distribution unlimited: 88ABW-2009-3797, 27 August 09.

C.R. Kalmanek et al. (eds.), *Guide to Reliable Internet Services and Applications*,
Computer Communications and Networks, DOI 10.1007/978-1-84882-828-5_9,
© Springer-Verlag London Limited 2010

Thus, it is critical to develop validation tools that check whether a given configuration is consistent with the requirements it is intended to implement. Besides checking consistency, configuration validation has another interesting application, namely, network testing. The usual invasive approach to testing has several limitations. It is not scalable. It consumes resources of the network and network administrators and has the potential to unleash malware into the network. Some properties such as absence of single points of failure are impractical to test as they require failing components in operational networks. A noninvasive alternative that overcomes these limitations is analyzing configurations of network components. This approach is analogous to testing software by analyzing its source code rather than by running it. This approach has been evaluated for a real enterprise.

Configuration validation is inherently hard. Requirements can be on connectivity, security, performance, and reliability and span multiple components and protocols. A real infrastructure can have hundreds of components. A component's configuration file can have a couple of thousand configuration commands, each setting the value of one or more configuration parameters. In general, the correctness of a component's configuration cannot be checked in isolation. One needs to evaluate global relationships into which components have been logically integrated. Configuration repair is even harder, since changing configurations to make one requirement true may falsify another. The configuration change needs to be holistic in that all requirements must concurrently hold.

This chapter motivates the need for configuration validation in the context of a realistic collaboration network, proposes an abstract design of a configuration validation system, surveys current technologies for realizing this design, outlines experience with deploying such a system in a real enterprise, and outlines future research directions.

Section 9.2 discusses the challenges of configuring a realistic, decentralized collaboration network, the vulnerabilities caused by configuration errors, and the benefits of using a validation system. Requirements on this network are complex to begin with. Their manual implementation can cause a large number of configuration errors. This number is compounded by the lack of a centralized configuration authority.

Section 9.3 proposes a design of a system that can not only validate the above network but also evolve to validate even more complex ones. This design consists of four subsystems. The first is a Configuration Acquisition System for extracting configuration information from components in a vendor-neutral format. The second is a Requirement Library capturing best practices and design patterns that simplify the conceptualization of end-to-end requirements. The third is a Specification Language whose syntax simplifies the specification of requirements. The fourth is an Evaluation System for efficiently evaluating requirements, for suggesting configuration repair when requirements are false, and for creating visualizations of logical relationships.

Section 9.4 discusses the Telcordia® IP Assure product [38] and the choices it has made to realize this design. It uses a parser generator for configuration acquisition. Its Requirement Library consists of requirements on integrity of logical structures, connectivity, security, performance, reliability, and government policy. Its specification language is one of visual templates. Its evaluation system uses algorithms from graph theory and constraint solving. It computes visualizations of several types of logical topologies.

Section 9.5 discusses logic-based techniques for realizing the above validation system design. Their use is particularly important for configuration repair. They simplify configuration acquisition and specification. They allow firewall subsumption, equivalence, and rule redundancy analysis. These techniques are the languages Prolog, Datalog, and arithmetic quantifier-free forms [51, 53, 67], the Kodkod [41, 69] constraint solver for first-order logic of finite domains, the ZChaff [27, 46, 73] minimum-cost SAT solver for Boolean logic, and Ordered Binary Decision Diagrams (OBDDs) [12].

Section 9.6 outlines related techniques for realizing the above validation system design. These are type inference for configuration acquisition [47], symbolic reachability analysis [72], its implementation [3] with symbolic model checking [48], and finally, validation techniques for Border Gateway Protocol (BGP), the Internet-wide routing protocol, and one of the most complex.

Section 9.7 contains a summary and outlines future research directions.

9.2   Configuration Validation for a Collaboration Network

This section discusses the challenges of configuring a realistic, multi-enterprise *collaboration network*, the types of its vulnerabilities caused by configuration errors, the reasons why these arise, and the benefits that can be derived from using a configuration validation system. Multiple communities of interest (COIs) are set up as logically partitioned virtual private networks (VPNs) overlaid on a common IP network backbone. The "nodes" of this VPN are gateway routers at each enterprise that participate in the COI. An enterprise can participate in more than one COI, in which case it would have one gateway router for each COI. For each COI, agreement is reached between participating network administrators on the top-level connectivity, security, performance, and reliability requirements governing the COI. Configuration of routers, firewalls, and other network components to implement these requirements is up to administrators. There is no centralized configuration authority. The administrators at different enterprises in a COI negotiate with each other to ensure configuration consistency. Such decentralized networks exist in industry, academia, and government and are clear candidates for the application of configuration validation tools.

Typical COI requirements are now described. The connectivity requirement is that every COI site must be reachable from every other COI site. The security requirement is twofold. First, all communication between sites must be encrypted. Second, no packets from one COI can leak into another COI. This requirement is especially important since collaborating enterprises have limited mutual trust. A site can be a part of more than one COI but the information that site is willing to share with partners on one COI is distinct from that with partners in another COI. The performance requirement specifies the bandwidth, delay, jitter, and packet loss for various types of applications. The reliability requirement specifies that connectivity be maintained in the face of link or node failure.

Since these requirements are complex, large numbers of configuration errors can be made. This number is compounded by the lack of a centralized configuration authority. The complexity has the further consequence that –less experienced administrators, especially in an emergency, tend to statically route traffic directly over the IP backbone rather than correctly set up dynamic routing. But, when the emergency passes, static routes are not removed for concern of breaking the routing. Over time, this causes the COIs to become brittle in that routes cannot be automatically recomputed in the face of link or node failure.

While administrators are well aware of configuration errors and their adverse effects on the global network, they lack the tools to identify these, much less remove these. The decentralized nature of the network prevents them from obtaining a picture of the global architecture. A validation system that could identify configuration errors, make recommendations for repairing these and help understand the global relationships would be of immense value to administrators.

Figure 9.1 shows the architecture of a typical COI with four collaborating sites A, B, C, D. Each site contains a host, an internal router, and a gateway router. The first two items are shown only for sites A and C. Each gateway router is physically connected to the physical IP backbone network (WAN). Overlaid on this backbone is a network of IPSec [41] tunnels interconnecting the gateway routers. An IPSec tunnel is used to encrypt packets flowing between its endpoints. Overlaid on the IPSec network is a network of GRE [22] tunnels. A GRE tunnel provides the appearance of two routers being directly connected even though there may be many physical hops between them. The two overlay networks are "glued" together in such

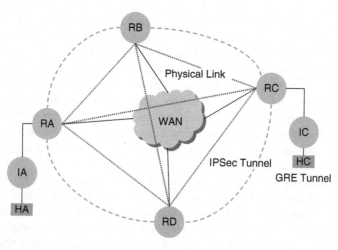

Fig. 9.1 Community of interest architecture

a way that all packets through GRE tunnels are encrypted. A routing protocol, e.g., BGP [33, 36], is run over the GRE network to discover routes on this overlay. If a link or node in this network fails, BGP discovers an alternate route if possible. A packet originating at host HA destined to host HC is first directed by its internal router IA to the gateway router RA. RA encrypts the packet, then finds a path to HC on the GRE network. When the packet arrives at RC, it is decrypted, decapsulated, and forwarded to IC. IC then forwards it to HC. All routers also run the internal routing protocol called OSPF [42]. OSPF discovers routes to destinations that are internal to a site. The OSPF process at the gateway router redistributes or injects internal routes into the BGP process. The BGP process then informs its peers at other gateway routers about these routes. Eventually, all gateway routers come to know about how to route packets to any reachable internal destination at any site.

   In summary, connectivity, security, and reliability requirements are satisfied by the use, respectively, of GRE, IPSec and BGP, and OSPF. The security requirement that data from one COI not leak into another is satisfied implicitly. GRE reachability to a different COI is disallowed, static routes to destinations in different COIs are not set up, gateway routers at the same enterprise but belonging to different COIs are not directly connected, and BGP sessions across different COIs are not set up.

   The performance requirement is satisfied by ensuring that GRE tunnels are mapped to physical links of the proper bandwidth, delay, jitter, and packet loss properties, although this is not always in control of COI administrators. Avoiding one cause of packet loss, is however, in their control. This is the blocking of Maximum Transmission Unit (MTU) mismatch messages. If a router receives a packet whose size is larger than the router's configured MTU, and the packet's Do Not Fragment bit is set, the router will drop the packet. The router will also warn the sender in an ICMP message that it has dropped the packet. Then, the sender can reduce the size of packets its sends. However, since ICMP is the same protocol used to carry ping messages, firewalls at many sites block ICMP. The result is that the sender will continue to send packets without reducing their size and they will all be dropped by the router [68]. Packets increase in size beyond an expected MTU because GRE and IPSec encapsulations add new headers to packets. To avoid such packet loss, the MTU at all routers is set to some fixed value accounting for the encapsulation. Alternatively, ICMP packets carrying MTU mismatch messages are not blocked.

   This design is captured by the following requirements:

Connectivity Requirements

1. Each site has a gateway router connected to the WAN.
2. There is a full-mesh of GRE tunnels between gateway routers.
3. Each gateway router is connected to an internal router at the same site.

Security Requirements

1. There is a full-mesh network of IPSec tunnels between all gateway routers.
2. Packets through every GRE tunnel are encrypted with an IPSec tunnel.
3. No gateway router in a COI has a static route to a destination in a different COI
4. No cross-COI physical, GRE, BGP connectivity, or reachability is permitted.

Reliability Requirements

1. BGP is run on the GRE tunnel network to discover routes to destinations in different sites.
2. OSPF is run within a site to discover routes to internal destinations.
3. OSPF and BGP route redistribution is set up.

Performance Requirements

1. MTU settings on all interfaces are set to be less than the expected packet size after taking into account GRE and IPSec encapsulation.
2. Alternatively, access-control lists at each gateway router permit ICMP packets carrying MTU messages.

Configuration parameters that must be correctly set to implement the above requirements include:

1. IP addresses and mask of physical and GRE interfaces
2. IP address of the local and remote BGP session end points and the autonomous system (AS) number of the remote end point
3. Names of GRE interface and IP address of associated local and remote physical tunnel end points
4. IP addresses of local and remote IPSec tunnel end points, encryption and hash algorithms to apply to protected packets, and the profile of packets to be protected
5. Destination, destination mask, and next hop of static routes
6. Interfaces on which OSPF is enabled and the OSPF areas to which they belong
7. Source and destination address ranges, protocols, and port ranges of packets for access-control lists
8. Maximum transmission units for router interfaces

As can be imagined, a large number of errors can be made in manual computation of configuration parameter values implementing these requirements. GRE tunnels may only configure in one direction or not at all. IPSec tunnels may only configure in one direction or not at all. GRE and IPSec tunnels may not be "glued" together. GRE tunnels or sequences of tunnels may link routers in distinct COIs. A COI gateway router may contain static routes to a different COI, so packets could be routed to that COI via the WAN. BGP sessions may be set up between routers in different COIs, so these routers may come to know about destinations behind each other. BGP sessions may only be configured in one direction or not at all. BGP sessions may not be supported by GRE tunnels, so these sessions will not be established. There may be single points of failure in the GRE and BGP networks. Finally, MTU settings on routers in a COI may be different leading to the possibility of packet loss. Such errors can be visualized by mapping various logical topologies. Two of these are shown below.

In Fig. 9.2, nodes represent routers and edges represent a GRE edge between routers. These edges have to be set up in both directions for a GRE tunnel to be established. This graph shows two problems. First, the edge labeled "Asymmetric" has no counterpart in the reverse direction. Second, the dotted line indicates a missing

Fig. 9.2   GRE tunnel
topology

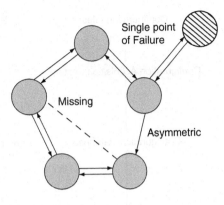

Fig. 9.3   BGP neighbor
topology

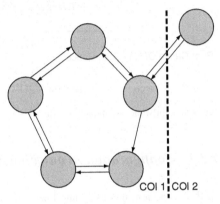

tunnel. Third, the hatched router indicates a single point of GRE failure. All GRE packets to destinations to the right of this router pass through this router.

In Fig. 9.3, nodes represent routers and links represent BGP sessions between nodes. This graph shows two problems. First, there is no full-mesh of BGP sessions within COI 1. Second, there is a BGP session between routers in two distinct COIs.

9.3   Creating a Configuration Validation System

This section outlines the design of a system that can not only validate the network of the previous section but also evolve to validate even more complex ones. As shown in Fig. 9.4, this consists of a Configuration Acquisition system to acquire configuration information in a vendor-neutral format, a Requirement Library containing fundamental requirements simplifying the task of conceptualizing administrator intent, an easy-to-use Specification Language in which to specify requirements, and an Evaluation System to efficiently evaluate specifications in this language. These subsystems are now described.

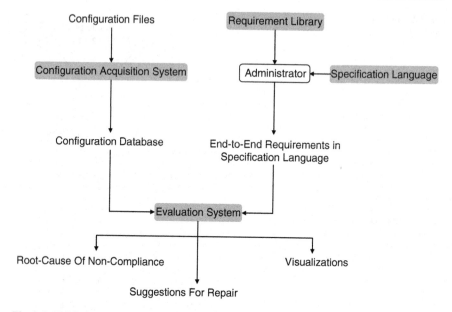

Fig. 9.4 Validation system architecture

9.3.1 Configuration Acquisition System

Each component has associated with it a configuration file containing commands that define that component's configuration. These commands are entered by the network administrator. The most reliable method of acquiring a device's configuration information is to acquire this file, manually or automatically. Other less-reliable methods are accessing the devices' SNMP agent and querying configuration databases. SNMP agents often do not store all of the configuration information one might be interested in. The correctness and completeness of a configuration database varies from enterprise to enterprise.

If configuration information is acquired from files, then these files have to be parsed. Configuration languages have a simple syntax and semantics, since they are intended to be used by network administrators who may not be expert programmers. Different vendors offer syntactically different configuration languages. However, the abstract configuration information stored in these files is the same, barring non-standard features that vendors sometimes implement. This information is associated with standardized protocols. Examples of it from the previous section are IP addresses, OSPF area identifiers, BGP neighbors, and IPSec cryptographic algorithms. This information needs to be extracted from files and stored in a vendor-neutral format database. Then, algorithms for evaluating requirements can be written just once against this database, and not once for every combination of vendor configuration language. However, configuration languages are vast, each with a very large set of features. Their syntax can change from one product release to another. Some vendors do not supply APIs to extract the abstract information. It should be possible to extract configuration information without having to understand all features of a configuration language. Extraction algorithms should be resilient to inevitable changes in configuration language syntax.

9.3.2   Requirement Library

The Requirement Library is analogous to libraries implementing fundamental algorithms in software development. The Library should capture design patterns and best practices for accomplishing fundamental goals in connectivity, security, reliability, and performance. Examples of these for security can be found in [18] and for routing in [33]. These patterns can be expressed as requirements. The administrator should be easily able to conceptualize end-to-end requirements as compositions of Library requirements.

9.3.3   Specification Language

The specification language should provide an easy-to-use syntax for expressing end-to-end requirements. Specifications should be as close as possible in their forms to their natural language counterparts. The syntax can be text-based or visual. Since requirements are logical concepts, the syntax should allow specification of objects, attributes, and constraints between these and compositions of constraints via operators such as negation, conjunction, disjunction, and quantification. For example, all of these constructs appear in the Section 9.2 requirement "No gateway router in a COI has a static route to a destination in a different COI."

9.3.4   Evaluation System

The Requirement Evaluation system should contain efficient algorithms to evaluate a requirement against configuration. These algorithms should output not just a yes/no answer but also explanations or counterexamples to guide configuration repair. Configuration repair is harder than evaluation. A set of requirements can be independently evaluated but if some are false, they cannot be independently made true. Changing the configuration to make one requirement true may falsify another. To provide further insight into reasons for truth or falsehood of requirements, this system should compute visualizations of logical relationships that are set up via configuration, analogous to visualizations of quantitative data [70].

9.4 IP Assure Validation System

This section describes the Telcordia® IP Assure product and discusses the choices made in it to implement the above abstract design of a validation system. This product aims to improve the security, availability, QoS, and regulatory compliance of IP networks. It uses a parser generator for configuration acquisition. Its Requirement Library consists of well over 100 requirements on integrity of logical structures, connectivity, security, performance, reliability, and government policy. Its specification language is one of visual templates. Its evaluation system uses algorithms from graph theory and constraint solving. It also computes visualizations of several types of logical topologies. If a requirement is false, IP Assure does compute a root-cause, although its computation is hand-crafted for each requirement. IP Assure does not compute a repair that concurrently satisfies all requirements.

9.4.1 Configuration Acquisition System

Section 9.3 raised three challenges in the design of a configuration acquisition system. The first was the design of a vendor-neutral database schema for storing configuration information. The second was extracting information from configuration files without having to know the entire configuration language for a given vendor. The third was making the extraction algorithms robust to inevitable changes in the configuration language. This section describes IP Assure's configuration acquisition system and sketches how well it meets these challenges.

IP Assure has defined a schema loosely modeled after DMTF [20] schemas. It uses the ANTLR [5] system to define a grammar for configuration files. The parser generated by ANTLR reads the configuration file and if successful returns an abstract syntax tree exposing the structure of the file. This tree is then analyzed by algorithms implemented in Java to create and populate tables in its schema. Often, information in a table is assembled from information scattered in different parts of the file.

The system is illustrated in the context of a configuration file containing the following commands in Cisco's IOS configuration language:

```
hostname router1
!
interface Ethernet0
 ip address 1.1.1.1 255.255.255.0
 crypto map mapx
!
crypto map mapx 6 ipsec-isakmp
 set peer 3.3.3.3
 set transform-set transx
 match address aclx
!
```

```
crypto ipsec transform-set transx esp-3des hmac
!
ip access-list extended aclx
  permit gre host 3.3.3.3 host 4.4.4.4
```

A configuration file is a sequence of command blocks consisting of a main command followed by zero or more indented subcommands. The first command specifies the name router1 of the router. It has no subcommands. Any line beginning with ! is a comment line. The second command specifies an interface Ethernet0. It has two subcommands. The first specifies the IP address and mask of this interface. The second specifies the name mapx of an IPSec tunnel originating from this interface. The parameters of the IPSec tunnel are specified in the next command block. The main command specifies the name of the tunnel, mapx. The subcommands specify the address of the remote endpoint of the IPSec tunnel, the set transx of cryptographic algorithms to be used, and the profile aclx of the traffic that will be secured by this tunnel. The next command block defines the set transx as consisting of the encryption algorithm esp-3des and the hash algorithm hmac. The last command block defines the traffic profile aclx as any packet with protocol, source address and destination address equal to gre, 3.3.3.3 and 4.4.4.4, respectively.

Part of an ANTLR grammar for recognizing the above file is:

```
commands: command NL (rest=commands | EOF)
          ->^(COMMAND command $rest?);
command: ('interface') => interface_cmd
       |('crypto')    => crypto_cmd
       |('ip')        => ip_cmd
       |unparsed_cmd;
interface_cmd: 'interface' ID (LEADINGWS interface_subcmd) *
          -> ^('interface' ID interface_subcmd *)
interface_subcmd:
       'ip' 'address' a1=ADDR a2=ADDR -> ^('address' $a1 $a2)
     |'crypto' 'map' ID -> ^(CRYPTO_MAP ID)
     |unparsed_subcmd;
```

The first grammar rule states that commands is a sequence of one or more command blocks. The ^ symbol is a directive to construct the abstract syntax tree whose root is the symbol COMMAND, whose first child is the command block just read, and second child is the tree representing the sequence of subsequent command blocks. The next rule states that a command block begins with the keywords interface, crypto, or ip. The symbol = > means no backtracking. The last line in this rule states that if a command block does not begin with any of these identifiers, it is skipped. Skipping is done via the unparsed_cmd symbol. Grammar rules defining it skip all tokens till the beginning of the next command block. The last two rules define the structure of an interface command block. ANTLR produces a parser that processes the above file and outputs an abstract syntax tree. This tree is then analyzed to create the tables below. Note that the ipsec table assembles information from the interface, crypto map, crypto ipsec, and ip access-list command blocks.

ipAddress Table			
Host	Interface	Address	Mask
router1	Ethernet0	1.1.1.1	255.255.255.0

ipsec Table					
Host	SrcAddr	DstAddr	EncryptAlg	HashAlg	Filter
router1	1.1.1.1	3.3.3.3	esp-3des	hmac	aclx

acl Table					
Host	Filter	Protocol	SrcAddr	DstAddr	Perm
router1	Aclx	gre	3.3.3.3	4.4.4.4	permit

IP Assure's vendor-neutral schema captures much of the configuration information for protocols it covers. Its skipping idea allows one to parse a file without recognizing the structure of all possible commands and command blocks. However, the idea is quite hard to get right in the ANTLR framework. One is trying to avoid writing a grammar for the skipped part of the language, yet the only method one can use is to write rules defining unparsed_cmd.

9.4.2 Requirement Library

9.4.2.1 Requirements on Integrity of Logical Structures

A very useful class of requirements is on the integrity of logical structures associated with different protocols. Before a group of components executing a protocol can accomplish an intended joint goal, various logical structures spanning these components must be set up. These structures are set up by making component configurations satisfy definite constraints. For example, before packets flowing between two interfaces can be secured via IPSec, the IPSec tunnel logical structure must be set up. This is done by setting IPSec configuration parameters at the two interfaces and ensuring that their values satisfy definite constraints. For example, the two interfaces must use the same hash and encryption algorithms, and the remote tunnel endpoint at each interface must equal the IP address of its counterpart.

An Hot Standby Routing Protocol (HSRP) [44] router cluster is another example of a logical structure. It allows two or more routers to behave as a single router by offering a single virtual IP address to the outside world, on a given subnet. This address is mapped to the real address of an interface on the primary router. If this router fails, another router takes over the virtual address. Before the cluster correctly functions, however, the same virtual address and HSRP group identifier must be configured on all interfaces and the virtual and all physical addresses must belong to the same subnet.

Much more complex logical structures are set up for BGP. Different routers in an autonomous system (AS) connect to different neighboring ASes, giving each router only a partial view of BGP routes. To allow all routers in an AS to construct a complete view of routes, routers exchange information between themselves via iBGP (internal BGP) sessions. The simplest logical structure for accomplishing this exchange is a full-mesh of iBGP sessions, one for each pair of routers. But a full-mesh is impractical for a large AS, since the number of sessions grows quadratically with the number of routers. Linear growth is accomplished with a hub-and-spoke structure. All routers exchange routes with a spoke called a route reflector. If these structures are incorrectly set up, protocol oscillations, forwarding loops, traffic blackholes, and violation of business contracts can arise [6,31,74]. See Section 9.6.4 for more discussion of BGP validation.

IP Assure evaluates requirements on integrity of logical structures associated with all common protocols. These structures include IP subnets, GRE tunnels, IPSec tunnels, MPLS [60] tunnels, BGP full-mesh or hub-and-spoke structures, OSPF subnets and areas, and HSRP router clusters.

9.4.2.2 Connectivity Requirements

Connectivity (also called reachability) is a fundamental requirement of a network. It means the existence of a path between two nodes in the network. The most obvious network is an IP network whose nodes represent subnets and routers and links represent direct connections between these. But as noted in Section 9.2, connectivity requirements are also meaningful for many other types of networks such as GRE, IPSec, and BGP. IP Assure evaluates connectivity for IP, VLANs, GRE, IPSec, BGP, and MPLS networks.

IP Assure also evaluates reachability in the presence of access-control policies, or lists, configured on routers or firewalls. An access-control list is a collection of rules specifying the IP packets that are permitted or denied based on their source and destination address, protocol, and source and destination ports. These rules are order-dependent. Given a packet, the rules are scanned from the top-down and the permit or deny action associated with the first matching rule is taken. Even if a path exists, a given packet may fail to reach a destination because an access-control list denies that packet.

9.4.2.3 Reliability Requirements

Reliability in a network means the ability to maintain connectivity in the presence of failures of nodes or links. A single point of failure for connectivity between two nodes in a network is said to exist if a single failure causes connectivity between the two nodes to be lost. Reliability is achieved by provisioning backup resources and setting up a reliability protocol. This protocol monitors for failures and when one occurs, finds backup resources and attempts to restore connectivity using those.

Configuration errors may prevent backup resources from being provisioned. For example, in Section 9.2, some GRE tunnels were only configured in one direction, not in the other, so they were unavailable for being rerouted over. Even if backup resources have been provisioned, configuration errors in the routing protocol can prevent these resources from being found. For example, in Section 9.2, BGP was simply not configured to run over some GRE tunnels, so it would not find these links to reroute over.

The architecture of the fault-tolerance protocol itself can introduce a single point of failure. For example, a nonzero OSPF area may be connected to OSPF area zero by a single area-border-router. If that router fails, then OSPF will fail to discover alternate routes to another area [36] even if these exist. Similarly, unless BGP route reflectors are replicated, they can become single points of failure [7].

Furthermore, redundant resources at one layer must be mapped to redundant resources at lower layers. For example, if all GRE tunnels originate at the same physical interface on a router, then if that interface fails, all tunnels would simultaneously fail. Ideally, all GRE tunnels originating at a router must originate at distinct interfaces on that router.

Single points of failure can also arise out of the dependence between security and reliability.

As shown in Fig. 9.5, routers R1 and R2 together constitute an HSRP cluster with R1 as the primary router. This cluster forms the gateway between an enterprise's internal network on the right and the WAN on the left. For security, an IPSec tunnel is configured from R1 to the gateway router C of a collaborating site. However, this tunnel is not replicated on R2. Consequently, if R1 fails, then R2 would take over the cluster's virtual address; however, IPSec connectivity to C would be lost.

Reliability requirements that IP Assure evaluates include absence of single points of failure in IP networks, with and without access-control policies; absence of single OSPF area-border-routers; and replication of IPSec tunnels in an HSRP cluster.

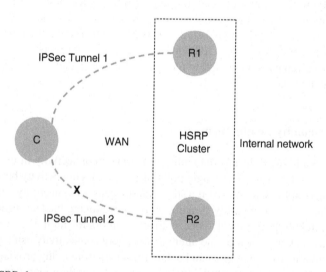

Fig. 9.5 HSRP cluster

9.4.2.4   Security Requirements

Typical network security requirements are about data confidentiality, data integrity, authentication, and access-control. IPSec is commonly used to satisfy the first three requirements and access-control lists are used to satisfy the last one. Access-control lists were discussed in Section 9.4.2.2. Components dedicated just to processing access-control lists are called firewalls. IP Assure evaluates requirements for both these technologies. For IPSec, it evaluates the tunnel integrity requirements in Section 9.4.2.1. For access-control lists, IP Assure evaluates two fundamental requirements. First, an access-control list subsumes another in that any packet permitted by the second is also permitted by the first. A related requirement is that one list is equivalent to another in that any packet permitted by one is permitted by the other. Two lists are equivalent if each subsumes the other. An enterprise may have multiple egress firewalls. Access-control lists on these may have been set up by different administrators over different periods of time. It is useful to check that the policy governing packets that leave the enterprise are equivalent. The second requirement that IP Assure evaluates on access-control lists is that a firewall has no redundant rules. A rule is redundant if deleting it will not change the set of packets a firewall permits. Deleting redundant rules makes lists compact and easier to understand and maintain.

9.4.2.5   Performance Requirements

The [19] protocol allows one to specify policies for partitioning packets into different classes, and then for according them differentiated performance treatment. For example, a packet with a higher DiffServ class is given transmission priority over one with a lower. Typically, voice packets are given highest priority because of the high sensitivity of voice quality to end-to-end delays. Performance requirements that IP Assure evaluates are that all DiffServ policies on all routers are identical, and that any policy that is defined is actually used by being associated with an interface.

IP Assure also evaluates the requirement that ICMP packets are not blocked. This is a sufficient condition for avoiding packet loss due to mismatched MTU sizes and setting of Do Not Fragment bits discussed in Section 9.2.

9.4.2.6   Government Regulatory Requirements

Government regulatory requirements represent "best practices" that have evolved over a period of time. Compliance to these is deemed essential for connectivity, reliability, security, and performance of an organization's network. Compliance to certain regulations such as the Federal Information Security Management Act (FISMA) [26] is mandatory for government organizations. Two examples of a FISMA requirement are (a) alternate communications services do not share a single point of failure with primary communication services, (b) all access between nodes internal to an enterprise and those external to it is mediated by a proxy server. IP Assure allows specification of a large number of FISMA requirements.

9.4.3 Specification Language

IP Assure's specification language is that of graphical templates. It offers a menu of more than 100 requirements in different categories. A user can select one or more of these to be evaluated. For each requirement, one can specify its parameters. For example, for a reachability requirement, one can specify the source and destination. For an access-control list equivalence requirement, one can specify the two lists. One cannot apply disjunction or quantification operators to requirements. The only way to define new requirements is to program in Java and SQL.

Figure 9.6 shows a few requirement classes that can be evaluated. These are QoS (DiffServ), HSRP, OSPF, BGP, and MPLS.

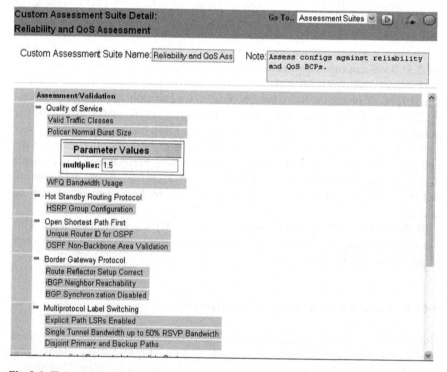

Fig. 9.6 IP Assure requirement specification screen

9.4.4 Evaluation System

Structural integrity requirements are evaluated with algorithms specialized to each requirement. In IP Assure, these algorithms are implemented with SQL and Java. The relevant tuples from the configuration database are extracted with SQL and analyzed by Java programs. For example, to evaluate whether an IPSec tunnel between two addresses `local1` and `local2` is set up, one checks that there are tuples `ipsec(h1, local1, remote1, ea1, ha1, filter1)` and `ipsec(h2, local2, remote2, ea2, ha2, filter2)` in the configuration database, and that `local1 = remote2`, `remote1 = local2`, `ea1 = ea2`, `ha1 = ha2` and `filter1` is a mirror image of `filter2`.

Reachability and reliability requirements for a network are evaluated by extracting the relevant graph information from the configuration database with SQL queries, then applying graph algorithms [63]. For example, given the tuple `ipAddress(host, interface, address, mask)`, one creates two nodes, the router `host` and the subnet whose address is the bitwise-and of `address` and `mask`, and then creates directed edges linking these in both directions. This step is repeated for all such tuples to compute an IP network graph.

To evaluate whether a node or a link is a single point of failure, one removes it from the graph and checks whether two nodes are reachable. If not, then the deleted node or link is a single point of failure. To check reachability in the presence of access-control lists, all edges at which these lists block a given packet are deleted, and then reachability analysis is repeated for the remaining graph.

Firewall requirements cannot be evaluated by enumerating all possible packets and checking for subsumption, equivalence, or redundancy. The total number of combinations of all source and destination addresses, ports, and protocols is astronomical: the total number of IPv4 source and destination address, source and destination port, and protocol combinations is 2^{104} (32 + 32 + 16 + 16 + 8). Instead, symbolic techniques are used. Each policy is represented as a constraint on the following fields of a packet: source and destination address, protocol, and source and destination ports. The constraint is true precisely for those packets that are permitted by the firewall, taking rule ordering into account. Let P1 and P2 be two policies and C1 and C2 be, respectively, the constraints representing them. The constraint can be constructed in time linear in the number of rules. Then, P1 is subsumed by P2 if there is no solution to the constraint $C1 \land \neg C2$. To check that a rule in P1 is redundant, delete it from P1 and check that the resulting policy is equivalent to P1.

For example, let a firewall contain the following rules that, for simplicity, only check whether the source and destination addresses are in definite ranges:

```
1, 2, 3, 4, deny
5, 6, 7, 8, permit
10, 15, 15, 20, permit
```

The first rule states that any packet with source address between 1 and 2 and destination address between 3 and 4 is denied. Similarly, for the second and third rules. These are represented by the following constraint C1 on the variables src and dst.

```
¬ (1=<src ∧ src=<2 ∧ 3=<dst ∧ dst=<4]) ∧
(5=<src ∧ src=<6 ∧ 7=<dst ∧ dst=<8) ∨
(10=<src ∧ src=<15 ∧ 15=<dst∧ dst=<20)
```

This constraint states that a packet is permitted if it is not the case that its source address is in $[1, 2]$ and destination address is in $[3, 4]$ and that these fields are either in $[5, 6]$ and $[7, 8]$, respectively, or in $[10, 15]$ and $[15, 20]$, respectively.

If there were another firewall with a single rule:

```
11, 12, 13, 14, permit
```

then the constraint C2 representing it would be

```
(11=<src∧src=<12 ∧ 13=<dst∧dst=<14)
```

To check whether the first firewall subsumes the second, check that C2∧¬C1 is unsolvable. A constraint solver will confirm that this is so. On the other hand, the solver will compute a solution to the constraint C1∧¬C2 as src = 5, dst = 7. Such constraints are solved by the ConfigAssure [51] system described in Section 9.5.

9.4.4.1 Proactive Evaluation

From just the configurations, IP Assure tries to guess requirements that the administrator intended and evaluates these. When its guess is correct, it saves the administrator the effort of explicitly specifying that requirement. When the guess is incorrect, the administrator can ignore the "false positive." For example, if IPSec is configured on an interface, then it is a good guess that IPSec should be configured on the remote endpoint of the tunnel. Then, the IPSec structural integrity requirement is evaluated. This approach has been implemented for a number of protocols. The intent for some requirements cannot be guessed. For example, in the FISMA requirement that all communication between internal and external subnets must pass through a firewall, one cannot guess what internal and external subnets are. IP Assure allows these to be explicitly specified.

9.4.4.2 Visualization

For visualization, IP Assure displays logical structures the way they are set up by configuration. Then, their integrity and defects both stand out. This approach has worked well for structures such as subnets, GRE tunnels, IPSec tunnels, OSPF areas, BGP full-meshes and hub-and-spoke structures, and HSRP router clusters. The relevant nodes and edges are extracted from the configuration database with SQL

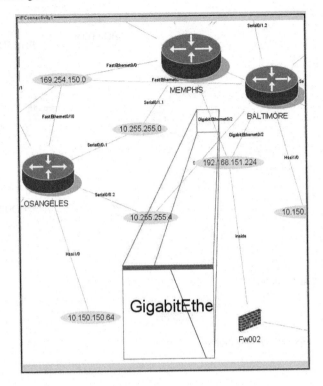

Fig. 9.7 Visualization of an IP network

queries and the Graphviz [30] layout tool is used. For example, in Fig. 9.7, nodes are routers and subnets, a link is only between a router and a subnet and represents that fact that the router has an interface on that subnet.

In Fig. 9.8, a link from a router to an area identifier means that the router has an interface in that area. This clearly shows that Area 10 has two border routers LOSANGELES and CHICAGO linking it to Area 0. Thus, there is no single point of failure due to a single ABR discussed above. However, the figure also shows that Area 17 has only a single ABR. This is a single point of failure as outlined in Section 9.4.2.3.

9.5 Logic-Based Techniques for Creating a Validation System

This section describes a suite of logic-based techniques that are particularly useful for creating a validation system. They simplify configuration acquisition and requirement specification. They allow firewall subsumption, equivalence, and rule redundancy analysis. Finally, they provide an efficient approach for solving the hard problem of configuration error repair. These techniques are the languages Prolog

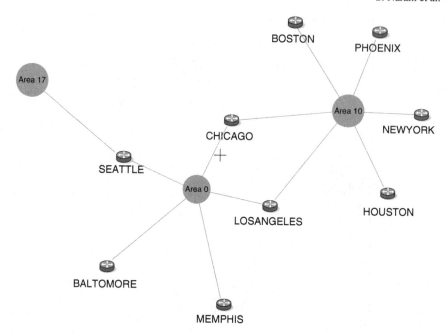

Fig. 9.8 OSPF topology visualization

and Datalog [53, 67] and arithmetic quantifier-free forms [51], the Kodkod [41] constraint solver for first-order logic, the minimum-cost ZChaff [73] SAT solver for Boolean logic, and Ordered Binary Decision Diagrams [12].

The Prolog language combines a rule-based programming language and a database into a single system. Its interpreter is based on the top-down SLD-resolution [53] inference procedure. Modern Prolog implementations are highly efficient and also have tight interfaces to external languages like C, C++, and Java. Algorithms that are best encoded in these languages can be so encoded, and then called from Prolog. Prolog databases of several million tuples can be efficiently queried [66]. Datalog is a restriction of Prolog to exclude data structures.

Kodkod is a Java API for solving a first-order logic constraint. While a Boolean constraint only contains Boolean variables, a first-order logic constraint can contain variables denoting data objects, relationships between these variables, and quantifiers on these variables. Kodkod solves a first-order logic constraint, in finite domains, by compiling it into a Boolean logic constraint, solving it with a SAT solver, and reflecting a solution back into a solution of the first-order logic constraint. If the constraint is unsolvable, Kodkod also computes a proof of unsolvability, inherited from the SAT solver. Typically, this is an unsolvable constraint that is much smaller than the original. The ZChaff SAT solver can solve millions of Boolean constraints in millions of Boolean variables in seconds. If costs are associated with the setting of a Boolean variable to true, then ZChaff can also be used to compute a minimum-cost solution to a constraint.

Any Boolean constraint can be transformed into a unique, equivalent form called an Ordered Binary Decision Diagram. Thus, equivalence between two Boolean constraints can be checked by checking that their OBDDs are identical. An OBDD also has the interesting property that if it is not trivially false, then it is satisfiable. The check for satisfiability is built into the algorithm to transform a Boolean constraint into its OBDD. However, OBDDs are efficiently constructed only for constraints with a few hundred Boolean variables although this size is ample for reasoning about firewalls.

The Service Grammar system used Prolog directly for specification and validation [50,58]. The ConfigAssure [51] system integrates Prolog with Kodkod. It allows fields in tuples in a configuration database to be variables. It computes values of these variables so that a given requirement becomes true of the database. It does so by transforming that requirement into an equivalent arithmetic quantifier-free form or QFF. A QFF is a Boolean combination of constraints formed from configuration variables, integers, the operators $+, -, <, =<, =, >, >=$, and bitwise logic operators. This QFF is then efficiently solved by Kodkod. If ConfigAssure is unable to find a solution, it outputs a proof of unsolvability, inherited from Kodkod. This proof is interpreted as a root-cause and guides configuration repair. Arithmetic quantifier-free forms constitute a good intermediate language between Boolean logic and first-order logic. Not only is it easy to express requirements in it, but it can also be efficiently compiled into Boolean logic. ConfigAssure was designed to avoid, where possible, the generation of very large intermediate constraints in Kodkod's transformation of first-order logic into Boolean.

If the fields that are responsible for making a requirement false are known, then one way to repair these is as follows: replace these fields with variables and use ConfigAssure to find new values of these variables that make the requirement true. Two approaches can be used to narrow down these fields. The first exploits the proof of unsolvability of the falsified requirement to compute a type of root-cause. The second exploits properties of Datalog proofs and ZChaff to compute that set of fields whose cost of change is minimal. The second approach has been developed in the MulVAL [35,55,56] system. More generally, MulVAL is a system for enterprise security analysis using attack graphs.

Ordered Binary Decision Diagrams are an alternative to SAT solvers for evaluating firewall policy subsumption and rule redundancy with a method conceptually similar to that in Section 9.4.4.

The use of these techniques for building different parts of a validation system is now illustrated with concrete examples based on the case study in Section 9.2.

9.5.1   Configuration Acquisition by Querying

When the structure of a configuration file is simple, as it is for Cisco's IOS, then it is not necessary to write a grammar with ANTLR or PADS/ML [47]. Instead, the structure can be put into a command database and then *queried* to construct the configuration database. The query needs to refer only to that part of the command database necessary to construct a given table. All other parts are ignored. This idea provides substantial resilience to insertion of new command blocks, insertion of new subcommands in a known command block, and insertion of new keywords in subcommands.

This idea is illustrated using Prolog, although any database engine could be used. Each command block is transformed into an ios_cmd tuple or Prolog fact, with the structure

```
ios_cmd(FileName, MainCommand, ListOfSubCommands)
```

where MainCommand and each item in ListOfSubCommands is of the form [NestingLevel | ListOfTokens]. [A|B] means the list with head A and tail B. For example, the IOS file of Section 9.4.1, named f here, is transformed into the following Prolog tuples:

```
ios_cmd(f, [0, hostname, router1], []).
ios_cmd(f,
    [0, interface, 'Ethernet0'],
    [   [1, ip, address, '1.1.1.1', '255.255.255.0'],
        [1, crypto, map, mapx] ]).
ios_cmd(f,
    [0, crypto, map, mapx, 6, 'ipsec-isakmp'],
    [   [1, set, peer, '3.3.3.3'],
        [1, set, 'transform-set', transx],
        [1, match, address, aclx]]).
ios_cmd(f,
    [0,crypto,ipsec,'transform-set',
        transx,'esp-3des',hmac], []).
ios_cmd(f,
    [0, ip, 'access-list', extended, aclx],
    [   [1, permit, gre, host, '3.3.3.3',
            host, '4.4.4.4']]).
```

Note the close correspondence between the structure of command blocks in the IOS file and associated ios_cmd tuples. One can now write Prolog rules to construct the configuration database. For instance, to construct rows for the ipAddress table, one can use:

```
ipAddress(H, I, A, M):-
        ios_cmd(File, [0, hostname, H|_], _),
        ios_cmd(File, [0, interface, I|_], Args),
        member(SubCmd, Args),
        subsequence([ip, address, A, M], SubCmd).
```

The syntactic convention followed in Prolog is that identifiers beginning with capital letters are variables, otherwise they are constants. The :- symbol is a shorthand for if. All variables are universally quantified. The rule states that ipAddress of an interface I on host H is A with mask M if there is a File containing a hostname command declaring host H, an interface command declaring interface I, and a subcommand of that command declaring its address and mask to be A and M, respectively.

Note that this definition is unaffected by subcommands of the `interface` command that are not of interest for computing `ipAddress`, or that are defined in a subsequent IOS release. It only tries to find a subcommand containing the sequence `[ip, address, A, M]`. It does not require that the subcommand be in a definite position in the block, or that the sequence `address A, M` appear in definite position in the `ip` subcommand. Now, where `H, I, A, M` are variables, the query `ipAddress(H, I, A, M)` will succeed with the solution `H = f`, `I = 'Ethernet0'`, `A = '1.1.1.1'` and `M = '255.255.255.0'`. Here `f` is a host, `I` is an interface on this host, and `A` and `M` its address and mask, respectively.

`ipsec` is more complex but querying simplifies the assembly of information from different parts of a configuration file. For each interface, one finds the name of a crypto map `Map` applied to that interface, and then finds the corresponding crypto map command, from which one can extract the peer address `Peer`, the filter `Filter`, and transform-set `Transform`. These values are used to select the `crypto ipsec` command from which the `Encrypt` and `Hash` values are extracted. Thus, the `ipSecTunnel(H, Address, Peer, Encrypt, Hash, Filter)` is constructed.

```
ipsec(H, Address, Peer, Encrypt, Hash, Filter):-
    ios_cmd(File, [0, interface, I |_], Args),
    member([_, crypto, map, Map |_], Args),
    ios_cmd(File, [0, hostname, H |_], _),
    ipAddress(H, I, Address, _),
    ios_cmd(File, [0, crypto, map, Map |_], CArgs),
    member([_, set, peer, Peer |_], CArgs),
    member([_, match, address, Filter|_], CArgs),
    member([_, set, 'transform-set',
          Transform |_], CArgs),
    ios_cmd(File, [0, crypto, ipsec,
          'transform-set', Transform, Encrypt, Hash],_).
```

The `ipAddress` and `ipsec` tuples are constructed in all possible ways via Prolog backtracking. Together, these form the configuration database for these protocols.

9.5.2   Specification Language

This section shows how Prolog can be used to specify the types of requirements in the case study of Section 9.2. It has already been used to validate VPN and BGP requirements [50, 58]

As shown in Fig. 9.9, routers RA and RB are in the same COI but RX is in a different COI. RA's configuration violates two security requirements and one connectivity requirement. First, RA has a GRE tunnel into RX. Second, RA has a default static route using which it can forward packets destined to RX, to the WAN. Third, RA does not have a GRE tunnel into RB. All these violations need to be detected and configurations repaired.

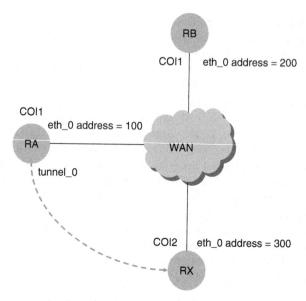

Fig. 9.9 Network violating security and connectivity requirements

A configuration database for the above network is represented by the following Prolog tuples:

```
static_route(ra, 0, 32, 400).
gre(ra, tunnel_0, 100, 300).
ipAddress(ra, eth_0, 100, 0).
ipAddress(rb, eth_0, 200, 0).
ipAddress(rx, eth_0, 300, 0).
coi([ra-coi1, rb-coi1, rx-coi2]).
```

The first tuple states that router ra has a default static route with a next hop of address 400. Normally, a mask is a sequence of 32 bits containing a sequence of ones followed by a sequence of zeros. In the ipAddress tuple, a mask is represented implicitly as the number of zeros at the end of the sequence. This simplifies the computations we need. The route is called "default" because any address matches it. The second states that router ra has a GRE tunnel originating from GRE interface tunnel_0 with local physical address 100 and remote physical address 300. The third tuple states that router ra has a physical interface eth_0 with address 100 and mask 0. Similarly, for the fourth and fifth tuples. The last tuple lists the community of interest of each router. Requirements are defined with Prolog clauses, e.g.:

```
good:-gre_connectivity(ra, rb).
gre_connectivity(RX, RY):-
    gre_tunnel(RX, RY),
    route_available(RX, RY).
```

```
gre_tunnel(RX, RY):-
    gre(RX, _, _, RemoteAddr),
    ipAddress(RY, _, RemoteAddr, _).
route_available(RX, RY):-
    static_route(RX, Dest, Mask, _),
    ipAddress(RY, _, RemotePhysical, 0),
    contained(Dest, Mask, RemotePhysical, 0).
contained(Dest, Mask, Addr, M):-
    Mask>=M,
    N is ((2^32-1)<< Mask)/\Dest,
    N is ((2^32-1)<< Mask)/\Addr.
bad:-gre_tunnel(ra, rx).
bad:-route_available(ra, rx).
```

The first clause states that good is true provided there is GRE connectivity between routers ra and rb since they are in the same COI. The second clause states that there is GRE connectivity between any two routers RX and RY provided RX has a GRE tunnel configured to RY and a route available to RY. The third clause states that a GRE tunnel to RY is configured on RX provided there is a GRE tuple on RX whose remote address is that of an interface on RY. The fourth clause states that a route to RY is available on RX provided an address RemotePhysical on RY is contained within the address range of a static route on RX. The fifth clause checks this containment. $<~<~$ is the left-shift operator and $/\backslash$ is the bitwise-and operator, not to be confused with the conjunction operator. The sixth clause states that bad is true provided there is a gre tunnel between ra and rx since ra and rx are *not* in the same COI. The last clause states that bad is also true provided a route on ra is available for packets with a destination on rx.

We now show how to capture requirements containing quantifiers. To capture the requirement all_good that between *every* pair of routers in a COI there is GRE connectivity, we can write:

```
all_good:-not(same_coi_no_gre).
same_coi_no_gre:-same_coi(X, Y), not(gre_connectivity (X, Y)).
same_coi(X, Y):-coi(L), member(X-C, L), member (Y-C, L).
```

The first rule states all_good is true provided same_coi_no_gre is false. The second rule states that same_coi_no_gre is true provided there exist X and Y that are in the same COI but for which gre_connectivity(X, Y) is false. The last rule states that X and Y are in the same COI provided there is some COI C such that X-C and Y-C are in the COI association list L.

Similarly, we can capture the requirement no_bad that *no* router contains a route to a router in a different COI.

As previously mentioned, the MulVAL system has proposed the use of Datalog for specification and analysis of attack graphs. Datalog is a restriction of Prolog in which arguments to relations are just variables or atomic terms, i.e., no complex terms and data structures. This restriction means, in particular, that predicates such as all_good and all_pairs_gre cannot be specified and neither can subnet_id since it needs bitwise operations. However, the first five Prolog tuples above and the first three rules can be specified. This restriction, however, permits MulVAL to perform fine-grained analysis of root-causes of configuration errors and to compute strategies for their repair. This is discussed in the next section.

9.5.3   Evaluation for Repair

If a configuration database and requirements are expressed in Prolog, then its query capability can be used to evaluate whether requirements are true. For example, the query route_available(ra, rb) is evaluated to be true by clauses for route_available, static_route, and contained. The query bad succeeds for two reasons. First, the static route on ra is a default route. It forwards packets to any destination, including to destinations in a different COI. Second, a GRE tunnel to router rx is configured on ra even though rx is in a different COI. On the other hand, the query good fails. This is because the predicate gre_tunnel(ra, rb) fails. The only GRE tunnel configured on ra is to rx, not to rb.

If requirement evaluation against a configuration database is the only goal, then a Prolog-based validation system is practical on a realistic scale. However, if a requirement is false for a configuration database and the goal is to change some fields in some tuples so that the requirement becomes true, then Prolog is not adequate. The Prolog query (good,not(bad)), representing the conjunction of good and not(bad), will simply fail. Prolog will not return new values of these fields that make the query true.

In order to efficiently compute new values of these fields, a constraint solver with the capability to compute a proof of unsolvability is needed. Such a capability is provided by the ConfigAssure system. ConfigAssure allows one to replace some fields in some tuples in a configuration database with configuration variables. These variables are *unrelated* to Prolog variables. ConfigAssure also allows one to specify a requirement R as an equivalent QFF RC on these configuration variables. Solving RC would compute new values of these fields, in effect repairing the fields.

For example, suppose we suspect that the query (good,not(bad)) fails because addresses and the static route mask are incorrect. We can replace all these with configuration variables to obtain the following database:

```
static_route(ra, dest(0), mask(0), 400).
gre(ra, tunnel_0, gre_a_local(0), gre_a_remote(0)).
ipAddress(ra, eth_0, ra_addr(0), 0).
ipAddress(rb, eth_0, rb_addr(0), 0).
ipAddress(rx, eth_0, rx_addr(0), 0).
coi([ra-coi1, rb-coi1, rx-coi2]).
```

Here, dest(0), mask(0), gre_a_local(0), gre_a_remote(0), ra_addr(0), rb_addr(0), rx_addr(0) are all configuration variables. In order that this database satisfy (good ∧ not(bad)), these configuration variables must satisfy the following constraint RC:

```
¬gre_a_remote(0)=rx_addr(0)∧
¬contained(dest(0),mask (0),
  rx_addr(0),0)
  ∧ gre_a_remote(0)=rb_addr(0)
  ∧ contained(dest(0),mask(0),rb_addr(0),0)
     ∧ ¬ ra_addr(0)=rb_addr(0) ∧ ¬rb_addr(0)=rx_addr(0) ∧
¬rx_addr(0)=ra_addr(0)
```

The constraint on the first two lines is equivalent to not(bad). It states that ra should neither have a GRE tunnel nor a static route to rx. The constraint on the next two lines is equivalent to good. It states that ra should have both a GRE tunnel and a static route to rb. The constraint on the last line states that all interface addresses are unique. Solving this constraint would indeed find new values of configuration variables and hence repair the fields. However, one may change fields, such as ra_addr(0), unrelated to the failure of (good,not(bad)). To change fields only related to failure, one can exploit the proof of unsolvability that ConfigAssure automatically computes when it fails to solve a requirement. This proof is a typically small and unsolvable part of the requirement, and can be taken to be a root-cause of unsolvability.

The idea is to generate a new constraint InitVal that is a conjunction of equations of the form x = c where x is a configuration variable that replaced a field and c is the initial value of that field. Now try to solve RC∧InitVal. Since R is false for the database without variables, ConfigAssure will find RC∧InitVal to be unsolvable and return a proof of unsolvability. If, in this proof, there is an equation x = c that is also in InitVal, then relax the value of x by deleting x = c from InitVal to create InitVal'. Reattempt a solution to RC∧InitVal' to find a new value of x. More than one such equation can be deleted in a single step. For example, the definition of InitVal for above configuration variables is:

```
dest(0)=0
∧ mask(0)=32
∧ gre_a_local(0)=100
∧ gre_a_remote(0)=300
∧ ra_addr(0)=100
∧ rb_addr(0)=200
∧ rx_addr(0)=300
```

Submitting RC∧InitVal to ConfigAssure generates a proof of unsolvability that ra should have a tunnel to rb but instead has one to rx:

```
gre_a_remote(0)=rb_addr(0) ∧ gre_a_remote(0)=300 ∧ rb_addr(0)=200
```

Deleting the second equation from InitVal to obtain InitVal' and solving RC∧InitVal' we obtain another proof of unsolvability that ra has a static route to rx:

```
rx_addr(0)=300 ∧ dest(0)=0 ∧ mask(0)=32 ∧
¬contained
   (dest(0),mask(0),rx_addr(0),0)
```

Deleting the second and third equations and solving, we obtain a solution that fixes both the GRE tunnel and the static route on `ra`:

```
dest(0)=200
mask(0)=0
gre_a_remote(0)=200
gre_a_local(0)=100
ra_addr(0)=100
rb_addr(0)=200
rx_addr(0)=300
```

Values of just the first three variables needed to be recomputed. Values of others do not need to be. Note that `ra_addr(0)` never appeared in a proof of unsolvability even though it did in RC. Thus, its value definitely does not need to be recomputed. This is not obvious from RC. Note also that repair is holistic in that it satisfies both `good` and `not(bad)`.

The remaining task is generation of the constraint RC. It is accomplished by thinking about specification as a method of computing an equivalent quantifier-free formula, i.e., defining the predicate `eval(Req, RC)` where `Req` is the name of a requirement and RC is a QFF equivalent to `Req`. The original Prolog specification of `Req` in Section 9.5.2 is no longer needed. It is replaced by a *metalevel* version as follows:

```
eval(bad, or(C1, C2)):-
    eval(gre_tunnel(ra, rx), C1),
    eval(route_available(ra, rx), C2).
eval(gre_tunnel(RX, RY), RemoteAddr=Addr):-
    gre(RX, _, _, RemoteAddr),
    ipAddress(RY, _, Addr, _).
eval(route_available(RX, RY), C):-
    static_route(RX, Dest, Mask, _),
    ipAddress(RY, _, RemotePhysical, _),
    C=contained(Dest, Mask, RemotePhysical, 0).
eval(addr_unique, C):-
    andEach([not(ra_addr(0)=rb_addr(0)),
            not(rb_addr(0)=rx_addr(0)),
            not(rx_addr(0)=ra_addr(0))], C).
eval(topReq, C):-
    eval(good, G),
    eval(bad, B),
    eval(addr_unique, AU),
    andEach([G, B, AU], C).
```

These rules capture the semantics of the Prolog rules. The first states that a QFF equivalent to `bad` is the disjunction of C1 and C2 where C1 is the QFF equivalent to `gre_tunnel(ra, rx)` and C2 is the QFF equivalent to `route_available(ra, rx)`. The second rule states that the QFF equivalent to `gre_tunnel(RX, RY)` is RemoteAddr= Addr where RemoteAddr is the remote physical address of a GRE tunnel on RX and Addr is the address of an interface on RY. The third rule states that the QFF equivalent to route_available(RX, RY) is C provided C is the constraint that RX contains a static route for an address on RY. The fourth rule computes the QFF for all interface addresses being unique. The last rule computes the QFF for the top-level constraint topReq.

Now, the Prolog query eval(topReq, RC) computes RC as above. As has been shown in [51], QFFs are much more expressive than Boolean logic, so it is not hard to write requirements using the eval predicate.

9.5.4 Repair with MulVAL

The MulVAL system proposes an alternative, precise method of computing the fields that cause the success of an undesirable requirement provided that requirement is expressed in Datalog. A requirement, such as bad, is said to be undesirable if it enables adversary success. This method is based on the observation that any tuple in a proof of an undesirable requirement is responsible for the truth of that requirement. These tuples contain all the fields that need to be replaced by configuration variables. For example, one proof of bad with the original Prolog specification in Section 9.5.2 is:

```
bad
gre_tunnel(ra, rx)
gre(ra, tunnel_0, 100, 300) ∧ ipAddress(rx, eth_0, 300, 0)
```

Here, each condition is implied by its successor by the use of a rule in the Prolog specification. The second proof of bad is:

```
bad
route_available(ra, rx)
static_route(ra,0,32,400) ∧ ipAddress(rx, eth_0,300,
  0) ∧ contained(0,32,300,0)
```

The tuples that contribute to the proof of bad are:

```
gre(ra, tunnel_0, 100, 300) -- from the first proof
ipAddress(rx, eth_0, 300, 0) -- from the first proof
static_route(ra, 0, 31, 400) -- from the second proof
```

The following tuples do not contribute to the proof of bad:

```
ipAddress(ra, eth_0, 100, 0).
ipAddress(rb, eth_0, 200, 0).
```

The three tuples in the proof of bad contain all the fields that need to be replaced by configuration variables. Note that the address of interfaces at ra and rb do not need to be replaced.

The MulVAL system does not actually compute new values of fields. It only computes the set of tuples that should be disabled to disable all proofs of the undesirable property. A tuple can be disabled by changing its fields to different values or deleting it. But, MulVAL computes the set in an optimal way. It first derives a Boolean formula representing all the ways in which tuples should be disabled, then solves this with a minimum-cost SAT solver. A solution represents a set of tuples to disable. For example, the Boolean formula for the above two proofs is:

```
¬ gre(ra, tunnel_0, 100, 300) ∨ ¬ipAddress(rx, eth_0,300, 0) ∧
¬ ipAddress(rx, eth_0, 300, 0) ∨ ¬static_route(ra, 0, 32, 400)
```

The first formula states that to disable the first proof, either the gre tuple or the ipAddress tuple must be disabled. The second formula states that to disable the second proof, either the ipAddress or the static_route tuple must be disabled. Costs are associated with disabling each tuple. The minimum-cost SAT solver computes that set of tuples whose cost of disabling is a minimum. For example, the cost of disabling the ipAddress tuple may be high because many requirements depend on this tuple. The cost of disabling the static_route and gre tuples may be a lot lower. It is not, in general, simple to assign cost to disabling a tuple. Furthermore, this approach only computes how to disable an undesirable requirement. It does not guarantee that disabled tuples will also not disable desirable requirements, unless these latter requirements are also expressed in Boolean logic and the combined constraint is solved.

9.5.5 Evaluating Firewall Requirements with Binary Decision Diagrams

Hamed et al. [34] evaluate firewall subsumption and rule redundancy using Ordered Binary Decision Diagrams [12]. Their algorithm is conceptually the same as in Section 9.4.4. It first transforms firewall policies into Boolean constraints upon source and destination addresses, source and destination ports, and the protocol. These constraints are true only for those packets that are permitted by the firewall. These fields are represented as sequences of Boolean variables, e.g., an address field as a sequence of 32 variables and a port field as a sequence of 16 bits. The algorithm then checks whether combinations of constraints for evaluating subsumption and redundancy have a solution. Since constraints are represented as Ordered Binary Decision Diagrams, this check is straightforward. By contrast, ConfigAssure represents the above fields as integer variables and represents a policy as an arithmetic quantifier-free form constraint. It lets Kodkod transform this into a Boolean constraint and use a SAT solver to check satisfiability.

9.6 Related Work

9.6.1 Configuration Acquisition by Type Inference

Another approach to parsing configuration files is with the use of PADS/ML system [47]. Based on the functional language ML, PADS/ML describes the accepted language as if it were a type definition. PADS/ML supports the generation of parser, printer, data structure representation, and a generic interface to this representation. The generated code is in OCAML [43] language and additional tools, written in OCAML, then manipulate the internal data structure. This internal data structure is traversed to populate the relational database in the same way that the ANTLR abstract syntax tree is traversed.

Adaptive parsers are reported in [17]. These can modify the language they recognize when given examples of legal input. The inference system recognizes commands that are only handled in the abstract, much as the ANTLR grammar of IP Assure skips over some commands. Repeated instances of commands are used to generate new PADS/ML types, which are then further refined to provide access to fields in the commands. This means that as the IOS language evolves, the parser can evolve to provide an ever richer internal representation.

9.6.2 Symbolic Reachability Analysis

Instead of performing reachability analysis for each packet, a system for reachability analysis for sets of packets is described in Xie et al. [72]. This makes it possible to evaluate a requirement such as "a change in static routes at one or more routers does not change the set of packets that can flow between two nodes." It is not feasible to evaluate such a requirement by enumerating all packets and checking reachability. In this system, the reachability upper bound is defined to be the *union* of all packets permitted by each possible forwarding path from the source to the destination. This bound models a security policy that denies some packets (i.e., those outside the upper bound) under all conceivable operational conditions. The reachability lower bound is defined to be the common set of packets allowed by *every* feasible forwarding path from the source to the destination. This bound models a resilience policy that assures the delivery of some packets despite network faults, as long as a backup forwarding path exists. Algorithms are created for estimating the reachability upper and lower bounds from a network's packet filter configurations. Moreover, the work shows that it is possible to jointly reason about how packet filters, routing, and packet transformations affect reachability.

An interesting implementation of reachability analysis for sets of packets is found in the ConfigChecker [3] system. It represents the network's packet forwarding behavior as a giant state machine in which a state defines what packets are at what routers. However, the state-transition relation is not represented explicitly but rather symbolically as a constraint that must be satisfied by two states for the network to transition between these. This constraint itself is represented as an Ordered Binary Decision Diagram and input to a symbolic model checker [48]. Reachability requirements such as that above are expressed in Computational Tree Logic [48] and the symbolic model checker used to evaluate these. The transition-relation also takes into account features such as IPSec tunnels, multicast, and network address translation.

9.6.3 Alloy Specification Language

Alloy [2, 39] is a first-order relational logic system. It lets one specify object types and their attributes. It also lets one specify first-order logic constraints on these attributes. These are more expressive than Prolog constraints. Alloy solves constraints by compiling these into Kodkod and using Kodkod's constraint solver. The use of Alloy for network configuration management was explored in [49].Alloy's specification language is very appropriate for specifying requirements. All the requirements in Section 9.2 can be compactly expressed in Alloy. However, its constraint solver is inappropriate for evaluating requirements. This is because the compilation of first-order logic into Boolean logic leads to very large intermediate constraints. Kodkod addresses this problem by its partial-model optimization that exploits knowledge about parts of the solution. If the value of a variable is already known, it does not appear in the constraint that is submitted to the SAT solver. ConfigAssure follows a related approach but at a higher layer. The intuition is that given a requirement, many parts of it can be efficiently solved with non-SAT methods. Solving these parts and simplifying can yield a requirement that truly requires the power of a SAT solver. This plan is carried out by transforming a requirement into an equivalent quantifier-free form by defining the eval predicate for that requirement. QFFs have the property that not only is it easy to write eval rules, but also that QFFs are efficiently compiled and solved by Kodkod. Evaluation of parts of requirements and simplification are accomplished in the definition of eval.

9.6.4 BGP Validation

The Internet is, by definition, a "network of networks," and the responsibility for gluing together the tens of thousands of independently administered networks falls to the Border Gateway Protocol (BGP) [59, 64]. A network, or AS uses BGP to tell neighboring networks about each block of IP addresses it can reach; in turn, neighboring ASes propagate this information to their neighbors, allowing the entire Internet to learn how to direct packets toward their ultimate destinations. On the surface, BGP is a relatively simple path-vector routing protocol, where each router selects a single best route among those learned from its neighbors, adds its own AS number to the front of the path, and propagates the updated routing information to its neighbors for their consideration; packets flow in the reverse direction, with each router directing traffic along the chosen path in a hop-by-hop fashion.

Yet, BGP is a highly configurable protocol, giving network operators significant control over how each router selects a "best" route and whether that route is disseminated to its neighbors. The configuration of BGP across the many routers in an AS collectively expresses a routing policy that is based on potentially complex business objectives [15]. For example, a large Internet Service Provider (ISP) uses BGP policies to direct traffic on revenue-generating paths through their own downstream customers, rather than using paths through their upstream providers. A small AS like a university campus or corporate network typically does not propagate a BGP route learned from one upstream provider to another, to avoid carrying data traffic between the two larger networks. In addition, network operators may configure BGP to filter unexpected routes that arise from configuration mistakes and malicious attacks in other ASes [14,52]. BGP configuration also affects the scalability of the AS, where network operators choose not to propagate routes for their customers' small address blocks to reduce the size of BGP routing tables in the rest of the Internet. Finally, network operators tune their BGP configuration to direct traffic away from congested paths to balance load and improve user-perceived performance [25].

The routing policy is configured as a "route map" that consists of a sequence of clauses that match on some attributes in the BGP route and take a specific action, such as discarding the route or modifying its attributes with the goal of influencing the route-selection process. The BGP defines many different attributes, and the route-selection process compares the routes one attribute at a time to ultimately identify one "best" route. This somewhat indirect mechanism for selecting and propagating routes, coupled with the large number of route attributes and route-selection steps, makes configuring BGP routing policy immensely complicated and error-prone. Network operators often use tools for automatically configuring their BGP-speaking routers [11, 21, 29]. These tools typically consist of a template that specifies the sequence of vendor-specific commands to send to the router, with parameters unique to each BGP session populated from a database; for example, these parameters might indicate a customer's name, AS number, address block(s), and the appropriate route-maps to use. When automated tools are not used, the network operators typically have configuration-checking tools to ensure that the sessions are configured correctly, and that different sessions are configured in a consistent manner [16,24].

Configuring the BGP sessions with neighboring ASes, while important, is not the only challenge in BGP configuration. In practice, an AS consists of multiple routers in different locations; in fact, a large ISP may easily have hundreds if not thousands of routers connected by numerous links into a backbone topology. Different routers connect to different neighbor ASes, giving each router only a partial view of the candidate BGP routes. As such, large ISPs typically run BGP *inside* their networks to allow the routers to construct a more complete view of the available routes. These internal BGP (iBGP) sessions must be configured correctly to ensure that each router has all the information it needs to select routes that satisfy the AS's policy. The simplest solution is to have a "full-mesh" configuration, with an iBGP session between each pair of routers. However, this approach does not scale, forcing large ISPs to introduce hierarchy by configuring *route reflectors* or *confederations* that limit the number of iBGP sessions and constrain the dissemination of routes. Each route reflector, for instance, selects a single "best route" that it disseminates to its clients; as such, the route-reflector clients do not learn all the candidate routes they would have learned in a full-mesh configuration.

When the "topology" formed by these iBGP sessions violates certain properties, routing anomalies like protocol oscillations, forwarding loops, traffic blackholes, and violations of business contracts can arise [6, 31, 74]. Fortunately, static analysis of the iBGP topology, spread over the configuration of the routers inside the AS, can detect when these problems might arise [24]. Such tools check, for instance, that the top-level route reflectors are fully connected by a "full-mesh" of iBGP sessions. This prevents "signaling partitions" that could prevent some routers from learning *any* route for a destination. Static analysis can also check that route reflectors are "close" to their clients in the underlying network topology, to ensure that the route reflectors make the same routing decisions that their clients would have made with full information about the alternate routes. Finally, these tools can validate an ISP's own local rules for ensuring reliability in the face of router failures. For instance, static analysis can verify that each router is configured with at least two route-reflector parents. Collectively, these kinds of checks on the static configuration of the network can prevent a wide variety of routing anomalies.

For the most part, configuration validation tools operate on the vendor-specific configuration commands applied to individual routers. Configuration languages vary from one vendor to another, – for example, Cisco and Juniper routers have very different syntax and commands, even for relatively similar configuration tasks. Even within a single company, different router products and different generations of the router operating system have different commands and options. This makes configuration validation an immensely challenging task, where the configuration-checking tools much support a wide range of languages and commands. To address these challenges, research and standards activities have led to new BGP configuration languages that are independent of the vendor-specific command syntax [1, 71], particularly in the area of BGP routing policy. In addition to abstracting vendor-specific details, these frameworks provide some support for configuring entire networks rather than individual routers. For example, the Routing Policy Specification Language (RPSL) [1] is object-oriented, where objects contain AS-wide policy and administrative information that can be published in Internet Routing Registries [37]. Routing policy can be expressed in terms of user-friendly keywords for defining actions and groups of address blocks or AS number. Configuration-generation tools can read these specifications to generate vendor-specific commands to apply to the individual routers [37]. However, while RPSL is used for publishing information in the IRRs, many ISPs still use their own configuration tools (or manual processes) for configuring their underlying routers.

In summary, the configuration of BGP takes place at many levels – within a single router (to specify a single end point of a BGP session with the appropriate route-maps and addresses), between pairs of routers (to ensure consistent configuration of the two ends of a BGP session), across different sessions to the same neighboring AS (to ensure consistent application of the routing policy at each connection point), and across an entire AS (to ensure that the iBGP topology is configured correctly). In recent years, tools have emerged for static analysis of router-configuration data to identify potential configuration mistakes, and for automated generation of the configuration commands that are sent to the routers. Still, many interesting challenges remain in raising the level of abstraction for configuring BGP, to move from the low-level focus on configuring individual routers and BGP sessions toward configuring an entire network, and from the specific details of the BGP route attributes and route-selection process to a high-level specification of an AS's routing policy. As the Internet continues to grow, and the business relationships between ASes become increasingly complex, these issues will only become more important in the years ahead.

9.6.5 Other Validation Systems

Netsys was an early software product for configuration validation. It was first acquired by Cisco Systems and then by WANDL Corporation. It contained about a 100 requirements that were evaluated against router configurations. OPNET offers validation products NetDoctor and NetMapper. These are not standalone but rather modules that need to be plugged into the base IT Sentinel system [54]. For more description of these, see [23]. None of these products offer configuration repair, reasoning about firewalls, or symbolic reachability analysis. The Smart Firewalls work [13] was an early attempt at Telcordia to develop a network configuration validation system. A survey of system, not network, configuration is found in [4]. Formal methods for jointly reasoning about IPSec and firewall polices are described in [32]. A high-level configuration language is described in [45].

9.7 Summary and Directions for Future Research

To set up network infrastructure satisfying end-to-end requirements, it is not only necessary to run appropriate protocols on components but also to correctly configure these components. Configuration is the "glue" for logically integrating components at and across multiple protocol layers. Each component has a finite number of configuration parameters, each of which can be set to a definite value. However, today, the large conceptual gap between end-to-end requirements and configurations is manually bridged. This causes large numbers of configuration errors whose adverse effects on security, reliability, and high cost of deployment of network infrastructure are well documented. See also [57, 62].

Thus, it is critical to develop validation tools that check whether a given configuration is consistent with the requirements it is intended to implement. Besides checking consistency, configuration validation has another interesting application, namely network testing. The usual invasive approach to testing has several limitations. It is not scalable. It consumes resources of the network and network administrators and has the potential to unleash malware into the network. Some properties such as absence of single points of failure are impractical to test as they require failing components in operational networks. A noninvasive alternative that overcomes these limitations is analyzing configurations of network components. This approach is analogous to testing software by analyzing its source code rather than by running it. This approach has been evaluated for a real enterprise.

Configuration validation is inherently hard. Whether a component is correctly configured cannot be evaluated in isolation. Rather, the global relationships into which the component has been logically integrated with other components have to be evaluated. Configuration repair is even harder since changing configurations to make one requirement true may falsify another. The configuration change should be holistic in that it should ensure that all requirements concurrently hold.

This chapter described the challenges of configuring a typical collaboration network and the benefits of using a validation system. It then presented an abstract design of a configuration validation system. It consists of four subsystems: configuration acquisition system, requirement library, specification language, and evaluation system. The chapter then surveyed technologies for realizing this design. Configuration acquisition systems have been built using three approaches: parser generator, type inference, and database query. Classes of requirements in their Requirements Library are logical structure integrity, connectivity, security, reliability, performance, and government regulatory. Specification languages include visual templates, Prolog, Datalog, arithmetic quantifier-free forms, and Computational Tree Logic. Evaluation systems have used graph algorithms, the Kodkod constraint solver for first-order logic constraints, the ZChaff SAT solver for Boolean constraints, Binary Decision Diagrams, and symbolic model checkers. Visualization of not just the IP topology but also of various other logical topologies provides useful insights into network architecture. Logic-based languages are very useful for creating a validation system, particularly for solving the hard problems of configuration repair and symbolic reasoning about requirements.

Future research needs to focus on all four components of a validation system. Robust configuration acquisition systems are critical to automated validation. The accumulated experience of building large networks is vast but largely unformalized. Formalizing these in a Requirement Library would not only raise the level of abstraction at which network requirements are written but also improve their precision. New classes of requirements, one on VLAN optimization and another on configuration complexity, are reported in [28, 65] and in [9], respectively. Specification languages that are easy to use by network administrators are also critical for broad adoption of validation systems. Logic-based languages are a good candidate despite the perception that these are too complex for administrators. These are closest in form to the natural language requirements in network design documents. The configuration languages administrators use are already declarative in that they do not contain side-effects and the ordering of commands is unimportant. Introducing logical operators, data structures, and quantifiers into these is a natural step toward making these much more expressive. See [71] for a recent example of using the Haskell functional language for specifying BGP policies. High-level descriptions of component configurations could then again be composed by logical operators to describe network-wide requirements. In the nearer term, even making an implementation of the Requirement Library available as APIs in system administration languages like Perl or Python should vastly improve configuration debugging. Much greater understanding is needed of useful ways to visualize logical structures and relationships in networks. One might derive inspiration from works such as [70]. Finally, a good framework for repairing configurations was described in Section 9.5.3, but it needs to be further explored. For example, one needs to understand how the convergence of the repair procedure is affected by choice of configuration variable to relax, and how ideas of MulVAL can be generalized and combined with those of ConfigAssure. Creating the trust in network administrators before they allow automated repair of their component configurations is an open problem.

Acknowledgments We are very grateful to Jennifer Rexford, Andreas Voellmy, Richard Yang, Chuck Kalmanek, Simon Ou, Geoffrey Xie, Yitzhak Mandelbaum, Ehab Al-Shaer, Sanjay Rao, Adel El-Atawy, and Paul Anderson for their contributions and comments.

References

1. Alaettinoglu, C., Villamizar, C., Gerich, E., Kessens, D., Meyer, D., Bates, T., et al. (1999). Routing Policy Specification Language. RFC 2622.
2. Alloy. http://alloy.mit.edu/
3. Al-Shaer, E., Marrero, W., El-Atawy, A., & ElBadawy, K. (2008). *Towards global verification and analysis of network access control configuration.* Technical Report, TR-08-008, DePaul University, from http://www.mnlab.cs.depaul.edu/projects/ConfigChecker/TR-08-008/paper.pdf
4. Anderson P (2006) System Configuration. In Short Topics in System Administration ed. Rick Farrow. USENIX Association.
5. ANTRL v3. http://www.antlr.org/
6. Basu, A., Ong, C.H., Rasala, A., Shepherd, F.B., & Wilfong, G. (2002). Route oscillations in I-BGP with route reflection. *ACM SIGCOMM.*
7. Bates, T., Chandra, R., & Chen, E. (2000). BGP route reflection – an alternative to full mesh IBGP. RFC 2796. http://www.faqs.org/rfcs/rfc2796
8. Bellovin, R., & Bush, R. (2009). Configuration management and security. *IEEE Journal on Selected Areas in Communications [special issue on Network Infrastructure Configuration],* 27(Suppl. 3).
9. Benson, T., Akella, A., & Maltz, D. (2009). Unraveling the complexity of network management. *USENIX Symposium on Network Systems Design and Implementation.*
10. Berkowitz, H. (2000). Techniques in OSPF-Based Network. http://tools.ietf.org/html/draft-ietf-ospf-deploy-00
11. Bohm, H., Feldmann, A., Maennel, O., Reiser, C., & Volk, R. (2005). Network-wide inter-domain routing policies: Design and realization. Unpublished report, http://www.net.t-labs.tu-berlin.de/papers/BFMRV-NIRP-05.pdf.

12. Bryant, R. (1986). Graph-based algorithms for Boolean function manipulation. *IEEE Transactions on Computers*, C-35(Suppl. 8), 677–691.
13. Burns, J., Cheng, A., Gurung, P., Martin, D., Rajagopalan, S., Rao, P., et al. (2001). Automatic management of network security policy. *Proceedings of DARPA Information Survivability Conference and Exposition (DISCEX II'01)*, volume 2, Anaheim, CA.
14. Butler, K., Farley, T., McDaniel, P., & Rexford, J. (2008). A survey of BGP security issues and solutions. Unpublished manuscript.
15. Caesar, M., & Rexford, J. (2005). BGP routing policies in ISP networks. *IEEE Network Magazine* [Special issue on Interdomain Routing], *19*, 5–11.
16. Caldwell, D., Gilbert, A., Gottlieb, J., Greenberg, A., Hjalmtysson, G., & Rexford, J. (2003). The cutting EDGE of IP router configuration. *ACM SIGCOMM HotNets Workshop*.
17. Caldwell, D., Lee, S., & Mandelbaum, Y. (2008). Adaptive parsing of router configuration languages. *Proceedings of the Internet Management Workshop*.
18. Cheswick, W., Bellovin, S., & Rubin, A. (2003). *Firewalls and Internet security: Repelling the Wily Hacker*. Reading, MA: Addison-Wesley.
19. Cisco Systems. (2005). DiffServ – The Scalable End-to-End QoS Model.
20. Distributed Management Task Force, from http://www.dmtf.org/home
21. Enck, W., Moyer, T., McDaniel, P., Sen, S., Sebos, P., Spoerel, S., et al. (2009). Configuration management at massive scale: System design and experience. *IEEE Journal on Selected Areas in Communications. 27*(Suppl. 3), 323–335.
22. Farinacci, D., Li, T., Hanks, S., Meyer, D., & Traina, P. (2000). Generic routing and encapsulation. RFC 2784.
23. Feamster, N. (2006). *Proactive techniques for correct and predictable Internet routing*. Doctoral dissertation, Massachusetts Institute of Technology, Boston, MA.
24. Feamster, N., & Balakrishnan, H. (2005). Detecting BGP configuration faults with static analysis. Symposium on Networked Systems Design and Implementation.
25. Feamster, N., & Rexford, J. (2007). Network-wide prediction of BGP routes. *IEEE/ACM Transactions on Networking, 15*(2), 253–266.
26. Federal Information Security Management Act. (2002). National Institute of Standards and Technology.
27. Fu, Z., & Malik, S. (2006). Solving the minimum-cost satisfiability problem using branch and bound search. *Proceedings of IEEE/ACM International Conference on Computer-Aided Design ICCAD*.
28. Garimella, P., Sung Y.W., Zhang, N., & Rao, S. (2007). Characterizing VLAN usage in an Operational Network. *ACM SIGCOMM Workshop on Internet Network Management*.
29. Gottlieb, J., Greenberg, A., Rexford, J., & Wang, J. (2003). Automated provisioning of BGP customers IEEE Network Magazine.
30. Graphviz. http://www.graphviz.org/
31. Griffin, T.G., & Wilfong, G. (2002). On the correctness of IBGP configuration. *Proceedings of ACM SIGCOMM*.
32. Guttman, J. (1997). Filtering postures: local enforcement for global policies. *Proceedings of the 1997 IEEE Symposium on Security and Privacy*.
33. Halabi, B. (1997). Internet routing architectures. Indianapolis, IN: New Riders Publishing.
34. Hamed, H., Al-Shaer, E., & Marrero, W. (2005). Modeling and verification of IPSec and VPN security policies. *Proceedings of IEEE International Conference on Network Protocols*.
35. Homer, J., & Ou, X. (2009). SAT-solving approaches to context-aware enterprise network security management. IEEE JSAC [Special Issue on Network Infrastructure Configuration].
36. Huitema, C. (1999). Routing in the Internet. Upper Saddle River, NJ: Prentice Hall.
37. Internet Routing Registry Toolset Project, from https://www.isc.org/software/IRRtoolset
38. IP Assure. Telcordia Technologies, Inc., from http://www.telcordia.com/products/ip-assure/
39. Jackson, D. (2006). Software abstractions: Logic, language, and analysis. Cambridge, MA: MIT Press.
40. Juniper Networks. (2008). What is behind network downtime? Proactive steps to reduce human error and improve availability of networks, from http://www.juniper.net/ solutions/literature/white_papers/200249.pdf

41. Kodkod, from http://web.mit.edu/emina/www/kodkod.html
42. Lampson, B. (2000). Computer security in real world. Annual computer security applications conference, from http://research.microsoft.com/en-us/um/people/blampson/64-securityinrealworld/acrobat.pdf
43. Leroy, X., Doligez, D., Garrigue, J., Rémy, D., & Vouillon, J. (2007). The objective caml system, release 3.10, documentation and user's manual.
44. Li, T., Cole, B., Morton, P., & Li, D. (1998). Cisco Hot Standby Router Protocol. RFC 2281.
45. Lobo, J., & Pappas, V. (2008). C2: The case for network configuration checking language. Proceedings of IEEE Workshop on Policies for Distributed Systems and Networks.
46. Mahajan, Y., Fu, Z., & Malik, S. (2004). Zchaff2004, An Efficient SAT Solver. Proceedings of 7th International Conference on Theory and Applications of Satisfiability Testing.
47. Mandelbaum, Y., Fisher, K., Walker, D., Fernandez, M., & Gleyzer, A. (2007). PADS/ML: A functional data description language. ACM Symposium on Principles of Programming Language.
48. McMillan, K. (1992). Symbolic model checking. Doctoral dissertation, Computer Science Department, Carnegie Mellon University, Pittsburgh, PA.
49. Narain, S. (2005). Network configuration management via model-finding. Proceedings of USENIX Large Installation System Administration (LISA) Conference.
50. Narain, S., Kaul, V., & Parmeswaran, K. (2003). Building autonomic systems via configuration. Proceedings of AMS Autonomic Computing Workshop.
51. Narain, S., Levin, G., Kaul, V., & Malik, S. (2008). Declarative infrastructure configuration synthesis and debugging. In E. Al-Shaer, C. Kalmanek, F. Wu (Eds), Journal of Network Systems and Management [Special issue on Security Configuration]
52. Nordstrom, O. & Dovrolis, C. (2004). Beware of BGP attacks. ACM SIGCOMM Computer Communications Review, 34(Suppl. 2), 1–8.
53. O'Keefe, R. (1990). The craft of prolog. Reading, MA: Addison Wesley.
54. OPNET IT Sentinel, from http://www.opnet.com/solutions/network_planning_operations/it_sentinel.html
55. Ou, X., Boyer, W., & McQueen, M. (2006). A scalable approach to attack graph generation. 13th ACM Conference on Computer and Communications Security (CCS).
56. Ou, X., Govindavajhala, S., & Appel, A. (2005). MulVAL: A logic-based network security analyzer. 14th USENIX Security Symposium, Baltimore, MD.
57. Pappas, V., Wessels, D., Massey, D., Terzis, A., Lu, S., & Zhang, L. (2009). Impact of configuration errors on DNS robustness. IEEE Journal on Selected Areas in Communication, 27(Suppl. 1), 275–290.
58. Qie, X., & Narain, S. (2003). Using service grammar to diagnose configuration errors in BGP-4. Proceedings of USENIX Systems Administrators Conference.
59. Rekhter, Y., Li, T., & Hares, S. (2006). A Border Gateway Protocol 4 (BGP-4), RFC 4271.
60. Rosen, E., Viswanathan, A., & Callon, R. (2001). Multiprotocol Label Switching Architecture. RFC 3031.
61. Schwartz, J. (2007). Who Needs Hackers? New York Times http://www.nytimes.com/2007/09/12/technology/techspecial/12threat.html
62. Securing Cyberspace for the 44th Presidency. (2008). CSIS Commission On Cybersecurity.
63. Sedgewick, R. (2003). Algorithms in Java. Reading, MA: Addison Wesley.
64. Stewart, J. (1999). BGP4: Inter-Domain Routing in the Internet. Reading, MA: Addison-Wesley.
65. Sung, E.Y., Rao, S., Xie, G., & Maltz, D. (2008). Towards systematic design of enterprise networks. ACM CoNEXT Conference.
66. SWI-Prolog Semantic Web Library, from http://www.swi-prolog.org/pldoc/package/semweb.html
67. SWI-Prolog, from http://www.swi-prolog.org/
68. TCP Problems with Path MTU discovery. RFC 2923.
69. Torlak, E., & Jackson, D. (2007). Kodkod: A Relational Model Finder. Tools and Algorithms for Construction and Analysis of Systems (TACAS '07).

70. Tufte, E. (2001). The visual display of quantitative information. Cheshire, CT: Graphics Press.
71. Voellmy, A., & Hudak, P. Nettle: A domain-specific language for routing configuration, from http://www.haskell.org/YaleHaskellGroupWiki/Nettle
72. Xie, G., Zhan, J., Maltz, D., Zhang, H., Greenberg, A., Hjalmtysson, G., et al. (2005). On static reachability analysis of IP networks. *IEEE INFOCOM*.
73. ZChaff, from http://www.princeton.edu/~chaff/
74. Zhang-Shen, R., Wang, Y., & Rexford, J. (2008). Atomic routing theory: Making an AS route like a single node. Princeton University Computer Science technical report TR-827-08.

Part V
Network Measurement

Chapter 10
Measurements of Data Plane Reliability and Performance

Nick Duffield and Al Morton

10.1 Introduction

10.1.1 Service Without Measurement: A Brief History

Measurement was not a priority in the original design of the Internet, principally because it was not needed in order to provide Best Effort service, and because the institutions using the Internet were also the providers of this network. A technical strength of the Internet has been that endpoints have not needed visibility into the details of the underlying network that connects them in order to transmit traffic between one another. Rather, the functionality required for data to reach one host from another is separated into layers that interact through standardized interfaces. The transport layer provides a host with the appearance of a conduit through which traffic is transferred to another host; lower layers deal with routing the traffic through the network, and the actual transmission of the data over physical links. The Best Effort service model offers no hard performance guarantees to which conformance needs to be measured. Basic robustness of connectivity – the detection of link failures and rerouting traffic around them – was a task of the network layer, and so need not concern the endpoints.

The situation described above has changed over the intervening years; the complexity of networks, traffic, and the protocols that mediate them, the separation of network users from network providers, coupled with customer needs for service guarantees beyond Best Effort now require detailed traffic measurements to manage and engineer traffic, and to verify that performance meets required goals, and to diagnose performance degradations when they occur. In the absence of detailed

N. Duffield (✉)
AT&T Labs, 180 Park Avenue, Florham Park, NJ 07901, USA
e-mail: duffield@research.att.com

Al Morton
AT&T Labs, 200 S Laurel Ave, Middletown, NJ 07748, USA
e-mail: acmorton@att.com

C.R. Kalmanek et al. (eds.), *Guide to Reliable Internet Services and Applications*,
Computer Communications and Networks, DOI 10.1007/978-1-84882-828-5_10,
© Springer-Verlag London Limited 2010

network monitoring capabilities integrated with the network, many researchers, developers, and vendors jumped into the void to provide solutions. As measurement methodologies become increasingly mature, the challenge for service providers becomes how to deploy and manage measurement infrastructure scalably. Indeed, to meet this need, sophisticated measurement capabilities are increasingly being found on network routers. Furthermore, all parties concerned with the provenance and interpretation of measurements – vendors of measurement systems, software and services, service providers and enterprises, network users and customers – need a consistent way to specify how measurements are to be conducted, collected, transmitted, and interpreted. Many of these aspects for both passive and active measurement are now codified by standard bodies.

We continue this introduction by briefly setting out the type of passive and active measurements that are the subject of this chapter, then previewing the broader challenges that face service providers in realizing them in their networks.

10.1.2 Passive and Active Measurement Methods

This chapter is concerned with two forms of dataplane measurement: passive and active measurements. These two types of measurement have generally focused on different aspects of network behavior, support different applications, and are accomplished by different technical means.

- *Passive measurement* comprises recording information concerning traffic as it passes observation points in the network. We consider three categories of passive measurement:

  - Link utilization statistics as provided by router interface counters; these are retrieved from a managed device by a network management station using the SNMP protocol.
  - Flow-level measurements comprising summaries of flows of packets with common network and transport header properties. These are commonly compiled by routers, then exported to a collector for storage and analysis. These statistics enable detailed breakdown of traffic volumes according to network and transport header fields, e.g., IP addresses and TCP/UDP ports.
  - Inspection of packet payloads in order to provide application-level flow measurements, or to support other payload-dependent applications such as network security and troubleshooting.

- In *active measurement*, probe traffic is inserted into the network, and the probe traffic, or the response of the network to it, is subsequently measured. Comparing the probe and response traffic provides a measure of network performance, as experienced by the probes. Active probing has been conducted by standalone tools such as `ping` and `traceroute` [53] that utilize or coerce IP protocols for measurement functionality. These and other methods are used for active measurement between hosts in special purpose measurement infrastructures, or between network routers, or from these to other endpoints such as application or other servers.

Although the correspondence between methods and applications – passive measurement for traffic analysis and active measurement for performance – has been the norm, it is not firm: passive measurement is used to observe probe packets, and there are purely passive approaches to performance measurement.

10.1.3   Challenges for Measurement Infrastructure and Applications

We now describe challenges facing design and deployment of active and passive measurement infrastructure by service providers and enterprises. As we discuss passive and active measurement methodologies in the following sections, we shall discuss their strengths and weaknesses in meeting these challenges. As one would expect, weaknesses in some of the more mature methods that we discuss have often provided the motivation for subsequent methods.

- *Speed*   Increasingly fast line rates challenge the ability of routers to perform complex per packet processing, including updating flow statistics, and packet content inspection.
- *Scale*   The product of network speed times the large number of devices producing measurements, gives rise to an immense amount of measurement data (e.g., flow statistics). In addition to consuming resources at the observation points, these data require transmission, storage, and processing in the measurement infrastructure and back-end systems.
- *Granularity*   Service providers and their customers increasingly require a detailed picture of network usage and performance. This is both to support individualized routine reporting, and also to support detailed retrospective studies of network behavior. These requirements reduce the utility of aggregate usage measurements, such as link-level counters, and simple performance measurement tools, such as `ping` and `traceroute`.
- *Scope*   For passive measurement: not all routers support granular measurement functionality, e.g, reporting flow statistics; or, the functionality may not be enabled due to resource constraints at the observation point or in the measurement collection infrastructure. When measurements are performed, information about protocol layers below IP (such as MPLS), or optical layer attributes (such as the physical link of an IP composite link) may be incompletely reported or even absent. Information above the network layer may be hidden as a result of endpoint encryption. For active measurement: not all network paths or links may be directly measured because of cost or other limitations in the deployment of active measurement hosts.

- *Timeliness* Measurement applications increasingly require short temporal granularity of measurements, either because it is desirable to measure events of short duration, such as traffic microbursts and sub-second timescale routing events, or because the reporting latency must be short, e.g., in real-time anomaly detection for security applications. The concomitant increase in measurement reporting or polling frequency increases load on measurement devices and increases the number of measurement data points.

- *Accuracy* In passive measurement, reduction of data volumes through sampling, in order to meet the challenges of speed and scale, introduces statistical uncertainty into measurements. In active measurement, bandwidth and scale constraints place a limit on active probing frequency and hence measurement accuracy is inherently dependent on the duration of the measurement period.

- *Management* There are several challenges for the management and administration of measurement infrastructure.

    - *Reliability* Measurement infrastructure components are subject to failure or outage, resulting in loss or corruption of measurements. The effects of component failure can be mitigated (i) at the infrastructure level (providing redundant capacity with fast detection of failure resulting in failover to backup subsystems), (ii) by employing reporting paradigms (e.g., sequence numbers) that facilitate automated checking, flagging, or workarounds for missing data, and (iii) reporting measurement uncertainty due to missing data or sampling to the consumer of the measurements.

    - *Correlation* Measurement applications may require correlation of measurements generated by different measurement subsystems, for example, passive and active traffic measurements, logs from application servers, and authentication, authorization, and accounting subsystems. A common case is when measurements are to be attributed to an entity such as an end host, but the mapping between measurement identifier (such as source IP address) and entity is dynamic (e.g., dynamic DHCP mappings). Correlation of multiple data sets presents challenges for data management, e.g., due to data size, diverse provenance, physical locations, and access policies. The measurement infrastructure must facilitate correlation by measures including the synchronization of timestamps set by different measurement subsystems.

    - *Consistency* The methodologies, reporting and interpretation of measurements must be consistent across different equipment and network management software vendors, service providers, and their customers.

In this chapter, Sections 10.2–10.6 cover passive measurement, including link-level aggregates, flow measurement, sampling, packet selection, and deep packet inspection (DPI). Sections 10.7–10.10 cover active measurements, including standardization of performance metrics, service level agreements, and deployment issues for measurement infrastructures. We conclude with an outlook on future challenges in Section 10.11. We shall make use of and refer to other chapters in this book that deal with specific applications of measurements, principally Chapter 5 on Network Planning and Chapter 13 on Network Security.

10.2 Passive Traffic Measurement

As previewed in Section 10.1.2, we consider three broad types of passive measurement: link statistics, flow measurements, and DPI. These encompass methods that are currently employed in provider networks, and also describe some newer approaches that have been proposed or may be deployed in the medium term. We now motivate and outline in more detail the material on passive measurement.

Section 10.3 describes SNMP measurements, or, more precisely, interface packet counters maintained in a router's Management Information Base (MIB) that are retrieved using the Simple Network Management Protocol (SNMP). The remote monitoring capabilities supported by the RMON MIB are also discussed.

SNMP measurements provide an undifferentiated view of traffic on a link. By contrast, measurement applications often need to classify traffic according to the values occurring in protocol header fields that occur at different levels of the protocol stack. They must determine the aggregate traffic volumes attributable to each such value, for example, to each combination of the network layer IP addresses and transport layer TCP/UDP ports. This information, and that relating to encapsulating protocols such as MPLS, has come to be known as "packet header" information. This is contrasted with "packet payload" or "packet content" information, which includes higher layer application and protocol information. This information may be spread across multiple network level packets.

The major development in passive traffic measurement over the last roughly 20 years, that serves these needs, has been traffic flow measurement. Traffic flows are sets of packets with common network/transport header values observed locally in time. Routers commonly compile summary statistics of flows (total packets, bytes, timing information) and report them, together with the common header values and some associated router state – but without any payload information – in a flow record that is exported to a collector. Cisco's NetFlow is the prime example. Flow records provide a relatively detailed representation of network traffic that supports many applications. Several of these are covered in detail in other chapters of this book: generation of traffic matrices and their use in network planning is described in Chapter 5; analysis of traffic patterns and anomalies for network security is described in Chapter 13. Related applications are the routine reporting of traffic matrices and trending of traffic volumes and application mix for customers and for service provider's network and business development organizations (see e.g. [5]).

Section 10.4 describes traffic flow measurement, including the operational formation of flow statistics, protocols for the standardization of flow measurement, flow measurement collection infrastructure, the use of sampling both packets and flow records themselves in order to meet the challenges of speed and scale and its impact on measurement accuracy, some recent proposals for traffic flow measurement and aggregation, and concludes with some applications of flow measurements.

Uniform packet sampling is one member of a more general class of packet selection primitives, that also includes filtering and more general sampling operations. In Section 10.5, we describe standardization of packet selection operations, their realization in routers, and applications of combined selection primitive for network management. We describe in detail the hash-based selection primitive, which allows for consistent selection of the same packet at different observation points, and discuss new measurement applications that this enables.

Packet header-based flow measurements provide little visibility into properties of the packet payload. However, network- and transport-level packet headers provide only a partial indication of traffic properties for the purposes of application characterization, security monitoring and attack mitigation, and software and protocol debugging. Section 10.6 reviews technologies for DPI of packet payload beyond the network- and transport-level headers, and shows how it serves these applications.

10.3 SNMP, MIBs, and RMON

In this section, we discuss traffic statistics that are maintained within routers and the methods and protocols for their recovery. A comprehensive treatment of these protocols and their realization can be found in [25].

10.3.1 Router Measurement Databases: MIBs

A MIB is a type of hierarchical database maintained by devices such as routers. MIBs have been defined by equipment vendors and standardized by the IETF. Currently, over 10,000 MIBs are defined. The MIB most relevant for traffic measurement purposes is MIB-II [60] that maintains counters for the total bytes and numbers of unicast and multicast packets received on an interface, along with discarded and errored packets. The Interface-MIB [59] further provides counts of multicast packets per multicast address. Protocol-specific MIBs, e.g., for MPLS [76], also provide counts of inbound and outbound packets per interface that use those protocols.

10.3.2 Retrieval of Measurements: SNMP

SNMP [77] is the Internet Protocol used to manage MIBs. A SNMP agent in the managed device is used to access the MIB and communicate object values to or from a network management station. SNMP has a small number of basic command types. Read commands are used to retrieve objects from the MIB. Write commands are used to write object values to the MIB. Notify commands are used to set conditions under which the managed device will autonomously generate a report. The most recent version of SNMP, SNMPv3, offers security functionality, including encryption and authentication, that were weaker or absent in earlier versions. For traffic measurement applications, the MIB interface-level packet and byte counters are retrieved by periodic SNMP polling from the management station; a polling interval of 5 min is common. The total packets and bytes transmitted between successive polls are then obtained by subtraction.

10.3.3   Remote Monitoring: RMON

The RMON MIB [81] supports a more detailed capability for remote monitoring than MIB-II, enabling the aggregation and notification over relatively complex events, e.g involving multiple packets. The original focus of RMON was in remote monitoring of LANs; resource limitations make RMON generally unsuitable for monitoring high rate packet streams in the WAN context, e.g., to supply greater detail than presented by SNMP/MIB-II measurements. Indeed, the limitations of RMON motivate the alternate flow and packet measurement paradigm in which samples or aggregates of packet header information are exported from the router to a collector which supports reporting, analysis, and alarming functionality, rather than the router performing these functions itself. We explore this paradigm in more detail in the following sections.

10.3.4   Properties and Applications of SNMP/MIB

We now review how SNMP/MIB measurements align with the general measurement challenges described in Section 10.1.3. *Scope:* The major strength of SNMP measurements is their ubiquitous availability from router MIBs. *Scale:* From the data management point of view, SNMP statistics have the advantage of being relatively compact, routinely comprising a fixed length data collected per interface at each polling instant, commonly every 5 min. *Granularity:* The main limitation of SNMP measurement is that they maintain packet and byte counters per interface only. *Timeliness:* The externally chosen and relatively infrequent polling times for SNMP measurements limit their utility for real-time or event-driven measurement applications.

Historically, SNMP measurements have been a powerful tool in the management of networks with undifferentiated service classes. SNMP statistics have been used to trend link utilization, and network administrators have used these trends to plan and prioritize link deployment and upgrades, on the basis of heuristics that relate link utilization to acceptable levels of performance. Active performance measurements using the ping and traceroute tools can also inform these decisions.

Although SNMP measurement do not directly report any constituent details within link aggregates, network topology and routing in practice constrain the set of possible edge-to-edge traffic flows that can give rise to the collection of measured traffic rates over all network links. This leads to the formulation of an inverse problem to recover the edge-to-edge traffic matrices from the link aggregates. A number of approaches have been proposed and some are sufficiently accurate to be of operational use; for further detail see Chapter 5. Knowledge of the traffic matrices provides powerful new information beyond simple trending, because it allows the prediction of link utilization under different scenarios for routing, topology, and spatially heterogeneous changes in demand.

10.4 Traffic Flow Measurement

This section describes traffic flow measurement, including the operational formation of flow statistics, protocols for the standardization of flow measurement, flow measurement collection infrastructure, the use of sampling both packets and flow records themselves in order to meet the challenges of speed and scale and its impact on measurement accuracy, some recent proposals for traffic flow measurement and aggregation, and concludes with some applications of flow measurements.

10.4.1 Flows and Flow Records

10.4.1.1 Flow and Flow Keys

A flow of traffic is a set of packets with a common property, known as the flow key, observed within a period of time. A set of interleaved flows is depicted in Fig. 10.1. Many routers construct and export summary statistics on flows of packets that pass through them. A flow record can be thought of as summarizing a set of packets arising in the network through some higher-level transaction, e.g., a remote terminal session, or a web-page download. In practice, the set of packets that are included in a flow depends on the algorithm used by the router to assign packets to flows. The flow key is usually specified by fields from the packet header, such as the IP source and destination address and TCP/UDP port numbers, and may also include information from the packet's treatment at the observation point, such as router interface(s) traversed. Flows in which the key is specified by individual values of these fields are often called *raw* flows, as opposed to *aggregate* flows in which the key is specified by a range of these quantities. As we discuss further in Section 10.4.3.2, routers commonly create flow records from a sampled substream of packets.

10.4.1.2 Operational Construction of Flow Records

Flow statistics are created as follows. A router maintains a cache comprising entries for each active flow, i.e., those flows currently under measurement. Each entry includes the key and summary statistics for the flow such as total packets and bytes,

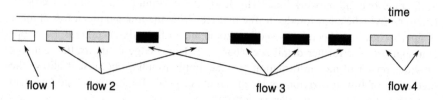

Fig. 10.1 Flows of observed packets, key indicated by shading

and times of observation of the first and last packets. When the router observes a packet, it performs a cache lookup on the key to determine if the corresponding flow is active. If not, it instantiates a new entry for that key. The flow statistics are then updated accordingly. A router terminates the recording of a flow according to criteria describe below; then the flow's statistics are exported in a flow record, and the associated cache memory released for use by new flows. Flow termination criteria include: (i) inactive flow or interpacket timeout: the time since the last packet observed for the flow exceeds some threshold; (ii) protocol-level information, e.g., a TCP FIN packet that terminates a TCP connection; (iii) memory management: termination to release memory for new flows; and (iv) active flow timeout: to prevent data staleness, flows are terminated after a given elapsed time since the arrival of the first packet of the flow.

The summary information in the flow record may include, as well as the flow key, and summary statistics of packet timing and size, other information relating to the packet treatment in the router, such as interfaces traversed, next hop router, and routing state information. Additionally, lower layer protocol information from the packet header may be included. For example, Cisco's NetFlow has a partial ability to report the MPLS label stack: it can report up to three labels from the MPLS label stack, with position in stack configurable. NetFlow can in some cases report the loopback address of the certain tunnel endpoints.

10.4.1.3 Commercial and Standardized Flow Reporting

The idea of modeling traffic as packets grouped by a common property seems first to have appeared in [54], and the idea was taken up in support of internet accounting in [62], and systematized as a general measurement methodology in [22]. Early standardization efforts within the Real Time Flow Measurement working group of the Internet Engineering Task Force (IETF) has now been supplanted by the work of the IP Flow Information eXport working group (IPFIX) [49]. In practice flow measurement has become largely identified with Cisco's NetFlow [18] due to (i) the large installed base; (ii) its emulation in other vendors' products, and (iii) its effective standardization by the use of NetFlow version 9 [23] as the starting point for the IPFIX protocol. NetFlow v9 offers the ability to administrators to define and configure flow keys, aggregation schemes, and the information reported in flow records.

An alternative reporting paradigm is provided by sFlow [71], in which header-level information from a subset of sampled packets are exported directly without aggregating information from packet bearing the same key. sFlow reports include a position count of the sampled packet within the original traffic stream; this facilitates estimating traffic rates.

10.4.2 Flow Measurement Infrastructure

10.4.2.1 Generation and Export of Flow Records

Cisco originated NetFlow as a by-product of IP route caching [17], but it has subsequently evolved as a measurement and reporting subsystem in its own right. Other router vendors now support the compilation of flow statistics, e.g., Juniper's JFlow [55], with the flow information being exported using the NetFlow version 9 format or according to the IPFIX standard. Note that implementation differences may lead to different information being reported across different routers. Standalone monitoring devices as discussed in Section 10.6.2 may also compile and export flow records.

Cisco Flexible NetFlow [14] provides the ability to instantiate and separately configure multiple flow compilers that operate concurrently. This allows a single router to serve different measurement applications that may have different requirements: traffic can be selected by first filtering on header fields; parameters such as sampling granularity, spatial and temporal aggregation granularity, reporting detail and frequency, and collector destination can be specified for each instantiation. We discuss packet selection operations more generally in Section 10.5.

10.4.2.2 Collection and Mediation of Flow Records

Flow records are exported from the observation point, either directly to a collector, or through a mediation device. NetFlow collection systems are available commercially [15] or as freeware [10], either in a basic form that receives and writes flow records to storage, or as part of larger traffic analysis system to support network management functions [5, 69], or focused on specific applications such as security [68]. Although export of flow records may take place directly to the ultimate collector, there are two architectural reasons that favor inserting mediation devices in the export path: scalability and reliability. The primary reason is scalability. Even with the compression of information that summarizes a set of packets in a fixed length flow record, the volumes of flow records produced by large-scale network infrastructure are enormous. As a rough example, a network comprising 100 10 Gb/s links that are 50% loaded in each direction, and in which each flow traverses ten routers, each of which compiles flow statistics after packet sampling at a rate of 1 in several hundred (see Section 10.4.3.2), would produce 1Gb/s of flow records, i.e., roughly 10 TeraBytes per day.

A secondary reason for using mediation boxes has been transmission reliability. Until recently, NetFlow has exclusively used UDP for export, in part to avoid the need for buffer flow records at the exporter, as would be required by a reliable transport protocol. But the use of UDP exposes flow records to potential loss in transit, particularly over long WAN paths. Due to skew in flow length distributions (see Section 10.4.3.3) uncontrolled loss of the records of long flows could severely reduce measurement accuracy.

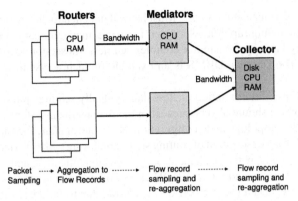

Fig. 10.2 Flow measurement collection infrastructure: hardware elements, their resources, and sampling and aggregation operations that act on the measurements

Mediation devices can address these issues and provided additional benefits:

- *Data Reduction*   By aggregating and sampling flow records, then exporting the reduced data to a central collector.
- *Reliable Staging*   The mediator can receive flow records over a LAN with controlled loss characteristics, then export flow records (or samples or aggregates) to the ultimate collector using a reliable transport protocol such as TCP. NetFlow v9 and the IPFIX protocol both support SCTP [78] for export, which gives administrators flexibility to select a desired trade-off between reliability and buffer resource usage at the exporter.
- *Distributed Query*   The mediation devices may also support queries on the flow records that traverse them, and thus together constitute a distributed query system.
- *Selective Export*   Multiple streams of flow records selected according to specified criteria may be exported to collectors serving different applications.

An example of such an architecture is illustrated in Fig. 10.2; see also [39]. In each of a number of geographically distributed router centers, a mediation device receives flow records from its colocated routers; aggregates and samples are then exported to ultimate collector. Protocols for flow mediators are currently under standardization in the IPFIX working group of the IETF [49].

10.4.2.3   Collection and Warehousing of Flow Records

The final component of the collection infrastructure is the repository that serves to receive and store the flow records, and serve as a database for reporting and query functions. Concerning the attributes of a data store:

- *Capacity*   Must be extensive; even with packet and flow sampling, a large service provider network may generate many GB of flow records per day.

- *DataBase Management System* Must be well matched to the challenges of large datasets, including rapid ingestion and indexing, managing large tables, a high-level query language to support complex queries, transaction logging, and data recovery. The Daytona DBMS is an example of such a system in current use; see [44].
- *Data Sources* Interpretation of flow data typically requires joining with other datasets, which should also be present in the management system, including but not limited to, topology and configuration data, control plane measurements (see Chapter 11 for a description of routing state monitoring), MIB variables acquired by SNMP polling, network elements logs from authentication, authorization, and accounting servers, and logs from DHCP and other network servers.
- *Data Quality* Data may be corrupt or missing due to failures in the collection and reporting systems. The complexity and volume of measured data necessitate automated mechanisms to detect, mark, and mitigate unclean data; see e.g. [30].
- *Data Security and Customer Privacy* Flow measurements and other data listed should be considered as sensitive customer information. Service provider policies must specify practices to maintain the integrity of the data, including controlled and auditable access restricted to individuals needing to work with the data, encryption, anonymization, and data retention policies.

10.4.3 Sampling in Flow Measurement and Collection

10.4.3.1 Sampling as a Data Reduction Method

In the previous sections, we have touched on the fact that the speed of communications links provides a challenge for the formation of flow records at the router, and both speed and the scale of networks – the large number of interfaces that can produce flow records – provide a challenge for the collection and storage of flow records. Figure 10.2 illustrates the relevant resources at the router, mediator, and collector. To meet these challenges, data reduction must be performed. The reduction method must be well matched to the uses to which the reduced data is put. Three reduction methods are usually considered:

- *Aggregation* Summarizing measurements that share common properties. In the context of traffic flow measurement, header-level information on packets with the same key is aggregated into flows. Subsequent aggregation of flow records into predefined aggregates (e.g., aggregate traffic to each routing prefix) is a powerful tool for routine reporting.
- *Filtering* Selection of a subset of measurement that matches a specified criterion. Filtering is useful for drill down (e.g., to a traffic subset of interest).
- *Sampling* Selection of data points according to some nondeterministic criterion.

A limitation for aggregation and filtering as general data reduction methods is the manner in which they lose visibility into the data: traffic not matching a filter is discarded; detail within an aggregate is lost (while flow records aggregate packets over time, they need not aggregate spatially, i.e., over packet header values). Of the three methods, only sampling retains the spatial granularity of the original data, and thus retains the ability to support arbitrary aggregations of the data, include those formulated after the measurements were made. This is important to support exploratory, forensic, and troubleshooting functions, where the traffic aggregates of interest are typically not known in advance. The downside of sampling is the statistical uncertainty in the resulting measurements; we address this further in Section 10.4.3.4.

We now discuss sampling operations used during the construction and recovery of flow measurements. As illustrated in Fig. 10.2, packet sampling (see Section 10.4.3.2) is used in routers in order to reduce the rate of the stream of packet header information from which flow records are aggregated. The complete flow records are then subjected to further sampling (see Section 10.4.3.3) and aggregation within the collection infrastructure, at the mediator to reduce data volumes, or in the collector, for example, dynamically sampling from a flow record database in order to reduce query execution times, or permanently in order to select a representative set of flow records (or their aggregates) for archiving. We discuss the ramifications of sampling for measurement accuracy in Section 10.4.3.4, and some more recent developments in stateful sampling and aggregation the straddle the packet and flow levels in Section 10.4.3.5. Finally, we look ahead to Section 10.5, which sets random packet sampling in the broader context of packet selection operations and their applications, including filtering, both in the sense understood above, and also consistent packet selection as exemplified by hash-based sampling.

10.4.3.2 Random Packet Sampled Flows

The main resource constraint for forming flow records is at the router flow cache in which the keys of active flows are maintained. To lookup packet keys at the full line rate of the router interfaces would require the cache to operate in fast, expensive memory (SRAM). Moreover, routers carry increasingly large numbers of flows concurrently, necessitating a large cache. By sampling the packet stream in advance of the construction of flow records, the cache lookup rate is reduced, enabling the cache to be implemented in slower, less expensive, memory (DRAM).

A number of different sampling methods are available. Cisco's Sampled NetFlow samples packets every Nth packet systematically, where N is a configurable parameter. Random Sampled NetFlow [21] feature employs stratified sampling based on arrival count: one packet is selected at random out of every window on N consecutive arrivals. Although these two methods have the same average sampling rate, there are higher-order differences in the way multiple packets are sampled; for example, consecutive packets are never selected in Sampled NetFlow, while they can be in Random Sampled NetFlow. However, the effect of such differences on flow statistics is expected to be small except possibly for flows which that represent noticeable proportion (greater than $1/N$) of the load, since the position of a given flow's packets in the packet arrival order at an interface is then effectively randomized by the remaining traffic. In distinction, Juniper's J-flow [55] offers the ability to sample runs of consecutive packets.

Sampling and other packet selection methods have been standardized in the PSAMP working group of the IETF [24,32,33,82]. We review these in greater detail in Section 10.5. PSAMP is positioned as a protocol to select packets for reporting at an observation point, with IPFIX as the export protocol. For example, selected packets could be reported on as single packet flow records, using zero active timeout for immediate reporting.

If sampling 1 out of N packets on average, then from a flow with far fewer than N packets, if any packets are sampled, typically only one packet will be sampled. In this case one might just as well sample packets without constructing flow records; this would save resources at the router since there would be no need to cache the single packet flows until expiration of the interpacket timeout. Indeed, there are many short flows: web traffic is a large component of Internet traffic, in which the average flow length is quite short, around 16 packets in one study [42]. However, there are several reasons to expect that longer flows will continue to account for much traffic. First, several prevalent applications and application classes predominantly generate long-lived flows, for example, multimedia downloads and streaming, and VoIP. Secondly, tunneling protocols such as IPSEC [56] may aggregate flows between multiple endpoints into a packet stream in which the endpoint identities are not visible in the network core; from the measurement standpoint, the stream will thus appear as a single longer flow. For these reasons, unless packet sampling periods becomes comparable with or larger than the number of packets in these flows, flow statistics will still afford useful compression of information.

10.4.3.3   Flow Record Sampling

Sampling flow records present a challenge, because of the highly skewed distribution of flow sizes found in network traffic. Experimental studies have shown that the distribution of flow lengths is heavy tailed; in particular, a large proportion of the total bytes and packets in the traffic stream occur in a small proportion of the flows; see, e.g. [42]. This makes the requirements for flow record sampling fundamentally different to those for packet sampling. While packets have a bounded size, uniform and uncontrolled sampling due to transmission loss are far more problematic for flow records than for sampled packets, since omission of a single flow report can have huge impact on measured traffic volumes. This motivates sampling dependent on the size of the flow reported on. A simple approach would be to discard flow records whose byte size falls below a threshold. This gives a conservative, and hence biased measure of the total bytes, and is susceptible to subversion: an application or user that splits its traffic up into small flows could evade measurement altogether. This would be a weakness for accounting and security applications.

Smart Sampling can be used to avoid the problems associated with uniform sampling of flow records. Smart Sampling is designed with the specific aim of achieving the optimal trade-off between the number of flow records actually sampled, and the accuracy of estimates of underlying traffic volumes derived from those samples.

In the simplest form of Smart Sampling, called *Threshold Sampling* [36], each flow record is sampled independently with a probability that depends on the reported flow bytes: all records that report flow bytes greater than a certain threshold z are selected; those below threshold are selected with a probability proportional to the flow bytes. Thus, the probability to sample a flow record representing x bytes is

$$p_z(x) = \min\{1, x/z\}$$

The desired optimality property described above holds in the following sense. Suppose X bytes are distributed over some number m of flows of size $x_1, \ldots, x_m$ so that $X = \sum_{i=1}^{m} x_i$. We consider unbiased estimates $\widehat{X}$ of X, i.e., $\widehat{X}$ is a random quantity whose average value is X. Suppose $\widehat{X}$ is an unbiased estimate of X obtained from a random selection of a subset of $n < m$ of the original flows, having sizes $x_1, \ldots, x_n$, where selection is independent according to some size-dependent probability $p(x)$. A standard procedure to obtain unbiased estimates is to divide the measured value by the probability that it was sampled [47]. Thus in our case each sampled flow size is normalized by its sampling rate, so that $\widehat{X} = \sum_{i=1}^{n} x_i / p(x_i)$ is an unbiased estimate of X. We express the optimal trade-off as trying to minimize a total "cost" that is a linear combination

$$C_z = z^2 \mathsf{E}[n] + \mathsf{Var}[\widehat{X}]$$

of the average number of samples and the estimation variance, where z is a parameter that expresses the relative importance we attach to making the number of samples small versus making the variance small. For example, when z is large, making $\mathsf{E}[n]$ small has a larger effect on reducing C_z. It is proved in [36] that the cost C_z is minimized for *any* set of flow sizes $x_1, \ldots, x_m$ by using the sampling probabilities $p(x) = p_z(x)$. With the probabilities p_z, each selected flow x_i gives rise to an estimate $x_i / p_z(x_i) = \max\{x_i, z\}$.

Although optimal as stated, Threshold Sampling does not control the exact number of samples taken. For example, if the number of flows doubles during a burst, then on average, the number of samples also doubles (assuming the same flow size distribution). However, exact control may be required in some applications, e.g., when storage for samples has a fixed size constraint, or for sampling a specified number of representative records for archiving. A variant of Smart Sampling, called Priority Sampling [37], is able to achieve a fixed sample of size $n < m$, as follows. Each flow of size x_i is assigned a random *priority* $w_i = x_i / a_i$ where a_i is a uniformly distributed random number in $(0, 1]$. Then the k flows of highest priority are selected for sampling, and each of them contributes an estimate $\max\{x_i, z'\}$ where z' is now a *data-dependent* threshold z' set to be $(k + 1)$st largest priority. It is shown in [37] that this estimate is unbiased.

Priority Sampling is well suited for back-end database applications serving queries that require estimation of total bytes in an arbitrary selection of flows (e.g., all those in a specific matrix element) over a specified time period. A random priority is generated once for each flow, and the records are stored in descending order of priority. Then an estimate based on k flows proceeds by reading $k + 1$ flow records of highest priority that match the selection criterion, forming an unbiased estimate as above. Because the flow records already are in priority-sorted order, selection is very fast (see [4]).

10.4.3.4 Estimation and the Statistical Impact of Sampling

Whether sampling packets or flow records, the measured numbers of packet, bytes, or flows must be normalized in order to give an unbiased estimate of the actual traffic from which they were derived; we saw how this was done for threshold sampling in Section 10.4.3.3. For 1 in N packet sampling, byte estimates from selected packets are multiplied by N. The use of sampling for measuring traffic raises the question of how accurate estimates of traffic volumes will be. The statistical nature of estimates might be thought to preclude their use for some purposes. However, for many sampling schemes, including those described above, the frequency of estimation errors of a given size can be computed or approximated. This can help answer questions such as "if no packets matching a given key were sampled, then how likely is it that there were X or more bytes in packets with this key that were missed".

A rough indication of estimation error is the relative standard deviation (RSD), i.e, the standard deviation of the estimator $\widehat{X}$ divided by the true value X. The RSD for estimating an aggregate of X bytes of traffic using independent 1 in N packet sampling is bounded above by $\sqrt{N x_{\max}/X}$ where $x_{\max}$ is the maximum packet size. For flow sampling with threshold z, the RSD is bounded above by $\sqrt{z/X}$. Observe the RSD decreases as the aggregate size increases. In cases where multiple stages of sampling and aggregation are employed – for example, packet sampled NetFlow followed by Threshold Sampling of flow records – the sampling variance is additive. In the example, the RSD becomes

$$\sqrt{(z + N x_{\max})/X}$$

As an example, consider 1 in $N = 1,000$ sampling of packets of maximum size $x_{\max} = 1,500$ bytes with a flow sampling threshold of $z = 50$ MB. In this case $z \gg N x_{\max} = 1.5$ MB , and so Smart Sampling contributes most of the estimation error. With these sampling parameters, estimating the 10 min average rate of a 1 Gb/s backbone traffic stream on a backbone would incur a typical relative error of 3%. In fact, rigorous confidence intervals for the true bytes in terms of the estimated values can be derived (see [26, 79]), including for some cases of multistage sampling.

Using an analysis of the sampling errors, the impact of flow sampling on usage-based charging, and ways to avoid or ameliorate estimation error, are described in [35]. The key idea is that a combination of (i) systematic undercounting of customer traffic by a small amount, and (ii) using sufficiently long billing periods, can reduce the likelihood over over-billing customers to an arbitrarily small probability.

10.4.3.5   Stateful Packet Sampling and Aggregation

The dichotomy between packet sampling on a router and flow sampling in the measurement infrastructure, while architecturally simple, does not necessarily result in the best trade-off between resource usage and measurement accuracy. We briefly review some recent research that proposed to maintain various degrees of router state in order to select and maintain flow records for subsets of packets.

- *Sample and Hold [41]*   All packets arriving at the router whose keys are not currently in the flow cache are subjected to sampling; packets that are selected in this manner have a corresponding flow cache entry created, and all subsequent packets with the same key are selected (subject to timeout). Thus, long flows are preferentially sampled over short flows, since the flow cache tends to be populated only by the longer flows. This achieves similar aims to Smart Sampling but in a purely packet-based solution. While the cache can be made smaller than would be required to measure all flows, a cache lookup is still required for each packet.
- *Adaptive Sampling Methods*   Both NetFlow and Sample and Hold can be made adaptive by adjusting their underlying sampling rate and flow termination criteria in response to resource usage, e.g., to control cache occupancy and flow record export rate. Now recall from Section 10.4.3.3 that construction of unbiased estimators required normalization of sample bytes and packet counts by dividing by the sampling rate. Adjustment of the sampling rate requires matching renormalization in estimators in order to maintain unbiasedness. Partial flow records may be resampled (and further renormalized) and may be discarded in some cases (see [40]). In one variant of this approach the router maintains and exports a strictly bounded number of flow records, providing unbiased estimates of the original traffic bytes.
- *Stepping Methods*   Stepping is an extension of the adaptive method in which, when downward adjustments of the sampling rate occur, estimates of the total bytes in packets of a given key that arrived since the previous such adjustment – the steps – are sampled and exported from the flow cache. Such exports can take place from the flow cache into DRAM, where the steps can be aggregated. The payoff is higher estimation accuracy, because once exported, the steps are not subject to loss (see [27]).
- *Run-Based Estimation*   In its simplest form, run-based estimation involves caching in SRAM only the key of the last observed packet. If the current packet matches the key, the run event is registered in a cache in DRAM. Using a time-series model, the statistics of the original traffic are estimated from those of the runs. A generalization of the approach can additionally utilize longer runs [45].

10.5 Packet Selection Methods for Traffic Flow Measurement

10.5.1 Packet Selection Primitives and Standards

In Section 10.4.3.2 random packet sampling was presented as a necessity for reducing packet rates prior to the formation of flow statistics; moreover, random sampling has significant advantages over filtering and aggregation as a continuously operating general data reduction method. In this chapter we shift the emphasis somewhat and consider a set of packet selection primitives, and their ability to serve a variety of specific measurement applications. Following [33] we classify selection primitives as follows:

- *Filtering*   Selection of packets based deterministically on their content. There are two important subcases:

  - *Property Match Filtering*   Selection of a packet if a field or fields match a predefined value.
  - *Hash-Based Selection*   A hash of the packet is calculated and the packet is selected if it falls in a certain range.

- *Sampling*   Selection of packets nondeterministically.

Some primitives of this type are provided by Cisco Flexible NetFlow [14] that allows combinations of certain random sampling and property match filters. The framework above was standardized in the Packet Sampling (PSAMP) working group of the IETF [33]. A collection of sampling primitives is described in [82], including but not limited to the fixed rate sampling from Section 10.4.3.2. Property match filtering can be based on packet header fields (such as IP address and port) and the packet treatment by the router, including interfaces traversed, and the routing state in operation during the packet's transit of the router. Hash-based selection, including specific hash functions, is also standardized in [82]. We describe the operation and applications of hash-based selection in Section 10.5.2.

From both at the implementation and standards viewpoint, packet selection is positioned as a front-end process that passes selected packets to a process that compiles and exports flow statistics. Thus, a PSAMP packet selector passes packets to an IPFIX flow reporting process. A flow record can report on single selected packets by setting the inactive flow timeout to zero. A key development in support of network management is the ability of routers and other measurement devices to support simultaneous operation of multiple independent measurements, each of which is composed of combinations of packet selection primitives. This type of capability is already present in Cisco Flexible NetFlow [14] and standardized in PSAMP/IPFIX. Each packet selection process can, in principle, be associated with its own independently configurable flow reporting process. The ability to dynamically configure or reconfigure packet selection provides a powerful tool for a variety of applications, from low-rate sampling of all traffic to supply routine reporting for Network Operation Center (NOC) wallboard displays, to targeted high-rate sampling that drills down on an anomaly in real time (see Fig. 10.3).

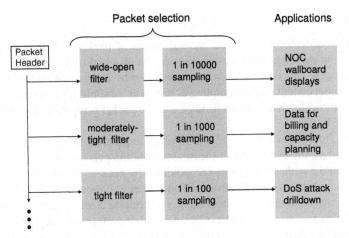

Fig. 10.3 Concurrent combinations of sampling and filtering packet selection primitives

10.5.2   Consistent Packet Sampling and Hash-Based Selection

The aim of consistent packet sampling (also called Trajectory Sampling) is to sample a subset of packets at some or all routers that they traverse. The motivation is new measurement applications that are enabled or enhanced; see below. Consistent packet sampling can be implemented through hash-based selection. Routers calculate a hash of packet content that is invariant along the packet path, and the packet is selected for reporting if the hash values falls in a specified range. When all routers use the same hash function and range, the sampling decisions for each packet are identical at all points along its path. Thus, each packet signals implicitly to the router whether it should be sampled. Information on the sampled packet can be reported in flow records, potentially one per sampled packet. In order to aid association of different reports on the same packet by the collector, the report can include not only packet header fields, but also a packet label or digest, taking the form of a hash (distinct from that used for selection) whose input includes part of the packet payload.

An ideal hash function would provide the appearance of uniform random sampling over the possible hash input values. This is important both for accurate traffic estimation purposes, and for integrity: network attackers should not be able to predict packet sampling outcomes. Use of a cryptographic hash function with private parameter provides the strongest conformance to the ideal. In practice, implementation constraints on computational resources may require weaker hash functions to be used. Hash-based packet selection has been proposed in [38], with further work on its applications passive performance monitoring in [34, 83]. Security ramifications of different hash function choices are discussed in [43]. Hash-based sampling has been standardized as part of the PSAMP standard in the IETF [82].

Applications of consistent sampling include:

- *Route Troubleshooting* Direct measurements of packet paths can be used to detect routing loops and measure transient behavior of traffic paths under routing changes. This detailed view is not provided by monitoring routing protocols alone. Independent packet sampling at different locations does not provide such a fine timescale view in general, since a given packet is typically not sampled at multiple locations.
- *Passive Performance Measurement* Correlating packet samples at two or more points on a path enables direct measurement of the performance experienced by traffic on the path, such as loss (as indicated by packets present at one point on the path that are missing downstream) and latency (if reports on sampled packets include measurement timestamps from synchronized clocks). This is an attractive application for service providers since it can alert performance degradation at the level of individual customers, reflecting the same packet transit performance that customers themselves experience.

10.6 Deep Packet Inspection

Sections 10.4 and 10.5 are concerned with the measurement and characterization of traffic at the granularity of a flow key that depends on the packet only through header fields. However, there are important network management tasks that depend on knowledge of packet payloads, and hence for which traffic flow monitoring is insufficient. The term DPI denotes measurement and possible treatment of packets based on their payload. We describe some broad designs policy issues associated with the deployment of DPI in Section 10.6.1; specific technologies for DPI devices are described in Section 10.6.2, and three applications of DPI for network management in Section 10.6.3: application-specific bandwidth management, network security monitoring, and troubleshooting.

10.6.1 Design and Policy Issues for DPI Deployment

DPI functions are not uniformly featured in routers, and hence some uses will require additional infrastructure deployment. DPI is extremely resource intensive due to the need to access and process packet payload at line rate. This makes DPI expensive compared with flow measurement, which hinders its widespread deployment. A limited deployment may be restricted to important functional sites, or at a representative subset of different site types, e.g., a backbone link, an aggregation router, or in front of datacenter.

Like all traffic measurements, DPI must maintain privacy and confidentiality of customer information throughout the measurement collection and analysis process. Although flow measurements already encode patterns of communications through source and destination IP addresses, DPI of packet payload may also encompass the content of the communications. Service provider policies must specify practices to maintain the privacy of the data, including controlled and auditable access restricted to individuals needing to work with the data, encryption, anonymization, and data retention policies. See also the discussion specific to DPI for security monitoring in Section 13.4. Furthermore, any use of DPI data must be conducted in accordance with legal regulations in force. Similar issues exist for providers of host-based services as opposed to communications services, where servers intrinsically have access to user-specific data that may be presented by the customer in the course of using those services, e.g., email, search, or e-commerce transactions.

10.6.2   Technologies for DPI

DPI functionality is realized in dedicated general-purpose traffic monitors [28], and within vendor equipment targeted at specific applications such as security monitoring [68] and application-specific bandwidth management [19]. As the value of DPI-based applications for service providers grows, DPI functionality has also appeared in some routers and switches [16]. General-purpose computing platforms have been used for DPI, e.g., using Snort [74], an open-source intrusion detection system. Some DPI devices operate in line where they perform network management functions directly, such as security-based filtering or application bandwidth management. Others act purely as monitors and require a copy of the packet stream to be presented at an interface. There are several ways by which this can be accomplished: (i) by copying the physical signal that carries the packets, e.g., with an optical splitter; (ii) by attaching the monitor to a shared medium carrying the traffic, or (iii) by having a router or switch copy packets to an interface on the monitor.

The architectural challenges for all DPI platforms are: (i) the high incoming packet rate; (ii) the large number of distinct signatures against which each packet is to be matched – Snort has several hundred – and (iii) signatures that match over multiple packets, and hence require flow-level state to be maintained in the measurement device. These factors have tended to favor the use of dedicated DPI devices ahead of router-based integration in the past. They also drive architectural design for DPI devices in which aggregation and analysis if pushed down as close to the data stream as possible.

Coupled with general-purpose computational platforms, tcpdump [52] is a public domain software that captures packets at an interface of the host on which it executes. Tcpdump has been widely used as both a diagnostic tool, and also to capture packet header traces in order to conduct reproducible exploratory studies. However, the enormous byte rates of network data in comparison with storage and transmission resources, generally preclude collecting packet header traces longer than a few minutes or perhaps hours. A number of anonymized packet header traces have been made available by researchers; see e.g., ([9]). Software for removal of confidential information from packet traces, including anonymization, is available (see [63]).

10.6.3   Applications of DPI

In this section, we motivate the importance of DPI by describing network management applications that require detail from packet payload: application characterization and management, network security, and network debugging.

10.6.3.1   Application Demand Characterization and Bandwidth Management

Applications place diverse service requirements on the network. For example, real-time applications such as VoIP require relatively small bandwidth but have stringent latency requirements. Video downloads require high throughput but are elastic in terms of latency. Service providers can differentiate resources among the different service classes according to the size of the demands in each class. Hence a crucial task for network planning is to characterize and track changes in the traffic mix across application classes.

In the past, application and application class could be inferred reasonably well from TCP/UDP port numbers on the basis of IANA well-known port assignments [50]. However, purely port-based identification is becoming less easy due to factors including (i) lack of adherence to port conventions by application designers, (ii) piggybacking of applications on well-known ports, such as HTTP port 80, in order to facilitate firewall traversal; and (iii) separation of control and data channels with dynamic allocation of data port during control level handshaking (see Chapter 5 for further details). On the other hand, knowledge of application operation can be used to develop packet content-level signatures. In some cases, this would involve matching strings of an application-level protocol across one or more network packets. For applications that use separate data and control channels, this could entail (a) matching a signature of the control channel in the manner just described with further inspection, then (b) identifying the data channel port communicated in the control channel, (c) using the identified data channel port to classify further packet or flow level measurements taken (see [80]).

Application-based classification can be used purely passively. Knowledge of the mix and relative growth between different application classes is necessary for network planning. It can also be used actively to apply differentiated resource allocation policies to different application classes, concerning traffic shaping, dropping of out-of-profile packets, or restoration priority after failures. As an example, access to a customer access channel can be prioritized so that the performance of delay-sensitive VoIP traffic is not impaired by other traffic. A number of vendors supply equipment with such capabilities (see e.g. [19, 75]).

10.6.3.2   Network Security

While some network attacks can be identified based on header-level information this is not true in general. As a counterexample, the well-known Slammer worm

[64] was evident due to (i) its rapid growth leading to sharp increases in traffic volume; (ii) the increase was associated with particular values of the packet header field, and (iii) contextual information that the application exploited predominantly exchanges traffic across LANs or intranets rather than across the WAN. This combination of factors made it relatively easy to identify the worm and block its spread by instantiating header-level packet filters, without significantly impacting legitimate traffic.

However, these conditions do not hold in general. Many network attacks exploit vulnerabilities in common applications such email, chat, p2p, and web-browsing mediated by network communications that, in contrast with the Slammer example [64], (i) are relatively stealthy, not exhibiting large changes in network traffic volume at least during the acquisition phase, (ii) are not distinguished from legitimate traffic by specific header field values, and hence (iii) blend into the background of legitimate traffic at the flow level. Examples include installation of malware such as keystroke loggers, or the acquisition and subsequent control of zombie hosts in botnets.

To detect and mitigate these and other attacks, packet inspection is a powerful tool to enable matching against known signatures of malware, including viruses, worms, trojans, botnets. Indeed, a sizable proportion of the attack detection signatures commonly used in the public domain Snort packet inspection system [74] match only on the packet payload rather than the header.

Similarly to Section 10.6.3.1, a network security tool may operate purely passively in order to gain information about unwanted traffic, or may be coupled to filtering functions that block specific flows of traffic (see Chapter 13 for further details).

10.6.3.3 Debugging for Software, Protocols, and Customer Support

Both networking hardware and software that implement services can contain subtle dependencies and display unexpected behavior that, despite pre-deployment testing, only becomes evident in the live network. DPI permits network operators to monitor, evaluate, and correct such problems. To troubleshoot specific network or service layer issues, DPI devices could be deployed at a concentration point where specific protocol exchanges or application-layer transactions can be monitored for correctness. Operators might also use portable DPI devices, which would allow them deploy devices in specific locations to investigate suspected hardware or software bugs. Similarly, DPI enables technicians to assist customers in debugging customer equipment, and software installations and configurations. This can enable technicians to rapidly determine the nature of problems rated to network transmissions, rather than rely on potentially incomplete knowledge derived from customer dialogs.

10.7 Active Performance Measurement

This section is concerned with the challenges and design aspects of providing active performance measurement infrastructures for service providers. The four metric areas of common interest are:

- *Connectivity* Can a given host be reached from some set of hosts?
- *Loss* What proportion of a set of packets are lost on a path (or paths) between two hosts? Loss may be considered in an average sense (all packets over some period of loss) or granular in time (burst loss properties) or space (broken down, e.g., by customer or application).
- *Delay* The network latency over a path (or paths) between two hosts, viewed at the same granularity as for loss measurements.
- *Throughput* Bytes or packets successfully transmitted between two hosts, potentially broken down by application or protocol (e.g., TCP vs. UDP).

Historically, active measurement tools such as `ping` and `traceroute` have long been used to baseline roundtrip loss and delay and map IP paths, either as standalone tools, or integrated into performance measurement systems. Bulk throughput has been estimated using the `treno` tool [58], which creates a probe stream that conforms to the dynamics of TCP. There is a large body of more recent research work proposing improved measurement methods and analysis (see, e.g., [29]). However, the focus of the remainder of this chapter concerns more the design and deployment issues for the components of an active measurement and reporting infrastructure of the type increasingly deployed by service providers and enterprise customers. Specifically:

- *Performance Metric Standardization* This is required in order for all parties involved in the measurement, dissemination and interpretation of results to agree on the methods of acquiring performance measurements, and their meaning. Such parties include network service providers, their customers, third-party measurement service providers, and measurement system vendors. Performance metric standardization is described in Section 10.8.
- *Service Level Agreements* Service providers must offer specific performance targets to their customers, based upon agreed metrics. Section 10.9 describes processes for establishing SLAs between service providers and customers.
- *Deployment of Active Measurement Infrastructures* Deployment issues for large-scale active measurement infrastructures are discussed in Section 10.10, together with some examples of different deployment modes.

10.8 Standardization of IP Performance Metrics

In this section, we give an overview of standardization activities on IP performance metrics. There are not one, but two standard bodies that provide the authoritative view of IP network performance and on packet performance metrics in general.

They are the IETF (primarily the IP Performance Metrics IPPM working group), and the International Telecommunications Union - Telecommunications Sector Study Group 12 (ITU-T SG 12, specifically the Packet Network Performance Question 17). Although there are some differences in the approaches and the metric specifications between these two bodies, they are relatively minor.

The critical advantage of using standardized metrics is the same as for any good standard: the metrics can be implemented from unambiguous specifications, which ensure that two measurement devices will work the same way. They will assign timestamps at the same defined instants when a packet appears at the measurement point (such as first bit in, or the last bit out). They will use a waiting time to distinguish between packets with long delays and packets that do not arrive (because one cannot wait forever to report results, and for many applications a packet with extremely long delay is as good as lost). They will perform statistical summary calculations the same way, and when presented with identical network conditions to measure, they produce the same results.

The ITU-T has defined its IP performance metrics in one primary Recommendation, Y.1540. The general approach is to define basic sections bounded by measurement points, which are

- Hosts at the source and destination(s)
- Network Sections (composed of routers and links, and usually defined by administrative boundaries)
- Exchange Links (between the other entities)

The next step is to define packet transfer reference events at the various section boundaries. There are two main types of reference events:

- Entry event to a host, exchange link, or network section
- Exit event from a host, exchange link, or network section

Then, the fundamental outcomes of successful packet transfer and lost packet are defined, followed by performance parameters that can be calculated on a flow of packets (referred to using the convention "population of interest"). ITU-T's metrics are useful in either active or passive measurement, and do not specify sampling methods.

The IETF began work on network performance metrics in the mid-1990s, by first developing a comprehensive framework for active measurement [70]. The framework RFC established many important conventions and notions, including:

- The expanded use of the metric definition template developed in earlier IETF work on Benchmarking network devices [6].
- The general concept of "packets of Type-P" to reflect the possibility that packets of different types would experience different treatment, and hence, performance as they traverse the path. A complete specification of Type-P and the source and destination addresses are usually equivalent to the ITU-T's "population of interest".

- The notion of "wiretime", which recognizes that physical devices are needed to observe packets at the IP-layer, and these devices may contribute to the observed performance as a source of error. Other important time-related considerations are detailed, too.
- The hierarchy of singletons ("atomic" results), samples (sets of singletons), and statistics (calculations on samples).

A series of RFCs followed over the next decade, one for each fundamental metric that was identified. The IETF wisely put the various metric RFCs (RFC 2679 [2] and RFC 2680 [3]) on the Standards Track, so that the implementations could be compared with the specifications and used to improve their quality (and narrow-down some of the flexibility) over time. RFC 2330 [70] and RFC 3432 [72] specify Poisson and Periodic sampling, respectively. Throughput-related definitions are in RFC 5136 [12].

One area in which IETF was extremely flexible was its specification for delay variation, in RFC 3393[31]. This specification applies to almost any form of delay variation imaginable, and was endowed with this flexibility after considerable discussion and comparisons between the ITU-T preferred form and other methods (some of which were adopted in other IETF RFCs). This flexibility was achieved using the "selection function" concept, which allows the metric designer to compare any pair of packets (as long as each is unambiguously defined from a stream of packets). Thus, this version of the delay variation specification encouraged practitioners to gain experience with different metric formulations on IP networks, and facilitated comparison between different forms by establishing a common framework for their definition. A common selection function uses adjacent packets in the stream, and this is called "Inter-Packet Delay Variation".

In contrast, the ITU-T Recommendations of the early 1990s (for ATM networks) used essentially the same form of delay variation metric as in Y.1540 and as used today in Recommendations for the latest networking technologies. It is called the "2-point Packet Delay Variation" metric. This metric defines delay variation as the difference between a packet's one-way delay and the delay for a single reference packet. The recommended reference is the packet with the minimum delay in the test sample, removing propagation from the delay distribution and emphasizing only the variation. This definition differs significantly from the inter-packet delay variation definition. Fortunately, an IETF project has rather completely investigated the two main forms of delay variation metrics, and is available to provide guidance on the appropriate form of metric for various tasks [66]. The comparison approach was to define the key tasks (such as de-jitter buffer size and queuing time estimation) and challenging measurement circumstances for delay variation measurements (such as path instability and packet loss), and to examine relevant literature. In summary, the ITU-T definition of "2-point Packet Delay Variation" was the best match to all tasks and most circumstances, but with a requirement for more stable timing being its only weakness.

10.9   Performance Metrics in Service-Level Agreements

In this section, we discuss Service-Level Agreements, or SLA, and how the key metrics defined above contribute to a successful relationship between customers and their service providers.

10.9.1   Definition of a Service-Level Agreement (SLA)

For our purposes, we define a Service-Level Agreement as:

> A binding contract between Customer and Service Provider that identifies all important aspects of the service being delivered, constrains those aspects to a satisfactory performance level which can be objectively verified, and describes the method and format of the verification report.

This definition makes the SLA-supporting role and design of active measurement systems quite clear. The measurement system must assess the service on each of the agreed aspects (metrics) according to the agreed reporting schedule and determine whether the performance thresholds have been met. The details of the SLA may even specify the points where the active measurement system will be connected to the network, the sending characteristics of the synthetic packets dedicated for verification testing, and the confidence interval beyond which the results conclusively indicate that the threshold was met/not met.

10.9.2   Process to Develop the Elements of an SLA

This section describes a process to develop the critical performance aspects of an SLA. Typically, a network operator establishes a standard set of SLAs for a network service by conducting this process internally, using a surrogate for the customer. The specific details of the SLA may differ for different services, e.g., an enterprise Internet access service might have a different SLA from a premium VPN service. An SLA might specify performance metrics such as data delivery (the inverse of packet loss), site-to-site latency by region or location, delay variation or jitter, availability, etc. as well as a number of nonperformance metrics such as provisioning intervals. There are also cases in which a network operator may develop a customized SLA for a particular customer (e.g., because the size of their network or other special circumstances demand it). The process that a service provider and the customer would go through to develop a customized SLA illustrates the issues that need to be addressed when developing an SLA. We present an example of such a process here.

In principle, the SLA represents a common language between the customer and service provider. The process involves collection of requirements and a meeting of peers to compare the view from each side of the network boundaries. One set of steps to create agreeable requirements is given below.

1. The customer identifies the locations where connectivity to the communications service is required (Customer–Service Interfaces), and the service provider compares the location list with available services.
2. The customer and service provider agree on the performance metrics that will be the basis for the SLA. For example, a managed IP network provides a very basic service – packet transfer from source to destination. The SLA is based on packet transfer performance metrics, such as delay, delay variation, and loss ratio. If higher-layer functions are also provided (e.g., domain name to address resolution), then additional metrics can be included.
3. The customer must determine exactly how they plan to use a communications network to conduct business, and express the needs of their applications in terms of the packet performance metrics. The performance requirements may be derived from analysis of the component protocols of each customer application, from tests with simulated packet transfer impairments, or from prior experience. Sometimes, the service provider will consult on the application modeling.
4. In parallel, the service provider collects (or estimates) the levels of packet transfer performance that can be delivered between geographically dispersed service interfaces. Active measurements often serve this aspect of the process, by revealing the network performance possible under current conditions.
5. When the customer and service provider meet again, the requested and feasible performance levels for all of the performance metrics are compared. Where the requested performance levels cannot be met, revised network designs or a plan to achieve interim and long-term objectives in combination with deployment of new infrastructure may be developed, or the customer may relax specific requirements, or a combination of the two.
6. Once the performance levels of the SLA are agreed upon, it remains to decide on the formal reporting intervals and how the customer might access the ongoing measurement results. This aspect is important because formal reporting intervals are often quite long, on the order of a month.
7. If the customer needs up-to-date performance status to aid in their troubleshooting process, then monthly reports might be augmented with the ability to view a customized report of recent measurements. The active measurement system would communicate measured results on a frequent basis to support this monitoring function, as well as longer-term SLA reports.

There are several process complexities worth mentioning. First, the customer may be able to easily determine the performance requirements for a single application flow, but the service providers' measurements will likely be based on a test flow, which experiences the same treatment as the rest of the flows. The test packet flow may not have identical sending characteristics as customer flows, and will certainly represent only a small fraction of the aggregate traffic. Thus, the active test flow performance will represent the customer flow performance only on a long-term basis. Second, active measurements of throughput may have a negative affect on live traffic while they are in-progress. As a result, the throughput metric may be specified through other means, such as the information rate of the access link on each service interface, and not formally verified through active measurement.

10.10 Deployment of Active Measurement Infrastructures

In this section, we describe several ways in which active measurement systems can be realized. One of the key design distinctions is the measurement device topology. We describe and contrast several of the topologies that have seen deployment, as this will be an important consideration for any system the reader might devise. We categorize the topologies according to where the devices conducting measurements are physically located.

10.10.1 Geographic Deployment at Customer–Service Interfaces

In this topology, measurement devices (or measurement processes in multipurpose devices) are located as close as possible to the service interfaces. Figure 10.4a

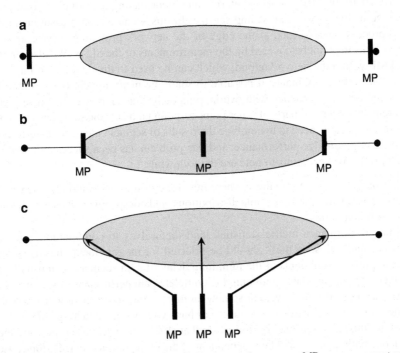

Fig. 10.4 Deployment scenarios for active measurement infrastructure. MP = measurement point. (a) MP at ends of path in point-to-point service. (b) MP at network edge; no coverage of access links. (c) MP at central location with connectivity to remote locations

depicts this topology for a point-to-point service, with a Measurement Point (MP) at each end of the path. The Cisco Systems IP SLA™ product embeds an active measurement system at routers and switches that often resides in close proximity to the Customer–Service Interfaces. The measurement results can be collected by accessing specific MIB modules using SNMP. The utility of IP SLA™ capabilities was recognized for multi-vendor scenarios, and the Two-way Active Measurement Protocol (TWAMP) [46] standardizes a fundamental test control and operation capability.

The primary advantage of this topology is that the measurement path covers the entire service in a single measurement, so the active test packets will experience conditions very similar to customer traffic. However, the measurement device/process must be located at a remote (customer) site to provide such coverage, so their cost is not shared across multiple services and it must be managed (and have results collected) remotely. The scale of the measurement system is also an issue. A full-mesh of two-way active measurements grows exponentially with the number of nodes, N, according to $N * (N - 1)/2$.

10.10.2   Geographic Deployment at Network Edges

In Fig. 10.4b, the MPs move to intermediate nodes along the point-to-point path, the edge of the network providing service. In this scenario, the measurement devices/processes are located at the edge of the network providing service and the access links may not be covered by the measurements or the SLAs. We also show a third MP within the network cloud, which can be used to divide the path into segments. This topology makes it possible to share the measurement devices and the measurements they produce with overlapping paths that support different services, different customers, or parts of other point-to-point paths for the same customer. Of course, a process is needed to combine the results of segment measurements to estimate the edge-to-edge performance, and this problem has been successfully solved [51, 65, 67]. The key points to note are the following:

- The interesting cases are those where impairments are time-varying, thus we expect to estimate features of time distributions, and not specific values (singletons) at particular times.
- Some performance metric statistics lend themselves to combination, such as means and ratios, so these should be selected for measurement and SLAs. For example, measurements of the minimum delay of path segments can usually be taken as additive when estimating the complete path performance. Average one-way delay is also additive, but somewhat more prone to estimation errors when the segment distributions are bimodal or have wide variance (a long tail).
- There must be a reasonable case made that (for each metric used) performance on one path segment will be independent of the other, because correlation causes the estimation methods to fail. An obvious correlation example is any metric

that evaluates packet spacing differences – the measurement is dependent on the original spacing, and that spacing will change when there is any delay variation present on the path segments.

We note that it is also possible to obtain complete path coverage using this topology, with assistance from low-cost test reflector devices/processes located at the service interfaces (such as those described in RFC 5357 [46]) (see [13] for more details).

10.10.3   Centralized Deployment with Remote Connectivity

As alternative to remote deployment of measurement devices/processes, Fig. 10.4c shows all MPs moved to a central location with connectivity to strategic locations in the network (such as the network edges in key cities). This topology offers the advantage of easy access to the measurement devices at the central location, thus affording rapid reconfiguration and upgrade. However, reliable remote access links are needed between this single location and every network node that requires testing. Also, even if the remote access links are transparent from a packet loss perspective, they will still introduce delay that is not present on the customer's path through the network. The mere cost of the remote access links may make remote device deployment in Fig. 10.4b more attractive. Thus, topologies like this have been deployed for remote connectivity monitors when the devices implementing a network technology do not have sufficient native support for remote device deployment (e.g., Frame Relay networks).

A system exploiting this approach is described in [8] where tunneling is used to steer measurement packets on round-trip paths from a central host, via the access links. In this sense, virtual measurements are conducted between different pairs of hosts in the network core. A related approach for multicast VPN monitoring is described in [7].

10.10.4   Collection for Infrastructure Measurements

When measurement devices are geographically dispersed, there must be a means to collect the results of measurements and make them available for monitoring, reporting, and SLA compliance verification. This requires some form of protocol to fetch either the per-packet measurements, or the processed and summarized results for each intermediate measurement interval (e.g., 5–15 min). Once the measurement results have been collected at a central point, they should be stored in a database system and made available for on-going display, detailed analysis, and SLA verification/reporting.

10.10.5 Other Types of Infrastructure Measurements

10.10.5.1 Independent Measurement Networks

Measurement service vendors, such as Keynote [57], station measurement devices in locations of ISPs representing, e.g., typical customer access points, and conduct a variety of measurements between measurement devices or between them and service hosts, including, web and other server response times, access bandwidth, VoIP, and other access performance. Comparative performance measures are published and detailed results are made available through subscription.

10.10.5.2 Cross Provider and Network-Wide Measurements

End-to-end paths commonly traverse multiple service providers. Thus, it is natural to measure the inter-provider components to performance. The most prominent example is the RIPE network [73], which has stationed measurement devices in a number of participating ISPs, conducts performance measurements between them, and disseminates selected views to the participants. Novel active measurement infrastructure is being deployed in advanced research and development networks (e.g., MeasurementLab/PlanetLab [61]), including work in developing architectures for managing access to and data recovery from measurement infrastructures.

10.10.5.3 Performance Measurement and Route Selection

Router measurement capabilities may also be coupled to the operation of routing protocols themselves. Cisco Performance Routing [20] enables routers in a multiply-homed domain to conduct performance measurements to external networks. The measurements are then compared in order to determine the best egress to that network and adjust route parameters accordingly.

10.11 Outlook

The challenges described in Section 10.1.3 will grow with network size and complexity. The fundamental challenges for passive measurement, that of large data volumes caused by network scale and speed, are usually addressed by sampling. Going forward, there are three related trade-offs for the measurement infrastructure. Unless the capacity of the measurement infrastructure grows commensurate with the growth in network speed and scale grows, sampling rates must decrease in order to fit the measurements within the current infrastructure. But decreasing sampling rates reduces the ability to provide an accurate fine-grained view the traffic. Although loss of detail and accuracy can be ameliorated by aggregation, that would go against the increasing demand for detailed measurements differentiated by customer, application, and service class. On the other hand, growing the infrastructure and retaining current sampling rates present its own challenges, and not just for in equipment and administration costs. Distributed measurement architectures are an attractive way to manage scale, enabling local analysis and aggregation rather than requiring recovery of data to a single central point. Then, the challenge becomes the design of distributed analysis and efficient communication methods between components of measurement infrastructure. This is particularly challenging for network security applications, which need a network-wide view in order to identify stealthy unwanted traffic.

Active measurement presents analogous challenges in viewing network performance differentiated by, e.g., customer, application, traffic path, and network element. Aggregate performance measurements are no longer sufficient. There are a number of approaches to target probe packets on or onto particular paths: (i) the probe may craft the packet in order that network elements select the packet on the desired path; this approach was taken in [7, 8], or (ii) passively measuring customer traffic directly, e.g., by comparing timestamps between different points on the path to determine latency (see Section 10.5.2). Both these approaches require knowledge of the mapping between the desired entity to be measured from (customer, service class) and the observable parts of the packets. A challenge is that this mapping may be difficult to elucidate, or depend on network state that may become unstable precisely at the time a performance problem needs to be diagnosed.

Tomographic methods have been proposed to infer performance on links from performance on sets of measured path that traverse them (see [1, 11]), typically under simplifying independence assumptions concerning packet loss, latency, and link failure. These approaches aim to supply indirectly, performance measurements that are not available directly. It remains a challenge to bring the early promise of these methods to fruition in production-level tools under general network conditions (see e.g. [48]). The relative utility of performance tomographic approaches will depend on the extent to which the detailed network performance measurements can be provided directly by router-based measurements in the future.

This outlook stands in contrast to the state described in the opening section, where little measurement functionality was provided in the network infrastructure. As the best ideas in measurement research and development mature into standard equipment features, the challenge will be to manage the complexity and scale of the infrastructure and the data itself.

References

1. Adams, A., Bu, T., Caceres, R., Duffield, N., Friedman, T., Horowitz, J., Lo Presti, F., Moon, S. B., Paxson, V., & Towsley. D. (2000). The use of end-to-end multicast measurements for characterizing internal network behavior. *IEEE Communications Magazine, May 2000, 38*(5), 152–159.
2. Almes, G., Kalidindi, S., & Zekauskas, M. (1999). A one-way delay metric for IPPM. RFC 2679, September 1999.

3. Almes, G., Kalidindi, S., & Zekauskas, M. (1999). A one-way packet loss metric for IPPM. RFC 2680, September 1999.
4. Alon, N., Duffield, N., Lund, C., & Thorup, M. (2005). Estimating arbitrary subset sums with few probes. In *Proceedings of 24th ACM Symposium on Principles of Database Systems (PODS)* (pp. 317–325). Baltimore, MD, June 13–16, 2005.
5. AT&T Labs. Application traffic analyzer. http://www.research.att.com/viewProject.cfm?prjID=125.
6. Bradner, S. (1991). Benchmarking terminology for network interconnection devices. RFC 1242, July 1991.
7. Breslau, L., Chase, C., Duffield, N., Fenner, B., Mao, Y., & Sen, S. (2006). Vmscope: a virtual multicast vpn performance monitor. In *INM '06: Proceedings of the 2006 SIGCOMM Workshop on Internet Network Management* (pp. 59–64). New York, NY, USA: ACM.
8. Burch, H., & Chase, C. (2005). Monitoring link delays with one measurement host. *SIGMETRICS Performance Evaluation Review, 33*(3):10–17.
9. CAIDA. The CAIDA anonymized 2009 internet traces dataset. http://www.caida.org/data/passive/passive_2009_dataset.xml.
10. CAIDA. cflowd: Traffic flow analysis tool. http://www.caida.org/tools/measurement/cflowd/.
11. Castro, R., Coates, M., Liang, G., Nowak, R., & Yu, B. (2004). Network tomography: recent developments. *Statistical Science, 19*, 499–517.
12. Chimento, P., & Ishac, J. (2008). Defining network capacity. RFC 5136, February 2008.
13. Ciavattone, L., Morton, A., & Ramachandran, G. (2003). Standardized active measurements on a tier 1 IP backbone. *IEEE Communications Magazine*, pp. 90–97, June 2003.
14. Cisco Systems. Cisco IOS Flexible NetFlow. http://www.cisco.com/web/go/fnf.
15. Cisco Systems. Cisco NetFlow Collector Engine. http://www.cisco.com/en/US/products/sw/netmgtsw/ps1964/.
16. Cisco Systems. Delivering the next generation data center. http://www.cisco.com/en/US/products/ps9402/.
17. Cisco Systems. IOS switching services configuration guide. http://www.cisco.com/en/US/docs/ios/12_1/switch/configuration/guide/xcdipsp.html.
18. Cisco Systems. NetFlow. http://www.cisco.com/warp/public/732/netflow/index.html.
19. Cisco Systems. Optimizing application traffic with cisco service control technology. http://www.cisco.com/go/servicecontrol.
20. Cisco Systems. Performance Routing. http://www.cisco.com/web/go/pfr/.
21. Cisco Systems. Random Sampled NetFlow. http://www.cisco.com/en/US/docs/ios/12_0s/feature/guide/nfstatsa.html.
22. Claffy, K. C., Braun, H.-W., & Polyzos, G. C. (1995). Parameterizable methodology for internet traffic flow profiling. *IEEE Journal on Selected Areas in Communications, 13*(8), 1481–1494, October 1995.
23. Claise, B. (2004). Cisco Systems NetFlow Services Export Version 9. RFC 3954, October 2004.
24. Claise, B., Johnson, A., & Quittek, J. (2009). Packet sampling (psamp) protocol specifications. RFC 5476, March 2009.
25. Claise, B., & Wolter, R. (2007). *Network management: accounting and performance strategies.* Cisco.
26. Cohen, E., Duffield, N., Lund, C., & Thorup, M. (2008). Confident estimation for multistage measurement sampling and aggregation. In *ACM SIGMETRICS*. June 2–6, 2008, Maryland, USA: Annapolis.
27. Cohen, E., Duffield, N. G., Kaplan, H., Lund, C.,& Thorup, M. (2007). Algorithms and estimators for accurate summarization of internet traffic. In *IMC '07: Proceedings of the 7th ACM SIGCOMM Conference on Internet Measurement* (pp. 265–278). New York, NY, USA: ACM.
28. Cranor, C., Johnson, T., Spataschek, O., & Shkapenyuk, V., (2003). Gigascope: a stream database for network applications. In *SIGMOD '03: Proceedings of the 2003 ACM SIGMOD International Conference on Management of Data* (pp. 647–651). New York, NY, USA: ACM.
29. Crovella, M., & Krishnamurthy, B. (2006). *Internet measurement: infrastructure, traffic and applications.* New York, NY: Wiley.

30. Dasu, T., & Johnson, T. (2003). *Exploratory data mining and data cleaning.* New York, NY, USA: Wiley.

31. Demichelis, C., & Chimento, P. (2002). Ip packet delay variation metric for ip performance metrics (ippm). RFC 3393, November 2002.

32. Dietz, T., Claise, B., Aitken, P., Dressler, F., & Carle, G. (2009). Information model for packet sampling export. RFC 5477, March 2009.

33. Duffield, N.G., Claise, B., Chiou, D., Greenberg, A., Grossglauser, M., & Rexford, J. (2009). A framework for packet selection and reporting. RFC 5474, March 2009.

34. Duffield, N.G., Gerber, A., & Grossglauser, M. (2002). Trajectory engine: A backend for trajectory sampling. In *IEEE Network Operations and Management Symposium (NOMS) 2002.* Florence, Italy, 15–19 April 2002.

35. Duffield, N.G., Lund, C., & Thorup, M. (2001). Charging from sampled network usage. In *Proceedings of 1st ACM SIGCOMM Internet Measurement Workshop (IMW)* (pp. 245–256). San Francisco, CA, November 1–2, 2001.

36. Duffield, N.G., Lund, C., & Thorup, M. (2005). Learn more, sample less: control of volume and variance in network measurements. *IEEE Transactions on Information Theory, 51*(5), 1756–1775.

37. Duffield, N.G., Lund, C., & Thorup, M. (2007). Priority sampling for estimation of arbitrary subset sums. *Journal of ACM, 54*(6), Article 32, December 2007. Announced at SIGMETRICS'04.

38. Duffield, N., & Grossglauser, M. (2001). Trajectory sampling for direct traffic observation. *IEEE/ACM Transactions on Networking, 9*(3), 280–292, June 2001.

39. Duffield, N., & Lund, C. (2003). Predicting resource usage and estimation accuracy in an IP flow measurement collection infrastructure. In *Proceedings of Internet Measurement Conference.* Miami, FL, October 27–29, 2003.

40. Estan, C., Keys, K., Moore, D., & Varghese, G. (2004). Building a better netflow. In *Proceedings of the ACM SIGCOMM 04.* New York, NY, 12–16 June 2004.

41. Estan, C., & Varghese, G. (2002). New directions in traffic measurement and accounting. In *Proceedings of ACM SIGCOMM '2002.* Pittsburgh, PA, August 2002.

42. Feldmann, A., Rexford, J., & Cáceres, R. (1998). Efficient policies for carrying web traffic over flow-switched networks. *IEEE/ACM Transactions on Networking, 6*(6), 673–685, December 1998.

43. Goldberg, S., & Rexford, J. (2007). Security vulnerabilities and solutions for packet sampling. In *IEEE Sarnoff Symposium.* Princeton, NJ, May 2007.

44. Greer, R. (1999). Daytona and the fourth-generation language cymbal. In *SIGMOD '99: Proceedings of the 1999 ACM SIGMOD International Conference on Management of Data* (pp. 525–526). New York, NY, USA: ACM.

45. Hao, F., Kodialam, M., & Lakshman, T.V. (2004). Accel-rate: a faster mechanism for memory efficient per-flow traffic estimation. In *SIGMETRICS '04/Performance '04: Proceedings of the Joint International Conference on Measurement and Modeling of Computer Systems* (pp. 155–166). New York, NY, USA: ACM.

46. Hedayat, K., Krzanowski, R., Morton, A., Yum, K., & Babiarz, J. (2008). A two-way active measurement protocol (twamp). RFC 5357, October 2008.

47. Horvitz, D. G., & Thompson, D. J. (1952). A generalization of sampling without replacement from a finite universe. *Journal of the American Statistical Association, 47*(260), 663–685.

48. Huang, Y., Feamster, N., & Teixeira, R. (2008). Practical issues with using network tomography for fault diagnosis. *SIGCOMM Computer Communication Review, 38*(5), 53–58.

49. IETF. IP Flow Information Export (ipfix) charter. http://www.ietf.org/html.charters/ipfix-charter.html. Version of 16 December 2008.

50. Internet Assigned Numbers Authority. Port numbers. http://www.iana.org/assignments/port-numbers.

51. ITU-T Recommendation Y.1540. Network performance objectives for IP-based services, February 2006.

52. Jacobson, V., Leres, C., & McCanne, S. tcpdump.

53. Jacobson V. Traceroute. ftp://ftp.ee.lbl.gov/traceroute.tar.gz.
54. Jain, R., & Routhier, S. (1986). Packet trains – measurements and a new model for computer network traffic. *IEEE Journal on Selected Areas in Communications, 4*(6), 986–995, September 1986.
55. Juniper Networks. Junose 8.2.x ip services configuration guide: Configuring j-flow statistics. http://www.juniper.net/techpubs/software/erx/junose82/swconfig-ip-services/html/ip-jflow-stats-config.html.
56. Kent, S., & Atkinson, R. (1998). Security architecture for the Internet Protocol. RFC 2401, November 1998.
57. Keynote Systems. http://www.keynote.com.
58. Mathis, M., & Mahdavi, J. (1996). Diagnosing internet congestion with a transport layer performance tool. In *Proceedings of INET 96*. Montreal, Quebec, 24–28 June 1996.
59. McCloghrie, K., & Kastenholz, F. The interfaces group mib. RFC 2863, June 2000.
60. McCloghrie, K., & Rose, M. (1991). Management Information Base for Network Management of TCP/IP-based internets: MIB-II. *RFC 1213*, available from http://www.ietf.org/rfc, March 1991.
61. MeasurementLab. http://www.measurementlab.net/.
62. Mills, C., Hirsh, D.,& Ruth, D. (1991). Internet accounting: background. RFC 1272, November 1991.
63. Greg Minshall. tcpdpriv. http://ita.ee.lbl.gov/html/contrib/tcpdpriv.html.
64. Moore, D., Paxson, V., Savage, S., Shannon, C., Staniford, S., & Weaver, N. (2003). Inside the slammer worm. *IEEE Security and Privacy, 1*(4), 33–39.
65. Morton, A. (2008). Framework for metric composition, June 2009. draft-ietf-ippm-framework-compagg-08 (work in progress).
66. Morton, A., & Claise, B. (2009). Packet delay variation applicability statement. RFC 5481, March 2009.
67. Morton, A., & Stephan, E. (2008). Spatial composition of metrics, October 2009. draft-ietf-ippm-spatial-composition-10 (work in progress).
68. Narus, Inc. Narusinsight secure suite. http://www.narus.com/products/security.html.
69. Packetdesign. Traffic explorer. http://www.packetdesign.com/products/tex.htm.
70. Paxson, V., Almes, G., Mahdavi, J., & Mathis, M. (1998). Framework for ip performance metrics. RFC 2330, May 1998.
71. Phaal, P., Panchen, S., & McKee, N. (2001). Inmon corporation's sflow: A method for monitoring traffic in switched and routed networks. RFC 3176, September 2001. http://www.ietf.org/rfc/rfc3176.txt.
72. Raisanen, V., Grotefeld, G., & Morton, A. (2002). Network performance measurement with periodic streams. RFC 3432, November 2002.
73. RIPE. http://www.ripe.net.
74. Roesch, M. (1999). Snort – Lightweight Intrusion Detection for Networks. In *Proceedings of USENIX Lisa '99*, Seattle, WA, November 1999.
75. Sandvine. http://www.sandvine.com/.
76. Srinivasan, C., Viswanathan, A., & Nadeau, T. (2004). Multiprotocol label switching (MPLS) label switching router (LSR) management information base (MIB). RFC 3813, June 2004.
77. Stallings, W. (1999). *SNMP, SNMP v2, SNMP v3, and RMON 1 and 2 (Third Edition)*. Reading, MA: Addison-Wesley.
78. Stewart, R., Ramalho, M., Xie, Q., Tuexen, M., & Conrad, P. (2004). Stream control transmission protocol (sctp) partial reliability extension. RFC3758, May 2004.
79. Thorup, M. (2006). Confidence intervals for priority sampling. In *Proceedings of ACM SIGMETRICS/Performance 2006* (pp. 252–263) Saint-Malo, France, 26–30 June 2006.
80. van der Merwe J., Cáceres, R., Chu, Y.-H., & Sreenan, C. (2000). mmdump: a tool for monitoring internet multimedia traffic. *SIGCOMM Computer Commununication Review, 30*(5), 48–59.
81. Waldbusser, S. (2000). Remote network monitoring management information base. *RFC 2819*, available from http://www.ietf.org/rfc, May 2000.

82. Zseby, T., Molina, M., Duffield, N.G., Niccolini, S., & Raspall, F. (2009). Sampling and filtering techniques for ip packet selection. RFC 5475, March 2009.
83. Zseby, T., Zander, S., & Carle, G. (2001). Evaluation of building blocks for passive one-way-delay measurements. In *Proceedings of Passive and Active Measurement Workshop (PAM 2001)*. Amsterdam, The Netherlands, 23–24 April 2001.

Chapter 11
Measurements of Control Plane Reliability and Performance

Lee Breslau and Aman Shaikh

11.1 Introduction

The control plane determines how traffic flows through an IP network. It consists of routers interconnected by links and routing protocols implemented as software processes running on them. Routers (or more specifically routing protocols) communicate with one another to determine the path that packets take from a source to a destination. As a result, the reliability and performance of the control plane is critical to the overall performance of applications and services running on the network. This chapter focuses on how to measure and monitor the reliability and performance of the control plane of a network.

The original Internet service model supported only unicast delivery. That is, a packet injected into the network by a source host was intended to be delivered to a single destination. Multicast, in which a packet is replicated inside the network and delivered to multiple hosts was subsequently introduced as a service. While certain multicast routing protocols leverage unicast routing information, unicast and multicast have very distinct control planes. They are each governed by a different set of routing protocols, and measurement and monitoring of these protocols consequently take different forms. Therefore, we cover unicast and multicast control plane monitoring separately in Sections 11.2 and 11.3, respectively.

We start Section 11.2 with a brief overview of how unicast forwarding works, describing different routing protocols and how they work to determine paths between a source and a destination. We then look at two key components of performance monitoring: instrumentation of the network for data collection in Section 11.2.2, and strategies and tools for data analysis in Section 11.2.3. More specifically, the instrumentation section describes what data we need to collect for route monitoring along with mechanisms for collecting the data needed. The analysis section focuses on various techniques and tools that show how the data is used for monitoring the

L. Breslau and A. Shaikh (✉)
AT&T Labs – Research, Florham Park, NJ, USA
e-mail: breslau@research.att.com; ashaikh@research.att.com

C.R. Kalmanek et al. (eds.), *Guide to Reliable Internet Services and Applications*, Computer Communications and Networks, DOI 10.1007/978-1-84882-828-5_11, © Springer-Verlag London Limited 2010 performance of the control plane. While the focus of the section is on management and operational aspects, we also describe some of the research enabled by this data that has played a vital role in enhancing our understanding of the control plane behavior and performance in real life. We follow this up with a description of the AT&T OSPF Monitor [1] in Section 11.2.4 as a case study of a route monitor in real life. In Section 11.2.5, we describe control plane monitoring of MPLS, which has been deployed in service provider networks in the last few years and is a key enabler of Traffic Engineering (TE) and Fast Re-route (FRR) capabilities, as well as new services such as VPN and VPLS.

Section 11.3 follows a similar approach in its treatment of multicast. We begin with a motivation for and historical perspective of the development and deployment of multicast. In Section 11.3.1, we provide a brief overview of the multicast routing protocols commonly in use today, PIM and MSDP. We then outline some of the challenges specific to monitoring the multicast control plane in Section 11.3.2. Section 11.3.3 provides detailed information about multicast monitoring. This includes an overview of early multicast monitoring efforts, a discussion of the information sources available for multicast monitoring, and a discussion of specific approaches and tools used in multicast monitoring.

At the end of the chapter, in Section 11.4, we provide a brief summary and avenues for future work.

11.2 Unicast

In this section, we focus on monitoring of unicast routing protocols. We begin by providing a brief overview of how routers forward unicast packets and the routing protocols used for determining the forwarding paths before delving into details of how to monitor these protocols.

11.2.1 Unicast Routing Overview

Let us start with the description of how routing protocols enable the forwarding of unicast packets in IP networks. With unicast, each packet contains the address of the destination. When the packet arrives at a router, a table called the *Forwarding Information Base (FIB)*, also known as the forwarding table, is consulted. This table allows the router to determine the next-hop router for the packet, based on its destination address. Packets are thus forwarded in a hop-by-hop fashion, requiring look-ups in the forwarding table of each router hop along its way to the destination. The forwarding table typically consists of a set of prefixes. Each prefix is represented by an IP address and a mask that specifies how many significant bits of a destination address need to match the address of the prefix. For example, a prefix represented as 10.0.0.0/16 would match a destination address whose first 16 bits are the same as the first 16 bits of 10.0.0.0 (i.e., 10.0). Thus, the address 10.0.0.1 matches this prefix, so do 10.0.0.2 and 10.0.1.1. It is possible, and is often the case that, more than one prefix in a FIB match a given (destination) address. In such a case, the prefix with the highest value of the mask length is used for determining the next-hop router. For example, if a FIB contains 10.0.0.0/16 and 10.0.0.0/24, and the destination is 10.0.0.1, prefix 10.0.0.0/24 is used for forwarding the packet even though both prefixes match the address. For this reason, IP forwarding is based on the *longest prefix*.

Routers run one or more *routing protocols* to construct their FIBs. Every routing protocol allows a router to learn the network topology (or some part of it) by exchanging messages with other routers. The topology information is then used by a router to determine next hops for various prefixes, i.e., the FIB.

Learning Topology Information

Depending on how much topology information each router learns, the routing protocols can be divided into two main classes: *distance-vector* and *link-state*.

In a distance-vector routing protocol at each step, every router learns the distance of each adjacent router to every prefix. Every prefix is connected to one or more routers in the network. The distance from a router to a prefix is the sum of weights of individual links on the path, where the weight of every link is assigned in the configuration file of the associated router. A router, upon learning distances from neighbors, chooses the one that is closest to a given prefix as its next-hop, and subsequently propagates its own distance (which is equal to the neighbor's distance plus the weight of its link to the neighbor) to the prefix to all other neighbors. When a router comes up, it only knows about its directly connected prefixes (e.g., prefixes associated with point-to-point or broadcast links). The router propagates information about these prefixes to its neighbors, allowing them to determine their routes to them. The information then spreads further, and ultimately all routers in the network end up with next-hops for these prefixes. In a similar vein, the newly booted router also learns about other prefixes from its neighbors, and builds its entire FIB. The distance-vector protocols essentially implement a distributed version of the Bellman Ford shortest-path algorithm [2]. RIP [3] is an example of a distance-vector protocol. EIGRP, a Cisco-proprietary protocol, is another example. It contains mechanisms (an algorithm called DUAL [4]) to prevent forwarding loops that can be formed during network changes when routers can become inconsistent in their views of the topology. A subclass of distance-vector, called *path-vector protocols* include the actual path to the destination along with the distance in the updates sent to neighbors. The inclusion of the path helps in identifying and avoiding potential loops from forming during convergence. BGP [5] is an example of a path-vector protocol.

With link-state routing protocols, each router learns the entire network topology. The topology is conceptually a directed graph – each router corresponds to a node in this graph, and each link between neighboring routers corresponds to a unidirectional edge. Just like distance-vector protocols, each link also has an administratively assigned weight associated with it. Using the weighted topology graph, each router computes a shortest-path tree with itself as the root, and applies the results to compute next-hops for all possible destinations. Routing remains consistent as long as all the routers have the same view of the topology. The view of the topology is built in a distributed fashion, with each router describing its local connectivity (i.e., set of links incident on it along with their weights) in a message, and flooding this message to all routers in the network. OSPF [6] and IS-IS [7] are examples of link-state protocols.

Autonomous Systems (ASes) and Hierarchical Routing

The Internet is an inter-network of networks. By design, these networks are envisioned to be administered by independent entities. In other words, the Internet is a collection of independently administered networks. Roughly speaking, such networks are known as *Autonomous Systems (ASes)*. Each autonomous system consists of a set of routers and links that are usually managed by a single administrative authority. Every autonomous system can run one or more routing protocols of its choice to route packets within the system. RIP, EIGRP, OSPF and IS-IS are typically used for routing packets within an AS and are, therefore, known as *intradomain* or *Interior Gateway Protocols (IGPs)*. In addition, a routing protocol is needed to forward packets between ASes. BGP is used for this purpose and is known as an *interdomain* or an *Exterior Gateway Protocol (EGP)*.

Next, we present an overview of BGP and OSPF as they come up a lot in the subsequent discussions. For details on other routing protocols, please refer to [8].

11.2.1.1 BGP Overview

As mentioned in Section 11.2.1.1, BGP is the de facto routing protocol used to exchange routing information between ASes. BGP is a path-vector protocol (a subset of distance-vector protocols). In path-vector protocols, a router receives routes from its neighbors that describe their distance to prefixes, as well as the path used to reach the prefix in question. Since BGP is used to route packets between ASes, the path is described as a sequence of ASes traversed along the way to the prefix, the sequence being known as an *ASPath*. Thus, every route update received at a router contains the prefix and the ASPath indicating the path used by the neighbor to reach the prefix. The distance is not explicitly included; rather it implicitly equals the number of ASes in the ASPath.

Apart from ASPath, BGP routes also contain other attributes. These attributes are used by a router to determine the most preferred route from all received routes to a destination prefix. Figure 11.1 shows the steps of a decision process that a

Fig. 11.1 The decision
process used by BGP to select
the best route to every prefix.
Vendor-dependent steps are
not included

1. Highest Local Preference
2. Shortest ASPath Length
3. Lowest Origin Type
4. Lowest MED
5. Prefer Closest Egress (based on IGP distance)
6. Arbitrary Tie Breaking

BGP-speaking router follows to select its most preferred route. The process is run independently for each prefix, and starts with all the available routes for the prefix in question. At every step, relevant attributes of the routes are compared. Routes with the most preferred values pass onto the next step while other routes are dropped from further consideration. At the end of the decision process, a router ends up with a single route for every prefix, and uses it to forward data traffic. Note that the second step of the decision process compares the length of ASPath of the routes that survived the first step, keeps the ones with the shortest ASPaths, while discarding the rest. We will not go into details of other steps except to point out that if faced with more than one route in step 5, the router selects route(s) which minimize the IGP distance a packet will have to travel to exit its AS. This process of preferring the closest egress is known as *hot-potato* or *closest-egress* routing.

A router forms BGP sessions with other routers to exchange route updates. The two ends of a session can either belong to the same AS or a different AS. When the session is formed between routers in the same AS, it is known as an *internal BGP (IBGP)* session. In contrast, when the routers are in different ASes, the session is known as *external BGP (EBGP)* session. For example, in Fig. 11.2, which shows multiple interconnected ASes and routers in them, solid lines depict IBGP sessions, whereas dashed lines represent EBGP sessions. The EBGP sessions setup between routers in neighbor ASes allow them to exchange routes to various prefixes. The routes learned over EBGP sessions are then distributed using IBGP sessions within an AS. For example, AS 2 in Fig. 11.2 learns routes from ASes 1, 3, and 4 over EBGP sessions, which are then distributed among its routers over IBGP sessions.

In order to disseminate all routes learned via EBGP to every router, routers inside an AS like AS 1 need to form a full-mesh of IBGP sessions. A router receiving a route update over an EBGP session propagates it to all other routers in the mesh, however, route updates received over IBGP sessions are not forwarded back to the routers in the mesh (see [9] for full details). An IBGP full-mesh does not scale for ASes with a large number of routers. To improve scalability, large ASes use an IBGP hierarchy such as route reflection [10]. Route reflection allows the re-announcement of some routes learned over IBGP sessions. However, it sacrifices the number of candidate routes learned at each router for improved scalability. For example, AS 2 in Fig. 11.2 employs a route reflector hierarchy.

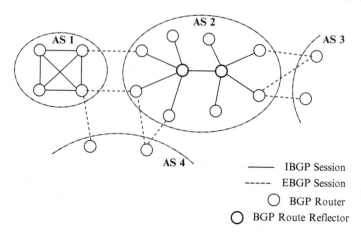

IBGP Session

EBGP Session

BGP Router

BGP Route Reflector

Fig. 11.2 Example topology with multiple ASes and BGP sessions

11.2.1.2 OSPF Overview

As noted in Section 11.2.1.1, OSPF is a link-state protocol, which is widely used to control routing within an Autonomous System (AS).[1] With link-state routing protocols, each router learns the entire view of the network topology represented as a weighted graph, uses it to compute a shortest-path tree with itself as the root, and applies the results to construct its forwarding table. This assures that packets are forwarded along the shortest paths in terms of link weights to their destinations [11]. We will refer to the computation of the shortest-path tree as an *SPF computation*, and the resultant tree as an *SPF tree*.

For scalability, an OSPF network may be divided into areas determining a two-level hierarchy as shown in Fig. 11.3. Area 0, known as the *backbone area*, resides at the top level of the hierarchy and provides connectivity to the non-backbone areas (numbered 1, 2, etc.). OSPF assigns each link to one or more areas.[2] The routers that have links to multiple areas are called *border routers*. For example, routers C, D, and G are border routers in Fig. 11.3. Every router maintains a separate copy of the topology graph for each area to which it is connected. The router performs the SPF computation on each such topology graph and thereby learns how to reach nodes in all adjacent areas.

A router does not learn the entire topology of remote areas. Instead, it learns the total weight of the shortest paths from one or more border routers to each prefix in

---

[1] Even though an IGP like OSPF is used for routing within an AS, the boundary of an IGP domain and an AS do not have to coincide. An AS may consist of multiple IGP domains; conversely, a single IGP domain may span multiple ASes.

[2] The original OSPF specification [6] required each link to be assigned to *exactly* one area, but a recent extension [12] allows a single link to be assigned to multiple areas.

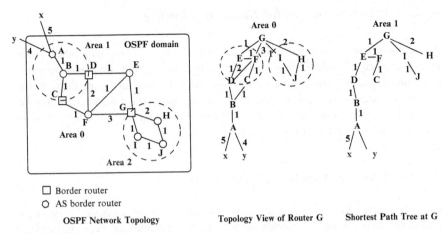

□ Border router
○ AS border router

OSPF Network Topology   Topology View of Router G   Shortest Path Tree at G

Fig. 11.3 An example OSPF topology, the view of the topology from router G, and the shortest-path tree calculated at G. Although we show the OSPF topology as an undirected graph here for simplicity, the graph is directed in reality

remote areas. Thus, after computing the SPF tree for each area, the router learns which border router to use as an intermediate node for reaching each remote node. In addition, the reachability of external IP prefixes (associated with nodes outside the OSPF domain) can be injected into OSPF (e.g., X and Y in Fig. 11.3). Roughly, reachability to an external prefix is determined as if the prefix was a node linked to the router that injects the prefix into OSPF. The router that injects the prefix into OSPF is called an *AS Border Router (ASBR)*. For example, router A is an ASBR in Fig. 11.3.

Routers running OSPF describe their local connectivity in *Link State Advertisements (LSAs)*. These LSAs are *flooded* reliably to other routers in the network. The routers use LSAs to build a consistent view of the topology as described earlier. Flooding is made reliable by mandating that a router acknowledge the receipt of every LSA it receives from every neighbor. The flooding is hop-by-hop and hence does not itself depend on routing. The set of LSAs in a router's memory is called the *link-state database* and conceptually forms the topology graph for the router.

Two routers are neighbor routers if they have interfaces to a common network (i.e., they have a direct path between them that does not go through any other router). Neighbor routers form an *adjacency* so that they can exchange LSAs with each other. OSPF allows a link between the neighbor routers to be used for forwarding only if these routers have the same view of the topology, i.e., the same link-state database for the area the link belongs to. This ensures that forwarding data packets over the link does not create loops. Thus, two neighbor routers make sure that their link-state databases are in sync by exchanging out-of-sync parts of their link-state databases when they establish an adjacency.

11.2.2 Instrumentation for Route Monitoring

As mentioned, routers exchange information about the topology with other routers in the network to build their forwarding tables. As a result, understanding control plane dynamics requires collecting these messages and analyzing them. In this section, we focus on the collection aspect, leaving analysis for the next section. We first focus on how to instrument a single router, before turning our attention to the network-wide collection of messages.

11.2.2.1 Collecting Data from a Single Router

Even though the kind of information exchanged in routing messages varies from protocol to protocol, the flow of messages through individual routers can be modeled in the same manner, as depicted in Fig. 11.4. Every router basically receives messages from its neighbors from time to time. These messages are sent by neighbors in response to events occurring in the network or expiration of timers; again, the exact reasons are protocol specific. As described in Section 11.2.1, the message describes some aspect of the network topology or reachability to a prefix along with a set of attributes. Upon receiving the message, the router runs its route selection procedure taking the newly received message into account. The procedure can change the best route to one or more prefixes in the FIB. A router also sends messages to neighbors as network topology and/or reachability to prefixes change – the trigger and contents of the messages depend on the protocol. Given this, to understand routing dynamics of a router would require instrumenting the router to collect (i) incoming messages into a router over all its links, (ii) the changes induced to the FIB, and (iii) outgoing messages to all the neighbors.

Some protocols such as BGP allow routers to apply *import policies* to incoming messages; applying these policies results in either dropping of messages or modifications to the attributes. In such a scenario, it might be beneficial to collect incoming messages before and after application of import policies. In a similar vein, BGP

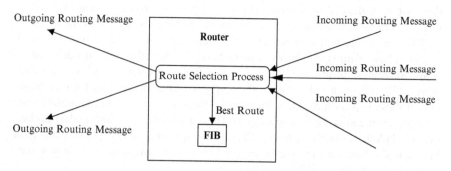

Fig. 11.4 Message flow through a router

applies *export policies* to outgoing messages before they are sent to neighbors in which case messages can be collected before and after the application of export policies.

Ideally, one would like the router to "copy" every incoming and outgoing message, as well as changes to the FIB to a management station. In reality, no standardized way for achieving this exists, and as a result no current router implementations support it. Despite this, one could get an approximate version of the required information in several different ways. One such way is to use splitters to read messages directly off a link. Unfortunately, this option is often impractical, expensive, and does not scale beyond a few routers and links. For this reason, this option is rarely used in practice. Another option is to log into the router through its CLI (Command Line Interface) or query SNMP MIBs [13] to extract the required information. Routers and (routing protocols running on them) often store a copy of the most recently received and transmitted messages in memory and allow them to be queried via CLI or SNMP MIBs. Thus, a network management station can periodically pull the information out of a router. Unfortunately, it is almost impossible to capture every incoming/outgoing message this way since even the most frequent polling supportable by routers fall far short of the highest frequency at which routing messages are exchanged. Even so, this option is used in practice at times since it provides a fairly inexpensive and practical way of getting some information about the routing state of a router. For example, the Peer Dragnet [14] tool uses information captured via the CLI to analyze inconsistent routes sent by EBGP peers of an AS.

A third option to collect routing messages is to establish a routing session with a router just like any other router. This forces the router to send messages as it would to any other router.[3] Obviously, this approach does not give information about incoming messages and changes to the FIB. Even for an outgoing message, the management station does not receive the message at the time a router sends it to other neighbors. Despite this, the approach provides valuable information about route dynamics. For distance-vector protocols, the outgoing message is usually the route selected by the router and for link-state protocols, these messages describe updates to the topology view of the router. As a result, this approach is used quite extensively in practice. For example, RouteViews [15] and RIPE [16] collect BGP updates from several ASes and their routers, as does the OSPF Monitor described in [1], and later in Section 11.2.4. One serious practical issue with this approach is the potential injection of routing messages from the management station, which could disrupt the functioning of the control plane. For protocols that allow import policies (e.g., BGP) one could apply a policy to drop any incoming messages from the management station, but for other protocols (e.g., OSPF, IS-IS) the only way to protect against injection of messages is to rely on the correctness of the software running on the management station.

---

[3] A router running a distance-vector protocol sends its selected route for a given prefix to all its neighbors, except the next-hop of the route when split horizon [8] is implemented. It is this selected route that we are interested in, and will receive, at the management station.

11.2.2.2   Collecting Network-Wide Data

In Section 11.2.2.1, we discussed ways in which routing messages can be collected from a single router. In this section, we expand our focus to the entire network. The key question we focus on is: how many routers does one need to collect routing messages from? The naive answer is: from *all* routers of the network. Indeed, if the aim is to learn about each and every message flowing between routers and the exact state of routers at every instance of time, then there is no choice but to collect messages from all routers. In reality, collecting messages from all routers is extremely challenging due to scale issues. Thus, in practice the answer depends on the kind of routing protocol and the analysis requirement. Let's go into some details.

The kind of routing protocol – whether link-state or distance-vector – plays a major role in deciding how many routers one needs to collect data from. In a link-state protocol, every router learns the entire view of the network topology, and so collecting messages from even a single router is enough to determine the overall state of the network topology. As we will see later in Sections 11.2.3 and 11.2.4, even this seemingly "limited" data enables a rich set of management applications. Some examples are (and we will talk about these in more detail in subsequent sections): (i) ability to track network topology and its integrity (against design rules) in real-time, (ii) ability to determine events such as router/link up/downs and link weight changes as they unfold, (iii) ability to determine how forwarding paths evolve in response to network events, and (iv) ability to determine workload imposed by the routing messages. We should emphasize here that for all the applications, the data is providing the "view" from the router from which the data is being collected at that point of time. Other routers' views can be somewhat different due to message propagation and processing delays. The exact nature of these delays, how they are affected by other events in the network, and their implications for the analysis/application at hand are poorly understood. Our belief is that these delays are small (on the order of milliseconds) in most cases, and thus can be safely ignored for all practical purposes.

The story is different for distance-vector protocols since every router gets a partial view of the topology: only the distance of prefixes from neighbors. As a result, one often needs views from multiple, if not all, routers. The exact set depends on the network configuration and on the kind of analysis being performed. For example, if one wants to learn external routes coming into an AS, it suffices to monitor BGP routes from the routers at the edge of the network. In fact, numerous studies on BGP dynamics, inter-AS topology and relationships between ASes have been carried out based on BGP data collected from a fairly small set of ASes at RouteViews and RIPE. Although the completeness and representativeness of these studies is debatable, there is no doubt that such studies have tremendously increased awareness about BGP and its workings in the Internet. Furthermore, by combining routing data collected from a subset of routers with other network data, one can often determine routing state of other routers – at least in steady state once routing has converged after a change. For example, a paper by Feamster and Rexford [17] describes a methodology to determine BGP routes at every router inside an AS based on routes learned at the edge of the network, and configuration of IBGP sessions.

11.2.3   Applications of Route Monitoring

In this section, we demonstrate the utility of the data collected by route monitors. We first describe the basic functionality enabled by the data. We then describe how this basic functionality can be used in various network management tasks. Finally, we describe how the data has been used in advancing the understanding of the behavior of routing protocols in real life.

11.2.3.1   Information Provided by Route Monitors

Routing State and Dynamics   Route monitors capture routing messages, and so they naturally provide information about the current state of routing and how it evolves over time. This information is useful for a variety of network management tasks such as troubleshooting and forensics, capacity planning, trending, and traffic engineering to name a few. For link-state protocols, the routing messages provide information about the topology (i.e., set of routers, links and link weights), whereas for distance-vector protocols, the information consists of route tables (i.e., set of destinations and the next-hop and distance from the router in question). Both pieces of information are useful. Furthermore, calculating routing tables from topology is straightforward: one just needs to emulate route calculation for every router in the topology. Going in the other direction from routing tables to topology is easy if information from all routers (running the distance-vector protocol) is available. In practice though, information is often collected from a subset of routers, in which case, deriving a complete topology view may not be possible.

End-to-End Paths   Knowing what path traffic takes in the network (from one router to another) is crucial for network management tasks such as fault localization and troubleshooting. For example, a link failure can affect performance of all paths traversing the link. If the only way of detecting such failures is through end-to-end active probing, then knowing paths would allow operators to quickly localize the problem to the common link. Routing messages collected by route monitors allow one to determine these paths and how they evolve in response to routing events. Note that active probes (e.g., traceroute) also allow one to determine end-to-end paths in the network. However, tracking path changes in response to network events using active probing suffers from major scalability problems. First of all, the number of router pairs in a large network can be in the range of hundreds of thousands to millions. This makes probing every path at a fine time scale prohibitively expensive. A second problem arises due to the use of multiple equal cost paths (known as ECMP) between router pairs. ECMP arises when more than one path with smallest weight exist between router pairs. Most intradomain protocols such as OSPF use all the paths by spreading data traffic across them.[4] Since service providers often have redundant links in their networks, router pairs are more likely to have multiple paths than not. ECMP unfortunately exacerbates the scalability problem for active probing. Furthermore, engineering probes so that all ECMPs are covered is next to impossible since how routers would spread traffic across multiple paths is almost impossible to determine a priori.

11.2.3.2 Utility of Route Monitors in Network Management

The data provided by route monitors and the basic information gleaned from them aid several network management tasks such as troubleshooting and forensics, network auditing, and capacity planning. Below we provide a detailed account of how this is done for each of these three tasks.

Network Troubleshooting and Forensics Route monitors provide a view into routing events as they unfold. This view can be in the form of topology, routing tables, or end-to-end paths as mentioned in the previous sections; which form proves useful often depends on the specific troubleshooting task at hand. For example, if a customer complains about loss of reachability to certain parts of the Internet, looking at BGP routes and their history can provide clues about causes of the problems. Similarly, if performance issues are seen in some parts of the network, knowing what routing events are happening and how they are affecting paths can provide an explanation for the issues. Note that the route monitors' utility not only stems from the current view of routing they provide (after all operators can always determine the current view by logging into routers), but from the historical data they provide which allows operators to piece together sequence of events leading to the problems. Routers do not store historical state, and so cannot provide such information. Going back to the debugging of customer complaining about lost reachability, it is rarely enough to determine the current state of the route, especially if no route exists to the prefix. To effectively pinpoint the problem, the operator might also need to know the history of route announcements and withdrawals for the prefix, and that data can only be provided by route monitors. Figure 11.5 shows snapshot of a tool that allows operators to view sequence of BGP route updates captured by a monitor deployed in a tier-1 ISP.

Network Auditing and Protocol Conformance Another use of route monitors is for auditing the integrity of the networks and conformance of routing protocols to their specifications. To audit the integrity of the network, one needs to devise rules against which the actual routing behavior can be checked. For example, network administrators often have conventions and rules about weights assigned to links.

---

[4] The exact algorithm for spreading traffic across ECMPs is implemented in the forwarding engine of routers.

		BGP Route History for 0.0.0.0/0 and its Subnets							
Count	Time (GMT)	Router	Event	Prefix	ASPath	Local Pref	Origin	MED	Next-hop
1	Wed Apr 1 18:32:50 2009	10.0.0.1	WITHDRAW	192.168.0.0/24	--	--	--	--	--
2	Wed Apr 1 18:32:50 2009	10.0.0.1	ANNOUNCE	172.16.3.0/23	65001 65010 65145	90	IGP	0	10.0.1.3
3	Wed Apr 1 18:32:52 2009	10.0.0.1	ANNOUNCE	10.1.123.0/12	65001 65126	80	IGP	25	10.0.1.8
4	Wed Apr 1 18:32:55 2009	10.0.0.1	ANNOUNCE	192.168.3.0/18	65001 65324 65002 65121 65084	80	IGP	0	10.0.2.1
5	Wed Apr 1 18:32:58 2009	10.0.0.1	ANNOUNCE	192.168.0.0/24	65001 65223 65145	65	IGP	100	10.0.1.1
6	Wed Apr 1 18:33:31 2009	10.0.0.1	ANNOUNCE	172.23.4.0/21	65001 65132	90	IGP	10	10.0.2.1
7	Wed Apr 1 18:33:44 2009	10.0.0.1	ANNOUNCE	10.231.34.64/20	65001 65010 65192 65034	65	IGP	12	10.0.1.45
8	Wed Apr 1 18:33:47 2009	10.0.0.1	ANNOUNCE	192.168.0.0/24	65001 65023 65145	90	IGP	0	10.0.1.1
9	Wed Apr 1 18:34:08 2009	10.0.0.1	ANNOUNCE	172.22.73.0/25	65001 65420 65321 65005	70	IGP	0	10.0.2.12
10	Wed Apr 1 18:34:21 2009	10.0.0.1	ANNOUNCE	172.172.72.0/21	65001 65014 65105	110	IGP	10	10.0.1.109

Fig. 11.5   Screen-shot of a tool to view BGP route announcement/withdrawals

It then becomes necessary to monitor the network for potential deviations (that happen intentionally or due to mistakes) from these rules. Since (intradomain) routing messages provide current information about link weights, they provide a perfect source for checking whether network's actual state conforms to the design rules or not. Checking that the network state matches the design rules is especially crucial during maintenance windows when a network undergoes significant change. Similar to network auditing, routing messages can also be used to verify that protocol implementations conform to the specifications. At the very least, one could check whether message format is correct as per the specifications or not. Another check is to compare the rate and sequence of messages against the expected behavior. The "Refresh LSA bug" caught by the OSPF Monitor [1] where OSPF LSAs were being refreshed much faster than the recommended value [6] is an instance of this.

Capacity Planning Capacity planning, where network administrators determine how to grow their network to accommodate growth, is another task where routing data is extremely useful. In particular, the data allows planners to see how routing traffic is growing over time, which can then be used to predict resources required in the future. As such, the growth of two parameters is very important: the number of routes in the routing table, and the rate at which routing messages are disseminated. The former has significant bearing on the memory required on the routers, whereas the latter affects the CPU (and sometimes bandwidth) requirements for routers. For service providers, accurately knowing how long current CPU/memory configuration on routers can last, and when upgrades will be needed is extremely important for operational and financial planning. The growth patterns revealed by routing data play a key role in forming these estimates. These estimates also allow service providers to devise optimization techniques to reduce resource consumption. For example, consider layer-3 MPLS VPN [18] service, which allows enterprise customers to interconnect their (geographically distributed) sites via secure, dedicated tunnels over a provider network. Over the last few years, this service has witnessed a widespread deployment. This has led to tremendous growth in the number of BGP routes a VPN service provider has to keep track of, resulting in heavy memory usage on its routers. Realizing this scalability problem, Kim et al. [19] have proposed a solution that allows a service provider to tradeoff direct connectivity between sites (e.g., from any-to-any to a more restricted hub-and-spoke where traffic between two sites now has to go through one or more hub sites) with number of routes that need to be stored. The data collected by the route monitors was crucial in this work: first, to realize that there is a problem, and next, to evaluate the efficacy of the scheme in realistic settings. In particular, Kim et al. show 90% reduction in the memory usage while limiting path stretch between sites to only a few hundred miles, and extra bandwidth usage by less than 10%.

11.2.3.3 Performance Assessment of Routing Protocols

Routing data is key to understanding how routing protocols behave and perform in real life. We have already talked about one aspect of this behavior above, namely conformance to the specifications. Here we would like to talk about other aspects of the performance such as stability and convergence, which are key to quantifying the overall performance of the routing infrastructure. For example, numerous BGP studies detailing its behavior in the Internet have been enabled thanks to the data collected by RouteViews [15], RIPE [16], and other BGP monitors. We briefly describe some studies to illustrate the point.

Route updates collected by BGP monitors have led to several studies analyzing the stability (or lack thereof) of BGP routing in the Internet.[5] Govindan and Reddy [20] were the first to study the stability of BGP routes back in 1997 – a couple of years after commercialization of the Internet started. Their study analyzed BGP route updates collected from a large ISP and a popular Internet exchange point (where several service providers are interconnected to exchange routes and traffic). The study found a clear evidence of deteriorating stability of BGP routes which it attributed to the rapid growth – doubling of the number of ASes and prefixes in about 2 years – of the Internet. Subsequently, Labovitz et al. [21] observed a higher than expected number of BGP updates in the data collected at five US public Internet exchange points. The real surprising aspect of their study was the finding that about 99% of these updates did not indicate real topological changes, and had no reason to be there. The authors found that some of these updates were due to bugs in the BGP software of a router vendor at that time. Fixing of these bugs by the vendor led to an order of magnitude reduction in the volume of BGP route updates [22].

Convergence, the time taken by a routing protocol to recalculate new paths after a network change, is another critical performance metric. Labovitz et al. [23] were the first to systematically study this metric for BGP in the Internet. They found that BGP often took tens of seconds to converge – an order of magnitude more than what was thought at that time. The problem as they showed stems from the

---

[5] The term stability refers to the stability of BGP routes, which roughly corresponds to how frequently they undergo changes.

inclusion of ASPath in BGP route announcements (i.e., the very thing that makes BGP a path-vector protocol). The purpose of including the ASPath is to prevent loops and "count-to-infinity" problem[6] that BGP's distance-vector brethren (e.g., RIP) suffer from. However, this leads to "path exploration" as shown by Labovitz et al., where routers might cycle through multiple (often transient) routes with different ASPaths before settling on the final (stable) routes, thereby exacerbating the convergence times. Several ways of mitigating this problem have been proposed since then, essentially by including more information in BGP routes [24–28], but none of them have seen deployment to date.

Mao et al. [29] tied hitherto independently explored stability and convergence aspects of BGP together by showing how route flap damping (RFD) [30] used for improving stability of BGP could interact with path exploration to adversely impact convergence of BGP. RFD is a mechanism that limits propagation of unstable routes, thereby mitigating adverse impact of persistent flapping of network elements and mis-configurations, which improves overall stability of BGP, and was a recommended practice [31] in early 2000. Unfortunately, as Mao et al. showed, RFD can also suppress relatively stable routes by treating route announcements received during path exploration as evidence of instability of a route. Specifically, the study showed that a route needs to be withdrawn only once and then re-announced for RFD to suppress it for up to an hour in certain circumstances. This work coupled with manifold increase in router CPU processing capability resulted in a recommendation by RIPE [32] to disable RFD.

Routing data is not only valuable in analyzing performance of protocol separately, but also useful for understanding how they interact with one another as Teixeira et al. [33] did by focusing on how OSPF distance changes in a tier-1 ISP affected BGP routing. Their study showed that despite the apparent separation between intra and interdomain routing protocols, OSPF distance changes do affect BGP routes due to what is known as the "hot-potato routing". [7] The extent of the impact depended on several factors including location and timing of a distance change. Even more surprisingly, BGP route updates resulting from such changes could lag by as much as a minute in some cases, resulting in large delays in convergence.

In closing, these and numerous other studies have not only enhanced our knowledge of how routing protocols behave in the Internet, but have also led to improvements in their performance (such as reduction in unwarranted BGP updates or disabling of RFD as mentioned earlier).

---

[6] With distance-vector protocols, two or more routers can get locked into a cyclical dependency where each router in the cycle uses the previous router as a next-hop for reaching a destination. The routers then increment their distance to the destination in a step-wise fashion until all of them reach infinity, which is termed as "counting to infinity". For more details, refer to [8].

[7] As explained in Section 11.2.1.1, hot-potato routing refers to BGP's propensity to select the shortest way out of its local AS to a prefix when presented with multiple equally good routes (i.e., ways out of the AS). This allows an AS to hand off data packets as quickly as possible to its neighboring AS much like a hot potato.

11.2.4   Case Study of a Route Monitor: The AT&T OSPF Monitor

Several route monitoring systems are available both as academic/research endeavors as well as commercial products. RouteViews [15] and RIPE [16] collect BGP route updates from several ISPs and backbones around the world. The data is used extensively for both troubleshooting and academic studies of the interdomain routing system. The corresponding web sites also list several tools for analysis of the data. On the intradomain side, a paper by Shaikh and Greenberg [1] describes an OSPF monitor. The paper provides detailed description of the architecture and design of the system and follows it up with a performance evaluation and deployment experience. On the commercial side, Packet Design's Route Explorer [34] and Packet Storm's Route Analyzer [35] are route monitoring products. The Route Explorer provides monitoring capability for several routing protocols including OSPF, IS-IS, EIGRP and BGP, whereas Route Analyzer provides similar functionality for OSPF.

Out of various route monitoring systems mentioned above, we focus on the OSPF Monitor described by Shaikh and Greenberg [1] as a case study in this section since the paper provides extensive details about system architecture, design, functionality, and deployment. This is something not readily available for other route monitoring systems, especially the architecture and design aspects, which are key to understanding how control plane monitoring is realized in practice. From here on, we will refer to the OSPF Monitor described in [1] as the AT&T OSPF Monitor, and go into details of the system in terms of data collection and analysis aspects next.

The AT&T OSPF Monitor separates data (specifically, LSAs) collection from data analysis. The main reasoning behind this is to keep data collection as passive and simple as possible due to the collector's proximity to the network. The component used for LSA collection is called an *LSA Reflector (LSAR)*. The data analysis on the other hand is divided into two components: LSA aGgregator (LSAG) and OSPF-Scan. The LSAG deals with LSA streams in real time, whereas OSPFScan provides capabilities for off-line analysis of the LSA archives. This three component architecture is illustrated in Fig. 11.6. We briefly describe these three components now.

The LSAR supports three modes for capturing LSAs: the host mode, the full adjacency mode, and the partial adjacency mode. With the host mode, which only works on a broadcast media such as Ethernet LAN, the LSAR subscribes to a multicast group to receive LSAs being disseminated. This is a completely passive way of capturing LSAs, but suffers from reliability issues, slow initialization of link-state database and only works on broadcast media. With the full adjacency mode, the LSAR establishes an OSPF adjacency with a router to receive LSAs. This allows LSAR to leverage OSPF's reliable flooding mechanism, thereby overcoming both the disadvantages of the host mode. However, the main drawback of this approach is that instability of LSAR or its link to the router can trigger SPF calculations in the entire network, potentially destabilizing the network. The reason for SPF calculation stems from the fact that with a full adjacency, the router includes a link to the LSAR in its LSA sent to the network. The partial adjacency mode of collecting LSAs provides a way to circumvent this problem while retaining all the benefits of having an adjacency. In this mode, the LSAR establishes adjacency with a router,

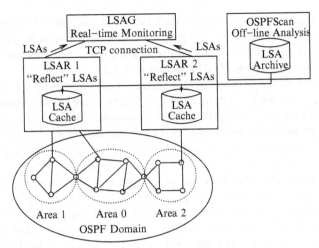

Fig. 11.6 The architecture of the AT&T OSPF monitor described in [1]

but only allows it to proceed to a stage where LSAs can be received over it from the router, but it cannot be included in the LSA sent by the router to the network. To keep the LSAR-router adjacency in the intermediate state, the LSAR describes its own Router-LSA[8] to the router during the link-state database synchronization process but never actually sends it out to the router. As a result, the database is never synchronized, the adjacency stays in OSPF's *loading* state [6], and is never fully established. Keeping the adjacency in the loading state protects the network from the instability of the LSAR or its link to the router.

Having described data collection by the LSAR, let us now turn our attention to the LSAG, which processes LSAs in real time. The LSAG populates a model of the OSPF network topology as it processes the LSAs. The model captures elements such as OSPF areas, routers, subnets, interfaces, links, and relationship between them (e.g., an area object consists of a set of routers that belong to the area, a router object in turn consists of a set of interfaces belonging to the router, etc.). Using the model as a base, the LSAG identifies changes (such as router up/down, link up/down, link cost changes, etc.) to the network topology and generates messages about them. Even though there are only about five basic network events, about 30 different types of messages are generated by the LSAG because of how broadcast media (such as Ethernet) are supported in OSPF, how a change in one area propagates to other areas, and how external information is redistributed into OSPF. In addition to identifying changes to the network topology, the LSAG also identifies elements that are unstable, and generates messages about such flapping elements. The LSAG also generates messages for non-conforming behavior, such as when

---

[8] A Router-LSA in OSPF is originated by every router to describe its outgoing links to adjacent routers along with their associated weights.

refresh LSAs are observed too often. Apart from using the topology model to identify changes, the LSAG also uses it to produce snapshots of the topology periodically and when network changes occur. One use of these snapshots is for performing an audit of link weights as described in Section 11.2.3.2.

Finally, we turn our attention to OSPFScan, which supports off-line analysis of LSA archives. One thing worth mentioning about the AT&T OSPF Monitor is that the capabilities supported by OSPFScan for off-line analysis are mostly a superset of the ones supported in real time by the LSAG with the underlying idea being anything that can be done in real time can be performed off-line as a playback. In terms of processing of LSAs, OSPFScan follows a three-step process: parse the LSA, test the LSA against a user-specified query expression, and analyze the LSA according to user interest if it satisfies the query. The parsing step converts each LSA record into what is termed a *canonical form* to which the query expression and subsequent analysis is applied. The use of a canonical form makes it easy to adapt OSPFScan to support LSA archive formats other than the native one used by the LSAR.

The query language resembles C-style syntax; an example query expression is "areaid == '0.0.0.0'". When a query is specified, OSPFScan matches every LSA record against the query, carrying out subsequent analysis for the matching records, while filtering out the non-matching ones. For example, the expression above would result in the analysis of only those LSAs that were collected from area 0.0.0.0.

In terms of analysis, OSPFScan provides the following capabilities:

1. **Modeling Topology Changes** Recall that OSPF represents the network topology as a graph. Therefore, OSPFScan allows modeling of OSPF dynamics as a sequence of changes to the underlying graph where a change represents addition/deletion of vertices/edges to this graph. Furthermore, OSPFScan allows a user to analyze these changes by saving each change as a single topology change record. Each such record contains information about the topological element (vertex/edge) that changed along with the nature of the change. For example, a router is treated as a vertex, and the record contains the OSPF router-id to identify it. We should point out that the topology change records and LSAG message logs essentially describe the same thing, but the former is geared more for computer processing, whereas the latter is aimed at humans.

2. **Emulation of OSPF Routing** OSPFScan allows a user to reconstruct a routing table of a given set of routers at any point of time based on the LSA archives. For a sequence of topology changes, OSPFScan also allows the user to determine changes to these routing tables. Together, these allow calculation of end-to-end paths through the OSPF domain at a given time, and see how this path changed in response to network events over a period of time. The routing tables also facilitate analysis of OSPF's impact on BGP through hot-potato routing [33].

3. **Classification of LSA Traffic** OSPFScan allows various ways of "slicing-and-dicing" of LSA archives. For example, it allows isolating LSAs indicating changes from the background refresh traffic. As another example, it also allows classification of LSAs (both change and refresh) into new and duplicate instances. This capability was used in a case study that analyzed one month LSA traffic for an enterprise network [36].

11.2.5 MPLS

Recall that MPLS has been deployed widely in service provider networks over the last few years. It has played a key role in evolving best-effort service model of IP networks by enabling traffic engineering (TE), fast reroute (FRR), and class of service (CoS) differentiation. In addition, MPLS has also allowed providers to offer value-added services such as VPN and VPLS.

Unlike traditional unicast forwarding in IP networks where routers match destination IP address to the longest matching prefix, MPLS uses a label switching paradigm. Each (IP) packet is encapsulated in an MPLS header, which contains among other things the label which is used by a router to determine the outgoing interface. The value of the label changes along every hop. Thus, while determining the outgoing interface, the router also determines the label with which it replaces the incoming label of the packet. This means that a router running MPLS has to maintain an *LFIB* (*Label Forwarding Information Base*), which contains mapping between incoming label and (outgoing interface, outgoing label) pairs. The sequence of routers an MPLS packet follows is known as an *LSP* (*Label Switched Path*). The first router along the LSP encapsulates a packet into an MPLS header, while the last router removes the MPLS header and forwards the resulting packet based on the underlying header.

The LFIB used for MPLS switching is populated by its control plane. This is done by creating and distributing mapping between a label and an *FEC* or a *Forwarding Equivalence Class*. An FEC is defined as a set of packets that need to receive the same forwarding treatment inside an MPLS network. A router running MPLS first generates a unique label for each FEC it supports, and uses one of the control plane protocols to distribute the label-FEC mappings to other routers. The dissemination of this information allows each router to determine incoming and outgoing labels and outgoing interface for each FEC, and thereby populate its LFIB.

MPLS currently uses three routing protocols for distributing label-FEC mappings: LDP (Label Distribution Protocol) [37], RSVP-TE (Resource reSerVation Protocol) [38], and BGP [39, 40]. With LDP, a router exchanges label-FEC mappings with each of its neighbors using a persistent session. FECs, in case of LDP, are generally IP prefixes. The labels learned from the neighbors allow the router to determine mapping between incoming and outgoing labels. To determine the outgoing interface, LDP relies on the IGP (such as OSPF, IS-IS etc.) running in the underlying IP network. Thus, LSPs created by LDP follow the paths calculated by the IGP from source router to the destination prefix. RSVP, on the end, is used for "explicitly" created and routed LSPs between two end points; the path need not follow the IGP path. The first router of the LSP initiates path setup by sending an RSVP message. The message propagates along the (to be established) LSP to the last router. Every intermediate router processes the message, creating an entry in its LFIB for the LSP. RSVP also allows reservation of bandwidth along the LSP, making it ideal for TE and CoS routing. Finally, BGP is used for distributing prefix to label mappings (mostly) in the context of VPN services. With VPNs, different customers of a VPN service provider can use overlapping IP address blocks, and BGP-distributed label to prefix mapping allows a provider's egress edge router to determine which customer a given packet belongs to.

The flow of control messages through individual routers running LDP and RSVP-TE can be modeled in the same manner as traditional unicast routing protocols as shown in Fig. 11.4. Thus, to monitor these protocols, one needs to collect incoming messages, outgoing messages, and changes occurring to the LFIB at every router. As a result, various techniques described in Section 11.2.2 for data collection apply to these protocols as well. One caveat applies to RSVP though since it does not have a notion of a protocol session. Given this, it is not possible to collect information about RSVP messages through a session with an RSVP router. To collect information about RSVP dynamics thus requires some mechanism for routers to send messages to a monitoring session when tunnels are setup and torn down – SNMP traps defined in RFC 3812 [41] provide such a capability.

Once routing data is collected from LDP or RSVP routers, it can be used in similar fashion as described in Section 11.2.3. For example, knowing label binding messages sent by LDP routers allows an operator to know if LSPs are established correctly or not. As another example, knowing the size of an LFIB (i.e., the number of LSPs traversing a router) and how it is evolving can be a key parameter in capacity planning.

11.3 Multicast

Throughout its relatively brief but rapidly evolving history, the Internet has primarily provided unicast service. A datagram is sent from a single sender to a single receiver, where each endpoint is identified by an IP address. Many applications, however, involve communication between more than two entities, and often the same data needs to be delivered to multiple recipients. As examples, software updates may be distributed from a single server to multiple recipients, and streaming content, such as live video, may be transmitted to many receivers simultaneously. When the network layer only supports one-to-one communication, it is the responsibility of the end systems to replicate data and transmit multiple copies of the same packet. This solution is inefficient both with respect to processing overhead at the sender and bandwidth utilization within the network.

Multicast [42], on the other hand, presents an efficient mechanism for network delivery of the same content to multiple destinations. In IP multicast, the sender transmits a single copy of a packet into the network. The network layer replicates the packet at appropriate routers in the network such that copies are delivered to all interested receivers and at most one copy of the packet traverses any network link. Multicast is built around the notion of a multicast group, which is a 32-bit identifier taken from the Class D portion of the IP address space (224.0.0.0 – 239.255.255.255). In multicast packets, the group address is contained in the destination IP address field in the header. Receivers make known their interest in receiving packets sent to the group address via a group membership protocol such as IGMP [43], and multicast routing protocols enable multicast packets to be delivered to the interested receivers.

Multicast was first proposed in the 1980s and was deployed on an experimental basis in the early 1990s. This early deployment, known as the MBone [44] (for Multicast Backbone), consisted of areas of the Internet in which multicast was deployed. These areas were connected together using IP-in-IP tunnels enabling multicast packets to traverse unicast-only portions of the Internet. The predominant applications used in the MBone, videoconferencing and video broadcast, primarily supported small group collaboration and broadcast of technical meetings and conferences.

After rapid initial growth, the MBone peaked and then began to flounder. The technology, while initially promising, did not find its way into service provider networks. Several reasons have been given for this. These include the lack of a clear business model (i.e., who would be charged for packets that are replicated and delivered to many receivers), security concerns (i.e., the original any-to-any IP multicast service model allowed any host in the network to transmit packets to a multicast group), and concerns about manageability (i.e., lack of tools to monitor, troubleshoot and debug this new technology).

More recently, deployment of network layer multicast service within IP networks has been increasing. This deployment has occurred primarily in enterprise networks, in which some of the earlier concerns with multicast (e.g., security, business model) are more easily mitigated. Common multicast applications in enterprise networks include software distribution and dissemination of financial trading information. The deployment of multicast within enterprise networks has also driven deployment in service provider networks in order to support the needs of Virtual Private Network (VPN) customers who use multicast in their networks. The Multicast VPN solution defined for the Internet [45, 46] requires customer multicast traffic to be encapsulated in a second instance of IP multicast for transport across the service provider backbone. Finally, the widespread deployment of IPTV, an application that benefits greatly from multicast service, is creating further growth of IP multicast.

Forwarding multicast packets within a network makes use of a separate FIB from the unicast FIB and depends on a new set of routing protocols to create and maintain these FIB entries. As such, the set of tools used to monitor unicast routing cannot be used. In this section, we review the basics of multicast routing, identify issues that make monitoring and managing multicast more difficult than monitoring unicast routing, and finally describe tools and strategies for monitoring this technology.

11.3.1 Multicast Routing Protocols

A multicast FIB entry is indexed by a multicast group and a source specification, where the latter consists of an address and mask. Packets that match the group address and source specification will be routed according to the FIB entry. The FIB entry itself contains an incoming interface over which packets matching the source and group are expected to arrive, and a set of zero or more outgoing interfaces over which copies of the packets should be transmitted. The union of FIB entries pertaining the same group and source(s) across all routers forms a tree, denoting the set of links over which a packet is forwarded to reach the set of interested receivers. It is the job of multicast routing protocols to establish the appropriate FIB entries in the routers and thereby form this multicast tree.

Over the last two decades, several multicast routing protocols have been proposed and in some cases implemented and deployed. These include DVMRP [47], MOSPF [48], CBT [49], MSDP [50], and PIM [51, 52]. In this section, we give an overview of PIM and MSDP as they are the most widely deployed multicast routing protocols.

11.3.1.1 PIM

Protocol Independent Multicast, or PIM, is the dominant multicast routing protocol deployed in IP networks. PIM does not exchange reachability information in the sense that unicast routing protocols, such as OSPF and BGP, do. Rather, it leverages information in the unicast FIB in order to construct multicast trees, and it is agnostic as to the source of the unicast routing information. There are multiple variants of PIM, including PIM Sparse Mode (PIM-SM), PIM Dense Mode (PIM-DM), Source Specific PIM (PIM-SSM), and Bidirectional PIM (PIM-Bidir). In this section, we present a brief overview of the basic operation of PIM-SM and PIM-SSM, as they are the most commonly deployed variants of PIM, in order to motivate the challenges in multicast monitoring and their solutions.

Before turning to PIM we discuss one key aspect of multicast trees and the protocols that construct them. Multicast trees can be classified as *shared trees* or *source trees*. A shared tree is one that is used to forward packets from multiple sources. In this case, the multicast routing entry is denoted by a group and a set of sources (e.g., using an address and a mask). For a shared tree, the set of sources usually includes all sources, and the routing table entry is denoted by the $(*, G)$ pair, where G denotes the multicast group address and '*' denotes a wildcard (indicating all sources). A source tree, on the other hand, is used to forward packets from a single source, and is denoted as (S, G), where G again refers to the multicast group and S refers to a single source.

PIM-SM uses both shared and source trees, depending on both the variant and how it is configured. In both cases, multicast trees are constructed by sending *Join* messages from the leaves of the tree (the routers that are directly connected to hosts that want to receive packets transmitted to the multicast group) toward the root of the tree. In the case of a source tree, the root is a source that transmits data to the multicast group and the *Join* message is referred to as an (S, G) *Join*. For a shared tree, the root is a special node referred to as a *Rendezvous Point*, or RP, and the *Join* message is referred to as a $(*, G)$ *Join*. The RP for a group, which can be configured statically at each router or determined by a dynamic protocol such as BSR [53], must be agreed upon by all routers in a PIM domain.[9]

PIM *Join* messages are transmitted hop-by-hop toward the root of the tree. At each router, the next hop is determined using the unicast FIB. Specifically, the *Join* message is transmitted to the next hop on the best route (as determined by the unicast routing table) toward the root (i.e., source or RP). As such, the *Join* message follows the shortest path from the receiver to the root of the tree. At each hop, the router keeps track of the neighbor router from which the *Join* message was received and the neighbor router to which it was forwarded. The latter is denoted as the upstream neighbor in the multicast FIB and the former is denoted as a downstream neighbor. When subsequent multicast data packets are received from the upstream neighbor, they will be forwarded to the downstream neighbor.

When a router receives a subsequent $(*, G)$ or (S, G) *Join* message for a FIB entry that already exists, the router from which the *Join* message is received is added to the list of downstream neighbors. However, the *Join* message need not be forwarded upstream as a *Join* message will have already been forwarded toward the root of the tree. In this way, *Join* messages from multiple downstream neighbors are merged, and when data packets are received, they will be replicated with a copy forwarded to each downstream neighbor. PIM uses *soft state*, so that *Join* messages are retransmitted hop-by-hop periodically, and state that is not refreshed is deleted when an appropriate timer expires.

In PIM-SM, all communication begins on a shared tree. Last hop routers transmit *Join* messages toward the RP, forming a shared tree with the RP at the root and last hop routers as leaves. This process is depicted in Steps 1–3 in Fig. 11.7a, in which router R2 transmits a *Join* message toward the RP. This message is then forwarded by R1 to the RP. R3 subsequently transmits a *Join* message toward the RP, which is received by R1 and not forwarded further. When a source wants to transmit packets to the group, it encapsulates these packets in PIM *Register* messages transmitted using unicast to the RP. The RP decapsulates these packets and transmits them on the shared tree, so that they are delivered to all routers that joined the tree. The RP then sends an (S, G) *Join* message toward the source, building a source tree from the source to the RP. Steps 4–5 in Fig. 11.7a depict a *Register* message from a source S to the RP followed by a subsequent *Join* from the RP to S. Once this source tree is established, packets are sent using native multicast from the source to the RP and from the RP to the leaf routers, as shown in Fig. 11.7b. When multiple sources have data to send to the multicast group, each will send PIM *Register* messages to the RP, which in turn will send PIM *Join* messages to the sources, thereby creating multiple (S, G) trees.

While all communication, in PIM-SM begin on shared trees, the protocol allows for the use of source trees. Specifically, when a last hop router receives packets from a source, it has the option to switch to a source tree for that source. It does this by

---

[9] A PIM domain is defined as a contiguous set of routers all configured to operate within a common boundary. All routers in the domain must map a group address to the same RP.

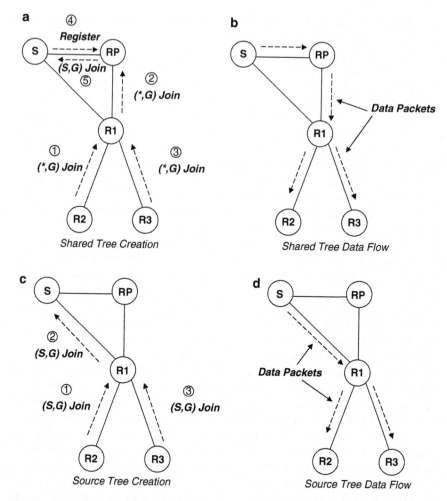

Fig. 11.7 Example PIM Operation: (**a**) Sequence of control messages for shared tree creation. (**b**) Resulting flow of data packets. (**c**) Sequence of control messages for switchover to source tree. (**d**) Resulting flow of data packets

sending an (S, G) *Join* toward the source, joining the source tree (just as the RP did in the description above). Once it has received packets on the source tree, it then sends a *Prune* message for the source on the shared tree, indicating that it no longer wants to receive packets from that source on the shared tree. The *Join* messages needed to switch from the shared to source tree are shown in Fig. 11.7c, and the resulting flow of data packets is shown in Fig. 11.7d. Source trees allow for more efficient paths from the source to receiver(s) at the expense of higher protocol and state overhead.

PIM-SSM (Source Specific Multicast) does away with the need for RPs, thereby simplifying multicast tree construction and maintenance while using a subset of the PIM-SM protocol mechanisms. PIM-SSM only uses source trees. The source of traffic is known to hosts interested in joining the multicast group (e.g., via an out-of-band mechanism). These receivers signal their interest in the group via IGMP, and their directly connected routers send (S, G) *Join* messages directly to the source, thereby building a source tree rooted at the sender.

11.3.1.2 MSDP

In PIM-SM, there is a single RP that acts as the root of a shared tree for a given multicast group. (Note that a single router may act as an RP for many groups.) This provides a mechanism for rendezvous and subsequent communication between sources and receivers without either having any pre-existing knowledge of the other. However, there are two situations in which multiple RPs for a group may be desirable. The first involves multicast communication between domains. Specifically, two or more service providers may wish to enable multicast communication between them. If there is only a single RP for a group, failure of the RP in one provider's network may impact service in the other's network, even if all of the sources and receivers are located in the latter's network. Service providers may not be willing to depend on a critical resource (e.g., the RP) located in another service provider's network for what may be purely intradomain communication. Further, even without RP outages, performance may be suboptimal if purely intradomain communication is required to follow interdomain paths. That is, a multicast tree between senders and receivers in one ISP's network may traverse another ISP's network. Thus, each provider may wish to have an RP located within its own domain.

The second situation in which multiple RPs may be useful involves communication within a single PIM domain. Specifically, redundant RPs provide a measure of robustness, and this can be implemented using IP anycast [54]. Each RP is configured with the same IP address, and the RP mapping mechanism identifies this anycast address as the RP address. Each router wishing to join a shared tree sends a $(*, G)$ *Join* message toward the RP address. By virtue of anycast routing, which uses unicast routing to route the message to the "closest" RP, the router will join a shared tree rooted at a nearby RP. As a result, multiple disjoint shared trees will be formed within the domain. Similarly, when a source transmits a PIM *Register* message to an anycast RP address, this message will only reach the nearest RP. As such, sources and receivers will only communicate with those subsets of routers closest to the same RP, and the required multicast connectivity will not be achieved.

The problem of enabling multicast communication when multiple RPs exist for the same group (whether within or between domains) is solved by the Multicast Source Discovery Protocol (MSDP) [50]. MSDP enables multicast communication between different PIM-SM domains (e.g., operated by different service providers) as well as within a PIM-SM domain using multiple anycast RPs. MSDP-speaking RPs form peering relationships with each other to inform each other of active sources. Upon learning about an active source for a group for which there are interested receivers, an RP joins the source tree of that source so that it can receive packets from the source and transmit them within its own domain or on its own shared tree.

We give a brief overview of MSDP. Each RP forms an MSDP peering relationship with one or more other RPs using a TCP connection. These MSDP connections form a virtual topology among the various RPs. RPs share information about sources as follows. For each source from which it receives a PIM *Register* message, an RP transmits an MSDP *Source-Active (SA)* message to its MSDP peers. This *SA* message, which identifies a source and the group to which it is sending, is flooded across the MSDP virtual topology so that it is received by all other MSDP-speaking RP routers.

Upon receipt of an *SA* message, an RP (in addition to flooding the message to its other MSDP peers) determines whether there are interested receivers in its domain. Specifically, if the RP has previously received a *Join* message for the shared tree indicated by the group in the *SA* message, the RP will transmit a PIM *Join* message to the source. In this way, the RP joins the source tree rooted at the source in question, receives multicast packets from it, and multicasts these packets on the shared tree rooted at the RP. Thus, multicast communication is enabled when multiple RPs exist for the same group, whether within or across domains.

11.3.2   Challenges in Monitoring Multicast

In the early days of multicast, one of the often cited reasons for its slow deployment was the difficulty of monitoring and managing the service; commercial routers implemented the protocols, but network operators had little way of knowing how the service was working when they deployed it. While this was by no means the only impediment to its deployment, it did present a significant challenge to network operators. To some degree, the problems cited early on with multicast management remain true today. Before turning to specific tools and techniques used to monitor and manage multicast in order to provide a stable and reliable network service, we identify some of the generic challenges for managing the technology, while deferring some of the protocol-specific issues to Section 11.3.3.

While multicast is by no means a new technology, it is not yet mature. Because it has only been deployed in a significant way in the last few years, there does not yet exist the experience and knowledge surrounding it as exists with unicast service. This manifests itself in two related ways. First, engineers and operators in many cases are unfamiliar with the technology and face a steep learning curve in troubleshooting and monitoring multicast. Second, due to a rather limited deployment experience, the kinds of tools that have evolved in the unicast world and that have been essential in route monitoring do not yet exist for multicast.

Putting aside the relative newness of the technology, there are aspects of multicast that make it inherently more challenging to manage than unicast. Most obviously, the nature of what constitutes a route followed by a packet has changed. In unicast routing, the path taken by a packet from source to destination consists of a sequence of routers (usually no more than 20 or 30). This path is easily identifiable (e.g., using tools such as *traceroute*) and can be presented to a network operator in a way that is easy to understand. In multicast routing, a packet no longer traverses an ordered sequence of routers, but rather follows a tree of routers from a source to multiple destinations. The tree can be very large, consisting of hundreds of routers. Identifying the tree becomes more challenging, and perhaps more significantly, presenting it to a network operator in a useful manner is difficult.

In addition to being large, multicast trees are not static. That is, they are driven by application behavior, and the set of senders and receivers may change during the lifetime of an application. As such, branches may be added to and pruned from multicast trees over time, and these changes can happen on short timescales. Thus, understanding the state of multicast is made more difficult by the dynamic nature of the multicast trees.

Finally, the multicast routing state used to forward a packet from a source to a set of receivers can be data driven. That is, the state may not be instantiated until an application starts sending traffic or expresses interest in receiving it. In contrast, with unicast routing, the FIB entries used to route a packet from a source to a destination are independent of the existence of application traffic. Thus, routing table entries can be queried (either directly with SNMP or indirectly with a utility like *traceroute*) in order to discover or verify a route. With multicast the analogous routing state may not exist until applications are started. Using PIM-SM as an example, the shared tree from the RP to receivers is formed as a result of receivers joining a multicast group. Similarly, the state needed to route a packet from a source to the RP is not created until the source sends a PIM *Register* message to the RP and the RP subsequently sends an (S, G) *Join* to the source. Given this, answering such questions (as one might want to do in advance of a streaming broadcast) as "how would packets be routed from the source to receivers" is problematic.

Given the inherent difficulties in monitoring and managing multicast routing, there exists a need for new tools, methods and capabilities to assist in this process. We now turn to the challenges of monitoring specific protocols and the ways in which these challenges can be met.

11.3.3 Multicast Route Monitoring

Multicast routing involves complex protocols. In order to understand, troubleshoot and debug the state of multicast in a network, operators need to be able to answer several key questions. These include:

- What is the FIB entry for a particular source and group at a router?
- What is the multicast tree for a (S, G) or $(*, G)$ pair?
- What route will a packet take from a source to one or more receivers? (As will be explained below, this question differs subtly from the preceding one.)
- Are multicast trees stable or dynamic?

- Are packets transmitted by source S to group G being received where they should be?
- Is multicast routing properly configured in the network?

Answering these and other questions about multicast requires a new set of management tools and capabilities. In this section, we describe how monitoring tools can be used to answer these questions. Before doing so, we briefly review the network management capabilities developed during earlier experiences with multicast.

11.3.3.1 Early MBone Tools

The MBone grew from a few dozen subnets in 1992 to over 3,000 four years later [55]. At its inception, it connected a small community of collaborating researchers, but it expanded to include a much broader set of users and applications. It was initially maintained by a few people who knew administrators at all the participating sites. Therefore, monitoring and debugging of the infrastructure developed in an ad hoc manner.

As the MBone grew, it faced an increasing set of management challenges. To meet these challenges, the researchers who managed and used it developed a broad set of tools. While we avoid an exhaustive review of these tools we give a few representative examples here which encompass both application and network layer tools.

- *mrinfo* discovered the multicast topology by querying multicast routers for their neighbors.
- *mtrace* was used to discover the path packets traversed to reach a receiver from a source.
- *rtpmon* was an application-level monitoring tool that provided end-to-end performance measurements for a multicast group.
- The DVMRP Route Monitor [56] monitored routing exchanges between multicast routers in the MBone.

The tools mentioned here, and the many others that were developed (see [57,58] for a more complete list) provided great value to the early MBone users. They addressed real problems and allowed operators and users to understand, monitor, and troubleshoot the experimental network. While in many cases they provided insight and lessons, which inform current efforts, they are unable to form the basis for a current multicast management strategy. Many of the tools use RTCP and monitor application performance. Others were built specifically to monitor *mrouted*, the public domain multicast routing daemon used in the early MBone. Neither of these support the needs of large ISPs to monitor their multicast infrastructure. Instead, today's multicast management and monitoring strategy must be built around tools that work in the context of the multi-vendor commercial routers managed by the ISPs.

11.3.3.2 Information Sources

While the earlier experience with the MBone provided some valuable insight as to the challenges with managing multicast, it also showed the need for tools that worked with commercial routers and that could be deployed by service providers at scale. Such tools must work in the confines of the capabilities available on the routers that support multicast. We discuss the options for gathering information about multicast in this section, in order to motivate the kinds of solutions described later.

As described in Section 11.2.3, route monitors provide enormous capability with respect to monitoring unicast routing. BGP monitors peer with BGP speaking routers to collect routing updates and thereby monitor network reachability and stability, possibly from multiple vantage points. Similarly, OSPF monitors collect flooded LSAs to learn the topology of a network and emulate its route computation. Unfortunately, analogous route monitoring is more difficult with multicast.

PIM is not a conventional routing protocol per se. That is, PIM routers do not exchange reachability information, nor do they flood information about their local topology or routing state. Instead, PIM makes use of the routes computed by another routing protocol, such as OSPF. Specifically, PIM uses the routes in a unicast FIB to forward PIM *Join* messages toward the root of a multicast tree. These *Join* messages cause the router to instantiate the multicast FIB entries needed to forward multicast packets.

We do note that in contrast, MSDP is amenable to monitoring akin to what is feasible with unicast. It is built upon information exchanges over peering connections (themselves using TCP). These advertisements are flooded to all MSDP speakers, therefore an MSDP monitor could collect (possibly from multiple other routers) and analyze these exchanges.

Since a route monitor cannot collect information about a PIM domain, other sources of information are needed upon which to build appropriate multicast monitoring and management capabilities. We review the two most readily available sources of information here: SNMP and CLI.

SNMP provides a mechanism upon which to build multicast management applications. It is an Internet standard presenting a common interface upon which to access information from routers. Service providers use it in other network management functions. Therefore, libraries, pollers and related expertise are abundant. Several multicast-related MIBs have been defined providing extensive information about multicast routing (e.g. [59, 60]). These MIBs provide information about interfaces on which multicast is enabled, multicast routing adjacencies, and multicast FIB entries.

SNMP is not without its shortcomings. We identify three in particular. First, except for a relatively small number of traps defined in multicast-related MIBs, all SNMP-related information must be polled. Hence, changes in multicast routing entries, as occur when a tree changes, can only be discovered through polling. Learning about such changes in a timely and scalable manner may be challenging. Second, while SNMP is defined as an Internet standard, vendors can define and implement their own proprietary MIBs. By availing themselves of this option, vendors make the development of vendor-independent management tools more difficult. Finally, a single vendor may support different MIBs on different devices, as can be the case when a vendor undergoes a major revision of its operating system.

Scripts that directly access the command line interfaces of routers present an alternative way of collecting multicast related information from routers. However, the command line interface does not return information in a structured machine readable format (as SNMP does) and therefore requires parsing of the output to obtain specific items. Further, because the command line interfaces are not standardized, building portable vendor-independent tools (and even tools that work with different platforms of a single vendor) can be difficult.

11.3.3.3 Multicast Monitoring

SNMP is generally a more useful and flexible platform upon which to base multicast-related management and monitoring tools. Using SNMP, monitoring tools can retrieve relevant multicast routing information from routers and produce the kinds of reports and output that one might get from a conventional route monitor. In this section, we present examples of the kind of functionality that can be implemented.

As a first example, SNMP-based tools can discover the multicast topology, i.e., the contiguous set of routers that implement PIM within a domain. Specifically, each PIM router will report its set of PIM neighbors (those adjacent routers that also run PIM). By starting at any router within a domain and recursively querying for lists of PIM neighbors, the entire topology can be discovered. The multicast topology can be used to verify that multicast is configured as expected (e.g., all routers are reachable in the multicast topology) and to track topology changes as they occur.

As a next example, multicast-related MIBs can be mined to report and explore specific multicast FIB entries at a router. When multicast was first deployed on commercial routers, a common monitoring and debugging technique employed by operators was to logon to a router and to use the command-line interface to observe routing table entries. In particular, the *show ip mroute* command provides detailed information about one or more (S, G) or $(*, G)$ entries. This includes information about the upstream router, outgoing interfaces by which downstream neighbors are reached, the RP (in the case of PIM-SM), and various timers related to the entry. In fact, much of the information provided by the command line is also exported in MIBs. Gathering the information in machine-readable format provides an ability to emulate the existing command-line output, while at the same time augmenting it and producing more valuable output using a graphical or web-based interface. Further, when gathering MIB data from a router, output need not be constrained to the format provided on router command lines. Groups can be filtered, for example, based on their importance, traffic volume or dynamicity, and automatic reports on critical information can be generated. Figure 11.8 depicts an example of

```
Router: attga-rtr1 (10.20.1.1)
IP Multicast Routing Table
Flags: D - Dense, S - Sparse, s - SSM Group
       C - Connected, L - Local, P - Pruned
       R - RP-bit set, F - Register Flag, T - SPT-bit set, J - Join SPT
Timers: Uptime/Expires
Interface state: Interface, Next-Hop, State/Mode
Application: Customer 1 VPN
(*, 239.1.23.5), uptime 49d17h, expires 00:02:56, AnycastRP is stlmo-rtr3 (10.21.3.2)
  Incoming interface: POS15/0, RPF neighbor attga-rtr2 (10.21.17.1)
  Outgoing interface list:
    Loopback0, Forward/Sparse, 49d17h/00:00:00
Source: attga-rtr1
(10.20.1.1, 239.1.23.5), uptime 49d17h, expires 00:03:29
  Incoming interface: Loopback0, RPF neighbor 0.0.0.0
  Outgoing interface list:
    attga-rtr2 (POS0/0), Forward/Sparse, 42d15h/00:02:51
    attga-rtr3 (POS15/0), Forward/Sparse, 44d12h/00:03:10
```

Fig. 11.8 SNMP-generated (*, G) and (S, G) multicast routing table entries

SNMP-generated multicast routing state at a router. Adjacent routers in the display, as well as the Rendezvous Point, are clickable, yielding the analogous routing state at those routers.

While viewing multicast routing information gathered from a single router is valuable, the real power of SNMP comes from its ability to collect and synthesize data from multiple routers simultaneously. In the case of multicast, it can be used to discover multicast distribution trees in the network. This is critical in giving operators the ability to understand their networks, locate problems and develop solutions. The automated collection of information from many routers simultaneously enables tree discovery at a scale not feasible using a manual router-by-router approach.

Multicast tree discovery works as follows. A management application using SNMP can gather local state for a multicast FIB entry starting at any router on the tree (the router can be a known source, receiver, or a transit router such as an RP). The key pieces of state here include the upstream neighbor of the router, the downstream routers to which it will forward packets, and perhaps the identity of the RP (in the case of shared trees as in PIM-SM). Beginning from this initial router, the entire tree can be discovered by repeating queries recursively at upstream and downstream routers until the source and all leaf routers are reached. An example of the output of such a tree discovery is shown in Fig. 11.9. The routers in this tree display are clickable, allowing the user to drill down to router-specific state for the group (like that shown in Fig. 11.8).

The ability to easily discover an entire tree is invaluable. It enables operators to see how packets will be forwarded, and in the case of problems, provides guidance as to where faults may be located and troubleshooting should begin. In the case of very large trees, graphical displays (like that shown in Fig. 11.10) are needed. In addition, zooming, panning and searching become critical as the number of routers on a tree exceeds a few tens.

Initial Router: **nycny-rtr1 (10.20.167.22)**

Source: **0.0.0.0**

Group: **239.16.88.39**

Application: **Customer 2 VPN**

```
--cgcil-rtr2 (10.20.14.27) *Anycast RP (10.21.3.2)*
 |
 +--seawa-rtr1 (10.20.121.12)
 |  |
 |  +--ptdor-rtr4 (10.20.33.15)
 |  |  |
 |  |  +--ptdor-rtr7 (10.20.33.87)
 |  |
 |  +--seawa-rtr8 (10.20.52.119)
 |  |  |
 |  |  +--seawa-rtr10 (10.20.51.42)
 |  |
 |  +--ptdor-rtr6 (10.20.16.100)
 |     |
 |     +--ptdor-rtr15 (10.20.61.115)
 |
 +--cgcil-rtr2 (10.20.122.14)
    |
    +--nycny-rtr1 (10.20.14.188)
       |
       +--nycny-rtr6 (10.20.4.110)
          |
          +--nycny-rtr5 (10.20.121.106)
             |
             +--nycny-rtr10 (10.20.52.27)
```

Fig. 11.9 SNMP-generated multicast tree

Monitoring PIM-SM presents challenges beyond discovering a single multicast tree. Recall that receivers join a shared tree rooted at an RP and that the RP independently joins a source-specific tree rooted at each source. Thus, for a single multicast group, multiple FIB entries may exist at each router, corresponding to one or more (S, G) pairs and a $(*, G)$ entry. Each entry may have different sets of incoming and outgoing interfaces. Since the packet forwarding rules are extremely complex, it may not always be easily understood how a particular packet will be forwarded. A packet may initially be forwarded along a source-specific tree, and then be replicated and transition to a shared tree at one or more points.

This challenge can be addressed through the simultaneous discovery and display of multiple multicast trees, as shown in Fig. 11.11. This shows the source tree from a single sender to multiple *RPs* and shared trees from each of the *RPs* to associated last hop routers. Note that the trees may overlap and in many cases branches from different trees will flow in different directions on the same link. Use of a display

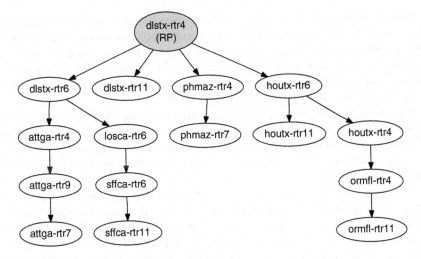

Fig. 11.10   Graphical display of a multicast tree

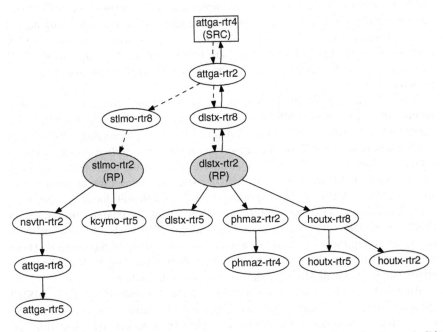

Fig. 11.11   Tree display depicting a single source tree (*dashed lines*) and two shared trees (*solid lines*) for a single multicast group

like this can show how packets are transmitted from a sender to a receiver, and can illustrate where problems in the tree(s) exist.

The multicast-related MIBs provide a level of detail not available with unicast. Specifically, whereas unicast MIBs provide information about destination networks, the multicast MIB entries, identified by the combination of a source and a group, or just a group, provide information about a particular application since at any point in time, a multicast group is generally used by a single application instance. This level of detail would be akin in the unicast world to a MIB entry per TCP connection. Hence, instead of asking a router about unicast routes to a destination, we can look at multicast routes used by a particular application.

Such fine-grained information will clearly present scaling challenges as the scope of multicast deployment continues. However, it also presents real opportunities in the area of multicast monitoring. This becomes especially relevant as network operators transition from viewing their jobs as monitoring routers and links to managing end-to-end services.

Given the ability to associate a multicast group with an application, the provider can perform application-specific monitoring. In fact, the tools outlined above already do this to some extent – the multicast trees being discovered and displayed give information about routing for the specific applications that use them. In addition, traffic or performance monitoring is also possible. That is, a provider can monitor a well-known application to verify both that multicast routing state exists, and that traffic is being received. For example, in an IPTV network, each TV channel is generally transmitted on its own multicast group. If the network is engineered so that groups are statically joined at certain routers, or if routers are monitored to dynamically determine where channels are being distributed, group-specific MIB variables, such as packet and byte counters, can be gathered to monitor application performance.

While the majority of attention in the area of multicast management is focused on PIM, the deployment of MSDP will likely expand, as multicast grows within domains and as providers explore interdomain multicast. As a protocol, MSDP bears some resemblance to BGP (in the sense that routers form explicit peering connections), and lessons and techniques that have evolved in the management of BGP can be applied to MSDP. Recall that MSDP routers share information about active sources across domains. MSDP speaking routers in different domains form peering relationships and exchange information over reliable TCP connections (as with BGP). An MSDP router (which is generally also an RP), sends *SA* messages to its peers, informing them of the active sources for each group in the domain. These messages are flooded throughout the virtual topology formed by the MSDP peering relationships so that all MSDP routers have global information.

An MSDP monitor can form a peering relationship with one or more MSDP speaking routers. The peering relationships would be entirely passive, so that the monitor learns information, but does not inject announcements into the network. The monitor could thus learn about active sources in other domains. This dynamically learned information could be used to drive other monitoring functions, such as tree discovery or per-application monitoring. In addition, peerings with multiple MSDP speakers could be used to verify the consistency of views at different vantage points in the network.

11.4 Summary and Future Directions

In this chapter, we have described tools and techniques to monitor the control plane for unicast as well as multicast services. The control plane, consisting of the routing protocols running in the network, determines how packets flow from a source to a destination. The proper functioning of the control plane is key to the overall functioning of the Internet, and as a result it is critical to monitor its performance on an ongoing basis. This chapter in particular focused on what data needs to be collected and how it can be used for effective monitoring of the control plane.

Although we have come a long way from the early days of the Internet when routing protocols were deployed with little thought given to their management, many challenges remain. This is due in part to the fact that network management needs to continually catch up with a constantly evolving infrastructure. The advent of MPLS and multicast are cases in point. Control plane monitoring for these new services could borrow techniques and lessons learned from earlier experiences, but they present their own unique requirements as well. Similarly, while we expect today's tools to provide a foundation to support future control plane monitoring as the Internet evolves, new challenges demand additional tools and strategies. We provide a few examples of what we see as likely future challenges and requirements before closing the chapter.

As the Internet continues its explosive growth, scale remains a major challenge. The number of routing table entries and messages in the control plane has been increasing rapidly as more and more people and businesses come online. This growth not only poses scalability challenges to the control plane itself, but also to the systems that monitor and manage it. Imagine monitoring and maintaining end-to-end paths between hundreds of thousands of router pairs in real time, and updating them as the network undergoes changes. Similarly, consider current SNMP-based tools that can query the entire multicast routing tables of a router. As the use of multicast expands and consequently multicast routing tables grow (e.g., to rival the size of unicast routing tables), the existing tools and techniques will not scale. The ability of network operators to gain information about individual groups and applications will diminish, and existing tools will need to be extended or replaced.

Another challenge, related in part to scale, lies in the area of inter-provider monitoring. Most control plane monitoring today takes place within the context of a single provider. There do exist facilities like RouteViews [15] for monitoring interdomain BGP changes across providers. However, understanding control plane behavior across providers could benefit from advances in tools to support inter-provider monitoring. Such tools would, of necessity, preserve privacy across providers and adhere to strict security requirements.

The Internet's best-effort service model works well for applications such as file transfer and electronic mail. However, many new applications running on the Internet have significantly more stringent performance requirements. These performance requirements place additional requirements on the control plane as well. For example, as we saw in this chapter, traditional unicast routing protocols often take several tens of seconds to converge after a change. This, unfortunately, is totally inadequate for applications such as VoIP and IPTV. To fill this gap, service providers have attempted to improve the convergence time of existing routing protocols through better implementation and configurations. In addition, they have introduced new technologies such as IP and MPLS-based fast reroute (FRR) schemes. As providers deploy technology aimed to improve routing protocol behavior, there is a corresponding need for more advanced tools to monitor the performance and reliability of the control plane so that the results of routing protocol changes can be verified or measured.

During the last decade we have made substantial progress in our ability to monitor and measure the performance of the control and data planes. An exciting avenue for future work lies in closing the feedback loop by automatically adjusting network configuration to optimize its performance as information is gleaned from the monitoring systems. Achieving this will require sophisticated models to represent current network performance, and its performance under various "what-if" scenarios. These models then need to be translated into mechanisms for reliably and scalably adjusting device configurations and resource allocations, as well as for redesigning and re-architecting networks at various timescales in an automated fashion. Apart from application performance and resource usage, an automated "measure-model-control" loop will be crucial in running the networks in a more efficient and reliable manner.

References

1. Shaikh, A., & Greenberg, A. (2004). OSPF monitoring: architecture, design and deployment experience. In *Proceedings of USENIX Symposium on Networked Systems Design and Implementation (NSDI)*, San Francisco, California, March 2004.
2. Cormen, T. H., Leiserson, C. E., Rivest, R. L., & Stein, C. (2001). *Introduction to algorithms*, second ed. Cambridge, MA: MIT Press.
3. Malkin, G. (1998). RIP Version 2. IETF Request for Comments (RFC) 2453, November 1998.
4. Garcia-Luna-Aceves, J. (1989). A unified approach to loop-free routing using distance vector or link states. In *Proceedings of ACM SIGCOMM*, Austin, Texas, September 1989.
5. Rekhter, Y., Li, T., & Hares, S. (2006). A border gateway protocol 4 (BGP-4). IETF Request for Comments (RFC) 4271, January 2006.
6. Moy, J. (1998). OSPF Version 2. IETF Request for Comments (RFC) 2328, April 1998.
7. Callon, R. (1990). Use of OSI IS-IS for routing in TCP/IP and dual environments. IETF Request for Comments (RFC) 1195, December 1990.
8. Huitema, C. (1999). *Routing in the Internet*. Prentice Hall PTR, second ed., Upper Saddle River, New Jersey, December 1999.
9. Stewart, J. W. (1998). *BGP4: inter-domain routing in the Internet*. Addison-Wesley, Upper Saddle River, New Jersey, December 1998.
10. Bates, T., Chen, E., & Chandra, R. (2006). BGP route reflection: an alternative to full mesh Internal BGP (IBGP). IETF Request for Comments (RFC) 4456, April 2006.
11. Moy, J. (1998). *OSPF: Anatomy of an Internet routing protocol*. Addison-Wesley, Reading, Massachusetts, February 1998.
12. Mirtorabi, S., Psenak, P., Lindem, A., & Oswal, A. (2008). OSPF multi-area adjacency. IETF Request for Comments (RFC) 5185, May 2008.
13. Mauro, D., & Schmidt, K. (2005). *Essential SNMP*. O'Reilly & Associates, second ed., Sebastopol, California, September 2005.

14. Patrick, N., Scholl, T., Shaikh, A., & Steenbergen, R. (2006). Peering dragnet: examining BGP routes received from peers. North American Network Operators' Group (NANOG) presentation, October 2006.
15. University of Oregon Route Views Project. http://www.routeviews.org/.
16. RIPE Routing Information Service (RIS). http://www.ripe.net/ris/index.html.
17. Feamster, N., & Rexford, J. (2007). Network-wide prediction of BGP routes. *IEEE/ACM Transactions on Networking*, pp. 253–266, April 2007.
18. Rosen, E., & Rekhter, Y. (2006). BGP/MPLS IP Virtual Private Networks (VPNs). IETF Request for Comments (RFC) 4364, February 2006.
19. Kim, C., Gerber, A., Lund, C., Pei, D., & Sen, S. (2008). Scalable VPN routing via relaying. In *Proceedings of ACM SIGMETRICS*, Annapolis, Maryland, June 2008.
20. Govindan, R., & Reddy, A. (1997). An analysis of Internet inter-domain topology and route stability. In *Proceedings of IEEE INFOCOM*, Kobe, Japan, pp. 850–857, 1997.
21. Labovitz, C., Malan, G. R., & Jahanian, F. (1998). Internet routing instability. *IEEE/ACM Transactions on Networking, 6*, pp. 515–528, October 1998.
22. Labovitz, C., Malan, G. R., & Jahanian, F. (1999). Origins of Internet routing instability. In *Proceedings of IEEE INFOCOM*, New York, New York, pp. 218–226, 1999.
23. Labovitz, C., Ahuja, A., Bose, A., & Jahanian, F. (2001). Delayed Internet routing convergence. *IEEE/ACM Transactions on Networking, 9*, pp. 293–306, June 2001.
24. Pei, D., Zhao, X., Wang, L., Massey, D., Mankin, A., Wu, S. F., & Zhang, L. (2002). Improving BGP convergence through consistency assertions. In *Proceedings of IEEE INFOCOM*, New York, New York, 2002.
25. Bremler-Barr, A., Afek, Y., & Schwarz, S. (2003). Improved BGP convergence via ghost flushing. In *Proceedings of IEEE INFOCOM*, San Francisco, California, 2003.
26. Pei, D., Azuma, M., Massey, D., & Zhang, L. (2005). BGP-RCN: improving BGP convergence through root cause notification. *Computer Networks Journal, 48*, pp. 175–194, June 2005.
27. Chandrashekar, J., Duan, Z., Krasky, J., & Zhang, Z.-L. (2005). Limiting path exploration in BGP. In *Proceedings of IEEE INFOCOM*, Miami, Florida, 2005.
28. Pei, D., Zhang, B., Massey, D., & Zhang, L. (2006). An analysis of path-vector convergence algorithms. *Computer Networks Journal, 50*, February 2006.
29. Mao, Z. M., Govindan, R., Varghese, G., & Katz, R. (2002). Route flap damping exacerbates Internet routing convergence. In *Proceedings of ACM SIGCOMM*, Pittsburgh, Pennsylvania, 2002.
30. Villamizar, C., Chandra, R., & Govindan, R. (1998). BGP route flap damping. IETF Request for Comments (RFC) 2439, November 1998.
31. Panigl, C., Schmitz, J., Smith, P., & Vistoli, C. (2001). RIPE routing-WG recommendations for coordinated route-flap damping parameters. RIPE document ripe-229, October 2001. ftp://ftp.ripe.net/ripe/docs/ripe-229.txt.
32. Smith, P., & Panigl, C. (2006). RIPE routing working group recommendations on route-flap damping. RIPE document ripe-378, May 2006. http://www.ripe.net/ripe/docs/ripe-378.html.
33. Teixeira, R., Shaikh, A., Griffin, T. G., & Rexford, J. (2008). Impact of hot-potato routing changes in IP networks. *IEEE/ACM Transactions on Networking, 16*, pp. 1295–1307, December 2008.
34. Route Explorer from Packet Design Inc. http://www.packetdesign.com/products/rex.htm.
35. Route Analyzer from PacketStorm Communications, Inc. http://www.packetstorm.com/route.php.
36. Shaikh, A., Isett, C., Greenberg, A., Roughan, M., & Gottlieb, J. (2002). A case study of OSPF behavior in a large enterprise network. In *Proceedings of ACM SIGCOMM Internet Measurement Workshop (IMW)*, Marseille, France, November 2002.
37. Andersson, L., Minei, I., & Thomas, B. (2007). LDP specification. IETF Request for Comments (RFC) 5036, October 2007.
38. Awduche, D., Berger, L., Gan, D., Li, T., Srinivasan, V., & Swallow, G. (2001). RSVP-TE: extensions to RSVP for LSP tunnels. IETF Request for Comments (RFC) 3209, December 2001.

39. Rekhter, Y., & Rosen, E. (2001). Carrying label information in BGP-4. IETF Request for Comments (RFC) 3107, May 2001.

40. Rosen, E., & Rekhter, Y. (2006). BGP/MPLS IP virtual private networks (VPNs). IETF Request for Comments (RFC) 4364, February 2006.

41. Srinivasan, C., Viswanathan, A., & Nadeau, T. (2004). Multiprotocol label switching (MPLS) traffic engineering (TE) management information base (MIB). IETF Request for Comments (RFC) 3812, June 2004.

42. Deering, S. (1988). Multicast routing in internetworks and extended LANs. In *Proceedings of ACM SIGCOMM*, Stanford, California, pp. 55–64, August 1988.

43. Cain, B., Deering, S., Kouvelas, I., Fenner, B., & Thyagarajan, A. (2002). Internet group management protocol, Version 3. IETF Request for Comments (RFC) 3376, October 2002.

44. Casner, S., & Deering, S. (1992). First IETF Internet audiocast. *ACM Computer Communication Review, 22*, July 1992.

45. Multicast in MPLS/BGP IP VPNs. Internet draft, July 2008. http://www.ietf.org/internet-drafts/draft-ietf-l3vpn-2547bis-mcast-07.txt.

46. Multicast virtual private networks. White paper, Cisco Systems, 2002. http://www.cisco.com/warp/public/cc/pd/iosw/prodlit/tcast_wp.pdf.

47. Waitzman, D., Partridge, C., & Deering, S. (1988). Distance vector multicast routing protocol. IETF Request for Comments (RFC) 1075, November 1988.

48. Moy, J. (1994). Multicast Extensions to OSPF. IETF Request for Comments (RFC) 1584, March 1994.

49. Ballardie, T., Francis, P., & Crowcroft, J. (1993). Core based trees (CBT): an architecture for scalable inter-domain multicast routing. In *Proceedings of ACM SIGCOMM*, San Francisco, California, pp. 85–95, September 1993.

50. Fenner, B., & Meyer, D. (2003). Multicast source discovery protocol (MSDP). IETF Request for Comments (RFC) 3618, October 2003.

51. Fenner, B., Handley, M., Holbrook, H., & Kouvelas, I. (2006). Protocol independent multicast – sparse mode (PIM-SM): protocol specification (Revised). IETF Request for Comments (RFC) 4601, August 2006.

52. Adams, A., Nicholas, J., & Siadak, W. (2005). Protocol independent multicast – dense mode (PIM-DM): protocol specification (Revised). IETF Request for Comments (RFC) 3973, January 2005.

53. Bhaskar, N., Gall, A., Lingard, J., & Venaas, S. (2008). Bootstrap router (BSR) mechanism for protocol independent multicast (PIM). IETF Request for Comments (RFC) 5059, January 2008.

54. Partridge, C., Mendez, T., & Milliken, W. (1993). Host anycasting service. IETF Request for Comments (RFC) 1546, November 1993.

55. McCanne, S. (1999). Scalable multimedia communication using IP multicast and lightweight sessions. *IEEE Internet Computing, 3*(2), pp. 33–45.

56. Massey, D., & Fenner, B. (1999). Fault detection in routing protocols. In *Proceedings of International Conference on Network Protocols (ICNP)*, Toronto, Canada, 1999.

57. Saraç, K., & Almeroth, K. C. (2000). Supporting multicast deployment efforts: a survey of tools for multicast monitoring. *Journal of High Speed Networks, 9*(3,4), pp. 191–211.

58. Namburi, P., Saraç, K., & Almeroth, K. C. (2006). Practical utilities for monitoring multicast service availability. *Computer Communications Special Issue on Monitoring and Measurement of IP Networks, 29*, pp. 1675–1686, June 2006.

59. McCloghrie, K., Farinacci, D., Thaler, D., & Fenner, B. (2000). Protocol independent multicast MIB for IPv4. IETF Request for Comments (RFC) 2934, October 2000.

60. McCloghrie, K., Farinacci, D., & Thaler, D. (2000). IPv4 multicast routing MIB. IETF Request for Comments (RFC) 2932, October 2000.

Part VI
Network and Security Management, and Disaster Preparedness

Chapter 12
Network Management: Fault Management, Performance Management, and Planned Maintenance

Jennifer M. Yates and Zihui Ge

12.1 Introduction

As the Internet grew from a fledgling network interconnecting a few University computers to a massive infrastructure deployed across the globe, the focus was primarily on providing connectivity to the masses. And IP has certainly achieved this. IP is used today to connect businesses and consumers across the globe. An increasingly diverse set of services have also come to use IP as the underlying communications protocol, including e-commerce, voice, mission-critical business applications, TV (IPTV), as well as e-mail and Internet web browsing. Nowadays, even people's lives depend on IP networks – as IP increasingly supports emergency services and other medical applications.

This tremendous diversity in applications places an equally diverse set of requirements on the underlying network infrastructure, particularly with respect to bandwidth consumption, reliability, and performance. At one extreme, e-mail is resilient to network impairments – the key requirement being basic connectivity. E-mail servers continually attempt to retransmit e-mails, even in the face of potentially lengthy outages. In contrast, real-time video services typically require high bandwidth and are sensitive to even very short-term "glitches" and performance degradations.

IP is also a relatively new technology – especially if we compare it with technology such as the telephone network, which has now been around for over 130 years. As IP technology has matured over recent years, network availability has been driven up – a result of maturing hardware and software, as well as continued improvements in network management practices, tools, and network design. These improvements have enabled a shift in emphasis to focus beyond availability and faults to managing performance – for example, eliminating short-term "glitches," which may not be at all relevant to many applications (e.g., e-mail), but can cause

J.M. Yates (✉) and Z. Ge
AT&T Labs – Research, Florham Park, NJ, USA
e-mail: jyates@research.att.com; gezihui@research.att.com

C.R. Kalmanek et al. (eds.), *Guide to Reliable Internet Services and Applications*,
Computer Communications and Networks, DOI 10.1007/978-1-84882-828-5_12,
© Springer-Verlag London Limited 2010

degradation in service quality to applications such as video streaming and online gaming. The transformation of IP from a technology designed to support best-effort data delivery to one that supports a diverse range of sensitive real-time and mission-critical applications is a testament to the industry and to the network operators who have created technologies, automation, and procedures to ensure high reliability and performance.

In this chapter, we focus on the network management systems and the tasks involved in supporting the day-to-day *operation* of an ISP network. The goal of network operations is to keep the network up and running and performing at or above designed levels of service performance. Achieving this goal involves responding to issues as they arise, proactively making network changes to prevent issues from occurring, and evolving the network over time to introduce new technologies, services, and capacity. We can loosely classify these tasks into categories using traditional definitions discussed within the literature – namely, fault management, performance management, and planned maintenance.

At a high level, fault management is easy to understand: it includes the "break/fix" functions – if something breaks, fix it. More precisely, fault management encompasses the systems and workflows necessary to ensure that faults are rapidly detected, the root causes are diagnosed, and the faults are rapidly resolved. It can also include predicting failures before they occur, and remediating the problem before it actually happens.

Performance management can be defined in several different ways: for example, (1) designing, planning, monitoring, and taking action to prevent and recover from overload conditions once they happen, and (2) monitoring both end-network performance and per element performance and taking actions to address performance degradation. Performance can be measured and managed on the links between network elements (e.g., bandwidth utilization), on the network elements themselves (e.g., CPU utilization), on the traffic flow (e.g., packet loss, latency, or jitter), or on the quality of the service transactions (e.g., voice call quality or time to deliver a text message). The first definition focuses on traffic management and encompasses roles executed by network engineering organizations (capacity planning) and operations (real-time responses to network conditions). In this chapter, we will focus on the second definition of performance management: monitoring network performance and taking appropriate actions when performance is degraded. This performance degradation may be the result of an unplanned surge in traffic that exceeds engineered capacity (whether legitimate traffic or "attack traffic" from a Distributed Denial-of-Service attack), loss of available capacity (e.g., owing to a hardware failure), intermittent problems that cause high bit error rates on a link, or logical problems such as incorrect configurations or software errors that create a "black hole."

Both network faults and degraded performance may require intervention by network operations, and the line between fault and performance management is blurred in practice. Sometimes, a fault can occur with no performance degradation, such as when a circuit board fails but its function is taken over by a redundant card. Alternatively, a performance problem can occur without any corresponding hardware fault, such as when a surge of customer traffic exceeds available capacity. Then in other situations, a fault can occur and result in degraded performance, such as when a link fails and results in the network's inability to carry all customer traffic without traffic loss or degradation. In this chapter, we refer to a network condition that may require the intervention of network operations as a network *event*. Events are triggered by an underlying *incident*; a single incident can result in multiple network events (e.g., link down, congestion, and packet loss). The events in question may have a diverse set of causes, including hardware failures, software bugs, external factors (e.g., flash crowds, outages in peer networks), or combinations of these. The impact resulting from different incidents also varies drastically, ranging from outages during which affected customers have no connectivity for lengthy periods of time (known as "hard outages"), through to those which result in little or no customer impact (e.g., loss of network capacity where traffic re-routes around it). In between these two extremes lie incidents which result in customers experiencing degraded performance to differing extents – e.g., sporadic packet loss, or increased delay and/or jitter.

In addition to rapidly reacting to issues that arise, daily network operation also incorporates taking planned actions to proactively ensure that the network continues to deliver high service levels, and to evolve network services and technologies. We refer to such scheduled activities as *planned maintenance*. Planned maintenance includes a wide variety of activities, such as changing a fan filter in a router, hardware or software upgrades, capacity augmentation, preventive maintenance, or rearranging connections in response to external factors, including even highway maintenance being carried out where cables are laid. Such activities are usually performed at a specific, scheduled time, typically during nonbusiness hours when network utilization is low and the impact of the maintenance activity on customers can be minimized.

This chapter covers both fault and performance management, and planned maintenance. Section 12.2 focuses on fault and performance management – predicting, detecting, troubleshooting, and repairing network faults and performance impairments. Section 12.3 examines how process automation is incorporated in fault and performance management to automate many of the tasks that were originally executed by humans. Process automation is the key ingredient that enables a relatively small operations group to manage a rapidly expanding number of network elements and customer ports, and growing network complexity. Section 12.4 discusses tracking and managing network availability and performance over time, looking across large numbers of network events to identify opportunities for performance improvements. Section 12.5 then focuses on planned maintenance. Finally, in Section 12.6, we discuss opportunities for new innovations and technology enhancements, including new areas for research. We conclude Section 12.7 with a set of "best practices."

12.2 Real-Time Fault and Performance Management

Fault and performance management comprise a large and complex set of functions that are required to support the day-to-day operation of a network. As mentioned in the previous section, network events can be divided into two broad categories: faults and performance impairments. The term fault is used to refer to a "hard" failure – for example, when an interface goes from being operational (up) to failed (down). Performance events denote situations where a network element is operating with degraded performance – for example, when a router interface is dropping packets, or when there is an undesirably high loss and/or delay experienced along a given route. We use the term "event management" to generically define the set of functions that detect, isolate, and repair network malfunctions – covering both faults and performance events.

The primary goal of event management is to rapidly respond to network incidents as they occur so that any resulting customer impact can be minimized. However, achieving this within the complex environment of ISP networks today requires a carefully designed and scalable *event management framework*. Figure 12.1 presents a simplified view of such a framework. The goal of the design is to enable rapid and reliable detection and notification of network events, so that action can be taken to troubleshoot and mitigate them. However, as anyone who has experience with large networks can attest, this is in itself a challenging problem.

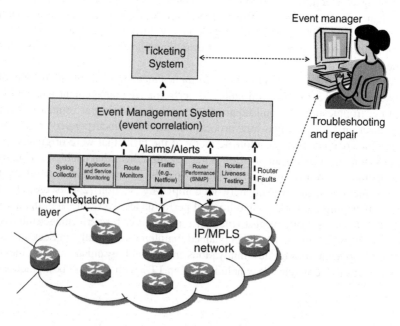

Fig. 12.1 Simplified event management framework

At the base of the event management framework lies an extensive and diverse network *instrumentation layer*. The instrumentation layer illustrated in Fig. 12.1 collects network data from both network elements (routers, switches, lower-layer equipment) and network monitoring systems designed to monitor network performance from vantage points across the network. The measurements collected are critical for a wide range of different purposes, including customer billing, capacity planning, event detection and notification, and troubleshooting. The latter two functions are critical parts of daily network operations. With regard to this, the goal is to ensure that the wide range of potential fault and performance events are reliably *detected* and that there are sufficient measurements available to troubleshoot network incidents.

Both the routers and the collectors contained within the instrumentation layer detect events that can trigger notifications to the central *event management system*. Events detected include faults (e.g., link or router down) and performance impairments (such as excessive network loss or delay). These performance events are identified by looking for anomalous, "bad" conditions among the mounds of performance data, and logs collected within the instrumentation layer.

Given the diversity of the instrumentation layer, any given network incident will likely be observed as multiple different events. For example, a fiber cut (the incident) could result in events detected in the lower layer (e.g., SONET layer failures) and in events detected in the IP/MPLS network layer (router links failing and potentially congestion, packet loss, and excessive end-to-end delay). Each event, in turn, could be detected by multiple monitoring points. Thus, it is likely that a single incident will result in a deluge of *event notifications*, which would swamp the operations personnel trying to investigate. Significant automation is thus introduced in the event management system to *suppress and correlate* multiple event notifications associated with the same incident. The resulting *correlated event* is used to trigger the creation of a *ticket* in the network *ticketing system* – these tickets are used to notify operations personnel about the occurrence of the incident.

Once notified of an issue, operations personnel are responsible for *troubleshooting, restoration,* and *repair*. Troubleshooting, restoration, and repair have two primary goals: (1) restoring customer service and performance, and (2) fully resolving the underlying issue and returning network resources into service. These two goals may or may not be distinct – where redundancy exists, the network is typically designed to automatically reroute around failed elements, thus negating the need for manual intervention in restoring customer service. Troubleshooting and repair can then instead focus on returning the failed network resources into service so that there is sufficient capacity available to absorb future failures. In other situations, operations must resolve the issue to restore customer service. Rapid action from operations personnel is then imperative – until they can identify what is causing the problem and repair it, the customer may be out of service or experiencing degraded performance. This typically occurs at the edge of a network, where the customer connects to the ISP and redundancy may be limited. For example, if the nonredundant line-card to which a customer connects fails, the customer may be out of service until a replacement line-card can be installed.

We next delve into each of the different layers and functions of the event management framework in greater detail.

12.2.1 Instrumentation Layer, Event Detection, and Event Notification

The foundation of an event management system is the reliable detection and notification of network faults and performance impairments. We thus start by considering how these network events are detected, and how the corresponding event notifications are generated.

The primary goal is to ensure that the event management system is timely and reliably informed of network events. But each underlying incident may trigger a number of different events, and may occur anywhere across the vast network(s) being monitored. Depending on the impairments at hand, it may be that the routers themselves observe the events and report them accordingly. However, limitations in router monitoring capabilities, the inability to incorporate new monitoring capabilities without major router upgrades, and the need for independent network monitoring have driven a wide range of external monitoring systems into the network. These systems have the added benefit of being able to obtain different perspectives on the network when compared with the individual routers. For example, end-to-end performance monitoring systems obtain a network-wide view of performance; a view not readily captured from within a single router.

Chapters 10 and 11 have discussed the wide range of network monitoring capabilities available in large-scale operational IP/MPLS networks. These are incorporated within the instrumentation layer to support a diverse range of applications, ranging from network engineering (e.g., capacity planning), customer billing, to fault and performance management. Within fault and performance management, these measurements support real-time event detection, as well as other tasks such as troubleshooting and postmortem analysis, which are discussed later in this chapter.

The instrumentation layer, as illustrated in Fig. 12.1, is responsible for collecting measurements from both network elements (e.g., routers) and from external monitoring devices, such as route monitors and application/end-to-end performance measurement tools. Although logically depicted as a single layer, the instrumentation layer actually consists of multiple different collectors, each focused on a single monitoring capability. We next discuss these collectors in more detail.

12.2.1.1 Router Fault and Event Notifications

Network routers themselves have an ideal vantage point for detecting failures local to them. They are privy to events that occur on inter-router links terminating on them, and also to events that occur inside the routers themselves. They can thus identify all sorts of hardware (link, line–card, and router chassis failures) and software issues (including software protocol crashes and routing protocol failures). Routers themselves detect events and notify the event management systems – one can view the instrumentation layer for these events as residing directly within the routers themselves as opposed to in an external instrumentation layer.

In addition to creating notifications about events detected in the router, routers also write log messages, which describe a wide range of events observed on the router. These are known as *syslogs*; they are akin to the syslogs created on servers. The syslog protocol [1] is used to deliver syslog messages from network elements to the syslog collector depicted in Fig. 12.1. These syslog messages report a diverse range of conditions observed within the network element, such as link and protocol-related state changes (down, up), environment measurements (voltage, temperature), and warning messages (e.g., denoting when customers send more routes than the router is configured to allow). Some of these events relate to conditions that are then reported to the event management system, while others provide useful information when it comes to troubleshooting a network incident. Syslog messages are basically free-form text, with some structure (e.g., indicating date/time of event, location, and event priority). The form and format of the syslog messages vary between router vendors. Figure 12.2 illustrates some example syslog messages taken from Cisco routers – details regarding Cisco message formats can be found in [2].

12.2.1.2   External Fault Detection and Route Monitoring

Router fault detection mechanisms are complemented by other mechanisms to identify issues that may not have been detected and/or reported by the routers – either because the routers do not have visibility into the event, their detection mechanisms fail to detect it (maybe due to a software bug), or because they are unable to report the issue to the relevant systems. For example, basic periodic ICMP

Mar 15   00:00:06   ROUTER_A   627423:   Mar   15   00:00:00.554:   %CI-6-ENVNORMAL:+24 Voltage measured at 24.63
Mar 15   00:00:06   ROUTER_B   289883:   Mar   15   00:00:00.759:   %LINK-3-UPDOWN: Interface Serial13/0.6/16:0, changed state to up
Mar   15   00:00:13   ROUTER_C   2267435:   Mar   15   00:00:12.473: %CONTROLLER-5-UPDOWN: Controller T3 10/1/1 T1 18, changed state to DOWN
Mar 15   00:00:06   ROUTER_D   852136:   Mar   15   00:00:00.155:   %PIM-6-INVALID_RP_JOIN: VRF 13979:28858: Received (*, 224.0.1.40) Join from 1.2.3.4 for invalid RP 5.6.7.8
Mar 15 00:00:07 ROUTER_E 801790: -Process= "PIM Process", ipl= 0, pid=218
Mar 15 00:25:26 ROUTER_Z bay0007:SUN MAR 15 00:25:24 2009 [03004EFF] MINOR:snmp-traps:Module in bay 4 slot 6, temp 65 deg C at or above minor threshold of 65 degC.

Fig. 12.2 Example (normalized) syslog messages

"ping" tests are used to validate the liveness of routers and their interfaces – if a router or interface becomes unexpectedly unresponsive to ICMP pings, then this warrants concern and an event notification should be generated.

Route monitors, as discussed in Chapter 11, also provide visibility into control-plane activity; activity that may not always be reported by the routers. IGP monitors, such as OSPFmon [3], learn about link and router up/down events and can be used to complement the same events reported by routers. However, route monitors extend beyond simple detection of link up/down events, and can provide information about logical routing changes affecting traffic routing. Even further, the route(s) between any given source/destination can be inferred using routing data collected from route monitors. This information is vital when trying to understand the events that have affected a given traffic flow.

12.2.1.3 Router-Reported Performance Measurements

Although hardware faults have traditionally been the primary focus of event man-agement systems, performance events can also cause significant customer distress, and thus must be addressed. The goal here is to identify and report when network performance deviates from desired operating regions and requires investigation. However, the reliable detection of performance issues is really quite different from detecting faults. Performance statistics are continually collected from the network; from these measurements, we can then determine when performance departs from the desired operating regions.

As discussed in Chapter 10, routers track a wide range of different performance parameters – such as counts of the number of packets and bytes flowing on each router interface, different types of interface error counts (including buffer overflow, malformatted packets, CRC check violations), and CPU and memory utilization on the central router CPU and its line-cards. These performance parameters are stored within the router in the *Simple Network Management Protocol (SNMP) Management Information Bases (MIBs)*. SNMP [4] is the Internet community's de facto standard management protocol. SNMP was defined by the IETF, and is used to con-vey management information between software *agents* on managed devices (e.g., router) and the managing systems (e.g., event management systems in Fig. 12.1).

External systems poll router MIBs on a regular basis, such as every 5 minutes. Thus, with a 5-min polling interval, the CPU measurement represents the average CPU utilization over a given 5-min interval; in polling packet counts, the poller can create measurements representing the total number of packets that have flowed on the interface in the given 5-min interval.

The SNMP information collected from routers is used for a wide variety of purposes, including customer billing, detecting anomalous network conditions that could impact or risk impacting customers (congestion, excessively high CPU utilization, router memory leaks), and troubleshooting network events.

12.2.1.4 Traffic Measurements

While SNMP measurements provide aggregate statistics about link loads – e.g., counts of total number of bytes or equivalently link utilization over a fixed time interval (e.g., 5 min), they provide little insight into how this traffic is distributed across different applications or different source/destination pairs. Instead, as discussed in Chapter 10, Netflow and deep packet inspection (DPI) are used to obtain much more detailed measurements of how traffic is distributed across applications, network links, and routes. These measurement capabilities are especially critical in troubleshooting various network conditions. DPI, in particular, can be used to obtain unique visibility into the traffic carried on a link, which is useful in trying to understand what and how traffic may be related to the given network issues. For example, DPI could be used to identify malformed packets and where they came from, or identify what traffic is destined to an overloaded router CPU.

12.2.1.5 End-to-End Network, Application and Service Monitoring

Although monitoring the state and performance of individual network elements is critical to managing the overall health of the network, it is not in itself sufficient to understanding the performance as perceived by customers. It is imperative to monitor and detect events based on the *end-to-end network and service-level performance*.

End-to-end measurements – even as simple as that achieved by sending test traffic across the network from one edge of the network to another – provide the closest representation of what customers experience as can be measured from within the ISP network. End-to-end measurements were discussed in more detail in Chapter 10. In the context of fault and performance management, they are used to identify anomalous network conditions, such as when there is excessive end-to-end packet loss, delay, and/or jitter. These events are reported to the event management system, and used to trigger further investigation.

As discussed in Chapter 10, performance monitoring can be achieved using either active or passive measurements. Active measurements send test probes (traffic) across the network, collecting statistics related to the network and/or service performance. In contrast, passive measurements examine the performance of traffic being carried across the network, such as customer traffic. Ideally, such measurements would be taken out as close to the customers as possible, even into the customer domains. However, this is not always possible, particularly if the ISP does not have access to the customer's end device or domain.

End-to-end performance measurements can be used both to understand the impact of known network incidents, and to identify events that have not been detected via other means. When known incidents occur, end-to-end performance measurements provide direct performance measures, which present insight into the incident's customer impact. In addition end-to-end measurements also provide an overall test of the network health, and can be used to identify the rare but potentially critical issues (e.g., faults) which the network may have failed to detect. When it comes to faults, these are known as *silent failures*, and have historically been an artifact of immature router technologies – where the routers simply fail to detect issues that they should have detected. For example, consider an internal router fault (e.g., corrupted memory on a line-card), which is causing a link to simply drop all traffic. If the router fails to detect that this is occurring, then it will fail to reroute the traffic away from the failed link, and to report this as a fault condition. Thus, traffic will continue to be sent to a failed interface and be dropped – a condition known as *black-holing*. End-to-end measurements provide a means to proactively detect these issues; in the case of active measurements, the test probes will be dropped along with the customer traffic – this would be detected and appropriate notifications would be generated. Thus, the event can be detected even when the network elements fail to report them and (hopefully!) before customers complain.

In addition to auditing the integrity of the network, simple test probes can also be used to estimate service performance (e.g., estimating how well IPTV services are performing). However, extrapolating from simple network loss and delay measures to understand the impact of a network event on any given network-based application is most often an extremely complex, if not impossible, task involving the intimate details of the application in question. For example, understanding how packet loss, delay and jitter impact the video streams is an area of active research.

Ideally, we would like to directly measure the performance of each and every application that operates across a network. This may be an impossible task in networks supporting a plethora of different services and applications. However, if a network is critical to a specific application – such as IPTV – then that application also needs to be monitored, and appropriate mechanisms must be in place to detect issues. After all, the goal is to ensure that the service is operating correctly – ascertaining this requires direct monitoring of the service of interest.

12.2.1.6 Event Detection and Notification

The instrumentation layer thus provides network operators with an immense volume of network measurements. How do we transform these data to identify network issues that require investigation and action?

Let us start by identifying the events that we are interested in detecting. We clearly need to detect faults – conditions that may be causing customer outages or taking critical network resources out of service. We also aim to detect performance issues that may be causing degraded customer experiences. And finally, we wish to detect network element health concerns, which are either impacting customers or are risking customer impact.

The majority of faults are relatively easy to detect – we need to be able to detect when network elements or components are out of service (down). It gets a little more complicated when it comes to defining performance impairments of interest. If we are too sensitive in the issues identified – for example, reporting very minor, short conditions – then operations personnel risk expending tremendous effort attempting to troubleshoot meaningless events, potentially missing events that are of great significance among all the noise and false alarms. Short-term impairments, such as packet losses or CPU anomalies, are often too short to even enable real-time investigation – the event has more often than not cleared before operations personnel could even be informed about it, let alone investigate. And short-term events are expected – no matter how careful network planning and design is, occasional short-term packet losses, for example, will occur. However, even a transient problem might warrant attention if it is recurring and/or a leading indicator of a more serious incident that is likely to occur.

Instead, we need to focus on identifying events that are sufficiently large, chronic (recurring), or persist for a significant period of time. Simple thresholding is typically used to achieve this – an event is identified when a parameter of interest exceeds a predefined value for a specified period of time. For example, an event may be declared when packet loss exceeds 0.3% over three consecutive polling periods across an IP/MPLS backbone network. However, note that more complicated signatures can be and are indeed used to detect some conditions. Section 12.4.1 discusses this in more detail, including how appropriate thresholds can be identified.

Once we have detected an issue – whether it is a fault or performance impairment – our goal is to report it so that appropriate action can be taken. Event notification is realized through the generation of an *alarm* or an *alert,* which is sent to the event management platform as illustrated in Fig. 12.1. We distinguish between these two – an alarm traditionally describes the notification of a fault, while an alert is a notification of a performance event. Alarms and alerts themselves have a life span – they start with a SET and typically end through an explicit CLEAR. Thus, explicit notifications of both the start of an event (the SET) and the end of an event (CLEAR) generally need to be conveyed to the event management system.

SNMP traps or *informs* (depending on the SNMP version) are used by routers to notify the event management system of events. Given the predominance of SNMP in IP/MPLS, this same mechanism is also often used between other collectors in the instrumentation layer and the event management layer. Traps/informs represent asynchronous reports of events and are used to notify network management systems of state changes, such as links and protocols going down or coming up. For example, if a link fails, then the routers at either end of the link will send SNMP traps to the network management system collecting these. These traps typically include information about the source of the event, the details of the type of event, the parameters, and the priority. Figure 12.3 depicts logs detailing traps collected from a router. The logs report the time and location of the event, the type of event that has occurred and the SNMP MIB Object ID (OID). In this particular case, we are observing the symptoms associated with a line-card failure, where the line-card contains a number of physical and logical ports. Each port is individually reported as having failed. This includes both the physical interfaces (denoted in the Cisco router example below as T3 4/0/0, T3 4/0/1, Serial4/1/0/3:0, Serial4/1/0/4:0, Serial4/1/0/5:0, Serial4/1/0/23:0, Serial4/1/0/24:0, Serial4/1/0/25:0 and the logical interfaces (denoted in the example below as Multilink6164 and Multilink6168). In the example shown in Fig. 12.3, the OID that denotes the link down event is "4.1.3.6.1.6.3.1.1.5.3.1.3.6.1.4.1.9.1.46 0" – and can be seen on each event notification.

1238081113 10 Thu Feb 21 03:10:07 2009 Router_A- Cisco LinkDown Trap on Interface T3 4/0/0;4.1.3.6.1.6.3.1.1.5.3.1.3.6.1.4.1.9.1.46 0

1238081117 10 Thu Mar 26 15:25:17 2009 Router_A - Cisco LinkDown Trap on Interface T3 4/0/1;4.1.3.6.1.6.3.1.1.5.3.1.3.6.1.4.1.9.1.46 0

1238081118 10 Thu Mar 26 15:25:18 2009 Router_A - Cisco LinkDown Trap on Interface Serial4/1/0/3:0;4.1.3.6.1.6.3.1.1.5.3.1.3.6.1.4.1.9.1.46 0

1238081118 10 Thu Mar 26 15:25:18 2009 Router_A - Cisco LinkDown Trap on Interface Serial4/1/0/4:0;4.1.3.6.1.6.3.1.1.5.3.1.3.6.1.4.1.9.1.46 0

1238081119 10 Thu Mar 26 15:25:19 2009 Router_A - Cisco LinkDown Trap on Interface Serial4/1/0/5:0;4.1.3.6.1.6.3.1.1.5.3.1.3.6.1.4.1.9.1.46 0

1238081124 10 Thu Mar 26 15:25:24 2009 Router_A - Cisco LinkDown Trap on Interface Serial4/1/0/23:0;4.1.3.6.1.6.3.1.1.5.3.1.3.6.1.4.1.9.1.46 0

1238081124 10 Thu Mar 26 15:25:24 2009 Router_A - Cisco LinkDown Trap on Interface Serial4/1/0/24:0;4.1.3.6.1.6.3.1.1.5.3.1.3.6.1.4.1.9.1.46 0

1238081125 10 Thu Mar 26 15:25:25 2009 Router_A - Cisco LinkDown Trap on Interface Serial4/1/0/25:0;4.1.3.6.1.6.3.1.1.5.3.1.3.6.1.4.1.9.1.46 0

1238081125 10 Thu Mar 26 15:25:25 2009 Router_A - Cisco LinkDown Trap on In terface Multilink6164;4.1.3.6.1.6.3.1.1.5.3.1.3.6.1.4.1.9.1.46 0

1238081125 10 Thu Mar 26 15:25:25 2009 Router_A - Cisco LinkDownTrap on Interface Multilink6168;4.1.3.6.1.6.3.1.1.5.3.1.3.6.1.4.1.9.1.46 0

Fig. 12.3 Example logs from (anonymized) SNMP traps

12.2.2 Event Management System

The preceding section discussed the vast monitoring infrastructure deployed in modern IP/MPLS networks and used to detect network events. However, the number of event notifications created by such an extensive monitoring infrastructure would simply overwhelm a network operator – completely obscuring the real incident in an avalanche of alarms and alerts. Manually weeding out the noise from the true root cause could take hours or even longer for a single incident – time during which critical customers may be unable to effectively communicate, watch TV, and/or access the Internet. This is simply not an acceptable mode of operation.

By way of a simple example, consider a fiber cut impacting a link between two adjacent routers. The failure of this link (the fault) will be observed at the physical layer (e.g., SONET) on the routers at both ends of the link. It will also be observed in the different protocols running over that link – for example, in PPP, in the intradomain routing protocol (OSPF or IS-IS), in LDP and in PIM (if multicast is enabled), and potentially even through BGP. These will all be separately logged via syslog messages; failure notifications (traps) would be generated by the routers at both ends of the link in question to indicate that the link is down. The same incident would be captured by route monitors (in this case, by the intradomain route protocol monitors [3]). Network management systems monitoring the lower-layer (e.g., layer one/physical layer) technologies will also detect the incident, and will alarm. Finally – should congestion result from this fault – performance monitoring tools may report excessively high load and packet losses observed from the routers, end-to-end performance degradations may be reported by the end-to-end performance monitoring, and application monitors would send alerts if customer services are impacted. Thus, even a single fiber cut can result in a plethora of event notifications. The last thing we need is for the network operator to manually delve into each one of these to identify the one that falls at the heart of the issue – in this case, the alarm that denotes a loss of incoming signal at the physical layer.

Instead, automated event management systems as depicted in Fig. 12.1 are used to automatically identify both an incident's *origin* and its *impact* from among the flood of incoming alarms. The key to achieving this is *event correlation* – taking the incoming flood of event notifications, automatically identifying which notifications are associated with a common incident, and then analyzing them to identify the most likely explanation and any relevant impact. The resulting correlated events are input to the ticket creation process; tickets are used to notify operations personnel of an issue requiring their attention. In the above example, the event's origin can be crisply identified as being a physical layer link failure; the impact of interest to the network operator being any resulting congestion and the extent to which any service and/or network performance degradation is impacting customers, and how many and which customers are impacted. The greater the impact of an event, the more urgent is the need for the network operator to instigate repair.

12.2.2.1 Managing Event Notification Floods: Event Correlation

So how can we effectively and reliably manage this onslaught of event notifications? First of all, not all notifications received by an event management system need to be correlated and translated into tickets to trigger human investigation. For example, expected notifications corresponding to known maintenance events can be logged and discarded – there is no need to investigate these, as they are expected side-effects of the planned activities. Similarly, duplicate notifications can be discarded – if a notification is received multiple times for the same condition, then only one of these notifications needs to be passed on for further analysis. Thus, as notifications are received by the event management system, they are filtered to identify those which should be forwarded for further correlation.

Similarly, notifications of one off events that are very short in nature – effectively "naturally" resolving themselves – can often be discarded as there is no action to be taken by the time that the notification makes it for further analysis. Thus, if an event notification SET is followed almost immediately by a CLEAR, then the event management system may chose to discard the event entirely. Such events can occur, for example, because of someone accidentally touching a fiber in an office, causing a very rapid, one off impairment. There is little point to expending significant resources investigating this event – it has disappeared and is not something that someone in operations can do anything about – unless it continues to happen. Short conditions that continually reoccur are classified as *chronics*, and do require investigation. Thus, if an event keeps occurring, then a chronic event is declared and a corresponding ticket is created so that the incident can be properly investigated.

Event correlation, sometimes also referred to as *root cause analysis*[1] within the event management literature, follows the event filtering process. Put simply, event correlation examines the incoming stream of network event notifications to identify those which occur at approximately the same time and are physically or logically related, and can be associated with a common explanation. These are then grouped together as being a *correlated event*. The goal here is to identify the *originating event* – effectively identifying the type and location of the underlying incident being reported. Note that the originating event may not have been directly observed – it is entirely possible that only symptoms of the incident were reported, without a direct event reporting the origin. For example, consider a router line-card that supports multiple different interfaces. It may not actually be possible to directly detect a line-card failure. Instead, a line-card failure may be inferred from the observation of multiple (or all) interfaces failing within that line-card. The events reported to the event management system are thus the individual interface failures; the originating event is the line-card failure and must be inferred through event correlation.

There are numerous commercial products available that implement alarm correlation for IP/MPLS networks, including HP's Operations Center (previously Open-View) [5], EMC's Ionix [6], and IBM's Tivoli [7]. The basic idea behind these tools is the notion of causal relationships – understanding what underlying events cause what symptoms. Building this model requires detailed real-time knowledge and understanding of the devices and network behavior, and of the network topology. Given that network topology varies over time, the topology must be automatically derived. An event correlation engine then uses the discovered causal relationships to correlate the event notifications received. However, how the products implement event correlation varies. Some tools use defined rules or policies to perform the correlation. The rules are defined as "if condition(s) then conclusion" – conditions relate to observed events and information about the current network state, while the conclusion here for any given rule is the correlated event. These rules capture domain expertise from humans and can become extremely complex.

The Codebook approach [8, 9] applies experience from graphs and coding to event correlation. A *codebook* is precalculated based on network topology and models of network elements and network behavior to model the *signatures* of different possible originating events. The event notifications received by an event management system implemented using codebooks are referred to as *symptoms*.

---

[1] Note that although root cause analysis is a term often used by event management system vendors, we prefer to use the term "event correlation" here, as root cause more generally implies a far more detailed explanation than can be provided by event management systems. More details are provided later in this chapter.

These symptoms are compared against the set of known signatures; the signature that best matches the observed symptoms is selected to identify the originating event.

Event signatures are created by determining the unique combination of event notifications that would be received for each possible originating event. This can be inferred by looking at the network topology and how components within a router and between routers are connected. A model of each router is (automatically) created – denoting the set of line-cards deployed within a router, the set of physical ports in existence on a line–card, and the set of logical interfaces that terminate on a given physical port. The network topology then indicates which interfaces on which line-cards on which routers are connected together to form links. In large IP/MPLS networks, such information is automatically discovered. Once the set of routers in the network is known (either through external systems or via autodiscovery), SNMP MIBs can be *walked* to identify all the interfaces on the router, and the relationships between interfaces (for example, which interfaces are on which port and which ports are on which line-card).

Given knowledge of router structure and topology, event signatures can be identified by examining which symptoms would be observed upon each individual component failure. To illustrate this, let us consider the simple four-node scenario depicted in Fig. 12.4. In this example, we consider what would be observed if line-card C1 failed on router 2. Such a failure would be observed on all of the four interfaces contained within the first line-card on router 2 (card C1), and also on interface I1 on port P1 and interface I1 on port P2 on card C1 of router 1, and on interface I2 on port P1 and interface I2 on port P2 on card C1 of router 3. These are all interfaces that are directly connected to interfaces on the failed line-card on router 2. If the failure of line-card C1 on router 2 were to happen, then alarms would be generated by the three routers involved and sent to the event management system. This combination of symptoms thus represents the *signature* of the line-card failure

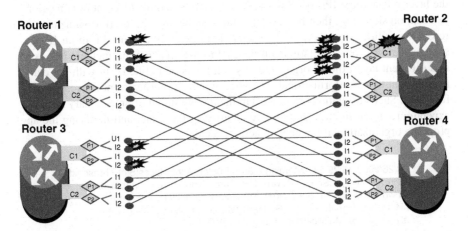

Fig. 12.4 Signature identification

on router 1. This signature, or combination of event notifications, is unique – if this is observed, we conclude that the incident relates to the failure of line-card 1 on router 2.

Let us now return to the SNMP traps provided in Fig. 12.3. This example depicted the traps sent by an ISP router *Router_A* to the event management system upon detecting the failure of a set of interfaces. Traps were sent corresponding to eight physical interfaces and two logical (multilink) interfaces – in this example, all of these interfaces connect to external customers, as opposed to other routers within the ISP. The ISP thus has visibility into only the local ISP interfaces (the ones reported in the traps in Fig. 12.3), and does not receive traps from the remote ends of the links – the ends within customer premises. Thus, the symptoms observed for the given failure mode are purely those coming from the one ISP router – nothing from the remote ends of the links as was the case for the previous example illustrated in Fig. 12.4. This set of received alarms is compared with the set of available signatures; comparison will provide a match between this set of alarms (symptoms) and the signature associated with the failure of a line-card (Serial4) on Router_A. The resulting correlated event output from the event management system identifies the line-card failure, and incorporates the associated symptoms (namely the individual interface failures). Figure 12.5 depicts an example log of the correlated event that would have been output by an event management system for this failure example. The format of the alarm log here is consistent with alarms generated by a production event management system. In this particular example, slot (line-card) Serial4 on Router_A was reported to be down. Supporting information included in the alarm log indicates that ten out of a total of ten configured interfaces on this line–card were down. This is a critical alarm, indicating that immediate attention was required.

Correlation can also be used across layers or across network domains to effectively localize events for more efficient troubleshooting. Consider the example illustrated in Fig. 12.6. Let us consider an example of a fiber cut – this occurs in the layer one (L1) network, which is used to directly interconnect two routers. If the layer one and the IP/MPLS networks are maintained by different organizations (a common situation), then there is little that can be done in the IP organization to repair the failure. However, the IP routers both detect the issue. From an IP perspective, cross-layer correlation can be used to identify that the incident occurred in a different layer; the IP organization should thus be notified, but with the clarification that this is informational – another organization (layer one) is responsible for repair. Such correlations can save a tremendous amount of unnecessary resource expenditure, by accurately and clearly identifying the issue, and notifying the appropriate organization of the need to actuate repair.

03/26/2009 15:25:28: Incoming Alarm: Router_A:Interfaces|Slot Threshold Alarm: Router_A:Serial4 Down. There are 10 out of 10 interfaces down. Down Interface List: Serial4/0/0, Serial4/0/1, Serial4/1/0/3:0, Serial4/1/0/4:0, Serial4/1/0/5:0, Serial4/1/0/23:0, Serial10/1/0/24:0, Serial10/1/0/25:0, Multilink6164, Multilink6168|Critical

Fig. 12.5 Correlated event associated with the traps illustrated in Fig. 12.3

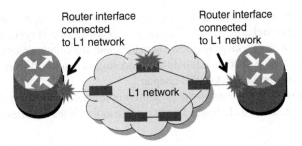

Router interface
connected
to L1 network

Router interface
connected
to L1 network

L1 network

Fig. 12.6 Cross-layer correlation

The correlated (originating) event output by the event management system effectively identifies approximately where an event occurred and what type of event it was. However, this is still a long way from identifying the true root cause of an incident, and thus being able to rectify it. If we consider the example depicted in Fig. 12.4, event correlation is able to successfully isolate the problem as being related to line-card 1 on router 2. However, we still need to determine how and why the line-card failed. Was the problem in hardware or software? What in the hardware or software failed and why? Tremendous work is still typically required before reaching true issue resolution. Assuming that human investigation is required, this is achieved by automatically opening a ticket.

12.2.3 Ticketing

Tickets are used to notify operations personnel of events that require investigation, and to track ongoing investigations. Tickets are at the heart of troubleshooting network events, and record actions taken and their results.

If the issue being reported has been detected within the network, then the tickets are automatically opened by the event management systems. However, if the issue is, for example, first reported by a customer before it has been detected by the event management systems, then the ticket will likely have been opened by a human, presumably the customer or a representative from the ISP's customer care organization.

The tickets are opened with basic information regarding the event at hand, such as the date, time, and location of where the issue was observed, and the details of the correlated events and original symptoms that triggered the ticket creation. From there, operations personnel carefully record in the ticket the tests that they execute in troubleshooting the event, and the observations made. They record interactions with other organizations, such as operations groups responsible for other technologies in the network, or employees from equipment manufacturers (vendors). Clearly, carefully tracking observations made while troubleshooting a complex issue is critical for the person(s) investigating. Moreover, the tickets also serve the purpose of allowing easy communication about investigations across personnel, such as between the network management team and the customer service team, or to hand off across, say, a change of shift.

Once an investigation has reached its conclusion and the issue has been rectified, the corresponding ticket is closed. A resolution classification is typically assigned, primarily for use in tracking aggregate statistics and for offline analysis of overall network performance. Network reliability modeling is discussed in more detail in Chapter 4 and in Section 12.4 of this chapter.

Tickets provide the means to track and communicate issues and their current status. However, the real challenge lies in troubleshooting these issues.

12.2.4 Troubleshooting

Troubleshooting a network issue is analogous to being a private investigator – hunting down the offender and taking appropriate action to rectify the issue. Drilling down to root cause can require keen detective instincts, knowing where to look and what to look for. Operations teams often draw upon vast experience and domain knowledge to rapidly delve into the vast depths of the network and related network data to crystallize upon the symptoms, and theorize over potential root causes. This is often under extreme pressure – the clock is ticking; customer service may be impaired until the issue is resolved.

The first step of troubleshooting a network incident is to collect as much information about the event as possible that may help with reasoning about what is happening or has happened. Clearly, a fundamental part of this involves looking at the event symptoms and impact. The major symptoms are generally provided in the correlated event that triggered the ticket's creation. Additional information can be collected as the result of tests that the operator performs in the network during further investigation of the issue. This can also be complemented by historical data pulled from support systems or from analysis of actions taken previously within the network (e.g., maintenance activities) that could be related.

The tests invoked by the network operator range considerably in nature, depending on the type of incident being investigated. In general, they may include ping tests ("ping" a remote end to see if it is reachable), different types of status checks (executed as "show" commands on Cisco routers, for example), and on-demand end-to-end performance tests. In addition to information about the event, it may also be important to find out about potentially related events and activities – for example, did something change in the network that could have invoked the issue? This could have been a recent change, or something that changed a while ago, waiting like a ticking time bomb until conditions were ripe for a dramatic appearance.

Armed with this additional information, the network operator works toward identifying what is causing the event, and how it can be mitigated. In the majority of situations, this can be achieved quickly – leading to rapid, permanent repair. However, some incidents are more complex to troubleshoot. This is when the full power of an extended operations team comes into force.

Let us consider a hypothetical example to illustrate the process of troubleshooting a complex incident. In this scenario, let us assume that a number of edge routers across the network fail one after another over a short period of time. As these are the routers that connect to the customers, it is likely that the majority of customers connected to these routers are out of service until the issue is resolved – the pressure is really on to resolve the issue as fast as possible!

Given that we are assuming that routers are failing one after another, it takes two or more routers to fail before it becomes apparent that this is a cascading issue, involving multiple routers. Once this becomes apparent, the individual router issues should be combined to treat the event as a whole.

As discussed earlier, the first goal is to identify how to bring the routers back to being operational and stable so that customer service is restored. Achieving this requires at least some initial idea about the incident's underlying root cause. Then, once the routers have been brought back in service, it is critical to drill down to fully understand the incident and root cause so that permanent repair can be achieved – ideally permanently eliminating this particular failure mode from the network.

The first step in troubleshooting such an incident is to collect as much information as possible regarding the symptoms observed, identify any interesting information that may shed light on the trouble, and create a timeline of events detailing when and where they occurred. This information is typically collated from the alarms, alerts, and tickets, by running diagnostic commands on the router, and from information collected within the various collectors contained within the instrumentation layer. Syslogs provide a huge amount of information about events observed on network routers. This information is complemented by that obtained from route monitors and performance data collected over time, and from logs detailing actions taken on the router by operations personnel and automated systems.

The biggest challenge now becomes how to find something useful among the huge amount of data generated by the network. Operations personnel would painstakingly sift through all these data, raking through syslogs, examining critical router statistics (CPU, memory, utilization, etc.), identifying what actions were performed within the network during the time interval before the event, and examining route monitoring logs and performance statistics. Depending on the type of incident, and whether the routers are reachable (e.g., out of band), diagnostic tests and experimentation with potential actions to repair the issue are also performed within the network.

In a situation where multiple elements are involved, it is also important to focus on what the routers involved have in common and how they may be different from other routers that were not impacted. Are the impacted routers all made by a common router vendor, are they a common router model? Do they share a common software version? Are they in a common physical or logical location within the network? Do they have similar number of interfaces, or load, or anything that may relate to the issue at hand? Has there been any recent network changes made on these particular routers that could have triggered the incident? Are there customers that are in common across these routers? Identifying the factors that are common and those that are not can be critical in focusing into what may be the root cause of the issue at hand. For example, if the routers involved are from different vendors, then it is less likely to be a software bug causing the issue. And if there is a common customer associated with all the impacted routers, then it would make sense to look further into whether there is anything about the specific customer that may have induced the issue or contributed in some way. For example, was the customer making any significant changes at the time of the incident?

The initial goal is to extract sufficient insight into the situation at hand to indicate how service can be restored. Once this is achieved, appropriate actions can be taken to rectify the solution. However, in many situations, such as those induced by router bugs, the initial actions may restore service, but do not necessarily solve the underlying issue. Further (lengthy) analysis – potentially involving extensive lab reproduction and/or detailed software analysis – may be necessary to truly identify the real root cause. This is often known as *postmortem analysis*.

Large ISPs typically maintain labs containing scaled down networks containing the same types of hardware and software configurations as are operating in production. The labs provide a controlled environment in which to experiment without the risk of impacting customer traffic. The labs are used both to extensively test the hardware and software before it is deployed in the production network, and to understand issues as they arise in the production network. When it comes to troubleshooting issues, testers use the lab environment to reproduce the symptoms observed in the field, evaluate the conditions under which they occur and take additional measurements in a bid to uncover the underlying root cause. The lab environment is also often used to experiment with potential solutions to address the issue, and to certify solutions before they are deployed in the production network.

Detailed analysis of software and hardware designs and implementations can also provide tremendous insight into why problems are occurring and how they can be addressed. These are typically done by or in collaboration with the vendor in question.

12.2.5 Restore Then Repair

As discussed previously, recovering from an incident typically involves two goals: (1) restoring customer service and performance, and (2) fully resolving the underlying issue and returning network resources into service. These two goals may or may not be distinct – where redundancy exists, the network is typically designed to automatically reroute around failures, thus negating the need for manual intervention in restoring customer service. Troubleshooting and repair can instead focus on returning the failed network resources into service so that there is sufficient capacity available to absorb future failures. In other situations, customer service restoral and failure resolution may be one and the same. Let us consider two examples in more detail.

12.2.5.1 Core Network Failure

Consider the example of a fiber cut impacting a link between two routers in the core of an IP/MPLS network. IP network cores are designed with redundancy and

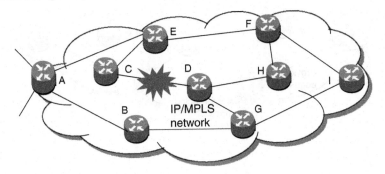

Fig. 12.7 Core network fiber cut

spare capacity, so that traffic can be rerouted around failed network resources. This rerouting is automatically initiated by the routers themselves – the exact details of which depend on the mechanisms deployed, as discussed in Chapter 2. In the example in Fig. 12.7, traffic between the routers E and D is normally routed via router C. However, in the case where the link between routers C and D fails, the traffic is then rerouted via F and H.

Assuming that the network has successfully rerouted all traffic without causing congestion, the impetus for rapidly restoring the failed resources is to ensure that the capacity is available to handle future failures and/or planned maintenance events. If, however, congestion results from the failure, then immediate intervention is required by operations personnel to restore the customer experience. Immediate action would likely be taken to reroute or load-balance traffic, in a bid to eliminate the performance issues while the resources are being repaired – for example, by tuning the IGP weights (e.g., OSPF weight tuning). In the example of Fig. 12.7, if there were congestion observed on, say, the link between routers F and H, then operations personnel may need to reroute some of the traffic via routers F, I, and G. Note that this requires that operations have an appropriate network modeling tool available to simulate potential actions before they are taken. This is necessary to ensure that the actions to be taken will achieve the desired result of eliminating the performance issues being observed.

In this example, permanent repair is achieved when the fiber cut is repaired. This requires that a technician travel to the location of the cut, and resplice the impacted fiber(s).

12.2.5.2 Customer-Facing Failure

Let us now consider the failure of a customer-facing line-card in a service provider's edge router. We focus on a customer that has only a single connection between the customer router and the ISP edge router, as illustrated in Fig. 12.8.

Cost-effective line-card protection mechanisms simply do not exist for router technologies today. Instead, providing redundancy on customer-facing interfaces requires that an ISP deploy a dedicated backup line-card for each working line-card.

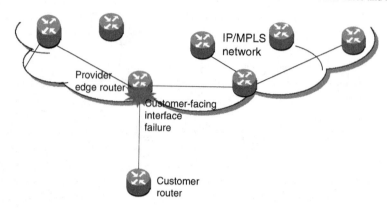

Fig. 12.8 Failure on customer-facing interface

However, this may be prohibitively expensive; instead customers that need higher reliability can choose a multihomed redundancy option where the customer purchases two separate connections to either a common ISP or two different ISPs. In situations where redundancy is not deployed and customers are not multihomed, a failure of the ISP router line-card facing the customer will result in the customer being out of service until the line-card can be returned to service.

If the line-card failure is caused by faulty hardware, the customer may be out of service until the failed hardware can be replaced, necessitating a rapid technician visit to the router in question. However, if the issue is in software, for example, service can potentially be restored via software rebooting of the line-card. Although this apparently fixes the issue and restores customer service, it is not a permanent repair. If this is likely to occur again, then the issue must be permanently resolved – the software must be debugged, recertified (tested) for network deployment, and then installed on each relevant router network-wide before permanent repair is achieved. This could involve upgrading potentially hundreds of routers – a major task, to say the least. In this case, the repair of the underlying root cause takes time, but is necessary to ensure that the failure mode does not occur again within the network. If the issue is extreme and a result of a newly introduced software release on the router, then the software may be "rolled back" to a previous version that does not suffer from the software bug. This can provide a temporary solution while the newer software is debugged.

12.3 Process Automation

The previous section described the basic systems and processes involved in detecting and troubleshooting faults and performance impairments. These issues often need to be resolved under immense time pressure, especially when customers are being directly impacted.

However, humans are inherently slow at many tasks. In contrast, computer systems can perform well-defined tasks much more rapidly, and are necessary to support the scale of a large ISP network. Although human reasoning about extremely complex situations is often difficult, if not impossible, to automate; automation can be used to support human analysis and to aid in performing simple, well-defined and repetitive tasks. This is referred to here as *process automation*.

Process automation is widely used in many aspects of network management, such as in customer service provisioning. Relevant to this chapter, it is also applied to the processes executed in network troubleshooting and even repair. Process automation in combination with the event filtering and correlation discussed in Section 12.2.2.1 are what enable a small operations team to manage massive networks that are characterized by tremendous complexity and diversity. The automation also speeds trouble resolution, thereby minimizing customer service disruptions, and eliminates human errors, which are a fact of life, no matter how much process is put in place in a bid to minimize them.

Over time, operations personnel have identified a large number of tasks that are executed repeatedly and are very time-consuming when executed by hand. Where possible, these tasks are automated in the process automation capabilities illustrated in the modified event management framework of Fig. 12.9.

The process automation system lies between the event management system and the ticketing system. One of its major roles is to provide the interface between these two systems – listening to incoming correlated events and opening, closing, and

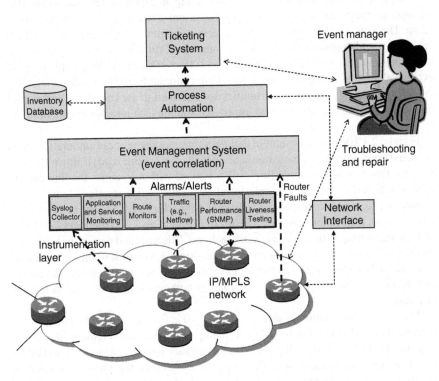

Fig. 12.9 Event management framework incorporating process automation

updating tickets. But rather than simply using the output of the event management system to trigger ticket creation and updates, process automation can take various actions based on network state and the situation at hand. The system implementing the process automation collects additional diagnostic information, and reasons about relatively complex scenarios before taking action. On creating or updating a ticket, the process automation system automatically populates the ticket with relevant information that it collected in evaluating the issue. This means that there is already a significant amount of diagnostic information available in the ticket as it is opened by a human being to initiate investigation into an incident. This can dramatically speed up incident investigation, by eliminating the need for humans to go out and manually execute commands on the network elements to collect initial diagnostic information.

The process automation system interfaces with a wide range of different systems to execute tasks. In addition to the event management and ticketing systems, a process automation system also interacts closely with network databases and with the network itself (either directly, or indirectly through another system). For example, collecting diagnostic information related to an incoming event will likely involve reaching out to the network elements and executing commands to retrieve the information of interest. This could be done either directly by the process automation system, or via an external network interface, as is illustrated in Fig. 12.9.

Process automation is often implemented using an expert system – a system that attempts to mimic the decision-making process and actions that a human would execute. The logic used within the expert system is defined by *rules* or *policies*, which are created and managed by *experts*. The number of rules in a complex process automation system is typically in the order of 100s–1,000s given the complexity and extensive range of the tasks at hand. Rules are continually updated and managed by the relevant experts as new opportunities for automation are conceived and implemented, processes are updated and improved, and the technologies used within the network evolve and change.

Figure 12.10 depicts an example that demonstrates the process automation steps executed upon receipt of a basic notification that a slot (or line card) is down (failed). A slot refers to where a single line card is housed within a router; the line-card in turn is assumed to support multiple interfaces. Each active interface terminates a connection to a customer, peer, or adjacent network router. As can be seen from this example, the system executes a series of different tests and then takes different actions depending on the outcome(s) of each test. The tests and actions executed are specific to the type of event triggering the automation, and also to the router model in question. Note that in this particular case, the router in question is a Cisco router, and thus Cisco command line interface (CLI) commands are executed to test the line-card.

The process automation example in Fig. 12.10 is for supporting the network operations team. This team is focused on managing the network elements and is not responsible for troubleshooting individual customer issues – those are handled by the customer care organization. Thus, a primary goal of the process automation in this context is to identify issues with network elements; weeding out individual

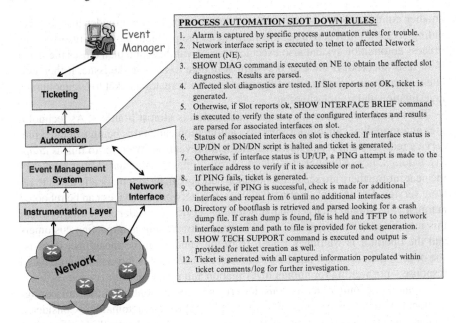

Fig. 12.10   Example process automation rule – router "slot down"

customer issues (and not creating tickets on them for this particular team). In this example of a customer-facing line-card with multiple customers carried on different interfaces on the same card, the automation ensures that there are multiple interfaces that are simultaneously experiencing issues, as opposed to being associated with a single customer. This makes it likely that the issue at hand relates to the line-card (part of the network), rather than the customer(s).

The results of the tests executed by the process automation system are presented to the operations team through the ticket that is created or updated. Thus, as an operations team member opens a new ticket ready to troubleshoot an issue, he/she is immediately presented with a solid set of diagnostic information, eliminating the trouble and delay associated with logging into individual routers and running these same tests. This significantly reduces the investigation time, the customer impact, and the load on the operations team.

In addition to ensuring that only relevant tickets are created, process automation also distinguishes between new issues and new symptoms associated with an existing, known problem. Thus, if a ticket has already been created for a current incident, when a new symptom is detected for this same ongoing event, the process automation will associate the new information with the existing ticket, as opposed to creating a new ticket.

For a more complex scenario, now consider a customer-initiated ticket, created either directly by the customer or by a customer's service representative. The process automation system picks up the ticket automatically and, with support from other systems, launches tests in an effort to automatically analyze the issue. If the system can localize the issue, it may either automatically dispatch workforce to the field or refer the ticket to the appropriate organization, which may even be another company (e.g., where another telecommunications provider may be providing access). On receiving confirmation that the problem has been resolved, the process automation system also executes tests to validate, and then closes the ticket if all tests succeed. If the expert system is unable to resolve the issue, it then collates information regarding the diagnostic tests and creates a ticket to trigger human investigation and troubleshooting.

The opportunity space for process automation is almost limitless. As technologies and modeling capabilities improve, automation can and is being extended into service recovery and repair and even incident prevention. We refer to this as *adaptive maintenance*. Although it is clearly hard to imagine automated fiber repairs in the near future, there are scenarios in which actions can be automatically taken to restore service. For example, network elements or network interfaces can be rebooted automatically should such action likely restore service. Consider one scenario where this may be an attractive solution – a known software bug is impacting customers and the operator is waiting for a fix from the vendor; in the meantime, if an issue occurs, then the most rapid way of recovering service is through the automated response – not waiting for human investigation and intervention.

As another example, let us consider errors in router configurations (misconfigurations), which can be automatically fixed via process automation. Consider a scenario where regular auditing such as that discussed in Chapter 9 identifies what we refer to as "ticking time bombs" – misconfigurations that could cause significant customer impact under specific circumstances. These misconfigurations are automatically detected, and can also be automatically repaired – the "bad" configuration being replaced with "good" configuration, thereby preventing the potentially nasty repercussions.

While adaptive maintenance promises to greatly reduce recovery times and eliminate human errors that are inevitable in manual operations, a flawed adaptive maintenance capability can create damage at a scale and speed that is unlikely to be matched by humans. It is thus crucial to carefully design and implement such an adaptive maintenance system, and ensure that safeguards are introduced to prevent potentially larger issues from arising with the wrong automated response. Meticulous tracking of automated actions is also critical, to ensure that automated repair does not hide underlying chronic issues that need to be addressed. However, even with these caveats and warnings, automation often offers an opportunity for far more rapid recovery from issues than a human being could achieve through manually initiated actions.

The value of automation throughout the event management process (from event detection through to advanced troubleshooting) is unquestionable – reducing millions of event notifications to a couple of hundred or fewer tickets that require human investigation and intervention. This automation is what allows a small network operations team to successfully manage a massive network, with rapidly growing numbers of network elements, customers, and complexity.

12.4   Managing Network Performance Over Time

The event management systems discussed in Section 12.2 and 12.3 primarily focus on real-time troubleshooting of *individual* large network events that persist over extended periods of time, such as link failures, or recurring intermittent (chronic) flaps on individual links. However, this narrow view of looking at each individual event in isolation risks leaving network issues flying under the event management radar, while potentially impacting customers' performance.

Let us consider an analogy of financial management within a large corporate or government organization. In keeping a tight reign over a budget, an organization would likely be extremely careful about managing large transactions – potentially going to great lengths to approve and track each of the individual large purchases made across the organization. However, tracking large transactions without considering the broader picture can result in underlying issues flying under the radar. A single user's individual transaction may appear fine in isolation, but analysis over a longer time interval may uncover an excessively large number of such transactions – something that may justify further investigation. Focusing only on the large transactions, and allowing smaller transactions to proceed without attention allows the system to scale – it would simply be impractical to have each individual request approved, independent of its cost. However, if no one is tracking the bottom line – the total expenditure – it may well be that the small expenditures add up considerably, and could lead to financial troubles in the long run. Instead, careful tracking of how money is spent across the board is critical, characterizing at an aggregate level how, where, and why this money is spent, whether it is appropriate and (in situations where money is tight) where there may be opportunities for reductions in expenditure. New processes or policies may well be introduced to address issues identified. However, this can only be seen with careful analysis of longer-term spending patterns covering both large and small expenditures.

Returning to the network, carefully managing network performance also requires examining network events holistically – exploring series of events – large and small – instead of purely focusing on each large event in isolation. The end goal is to identify actions that can be taken to improve overall network performance and reliability. Such actions can take many forms, including software bug fixes, hardware redesigns, process changes, and/or technology changes.

An important step toward driving network performance is to carefully track performance over time, with periods of poor performance identified so that intervention can be initiated. For example, if it is observed that the network has recently been demonstrating unacceptably high unavailability due to excessive numbers of line-card failures, then investigation should be initiated in an effort to determine why this is occurring, and to take appropriate actions to rectify the situation. However, we do not need to wait for performance to degrade – regular root cause analysis of network impairments can identify areas for improvements, and potentially even uncover previously unrecognized yet undesirable network behaviors that could be eliminated. For example, consider a scenario where ongoing root cause analysis of network packet loss uncovered chronic slower-than-expected recovery times in the face of network failures. Once identified, efforts can be initiated to identify why this is occurring (router software bug?, hardware issue?, fundamental technology limitations?), and to then drive either new technologies or enhancements to existing technologies into the network to permanently rectify this situation.

Tracking network performance over time and drilling into root causes of network impairments typically involves delving into large amounts of historical network data. Exploratory Data Mining (EDM) is thus used to complement real-time event management through detailed analysis across large numbers of events, identifying patterns in failures and performance impairments and in the root causes of these network events. However, this is clearly a challenging goal; the volumes of network data are tremendous, the data sources are very diverse, and the patterns to be identified can be complex.

12.4.1 Trending Key Performance Indicators (KPIs)

So let us start by asking a seemingly simple question – how well is my network performing? The first step here is to clearly define what we mean by network performance, so that we can provide metrics that can be evaluated using available network measurements. We refer to these metrics as *Key Performance Indicators*, or *KPIs*.

When tracking how well the network is performing, it is important to ensure that metrics obtain a view that is as close as possible to what customers are experiencing. However, how well the network is performing is in the eye of the beholder – and different beholders have different vantage points, and different criteria. Some applications (e.g., e-mail or file transfers) are extremely resilient to short outages while others, such as video, are extremely sensitive to even very short-term impairments. Thus, KPIs need to capture and track a range of different performance metrics, which reflect the diversity of applications being supported. KPIs should track application measures, such as the frequency and severity of video impairments that would be observable to viewers. However, network-based metrics are also critical, particularly in networks where there is a vast array of different applications being supported. Thus, KPIs should include, but not be limited to, metrics tracking network availability (DPM – see Chapter 3 for details), application performance, and end-to-end network performance (packet loss, delay, and jitter).

KPIs can also capture noncustomer-impacting measures of network health, such as the utilization of network resources. These provide us with the ability to track network health before we hit customer-impacting issues. There are many limited resources in a router – link capacity is an obvious one; router processing power and memory are two other key examples. Link capacity is traditionally tracked as part of the capacity management process discussed in Chapter 5, and is therefore not discussed further here. However, router CPU and memory utilization – both on the router's central route processor and on individual line-cards – are also limited yet critical resources that are often less well analyzed than link capacity. One of the most critical functions that the central route processor is responsible for is control-plane management – ensuring that routing updates are successfully received and sent by the router, and that the internal forwarding within the router is appropriately configured to ensure successful routing of traffic across the network. Thus, the integrity of the network's control plane is very much dependent on router CPU usage – if CPUs become overloaded with high-priority tasks, the integrity of the network control plane could be put at risk. Router memory is similarly critical – if memory becomes fully utilized within a router, then the router is at risk of crashing, causing a nasty outage. Thus, these limited resources must be tracked to ensure that they are not approaching exhaust either over the long-term, or over shorter periods of time.

KPIs must be measurable – thus, a given KPI must map to a set of measurements that can be made on an ongoing basis. Availability-based KPIs can be readily calculated based on logs from the event management system and troubleshooting analyses. Chapters 3 and 4 discuss availability modeling and associated metrics; they are thus not discussed further here.

Application-dependent performance metrics can be obtained through extensive monitoring at the application level. Such measurements can be implemented either using "test" measurements executed from sample devices strategically placed across the network (active measurements), or by collecting statistics from network monitors or from user devices where accessible (passive measurements). Such application measurements are a must for networks that support a limited set of critical applications – such as an IPTV distribution network. However, it is practically impossible to scale this to every possible application type that may ride over a general-purpose IP/MPLS backbone, especially if application performance depends on a plethora of different customer end devices.

Instead, end-to-end measurements of key network performance criteria, namely packet loss, delay, and jitter, are the closest general network measures of customer-perceived network performance. These measurements provide a generic, application-independent measure of network performance, which can (ideally) be applied to estimate the performance of a given application.

End-to-end packet loss, delay, and jitter would likely be captured from an end-to-end monitoring system, such as described in Chapter 10 and [10]. In an active monitoring infrastructure, for example, large numbers of end-to-end test probes are sent across the network; loss and delay measurements are calculated based on whether these probes are successfully received at each remote end, and how long they take to be propagated across the network. From these measurements, network loss, delay, and jitter can be estimated over time for each different source and destination pair tested. By aggregating these measures over larger time intervals, we can calculate a set of metrics, such as average or 95th percentile loss/delay for each individual source/destination pair tested. These can be further aggregated across source/destination pairs to obtain network-wide metrics. However, how loss is distributed over time can really matter to some applications – a continuous period of loss may have greater (or lesser) impact on a given application than the same total loss distributed over a longer period of time. KPIs can thus also examine other characteristics of the loss beyond simple loss rate measurements – for example, tracking loss intervals (continuous periods of packet loss). Metrics that track the number of "short" versus "long" duration outages may be used to characterize network performance and its impact on various network-based applications.

Ideally, end-to-end measurements should extend out as far to the customer as possible, preferably into the customer domain. However, this is often not practical – scaling to large numbers of customers can be infeasible, and the customer devices are often not accessible to the service provider. Thus, comprehensive end-to-end measurements are often only available between network routers, leaving the connection between the customer and the network beyond the scope of the end-to-end measurements. Tracking performance at the edge of the ISP network thus requires different metrics. One popular metric is BGP flap frequency aggregated over different dimensions (e.g., across the network, per customer, etc.). However, it is important to note that by definition the ISP/customer and ISP/peer interfaces cross trust domains – the ISP often only has visibility and control over its own side of this boundary, and not the customer and peer domains. It is actually often extremely challenging to distinguish between customer/peer-induced issues and ISP-induced issues. Thus, without knowing about or being responsible for customer and peer activities on the other side of trust boundaries, BGP event measures and other similar metrics can be seriously skewed. A customer interface that is flapping incessantly can significantly distort these metrics, making it extremely challenging to distinguish patterns that may be attributed to the ISP.

Once we have defined our key metrics, we can then track how these change over time. This is known as *trending*. Trending of KPIs is critical for driving the network to higher levels of reliability and performance, and for identifying areas and opportunities for improvement. The goal is to see these KPIs improve over time, corresponding to network and service performance improvements. However, if KPIs turn south, indicating worsening network and service conditions, investigation would likely be required. KPIs can thus be used to focus operations' attention to areas that need most immediate attention.

Let us consider a simple example of end-to-end loss. If the loss-related KPIs (e.g., average loss) degrade, then investigation would be required to understand the underlying root cause(s) and to (hopefully) initiate action(s) to reverse the negative trend. Obviously, the actions taken depend on the root cause(s) identified – but could include capacity augments, elimination of failure modes (e.g., if loss may be introduced by router hardware or software issues), or may even require the introduction of a new technology, such as faster failure recovery mechanisms.

Careful tracking of KPIs over time can also enable the detection of anomalous network conditions – thereby detecting issues that may be flying under the radar of the event management systems described in Section 12.2. Let us consider an example where the rate of protocol flaps has increased within a given region of the network. The individual flaps are too short to report on – each event has cleared even before a human can be informed of it, let alone investigate. Thus, the real-time event management system would only detect an issue if the number of flaps occurring during a given time duration and in a given location exceeds a predefined threshold, upon which the flapping is defined to be chronic. If the number of flaps on individual interfaces does not cross this threshold, then an aggregate increase in flaps across a region may go undetected by the event management system. However, this aggregate increase could be indicative of an unexpected condition, and be impacting customers. It would thus require investigation.

Careful trending and analysis of KPIs can also be used to identify new and improved event signatures, which can be incorporated in the real-time event management system discussed in Section 12.2. These new signatures are designed to better detect individual events that should be reported to operations personnel. The identification of new signatures is a continual process, typically leveraging the vast and evolving experience gained by network operators as they manage the network on a day-to-day basis. However, this human experience can be complemented by data mining. It is far from easy to specify what issues should be reported amidst the mound of performance data collected from the routers. For example, under what conditions should we consider CPU load to be excessive, and thus alarm on it to trigger intervention? At what point does a series of "one off" events become a chronic condition that requires immediate attention?

Individual performance events used to trigger event notifications are typically detected using simple threshold crossings – an event is identified when the parameter of interest exceeds a predefined value (threshold) for a given period of time. However, even selecting this threshold is often extremely challenging. How bad and for how long should an event persist before operations should be informed for immediate investigation? Low level events often clear themselves; if we are overly sensitive at picking up events to react to, then we risk generating too many false alarms, causing operations personnel to spend most of their time chasing false alarms and risking them missing the critical issues among the noise. If we are not sensitive enough, then critical issues may fly under the radar and not be appropriately reacted to in a timely fashion. Analysis of vast amounts of network data can be key to selecting suitable thresholds so as to carefully manage the rate of false positives and false negatives. However, note that the thresholds selected may not actually be constant values – in some cases they could vary over time, or may vary over different parts of the network. Thus, it may actually be sensible to have these thresholds be automatically learned and adjusted as the network evolves over time.

Simple thresholding techniques can also be complemented by more advanced anomaly detection mechanisms. For example, consider a router experiencing a process memory leak. In such a situation, the available router memory will (gradually) decrease – the rate of decrease being indicative of the point at which the router will hit memory exhaust and likely cause a nasty router crash. Under normal conditions, router memory utilization is relatively flat; a router with a memory leak can be detected with a nonzero gradient in the memory utilization curve. Predicting the impending issue well in advance provides network operations with the opportunity to deal with the issue before it becomes customer impacting. These are known as *predictive alerts*, and can be used to nip a problem in the bud, thereby entirely preventing a potentially nasty issue. Again, detailed analysis of vast amounts of data is required to identify appropriate anomaly detection schemes, which can accurately detect issues, with minimal false alerts. There is a vast array of publications focused on anomaly detection on network data [11–15], although much of the work focuses on traffic anomalies.

12.4.2   Root Cause Analysis

KPIs track network performance; they do not typically provide any insight into what is *causing* a condition or how to remediate it. However, driving network improvements necessitates understanding the root cause of recurring network issues – potentially down to the smallest individual events.

Characterizing the root causes of network events (e.g., packet loss) and then creating aggregate views across many such events can enable insights into the underlying behavior of the network and uncover opportunities for longer-term improvements. However, investments made in improving network performance should ideally be focused on the opportunities with the greatest impact. By quantifying the contribution of different root causes for a given type of recurring network event (e.g., packet loss), a network operator can identify the most common root causes, and focus energies on addressing these. In the case of packet loss, for example, if a significant portion of the loss was determined to be congestion-related, then additional network capacity may be required. If significant loss was alternatively attributed to a previously unidentified issue within the network elements (e.g., routers), then the response will ideally involve actions that could permanently eliminate the issue. A Pareto analysis [16, 17] is a formal technique used to guide this process – it evaluates the benefits of potential actions, and identifies those that have the maximal possible impact.

Troubleshooting individual network events was discussed in detail in Section 12.2.4. To identify the root causes of a class of events, such as hardware failures, packet losses, or protocol flaps, we need to drill down into multiple individual events in a bid to come up with the best explanation of their likely root causes. Root cause analysis here is similar to that described in Section 12.2.4 – with a couple of important distinctions. Specifically, we are typically examining large numbers of individual events, as opposed to a single large event, and we are typically examining historical events, as opposed to real-time events.

As with troubleshooting individual real-time issues, root cause analysis of recurring events typically commences with a detailed analysis of available network data. Scalable data mining techniques are key to effectively making the most of the wealth of available data, given the large number of events generally involved, and the diversity of possible root causes. But data mining alone does not always reveal the underlying root cause(s) – especially in scenarios where anomalous network conditions or unexpected network behaviors are identified. Instead, such analysis would be complemented by targeted network measurements, lab reproduction, and detailed software and/or hardware analysis.

Targeted network measurements can be used to complement the regular network monitoring infrastructure in situations where the general monitoring is insufficiently fine-grained or focused to provide the detailed information required to troubleshoot a specific recurring issue. Obtaining additional measurements – particularly when trying to capture recurring events with very short symptoms (e.g., short bursts of packet losses) – may involve establishing an ad hoc measurement infrastructure or augmenting an existing infrastructure to make targeted measurements pursuant to the issue being investigated. For example, when troubleshooting a recurring issue related to router process (CPU) management, very fine-grained CPU measurements may be temporarily obtained from a small subset of network routers through targeted measurements (e.g., recording measurements every 5 seconds instead of every 5 minutes). Such measurements could not be obtained across the entire network on an ongoing basis (simply due to scale), but could be critical in getting to the bottom of an elusive recurring issue. As another example, if malformed packets are causing erroneous network behavior, then detailed inspection of specific traffic carried over a network link could identify what this traffic is and where it is coming from, information which is likely to be critical to troubleshooting the issue. However, such measurements are not going to be collected on a regular basis; they simply do not scale and are too targeted to a specific issue. Note also that targeted measurements will likely need to be taken during the occurrence of an event of interest – which could be challenging to capture for an intermittent issue with very short symptoms (e.g., short bursts of packet loss). But once such measurements are available, they can complement the regularly collected data and be fed into the network analyses.

Lab testing and hardware/software analysis to troubleshoot recurring issues are similar to that discussed in Section 12.2.4 for troubleshooting individual issues. However, lab testing and detailed software/hardware analysis are more often than not immense and extremely time-consuming efforts, which should not be entered into lightly. It is thus critical to glean as much information from available network data as possible to effectively guide these other efforts. EDM techniques are at the heart of this. We thus return our focus to how we can effectively use EDM in analyzing recurring network conditions.

12.4.2.1   Data Integration

Constructing a good view of what is happening in a network requires looking across a wide range of different data sources, where each data source provides a different perspective and insight. Manually pulling all these data together and then applying reasoning to hypothesize about an individual event's root cause is excessively challenging and time-consuming. The data are typically available in a range of different tools, as depicted in Fig. 12.11. These tools are often created and managed by different teams or organizations, and often present information in different formats and via different interfaces. In the example in Fig. 12.11, performance data collected from SNMP MIBs is accessed via one web site, router syslogs may be obtained from an archive stored on a network server, a different server collates workflow logs, and end-to-end performance data are available in yet another web site. Thus, manually collecting data from all these different locations and then correlating it to build a complete view of what was happening in any given situation can be a painstaking process, to say the least. This situation may be further complicated in scenarios that involve multiple network layers or technologies, which are managed by different organizations. It is entirely possible that information across network layers/organizations is only accessible via human communication with an expert in

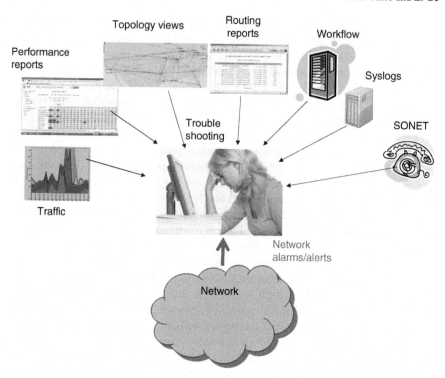

Fig. 12.11 Troubleshooting network events is difficult if data are stored in separate "data silos"

the other organization. For example, obtaining information about lower-layer network performance (e.g., SONET network) may involve reaching out via the phone to a layer one specialist. Of course, different data sources also use different conventions for timestamps (e.g., different time zones) and in naming network devices (e.g., router names may be specified as IP addresses, abbreviated names, or use domain name extensions). These further compound the complexity of correlating across different data sources. Thus, analyzing even a single event could potentially take hours by hand – simply in pulling the relevant data together. This is barely practical when troubleshooting an individual event, but becomes completely impractical when troubleshooting recurring events with potentially large numbers of root causes. However, it has historically been the state of the art.

Data integration and automation is thus absolutely critical to scaling data mining in support of root cause analysis. It would be difficult to overstate the importance of data integration: making all the relevant network and systems data readily accessible. The data should be made available in a form that makes it easy to correlate significant numbers of very diverse data sources across extended time intervals. AT&T Labs have taken a practical approach to achieving this [18] – collecting data from large numbers of individual "data silos" and integrating them into a common

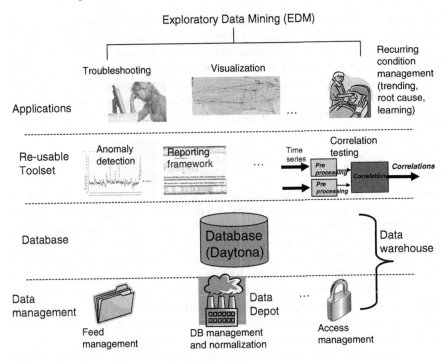

Fig. 12.12 Scaling network troubleshooting and root cause analysis

database. Above this common database is a set of tools and applications. This architecture is illustrated in Fig. 12.12. Scalable and automated feed management and database management tools [19, 20] are used to amass data into a common infrastructure and to load data into a massive data warehouse. The data warehouse archives data collected from various configuration-, routing-, fault-, performance-, and application-measurement tools, across multiple networks. Above the data warehouse resides a set of scalable and reusable analysis and reporting modules, which provide core capabilities in support of various applications. These components include a reporting engine (used for making data and more complex analyses available via web reports to end-users), anomaly detection tools, and different correlation capabilities (rules-based correlations and techniques for correlation testing and learning [18, 21, 22]). Above the reusable components lie a rapidly expanding set of data mining applications – ranging from web reports designed simply to expose the data to operations through a set of integrated data browsing and visualization tools, through to sophisticated trending reports and advanced statistical correlation testing and automated learning for root cause analysis [18].

The key to the infrastructure is scale – both in terms of the amount and the diversity of the network data being collated, and the range of different applications being supported. One of the key ingredients to achieving this is simple normalization of the incoming data, which is performed as the data are ingested into the database.

This normalization ensures, for example, that a common time zone is used across all data sources, and common naming conventions are used to describe network elements, networks, etc. By performing data normalization and preprocessing as the data is ingested into the database, it removes the burden and corresponding complexity of continual data conversions by applications and human users alike. Although an enormous undertaking, such an infrastructure enables scale in terms of the very diverse analyses that can be performed [18–22].

12.4.2.2 Scaling Root Cause Analysis

So let us now return to the challenge of scaling root cause analyses for a series of recurring events. We specify these events as a time series, referred to as a "symptom time series." This time series is characterized by temporal and spatial information describing when and where an event was observed and event-specific information. For example, a time series describing end-to-end packet loss measurements would have associated timing information (when each event occurred and how long it lasted), spatial information (the two end points between which loss was observed) and event-specific information (e.g., the magnitude of each event – in this case, how much loss was observed). Note that the infrastructure depicted in Fig. 12.12 allows such a time series to be formed using a simple database query.

The most likely root cause of each of our symptom events is then identified by correlating each event with the set of diagnostic information (time series) available in the data warehouse. Domain knowledge is used to specify which events should be correlated and how. If we consider our packet loss example, then we would correlate loss observations with events such as congestion, traffic reroutes, and internal router conditions known to cause loss. The correlations would be constrained to those which could have caused each observed loss event – namely those events along the path of the traffic experiencing the loss. The analysis then effectively becomes an automation of what a person would have executed – taking each symptom event in turn and applying potentially very complex rules to identify the most likely explanation from within the mound of available data. Aggregate statistics can then be calculated across multiple events, to characterize the breakdown of the different root causes. Appropriate remedies and actions can then be identified. Again, the data infrastructure depicted in Fig. 12.12 makes scaling this root cause analysis far more practical, as the root causes are typically identified from a wide range of different data sources; a common data warehouse with normalized naming conventions ensures that the analysis infrastructure does not need to be painfully aware of the data origins and conventions.

However, it is often far from clear as to what all the potential causes or impacts of a given set of symptom events are. Take, for example, anomalous router CPU utilization events. Once CPU anomalies are defined (a challenge unto itself), we are then faced with the question of what *causes* these anomalous events, and what *impacts* – if any – do they have. Causes and impacts can also be further categorized as "expected" versus "unexpected." For example, we may know a priori to expect that a given router upgrade would result in an increase in average router CPU, or that other newly implemented features or services may increase CPU load. In contrast, unexpected causes of CPU anomalies may include software bugs or improper router configuration changes. As to impact – CPU anomalies should not result in any customer impact. If they have gotten to the point where routing protocols are timing out, for example, then immediate attention is imperative. However, identifying that such impact is occurring among the enormous number of ongoing events that are observed in large-scale networks is far from an easy task.

Domain knowledge can be heavily drawn upon in identifying potential causes and impacts – network experts can often deduce from both knowledge of how things should work and from their experience in operating networks to create an initial list. However, network operators will rapidly report that networks do not always operate as expected nor as desired – routers are complicated beasts with bugs which can result in behaviors that violate the fundamentals of "networking 101" principles. Examination of real network data, and lots of them, is necessary to truly understand what is really happening.

Domain knowledge can be successfully augmented through EDM, which can be used to automatically identify these relationships – specifically, to *learn* about the root causes and impacts associated with a given event time series of interest. Such analyses are instrumental in advancing the effectiveness of network analyses, both for troubleshooting recurring conditions and revealing issues that are flying under the radar. Although there are numerous data mining techniques available [23, 24], one approach that is being applied within AT&T Labs is to identify relationships or correlations between different time series and across different spatial domains [21, 22]. This approach identifies those time series that are *statistically* correlated with a given symptom time series; these are likely to be the root causes or impacts of the time series of interest (the symptoms). However, given the enormous set of time series and potential correlations involved here, domain knowledge is generally necessary to guide the analysis – where to look and under what spatial constraints to correlate events (e.g., testing correlations of events on a common router, common path, common router interface). When looking for anomalous or unexpected correlations, the real challenge is in defining what is normal/desired behavior and what is not.

Let us consider another hypothetical example here, this time to illustrate how we can use statistical correlation testing to automatically identify the root causes of a particular recurring event – in this case, BGP session flaps (where the BGP session goes down and then comes up again shortly afterwards). We focus here on the connectivity between customers and an ISP – specifically, between a customer router (CR) and a provider edge router (PER). In particular, we focus on customers who use the BGP routing protocol to share routes with the ISP, and thus establish a BGP session between the CR and the PER. BGP may be used here, for example, in the case where customers are multihomed; in the event of a failure of the link between the CR and PER, BGP reroutes traffic onto an alternate route.

The physical connectivity between the CR and PER is provided over metropolitan and access networks as illustrated in Fig. 12.13. These networks in turn may be

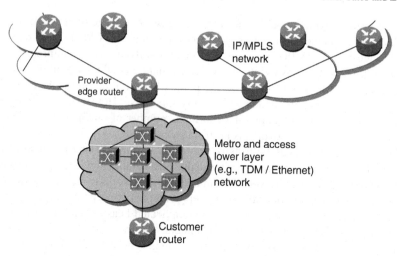

Fig. 12.13 Customer – ISP access

made up of a variety of layer one and layer two technologies (see Chapter 2). We refer to these as the lower-layer networks. These metro/access networks often have built-in mechanisms for rapidly and automatically recovering from failures. Thus, in these situations, failure recovery mechanisms may exist at both the upper layer (through BGP rerouting) and the lower layers. It is highly desirable to ensure that failure recovery is not invoked simultaneously at both layers [25]. This is achieved in routers today using timers – the IP routers are configured with a delay timer designed to allow the lower layer to attempt to recover from an issue first. If the lower layer restores connectivity within the defined timeout (e.g., 150 ms), then the routers do not react. However, if the lower layer fails to recover from the issue within the de-fined time interval, then the routers will attempt to restore service at the IP layer.

We can use correlation testing to help us investigate the potential root causes of BGP session flaps between PERs and CRs. Specifically, we can test the statistical correlation between the symptom time series (BGP session flaps) and a wide range of other time series, which correspond to a variety of other network events. We refer to these other events as *diagnostic events*. The goal is to identify those diagnostic time series that are statistically correlated with our symptom time series (BGP ses-sion flaps). However, rather than testing all possible time series across the entire network (an impractically large number of time series), we typically constrain our correlations to those in the same locality. In this case, we examine events either on the same router or on the same router interface as the BGP session flaps. Our diagnostic symptoms can be drawn from a range of different sources – workflow commands, router syslogs, lower-layer events, router performance events (e.g., high CPU, memory utilization, link loads, packet losses) and so on. The primary result of the correlation testing is a list of time series that are statistically correlated to the BGP session flaps; the idea being that these will reveal the root causes and impacts of the BGP session flaps.

So now let us consider a situation in which there is an underlying issue such that BGP sessions flap even when lower-layer failure recovery mechanisms rapidly recover from failures. This breaks the principle of layered failure recovery used here – as discussed, recovery actions at the lower layer should prevent IP links and BGP sessions between routers from failing during these events. Thus, domain knowledge would conclude that lower-layer failure recovery actions would not be related (correlated) to BGP session flaps. However, in the scenario we consider here, correlation testing would expose that the BGP session flaps are often occurring at the same time as lower-layer failure recovery events associated with the same link between the PER and the CR – more often than could be explained as pure coincidences. This would be revealed via strong statistical correlation between BGP flaps and failure recovery events on the corresponding lower layer – a correlation that violates normal operating behavior, and is indicative of erroneous network behavior. Correlation testing is in essence revealing that the network is not operating as designed – reality differs from intent. Erroneously failing the IP layer link and corresponding BGP session results in unnecessary customer impact – instead of seeing a few tens of milliseconds break in connectivity as the lower-layer recovery is performed, the customer may now be impacted for up to a couple of minutes. Also note the need here to bring in spatial constraints – we are explicitly interested in behavior happening across layers for each individual link between a PER and a given CR – it is this correlation that is not expected and indicates undesirable network behavior. It is entirely expected that failure recovery on a given PER – CR link correlates with BGP flaps on other links. This would be a result of a common lower-layer failure impacting both IP links that use lower-layer failure recovery mechanisms and those which do not. Those IP links without lower-layer recovery would experience the failure, causing their associated BGP session to fail. However, those with lower-layer failure recovery should not experience any impact on the higher layer protocols. Thus, the BGP failures on the links without failure recovery correlate with the lower layer failure recovery on the other, seemingly independent, links. This highlights the complexity here and the need for detailed domain knowledge and carefully designed spatial models in executing and analyzing correlation results.

Thus, statistical correlation testing can be used to expose failure modes that might otherwise go undetected, yet cause significant customer impact over time. Statistical correlation testing can also be used to delve deeper into network behavior, once revealed. For example, correlation testing can be used to identify how the strong correlation between BGP session flaps and lower-layer recovery events varies across technologies. Does it only exist for certain types of lower-layer technologies or certain types of router technologies (routers, line-cards)? If the same behavior is observed across lower-layer technologies from multiple vendors, then it is unlikely to be the result of an erroneous behavior in the lower-layer equipment (for example, slower than designed recovery actions). If, however, the correlation exists for only a single type of router, then it would be highly advisable to look closer at the given router type for evidence of a software bug that could explain the observed behavior. Thus, analysis of what is common and what is not common across the symptom observations can help in guiding troubleshooting. Targeted lab testing and detailed software analysis can then follow so that the underlying cause of the issue can be identified and rectified, with the intent that the failure mode will be permanently driven out of the network.

In general, the opportunity space for EDM is tremendous in large-scale IP/MPLS networks. The immense scale, complexity of network technologies, tight interaction across networking layers, and the rapid evolution of network software mean that we risk having critical issues flying under the radar, and that network issues are extremely complex to troubleshoot, particularly at scale. Driving network performance to higher levels will necessitate significant advances in applying data mining to the extremely diverse network data. This is an area ripe for further innovation.

12.5 Planned Maintenance

The previous sections focused on reacting to events and issues as they are identified. However, a large portion of the activity in a large operational network is actually a result of planned events. Managing a large-scale IP/MPLS network indeed requires regular planned maintenance – the network is continually evolving as network elements are added, new functionality is introduced, and hardware and software are upgraded. External events, such as major road works, can also impact areas where fibers are laid, and thus necessitate network maintenance.

There are two primary requirements of planned maintenance: (1) successfully complete the work required, and (2) minimize customer impact. As such, planned network maintenance is typically executed during hours when the expected customer impact and/or the network load is at its lowest. This typically equates to overnight and early hours in the morning (e.g., midnight to 6 a.m.). However, the extent to which customers would be impacted by any given planned maintenance activity also depends on the location of the resources being maintained, and what maintenance is being performed. Redundant capacity would be used to service traffic during planned maintenance activities – where redundancy exists, such as in the core of an IP network. However, as discussed in Section 12.2.5, such redundancy does not always exist and thus some planned maintenance activities can result in a service interruption. This is most likely to occur at the edge of an IP/MPLS network, where cost-effective redundancy is simply not available within router technologies today.

12.5.1 Preparing for Planned Maintenance Activities

Competing planned maintenance activities occurring across multiple network layers in a large ISP network could be a recipe for disaster, if not carefully managed. Meticulous preparation is thus completed in advance of each and every planned maintenance event, ensuring that activities do not clash, and that there are sufficient network and human resources available to successfully complete the scheduled work. Planning for network activities involves careful scheduling, impact assessment, coordination with customers and other network organizations, and identifying appropriate mechanisms for minimizing customer impact. We consider these in more detail here.

Scheduling of planned maintenance activities often requires juggling of a range of different resources, including operations personnel and network capacity, across different organizations and layers of the network. For example, in an IP/MPLS network segment where lower-layer network recovery does not exist, planned maintenance within the lower layer will likely impact the IP/MPLS network. If this is within the core of an IP/MPLS network (i.e., between ISP routers), the impacted IP/MPLS traffic will be rerouted, requiring spare IP network capacity. This same network capacity could also be required if, for example, IP router maintenance should occur simultaneously. This is illustrated in Fig. 12.14, where maintenance is required both on the link between routers C and D (executed by layer one technicians) and on router H (executed by layer 3 technicians). Much of the IP/MPLS traffic normally carried on the link between routers C and D may normally reroute over to the path E–F–H in the event of the link between C and D being unavailable. However, should router H also be unavailable (e.g., due to simultaneous planned maintenance), then this alternate path would not be available. The traffic normally carried on the link between routers C and D, and that normally carried via router H would all be competing for the remaining network resources. This has the potential to cause significant congestion and corresponding customer impact. This is clearly not an acceptable situation – the two maintenance activities must be coordinated so that they do not occur simultaneously, unless the network has adequate resources to successfully support them both. Thus, careful scheduling of planned maintenance within and across network layers is crucial. Such scheduling also necessitates carefully constructed processes to communicate and coordinate maintenance activities across organizations managing the different network layers.

However, how can a network operations team determine whether there are sufficient network resources to successfully execute planned maintenance activities with

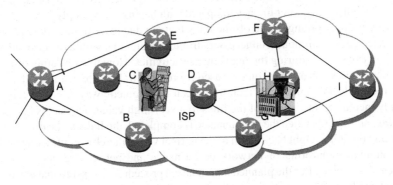

Fig. 12.14 Competing planned maintenance activities on a network link (between routers C and D) and a router (router H)

minimal customer impact? This is particularly complicated within the IP/MPLS core, where it is a nontrivial task to predict where and how much traffic will be rerouted in response to network events. Detailed "what if" simulation tools that can emulate the planned maintenance activities are key to ensuring that adequate resources are available for planned and unplanned activities. Such tools are used to evaluate the impact of planned activities in advance of the scheduled work, taking into account traffic, topology, planned activities, and ideally current network conditions. In situations where the planned maintenance activities would cause unacceptable impact, the simulation tools can also be used to evaluate potential actions that can be taken to ensure survivability (e.g., tweaking network routing).

If the planned maintenance is instead occurring at the provider edge router (the router to which customers connect), then it may be necessary to coordinate with or at least communicate the planned maintenance to the impacted customers. This is an especially important step when serving enterprise customers, who may need to make alternate arrangements during such activities. This communication is typically done well in advance of the planned activities – often many weeks. If the work needs to be repeated across many edge routers, as may occur when upgrading router software network-wide, then human resources must also be scheduled to manage the work across the different routers. This can become a relatively complex planning process, with numerous constraints.

12.5.2 Executing Planned Maintenance

Planning for scheduled maintenance activities generally occurs well in advance of the scheduled event, ensuring adequate time for customers to react and for internal network survivability evaluations to be completed. Maintenance can proceed after a successful last-minute check of current network conditions. However, service providers go to great lengths to carefully manage traffic in real time so as to further minimize customer impact. In locations where redundancy exists, such as in the core of the IP/MPLS network, gracefully removing traffic away from impacted network links in advance of the maintenance can result in significantly smaller (and potentially negligible) customer impact compared with having links simply fail while still carrying traffic. Forcing traffic off the links that are due to be impacted by planned maintenance also eliminates unnecessary traffic reroutes that would result should the link flap excessively during the maintenance activities. How this rerouting of traffic is achieved depends on the protocols used for routing traffic. For example, if simple IGP protocols are alone used, then traffic can be rerouted away from the links by simply increasing the weight of the links to a very high value. This act is known as *costing out* the link. Once the maintenance is completed, the link can be *costed in* by reducing the IGP weight back down to the normal value, thereby re-attracting traffic.

Continual monitoring of network performance and network resources is also critical during and after the planned maintenance procedure, to ensure that any unexpected conditions that arise are rapidly detected, isolated, and repaired. Think about taking your car to a mechanic – how often has a mechanic fixed one problem only to introduce another as part of their maintenance activities? Networks are the same – human beings are prone to make mistakes, even when taking the utmost care. Thus, network operators are particularly vigilant after maintenance activities, and put significant process and automated auditing in place to ensure that any issues that may arise are rapidly detected and addressed. For example, in the previously discussed scenario where links are costed out before commencing maintenance activities, it is critical that monitoring and maintenance procedures ensure that these network resources are successfully returned to normal network operation after completion of the maintenance activities. Accidentally leaving resources out of service can result in significant network vulnerabilities, such as having insufficient network capacity to handle future network failures. Additionally, for the larger-scale planned upgrades mentioned earlier, KPIs need to be monitored against expected impacts both during and after deployment. Undesired results, such as unexpectedly high CPU loads, can then be quickly investigated. Other unexpected results, such as a slow memory leak due to a bug in newly deployed software, may not be immediately apparent but can be detected through appropriate monitoring.

12.6   The Importance of Continued Innovation

The past 10 years or so have seen tremendous improvements in IP/MPLS network fault and performance management. However, there are still opportunities for exciting innovations. We herein outline a few directions in which we believe that further advances in the state of the art promise great operational benefits.

Router reliability remains an important area where innovation is needed. Although dramatic improvements have been achieved in recent years, router failures and maintenance are still the dominant cause of customer service outages. Router technologies must evolve to allow router software to be upgraded without impacting customers, to effectively manage control plane resources in the presence of overload conditions, and to support hardware monitoring and cost effective redundancy [26, 27] so that outage durations are minimized. Improvements in these areas depend on a combination of technical disciplines including real-time software systems, software engineering, as well as an increased emphasis on hardware "design for maintainability."

As demonstrated in earlier sections within this chapter, service providers have typically mastered the detection, troubleshooting, and repair of commonly occurring faults and performance impairments. However, the same cannot always be said for dealing with the more esoteric faults and performance issues. Significant advancements are crucial in detecting issues that "fly under the radar," and in troubleshooting complex network issues. Both of these present opportunities for advanced exploratory data mining. Tools for effectively and rapidly aiding in troubleshooting complex issues are particularly lacking; significant innovation is well overdue here. This is primarily because it is a challenging problem and one most understood by the small teams of highly skilled engineers to which such issues are escalated. These teams work in a demanding environment – each new line of investigation may be different from previous ones, and may (at least initially) defy understanding. Operations personnel, while under tremendous pressure, have to sift through immense quantities of data from diverse tools, collect additional information, and theorize over potential root causes. Arming these teams with appropriate data analysis tools for best achieving this is a challenging but necessary advancement. Significantly advancing the state of the art here will likely require a melding of data mining experts and network experts.

As a final topic, we consider process automation – specifically, how far can we and should we proceed with automating actions taken by operations teams? As highlighted in Section 12.3, process automation is already an integral part of at least some large ISP network operations. The ultimate goal may well be to fully automate common fault and performance management actions, closing the control loop of issue detection, troubleshooting, mitigation strategy identification and evaluation, and actuation of the devised responses in the network (e.g., rerouting traffic, repairing databases, fixing router configurations). There are vast opportunities for innovation in identifying new scenarios for such automated recovery and repair of both networks and supporting systems (e.g., databases, configuration). As such cases are revealed and proposed, it will undoubtedly often be challenging to replicate the complex logic that humans execute in identifying courses of actions to mitigate network issues, particularly dealing with the "corner cases" that arise in large networks. Creating appropriate safeguards to prevent potentially catastrophic actions should flawed reasoning be introduced into the system is also a challenge that must be addressed.

12.7 Conclusions

In this chapter, we described a wide range of network management and operational tasks designed to ensure that ISP networks operate at high levels of reliability and performance. We have organized these network operation activities into three threads, each serving a conceptually different purpose, although they overlap in practice. The first thread included a series of operations covering monitoring network health and service performance, detecting and notifying operations of fault and performance issues, localizing and troubleshooting issues, problem mitigation and service restoration, and finally repair and restoration of the impacted network resources. These tasks are typically handled in a "real-time" fashion, as they involve an ongoing service impact, pressing for immediate care. The second thread focused on offline exploratory data analysis for driving continued performance improvements. This includes defining and monitoring key performance indicators, conducting trending analyses to track network performance and health over time, applying root cause analysis and data mining to uncover underlying issues, conducting targeted measurement and lab testing to pinpoint the problem, and finally driving the problem out of the network where possible. These tasks are less time-pressured. However, they are often more complex as they require advanced analytic systems and experienced operations personnel to quickly focus on the anomalous network behaviors deeply hidden among a vast amount of network data.

While the first two threads deal with detecting and reacting to events that occur within the network and service, the third thread focused on planned events – activities that operations execute to maintain and evolve the network. These planned maintenance activities involve replacing equipment, upgrading software, and deploying new hardware and network capabilities. The major challenges in planned maintenance lie in the careful planning and preparation for planned events, and the prudent execution of these tasks such that customer impact is minimized.

We conclude with some final "best-practice" principles for both fault and performance management, and planned maintenance.

Fault and performance management "best-practice" principles for large IP/MPLS networks:

- Incorporate network management requirements whenever new technologies are being introduced – do not make network measurement, fault and performance management an afterthought
- Develop a comprehensive fault and performance data collection infrastructure
- Carefully design network alarms and alerts to ensure that network issues are rapidly detected and appropriate notifications are generated
- Deploy a scalable event management system, which effectively filters and correlates the onslaught of network alarms to rapidly isolate network issues
- Deploy a ticketing system, which is tightly integrated with the event management and process automation systems. The ticketing system is used to notify operations personnel of events requiring investigation, and to track analyses and final root cause
- Automate commonly executed operations tasks to speed issue resolution and free up staff for more complex tasks – but be careful and incorporate appropriate safeguards to protect the network
- Arm network operations teams with the necessary tools, network measurements, and skills for troubleshooting network issues
- Create and utilize lab environments for replicating and troubleshooting issues observed within the operational network
- Build close partnerships between vendors for collaborative troubleshooting of network events, particularly those related to vendor equipment
- Work closely with network engineering teams to ensure that automatic failure recovery is available where possible – this can (1) improve service availability through rapid failure recovery, and (2) remove the need for operations to respond in real time. Planned maintenance can then be scheduled at a convenient time
- Dedicate expert staff to ongoing analysis of recurring problems, and bring their learning back into the mainstream management systems

- Track and trend element-level and end-to-end key performance indicators over time – both those that indicate customer impact (e.g., network loss, delay, key service-level metrics) and those associated with network health (e.g., router CPU, memory utilization)
- Create scalable root cause analysis techniques and processes for investigating recurring performance issues
- Data integration: create a scalable infrastructure for exploratory data mining – where data can be readily accessed and correlated across multiple diverse time series.

Planned maintenance "best-practice" principles for large IP/MPLS networks:

- Instantiate processes that ensure that human beings "think twice" as they are touching the network to avoid unnecessary mistakes
- Plan and schedule maintenance activities carefully to minimize customer impact, including scheduling activities across network layers and across network organizations where necessary
- Execute careful validation of planned activities to ensure that there is sufficient spare network capacity to absorb load during core network maintenance
- Validate network state before executing planned maintenance to ensure that maintenance is not executed when the network is already impaired
- Minimize customer impact by taking routers and network resources "gracefully" out of service where possible (e.g., within the network core)
- Provide appropriate customer notifications (e.g., to enterprise customers) of upcoming planned maintenance activities, so that customers have the opportunity to take proactive actions where necessary
- Suppress relevant network alarms during planned maintenance activities to avoid operations chasing events, which they are in fact knowingly inducing
- Carefully monitor network and service performance before, during, and after maintenance, ensuring that all resources and services are successfully returned to operation
- Validate planned maintenance actions after completion (e.g., verify router configurations) to ensure that the correct actions were taken and that configuration errors or other bad conditions were not introduced during the activities
- Ensure where possible that mechanisms are available for rapid back out of maintenance activities, should issues be encountered during maintenance activities.

Acknowledgments The authors thank the AT&T network and service operations teams for invaluable collaborations with us, their Research partners, over the years. In particular, we thank Bobbi Bailey, Heather Robinett, and Joanne Emmons (AT&T) for detailed discussions related to this chapter and beyond. Finally, we acknowledge Stuart Mackie from EMC, for discussions regarding alarm correlation.

References

1. Gerards, R. (2009). *The Syslog Protocol*. IETF. RFC 5424.
2. Della Maggiora, P., Elliott, C., Pavone, R., Phelps, K., & Thompson, J. (2000). *Performance and fault management*. Cisco Press.
3. Shaikh, A., & Greenberg, A. (2004). *OSPF Monitoring: Architecture, Design and Deployment Experience*. USENIX. Symposium on Networked Systems Design and Implementation (NSDI).
4. Mauro, D., & Schmidt, K. (2005). *Essential SNMP*. O'Reilly.
5. HP's Operations Center. [Online] https://h10078.www1.hp.com/cda/hpms/display/main/hpms_content.jsp?zn = bto&cp = 1–11–15–28^1745_4000_100__
6. EMC's Ionix platform. [Online] http://www.emc.com/products/family/ionix-family.htm.
7. IBM's Tivoli. [Online] http://en.wikipedia.org/wiki/IBM_Tivoli_Framework.
8. Kliger, S., et al. (1995). *A Coding Approach to Event Correlation*. Fourth International Symposium on Integrated Network Management. pp. 266–277.
9. Yemini, S., Kliger, S., Mozes, E., Yemini, Y., & Ohsie, D. (May 1996). High speed and robust event correlation. *IEEE Communications Magazine, 34*, 82–90.
10. Ciavattone, L., Morton, A., & Ramachandran, G. (June 2003). Standardized active measurements on a Tier 1 IP backbone. *IEEE Communications Magazine*, 41.
11. Barford, P., Kline, J., Plonka, D., & Ro, A. (2002). *A Signal Analysis of Network Traffic*. ACM Internet Measurement Workshop. pp. 71–82.
12. Huang, Y., Feamster, N., Lakhina, A., & Xu, J. (2007). *Diagnosing Network Disruptions with Network-Wide Analysis*. ACM Sigmetrics. *35*, pp. 61–72.
13. Lakhina, A., Crovella, M., & Diot, C. (2005). *Mining Anomalies Using Traffic Feature Distributions*. ACM SIGCOMM. Vol. 35, pp. 217–228.
14. Zhang, Y., Ge, Z., Greenberg, A., & Roughan, M. (2005). *Network Anomography*. ACM Usenix. Internet Measurement Workshop. pp. 317–330.
15. Venkataraman, S., Caballero, J., Song, D., Blum, A., & Yates, J. (2006). *Black Box Anomaly Detection: Is It Utopian?*. ACM 5th Workshop on Hot Topics in Networking (HotNets). pp. 127–132.
16. Tague, N. R. (1995). *The Quality Toolbox*. Amer Society for Quality.
17. Juran, J., & Gryna, F. (1998). *Juran's quality control handbook*. New York: McGraw-Hill.
18. Kalmanek, C., Ge, Z., Lee, S., Lund, C., Pei, D., Seidel, J., Van der Merwe, J., & Yates, J. (October 2009). *Darkstar: Using Exploratory Data Mining to Raise the Bar on Network Reliability and Performance*. Design of Reliable Communication Networks International Workshop.
19. Golab, L., Johnson, T., Seidel, J., & Shkapenyuk, V. (2009). *Stream Warehousing with Data Depot*. ACM SIGMOD.
20. Golab, L., Johnson, T., & Shkapenyuk, V. (2009). *Scheduling Updates in a Real-Time Stream Warehouse*. IEEE International Conference on Data Engineering (ICDE). pp. 1207–1210.
21. Mahimkar, A., Yates, J., Zhang, Y., Shaikh, A., Wang, J., Ge, Z., & Ee, C. (2008). *Troubleshooting Chronic Conditions in Large IP Networks*. Madrid, Spain: ACM International Conference on Emerging Network Experiments and Technologies (CoNEXT).
22. Mahimkar, A., Ge, Z., Shaikh, A., Wang, J., Yates, J., Zhang, Y., & Zhao, Q. (2009). *Towards Automated Performance Diagnosis in a Large IPTV Network*. ACM SIGCOMM.
23. Dasu, T., & Johnson, T. (2003). *Exploratory data mining and data cleaning*. Wiley.
24. Nisbet, R., Elder, J., & Miner, G. (2009). *Handbook of statistical analysis & data mining applications*. Academic.

25. Demeester, P., Gryseels, M., Autenrieth, A., Brianza, C., Castagna, L., Signorelli, G., Clemente, R., Ravera, M., Jajszczyk, A., Janukowicz, D., Van Doorselaere, K., & Harada, Y. (August 1999). Resilience in multilayer networks. *IEEE Communications Magazine, 37*, pp. 70–76.
26. Sebos, P., Yates, J., Li, G., Greenberg, A., Lazer, M., Kalmanek, C., & Rubenstein, D. (2003). *Ultra-Fast IP Link and Interface Provisioning with Applications to IP Restoration*. IEEE/LEOS Optical Fiber Communications Conference. pp. 557–558.
27. Sebos, P., Yates, J., Li, G., Rubenstein, D., & Lazer, M. (2004). *An Integrated IP/Optical Approach for Efficient Access Router Failure Recovery*. IEEE/LEOS Optical Fiber Communications Conference.

Glossary of Terms and Acronyms

Term	Definition
Fault management	Set of functions that detect, isolate, and correct faults in a telecommunications network
Fault	"Hard" failure (e.g., link down)
Performance management	Set of functions that detect, isolate, and correct performance issues in a telecommunications network
Performance events	Situations where a network element or the network is operating with degraded performance (e.g., packet loss, excessive delay)
Event management	Set of functions that detect, isolate, and correct events in a telecommunications network
Incident	An occurrence that affects normal network operation
Event	A fault or performance anomaly or impairment. A single incident may result in multiple events
Originating event	The event directly associated with a given incident, as opposed to being a side-effect or symptom of the incident
Alarm	Notification of a fault
Alert	Notification of a performance event (e.g., threshold crossing, traffic anomaly)
Event notification	Generic term covering alarms and alerts
Event correlation	Taking multiple incoming events (observations related to an incident) and correlating them to identify a single *correlated event* to capture the incident
Event management system	A system that collects incoming event notifications, and filters and correlates these to output correlated events
Correlated event	Output from the event correlation
Ticket	A document that is used to notify operations of an issue that requires investigation and to track the analysis performed in diagnosing the issue
Ticketing system	System that manages tickets
Event manager	A person who manages event resolutions

(continued)

Term	Definition
Troubleshooting	A form of problem-solving applied to diagnosing the underlying root causes of network impairments
Silent failure	A condition where network elements fail to detect and report an impairment
Black hole	Traffic is dropped (lost) within the network. Black holes are often associated with silent failures
Process automation	Automation of process-related tasks
Trending	Track how parameters of interest (e.g., KPIs) behave over time
Key performance indicators	Metrics designed to measure network performance and health
Root cause analysis	Identifying the root cause of network event(s)
Pareto analysis	Statistical technique in decision-making that is used to select a limited number of tasks that produce significant overall effect
Planned maintenance	Planned activities in the network, such as for upgrading hardware and software, scheduled hardware replacements, and network growth and evolution

Acronym	Definition
IP	Internet Protocol
MPLS	Multi-Protocol Label Switching
ISP	Internet Service Provider
ICMP	Internet Control Message Protocol
IPTV	Internet Protocol Television
IGP	Interior Gateway Protocol
OSPF	Open Shortest Path First
IS-IS	Intermediate System to Intermediate System
BGP	Border Gateway Protocol
CPU	Central Processing Unit
CRC	Cyclic Redundancy Check
SNMP	Simple Network Management Protocol
IETF	Internet Engineering Task Force
MIB	Management Information Base
DPI	Deep Packet Inspection
LDP	Label Distribution Protocol
PIM	Protocol-Independent Multicast
PPP	Point-to-Point Protocol
CR	Customer Router
PER	Provider-Edge Router
KPI	Key Performance Indicator
EDM	Exploratory Data Mining
DPM	Defects Per Million

Chapter 13
Network Security – A Service Provider View

Brian Rexroad and Jacobus Van der Merwe

13.1 Introduction

In keeping with the theme of this book, this chapter on security, explores the actual and potential impact of security threats and concerns on network stability and robustness. We specifically take a *service provider* centric view of network security by considering the actions a service provider can take to ensure the integrity of the network and to protect network services and users.[1] Many of the security concerns providers and network users face are related to the fundamental fact that networks are shared resources, and their purpose is to provide connectivity and the means of interaction between network users and devices. Unfortunately, this very functionality also provides the means for unwanted interaction and exploitation. As an enabler for communications, this puts service providers in a unique position to also protect users and inhibit traffic unwanted by the indended recipient. Indeed protection against some network security threats, such as distributed denial of service (DDoS) attacks, is near impossible to achieve without network support.[2] Further, security services are enhanced by being network aware and utilizing network derived intelligence.

Dealing with security threats in the network by necessity requires monitoring of network activity and in some instances interfering with, or blocking, unwanted traffic. Traffic monitoring and manipulation are both important issues that may have legal and regulatory implications. We acknowledge this tension and argue that "the

B. Rexroad (✉) and J. Van der Merwe
AT&T Labs, Florham Park, NJ 07932, USA
e-mail: brian.rexroad@att.com; kobus@research.att.com

[1] We explicitly use the term *service provider* to emphasize the fact that, in addition to Internet access, other internet protocol (IP) based networks (e.g., virtual private networks (VPNs)) and IP-based services (e.g., hosting, VoIP, IPTV, content distribution, etc.), all relate to the security concerns of a provider and are therefore considered in scope.

[2] The brute force nature of many DDoS attacks means that access links are often overwhelmed, which renders premises based protection mechanisms ineffective.

C.R. Kalmanek et al. (eds.), *Guide to Reliable Internet Services and Applications*,
Computer Communications and Networks, DOI 10.1007/978-1-84882-828-5_13,
© Springer-Verlag London Limited 2010

network", or more generically cyberspace, has become such a critical part of our society that finding workable solutions to these non-technical issues is critical.

Our goal for this chapter is to first serve as a practical guide by identifying best-practices and describing specific monitoring and mitigation mechanisms that can be utilized. Second, we hope to aid the reader in developing a framework or philosophy for dealing with security from the point of view of a service provider, i.e., understanding which problems are inherent to the current Internet architecture, protocol suite and trust model, understanding the incentives, strengths and weaknesses of different role players and developing strategies of where to spend resources going forward.

Covering the complete network security subject in a single chapter is not feasible, not even if the coverage is perfunctory. Indeed, many excellent security books have been written to cover specific subsets of network security problems and solutions. *As such we will largely focus on security from a service provider perspective given the current Internet architecture, set of protocols and business relationships.* Within this context we will cover security related procedures, mechanisms, tools and services that can be utilized by service providers to protect the network infrastructure as well as the services that it enables. In the final section of the chapter we will, however, deviate somewhat from this near term focus to offer a more forward looking perspective.

The outline of the chapter is as follows.

In Section 13.2 we provide an exposition of the underlying network security threats and their causes. Some underlying security causes are technical in nature, e.g., the Internet best-effort service model. Others are the result of current business practices (e.g., service providers being both retail competitors with each other, as well as interconnection partners) and indeed the development of nefarious uses such as spam, phishing, data theft, and DDoS related extortion, which are enabled by broad use of the Internet. Because a single exploit can often be successfully launched against many Internet users, the economic balance tends to be weighted in the favor of bad actors.

In Section 13.3 we present an overall framework for service provider network security. We discuss the seven pillars that make up this framework.

Having the means to know when there is a security threat or incident, and having the necessary information to then deal with the problem is fundamental to any security strategy. Section 13.4 addresses the importance of developing good network security intelligence. We articulate a strategy for monitoring of network activity and systems to maintain security awareness.

In Section 13.5 we present a number of operational network security systems used for the detection and mitigation of security threats. A significant challenge for any network-based security system is the need for scalability. We describe several highly scalable systems, covering informational, compulsory and supplementary security services.

We consider the role of security operations as an essential part of the broader network operations in Section 13.6.

Finally, in Section 13.7 we summarize important insights and then briefly consider important new and developing directions and concerns in network security as an indication of where resources should be focused both tactically and strategically.

13.2   What Is the Problem?

Despite, or perhaps because of, its undeniable success and utility, the Internet and all networks that derive from the Internet architecture and protocols, are suffering from a litany of security concerns. In the best case these concerns are annoying and impede progress. However, because of the ever increasing use of networks for virtually all aspects of modern society, in the worst case, these security concerns have potential to negatively impact economies and governments at a global scale.

Interestingly the Internet can trace it roots, in part, to a desire to create more secure communications systems [16,54]. Specifically, concerns for physical attacks against centralized control systems motivated the conception of distributed communication networks [16]. Consequently, there was a decision to prioritize availability of the network over confidentiality and integrity. These protections were left to the end user to consider.

This and other design goals were articulated in a retrospective paper on the design philosophy of the DARPA internet protocols [24]. In priority order the design goals for the Internet architecture were:

1. Internet communication must continue despite loss of networks or gateways.
2. The Internet must support multiple types of communications service.
3. The Internet architecture must accommodate a variety of networks.
4. The Internet architecture must permit distributed management of its resources.
5. The Internet architecture must be cost effective.
6. The Internet architecture must permit host attachments with low level of effort.
7. The resources used in the Internet architecture must be accountable.

Given that its roots were in the defense community, it is not surprising that robustness against physical loss ranked highest in this list. This external threat model is, however, quite different from current day attacks, which come from *use of* the network. These attacks exploit protocol and architectural characteristics of the network itself and therefore effectively constitute an internal threat model.

Further, while interworking between different network technologies was part of the architectural thinking right from the start, the Internet predecessors mostly interconnected closed groups of trusted users. The architecture that emerged offered communication on a *best-effort basis, specifically limited the amount of per-flow information that network elements are required to maintain, instead relying on end systems to do that [24], and did not require global operational control [54].*

While providing a highly scalable system that is robust against physical failure, these guiding principles are somewhat problematic from a network security perspective. Best-effort delivery significantly simplifies the network forwarding mechanics because the network does not have to be [overly] concerned about dropping packets, i.e., transport protocols (e.g., Transmission Control Protocol (TCP)) take care of reliable delivery from the edge of the network. The fact that end-systems are entrusted to maintain connection state in effect means that they become part of the implied network trust model. This works well when end-systems can be trusted and when all traffic being forwarded to a particular destination is *wanted* by that destination, as would be the case in a closed community of trusted users. However, when end-systems are malicious and generate *unwanted* traffic, the best-effort delivery and the lack of per-flow information in network elements effectively becomes a conduit for delivering denial-of-service (DoS) attacks. Indeed DoS attacks (or their close cousin distributed denial of service (DDoS) attacks), remain a fundamental problem for the current Internet.

The fact that IP source addresses are not authenticated and therefore easily spoofed, exacerbates the situation because the perpetrators of the attack are effectively untraceable and therefore unaccountable. The implication is that the final goal in the above list has never been achieved. Dealing with unwanted traffic provides a strong argument for the need of source authentication and accountability. However, some argue that such measures would result in easy identification of endpoints and by association users, to which some have expressed privacy concerns. Such identifiability concerns present an inherent tension that will have to be addressed in network architectures that provide strong accountability [76].

Obviating the need for global operational control and instead allowing for distributed management was a great equalizer which allowed networks with different levels of operational sophistication (among other differences) to be interconnected with relative ease. From a network security perspective, this lack of formal *operational* interworking hampers the ability of service providers to deal with major security incidents. Further, the volume of minor security concerns is such that providers are left to fend for themselves via local approaches, especially when the root of the problem originates from a remote network with whom the provider has no formal relationship nor a vested interest to assist.

In the remainder of this section we will elaborate on these issues by first examining both the stated and actual Internet threat model, as well as the somewhat implied trust model of the Internet. We then consider the role of security protocols before looking at the incentives of different role players in network security, illustrating that the economic balance is heavily biased in favor of bad actors. Finally, we briefly consider the fact that cyberspace has become a critical infrastructure which impacts virtually all aspects of society, well beyond its cyber limits.

Effectively dealing with many of the concerns identified in this section might require architectural changes to the Internet, or changes to well entrenched business practices, and as such is well beyond the scope of this chapter.

13.2.1 Threat Model

The Internet Engineering Task Force (IETF) is an open international community concerned with the operation and evolution of the Internet. All IETF documents are required to specifically address security and the IETF provides guidelines for this in RFC 3552 [67]. The Internet threat model as defined in RFC 3552 in essence states that: (i) End-systems are assumed to *not* be compromised and (ii) attackers *are* assumed to have near complete control over the communication channel over which communication takes place.

This threat model is clearly unrealistic. First, security vulnerabilities in operating systems and applications (e.g., browsers) result in end-systems that are in fact *routinely* compromised and unwittingly utilized for nefarious activities. Despite end-system security receiving significant attention by operating system vendors and communities, the openness of these platforms and the plethora of applications that it enables suggest that end-system vulnerability will continue to be a concern for the foreseeable future.[3] Software piracy, among other things, exacerbates this situation since pirated software typically will not be updated with vendor patches. Consequently, vulnerabilities remain which can be exploited by attackers. Further, the ease with which end users can be lured into installing malware themselves, e.g., by downloading and executing electronic postcards from illegitimate websites [48], suggests that the social engineering aspect of the problem might be the most difficult challenge.

Second, while complete control of the communication channel by attackers remains a possibility, this has in practice proved to be much more difficult and unusual. Yes, end-systems and network elements, such as routers, contain software that are subject to flaws and bugs and are therefore not inherently more secure than end-systems. However, in general, commercial network providers have a vested interest to be more cautious [than end users] when deploying new software and more vigilant in working with vendors to identify and correct vulnerabilities. After all, commercial providers' business not only depends on the network, it is the network.

More realistic threat assumptions, from a service provider point of view would be:

- End-points (broadly defined) can and will be compromised and used to launch attacks against the network, its users and the services it provides.
- Necessary precautions must be taken to ensure the security of network elements that are under control of the provider.

These assumptions lead to a threat model where everything outside the periphery of the provider network is assumed to be potentially hostile and untrustworthy, while the objective is to make everything inside the network to be secure and trustworthy.

This simplistic threat model is, however, only part of the picture. In the Internet any single provider is only part of a set of interconnected networks that

---

[3] Data from the National Vulnerability Database (nvd.nist.gov), show a 25-fold increase in the annual number of published software flaws across all software systems from 1997 to 2007.

provide end-to-end connectivity. Therefore, to enable the most basic communication services between arbitrary hosts on the Internet, a provider has to trust, to some extent, entities that are outside of its sphere of control. We consider this somewhat implied trust model next.[4]

13.2.2 Trust Model

There is, somewhat surprisingly, no formal trust model for the Internet. However, by virtue of providing the means to communicate between different parties and across networks operated by different organizations there is an implied trust model. This implied trust model is largely defined first by the business and functional relationships between all involved parties and second by the underlying architecture, protocols and technologies.

13.2.2.1 Business and Functional Relationships

The Internet is a largely unaffiliated and loosely coupled set of organizations that interwork to realize its functionality. As such, every organization involved in the end-to-end delivery of a packet has to be relied upon to do "the right thing":

- Network equipment are assumed to be configured correctly and operators are assumed to follow best practice guidelines.
- Network equipment software is assumed to operate correctly and be bug free.
- Protocol endpoints are assumed to be who they claim to be.
- Internet users are assumed to act in good faith.

We know that these assumptions are not realistic. Incorrect network configuration routinely result in network incidents. For example, in a well known YouTube hijacking incident, an attempt by Pakistan Telecom to locally block access to YouTube prefixes in effect resulted in YouTube traffic from all over the Internet being redirected to Pakistan [68]. Like all software systems, network equipment software often has bugs that could have security implications [4]. Finally, while the owners of most network endpoints do act in good faith, their computers might be controlled by those who do not. And as a result, the protocol endpoint could exploit the unauthenticated nature of the IP protocol to claim any identity.

Further, these business and functional relationships are transitive in the sense that end-customers have to trust their access providers. Access providers (might) have to trust higher tier providers. All providers have to trust other providers

---

[4] In cases where the complete end-to-end path is under control of a single provider, e.g., in the case of virtual private network (VPN) services provided by a single provider, the simplified threat and trust model hold, and this results in higher confidence levels of security of the communications.

(technically, autonomous systems (ASes)) along the path to the ultimate destination. This transitive trust exists despite the fact that formal business arrangements are typically limited to the closest neighbors in this chain.

13.2.2.2   Technology Drivers

At the most basic level, the Internet best-effort unaccountable service model implies that the network should trust end-users to not send unwanted traffic. We have already discussed the fallacy of this misplaced trust which enables denial of service attacks. The inherent and implied Internet trust model can be explored (from an end-user perspective) by means of the common-place action of downloading a Web page [38]. First, the domain name system (DNS) is trusted to correctly map the domain name in the Uniform Resource Locator (URL) of the Web page (e.g., the "www.att.com" part of http://www.att.com/index.jsp) into an IP address. Second, in establishing a TCP session with the Web page in question, the Internet routing system is trusted to route packets along the intended path between the browser and the server. Third, all intermediate network elements are trusted to faithfully convey packets in transit. Finally, the end-systems in this interaction, i.e., the user host (client) that runs the browser and the server that provides the content, are both trusted to not be compromised so that the content intended by the content owners/creators (and only that content) be displayed to the user.

Unfortunately none of the elements in this chain of trust is built on solid ground as each element is subject to inherent vulnerabilities.

DNS can provide no guarantees about the validity of domain name to IP address mappings [2, 13]. DNS as currently deployed does not have any strong security protection of messages and is thus subject to modification in transit like all unprotected Internet protocols. The request/response nature of DNS queries, the fact that most DNS queries are conducted as connectionless transactions, the relatively small message identification space (which can be guessed relatively easily), and the capability to perform source address spoofing on the Internet allow an attacker to provide bogus responses to legitimate requests. The hierarchical caching nature of the DNS architecture, means that these types of attacks are particularly problematic as the (bogus) response may be cached until the time-to-live field in the response expire, which would typically be set to a long time period by an attacker. In fact, an attacker may originate the query in an effort to poison the cache of DNS servers with bogus answers. This is a technique that has been used to redirect victims to phishing sites.

Internet routing protocols and in particular BGP provide no guarantees about the correctness or validity of routes [17]. BGP messages could be tampered with in transit as there are no per-message or per-session security mechanisms. More serious though, is the fact that there is no guarantee that a BGP speaker advertising a route to a particular destination is authorized to advertise that route, or in fact has a route to the destination, or would be forwarding packets to the destination if it has a valid path [20]. In particular, an attacker could *hijack* a prefix belonging to another AS, to either intercept the traffic en route to the actual destination, or to send traffic while taking the identity of the hijacked address space. This would, for example, allow address-based firewall filters to be bypassed. It has been reported that this technique is used by email spammers to temporarily create the appearance that their mail servers are associated with reputable organizations and evade filtering techniques [66].

TCP provides no guarantees about the actual identity of the system that terminates the TCP connection. For example, TCP connections are routinely terminated by intermediate devices such as Web proxies, although that is not necessarily an indication of malicious activity. Further, TCP does not ensure that content is not tampered with in transit.

Finally, end-system exploits allow the compromise of both clients and servers. With a compromised server, even if the TCP session is terminated on the intended server and is not tampered with in transit, it is possible that the content on the server itself might have been tampered with. Compromised server content might cause a client's communication to download both the intended content, but also unintended content (i.e., malware) from a malicious website. Alternatively, a compromised client may be fooled into unknowingly visiting and disclosing data to a malicious server. (This attack might also be perpetrated via DNS exploits even when the client system is not compromised.) Finally, a compromised client computer, which is generally operated by someone that is not an IT professional, can be used as a tool to perform other compromises, to generate unwanted traffic, to serve as relay points, as temporary illegitimate servers, etc.

13.2.2.3   Towards an Internet Trust Model?

In an ITU recommendation [43] that deals with network security, trust is defined as follows:

> Generally, an entity can be said to "trust" a second entity when it (the first entity) assumes that the second entity will behave exactly as the first entity expects. This trust may apply only for some specific function.

Underlying this definition is an assumption that the entities in question can be reliably identified to be who they claim to be, i.e., can be authenticated. Based on how this original authentication is performed, three major trust models have been articulated [7]:

- **Direct Trust**   where the two entities involved validate each other's credentials without relying on a third party.
- **Transitive Trust**   where trust between two entities is imputed by virtue of a third party, or parties, trusted by one of the entities in question, having validated and established an original trust relationship. I.e., A validates and trusts B, B validates and trusts C, therefore A trusts C without performing any validation.
- **Assumptive (or Spontaneous) Trust**   where there is no mandatory explicit validation of credentials.

Above we have argued that many of the implied trust assumptions regarding business/functional relationships and the underlying technology that makes the Internet work, are in fact very weak at best. I.e., with respect to the "trust" definition provided above, many entities cannot be assumed to behave in the expected way. It is also clear from this discussion that the relationships and dependencies are very complicated so that, perhaps, it is not too surprising that there is no well defined trust model for the Internet. Depending on the functionality being considered, elements of all three trust models defined above are present in the Internet. For example, considering the monetary relationships between participants, service providers typically have a direct trust relationship with their paying customers and with other providers. As such there is a transitive trust relationship with the customers of other providers. However, because of lack of accountability and associated controls, this monetary relationship may fail to influence the way traffic flows across the Internet, so that an assumptive trust model will in effect be operational.

Finally, while the above discussion might seem dire, we note that this assumptive trust model works reasonably well where incentives do align. Specifically, many service providers generally work hard to do well by each other, thereby ensuring that the aggregate behavior is good. As we address below, however, assumptive trust breaks down when incentives are not aligned.

13.2.3 Secure Protocols to the Rescue?

Given the deeply embedded nature of the business/functional relationship component of the trust model described above, it is imperative that solutions to the weaknesses in the technical part be found. Of course the security vulnerabilities described above are well known in the networking and systems communities and a variety of counter measures have been developed over many years. Unfortunately, while solutions or partial solutions exist, they lack deployment for a variety of reasons.

For example, DNSSEC [11], the secure version of DNS, will eliminate many of the current known DNS vulnerabilities [13], mature implementations are available and there exist operational experience from several DNSSEC trials. However, widespread adoption of DNSSEC has not yet happened. This is due, in part, to technical and operational concerns: (i) DNSSEC make use of public-key cryptographic signatures and as such will require significantly more resources than current DNS systems. (ii) DNSSEC is a much more complex protocol than DNS and will therefore require more sophisticated operational support. (iii) There is a chicken-and-egg dilemma where lack of widespread deployment means the usefulness of DNSSEC is diminished which in turn hinders further deployment.

In addition, some of the theoretical attributes of DNSSEC may exacerbate several important practical security considerations. For example, one of the techniques used by DNS providers to protect users from visiting malicious sites or joining a malicious botnet is using a technique called DNS Sinkhole [70]. When implementing a DNS Sinkhole, domain name resolution is overridden from the authoritative response. DNSSEC will interfere with this protection technique. Other examples include DDoS attacks toward or related to DNS services, such as DNS amplification attacks. These attacks are much more insidious and frequently occurring problem than DNS cache poisoning or spoofing [5]. Since DNSSEC requires more processing resources and also will create larger query responses, it has become a mechanism to facilitate or worsen similar types of attacks.

Of far greater concern, there are vetting or accountability concerns associated with the DNS registry. It is well known that many DNS registry entries are incorrect [79]. DNSSEC only validates that the resolution of a domain name to IP address is consistent with what the authoritative name servers intended. Bogus registry information allows attackers to use domain names for malicious purposes and remain unaccountable. DNSSEC does little, or nothing, to maintain any enforcement of registry accuracy or integrity. The threat that the registry providers themselves may be compromised remains. This suggests a need to both rein-in the hierarchy to some set of trusted authorities, establishing standards for identity and authority management for domain names, and setting security standards for management of the systems that maintain the assignments of fully qualified domain names (FQDNs) to IP addresses.

Ironically, the greatest stumbling block in DNSSEC deployment, however, has been the controversial issue of which entity, or entities, would be responsible for signing of the root zone and how the management of the key signing key would be handled [52,85]. These issues concern Internet governance which is well beyond the scope of this chapter. At the time of writing there appears to be increased pressure for these issues to be resolved to pave the way for DNSSEC deployment.[5]

The picture is somewhat less promising for finding an imminent solution to the security concerns of BGP. A number of comprehensive architectures have been proposed to deal with BGP security [32, 50, 61], however, there currently appears to be no consensus on which, if any, of these solutions will be adopted [20]. Similar to DNS, many of the proposed solutions assume the existence of an accurate routing registry which would provide information concerning organizations and the autonomous system (AS) numbers and prefixes that are allocated to them. Unfortunately current registries are known to be highly inaccurate and fixing that presents significant problems in itself. Similar to DNSSEC, there are concerns about the processing resources that would be required to accommodate strong security mechanisms. In the case of BGP this concern is exacerbated by the dramatic increase in the number of routes that BGP is required to handle, as well as the fact that the control processors of deployed routers might be lacking in processing power.

---

[5] This change might have been helped along by recent publicity around the so-called Kaminsky DNS vulnerability [88]. The vulnerability involves a DNS cache poisoning attack, where an attacker (i) fakes a DNS response, e.g., by guessing the transaction identifier in the response, and (ii) provide incorrect information in the additional section (or "glue" section) of the response. While this attack can be mitigated through security analysis of DNS activity, there is no inherent solution without a change in the DNS protocol itself [81].

In the absence of comprehensive security mechanisms for critical infrastructure services like DNS and BGP, end-to-end application level security mechanisms provide significant protection. Specifically, in the case of client/server Web interaction, the use of HTTP over a secure transport protocol (e.g., Transport Layer Security (TLS)), provide cryptographic protection for Web sessions as well as server authentication in the form of a digital certificate that is typically signed by a certification authority. Certification authorities provide different levels of monetary guarantees for different strengths of certificates, with correspondingly more stringent identity verification by the certification authority.

While secure protocols are clearly needed and can eliminate some of the more basic problems, ultimately, secure protocols do not make systems secure. For example, as described above, a modern browser on an uncompromised host will be able to verify the validity of certificate issued by a certification authority. However, with this approach the end user in effect trusts the certification authority to validate and vouch for the identity of the server, or more correctly the identity of the organization or individual who buys the certificate. Similarly DNSSEC will be able to authenticate that a response originated from an authoritative name server, but will ultimately depend on some form of identity verification to allow DNS mappings to be entered into the system in the first place. The trust put into these verification steps then becomes the weakest links in the overall security chain [28].

Finally, the security mechanisms themselves do not necessarily provide iron-clad protection. For example, the practical feasibility of generating fake certification authority certificates has recently been demonstrated [75]. This, in combination with falsified DNS or BGP entries, can direct users to counterfeit sites which closely resemble the real sites and trick the users into providing private information.

13.2.4   Motivations, Incentives and Economics

Having looked at the technical and functional properties that make networks vulnerable to abuse and attack, we now briefly consider the motivations and incentives of different role players.

There appear to be at least three motivations for malicious network behavior namely mischief, economic/financial and political/ideological, perpetrated respectively by script kiddies, hackers/criminals and nation states/cyber terrorists.

From the attacker's side, early attacks were often performed by technically savvy villains who carried out their deeds for the associated boasting rights, or indeed to attack some of their fellow villains in the cyber equivalent of turf wars [30].

It is clear that there has been a progression from these early mischievous acts to economically motivated cyber attacks and activities. The prevalence of spam email, while not a security threat in itself, is evidence of the "success" of questionable economic practices and is often also the entry point for more serious attacks such as identity theft. There is also evidence that social engineering attacks via well crafted email campaigns have become an effective means for botnet operators to replenish their armies [48].

Other evidence of an underground economy enabled by the Internet include the trading of compromised hosts [56] which are then enlisted in botnet armies and used to attack targets, often with economic consequences for the target. Alternatively, such botnets are used as part of extortion threats against targets where short disabling attacks are used to convince the target to pay money to prevent a repeat attack [25]. Other economic incentives for cyber related attacks include the theft of intellectual property and identity theft. For example, some bots are harvested and/or purchased with the objective of extracting personal data or to be used as access points into otherwise closed networks.

We note that a significant factor in the booming underground cyber economy relates to the fundamental economics of Internet communication which are very favorable towards villains. Specifically, botnets can be hired cheaply [36] which translates to very insignificant business costs related to these activities. Flat-rate service models and the resulting always on-line practices that it enable, mean that consumer systems are easy targets for botnet recruiting and users are less vigilant about monitoring their network usage.

This situation is exacerbated by the difficulty of effective law enforcement against cyber criminals, which often requires an arduous process of coordinating with law enforcement agencies in different parts of the world. This essentially means that cyber criminals can operate with very small investment and risk. It is also interesting to note that these economically motivated cyber criminals need the network to remain operational, or at least to remain operational to the level where it enables their objectives. I.e., they have no incentive to bring down the network as a whole.

While it is in the interest of economically motivated miscreants to keep the network operational, the same is not necessarily the case for politically or ideologically motived cyber crimes. An example concerns multiple massive cyber attacks against web sites in Estonia in 2007 [82]. These attacks severely disrupted Internet functions. And they continued and evolved for an extended period of time. These attacks followed street violence after actions by the Estonian authorities which proved highly controversial with Estonians of Russian decent. For this reason some feared state involvement or endorsement by Russia. No such linkage has been proved, however, the incident does serve to illustrate the vulnerability of the Internet, or parts thereof, to concerted efforts by those with extreme political and ideological motivations. This is unfortunately not an isolated incident as evidenced by similar more recent cases. For example, in August 2008 Georgia accused Russia of launching cyber attacks against Georgian web sites [29], and in January 2009 DoS attacks from computers in Russia were launched against Kyrgyzstan ISPs [55]. Again, no government involvement has been proven, however, the attacks did coincide with political tension between the countries.

Since service providers are commercial endeavors, their incentives to deal with network security are also highly influenced by the fundamental economics involved. For providers, the economics are a difficult balance between commercial viability, flexibility, resiliency, and capacity. For example, while in principle it is feasible to build a network with enough capacity to withstand DDoS attacks (or more generally to add mitigation technology to that effect), such a network would be economically infeasible to operate [84]. Further, service providers need to provide network services to enable the legitimate traffic on its network, which involves significant operational costs. At the same time there are very limited means to prevent any unwanted/illegitimate traffic from using the same resources. As we will show in the remainder of this chapter, one way in which this economic imbalance can be addressed, at least in part, is to offer opt-in network security services which users pay for. Indeed, security services, like other services provided by a service provider, are provided in a competitive commercial environment. Like other service offers, the business reason for such an investment is typically that it would provide a competitive advantage and thus attract customers. Some security services might be provided on a subscription basis, thus directly garnering paying customer. In other cases, security services might be provided on-demand, e.g., to protect a customer against a massive DDoS attack. In such cases having the ability to provide on-demand protection services differentiate providers in the competitive landscape.

13.2.5 Critical Infrastructure Cyber-Security Concerns

We have already mentioned the fact that "the network" has become a critical part of our everyday lives. The extent to which this is true is well articulated in this quote from a U.S. Department of Homeland Security report [27]:

Without a great deal of thought about security, the Nation shifted the control of essential processes in manufacturing, utilities, banking, and communications to networked computers. As a result, the cost of doing business dropped and productivity skyrocketed. A network of networks directly supports the operation of all sectors of our economy – energy (electrical power, oil and gas), transportation (rail, air, merchant marine), finance and banking, information and telecommunications, public health, emergency services, water, chemical, defense industrial base, food, agriculture, and postal and shipping. The reach of these computer networks exceeds the bounds of cyberspace, They also control physical objects such as electrical transformers, trains, pipeline pumps, chemical vats, and radars.

This dependency between cyberspace and real world objects is exemplified by the 2003 power blackout in the northeastern U.S. and Canada [80]. This event was not caused by a network problem, nor were there any malicious actors, and indeed many different factors contributed to the final outcome. However, software (and hardware) malfunction in the alarm system that was used, were found to have contributed to the outage. In a more direct cyber/physical security incident, which fortunately had no ill effect, the Slammer worm was responsible for taking monitoring computers offline at a nuclear power plant [64].

There was a time when telecommunications in the United States was a completely regulated business. This may have enhanced the ability of the Government to influence how the telecommunications infrastructure was engineered and operated to protect it as a critical national infrastructure component. Since the Cold War, deregulation and a highly competitive telecommunications market have evolved. Prices have fallen dramatically. Technology has evolved. Further, in a highly competitive environment where service providers are accountable to their shareholders, the ability of the government to easily influence the strategic direction of telecommunications may be more limited.

The robustness of services is defined by customer preferences and private business models that seek maximum return on investment. Markets for telecommunications services are some of the most competitive. Consequently, the robustness of the buildings, equipment, software, security measures, bandwidth overhead, testing, personnel training, and a myriad of other measures becomes a function of the price and quality standards demanded by customers.

Dealing with these concerns is well beyond the scope of this chapter. However, the potential impact on national and, by extension, international security suggests that it is important for all role players to carefully consider the reliance of modern society on the Internet and the role they should be playing to ensure its continued robust operation. The way to influence the robustness of services is through purchasing practices – best services are not necessarily the cheapest.

13.3   Service Provider Network Security

Network security for service providers consists of establishing a basic foundation for security implementation and correctly executing on the details. The network needs to be architected and configured in a way to resist the myriad of security threats it faces. Some lessons are learned from experience. And since security threats evolve over time, other lessons can be learned through observation of smaller evolving threats and establishing protection mechanisms on a broad scale to prevent those threats from becoming customer affecting.

In this section we describe a general framework for service provider network security. Specifically, we describe a framework for network security that has been developed over time by the AT&T security organization and articulates some of AT&T's philosophy to network security. We elaborate with some of the configuration and protection mechanisms that can be used to help protect the infrastructure. Since each network environment is unique and depends on the equipment used, the architecture, the customers or users of the network, defining specific configurations is out of scope for this text. However, use of the framework should provide a foundation from which a solid network security program can be established. Generally, the network needs to be configured to be secure against attacks and exploits that can be prevented or neutralized. Similarly, there will remain inherent shortcomings in network infrastructure such as weaknesses in BGP that need to be overcome or compensated for as part of the network security framework.

13.3.1 A Framework for Network Security

The AT&T framework for network security defines seven pillars: *Separation, Testing, Control, Automation, Monitoring, Response & Recovery and Innovation* [14].[6] These pillars build upon having established security policy standards, engineering best practices, as well as being informed of network management practices recommended by vendors and operator groups such as NANOG [3]. All of these pillars are inter-dependent; they are all inter-related to each other. As we discuss the seven pillars below, these co-dependencies will be apparent, illustrating how the true strength of the approach derives from the framework as a whole.

- **Separation** This fundamental security principle dictates that things that do not belong together be separated both in terms of network functionality and in terms of duties performed by service provider personnel.
- **Testing** Testing and certification of all network elements and services, both before and after deployment, is crucial to ensure the functionality is as expected.
- **Control** The network needs to assure that authorized operators are the only ones in control of the network. Operators also need the ability to control the network both in terms of how traffic flows through the network and how the network is protected against protocol and architectural vulnerabilities.
- **Automation** The scale and complexity of provider networks, as well as the consistency and timeliness of actions compel automation of as many aspects as possible.
- **Monitoring** Measuring and monitoring network health, changes, and activity at different levels of granularity and from different viewpoints give operators insight into the normal and anomalous behavior of elements and traffic on the network.
- **Response and Recovery** Knowing what attacks and threats traffic or penetration attempts present to the network is of limited utility unless operators also have the necessary tools, mechanisms, and procedures to respond and mitigate the threats. In order to react to sometimes fast developing security events, 24/7 security analysis and remediation operations are required with well developed execution plans.
- **Innovation** Given the continually evolving nature of networking in general and networking security threats in particular, require a reciprocal continuous investment by providers in innovation to ensure robust and secure operation of their networks.

We now consider each pillar in turn.

---

[6] Note that the service provider context implies a broader operational approach compared to the more traditional CIA security principles of *confidentiality, integrity and availability*. For example: both *control* and *response* takes into account the need for dynamics in managing the security of a network, *separation* not only helps to maintain confidentiality of traffic on the network, but also helps to provide assurance of network management functions.

13.3.1.1 Separation

The *separation* principle finds application along several dimensions in a provider network. Two major categories are *separation of traffic* traversing the network and *separation of duties* involved in operating the network.

Separation of Traffic Traffic separation is used to maintain priority of various traffic types on the core network. Multi-protocol Label Switching (MPLS) technology provides a powerful capability to provide traffic separation on the network core. Separation of management (i.e., network command and control) traffic is the first priority. As we will discuss later, maintaining control of the network under all circumstances is a fundamental factor in maintaining services and operational continuity. MPLS networks can carry different protocol families, e.g., IPv4 and IPv6, on the same infrastructure while essentially keeping their operation separate. MPLS can be used to separate virtual private networks (VPNs) from other Internet traffic, and to provide separation between various customer networks. MPLS can be used to isolate traffic associated with specialized services such as VoIP and DDoS defense traffic. MPLS can also be used to prioritize delivery of certain traffic in times of stress (e.g., when segments of the network become overwhelmed with traffic floods.) Since MPLS provisioning and separation features are implemented logically in the network with minimal or no physical configuration changes, this lends itself to performing automation, which we will see is an important security attribute. Maintaining the separation of traffic sometimes necessitates the deployment of dedicated equipment at the edge of the network. For example dedicated equipment is needed when switching elements (e.g., routers or firewalls) do not provide inherent separation mechanisms and cannot support the appropriate delivery prioritization, or might have limited bandwidth and can be overwhelmed with traffic.

Separation of Duties Strict rules are enforced regarding who can view the status of network elements and who can modify them. With rare exceptions, only operations teams have direct access to network elements and support systems. Select development/engineering team members may have read-only access to operational systems for the purpose of helping to diagnose and reproducing behavior in the lab. But they are required to work through operations teams for any changes. This model helps to establish a consistent authorization model, which we will see is important to maintain secure control of the network and the association support systems. Those with access need to be appropriately trained and practiced in appropriate network operations. Similarly, operations teams are held accountable for the reliability and operations of the network. Therefore, they generally only support elements that have been "certified" through a battery of tests. Similarly, testing teams should be largely independent of engineering teams to assure no bias in compliance testing and to add an additional factor of variability in verification.

13.3.1.2 Testing

Testing is necessary to verify that the network will operate as expected in terms of operations and security. Testing applies to the certification of network elements as well as tests or audits of the configuration and installation environment in actual practice.

Certification Testing Certification tests are formulated for each element type (e.g., device, model, version, and patch) to assure products behave as they are supposed to. Service providers cannot depend on vendor marketing claims. Nor can vendors be expected to emulate all of the situations that are encountered in an operational environment. Therefore, independent tests help to validate devices are interoperable, reliable, maintainable, monitorable, replaceable and securable. Security specific tests are used to verify security requirements and adherence to security policy can be satisfied. Examples include, verifying access control and authentication compatibility, controls to limit exposure of management interfaces to user networks work as expected, and validation that the equipment behaves appropriately to unorthodox traffic. Naturally, this testing necessitates a reasonable amount of test facilities, effort, and time. But the effort is well worth it, and there are peripheral benefits such as the ability to provide rapid lab-reproduction for problems, patches, and installation processes when needed most. Many product vendors are willing to partner with large providers to support the testing since the testing process provides significant insight into the operational needs and "opportunities for improvement" to their products.

Configuration Testing and Audits Configuration testing and audits are also regularly performed on systems as they have been installed in or around the network. Security tests include vulnerability scanning with commercial security scanning products to help identify potential exposed access points. Occasional "white-hat" security penetration tests are performed that study the circumstances of installations and try to identify points of vulnerability that can be exploited. This includes social engineering exploitation attempts, which is a context that no scanning tool can consider. Audits come in multiple forms. Some aperiodic *regulatory audits* validate that the proper security practices are in place. Large network providers are frequently exposed to this type of audit in the course of providing communications services to certain industries such as financial and health. Regular *system configuration audits* are performed against systems by collecting the configuration of individual devices and vetting those configurations against expected configurations. Tests include validation that devices are at proper version and patch levels, appropriate access control lists (ACLs) are in place, only appropriate services are active, etc. In a very large network consisting of literally millions of manageable elements and literally thousands of configuration scenarios, there is no choice but to automate these types of checks.

13.3.1.3 Control

Network control functions can be categorized into several general and sometimes overlapping categories:

- *Operational availability controls* – measures taken to assure operations personnel have full control of the network at all times in terms of situational awareness and the ability to make changes to the network.
- *Device access controls* – measures taken to assure that only authorized network operations personnel and the tools they employ have access to devices in the network.
- *Passive router controls* – measures taken to avoid exposing network forwarding elements from protocol attacks or other denial of service attacks.
- *Traffic flow controls* – measures to control where traffic can and cannot go on the network, especially during security incidents.

Operational Availability Controls To the extent possible, operational tasks are scripted as Methods and Procedures (M&Ps) to establish and maintain consistency in practices and maintain positive control of the network. As we will discuss in the automation section, the need to provide automation of network management functions presents some important security attributes. However, there are still many scenarios that cannot be automated and require some form of human judgment and intervention. For example, when unexpected network events occur, M&Ps establish appropriate collaboration teams, scenario development, and operational change guidance to resolve any issue. During a security event, first order of business is to assure network control and operations are maintained. We detail some structure and methods for this response capability in Section 13.6.

To ensure operations staff can access network elements under all circumstances, both out-of-band and in-band access to network elements should be provided. Much of today's network management and operational tasks are performed in-band. I.e., network management traffic is carried like any other traffic through the network (possibly with a higher priority) and specifically addressed to an IP address associated with the device being managed, typically an interface address of the router. This arrangement simplifies network management tasks because tools can directly access routers without having to negotiate the intricacies of out-of-band access. In-band access to the control plane should, however, be restricted to specific trusted source address ranges to prevent access from external, untrusted parts of the network. While in-band operational access is preferred, all network devices should also be reachable via out-of-band means, which should not be dependent on the correct operation of network being managed. Out-of-band access is needed in cases where a severe network problem (not necessarily security related), prevents in-band device access. Typical out-of-band access is provided via dial-in access to terminal servers, which in turn provide device access via serial ports on network elements.

Devices Access Controls Device access controls are used to protect against the significant potential for abuse and service disruption through unauthorized access to network elements.

In the first instance this involves appropriate authentication, authorization and accounting (AAA). Network device access should be limited to authorized users to allow them to perform (only) the specific functions they are authorized to perform. Further, user actions should be logged for auditing and debugging purposes. The de-facto standard for providing AAA functions is the TACACS+ protocol. TACACS+ started out as a vendor proprietary protocol, but has since been widely adopted [21]. TACACS+ simplifies the management of AAA functions by utilizing a centralized database that defines the functions specific users can perform and further can be configured to log all configuration actions. To prevent a single point of failure, TACACS+ servers can be replicated and network elements can be configured to try them in turn.

While remaining a mainstay of network management, older versions of the simple network management protocol (SNMP), have poor security properties. For example, for SNMP versions prior to SNMPv3, SNMP access control is provided by clear text "community strings" which is susceptible to compromise via simple packet sniffing techniques. These shortcomings have been addressed through security mechanisms in SNMPv3, however, not all equipment are SNMPv3 capable. For such devices, SNMP security limitations can be addressed by: (i) limiting SNMP to read-only access, (ii) installing access control lists to limit SNMP access from specific SNMP server addresses and (iii) by compartmentalizing SNMP access between different SNMP based tools (i.e., providing each tool with separate and functional specific access).

Network devices generally use `telnet` as the default access protocol. Like SNMP community strings, `telnet` passwords are transmitted in clear text. Using `telnet` as an access protocol should be disabled and access should be provided via encrypted transport like `ssh`.

Passive Router Controls Network elements are in essence special purpose "computing devices" and are therefore subject to much of the same vulnerabilities as general purpose computing devices. Specifically, attackers can exploit software or other vulnerabilities to launch an attack against the functionality of the network element. At the most basic level protecting the router as a whole requires operators to explicitly use/allow what is needed while explicitly not using/allowing what is not needed. For example, because of the diverse services and configurations that they enable, routers are capable of a myriad of features and protocols and not even the most sophisticated networks make use of all such features. Routers should therefore specifically be configured with the services and protocols desired, and those that are not needed should be disabled. Further, physical router interfaces that are not currently in use should be explicitly disabled.

The router control plane provides functions that are typically too complicated to perform on linecards and thus constitute a so-called "slow path" through the router. As such, the control plane is a potential attack target. For example an attacker can attempt to exhaust the control plane resources by simply sending large numbers of packets that require processing in the router control plane. Similarly, an attacker might send malformed packets in an attempt to trigger bugs in the control plane software. Such attacks might cause protocol daemons, or the router itself, to crash, or might allow the network element to be compromised by allowing unauthorized access.

To protect the router control plane, again the basic approach is to allow all wanted and/or needed communication, while prohibiting all other communication. First, access control lists should be defined to restrict which network entities and which protocols are allowed to interact with the control plane. Second, within each allowed protocol, options with security concerns should be explicitly filtered out. For example, filtering packets with IP options set, filtering all fragmented packets, limiting ICMP to a safe subset of all ICMP packet types (Destination Unreachable, Time Exceeded, Echo Reply).

While a more obvious target, the router slow path is not the only potential attack target. Specifically, attacks against the router data-plane or "fast path" are also feasible. These attacks might take the form of resource exhaustion attacks against network elements that maintain state, e.g., stateful firewalls. Network elements in core provider networks typically do not maintain such state (by design), and data-plane attacks are therefore typically limited to edge devices.

In addition to per-router protection mechanisms, filtering, in the form of access control lists (ACLs), should be performed at the perimeter of the network to protect both the provider network as well as customers of the provider. Again only the limited safe subset of ICMP packet types should be allowed to cross the provider edge. Access to infrastructure IP addresses[7] within the provider network should not be allowed from external networks, i.e., from the Internet and from customer networks. On links from customer networks, source address validation should be performed to prevent address spoofing. Since network operations' traffic should only enter the network from the NOC, source address ranges associated with this function should be blocked from non-provider networks.

There need to be filters and policy management functions on routes that are received from other network providers. BGP filters should be deployed to defend the network against basic routing exploits. So called "bogon" routes, i.e., the default route, the loopback network, RFC 1918 routes and IANA-reserved routes [39], should be filtered out. In the same way, routes with private autonomous system numbers (ASNs) should not be accepted or announced. Since in practice AS path lengths are known to be constrained [78], limiting the acceptable BGP path length provides basic protection against exploit attempts. Further, as a basic measure against prefix hijacking, routers should be configured to not accept or announce routes with prefixes longer than a specific length, e.g., /24. (Recall that longer, or more specific, prefixes are more preferred and if accepted can therefore override legitimate shorter prefixes.) Similarly, for customer peering, only routes for prefixes that are assigned to the customer should be accepted. Route processing is compute intensive and uses memory on the router control plane. To prevent starvation of processor and memory resources, the rate and number of routes that are accepted from peers should be

---

[7] Infrastructure IP addresses refer to those addresses through which the equipment itself can be reached as an IP destination.

limited. Finally, all address space allocated to the provider should be *blackholed* in the aggregate (i.e., effectively dropped). Since all used address space will be specifically advertised via more specific addresses, this practice prevents abuse of currently unused but allocated address space.

Note that these measures provide a necessary first step in protecting the routing plane. However, because of the inability to precisely filter routes received across peering links, significant vulnerabilities remain. This was exemplified by the previously mentioned YouTube highjacking incident [68], where an incorrect route-map installed by a local provider caused a more specific route to be leaked to the Internet as a whole, thereby accidentally hijacking all traffic over the Internet that was destined for the content provider. To address these scenarios, current monitoring and analysis of routing data should be performed to determine when and where likely events occur. And operational processes are needed to coordinate the mitigation of rogue routes within the network as well as coordination with other providers to remediate rogue routes.

A summarization of some of the operational availability, devices access and passive router controls needed in a network are depicted in Fig. 13.1. The figure shows the separation of the different functional entities in the overall network operation and the security controls associated with each entity. While network-based services and the network operations center (NOC) are in a sense part of "the network", their specific higher level functions (compared with the basic packet forwarding functionality of the network) demands unique security concerns.

Traffic Flow Controls When security events do occur, appropriate dynamic traffic flow control mechanisms should be available to mitigate and/or eliminate the security threat. Examples include: Deploying access control lists (ACLs) to prevent the spread of an impending worm epidemic. Mitigating the effect of a DDoS traffic by dropping DDoS related traffic or redirecting it to a scrubbing complex (see Section 13.5.2). Adjusting routing policies in response to temporary peering link overload conditions.

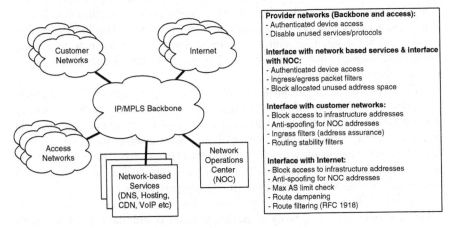

Fig. 13.1 Securing components of a provider network

13.3.1.4 Automation

Automation is imperative when operating a large network. Reliability and scalability are the primary influencing factors that necessitate automation. Operations support systems are implemented for provisioning, route policy management, billing, audit, network element scanning, log collection, security analysis and a myriad of other network operations functions. These systems provide consistency and accuracy to the process of managing millions of elements that make-up the network. They also provide a form of separation that assists with security. For example, it should be possible to designate specific operations support systems that are permitted and need to perform SNMP probes on network elements. This makes the activity patterns for the SNMP protocol somewhat predictable, and security analysis algorithms needed to evaluate the validity of SNMP probes should be relatively straight forward. Support systems also present security challenges since they tend to hold the keys to the kingdom. These platforms need to be engineered, tested, and operated with particular attention to security. Automation allows operators to concentrate on exceptions. As we outline in later sections, automated responses to security related events can be particularly challenging since the events are inherently not predictable and may be deliberately deceiving. In some cases, available network data alone may not be sufficient to determine if an event is a security issue. For example, distinguishing between a legitimate flash crowd and a DDoS attack may require application or services specific information [46].

13.3.1.5 Monitoring

In the context of security, monitoring can be categorized in two primary contexts: (i) analyzing traffic behavior on the network for security anomalies, (ii) analyzing control activities to assure there has been no breach of control systems.

Because network traffic monitoring in the context of large provider networks is a relatively complex subject, we deal with this topic separately in Section 13.4. Compared to monitoring and analyzing network traffic, monitoring the control activities of the network is more closely related to security analysis of business enterprise networks. When monitoring control activities, it is possible, for example, to perform much more focused checks for policy violations, or to flag specific exceptions to normal behavior in the latter case.

The AT&T *Threat Management Solution* is an example control activity monitoring system. This Security Information Management (SIM) system performs security analysis on data collected from a variety of sources related to network management and operations systems. A unique aspect of the system involves the use of a highly scalable data management system called Daytona [1] that allows the system to scale in depth and breadth. The Daytona technology also provides a means to perform analytical functions with significant flexibility and performance.

Scalability allows the system to not only collect security event data but also to collect a variety of other activity event data associated with the network management activities. Such inputs include firewall logs, flow data, alarms (e.g., intrusion detection systems (IDS) alarms), inputs from subordinate SIMs and `syslog` data collected from a variety of network elements. Performing security related analysis across such a broad range of sources allows the identification of security events that might go undetected in systems that perform specialized security detection. Scalability is also important to allow online retention of a significant history of activity, e.g., dating back many months. If there are any suspected events, they might be learned about weeks or months after the fact. The ability to forensically isolate specific suspect events can often help to determine the root cause and aid in resolution. Attackers will try to hide their tracks, but they will have difficult hiding from a system that collects and analyzes data from many points in an independent repository.

13.3.1.6   Response and Recovery

From the global nature of today's economy and the "flat world" nature of interactions on the Internet, it should be apparent that while provider networks experience well established daily peaks and valleys in terms of demand, these networks carry significant traffic volumes throughout the day. Providers are therefore required to have the necessary support in place to provide commensurate *response* on a 24×7 basis. Further, to ensure any event receives appropriate attention from technical experts, a tiered support structure is essential. Tiered support allows routine events to be handled through documented operational procedures, or ideally through automated operational procedures, thus leaving domain experts free to deal with unexpected and/or sophisticated events. This subject is explored in greater detail in Section 13.6.

Further, while to date most security incidents did not constitute disasters, it is conceivable that a massive security event might develop into the cyber equivalent of a physical disaster. Service providers should therefore have a well developed *recovery* program in place. This topic is dealt with in detail in Chapter 14.

13.3.1.7   Innovation

As we will outline in the remainder of this chapter, the unique requirements of each provider's network, service offerings and users, suggest that provider unique *innovations* are required to supplement security vendor offerings and to integrate vendor offerings into a comprehensive security solution.

13.4   Importance of Network Monitoring and Security Intelligence

A securely configured network is a necessary first step in service provider network security. Unfortunately, as outlined in Section 13.2 even a perfectly configured network remains vulnerable to attack and exploitation because of, for example, inherent protocol vulnerabilities and the fact that different role players and protocol components have inherent dependency and trust relationships. To address these concerns, diligent service providers are required to develop and deploy extensive network monitoring capabilities and to develop systems and algorithms to derive actionable intelligence from such data.

In this section we will first expound a number of principles associated with security related provider network monitoring. We will then consider sources of security monitoring and touch on the challenging aspect of implementing reliable monitoring mechanisms and tools. Finally, we will consider the use of network flow records as a specific source of data from which network intelligence can be derived. We will show real world examples of network intelligence derived from flow data which illustrates its utility but, more importantly, also shows how network intelligence can provide early indicators of potential future security events. We end this section by considering the importance of automated analysis of network intelligence.

13.4.1 Principles of Provider Network Monitoring

Network monitoring is a critical but challenging component in the security arsenal of network service providers. Below we discuss some of the challenges and opportunities associated with these actions and articulate a number of principles associated with security related network monitoring. These principles are listed in the text box titled "Principles of Provider Network Monitoring" and discussed in detail below.

Principles of Provider Network Monitoring

- Providers have broad visibility and coverage.
- Network monitoring is an integral part of network operations.
- Proper base-lining helps prevent false monitoring.
- Combine external information with analysis-derived intelligence.
- Perform only appropriate network monitoring.
- Security monitoring has broader benefits.
- Security monitoring helps providers understand the bigger context.

Providers Have Broad Visibility and Coverage While network monitoring is an essential part of simply keeping the network operational, we note that from a security perspective service providers are in a strong position to detect and react to security concerns. For example, compared to individual users and enterprises, provider networks with many client users have an entirely different perspective of network threats such as botnets, which are typically used as the platform for a variety of nefarious network activities. In the case of enterprise networks, visibility is typically restricted to activity in one's own address space where a relatively small number of addresses will generally be active. When a probe or exploit is attempted in this space, it is difficult to assess whether this is a random attack or whether this is a targeted attempt against a specific organization. Any statistical measurements could have significant error due to a lack of sufficient distribution.

Network Monitoring Is an Integral Part of Network Operations Service providers that do not perform the appropriate network monitoring are essentially blind to what is happening in their network, with potential dire consequences for them and their customers. Events such as self propagating network worms, email viruses, massive exploit events, distributed denial of service (DDoS) flooding attacks, and spam floods can occur at scales that can potentially congest network services. Many of these activities are associated with botnets either actively attacking or in the process of recruiting more bots. As long as botnets are able to generate revenue through DDoS attack extortion, spam campaigns, and other questionable activities, they will present a major and growing threat to network services.

Proper Base-Lining Helps Prevent False Monitoring It is crucially important for service providers to continuously perform network monitoring, not only when a network event is taking place. In cases where little or no monitoring is performed until an event happens, everything becomes an event. False monitoring is the result of not performing necessary monitoring during "normal" network conditions, which means that there is no baseline for comparing normal against abnormal when security events occur. The Internet continually has background noise of traffic due to exploit scans for new and old vulnerabilities, surveys & research probes, DDoS backscatter, and other unexplained activity. Consequently, it is possible to look at traffic at any time and conclude an attack is underway. It is important to conduct some sort of baseline monitoring at all times and assess the relative impact of the undesired activity to determine if an attack really is underway, or if the activity should simply be ignored. Ideally, this would be a science. But the Internet is not ideal, and consequently distinguishing "attack" from "noise" is somewhat of an art. As with any art, it requires practice and skill, which in the current context translates to service providers maintaining a staff of well trained security analysts.

Combine External Information with Analysis-Derived Intelligence In the past, computer attacks targeted select victims that had weak or flawed security. Now, botnets take advantage of anyone with even minor security weaknesses. Some attacks such as DDoS depend on no basic flaws in the target systems for the attacks to succeed. There are some sources of threat information based on honeypots/honeynets such as shadowserver.org and cymru.com. But information available regarding sizes of botnets and the threats they present are often predicted based on statistical models rather than actual measurements. There are few reliable sources of data that characterize the threats botnets present to network and application service providers. To understand the types and sizes of threats, it is necessary to merge externally available data with specific information about activity on your network. Examples of external security related data sources include organizations that track sources of spam, analyze malware or track nefarious activity across the Internet.

Perform Only Appropriate Network Monitoring It is important to establish a strictly enforced policy regarding network monitoring. It may not be permissible to perform traffic content analysis on carrier networks without appropriate justification.[8] And there may be legal differences between using monitoring systems to detect activity profiles that are indicative of malicious behavior and less discriminative perusal of traffic [62]. For example, it is a generally accepted (indeed expected) practice for ISPs to scan email content for virus attachments and/or links to malicious content. In general users are not complaining about email scanning, which scans content for virus and spam signatures, because the utility of such actions hugely outweigh potential customer concerns.

Security Monitoring Has Broader Benefits Some of the benefits of good network intelligence are somewhat peripheral to the operation of a robust network. The primary objective of operating a reliable and robust network is maintaining the service. DDoS attacks can threaten the service by clogging pipes. Spam originating from user clients can overload email systems and can result in other providers blocking email from your customers. On the other hand, phishing, identity theft, and to some extent network exploit attempts are things that are less likely to affect the network services, but they can have a derogatory affect on customers satisfaction. If early detection and mitigation results in fewer affected customers/clients, then customer satisfaction is improved, and subsequently, customer service calls and service cancellation may be reduced.

Security Monitoring Helps to Understand the Bigger Context Finally, it is important to understand the threats that affect services and your customers/users. Specifically, when a customer is under a DDoS attack it does not necessarily follow that the attack is negatively affecting the customer [84]. For example, large content providers are typically under constant attack and have to deal with it as part of staying in business. Unilaterally mitigating such attacks might make the situation worse, especially since many mitigation strategies have negative side effects. Also, the type of business customers are conducting will directly impact the type of traffic they expect to see on their network and will therefore impact the type of mitigation strategies that would be appropriate. For example, traffic in a corporate private network can be expected to be more predictable, lending itself to protection strategies that take advantage of that predictability [47, 59]. The business model of

---

[8] In the U.S, network monitoring is allowed by a provision in the so called wiretap law. Specifically, U.S. Code, Title 18, Chapter 119, § 2511 deals with "Interception and disclosure of wire, oral, or electronic communications prohibited" and states the following: *"(2) (a) (i) It shall not be unlawful under this chapter for an operator of a switchboard, or an officer, employee, or agent of a provider of wire or electronic communication service, whose facilities are used in the transmission of a wire or electronic communication, to intercept, disclose, or use that communication in the normal course of his employment while engaged in any activity which is a necessary incident to the rendition of his service or to the protection of the rights or property of the provider of that service, except that a provider of wire communication service to the public shall not utilize service observing or random monitoring except for mechanical or service quality control checks."*

e-commerce and content web sites, on the other hand, is built on the premise of attracting a less predictable audience, requiring alternative mitigation strategies [86].

13.4.2   Network Monitoring

Deriving good network intelligence builds on good basic network monitoring. As such, we will now in turn look at network monitoring, i.e., the mechanisms and infrastructure needed to collect network data, and then discuss how this data is used to derive network intelligence. We first consider the various sources of network related monitoring data and then discuss some of the practical issues related to developing the appropriate infrastructure for collecting such data.

13.4.2.1   Types and Sources of Security Monitoring

There is no single good source for network security data. Further, network security concerns often impose contradictory requirements on security data. For example, a global view of the security state of the network demands complete network coverage of all traffic on the network. Such complete coverage by necessity will have to be provided through an aggregate view (or a variety of aggregate views). On the other hand, determining the payload signature of an evolving worm epidemic requires very detailed monitoring of a subset of the traffic on the provider network. A good security monitoring approach will include all, or a significant subset, of the data sources discussed below and summarized in Table 13.1.

Monitoring of network node resources such as link bandwidth utilization, CPU load, and memory use, are all necessary and useful parts of network health monitoring. These SNMP-based monitoring mechanisms also have a purpose in security since some types of network events that can affect network performance are consequences of malicious activities in large scale. The objective is to recognize potential performance impact to the network and applications. Ideally, the goal is to recognize

Table 13.1 Types and sources of security related data

Category	Example source	Information
Infrastructure data	Asset databases	Node/link locations
	Node configuration	Configured protocols and services
Traffic dynamics	Flow records	Network wide traffic
	SNMP data	Node health
	Route monitors	Internal and external routing
	Packet inspection devices	Detailed traffic characterization
Service specific data	DNS logs	Botnet/phishing activity
	Spam traps	Spam sources
	Honeypots and honeynets	Malware characterization

events as they develop; prior to the point where impact has occurred. Infrastructure data includes information from asset databases and network element configuration information.

Other than highly aggregated information, SNMP derived node health data reveals little about the traffic dynamics on the network. Flow records collected by network elements provide significantly more granular information [15]. Specifically, flow based data analysis can provide insight into volume, protocol/port, source addresses, destination addresses, byte-to-packet ratios, and timing characteristics of events. Flow records can be generated with packet sampling and still provide useful insight into significant events such as DDoS attacks and network worms. Identification and characterization of some more subtle events such as network reconnaissance, attack forensics, and botnet controller identification require unsampled flow data generation. Sampling of flow data is considered in detail in Chapter 10 and we consider use of flow data to derive network security intelligence in more detail below in Section 13.4.3.

Given the crucial role of routing in the wellbeing and overall operation of the network, monitoring all aspects of routing is critically important both for normal network operations and from a network security perspective. Routing data aids the analysis of security incidents and supplements other data, i.e., to show where traffic might have entered or left the network. A number of route monitoring tools with a range of capabilities exist. In its most basic form monitoring tools partake in routing exchanges with routers in the network to allow an accurate real time view of routing. This includes tools to monitor interior gateway routing (IGP), such as OSPF [72] and ISIS [40]) and interdomain routing. More sophisticated monitoring tools allow the detection of inconsistent route advertisements across differing peering points from the same peer [31], looks for more general violations of peering agreements [63] or attempts to detect prefix hijacking attempts [90]. Route monitoring is covered in significantly more detail in Chapter 11.

Flow data necessarily does not provide any information regarding payload of packets. More granular data plane monitoring can be realized through so-called deep packet inspection (DPI) devices [26]. Such information might be crucial to understand, for example, the type of payload of a targeted infrastructure attack that is causing router malfunction [23]. As mentioned earlier, another example where payload information might be needed would be to understand the exploit method of an evolving worm outbreak. Unlike flow monitoring, the equipment and operational cost associated with DPI monitoring make ubiquitous deployment prohibitive. One approach to address this problem is to deploy DPI equipment at strategic locations in the network and to then redirect, e.g., by using a very specific BGP prefix, traffic of interest to these locations for further inspection. This approach has significant limitations though, as traffic of interest can not always be easily identified and redirected. An alternative is to utilize a mobile approach, whereby a DPI device is dynamically deployed to the physical network location from where detailed information is needed. This approach works best when the data collection of the DPI device is completely passive. The mobile DPI approach also has limitations because of the time involved for deployment, however, it could provide a practical compromise.

In addition to data derived directly from network traffic, data from network based services and security specific data sources fill out the quiver of potential data sources. An example service specific data source is logs from DNS caching resolvers. DNS is designed to translate domain names into IP addresses. It is much less effective at reversing the process, i.e., identifying domain names that point to known IP addresses. Internet registries have different requirements for maintaining reverse mapping information, reverse DNS is not uniformly implemented, and when implemented not always well maintained [71]. Attackers use this situation to their advantage. Botnets use domain names in malware to identify malware update sites and control points. Phishing sites create domain names that appear legitimate. As malicious IP addresses are identified and blocked by ISPs, or at enterprise firewalls, domain names can be pointed to new IP addresses – allowing attacks and operations to continue. By recording DNS logs or DNS response metadata from the network, it is possible to map IP addresses to the domain names used in these malicious activities [49]. It is also possible to perform a variety of analysis such as temporal analysis of domain names to identify fast-flux and transient domains [41], which can be used to help discover botnets and phishing activities.

Security specific data sources include various approaches to intentionally attract unwanted traffic or attacks to a controlled environment where it can be analyzed to make useful security related observations. Generically, these systems are called Honeypots and the basic concept is nicely captured by this definition [77]:

> A honeypot is an information system resource whose value lies in unauthorized or illicit use of that resource.

Honeypots present a popular way to gather information about malware. By hosting computers on the Internet or in enterprise networks with common vulnerabilities, eventually attackers will locate the machine and exploits will be executed against it. By hosting honeypots on many IP addresses, the probability of becoming a victim of attack increases. The objective is to capture malware, detect the event, and provide an opportunity to analyze and characterize the malware. This technique has limited utility if the honeypot does not have the correct vulnerability, or if user action is a factor in the infection process, as is the case with many application exploits. For example, the virtual honeypot framework [65] interacts with attack and exploit attempts only at the network level. This means that the actual end system software is never compromised, which reduces the risk associated with running the honeypot, but also limits the amount of information about malicious activity that can be learned from it. Honeypot technology that understands how to become a victim of social engineering attacks is still under development and probably will evolve for sometime to come.

To study attacks, exploits and malware behavior in a more holistic way requires that attackers be allowed more freedom on the honeypots, i.e., allowing the honeypots to become infected. Mechanisms need to be in place to prevent the honeypot from subsequently conducting attacks as a consequence of the infection. For example, Honeynets [37] have been developed as a means to allow honeypot end-systems to be completely compromised, and for the installed malware to be allowed to execute in order to study its behavior. This is achieved by selectively allowing interaction of the compromised honeypot with systems outside the honeynet through a filtering device called a honeywall [37]. Approaches to better scale honeynets have been developed to make use of virtual machines to host a large number of honeypots on a significantly smaller number of physical machines [87]. Unfortunately, in the ever evolving cat-and-mouse game between attackers and defenders, newer malware is capable of detecting execution in a virtual machine environment. This is taken as indication of a possible detection attempt so that the malware automatically disables itself [53]. The result is that honeynets had to evolve to detect virtual machine aware malware and facilitate execution of such malware on non-virtualized hardware [44].

Another form of honeypot is so called spam traps, or spam sinkholes, which create email accounts or complete email domains with the express purpose of attracting spam email [66, 77]. Obviously, there is no shortage of spam; roughly 90% of Internet email is characterized as spam [58]. In the effort to manage spam and understand the relationship to customers, there is value in understanding when characteristics of spam activity change, how they developed, the purpose or objectives of the spam, how that activity relates to customers. There are significant efforts by a variety of organizations to track sources of spam and use that information to identify problematic IP addresses, IP address blocks, and domains (e.g., http://www.spamhaus.org/). They also characterize attributes of the spam messages themselves for the purpose of detecting the spam. As a contribution to these efforts, and also for an ISP's own use, there is value in creating spam traps within the ISPs email systems.

By creating some proportion of spam trap accounts and seeding account information into a variety of places, it is possible to learn valuable information about spamming activity as it pertains to the ISPs network and email domain. By tracking spam associated with different account seeding techniques, it may be possible to determine how email addresses are being harvested by spammers. Spamming activities may come in surges. In some cases, spamming campaigns will seek to flood messages to the brink of an email system's capacity. Measuring changes in the volume of spam and whether that spam is detected as spam or not will help prepare appropriate mitigation strategies. It will be possible to quickly recognize the on-set of new spam campaigns.

Understanding the motives behind those campaigns can be valuable. Spam can be characterized in categories of malware, phishing, or mundane solicitation. Malware spam (or email viruses) may contain malware payload or may contain links to malware drop points. These emails are often cleverly crafted, with content related to current news events, to lure victims into downloading and executing malware. Understanding the malware that is being sent to customers will help understand threats against customers, which may result in customer service calls or could consequently impact the network. Phishing email payload typically contains a URL for a phishing site that attempts to convince recipients to divulge user credentials (username and password) for misuse. Again it is helpful to understand how customers are being targeted and how to prepare protections.

In the course of forensic analysis, spam analysis, and botnet analysis, encountering samples of malware is highly likely. Malware analysis is specialized, difficult, labor intensive, and time consuming. This challenge is not accidental. Malware developers are continually creating increasingly sophisticated techniques to hide their malware, mutate characteristics, change behavior, and prevent being analyzed.

Anti-virus vendors have developed some of the most advanced capabilities to analyze malware and the indicators that are left behind on infected computers. However, as a network provider, some of the most valuable characteristics are going to be the network observables associated with the malware behavior and activity. Understanding the functional capabilities of the malware such as back-door ports that might be opened, malware update capabilities, command and control mechanisms, DDoS tools they might contain and defensive actions the malware might utilize are valuable to a service provider. Using such information in conjunction with information about the quantitative presence of infected devices in and around the network will provide insights into the threat level they present to offered services. Understanding the command and control mechanisms and characteristics will provide insight into possible methods to surgically disable these threats without disrupting the services customers need. These indicators can also be used to help identify infected customers for notification and remediation assistance.

13.4.2.2 Implementation Considerations

Complete coverage of all implementation issues related to network security monitoring are well beyond the scope of this chapter. However, here we do address some of the concerns and contradictory requirements presented by a comprehensive security monitoring framework.

Perhaps the single most pressing implementation concern for provider based network monitoring is the tension between *scalability, fidelity, and coverage*. In an ideal world, fine grained measurements of all parts of the network would be available instantaneously and be archived over long periods of time. This is clearly not a feasible goal as the infrastructure needed to realize the monitoring system will be of similar (if not higher) complexity and cost as the network it is supposed to monitor.

We already mentioned the ubiquity of flow based monitoring. By definition flow monitoring is aggregated into per-flow measurements. However, despite this aggregation, traffic volumes are such that unsampled flow collection is still problematic, both from the point of view of the load imposed on network elements, as well as the capacity requirements of systems that process the flow data. A common approach to address this concern is to generate flow records based on packet sampled data. E.g., one in every 500 or 1,000 packets are used to generate flow records. This approach is attractive from a scalability point of view, but require caution when interpreting the data. We consider this in more detail is Section 13.4.3.1. Scalability concerns of the collected data volume might be significantly magnified when DPI data collection is utilized in a naive manner.

One of the primary objectives of security monitoring is to improve the reliability and availability of network services, it is therefore desirable to consider a passive implementation (e.g., physical-layer splitters). This adds other important attributes as well. Whereas network services require meticulous change control processes to maintain high levels of reliability, security monitoring and data analysis require the capability to remain very flexible and reactive to new attack techniques and investigation of suspect events. A passive approach provides valuable autonomy between the diverse operational requirements of the active network elements and the passive monitoring elements. The added costs of a passive approach can provide some clear benefits in a large network where reliability is a primary consideration.

Once captured, there is a trade-off between sending all captured data in unprocessed form to a centralized location for further analysis, versus performing initial processing locally and only sending processed data to a central point. One of the factors that play into the centralized versus distributed decision concerns the flexibility that is required in the post processing of the data. For example, if the ultimate network intelligence that will be extracted from the data is well known and well understood, it might be relatively simple to partition the work such that a distributed solution is feasible and provide good scalability properties. On the other hand, distributed processing invariably leads to a loss of information, and the lost information might be crucial in analyzing security incidents that are new or not well understood. While true for all network monitoring systems, flexibility is of particular concern for network security given the ever changing nature of network threats.

Another scalability concern involves the storage, processing and retention of security data. In the case of unsampled data, volumes are such that data typically cannot be stored in unaggregated form for very long periods of time.[9] There is a common tendency to put data into a database and then consider how to process that data. In many circumstances this is the right approach. But a large network can also generate a significant amount of metadata about network activity. Consequently, an attempt to insert and index all of the data can quickly become a task that consumes all of the available processing resources, and consequently accomplishs nothing. There is a balance that must be achieved between the types of analysis that are performed and the aspects of that data entered into a database. As a general rule, only enter data into a database when that data will be retrieved many more times than it is entered. For example, in the informational security system described in Section 13.5.1, no raw flow data is entered into a database as part of the unsampled flow data analysis. Rather, the flows are processed and then attributes regarding the volume of activity on each of the ports and protocols are stored in a database. Raw flows are retained for a short period of time and discarded, but the volumetric attributes are retained in a high-performance database and used for a variety of analysis functions. Further, off-the-shelf database technologies or naive processing methodologies are typically not sufficient for the data processing that needs to be performed. Instead specialized database technologies, such as the Daytona data management system [1], and streaming processing technologies, such as the Gigascope network stream database system [26], are often required.

Metadata is a generic term for data that is derived from other data. There is no fundamental beginning to metadata, and there is an even more ambiguous end. As analysis tools develop, the output from one analysis step starts as a report, but it invariably becomes the input to another analysis step. It is valuable to recognized this early, and consider a relatively standard format for all data that analysts, researchers, developers and downstream systems are comfortable with.

---

[9] Section 4.3 in Chapter 10 discusses the volume reduction associated with sampling.

Binary formats are the most compact, but they tend to be less flexible and more difficult to work with in ad-hoc ways since most Unix tools tend to manipulate ASCII files. A compromise may be to assure there are sufficient conversion tools to allow ad-hoc manipulation of data stored in binary format.

Finally, there is typically a trade-off between the robustness and scalability of a systems versus the flexibility it allows to enable prototyping and ad-hoc investigations. An ideal realization will allow scalable and reliable processing of well understood analyses, while at the same time facilitating ad-hoc investigations using the same data. For example, the informational security system described in Section 13.5.1 implemented four phases of analysis that are all connected. (i) Ad-hoc analysis is needed to perform analytical functions that have never been performed or need to address a new type of situation. The tools range from simple commands to use of complex analytical tools. (ii) As analytical needs are better understood and can be articulated in conceptual terms, researchers can apply mathematical tools to improve the accuracy and performance of the analysis. (iii) From this point, a proof-of-concept implementation is used by analysts in actual use to determine how effective the tool is and assess readiness. (iv) Finally, the tools are migrated to the production platform for life-cycle support, performance enhancements, and where applicable, automated reporting. This type of evolutionary model has been very successful by getting complex capabilities in the hands of analysts in the shortest possible time.

13.4.3   Network Intelligence

First-order analysis of network activity is to determine when there is an existing problem. Denial of service events can clog network bandwidths, overwhelm routers, and/or overwhelm servers on the network. While there has not been a massive network worm for a while, the possibility of events similar to Slammer, Blaster, and MyDoom still fundamentally exist.[10] Monitoring bandwidth usage, router buffer and CPU usage, firewall state space, and host performance can provide insights into the health of these resources as part of normal network analysis. These metrics are fairly reliable indicators of massive network events, whether security related or otherwise. However, by themselves these metrics do not provide enough information into why events are taking place nor how to mitigate them. Also, smaller events, that could still be customer impacting, might not necessarily be discernible in these metrics. Given the prevalence of flow-based monitoring capabilities in most network forwarding equipment, flow data is a particularly attractive source to form the basis of a comprehensive network intelligence infrastructure. In Section 13.4.3.1 we detail the types of network intelligence that can be readily derived from network flow data.

---

[10] While Conficker worm of 2009 exemplifies the continuing potential for massive network worms to exist, Conficker generally did not cause the same sort of network disruption as some of the earlier worms.

To complement reacting to security knowledge, there are definite benefits to taking a pro-active approach to the analysis. In Section 13.4.3.2, we present a history of cases where early indications of exploit development have been identified through generic traffic profiling of Internet activity. The objective is to detect threats as they develop rather than wait for events to have adverse effects on network or service application performance.

Given the massive amounts of monitoring data that large provider networks produce on a daily basis, automating procedures for deriving network intelligence is imperative. We discuss this topic in Section 13.4.3.3.

13.4.3.1   Intelligence from Flow Data

Commercial products are on the market to help measure activity on the network using flow data (e.g., netflow or cflowd). For coarse grained analysis, packet sampled flow data can be used to measure relative byte traffic levels at various access points in the network. It is important to realize that sampling results in loss of information. As a result sampled flow data cannot be used to accurately interpret certain events. For example, individual events that may have occurred are most likely not in the data, TCP flag information is not complete, packet and byte counts in individual flows are not correct. Even interpreting packet sampled or flow sampled records in aggregate can be difficult. These analysis points seem obvious, but they are easy to forget, and results from analyzing sampled data can be easily misinterpreted.

Below we describe how flow data can be interpreted to detect some types of security and non-security events, namely, DDoS attacks, flash crowds, address scanning and network worms. When an anomaly is detected (generally a relative increase in packets or bytes), analysis is used to help determine the origination points and destination points for the changes. Interpretations of the activity can help diagnose what might be happening as outlined below.

DDoS Attacks   Even with packet sampled flow data, the characteristics of *DDoS attacks* are such that most attacks can be detected with reasonably high confidence. The text box "Flow characteristics associated with DDoS attacks" list these characteristics.

Flow Characteristics Associated with DDoS Attacks

- *Large Increase in Packet Rate*   Changes in packet rate relative to normal are often an indicator of a denial of service attack. Attacks might use large packets in an attempt to overwhelm bandwidth resources and/or can use many connections in an attempt to overwhelm end-host or firewall session capacity.
- *Many Source IPs*   If there is a high proportion of source IP addresses in a given address block, then spoofing is likely. Determining a high proportion depends on a number of factors, so some experience comparing normal and

attack traffic is helpful. Identifying the presence of spoofed sources helps to develop greater confidence the activity is an attack (i.e., of malicious intent).

- *Consistent TCP Flag Combinations* If nearly all flows have the same flag combination (e.g., SYN only) in combination with a large increase in packets, this is a supporting indication of an attack where connections are generally unsuccessful. However, care should be taken concerning the interpretations of TCP flags when analyzing packet sampled flows. Some statistical analysis of many flows can be used to interpret typical TCP flag activity, but flag combinations for a single flow are obviously subject to the effects of sampling. I.e., the TCP flag field in a flow record is the logical "OR" of all TCP flags of sampled packets observed by the router and associated with that flow.

- *Consistent Single-Packet Flows* If nearly all flows have only one packet and/or have nearly all the same packet size, this suggests connection attempts are not being acknowledged. This might simply be the result of a non-DDoS related host failure. However, if the protocol is not TCP, then this may be the best indicator of a DDoS attack. But this is not a particularly strong indicator unless you can compare with a change from normal activity. There are protocols that use only one packet in a session and can have relatively consistent packet sizes in normal operation. DNS (53/udp) is an example.

- *Maximum Size Packets* If the attacker's objective is to flood the byte bandwidth capacity of the target, the attacker may choose to use maximum size packets. While maximum size packets are not unusual when transferring large amounts of data between two points, it is very unusual to see many long sequences of maximum size packets in UDP and particularly in ICMP for legitimate purposes. Traditionally, maximum packet size has been 1500 bytes as defined by Ethernet. Larger sizes will likely become more popular with higher access speeds.

- *Backscatter* Backscatter refers to the phenomena of observing unsolicited response traffic because some DDoS attacks use spoofed IP addresses [60]. Typical indications are TCP SYN-RST flows or ICMP "Destination unreachable" response flows sent from a target IP address and using the spoofed IP address as destination.

Flash Crowds It is not unusual to mistake a *flash crowd* for a DDoS attack. Flash crowds are caused by events that are generally not malicious such as a really good online sale or a very popular webcast. Many flows that appear to be successful connections could suggest a possible flash crowd, i.e., a rush of visitors to a particular website. Flows with a variety of flag combinations that in combination appear to show successful connections suggest an innocuous flash-crowd event. But there is a possibility that it is a DDoS attempt in progress. I.e., with a sufficiently large botnet,

B. Rexroad and J. Van der Merwe

a sophisticated attacker can emulate user behavior which can not be distinguished from a flash crowd simply from flow level characteristics.

Address Scanning Flow level information can be used to detect *scanning* which is used to identify potentially vulnerable machines on a network. Massive address scanning is performed by botnets or worms (which are not necessarily distinct scenarios). Again these activities have tell tale characteristics which are listed in the text box "Flow characteristics associated with address scanning".

Flow Characteristics Associated with Address Scanning

- Many flows from one or possibly many distinct source IP addresses to many destinations.
- Flows to darkspace (or greyspace) destinations as well as active destinations. (Darkspace refers to IP address blocks with no legitimate hosts but with advertised BGP routes on the Internet. Greyspace refers to unused addresses within address blocks that have active addresses.) Activity to darkspace and greyspace can manifest itself as ICMP "Destination unreachable" or ICMP "Time exceeded" backscatter messages from probed addresses toward the scanning sources.
- Most connections are unsuccessful with only occasional indications of successful connections. Successful connections might be determined based on the types of TCP flag combinations or identification of response traffic toward the IP addresses that are suspected to be scanning.

Network Worms The fundamental distinction between massive address scanning and a *network worm* is that worms demonstrate progressive increase in scanning activity and an increasing number of source addresses performing the scanning.

13.4.3.2 Early Indicators

Network intelligence derived from flow data might not be accurate enough to pinpoint specific security events, e.g., detect with high accuracy a DDoS attack against a specific customer. However, because of its ubiquitous coverage it serves as a very effective early warning system regarding the increase of suspicious activity in the network. Below we describe a number of such early indicators identified in real exploit scenarios, namely: intent to exploit, exploit trials and worm propagation.

Intent to Exploit When a vulnerability is announced for a network application, invariably there will be some reconnaissance activity (network scanning) for the associated application, i.e., *intent to exploit*. The reconnaissance is presumably a survey for hosts that might be potential targets for exploit. The activity may be collecting signatures of hosts that might indicate the version of application software and

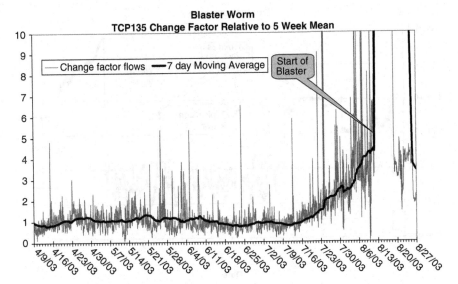

Fig. 13.2   Activity metrics on TCP port 135 in weeks prior to and including the Blaster worm

underlying operating system. The presence of sufficient hosts with potential vulnerabilities will likely guide the priority and amount of effort attackers will devote to
developing and refining an exploit. Indications of such efforts were very clear in the
case of the Blaster worm, where reconnaissance activity started immediately following the vulnerability announcement, and the level of reconnaissance increased
slowly over days until the presence of the worm was clearly evident. Figure 13.2
illustrates the increase in activity on port 135/tcp for the weeks prior and including
the Blaster worm event.

Exploit Trials   As an exploit is developed, it is often developed in stages and usually does not work to full potential in early phases. Such *exploit trials* can manifest
themselves in a few different ways, often as phases of on-again and off-again activity. For example, this occurred in the weeks leading to the Slammer worm with
activity on a MS-SQL port (1434/udp). Figure 13.3 shows packet counts for UDP
port 1434 in the weeks prior to the Slammer worm. Note that the y-axis is in log
scale. During the weeks of January 1, 2003 and January 8, 2003 there was more
than two orders of magnitude increase in packet counts. Some of these existed for
extended periods of time which might have been an initial worm attempt that fiz-
zled out. During the weeks of January 15, 2003 and January 22, 2003 there were two
short periods of increased activity which might again have been "test runs" before
the start of the actual Slammer event on January 25, 2003.

Worm Propagation   There have been some rare examples of very rapid *worm propagation*. Noted examples are the Slammer worm (once past the trials phase) and
the Witty worm. These worms have illustrated that it is not always possible to react to worm propagations once the worm is launched. However, these examples

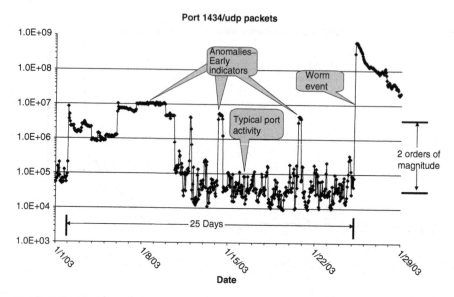

Fig. 13.3 Packet counts on UDP port 1434 in weeks prior to Slammer worm

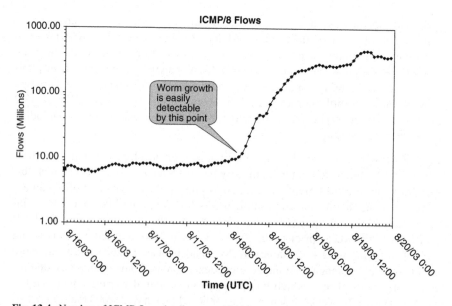

Fig. 13.4 Number of ICMP flows leading up to Nachi worm

were exceptionally aggressive/efficient worms, and most other worms have not been nearly as aggressive. The Nachi worm, for example, existed on the Internet for more than 8 hours before it became visible to even a small portion of the Internet (see Fig. 13.4). This is sufficient time to recognize the propagation, recognize a behavior profile, and prepare a mitigation plan. The activity is recognizable as a continual increase in the number of source IP addresses that are performing reconnaissance activity on a given port. In the case of the Nachi worm, the underlying behavior was a little more difficult to recognize since the reconnaissance was performed using icmp type 8 (echo request or ping) while the exploit was predominantly on port 135/tcp.

13.4.3.3 Automated Analysis

An important aspect of any data analysis effort is a need for automation. It is not practical to hire a team of analysts to continually assess traffic activity for millions of subscribers and billions of flows. Automated analysis functions are needed to help determine what is important and to lead a small team of analysts in the right direction to isolate relevant security events.

Below we describe considerations concerning automated analyses for developing security intelligence.

Ongoing Measurement of Key Parameters Select parameters need to be measured on a periodic basis. Some obvious parameters to measure are the number of packets and number of bytes on each IP protocol and port. It can be useful to count flows, which is defined as a unique source IP address destination IP address, IP protocol, source port, and destination port. Some less obvious measurements also include the number of active source IP addresses and the number of active destination IP addresses. Selection of parameters is a trade-off between simplicity and manageability of the data, system performance, and sacrificing information that might be useful. It is not possible to maintain all parameter information, but when dealing with unknown security concerns, it is desirable to err on the conservative side and maintain as much information as possible.

Baseline Generation A key aspect of identifying what is an anomaly is defining what is normal. We call the process of calculating the normal activity "baseline generation". As with selection of parameters to measure, there are a variety of ways to determine a baseline, which invariably involves some method of averaging over time. In traditional POTS phone call patterns, it has in general been possible to use the previous week of activity as a baseline measurement for call volume. But the Internet, in an era of multi-GigaByte transfers and DDoS attacks, is much more volatile than the metered 64 Kbps calls of POTS. Further, specific ports and protocols subdivide segments of activity into smaller and more volatile behaviors. Each hour of the day as well as each day of the week have unique characteristics. Methods that use decaying averages and compensate for diurnal behavior are effective for short-term averaging. For longer-term baselines, a moving average over several weeks for the same hour of day and same day of week have been shown to be effective. Another normalizing factor that we call "share value" can also be used in measurement. For example, rather than measuring the absolute count of packets on port 25/tcp, measure the share/percentage of 25/tcp packets relative to all packets on the network. This can help compensate for normal network changes or even anomalies in the availability of certain data in the analysis platform.

Alarm Detection Alarm detection becomes a comparison of current activity with the baseline. We already mentioned the volatility of measured parameters, and it is sometimes useful to consider how volatile data normally is in anomaly detection. To account for this, it can be useful to set alarm thresholds as multiples of standard deviation for a given measured parameter. For some ports and protocols, there is no defined application. But not surprisingly, there is occasionally traffic on nearly every port, protocol, and address possible. Some of this traffic may be accidental, but much has some sort of nefarious intent, so it is useful to monitor this activity. But measuring the relative change of activity from a baseline that is effectively zero presents a challenge. It may be sufficient to define a minimum measurement of activity that is considered important for alerting and investigation, and this can overcome some of the problems created by overly volatile or otherwise unused ports and protocols.

Threshold Management It is desirable to have a standard threshold set for all types of activity, but we have found some thresholds need to be more sensitive than others. For example, there are certain ports and protocols that are frequently targeted for attack, while other ports and protocols do not present a significant threat. Consequently, we have found it to be useful to set thresholds for certain special interest protocols to be tighter than the default group thresholds. None of this remains fixed, i.e., as the environment and attacks change, so should the measurements and the thresholds. It is useful to hold periodic analyst meetings that review thresholds along with current attack and exploit trends, and determine if, or what, threshold changes (upward or downward) are needed.

Reporting Generating reports is another activity highly amenable to automation. Specific examples include:

- *Alarms* Alarms are an obvious report type that are needed to raise attention to specific events. Depending on the users, it is useful to provide a summary console of recent alarms and also provide alerting subscription capability. Email seems to be the most flexible means for alarm delivery. If pertinent alarm information can be squeezed into the limits of SMS messages without inappropriate disclosure of information, analysts on call can easily receive pertinent alerts on a conventional cell phone.
- *Traffic Trending* Invariably, there will be a need to look at activity and traffic trends over short and long periods of time. Examples include reports on traffic volume attributes such as flows, packets, bytes, bytes per flow, bytes per packet.

13.5   Network Security Systems

In this section we consider several example network security systems that service providers utilize to protect network users from security threats. Such service provider actions are typically manifested as service offers or features. User protection services can be classified in three categories namely *Informational, Automated/Compulsory, and Supplementary/Optional*.

Informational services generally provide information to users about that status of the network and issues that may pertain to them. Acting on such information is, however, left up to the end user. Naturally, there must be sources of data to provide information to users, and this is necessarily the result of gathering and analyzing data from a variety of sources including abuse complaints, security advisories, traffic flow analysis, and sometimes some in-depth analysis of suspect activity. In Section 13.5.1 we describe the AT&T's Security Analysis Platform as a specific example of a sophisticated network security intelligence apparatus which, among other things, can be used to provide informational security services to users.

Automated or compulsory security services are normally realized in the form of filtering. It includes those that are performed to prevent collateral damage to users or services that might indirectly suffer as a result of an attack. For example, in order to provide quality service to all customers on a network, it is sometimes necessary to block the congestion caused by a denial of service flooding attack. Security services that are automatically provided as part of "standard" service offers also fall in this category. A canonical example is the filtering or tagging of suspected spam email when email services are provided. In Section 13.5.2 we describe DDoS blackholing as well as the AT&T email platform as specific examples in this category.

Supplementary or optional security services are those that customers specifically select or opt-in to use. Supplementary services often involve dedicated security infrastructure and as such often require service specific payment by customers. As noted earlier in this chapter, security as a service helps to correct the economic imbalance that is otherwise skewed in favor of bad actors. In Section 13.5.3, we describe customer specific DDoS filtering and network based firewall services as two specific service options in this category.

By necessity the categorization provided above is not absolute or perfect. For example, while derived network intelligence can be provided to customers as informational services, the same information might be utilized to trigger compulsory DDoS filtering, or customer specific DDoS filtering. Similarly, some informational services might be provided to all users as a default part of their service, or informational services might be offered as an optional service feature.

13.5.1   Informational Security Services

In this section we describe AT&T's Security Analysis Platform as a specific end-to-end example of how informational security intelligence is derived. As noted above,

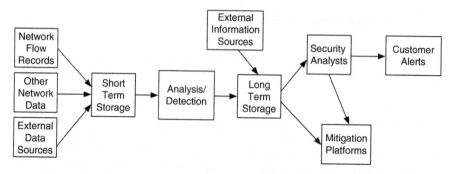

Fig. 13.5 Generic overview of AT&T's Security Analysis Platform

such security information is not only used for informational purposes, but also form the basis for mitigation actions.

A generic high level overview of the platform is depicted in Fig. 13.5. The primary source of dynamic network traffic information for this system is in the form of *network flow records*. Network flow records convey information regarding the source, destination, IP protocol, source port, destination, TCP flags, packet count, byte count, start time, and end time for activity on the network. In select portions of the AT&T Internet backbone, unsampled flow generation has been implemented and is processed in a variety of ways to help identify anomalies. The unsampled flow data complements packet sampled and smart sampled flow data that is more ubiquitously available.

As shown in Fig. 13.5, flow records are combined with *other network data*, e.g., topology information, as well as other *external data sources*, such as external sources of unwanted traffic, e.g., sources of spam email. Data from all these sources are saved in *short term storage* and an *analysis and/or detection* component combines all the data and performs automated analysis using predefined rules and algorithms. For simplicity we represent this component as a single entity, however, in reality it consists of a variety of sub-systems which we describe in more detail below. Further, the output of particular subsystems might be used as input to other sub-systems and is again not shown in the figure. For example, the output of port-scanning detection is used as input to botnet detection.

The output of the analysis/detection component is a set of alarms. These alarms are typically stored in *long term storage* and made available to a group of *security analysts* who investigate the alarms to determine whether action should be taken. The analysts also make use of other *external information sources*, for example CERT alerts or reports from virus protection vendors. Based on their domain knowledge and the intelligence provided by the platform, the analysts could generate detailed *customer alerts* to warn customers of emerging security concerns.

The analysts could also trigger appropriate mitigation actions to be performed in the available *mitigation platforms*. In some cases alarms generated from the analysis/detection component can directly feed into a mitigation system. We note, however, that because most mitigation activities have some negative side effects, and because all detection system are subject to false positives, automated response to network security threats is not trivial.

We will now describe various aspects of the analysis/detection component of the AT&T Security Analysis Platform in more detail.

13.5.1.1 Scan Detection and Trending

We consider several scanning related detection activities and/or algorithms namely, *general scanning, worm detection, scan volume alarming and summarization of scanning activity in a Reconnaissance Index.*

General Scanning General Scanning activity is characterized as source IP addresses that are making many, many connection attempts to destinations. This type of activity is generally suspect and usually represents an intent to exploit vulnerabilities in network applications. For this reason, the Security Analysis Platform detects and records the sources and some general characteristics of scanning activity on the Internet. The results of this analysis are used for a variety of subsequent analysis algorithms including worm detection, scan volume alarms, the reconnaissance index, and botnet detection. For example, the graphic in Fig. 13.6 depicts the number of unique source IPs that have been associated with scanning activity on port 445/tcp over a 200 day period leading into and through the evolution of the Conficker worm. The graphic was generated from data on the AT&T Internet Security Analysis Platform. Figure 13.6, clearly shows the evolution of the Conficker worm over time. The graph shows initial significant activity starting on

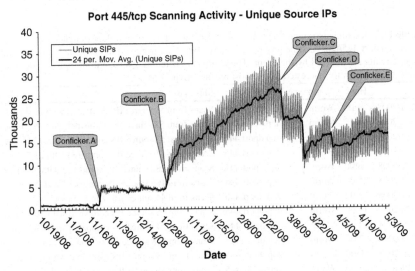

Fig. 13.6 Scan activity on port 445/tcp in Unique Source IP addresses/hour over a 200 day period

November 21. The graphic also shows the changes in Conficker behavior as new variants were released, and provides a relative measure of the worm's "success" at reaching previously infected hosts for update to later variants.

Worm Detection The Worm Detection algorithm provides early detection of worm activity on the Internet. When a worm propagates on a network, it performs the following steps: (i) Seeks exploitable hosts through scanning network addresses on target ports, (ii) performs an exploit against identified targets, (iii) replicates itself to the target, and (iv) repeats from step (i).

The worm detection algorithm tracks the number of unique hosts scanning, and alerts analyst to any significant increase in the number of hosts scanning on a given port. We perform this analysis at the Internet circuit level, i.e., physical links at the perimeter of the network. Worm alarms are valuable for identifying mass use of new exploits early in the deployment or even development phases. These types of events are attributable to a number of network disruptions and problems that have occurred on the Internet as well as within enterprises, making this unique capability invaluable for early warning and mitigation. Table 13.2 shows (in reverse chronological order) a sample of alarms that precipitated during the period leading to the Conficker worm event. Each line corresponds to an alarm being triggered on a specific circuit. These alarms are signifying an increase in the number of unique source IP addresses that are detected actively scanning on port 445/tcp. Specifically, for each circuit where an alarm has triggered, the number of detected source IPs scanning on this port is compared with the baseline average that has been observed on this circuit in previous periods. As the activity increases and becomes visible on more circuits with greater change, the frequency of alarms increases until the worm reached a saturation point. Interestingly, the alarms data in Table 13.2 show indications of developing activity on November 20 and perhaps as early as November 13.

Table 13.2 Example worm alarms which provided early indication of the Conficker worm propagating on port 445/tcp. As time progresses, more alarms are triggered in the same hour indicating more circuits are affected by the event. The alarms are listed in reverse chronological order since analysts are generally interested in the most recent activity first

Date	Hour	Alarm type	Target port	Message
11/21/2008	6:00	Worm	tcp.dport.445	Scans from 56 source IPs compared with 16.36 ave.
11/21/2008	6:00	Worm	tcp.dport.445	Scans from 53 source IPs compared with 15.81 ave.
11/21/2008	6:00	Worm	tcp.dport.445	Scans from 52 source IPs compared with 15.69 ave.
11/21/2008	6:00	Worm	tcp.dport.445	Scans from 61 source IPs compared with 21.76 ave.
11/21/2008	6:00	Worm	tcp.dport.445	Scans from 282 source IPs compared with 84.31 ave.
11/21/2008	5:00	Worm	tcp.dport.445	Scans from 196 source IPs compared with 56.39 ave.
11/21/2008	5:00	Worm	tcp.dport.445	Scans from 44 source IPs compared with 9.76 ave.
11/20/2008	13:00	Worm	tcp.dport.445	Scans from 35 source IPs compared with 10.00 ave.
11/20/2008	12:00	Worm	tcp.dport.445	Scans from 34 source IPs compared with 10.00 ave.
11/20/2008	7:00	Worm	tcp.dport.445	Scans from 158 source IPs compared with 55.91 ave.
11/19/2008	6:00	Worm	tcp.dport.445	Scans from 33 source IPs compared with 9.33 ave.
11/19/2008	6:00	Worm	tcp.dport.445	Scans from 33 source IPs compared with 9.18 ave.
11/13/2008	20:00	Worm	tcp.dport.445	Scans from 159 source IPs compared with 74.66 ave.

Scan Volume Alarms Another algorithm produce Scan Volume Alarms by evaluating changes in scanning activity across the Internet. As malicious botnets embark on efforts to draft new hosts into their control, network scanning is sometimes used to identify exploitable hosts. Scan activity increases on a given port or protocol can be indicative of a new exploit in use, which analysts can investigate prior to affecting an enterprise. Increases in scanning activity can also be indicative of botnet ramping-up efforts to draft new bots and facilitate malicious acts such as a spamming campaign or a DDoS attack.

Reconnaissance Index The AT&T Security Analysis Platform summarizes scanning activity measurements and normalizes these over time to generate a long term trending report called the Reconnaissance Index. The purpose of this index is to assess long-term changes in network exploit threat activity, in a manner analogous to a financial index. This index takes into account both the number of sources that are performing reconnaissance as well as the number of aggregate probes performed by those sources. A recent image of the AT&T Threat Reconnaissance Index is shown in Fig. 13.7. Not surprisingly, the reconnaissance index has shown a relative decrease over the past few years. This trend is indicative of efforts by attackers to deemphasize the rapid spread of network worms and minimize attention to their activities. Attackers are more motivated to gain control of computers without drawing attention so they can use the exploited computers for undesirable activities such as sending spam, DDoS attacks, identity theft, intellectual property theft, and even illegal distribution of media. In late 2006, as operating system vulnerabilities were starting to be patched more quickly, some exploit discoveries in applications

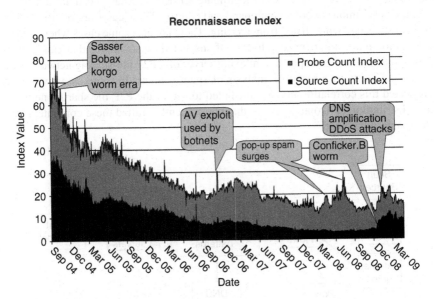

Fig. 13.7 Reconnaissance Index shows the contributions in the numbers of probes and the number of sources that are conducting the probes over time

initiated a surge in network scanning for vulnerabilities in applications including anti-virus software, weak database application passwords, and remote access applications. Some surges in pop-up spam activity to promote system scanning tools are noted. The rapid increase in the number of sources scanning increased significantly in late 2008 due to propagation of the Conficker worm. There have also been some recent surges in DNS amplification DDoS attacks that appear as probing activity to our analysis and affect the index.

13.5.1.2 Botnet Detection and Tracking

Based on the sources of malicious activity such as scanning for exploits and spam activity, analysis methods have been developed to correlate the activity of these malicious actors to likely control points and server hubs associated with botnets [49]. A high-level illustration of this analysis algorithm is shown in Fig. 13.8.

As shown in Fig. 13.8, the botnet detection analysis takes as input various reports of suspicious host activity, e.g., sources involved in scanning, spamming or DDoS attacks. These suspicious activity reports are further processed to extract the set of IP addresses that were involved in the suspicious activities. Next all flow records associated with the suspect IP addresses near the time of the activities are isolated. These flow records are then analyzed together to identify candidate botnet controllers. As shown in Fig. 13.8, DNS metadata is also used in the analysis. However, not all botnets use domain names as pointers to botnet servers; some point directly to IP addresses, therefore, we do not rely on the DNS metadata as a primary factor in detection. There are some types of legitimate services that have behavioral profiles that are very similar to botnet command and control. These cases are relatively few and can be easily white-listed from alerting. There are also some cases where a high correlation may exist between clusters of suspected bots/zombies that can lead to false-positives. For example, the indexing server of a P2P file-sharing network may trigger an alarm as a result of analysis of spam sources. In some cases, we have suspected this correlation may be attributed to use of the P2P file sharing network as a distribution of Trojan malware that consequently drafted these computers into the spamming botnet.

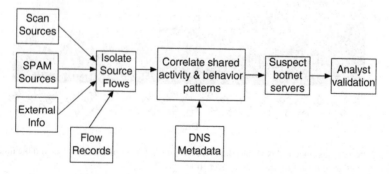

Fig. 13.8 Botnet detection algorithm summary

As shown in Fig. 13.8, the resulting suspect IP addresses are investigated by analysts to verify the type of function and validate association with botnet activities. Likely domain names and sometimes port information can be used to identify and track other control points of the botnets, and subsequent activity is used to help identify the members of the botnet(s) and further determine the types of activity the botnets are performing. These methods enable estimation of the relative sizes of botnets and validation of the intent to do harm through illegal and abusive activities such as exploits, DDoS attack, spamming activities, identity theft, etc.

The primary purpose of the botnet detection analysis is to determine if a given botnet presents a threat to network operations and services, customers, or to critical infrastructure. The information gained about the behavioral profiles of specific botnets, the malicious IP addresses, and associated domain names used can also be used to assist with isolation and blocking of malicious activity in the enterprise environment. General knowledge of the botnet technology, methods, and motives can be used to develop tools and operations functions that improve detection methods and automate the filter and/or alerting on suspected infections as part of routine network security operations.

Table 13.3 shows an example alarm from the botnet detection processing. A given alarm identifies an IP address and service port that is suspected to be supporting the botnet in some capacity. Triggers are identified as part of the alarm. For example, the first alarm indicates that 17 suspected botnet clients (zombies) associated, with this controller, were detected scanning (i.e., "sp:") on port 135 TCP (i.e., IP protocol 6). The range of analysis for this suspect is identified in a YYYYMMDDHH format, and the period of the latest alarm noted. Finally, a confidence score is provided that takes into account a number of additional flow characteristics that are generally indicative of botnet activity. A score that reaches a defined threshold is issued as an alarm to analysts for further investigation.

When botnet operators have purposeful tasks to perform, they are forced to engage in *botnet recruiting* in order to add new bots into their botnet(s). Fortunately, improvements in spam source controls and DDoS scrubbing technologies have caused increased volatility of bots engaged in these actions. Specifically, sustaining attacks requires a continual influx of new bots or at least a well established inventory. As the recruiting bots are exposed, so is the opportunity to defensively expose the command & control infrastructure of the associated botnet(s). While it is generally difficult to mitigate botnets, it is possible to squelch their strength and

Table 13.3 An example botnet alarm. For example, the first line shows a controller IP address (masked) with associated scanning activity ("sp") on port 135 TCP (protocol 6) from 17 zombies. Each alarm also contains times of activity and a confidence score

Server IP	Server port	Triggers	Earliest activity	Latest activity	Alarm time	Score
x.x.x.167	65146	sp:135-6(17)	2009050320	2009050704	2009050707	63
x.x.x.84	9517	sp:445-6(58),135-6(1)	2009050309	2009050707	2009050707	57.9
x.x.x.29	1122	sp:445-6(15)	2009050415	2009050619	2009050707	51.9

force activities on the part of botnet operators to maintain the botnet. I.e., force the botnet operator to perform botnet recruiting, which helps to reduce the attack power of the botnet.

13.5.1.3 Volumetric Anomaly Detection

Volumetric analysis is performed on each IP protocol, TCP port, UDP port, and ICMP type for changes in flow, packet, and byte volumes. This analysis measures significant changes in activity of each parameter relative to expected values. Generation of baseline or "expected" values is generally calculated based on historical activity. The baseline must account for the diurnal characteristics of network traffic activity and must also reasonably isolate any historical anomalies. Once anomalies are identified, further automated analysis is performed by the platform to identify contributing attributes that are reported to security analysts as alarm details for evaluation.

Volumetric analysis is a catch-all mechanism for detecting various types of events on the Internet. In addition to the alarming analysis, graphical tools provided by the platform allows analysts and customers the ability to look at short-term and long-term activity levels for specific ports and protocols. For example, Fig. 13.9 shows changes in network activity that resulted from patches that were applied to DNS servers in response to the recent disclosure of DNS cache poisoning attack techniques [88].

13.5.1.4 DDoS detection

The AT&T Security Analysis Platform also integrates commercial sub-systems to perform analysis and detection. In particular, multiple commercial DDoS detection systems [10] form part of the platform. One instance provides detection at a coarse "infrastructure" level. I.e., it is used to alert network operations and security analysts to significant traffic volume events that might have an impact on Internet service delivery. Because it is configured to look for large volume events in the core network of a Tier-1 ISP, this DDoS detection system will not detect smaller DDoS events, which, although not impacting on the network as a whole, might still be customer impacting. A second DDoS detection instance is therefore utilized to perform detection for customers who subscribe to this service, typically in combination with a DDoS mitigation service described below. This capability provides added sensitivity to customer designated network interfaces and address blocks, and it represents an analysis and reporting capability that complements the standard infrastructure DDoS detection. Finally, a third flow analysis platform is used to provide, among other types of analysis, intranet DDoS detection for private enterprise (VPN) customers. The alarms generated by these DDoS detection systems are ingested into the Security Analysis Platform for analysis and correlation with other detected anomalies.

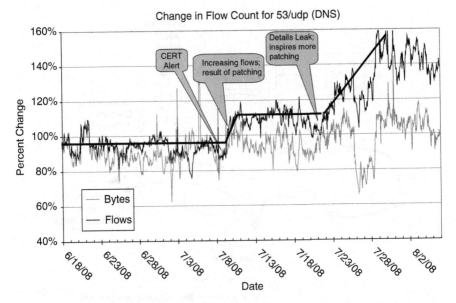

Fig. 13.9 Relative change in source-port 53/udp activity volume shows the effects of patching activities on the network in response to recent disclosure of recent DNS cache poisoning vulnerabilities. The solution to help alleviate the DNS cache poisoning threat was to force each query to assign a unique source port for DNS queries thus assigning a new session to each query. For performance reasons and simplicity of firewall rules, it had previously been common to use a fixed source port for DNS queries. This worked since DNS queries on port 53/udp are by definition single-packet sessions. As patches were installed in the wake of new information about the vulnerability and later exploit code, there were surges in patching efforts. These were revealed in network traffic behavior by a relative increase in the flow count on port 53/udp with no significant increase in byte count for the associated traffic. Randomization of the source port increased the number of flow records generated in DNS transactions

13.5.2 Automated or Compulsory Security Services

With the informational security services we dealt with in the preceding section, users were provided with information of possible or impending threats. Acting on such information, however, was largely left up to the users receiving the information with the service provider specifically not taking any mitigative action. There are, however, cases where service providers take unilateral action to prevent or mitigate specific security concerns. Below we consider two examples namely DDoS and spam mitigation.

13.5.2.1 DDoS Mitigation

In general service providers do not attempt autonomous mitigation of DDoS attacks. As we have indicated earlier, it is not always easy to distinguish between a DDoS

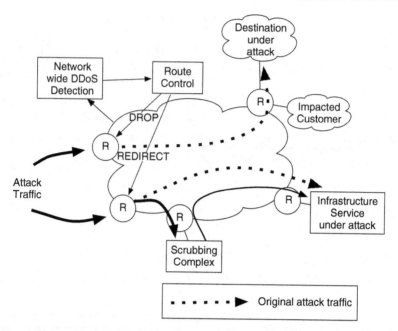

Fig. 13.10 DDoS mitigation techniques

attack and another legitimate surge in traffic, e.g., a flash crowd. DDoS mitigation techniques typically involve some negative side effects, therefore this possibility of a false positives in the DDoS detection mechanisms could be problematic. Further, some Internet destinations are almost constantly under attack and simply consider that as part of their operational costs.

There are, however, two scenarios where service providers do react to DDoS attacks as a normal course of action. One is when the attack in question is of such a magnitude that it starts to cause collateral damage in the network. A classic example involves an attack against a target that starts to indirectly impact other customers or network services. This example is depicted in the top part of Fig. 13.10. A second scenario involves an attack against a specific infrastructure service such as DNS. This example is illustrated in the bottom part of Fig. 13.10.

Figure 13.10 also shows two possible mitigation strategies that the provider might employ. As shown in the figure there is an implied DDoS detection mechanism, using techniques such as those described above, which precedes mitigation.

The simplest DDoS mitigation technique involves an approach called "blackholing" where the route to the attack target is tagged with a semantically "drop" label and distributed to ingress routers with a special route control function. Ingress routers in the provider network receive these routes and forward traffic to a specifically configured null interface, thus effectively dropping all traffic towards that destination. This approach is crude since *all* traffic destined for the advertised prefix will be dropped, whether attack traffic or wanted traffic. As such, this approach is best suited to the case where a very specific destination, e.g., a host specific route, is null routed. Of course all traffic to that specific destination will still be dropped, but the collateral damage is minimized. Fortunately, DDoS attacks are typically not as distributed as one might expect [57]. A more desirable approach is to surgically distribute the drop-labeled route to only those ingress routers that have the majority of attack traffic [83]. This approach is illustrated at the top of Fig. 13.10. Despite its shortcomings, blackholing is a useful mitigation mechanisms for service providers. In cases where significant DDoS traffic volumes cross boundaries between provider networks, smaller providers often seek blocking assistance from larger providers if the traffic is overwhelming their network. Unfortunately, this type of control does little to help the target of the attack. It is desirable to provide more surgical and more customer friendly mitigation services.

A more sophisticated DDoS mitigation strategy involves deploying dedicated DDoS mitigation devices [22] at strategic "scrubbing" locations in the provider network. In this case, the route control function advertises a prefix associated with the attack target to ingress routers in such a way that traffic towards the attack target is effectively "redirected" towards the scrubbing complex. This is shown in the bottom part of Fig. 13.10. This approach is attractive because in principle only attack traffic is filtered out at the scrubbing complexes so that wanted traffic can still be forwarded to the ultimate destination. On the flip side, the fact that dedicated infrastructure has to be deployed means that this approach can typically not be utilized for all provider traffic but is limited to protecting infrastructure services, or, as we will outline in Section 13.5.3, when it is offered as part of (paid for) supplementary security services.

13.5.2.2   Spam Mitigation

In addition to Internet access and basic services like DNS, ISPs typically provide a number of consumer or business-grade end user services to their customers including email services, Web-hosting, chat-rooms, Web portals, etc. Of these services, email typically has the highest take rate and also requires special care from a security perspective.

In this section we will describe the essential functionality of the security frontend to the AT&T consumer email platform as an example ISP email infrastructure which effectively adapts to ongoing email security concerns in a highly scalable manner.

Figure 13.11 depicts the major functional components of the multi-tiered AT&T email platform. External SMTP connections first encounter the *connection management* component. The connection management component maintains a reputation system whereby external SMTP connections are classified based on the historic and/or current behavior of their source IP addresses and are allocated resources accordingly. The resources of concern here are the number of SMTP processes that are allowed to be spawned. First, connections from known and trusted IPs (*friends*) are given unlimited resources. Connections from unknown source IPs are classified into a *default* class. The default class receives enough resources so that under normal operating conditions, e.g., when there are no email DoS attacks, no blocking occurs. However, the resources allocated to the default class are constrained to

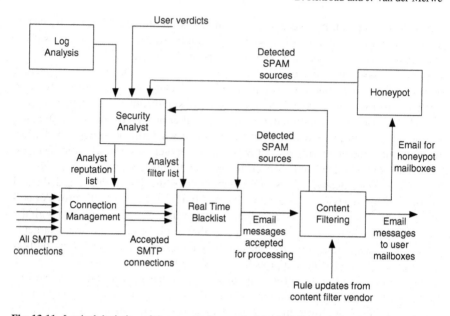

Fig. 13.11 Logical depiction of the security frontend of the AT&T email platform

prevent impact on the friends class when there are attacks. In the case of resource exhaustion, the sending SMTP connection may be terminated with a temporary unavailable SMTP response (i.e., response code 450: *Requested action not taken; mailbox unavailable or busy*). The third class of source IPs, which are generally known to be spam sources, fall in the *throttle* classification where the resources allocated to the set and/or to individual IPs are significantly constrained. Specifically, on average connections in this group would typically receive a 450 SMTP response 80–90% of the time.

SMTP connections that pass through this first level of defense are passed to the *real time blacklist (RBL)* component. The RBL parses and analyzes the SMTP protocol to determine the trustworthiness of an SMTP source. For example it performs reverse-DNS lookups on the domain name reported by the SMTP source and note discrepancies between this lookup and the SMTP source IP address. As the name suggests, the RBL is also dynamically updated based on feedback from subsequent tiers in the email platform. For example, information concerning detected spam sources is fed back from the next tier, so that this information can be used in ensuing rounds to decide whether or not to accept a connection from the same source. Based on this analysis, the RBL may terminate the connection with an SMTP unavailable response (i.e., response code 550: *Requested action not taken: mailbox unavailable*).

The RBL also receives a set of sieve filtering rules [33] from security analysts. These rules are utilized to queue accepted email messages for differential treatment. For example, most email messages are simply passed to the next defense layer, however, some might be queued as possible phishing attacks for analyst attention.

The third tier in the email processing platform consist of a commercial email *content screening* product. At this level email content is analyzed to determine whether any spam and or phishing rules are triggered. Like the RBL, the rules of the content filtering component are constantly updated. As mentioned above detected spam sources are fed back to the RBL tier for automatic inclusion in the RBL filter set, and the output is also provided to security analysts for further manual evaluation. Finally, email messages are delivered to user mailboxes, with an indication as to whether the email platform considered it spam or not.

The email processing platform also maintains *honeypot* or spamtrap [77] accounts. As we explained earlier, these are bogus email accounts, set up explicitly to attract spam email. As such, all email destined for a spamtrap is spam by definition. Sending this mail through the content filtering system therefore serves as an indication of spam that may have been missed by the content filters. This information is also made available to security analysts.

Users who are the final recipients of the email are ultimately the judges of the accuracy of the classification from the content filtering system. The email platform allows users to provide this judgment back to the system in the form of *user verdicts*. I.e., indicating that system classified spam was in fact not spam, or, conversely indicating that mail that passed through the system unflagged was spam.

In addition to all the sources of information already mention as informing them, security analysts also perform *log analysis* of the various system component logs. Indeed the human *security analysts* remain an integral component of this system. While well understood components of the analyses can and should be automated, the role of skilled analysts to react swiftly to changes in the strategy of perpetrators remain crucial to the success of dealing with unwanted email.

The success of this tiered approach is best appreciated by considering the fact that the platform receives in excess of 1.4 billion spam email messages on a typical day and is ordinarily successful in blocking more than 99.3% of it.

13.5.3 Supplementary or Optional Security Services

We now consider security services that users might specifically subscribe to. Service providers might offer these services as a means to differentiate their existing service offers, or might offer it as stand alone services. Either way, there is an implied economic incentive for service providers to provide these services.

13.5.3.1 Customer Specific DDoS Mitigation

Customer specific DDoS mitigation is technically accomplished in much the same way as the DDoS mitigation described earlier in Section 13.5.2. Traffic destined for attack targets is passed through scrubbers to allow only wanted traffic to pass to the subscribing customers. By subscribing to the service, the key difference is in the detection of DDoS attacks. Specifically, as shown in Fig. 13.12, a customer specific

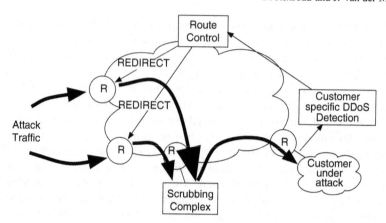

Fig. 13.12 Customer specific DDoS mitigation

DDoS detection mechanism is needed in order to detect attacks at the granularity where customer links might be impacted. (As opposed to the much higher capacity provider links.) This might involve deploying DDoS detection tools at the customer premises, or might be a network based detection capability that is tuned to detect attacks at the appropriate granularity. Since severe DDoS attacks might overload the regular customer links, a back channel might be needed to alarm on attacks when a customer premises deployment is performed.

As before, once an attack is detected, route control mechanisms are utilized to redirect customer traffic to an appropriate scrubbing complex, and "cleaned" traffic is sent on for delivery to the customer.

13.5.3.2 Network Based Security Services

The complexities of dealing with network security make the outsourcing of network policy enforcement to service providers as a network based managed security service an attractive option for customers. The acquisition, installation and maintenance of security equipment is handled by the service provider, while customers maintain the freedom to specify (and modify) their own security policies. Security services that can be provided in this manner provide bi-directional protection of customer networks from Internet-based security threats through stateful firewalls, network address translation (NAT), URL filtering, intrusion detection systems (IDSs) and content inspection.

Figure 13.13 depicts a high level view of an architecture that enables network based security services. As shown in the figure, security services are provided via security data centers that are directly connected to the provider network. Customer traffic to and from the Internet passes through these security data centers en route to the customer's network(s).

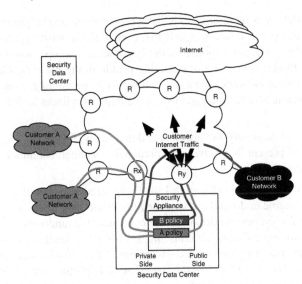

Fig. 13.13   Network based security services

It is critically important that individual customers private traffic remains separate as it routes to and traverses through the secure data center, where policy is applied. Another key concern is ensuring that individual customers security policies remain distinct (or virtualized) within the devices that are enforcing the set of security services, and that those policies can be easily and securely administered. As illustrated in the figure, separation of customer traffic is achieved by logically separate "connections" from the customer's network to the data center. The "connections" are realized in practice through tunneling or VPN technologies. Similarly, within the data center VLAN technologies are used to maintain the traffic separation. Modern security appliances [19, 34] are also capable of per-VLAN security policies and processing so that the per-customer separation is maintained all the way from the Internet gateway router, i.e., router R_y in Fig. 13.13, to the customer's network(s).

13.6   Security Operations

Network operations are a standard consideration in any environment where reliability is a factor. There are some added considerations when addressing the security operations needs of a network. The network security environment is continually changing. New attacks are created. Variations on old attacks are perfected. Human behavior is manipulated in creatively new ways to allow exploitation. New exploit methods are cumulative with old methods. Even as workarounds and patches are introduced, it is not unusual for old vulnerabilities to be reintroduced or similar ones to be created through the life-cycle of even stable systems. This suggests that an automation strategy is imperative to assist with detection and response methods as security threats evolve. It also suggests that even with the most aggressive strategy to automate detection and response methods, some manual operations are going to be necessary to maintain a secure operating profile in the network. Generally, the distinction between network operations and security operations comes down to the following characteristics, which stem from the malicious intent associated with security events:

- Failures occur randomly, but attacks are deliberately timed.
- Failures will present themselves in a predictable manner, but attacks may be intentionally deceiving.

Components of the network will fail somewhat randomly, but ultimately, the results are predictable and can be characterized. While new devices, software, and systems will develop new modes of failure over time, the randomness of the events generally do not have significant consequences on the overall performance of the network. Of course there are isolated exceptions.[11] Conversely, security events are malicious, and thus will be planned to occur at an opportune time to place the attacker at an advantage. For example, an attacker will attempt to take advantage of a newly discovered vulnerability before there is an opportunity to create and/or deploy a suitable patch.

As network failures will time themselves randomly, they will also present themselves in a predictable manner. While the diagnosis of a root cause of a network failure may not be straight forward, it is generally possible to create logical rules to diagnose the cause (see Chapter 12). Again, considering that security events are generally malicious, they can be intentionally disguised to appear as one thing while in reality being something different. Or events can be created to divert attention from the real event. For example, an attacker may launch a denial of service attack against one resource to divert attention from a penetration attack or to mask penetration probes against a target. Tactics such as diversion, concealment, and obscurity can and will be used to achieve the objective.

So while network operations will seek to find the simple explanation for a problem, a security operations team will need to dig deeper, always considering what motivation and technique may have been used by an attacker to trigger events. For this reason, it is generally recommended to have a security operations team represented in the analysis of root cause for network events, particularly if there is any suggestion of strange coincidences or unusual traffic activity.

13.6.1 Components of Security Operations

In this section we consider the components or entities involved in security operations and the relationships between those entities. Figure 13.14 depicts the organizational

---

[11] Case in point is an outage in the AT&T frame relay network in 1998, where a complete network outage resulted because of a software issue that propagated between switches [69].

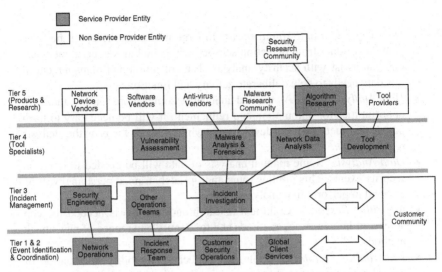

Fig. 13.14 Generic overview of the organizations involved in operations security

components involved in network security operations. The structure follows the typical tiered approach which, as we discussed in Section 13.3.1, ensures that security events can be responded to in timely fashion by the appropriate technical experts. Figure 13.14 also illustrates the fact that security operations is not a standalone function. In particular, security specific organizations (or functions) interact with other organizations within the service provider, interact with vendors and other relevant communities outside of the service provider organization, and of course interact with the customer community.

Having such a holistic view of network security operations is critically important to ensure its success. I.e., the complexity involved in any particular function represented in Fig. 13.14, implies that the function be fulfilled by a specialist, who might not necessarily be aware of the holistic view. E.g., network engineers tend to be focused on making the network operate, similarly, analysts tend to be focused on the activities they need to perform. Consequently, some of the tools that will be needed to help the analysts do their job and to help the network engineers be more successful can easily be overlooked without taking a more holistic approach.

To form a holistic view, below we list and discuss some of the functions that form part of security operations.

Functions Associated with Network Security Operations

- *Event Detection* Sensors that detect events that are either directly security related or provide information that contributes to identifying and understanding security events.

- *Data Collection and Management* In large networks, there will be large amounts of data from detection sensors, which includes general metadata that can assist with security analysis. The collection and management of this data needs to be a deliberate activity and function.
- *Data Analysis Tools* As manual analysis becomes more routine, there are opportunities for automation and refinement. It will be necessary to have people that focus on tools development while analysts focus on the analysis requirements.
- *Data Analysis* Some manual analysis of data will be needed to interpret security events. This implies some appropriately trained personnel will be on hand to perform that analysis.
- *Algorithm Research* Continual research and analysis is needed to keep abreast of known attack methods and to identify emergence of new attack methods.
- *Vulnerability Database* Tools that collect vulnerability information of many kinds that relate to hardware, operating systems, and application software used in and around the network environment.
- *Network Device Vendor Relationships* Ultimately, the creators of network and network security products know the most about their products. The product vendors do not always know the network environment. A cooperative relationship with vendors is necessary to merge the two.
- *Network Event Root Cause Analysis* When events occur, it may be easy to make the problem go away, but understanding the root cause with a balanced consideration of potential malice is important to recognizing and preventing future security issues.
- *Situational Awareness Tracking* This is the activity to be cognizant of events that are taking place in the world and how they might influence the security posture of the network and influence network activity.
- *Coordination and Collaboration Tools* As security analysis teams become more complex and disciplines become more specialized, tools are needed to exchange and preserve information efficiently.
- *Case Management* Tools that provide the capability to track and record the status of network and security events.
- *Customer/User Support* Customers and users of network services will depend on your network expertise, data, and controls to help maintain a good security posture.
- *Mitigation Mechanisms* It is not enough to simply identify and understand problems. Policies, tools and procedures need to be in place to remediate and hopefully prevent problems.
- *Network Engineers and Tools Development* Automation is paramount to recognizing relevant issues in large-scale networks.

Event Detection, Data Collection and Management and Data Analysis Tools   These functions are covered in detail in the earlier part of this chapter.

Data Analysis   Security Intelligence is discussed at length in this chapter. It is important to develop a team of analysts that are well acquainted with what various security attack events look like in the available data. Further, it is equally important to be able to recognize what normal traffic activity looks like. Every network is architected a little differently, data is collected a little differently, metadata is generated, collected, and managed differently, and traffic profiles vary depending on the user demographics. For these reasons, there is no substitute for training and practice of capable analysts. By detecting, characterizing, and addressing small network events, management of larger events become a matter of routine rather than a stressful experience, and the chances of accurate diagnosis and action are improved.

Algorithm Research   Network security is an arms race between the ability of attackers to exploit in competition with the ability to anticipate, detect, prevent, and remediate. In an enterprise environment, there are already a number of commercial tools that provide reasonably sophisticated analysis. In service provider environments, there are much fewer tools that are available commercially that can provide the appropriate perspective. Therefore, there may be a need to perform research and development into algorithms that characterize data, detect events, and help determine appropriate courses of action. Highly skilled and well trained analysts become very good at recognizing specific types of activities. But no analyst possesses all the skills necessary to recognize or characterize complex events, and analysts each possess different strengths. Researchers that have disciplines in mathematics, data presentation/visualization, and algorithm creation help to create the tools analysts will ultimately use. It is advisable to include algorithm researchers in a forensics activities. For example, when an event was not automatically detected but perhaps should have been, researchers should be employed to look for evidence of the event in the underlying historical data, develop algorithms or methods for detecting future events, and testing the algorithms against on-going activity to help validate the algorithm.

Vulnerability Database   Many security issues for systems are known. But there are many systems, network elements, operating system versions, and platforms that make it virtually impossible for any one person to know the full set of vulnerabilities and implications on network operations. Managing this complexity is paramount to managing a secure network. Collecting a database of potentially relevant vulnerability information (and exploit information when practical) is a helpful tool for engineers, systems managers, and security analysts alike. Theoretically, we should be able to identify all vulnerabilities for systems, fix those vulnerabilities as soon as they are discovered, and many of the security threats will be mitigated. In reality, not all vulnerabilities are known, and not infrequently vulnerabilities are exploited before they become public knowledge (so-called "zero-day" events). In other cases, vulnerabilities are known by a few and not disclosed to the users for lack of suitable fixes. The only practical defense is to engineer systems and networks using a defense in depth strategy. This type of engineering is regularly performed in the context of reliability engineering, which is commonly known as engineering for "no single point of failure". In security engineering, a similar strategy should be used to assure no single point of failure in a security mechanism will significantly compromise the assets that need to be protected.

Network Device Vendor Relationships There is a mutual benefit to developing a strong relationship with vendors that provide your network products. Most vendor designers do not actually use their products in real-world operations. While they may perform robust testing of their products, it is enormously difficult to anticipate all of the negative test cases that would be needed to thoroughly identify any issues in products. There is no substitute for reality, where many unanticipated circumstances will be encountered. Obviously, it will be desirable to report behavior that appears to be a direct security threat. But there is also benefit to reporting behavior that appears to be innocuous, since that behavior could be used to create a much more insidious problem. Similarly, having developed a strong relationship, vendors will become more comfortable and feel more obligated to communicate suspected issues that they have discovered such as vulnerabilities and exploits. One should never assume that a vendor's product is either secure or accurate, even if it is a security product.

Network Event Root Cause Analysis When network events occur, it is common practice to consider the "root cause" for the network event. Security representation should always be a part of network event analysis to consider the potential malicious motivations and techniques that could have been related to or the cause of the event. As stated previously, there may be malicious intent involved and attempts to make one type of event look like another. While network engineers and operators diagnose what appears to be the problem, security analysts should consider the possibility of other types of activities that may be taking place. In other words, it is the security analyst's role to act as a conspiracy theorist. Obviously, there is a balance that must be maintained. There is little value in disrupting normal operations and consuming excessive resources to investigate elaborate conspiracy theories. The security analysts should consider the possibilities and follow only those that have merit considering the likely impact to business risk and operations. Again, practice is the best way to develop an appropriate balance.

Situational Awareness Tracking There are activities and events that reside outside the network but can still affect the state of the network. Situational awareness is the practice or art of keeping abreast of conditions that could affect the network. For a service provider, national security status and terrorist threats, natural disasters, political events and other major events, personnel issues or threats, existing network events/outages, and other factors will all have a potential influence on the focus of security operations. Sometimes events can come from unlikely places. For example, Fig. 13.15 shows the effects of online viewing of the 2009 Inauguration event for President Barack Obama on UDP traffic volumes. This type of activity change could easily have been interpreted as either a DDoS attack or a worm had

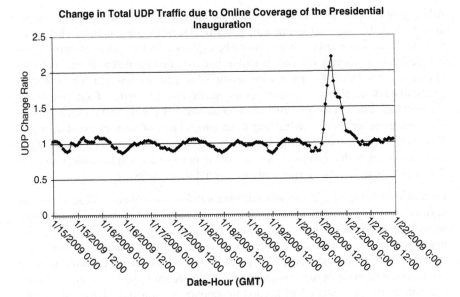

Fig. 13.15 UDP traffic change due to online viewing of the Inauguration of President Barack Obama

outside influences not been taken into consideration. Situational awareness and investigation of the event dynamics helped avert suspicions of malicious behavior in this case. The most common situational awareness "tools" in use likely are to have current affairs news casts, e.g., CNN and TWC, available on video monitors in the operations centers.

Coordination and Collaboration Tools While not discounting the value of this form of situational awareness, it is not sufficient. It will be useful to have some tools available that allows analysts to make notes on relevant events to track. Blogging tools might be adapted for this purpose. As new analysts start their work-day or shift, the situational awareness notes and recent cases provide a good starting point. At the end of each shift, analysts should check several internal and external sources of information that may have updates and relevant news that could have implications on network operations. Relevant points should be extracted from sites and included in the notes. Similarly, activities that have taken place during the shift which have been determined to be irrelevant, or more importantly, activities that need to be watched should be noted. Collaboration tools should keep a record of activities that extend beyond simple management of alerts and cases.

Case Management There will be a need for recording security events, delegating the investigation and/or the mitigation of those events and tracking them to closure. For a network of any significant size, there will be security issues and events that range from small and routine to large and complex. Issues might include situations or scenarios that are identified to help prevent security events from occurring.

Addressing issues to prevent events is a good thing and worthy of tracking. For example, it may be necessary to implement a critical security patch in network devices to assure a particular vulnerability cannot be exploited. In the course of implementing the patch, temporary mitigation actions may be implemented to assure attempts to exploit the vulnerability are not successful or at least are detected. There will be a need to track the status of security issues and events. A network of any significant size will have a case tracking system to address network events, and it may be possible to integrate security issue tracking as an integral part of network event tracking. However, since network security is often managed and functions as a distinct specialized discipline that complements network operations and engineering, it may be desirable to track security issues and cases as a distinct entity.

Customer/User Support Invariably, customers and/or users of network services will have security and operational difficulties. In the interest of maintaining customer satisfaction with the service, some amount of security support in the form of event management, data analysis, forensic & root cause analysis is needed to help customers resolve their issues. This seems somewhat obvious, but supporting customer events can become a burden on resources if the security operations costs do not account for the time and effort needed to support this function. There are significant peripheral benefits to providing this type of support since understanding the issues and concerns of customers can lead to developing services and functions in the network that address customer needs.

Network Engineers and Tools Development While not an intrinsic part of security operations, the people that develop tools that are used for monitoring, analyzing, and protecting the security of the network and network users often have the best knowledge about what works and what would constitute a misuse of tools that have been developed. Since security operations can be forced to extend outside the envelope of normal or expected use, it is best to plan for and include development representatives in the response execution for fringe events. For example, network devices, analytical tools, and systems almost always have features that may not have been fully tested or have not been integrated into normal network operations. Engineering may know what these features are and how they can be used. That could mean the difference between avoiding an event or having to recover from a disruptive outage.

13.7 The Indefinite Arms Race

More than any other aspect of networking, security appears set to be an indefinite arms race between those providing network services and services enabled by networks, and those who seek to use the same resources for illegitimate activities. Given the fact that a significant part (perhaps the majority) of such nefarious activity is economically motivated, plus the fact that the reliance of modern society on such networks continue to grow, suggest that this situation will persist. Indeed, realizing that service provider network security is as much a *process* and an *approach* as it is a technical discipline, is perhaps the single most important message in this chapter.

Below we summarize key insights from the approach to service provider network security presented in this chapter and provide thoughts on important future directions.

13.7.1 A Service Provider Approach to Network Security

Understand the Problem in Context A critical first step in dealing with network security is to understand the nature of the problem in the context of the specific provider network in question. I.e., understand intrinsic threats and how those are shaped by business relationships, fundamental technological dependencies or limitations and the incentives of different role players.

Develop and Follow a Comprehensive Framework to Network Security A comprehensive security framework is as much about technology as it is about structure, procedures and relationships. The most basic technical component of such a framework involves the configuration of network elements to be robust against exploitation and abuse.

Derive Actionable Network Intelligence Network monitoring at different granularities and timescales provide the raw data, which should be combined with other information sources, to derive security related network intelligence. Automation is crucial to support and enable analysis by security experts.

Pro-actively Deploy Network Security Services Acting on network intelligence to protect the network and to provide security services provides a "closed-loop" environment and to some extent offsets the economic imbalance between legitimate and illegitimate economies.

Take a Holistic Approach to Network Operations Network security operations should be performed within a holistic context with appropriate relationships and interactions between security functions, other service provider functions and non service provider functions like vendors and customers.

13.7.2 Future Directions

Safe Sharing of Security Intelligence We have emphasized the importance of each service provider developing good network security intelligence. To the extent that each provider is only part of the global network infrastructure, there is a need to share such security intelligence across service providers. There are some existing proposals and solutions along these lines [6, 8, 9]. One example is the anomaly

Fingerprint Sharing Alliance [9] which allows summary information about an attack (i.e., a fingerprint) to be shared between participants. Another example is the ATLAS initiative [8], whereby each service provider deploy devices in their network which runs a type of honeypot. Data collected from the honeypot is then shared with the third party ATLAS-service provider and made available to all participants. These initiatives are moving in the right direction, however, more work is needed especially to address the delicate balance between sharing richer information, while at the same time not running afoul of privacy concerns or revealing information that can be abused by a competitor.

Secure Protocols While we cautioned in Section 13.2 that secure protocols are not the proverbial "silver bullet", such initiatives should be encouraged and secure protocols should be developed and deployed where they address security needs.

Secure Network Architectures Despite receiving much attention from the networking research community [12,73,74,89], the security implications of the best-effort, unaccountable service model of the Internet architecture remains an unresolved problem. While the role of the network in mitigating other "higher layer" security concerns might be debatable, it seems clear that this problem can fundamentally only be solved "in the network". Some argue that these shortcomings can only be addressed in a clean-slate network design that is unencumbered by backwards compatibility with the current network [18].

Improve Incentives In the context of this chapter we have focused on one aspect of attempting to balance the playing field between good and bad actors, namely economics. Generalizing this to architectures and protocols that aim to provide mechanisms to correct the imbalance appears to be a promising direction. We consider a number of examples: At the transport protocol level "client puzzles" have been proposed [45] as a means for servers under DDoS attack to selectively accept connections from (presumably) legitimate clients that have successfully solved a puzzle. This approach shifts the balance of power as the client is required to perform work before any server resources are allocated to it. At the architectural level a DoS-resistant architecture has been proposed [35]. This architecture proposes to change the any-to-any service model of the Internet by being explicitly aware of whether a node acts as a client or a server and further explicitly aims to tilt the cost of communication in favor of the server. Economic disincentives have been proposed as a spam mitigation mechanism [51]. In essence this scheme associates cryptographic "stamps" to each sent email message, and canceled stamps (i.e., email that was deemed unwanted by the recipient) eventually results in the sender either having to pay to continue sending email, or, being blocked from sending email altogether. The adoption of these specific proposals remain uncertain, however, the fact that they all attempt to specifically address incentives appears to be a promising direction.

Scalability As we have indicated throughout this chapter, scalability is a significant network security concern, both in terms of the volumes of data used to derive network intelligence, and in terms of mitigation mechanisms and services employed to protect the network and its users. Most existing network security solutions are aimed at the enterprise market. This is expected because, first, enterprises are more security aware and are therefore willing to spend money to protect the applications they use. Second, enterprises present a sweet spot in terms of scalability. Finding scalable security solutions in the consumer market remains a significant challenge. The fact that this market is very price sensitive will further exacerbate the problem. However, it could be argued that the lack of security solutions in the consumer space is a significant contributor to the overall security problem as unmanaged home networks make easy prey for botnet recruiting effort. It is therefore important that security solutions be found in this space.

Internet Governance   We touched in passing on the role of Internet governance when considering DNSSEC in Section 13.2.3. Internet governance is largely orthogonal to core network security concerns. However, understanding the proper role for national and international bodies in governing the Internet and the potential impact on the security of the Internet, depending on how those roles are defined, is an important open question.

Cyber Critical Infrastructure   Similarly, we considered the fact that commercial entities are responsible for running and maintaining critical infrastructure in Section 13.2.5. Given the global dependence on this infrastructure, both economic and governmental, it would behoove governments and other role players to better understand the implications of this. In the U.S., recognition of these dependencies lead to the establishment of Information Sharing and Analysis Centers (ISACs) [42]. ISACs have been established on a per-sector basis to share information concerning cyber threats between critical infrastructure owners, operators and government. These industry initiatives might be complemented by government making the best quality security solutions available to commercial industry, and encouraging the special solutions that are being devised for protection of government to be used commercially as well. Similarly, government procurements of services should be helping to establish infrastructure that can be applied to help protect telecommunications of all of the critical infrastructure categories that depend on reliable communications in worst-case scenarios.

Acknowledgments   We would like to acknowledge the contributions of many of our colleagues in AT&T Labs and the AT&T Chief Security Office (CSO) organization. To a large extent we are simply reporting on their efforts over many years. We especially want to thank Steve Wood for explaining to us his work on the AT&T email platform, Adrian Cepleanu and Tom Scholl for expounding details of network security configuration, Joseph Blanda Jr. for sharing details about network based security services, Dave Gross who pioneered much of the security analysis work and Ed Amoroso, AT&T's Chief Security Officer whose technical leadership provides the structure in which much of this work takes place. We would also like to thank the editors as well as Bill Beckett, Dave Gross, Patrick McDaniel, Subhabrata Sen and Tom Scholl for providing insightful comments on earlier versions of this chapter.

References

1. Daytona Data Management System. Retrieved from http://www.research.att.com/~daytona/.
2. DNS Threats & DNS Weaknesses. Retrieved from http://www.dnssec.net/dns-threats.php.
3. North American Operator's Group. Retrieved from www.nanog.org.
4. US-CERT United States Computer Emergency Readiness Team. Retrieved from www.us-cert. gov.
5. The continuing denial of service threat posed by DNS recursion (v2.0). (2006). Retrieved from http://www.us-cert.gov/reading_room/DNS-recursion033006.pdf
6. Allman, M., Blanton, E., Paxson, V., & Shenker, S. (2006). Fighting coordinated attackers with cross-organizational information sharing. In *Workshop on Hot Topics in Networks (HotNets)*, Irvine, CA.
7. Andert, D., Wakefield, R., & Weise, J. (2002). Trust modeling for security architecture development. Retrieved from Sun BluePrints OnLine. Retrieved from http://www.sun.com/blueprints.
8. Arbor Networks. ATLAS initiative services & requirements – A service provider's guide to participating in the ATLAS initiative. Retrieved from www.arbornetworks.com.
9. Arbor Networks. Fingerprint sharing alliance – A community for coordinated, rapid attack resolution. Retrieved from www.arbornetworks.com.
10. Arbor Networks. (2009). Arbor peakflow SP pervasive network visibility, security and profitable managed services. Retrieved from http://www.arbornetworks.com/peakflowsp.
11. Arends, R., Austein, R., Larson, M., Massey, D., & Rose, S. (2005). Protocol modifications for the DNS security extensions. IETF RFC 4035.
12. Argyraki, K., & Cheriton, D. (2005). Network capabilities: The good, the bad and the ugly. In *Workshop on Hot Topics in Networks (HotNets)*, November 2005.
13. Atkins, D., & Austein, R. (2004). Threat analysis of the Domain Name System (DNS). IETF RFC 3833.
14. AT&T Laboratories, Information Security Center of Excellence. Seven pillars of carrier-grade security in the AT&T MPLS network.
15. Claise, B. (Ed.). (2004). Cisco systems NetFlow services export version 9. IETF RFC 3954. Retrieved from http://www.ietf.org/rfc/rfc3954.txt.
16. Baran, P. (1964). On distributed communications: I. Introduction to distributed communications networks. In *RAND Memorandum, RM-3420-PR*.
17. Barbir, A., Murphy, S., & Yang, Y. (2006). Generic threats to routing protocols. In *IETF RFC 4593*, October 2006.
18. Bellovin, S., Clark, D., Perrig, A., & D. S. (Eds.). (2005). A clean-slate design for the next-generation secure Internet. www.geni.net/documents.html. In *Community Workshop Report (GDD-05-02)*.
19. Bouchard, M., & Mangum, F. Beyond UTM – The value of a purpose-built network security platform. Available from http://www.fortinet.com.
20. Butler, K., Farley, T., McDaniel, P., & Rexford, J. (2007). A survey of BGP security issues and solutions. Retrieved from http://www.cs.princeton.edu/~jrex/papers/bgp-security08.pdf.
21. Carrel, D., & Grant, L. (1997). The TACACS+ Protocol. IETF draft: draft-grant-tacacs-02.txt, January 1997.
22. Cisco Systems. Defeating DDOS attacks. Retrieved from http://www.cisco.com/en/US/ products/ps5888/prod_white_papers_list.html.
23. Cisco Systems. (2009). Cisco security advisory: Cisco IOS software multiple features crafted UDP packet vulnerability. Retrieved from http://www.cisco.com/warp/public/707/cisco-sa-20090325-udp.shtml.
24. Clark, D. (1988). The design philosophy of the DARPA internet protocols. In *SIGCOMM '88: Symposium Proceedings on Communications Architectures and protocols* (pp. 106–114).
25. Computer Crime Research Center. (2005). Hackers: Companies encounter rise of cyber extortion. Retrieved from http://www.crime-research.org/news/24.05.2005/Hackers-companies-encounter-rise-cyber-extortion/.

26. Cranor, C., Johnson, T., Spatscheck, O., & Shkapenyuk, V. (2003). Gigascope: A stream database for network applications. In *Proc. ACM SIGMOD*, San Diego, CA (pp. 647–651).
27. Department of Homeland Security. (2003). The national strategy to secure cyberspace. Retrieved from http://www.dhs.gov/xlibrary/assets/National_Cyberspace_Strategy.pdf.
28. Ellison, C., & Schneier, B. (2000). Ten risks of PKI: What you're not being told about public key infrastructure. *Computer Security Journal, 16*(1), 17.
29. Espiner, T. (2008). Georgia accuses Russia of coordinated cyberattack. Retrieved from http://news.cnet.com/8301 1009_31001415083.html.
30. Evers, J. (2005). Is latest can of worms a cyber-crime turf war? Retrieved from http://software. silicon.com/malware/0,3800003100,39151483,00.htm.
31. Feamster, N., Mao, Z. M., & Rexford, J. (2004). BorderGuard: Detecting cold potatoes from peers. In *IMC '04: Proceedings of the 4th ACM SIGCOMM Conference on Internet Measurement*, New York, NY (pp. 213–218).
32. Goodell, G., Aiello, W., Griffin, T., Ioannidis, J., McDaniel, P., & Rubin, A. (2003). Working around BGP: An incremental approach to improving security and accuracy in interdomain routing. In *Proceedings of the NDSS*, San Diego, CA.
33. Guenther, P., & Showalter, T. (2008). Sieve: An email filtering language. IETF RFC 5228, January 2008.
34. Gupta, M. Single PAss Inspection Engine: The architecture for profitable MSSP services. Available from: http://www.ipolicynetworks.com/.
35. Handley, M., & Greenhalgh, A. (2004). Steps towards a DoS-resistant internet architecture. In *FDNA '04: Proceedings of the ACM SIGCOMM Workshop on Future Directions in Network Architecture*, Portland, OR.
36. Hellweg, E. (2004). When bot nets attack. Retrieved from http://www.technologyreview.com/ Infotech/13771/.
37. Honeynet Project. (2006). Know your enemy: Honeynets. Retrieved from http://www. honeynet.org/papers.
38. Huston, G. (2007). The ISP Column – Trust. Retrieved from http://www.isoc.org/pubs/isp/.
39. IANA. IANA IPv4 Address Space Registry. Available from http://www.iana.org/assignments/ ipv4-address-space/.
40. Iannaccone, G., Chuah, C.-N., Mortier, R., Bhattacharyya, S., & Diot, C. (2002). Analysis of link failures in an IP backbone. In *IMW '02: Proceedings of the 2nd ACM SIGCOMM Workshop on Internet Measurement*, New York, NY (pp. 237–242).
41. ICANN Security and Stability Advisory Committee. (2008). SSAC advisory on fast flux hosting and DNS. Retrieved from http://www.icann.org/en/committees/security/sac025.pdf.
42. ISACCOUNCIL.ORG. (2009). The role of information sharing and analysis centers (ISACs) in private/public sector critical infrastructure protection. Available from http://www.isaccouncil. org.
43. ITU-T telecommunication standardization sector of ITU. Series X: Data networks, open system communications and security. Information technology – Open systems interconnection – The directory: Public-key and attribute certificate frameworks. ITU-T Recommendation X.509, 2008.
44. John, J. P., Moshchuk, A., Gribble, S. D., & Krishnamurthy, A. (2009). Studying spamming botnets using botlab. In *Proceedings of the Second Symposium on Networked Systems Design and Implementation (NSDI)*.
45. Juels, A., & Brainard, J. (1999). Client puzzles: A cryptographic countermeasure against connection depletion attacks. In *Proceedings of the 1999 Network and Distributed System Security Symposium*.
46. Jung, J., Krishnamurthy, B., & Rabinovich, M. (2002). Flash crowds and denial of service attacks: Characterization and implications for CDNs and web sites. In *Proceedings of the 11th International Conference on World Wide Web*, ACM Press, Honolulu, Hawaii (pp. 252–262).
47. Kalafut, A. J., Van der Merwe, J., & Gupta, M. (2009). Communities of interest for Internet traffic prioritization. In *Proceedings of IEEE Global Internet Symposium*.

48. Kanich, C., Kreibich, C., Levchenko, K., Enright, B., Voelker, G., Paxson, V., & Savage, S. (2008). Spamalytics: An empirical analysis of spam marketing conversion. In *15th ACM Conference on Computer and Communications Security (CCS)*, Alexandria, VA.

49. Karasaridis, A., Rexroad, B., & Hoeflin, D. (2007). Wide-scale botnet detection and characterization. In *Conference on Hot Topics in Understanding Botnets (HotBots)*, Cambridge, MA.

50. Kent, S., Lynn, C., & Seo, K. (2000). Secure border gateway protocol (S-BGP). *IEEE JSAC, 18*(4), 582–592.

51. Krishnamurthy, B., & Blackmond, E. (2004). SHRED: Spam harassment reduction via economic disincentives. Retrieved from http://www.research.att.com/~bala/papers/shred-ext.ps.

52. Kuerbis, B., & Mueller, M. (2007). Securing the root: A proposal for distributed signing authority. Retrieved from http://internetgovernance.org/pdf/SecuringTheRoot.pdf.

53. Lau, B., & Svajcer, V. (2008). Measuring virtual machine detection in malware using DSD tracer. *Journal in Computer Virology*. Retrieved from http://www.springerlink.com/content/d71854121143m5j5/ and http://www.citeulike.org/article/3614541.

54. Leiner, B. M., Cerf, V. G., Clark, D. D., Kahn, R. E., Kleinrock, L., Lynch, D. C., Postel, J., Roberts, L. G., & Wolff, S. (2003). A Brief History of the Internet, version 3.32. Available from:www.isoc.org.

55. Lemos, R. (2009). Cyber attacks disrupt Kyrgyzstan's networks. Retrieved from http://www.securityfocus.com/brief/896.

56. Leyden, J. (2004). The illicit trade in compromised PCs. Retrieved from http://www.theregister.co.uk/2004/04/30/spam_biz/.

57. Mao, Z. M., Sekar, V., Spatscheck, O., van der Merwe, J., & Vasudevan, R. (2006). Analyzing large DDoS attacks using multiple data sources. In *SIGCOMM Workshop on Large Scale Attack Defense (LSAD)*.

58. Marshall8e6. TRACElabs. Retrieved from http://www.marshal8e6.com/TRACE/.

59. McDaniel, P., Sen, S., Spatscheck, O., Van der Merwe, J., Aiello, B., & Kalmanek, C. (2006). Enterprise security: A community of Interest based approach. In *Proceedings of Network and Distributed Systems Security 2006 (NDSS)*.

60. Moore, D., Voelker, G., & Savage, S. (2001). Inferring Internet denial-of-service activity. In *Proceedings of the USENIX Security Symposium* (pp. 9–22).

61. Ng, J. (2004). Extensions to BGP to Support Secure Origin BGP (soBGP). Internet Draft: draft-ng-sobgp-bgp-extensions-02.txt.

62. Ohm, P., Sicket, D., & Grunwald, D. (2007). Legal issues surrounding monitoring during network research. In *Internet Measurement Conference (IMC)*.

63. Patrick, N., Scholl, T., Shaikh, A., & Steenbergen, R. (2006). Peering dragnet: Examining BGP routes received from peers. North American Network Operators' Group (NANOG) presentation.

64. Poulsen, K. (2003). Slammer worm crashed Ohio nuke plant network. Retrieved from SecurityFocus, http://www.securityfocus.com/news/6767.

65. Provos, N. (2004). A virtual honeypot framework. *13th USENIX Security Symposium*.

66. Ramachandran, A., & Feamster, N. (2006). Understanding the network-level behavior of spammers. In *Proceedings of the ACM SIGCOMM*, Pisa, Italy.

67. Rescorla, E., & Korver, B. (2003). Guidelines for writing RFC text on security considerations. *IETF RFC 3552*.

68. RIPE NCC. (2008). YouTube Hijacking: A RIPE NCC RIS case study. Retrieved from http://www.ripe.net/news/study-youtube-hijacking.html.

69. Rohde, D., & Gittlen, S. (1998). AT&T frame relay net goes down for the count. Retrieved from http://www.networkworld.com/news/0414frame2.html.

70. Security and Prosperity Steering Group APEC Telecommunications and Information Working Group. (2008). Best Practice for cooperative response based on public and private partnership. Available from http://www.apec.org/.

71. Senie, D., & Sullivan, A. (2008). Considerations for the use of DNS reverse mapping. Internet draft: draft-ietf-dnsop-reverse-mapping-considerations-06.

72. Shaikh, A., & Greenberg, A. (2004). OSPF monitoring: Architecture, design, and deployment experience. In *Proceedings of the First Symposium on Networked Systems Design and Implementation (NSDI)*.

73. Simon, D. R., Agarwal, S., & Maltz, D. A. (2007). AS-based accountability as a cost-effective DDoS defense. In *Conference on Hot Topics in Understanding Botnets (HotBots)*.

74. Snoeren, A. C., Partridge, C., Sanchez, L. A., Jones, C. E., Tchakountio, F., Kent, S. T., & Strayer, W. T. (2001). Hash-based IP traceback. In *Special Interest Group on Data Communication (SIGCOMM) Conference*.

75. Sotirov, A., Stevens, M., Appelbaum, J., Lenstra, A., Molnar, D., Osvik, D. A., & de Weger, B. (2008). MD5 considered harmful today – Creating a rogue CA certificate. Retrieved from http://www.win.tue.nl/hashclash/rogue-ca/.

76. Spiekermann, S., & Faith Cranor, L. (2009). Engineering privacy. *IEEE Transactions on Software Engineering, 35*(1), 67–82.

77. Spitzner, L. (2003). Honeypots: Definitions and value of honeypots. Retrieved from http://www.tracking-hackers.com/papers/honeypots.html.

78. TEAM CYMRU. BGP/ASN Analysis Report. Retrieved from http://www.cymru.com/BGP/summary.html.

79. United States Government Accountability Office. (2005). Prevalence of false contact information for registered domain names. Retrieved from http://www.gao.gov/new.items/d06165.pdf.

80. U.S.-Canada Power System Outage Task Force. (2004). Final report on the August 14, 2003 blackout in the united states and Canada: Causes and recommendations. Available from https://reports.energy.gov/.

81. US-CERT. Vulnerability note VU#800113 – Multiple DNS implementations vulnerable to cache poisoning. Retrieved from http://www.kb.cert.org/vuls/id/800113.

82. Vamosi, R. (2007). Cyberattack in Estonia – What it really means. Retrieved from http://news.cnet.com/Cyberattack-in-Estonia-what-it-really-means/2008-7349_3-6186751.html.

83. Van der Merwe, J., Cepleanu, A., D'Souza, K., Freeman, B., Greenberg, A., Knight, D., McMillan, R., Moloney, D., Mulligan, J., Nguyen, H., Nguyen, M., Ramarajan, A., Saad, S., Satterlee, M., Spencer, T., Toll, D., & Zelingher, S. (2006). Dynamic connectivity management with an intelligent route service control point. *SIGCOMM Workshop on Internet Network Management (INM)*.

84. Vasudevan, R., Mao, Z. M., Spatscheck, O., & Van der Merwe, J. (2007). MIDAS: An impact scale for DDoS attacks. In *15th IEEE Workshop on Local and Metropolitan Area Networks (LANMAN)*.

85. VeriSign. (2008). Root zone signing proposal. www.ntia.doc.gov/DNS/VeriSign DNSSECProposal.pdf.

86. Verkaik, P., Spatscheck, O., van der Merwe, J., & Snoeren, A. (2006). PRIMED: A community-of-interest-based DDoS mitigation system. In *Proceedings of SIGCOMM Workshop on Large Scale Attack Defense (LSAD)*.

87. Vrable, M., Ma, J., Chen, J., Moore, D., Vandekieft, E., Snoeren, A., Voelker, G., & Savage, S. (2005). Scalability, fidelity and containment in the Potemkin virtual honeyfarm. In *Proceedings of ACM Symposium on Operating Systems Principles (SOSP)*.

88. Wright, C. (2008). Understanding Kaminsky's DNS Bug. Retrieved from http://www.linuxjournal.com/content/understanding-kaminskys-dns-bug.

89. Yu, W., Fu, X., Graham, S., Xuan, D., & Zhao, W. (2007). DSSS-based flow marking technique for invisible traceback. In *IEEE Symposium on Security and Privacy*.

90. Zheng, C., Ji, L., Pei, D., Wang, J., & Francis, P. (2007). A light-weight distributed scheme for detecting ip prefix hijacks in real-time. *SIGCOMM Computer Communication Review, 37*(4), 277–288.

Chapter 14
Disaster Preparedness and Resiliency

Susan R. Bailey

14.1 Introduction

The most important thing to remember in this chapter is its title. The previous working version of the title was "Disaster Recovery," which is certainly the most common phrase used to describe the set of activities associated with managing operations (including networks) through the most severe catastrophic incidents. Indeed, the kinds of activities that get publicity, make the headlines, and become the material for rewards and recognitions are the recovery activities that take place following a major disaster. The activities certainly do involve heroic acts and significant achievements worthy of credit. However, the problem with the term "Disaster Recovery" is the adjective, which places emphasis on the recovery activities that by definition take place *after* an event happens.

What is missing in the term "disaster recovery" are the events leading up to a disaster. To be most effective in recovering from a disaster, the bulk of investment of time and money, as well as the most significant point of leverage to substantially improve recovery performance, all should happen *before* the disaster occurs, so that we are prepared to act, and can act quickly and efficiently. This is true for any enterprise in any industry, and is most certainly true in running networks. Even industry's premier educational and certification program for those engaged in the practice of disaster management, formed in 1988 and known as the "Disaster Recovery Institute," has changed its name to "DRI International: The Institute for Continuity Management," signaling the important role in the full scope of activities that take place before, during, and after a disaster. The way to achieve successful disaster *recovery* is to implement disaster *preparedness*.

The terrorist attacks of September 11, 2001 demonstrate many of the dimensions of disaster planning and management, as well as the resiliency challenges that are involved in managing networks. The terrorist-piloted airplanes that crashed into the World Trade Center in New York City destroyed major communication hubs

S.R. Bailey (✉)
AT&T Global Network Operations
e-mail: srbailey@att.com

C.R. Kalmanek et al. (eds.), *Guide to Reliable Internet Services and Applications*,   517
Computer Communications and Networks, DOI 10.1007/978-1-84882-828-5_14,
© Springer-Verlag London Limited 2010

housed in the World Trade Center itself and its nearby buildings. These hubs were a core component of the network infrastructure serving lower Manhattan as well as the broader New York and East Coast area. At exactly the time when significant network capacity and connectivity was destroyed, a huge surge of traffic volume hit the network as people tried to reach their loved ones using any and all means possible, increasing volumes on the telecommunications infrastructure by double or more. And this volume was not nicely distributed around the USA and the world, but rather was primarily concentrated into and out of lower Manhattan. We call this phenomenon *focused overload*. This scenario is a network manager's nightmare: trying to handle an extraordinarily high traffic surge when you have less capacity available to handle the load. The same network that was being used for mass communications was also being used for many command-and-control activities by police, emergency management, and government officials, requiring real-time traffic prioritization decisions during the times of peak congestion. During times of peak-traffic volume on that day, phone calls destined for edge switches (known as "end offices"), which were known to be damaged and out of service, were restricted from entering the network and consuming capacity when it was clear that the phone calls could not complete successfully anyway. Phone traffic, which did not need to travel through the New York area (e.g., traffic destined from Atlanta to Boston), was redirected away from New York through the use of network management traffic controls. Yet, in the face of the enormously disastrous scenario, the network infrastructure did not collapse despite localized congestion. Ninety-six percent of AT&T's Government Emergency Telecommunications Services (GETS) traffic completed successfully even in the height of the event, AT&T's network hub was recovered and ready for service within 48 h, and the New York Stock Exchange and financial industry of lower Manhattan reopened in less than a week. Quite simply, this rate of recovery would have been impossible without the "silent heroes" who planned and practiced disaster preparedness well before that awful day.

A couple of years later, in October 2003, severe wildfires threatened the area surrounding San Diego, California. One of AT&T's mission critical network management work centers was dangerously close to the fire; so to protect its operational functions, the work center invoked its business continuity plan. Temporary operations were established at an alternate site several hundred miles away. Network managers were deployed to the alternate site, operational support system (OSS) access was established, and phone calls to the San Diego work center were redirected so that the staff at the alternate site could do all the mission critical work normally done in the San Diego work center. This was all done while still running the network, with no loss of operational functionality during the transition. The work center was ultimately not damaged by the fire. But if it were, the alternate location was prepared to operate indefinitely until a permanent replacement could be built.

Hence, the title of this chapter, and for that matter the content of the chapter, focuses on *disaster preparedness*, which includes creating, exercising, and ongoing management of disaster recovery plans. Maintaining a state of readiness enables quick, disciplined recovery to minimize service disruptions. With good disaster preparedness, *disaster recovery* becomes the disciplined management of the execution of disaster recovery plans.

Section 14.2 addresses the role of carrier networks as national critical infrastructure, and the resulting expectations for sustained operational service in the face of disasters. Section 14.3 reviews the types of considerations involved in sustaining continuity of operations in a network environment, pointing out that a full operational continuity program includes much more than simply protecting the network itself. Section 14.4 provides an overview of the discipline of business continuity management, including techniques to structure a business impact assessment and risk-management program.[1] Section 14.5 addresses some considerations for designing resiliency into the architecture of the network itself. Section 14.6 addresses preparations involved when a specific disaster such as a hurricane is predicted. Section 14.7 reviews the operational activities that come into play once a disaster happens. Section 14.8 highlights some important technologies associated with disaster recovery. The chapter closes with Section 14.9, a discussion of open questions and future research to further improve disaster preparedness and resiliency.

14.2   Networks as Critical Infrastructure

Network carriers have a lot of responsibility. The networks provide emergency lifeline communication for tens of millions of customers in the communities the carriers serve, including capabilities such as contacting fire and police departments or 9–1–1 emergency services. The fact that life and safety are involved makes it absolutely essential that these services operate continuously in spite of a disaster, because that is precisely when these services are needed the most.

Carrier networks carry huge volumes of daily communication traffic. In 2008 AT&T, for example, network traffic volume for all Internet Protocol (IP), transport, and voice services exceeded 16 petabytes per day. While all this traffic is valuable to those communicating, a relatively small but growing percentage of this huge volume is truly "mission critical." Government and other emergency management agencies such as FEMA and the Department of Defense depend on carriers' networks to perform the data and voice communication required for command, control, and communication functions activated to manage disasters.

In addition, as more industries become technology-based, communications networks become an increasingly mission critical component of other national "critical infrastructure" industries, such as the financial sector, and power generation and distribution. As the Internet backbone serves as an increasingly essential core for business operations and commerce, and infrastructure industries implement more electronics-enabled and automated processes, government and industry depend on the continuous availability of their network infrastructure and the carriers who provide it.

---

[1] The term "business continuity" is generally used to encompass aspects of planning and managing operational continuity for any type of operation, and in this chapter is not limited strictly to commercial businesses. The fundamental techniques are equally applicable for government, academic, and not-for-profit operations. In the government environment, business continuity is often referred to as Continuity of Government (COG) or Continuity of Operations (COOP).

14.3 Business Continuity in a Network Environment

Networks are subject to many kinds of threats, some obvious and well-known, others less obvious but equally as devastating. To characterize the threats, it is helpful to understand an abstract view of what a network entails. This section describes three major components: the network itself, network management work centers, and operational support systems (OSSs).

In simple terms, a network involves *links* and *nodes*. Nodes look like computing equipment housed in buildings of various shapes and sizes, ranging from small aggregation or regeneration equipment housed in tiny "huts" with a footprint of only tens of square feet, to huge data centers and central office buildings spanning tens of thousands of square feet. The links are the connections between the nodes, which are typically carried at a physical level on fiber cables that are buried underground, under the oceans, or in some cases strung aerially. The AT&T network, for example, involves more than 9,000 major buildings and another 200,000 smaller locations. There are about 900,000 sheath-miles of fiber just in the core of the AT&T backbone, and that does not even include the magnitudes of cabling to connect each customer to the AT&T backbone.

The network itself is not very useful without the operational functions that operate 24×7 to keep the network running, including maintenance and repair, configuration management, capacity management, and provisioning customer services. These functions are executed in *work centers*, which are typically administrative buildings staffed with network managers on a 24-h-per-day, 7-day-per-week basis. Work center functions can vary in their mission criticality, usually based on the requirement for these functions to be fully operational in order to keep a production network functioning. For example, an enterprise might determine that provisioning of new customer orders can be suspended temporarily at the time of a disaster, in which case work center functions involved with provisioning of orders might take days or weeks. By comparison, work center functions directly involved in maintaining network traffic flow and repairing network problems are usually deemed mission critical, and must be able to recover almost immediately.

These work centers interact with the network itself using operational support systems (OSSs), software applications, and their associated databases that perform functions such as alarm management and the tracking of individual work activities such as orders and tickets. Without the OSS, the people operating out of the work centers are unable to interact with the network to execute their required functions. The mission criticality of an OSS is correlated to the mission criticality of the work centers that use it.

So, a threat to the network can be anything that impacts the nodes and links of the network itself (whether physically or logically), the work centers and operational processes executed in them, or the OSS. The list of potential threats is practically endless, but some examples include:

- *Physical damage to network nodes* can be due to incidents such as fires and floods.
- *Physical damage to network links.* By their very nature of being geographically distributed and exposed to outdoor conditions, many network components

(especially fiber cable) are exposed to significant environmental and man-made threats such as train derailments, ships dragging anchor and snagging an undersea cable, earthquakes, or mudslides.

- *Widespread and extended loss of electrical power.* Since all the electronics in a network require electrical power, a loss of commercial electrical power can be a significant threat to the function of a network. The more widespread the power loss and the longer the duration, the more significant the disaster can be.
- *Denial-of-Service attacks,* or any other mass traffic event, injects mass traffic toward specific components of the network, disabling them by overloading them.
- *Worms and viruses* disable network components or OSS by destroying their logic or their databases.
- *Physical threats to work center buildings and their inhabitants,* which require the inhabitants to evacuate their normal operating environment. Work centers are subject to the same kinds of physical threats as network nodes (fires, floods, etc.). In addition, work centers can be impacted by threats that do not necessarily damage the building, but require the people who work in the building to evacuate and/or stay out of their normal operating environment. For example, a gas or chemical leak on the ground or in the air within a building or in the surrounding geographic area can require rapid evacuation. More severe examples can include bomb threats, or even worse, intentional attack using chemical, biological, or radiological weapons or "dirty bombs."
- *Other threats to work center personnel* can range from the loss of mass transit that impacts the movement of personnel between facilities, to a job action relation to union contract negotiations (commonly known as a "strike"), to a health pandemic that disables the workforce directly through illness (or death) or indirectly through the need to care for ill family members or fear of entering the work environment and becoming ill.
- *Failures in operational support systems used to run the network,* such as alarm management systems, ticketing systems, and remote testing platforms. These systems are subject to many of the same risks as the network itself, such as loss of power to data centers and other modes of failure to the flow of telemetry, the server hardware, and the application software.

To achieve a level of network resilience, a comprehensive disaster preparedness and business continuity program should encompass the physical components of the network itself (e.g., electronics and cabling), as well as work centers and their mission critical functions, and tools used. One way of representing this is in Fig. 14.1. The diagram shows a pyramid for each of the three major business continuity components: Work Centers, Network, and Operational Support Systems. Each step up the pyramid shows an increasingly significant recovery mechanism.

Many of these can share common foundational elements, at the base of each pyramid, which can be applied to any kind of asset, whether it is a work center, a component of the network, or the operational support systems and databases that are used to run the network. These include:

- *Business Continuity Discipline*: the disciplined approach to Business Impact Analysis and Risk Management that are described in much of this chapter,

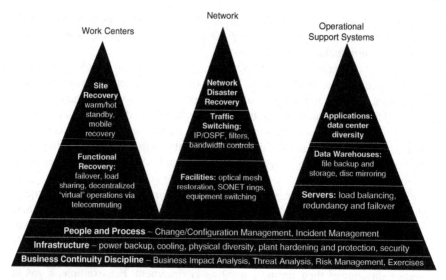

Fig. 14.1 Enterprise business continuity protocol

including the analysis of threats and vulnerabilities, risk mitigation, development disaster recovery plans, and ongoing exercising of those plans.

- *Infrastructure*: the technologies required to provide basic environmental and power conditions to an office. All buildings require power and air handling, whether they house network equipment such as routers and switches, operational support system servers and storage equipment, or work space for people.
- *People and Process*: a broad category covering the operational discipline in executing well-defined procedures, with vigilance and constant attention to the impact of any action on the network, its services, and its customers.

Above the shared foundation, the specific approaches to achieving business continuity can differ.

- In the center of the diagram, Network recovery focuses on moving service to diverse physical components, which are unaffected by a disaster. This can include recovery of service on alternate facilities such as backup equipment or alternate physical paths, or redirection of traffic onto alternative available capacity. Facility and traffic prioritization can be used to identify high-priority services, so that these services can be restored first with the least amount of downtime, as is discussed in more detail in Section 14.7.2. In situations of most extreme damage, rebuilding of components that are destroyed can be accomplished using specialized disaster recovery equipment.
- On the left of the diagram, Work Center recovery involves functional relocation and assuring the availability of skilled staff to pick up the operations when a primary work center is rendered unavailable. It can include the distribution of critical functions into alternative work centers or a telework model, or a full site

recovery, in which a dedicated backup site is maintained for purposes of recovering all of a work center's mission critical functionality.

- On the right of the diagram, Operational Support System recovery focuses on restoration of the applications in backup data centers, and also involves recovery of databases so that any data loss is minimized. It includes backup servers to recover from hardware failures, data backup and storage to protect against loss of data, and application-level recovery through diversifying the platform into multiple data centers.

14.4 Business Continuity Management

So, you have decided that you want to be prepared for disasters and resilient against their impact. Where do you start? The almost limitless list of potential disasters and the breadth of assets to worry about can make the task seem unwieldy. While it would be nice to protect *everything* from *any* disaster, that is virtually impossible. The key is understanding the most significant problem areas and effectively prioritizing investments in mitigation. The following terms are useful foundation to provide structure to this process.

Threats are factors that have the possibility of causing damage. Threats can take many forms, including physical, logical, economic, political, or social. Examples of threats include weather-related disasters such as hurricanes, floods, and tornadoes, financial disaster, disease pandemic, and the outbreak of war. One way of reducing the risk is to eliminate or reduce the possibility that a threat will occur. For example, a medical vaccine can reduce the possibility of a health pandemic occurring. Often, it is impossible to actually reduce or eliminate the probability of many kinds of threats, such as natural disasters; so the focus is on protection even in spite of the existence of the threat.

Vulnerabilities are characteristics of an asset that make it susceptible to damage by a threat. If it is difficult to eliminate a threat, another way of reducing an overall risk profile is to eliminate or reduce an asset's vulnerabilities. A classic example of reducing vulnerability is sandbagging to prevent the impact of a flood. The high water will still rise with the same probability whether or not there are sandbags, but the sandbags reduce vulnerability by physically holding back flood waters and protecting buildings, people, and equipment from damage.

Impact is the magnitude of damage to an asset in the event that a specific threat exploits a vulnerability. If you cannot adequately address a risk by eliminating threats and vulnerabilities, it can be possible to reduce risk exposure by providing mechanisms to control the impact. Continuing with the flood example mentioned above, an example would be providing pumps and other equipment to move water away once the flood waters have breached a vulnerable area.

14.4.1 Know What Is Important

The first step is to enumerate all the assets critical to sustained operation. Assets can be physical equipment, people and processes, customers, databases, or operational support systems. Assets can also include external assets including third-party suppliers and equipment vendors.

Not all assets are created equal, of course. An important step is to understand which assets are *mission critical*, meaning that it is impossible to sustain operation effectively without them. Assets that are not quite mission critical, but are important to recover within reasonable time can be assigned ratings of lower importance. Once assets are prioritized, this enables attention to be focused on those with the highest priority.

14.4.2 Analyze Risks

Business Impact Analysis is a formal process to provide structure to the identification and prioritization of threats based on understanding the potential impact to an operation or business. It starts with identifying credible threats that could cause an interruption to an organization's business. Each asset can be evaluated against each threat to determine whether that asset has a vulnerability associated with the threat. Those vulnerabilities can be evaluated and scored quantitatively or qualitatively on three measures:

- The *probability* that the threat will exploit the vulnerability
- The magnitude of the *service impact* if the above happens
- The ability to *control* the impacts.

These scores can then be rank-ordered and summarized into a risk matrix, such as the example shown in Fig. 14.2. This matrix is one of the most important elements

			Risk Exposure Results			
			Probability Factor (P)	Service Impact (S)	Controllability (C)	Risk Exposure
Risk Factor	Category	Weight (W)	High Low (5) (1)	High Low (5) (1)	Weak Strong (5) (1)	W x P x S x C
No single point of contact (SPOC) for all electrical equipment, as builts, and distribution infrastructure	Power	0.10	5	3	5	7.5
Collapsed SONET Ring (protection path rides same physical fiber as the primary path)	Transport	0.40	5	5	5	50.0
Network inventory database errors	Database Integrity	0.30	4	3	5	18.0
Unclear procedures and ownership/accountability for remediating hazardous materials conditions (e.g. fuel spill)	Procedure	0.30	3	2	5	9.0
Network equipment has insufficient battery life and no backup generator; batteries will discharge before generator can be dispatched and deployed	Power	0.80	5	5	5	100.0

Fig. 14.2 Risk matrix example

of a risk assessment, and is used to provide a prioritization in support of building plans to mitigate the most critical risks. In this example, the weight (W) is a judgment of the overall level of importance on a scale of 0–1.0, the probability factor (P) represents the likelihood that the vulnerability is exploited by a threat, the service impact (S) is the magnitude of the impact if a vulnerability is exploited, and controllability (C) represents the ability to control the impacts. These variables are then combined (in this case, multiplied, though other means of combining are possible) to provide an overall score, with a high score indicating the risk factor that poses the highest exposure, and therefore warranting the most focused attention to mitigate.

14.4.3   Develop a Plan

Risk mitigation involves identifying ways to reduce risk, by eliminating or reducing threats, eliminating or reducing vulnerabilities, or reducing impact by providing control mechanisms. The various proposed solutions can be evaluated by their overall impact on reducing risk, feasibility, and time and cost to implement.

When addressing the recovery of any asset, whether it is a network itself, a support system, or a work center that operates the network, two important variables can be considered when designing risk-mitigation solutions.

- *Recovery Time Objective (RTO)*: This is measured as the targeted duration of time between the occurrence of a disaster and the time that functionality is restored. For the network itself, this is measured as the outage downtime. For a work center, this would be the time between the declaration of a disaster impacting the work center and the recovery of its functionality in an alternate arrangement at one or multiple backup locations.
- *Recovery Point Objective (RPO)*: This involves the amount of data that is expected to be lost as a part of the recovery. It can be thought of as the point that you can roll back to and recover all critical configuration data. It is measured as the time between the start of the disaster and the time before the disaster when the databases and configurations were last updated and able to be recovered. For network components, this translates into the amount of provisioning activity prior to a disaster, which is lost after the network itself is recovered, and therefore must be reprovisioned.

RTO and RPO can be depicted visually in Fig. 14.3. Ideally, these variables would be near zero, indicating instantaneous recovery with no loss of data. Typically, shorter RTO and RPO require more expensive solutions. So, definition of RTO and RPO objectives require very careful consideration of exactly what an operation really needs and how much loss it can handle, based on the impact of downtime to the business. Once defined, they also provide a very straightforward measurement, useful during drills and exercises to evaluate the adequacy of the execution of disaster recovery plans.

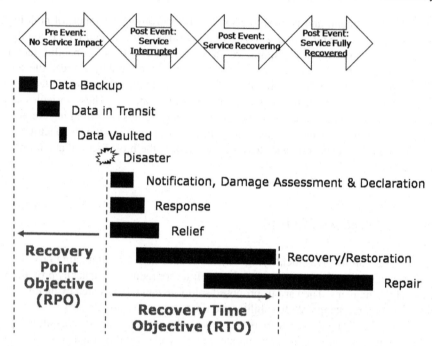

Fig. 14.3 Timeline of a disaster

	Current Risk	Mitigation Investments	
		Plan A	Plan B
Information Technology: Server and client platforms, LAN, MAN, WAN, data security, data management, applications, voice, storage, Disaster Recovery plans...			
Facility Security: Perimeter security, entrances / exits, loading dock, security cameras, alarm methods, remote monitoring, guard staffing, interior security systems...			
Infrastructure / Environmentals: Physical building structure, location, HVAC, water / plumbing, environment inspection...			
Facilities Safety: Fire exits, emergency procedures, fire suppression equipment (extinguishers, Halon, FM2000, dry & charged sprinklers), emergency lighting, test schedules...			
Power: Grounding, distribution, switching, dual grids, UPS installation, maintenance, capacity, load testing, generator installation, maintenance, DC battery plant...			
Other: Organizational structure, training & education, customer / supplier contracts...			

Fig. 14.4 Risk mitigation example

Frequently, an enterprise faces choices between alternative mechanisms to mitigate risk, which can vary in cost to implement and feasibility. One way to assess risk-mitigation options is to quantitatively compare their relative impact to the overall risk exposure. An example is shown in Fig. 14.4. Assume that there are two options for mitigating risks, portrayed in this figure as Plan A and Plan B. In this case, Plan B significantly improves the overall risk exposure compared to Plan A. Once risk-mitigation strategies are selected and implemented, a full disaster recovery or business continuity plan should be documented, outlining the exact procedural steps that should be taken. Anyone involved in managing or implementing the disaster recovery or business continuity plan needs to be advised and fully trained on what they are required to do in support of the plan.

14.4.4   Test and Manage the Plan

Conditions constantly change. New threats emerge as world events change. Asset bases evolve. New technologies are introduced. People move out and move in to organizations. To sustain a state of preparedness, life-cycle management of disaster recovery and business continuity plans is extremely important.

One aspect of life-cycle management is maintaining up-to-date documentation of disaster recovery and business continuity plans. Contact information, process updates, and other information must be kept current.

Another aspect is training and communication, to maintain overall awareness as well as more detailed training on specialized duties as people transition in and out of organizations. People need to be so familiar with what they need to do after a disaster that when it happens, they do what they need to do almost by habit.

Finally, practice, practice, practice! To maintain a state of preparedness, there is absolutely no substitute for actually invoking a business continuity and disaster recovery plan and seeing how it works. Simulate the actual implementation of disaster recovery and business continuity plans. Make it as real as possible.

- If equipment is involved, use the equipment and make sure it works.
- Measure RTO and RPO against organizational objectives.
- Make sure people are trained, including newcomers to an organization.
- Record problems and findings.
- Create a list of improvements and changes identified as a result of the exercise, with clear ownership and accountability.

Sometimes, it is impossible to actually test a business continuity and disaster recovery plan. Sometimes, the scenario being tested is too broad in scope to feasibly be exercised. Sometimes, the act of practicing the loss of functionality and the failover to an alternate arrangement introduces undue risk to customer service and network traffic. Where it is impossible to actually practice a real recovery situation, it might be necessary to practice on a testbed environment separate from the production network, or use traffic simulations based on mathematical models of network traffic across a network topology. Walk-throughs and "table-top exercises" can be used to approximate the movement of functions like work centers in a disaster scenario.

14.5 Design for Resiliency

Being prepared to handle a disaster scenario starts with the design and architecture of the network itself. If network traffic is impacted by the failure of a component, that component is identified as a *single point of failure (SPOF)*, and is a point of high vulnerability. Any component can be an SPOF, including network components, physical cabling within a building, long-distance fiber segments, undersea cable systems, power substations, or power cabling within an office. A component that is designed to have a backup or alternate arrangement, so that network traffic can persist even if the component fails, is said to have *diversity*. Generally speaking, the more simultaneous failures a particular platform can handle without impacting traffic, the more resilient is the network design. Applications with extremely high requirements for uninterrupted traffic flow under any circumstance, in a global design that contains many components spread across a wide variety of geographic environments, have been designed with eight or more layers of protection (meaning that the architecture can support seven simultaneous failures without impacting traffic flow).

It is painstaking work to design a resilient network, systematically eliminating all SPOFs, ranging from physical fiber diversity to software applications and the servers on which they ride. Traffic simulations based on specific real-time network topology and traffic patterns, such as those described in Chapter 2, can simulate the impact to network traffic under various failure conditions across a network topology.

Diversity and redundancy also apply to data storage and backup. Mission critical data, such as circuit layouts, routing policies, and customer configurations, can be replicated and stored in multiple diverse data centers, so that the data can be recovered even in spite of the complete loss of an entire data center and all the equipment in it. Data recovery is so important in the financial industry that it has regulatory guidelines issued by the Financial Industry Regulatory Authority (FINRA), requiring explicit plans for data backup and recovery (Financial Industry Regulatory Authority, FINRA Manual, section 3510).

Because of the significant dependence on uninterrupted power required to operate a carrier-grade network, carrier-grade network design normally includes the following elements:

- Completely redundant power cabling in major network buildings, with diverse building entrances and connectivity to geographically separated electrical substations on the power grid.
- Battery backup, with near seamless transfer to battery power.
- Diesel or natural gas-powered generators with autostart capabilities and switchgear so that the generators activate even if the office is unstaffed. Because batteries have limited storage, they are not sufficient for long-term power outages, lasting days or weeks. With proper maintenance and a well-run refueling program, generators can run almost indefinitely. Carrier network buildings have been known to operate for months on generator, for example after significant hurricanes.

- A typical power design engages the batteries immediately on loss of commercial power. The batteries provide power for the first few minutes until the generators can ramp up and are ready to carry the load, and which time the load switches over to the generators for longer-term service.
- Remote equipment installed in small nodes outside of major network offices pose significant challenges in the area of power protection. These small nodes serve as aggregation points or signal regeneration or amplification, and can number hundreds of thousands in a large network. The cost to install permanent generators to all these locations can be prohibitive, so these types of nodes often rely on battery backup, followed by dispatch and hookup of portable generators to power the nodes.

A work center without a business continuity plan can be an SPOF as well. Business continuity decisions factor into the design of work centers and their operational support systems. There are many approaches to designing work center business continuity. One possibility is to design a backup site, geographically distant from the primary work center location, which exists solely for the purpose of recovering the primary site. Another possibility is to build two or more centers that share the workload under normal operating conditions, with mechanisms to flow work inputs away from a center that is unable to operate due to a disaster, e.g. by redirecting phone calls, alarms, tickets, or other work drivers. Since many work centers perform multiple functions, another approach is to flow each function to an alternate arrangement, without necessarily moving all the work in the center as a whole to another work location.

The operational support systems and their associated databases used by employees in a work center should not be SPOFs either, and the time to work SPOFs out of the system architecture is during design and installation. Typically, this involves installation of servers at geographically distant data centers, with software designed so that it can fail over from one server or site to another.

14.6 When You See Disaster Coming

In many cases, we are lucky enough to see an impending disaster before it happens. For example, we can watch hurricanes form and travel across the water, and we are glued to the weather forecasts, which predict precisely when, where, and how severe the storm will be. This advance warning gives us precious lead time to take very specific preparatory actions, way beyond the broad planning and preparedness discussed so far.

It is helpful to maintain a checklist of pre-event activities to perform once a specific disaster risk is identified. Here are a few kinds of activities to do in preparation for a disaster.

Batten down the hatches. Take action to protect assets from physical damage. This can include sandbagging, boarding up windows and doors, and closing marine doors to prevent floodwaters from entering a building, installing chicken wire around roofing to help hold the shingles on, or welding manholes shut to prevent unauthorized access by those intending to do harm in preparation for mass political demonstrations. Work centers that are in harm's way might elect to activate disaster plans and move mission critical functions to other facilities outside of the risk area.

Lock down the network. Any time the network is being "touched," it is being put at risk. Any change can introduce a new problem. People can make mistakes, and software changes can introduce new bugs. During a disaster, the focus should be on handling the disaster, and any other problem is a distraction. The idea here is to call off as much unnecessary work as possible, planned or routine maintenance, software upgrades, etc., so that as much effort as possible is available to focus on handling the disaster itself. The scope of such a lock-down should include all assets at risk of damage, as well as any assets that might be needed to restore service due to other damage.

Fix everything possible. Anything that is broken in the network can be thought of as capacity that is not available to use, even if it is not directly service impacting. For example, if a line-card in a router is failed, but a redundant card is being used to sustain service, the failed line-card is not available to restore service in the event that the redundant card fails. Carriers call this situation a *simplex condition*, and all simplex conditions should be remediated before the disaster strikes. Even if the particular simplex component is not directly threatened by the disaster itself, disasters often result in difficulty of basic movement of equipment and suppliers, so the component would be difficult to replace even if it fails due to nondisaster-related conditions. Besides, that capacity might be needed to restore other service.

Know what is at risk. Take stock of what physical components (buildings, equipment, and cable routes) are at risk, and what services and what customers are riding on those components. When simulation tools are available, simulate the failure of those components to determine the potential service impact, and take preventive action where possible.

Move services out of harm's way. In many cases, services can be moved to alternate facilities and nodes that are not at the risk of damage, for example, by ring-switching synchronous optical (SONET) facilities or assigning an extremely high logical cost to IP backbone connections that are carried on fiber paths likely to sustain damage. The advantage of moving traffic in advance of an impending disaster, rather than waiting to see exactly what is damaged and triggering an automatic failover, is that the traffic move can be implemented under more controlled conditions, which can result in less overall service impact.

Stage emergency equipment and supplies. If repair and rebuilding is likely, identify the equipment and supplies that would be needed and stage them in preparation for deployment after the disaster. But be careful, you do not want your emergency supplies to be too close, or they can be subject to the same threats as your primary components. It can be prudent in some cases to leave the equipment in protected warehouses, to be dispatched after the threat has passed.

Preplan the recovery. Any design work that can be done in advance of a disaster eliminates precious time lost after a disaster doing "engineering on the fly." In some cases, network traffic can be rerouted to alternative equipment, which has been permanently installed in the network. For example, an IP-based application can reside on servers that are installed into geographically diverse data centers, with data backup and failover capabilities. In other cases, especially where connectivity needs to be re-established, equipment needs to be deployed near the disaster area. For this kind of scenario, AT&T's Network Disaster Recovery program utilizes software that preplans exactly which equipment and which trailers need to be deployed, with software that provides a design for the specific connections between the trailers and preprinted labels for the intertrailer cabling. In addition, configuration management software maintains current configurations of each component in the production network, so that the configuration can be downloaded en masse so that the trailerized disaster recovery equipment can take on the identity of the damaged equipment without the need to rebuild the mappings and configurations from scratch. This configuration management alone saves weeks (and potentially months) of restoration time.

Communicate to customers. In advance of a disaster, customer communication tends to focus on actions being taken to protect their service and to inform on special communications that the carrier will implement to keep their customers apprised as the event unfolds. It can be a calming influence for customers to know that their service is in professional hands and that the carrier is acting proactively and professionally to protect the network and customer traffic.

14.7   When Disaster Strikes

Regardless of the best efforts to prevent it, eventually a disaster will hit a network. That is when the network management team kicks into high gear, focusing all their energies on keeping the network alive, restoring any service that has been impacted, and addressing customer needs.

14.7.1   First and Foremost, Exercise-Disciplined Command and Control

Most network carriers have a command center or emergency management center that exists for the primary purpose of managing disasters of various sizes. AT&T's command center is its Global Network Operations Center (GNOC), as shown in Fig. 14.5. The GNOC has a military-style command-and-control structure, complete with predefined threshold-triggered actions and specific 24 × 7 duty officer assignments. A fundamental component of most command-and-control processes is

Fig. 14.5 AT&T Global Network Operations Center

an emergency management bridge, a secure conference call that serves as the focal point for critical communication of status, obtaining resources, and providing overall strategic priorities and direction. Kicking off this bridge is normally the very first order of business involved with almost any disaster recovery activity.

A good command-and-control process is structured with predefined actions based on identified scenarios including outages, incidents, attacks, crises, indicators, and threats. It should cast a wide net of information sources, including network management, government, customer, and other sources of information.

The control bridge serves a number of purposes, including:

- Ensuring proper flow of information and response decisions across the company
- Approving tactical plans and making critical decisions
- Ensuring that adequate resources are provided
- Coordinating incident response across organizations
- Assessing impact in near real time
- Prioritizing restoration
- Authorizing communications, including press releases and customer notifications.

Every person participating on the control bridge should have a specific assignment. Participants range from various functional organizations within a large carrier's company, including network operations, real estate, public relations, customer servicing, and security. Because 24 × 7 coverage and immediate response is fundamental to the success of a command-and-control structure, reachability is essential, and delegation is required for even brief times when a bridge member might be unreachable. The notification procedure itself requires significant preplanning, with the command center knowing alternate reach information, knowing personal schedules and delegations for all bridge participants. When an incident occurs, all participants whose functions are potentially involved should be notified to join the bridge, and those not required can be dismissed once the situation is understood sufficiently.

It is very helpful to separate those managing the command-and-control structure from those directly involved in fixing a problem. This is for two reasons. First, it enables those fixing a given problem to remain focused on their task of restoring service, without getting distracted by tasks such as crafting communications documents. Second, it is common for those extremely close to a problem to lose sight of the bigger picture, while a neutral oversight function can more easily see the overall view of priorities, service impacts, and response activities. Liaison functions often are established to bridge between those directly involved in repair and the command center.

Once a disaster situation is stabilized, the same command-and-control structure can take the lead in analyzing the event and capturing lessons learned after the fact. Every incident is an opportunity to learn, and lessons can range from prevention of future occurrences to improved response if the event ever happens again. Lessons learned can be translated into permanent improvements, including procedural changes and the creation or enhancement of preparedness checklists. It is helpful for these improvement opportunities to be captured and formalized on an action register, with clear ownership and accountability and time-bound expectations for implementing the identified improvements. Placing oversight of the implementation of the improvement program under the auspices of the formal command-and-control structure tends to ensure that the improvements are done quickly and completely, which ultimately makes the organization and the network more resilient in the face of future disasters.

It is important to consider resiliency of the functions and tools used for command and control, such as work centers, operational support systems, and conference bridges. They can themselves have single points of failure and be subject to threats. At a minimum, a strong command-and-control structure should have alternate backup notification and communication mechanisms, in case the primary mechanisms are failed. Backup arrangements can range from basics such as alternate conference bridges using geographically separated equipment, through to extreme cases such as radio backup in case all commercial telecommunications are failed.

14.7.2   Manage Traffic Congestion

Many disasters involve some form of traffic congestion, which is most simply described as too much traffic trying to go through too little capacity. Network nodes such as routers become congested by overrunning limits such as CPU capacity or memory. Links between nodes become congested when the traffic flowing down them exceeds the bandwidth of the connection. Just like a traffic jam on a highway, network congestion can disable network components that are overloaded, spread outwards to adjacent network components, and ultimately bring a network to its knees if not properly managed.

Traffic congestion is often an immediate after-effect that requires immediate action on the part of network managers. The basic approach is to service as much network traffic as possible, even if that means making difficult decisions to impact some traffic to keep the network from failing under the weight of the load. Traffic controls have developed on historical circuit-switched networks over decades, and include capabilities such as traffic redirection and bandwidth management. In today's IP networks, traffic adjustments require changes to traffic filters and routing policies, but can be utilized to achieve a similar goal.

In making traffic manipulation decisions, basic traffic management principles should be followed to protect the network

1. *Utilize all available resources.* During a congestion situation, all network capacity should be put into service to handle as much traffic as feasibly possible. To do this, traffic managers observe load conditions on nodes and links, simulate configuration changes, and implement routing changes to adjust traffic flows away from congestion bottlenecks and toward underutilized capacity. In the September 11 example cited in Section 14.1, there was no need for traffic traveling from Atlanta to Boston to go directly through New York because it was not originating or terminating there. Because network capacity in New York was congested and there was sufficient capacity outside of New York to handle additional load, network managers redirected this "via" traffic away from the congested area, so that all the network capacity in the New York area was being utilized to serve directly the traffic needing to get in or out of New York.

2. *Keep all available resources filled with traffic, which has the highest probability to result in effective communications.* In this principle, "effective communications" simply means that the traffic reaches its destination successfully. If a network manager has information that the destination is not able to receive traffic, there is no use consuming any network capacity to carry the traffic across the network only to fail at the end. Network managers attempt to restrict this traffic as it enters the network, so as to minimize unnecessary consumption of capacity for unsuccessful communications. In the traditional voice network, network management controls include "cancel-to," which are applied as traffic enters the network and direct the originating switch to fail phone calls destined for a terminating "end office" or terminating edge switch, for example if that switch is known to be down. Such controls do not yet exist in the IP network, other than brute-force application of things like Access Control Lists (ACLs), but they are a future opportunity as discussed in Section 14.9.2.

3. *In case of congestion and/or overload, give priority to traffic that makes the most efficient use of network resources.* The more network resources used to deliver a unit of traffic, the less overall traffic can be delivered on the available capacity. To apply this principle, network managers like to exercise directional bandwidth controls to enable traffic out of a disaster area, which greatly reduces the traffic

demand into the area. In the voice network, these controls can be applied to restrict fixed percentages of traffic headed directionally from one switch to another. This kind of control remains a future opportunity in IP networks of today.

4. *Inhibit traffic congestion and prevent its spread.* Ideally, all offered load would be completed, and that is indeed true at low and moderate load levels. At these levels, the entire offered load is easily completed. As the offered load increases further, network performance begins to degrade as the network components become more consumed in administrative tasks required to keep themselves up and running. Hence, the curve begins to drop off at high offered load levels, and not all that load is completed successfully. If offered load continues even further, performance continues to suffer gradually until a "break point" is reached, the load simply overwhelms the equipment, and the equipment becomes unable to service any traffic at all. Once this point is reached on one component on the network, the congestion spreads extremely quickly and other components are subsequently vulnerable to the same phenomenon. This scenario can get quickly out of hand. The network manager's task is to deliver traffic along this curve, completing as much traffic as possible on each network component without letting any component "fall off the cliff." This can mean intentionally failing some traffic so as to protect the broader infrastructure, which because it entails failing some amount of customer service, should be applied as much as is needed but as little as possible. While TCP offers endpoints the ability to throttle traffic based on perceived congestion between them, the underlying IP network operates largely on simple notions of links being up or down, with no ability to gate traffic volume in response to congestion. So congestion-related controls remain an opportunity for development in IP networks.

To support the prioritization of emergency communications, the US Department of Homeland Security works with network carriers to implement programs to support the prioritization of emergency communications for Government, Defense, emergency responder, and critical infrastructure communications. These include:

- Telecommunications Service Priority (TSP) is a program, which enables individual circuits on a backbone network to be identified as mission critical. This enables the circuit to be prioritized for restoration. Referring back to Fig. 14.1, TSP is an example of prioritization at the facility level.
- Government Emergency Telecommunications Service (GETS) has existed for many years on the circuit-switched voice network, and enables individual phone calls to be identified as "emergency" and prioritized above others when capacity is limited. Enhancements to GETS include expansion to Internet Protocol and Voice over Internet Protocol services. In Fig. 14.1, GETS is an example of Traffic-level service prioritization, since no circuits are actually restored, but individual traffic sessions are identified and prioritized for first treatment within the available capacity limits.
- Wireless Priority Service (WPS) operates similar to GETS, except that the voice calls that it operates on are wireless, cellular phone calls.

14.7.3 Restore First, Repair Later

When we encounter any type of problem, it is human nature that we try to diagnose and fix it. This is not necessarily the best course of action, in that diagnosis and repair can take a long time, during which customers are unable to use the network for their communication needs. An experienced network manager will keep in mind that the first priority is to restore customer service as quickly as possible, regardless of whether the root cause of the problem was found and fixed. In fact, often it is possible to restore customer service using alternate restoration mechanisms much faster than diagnosing and fixing the original problem that caused the service outage in the first place. Because of the long time that can be involved in repairing widespread damage, service restoration is almost always the preferred solution to bring back a network's ability to handle traffic immediately after a disaster. Because restoration takes advantage of equipment already deployed and ready to use, it requires little or no manual work, and can often be done remotely by network managers in a work center far from the disaster area. It takes a seasoned network manager to ensure that adequate attention is put toward restoration options, whether designed into the network architecture or designed in real time at the time of the disaster. This can be in parallel to (or instead of, if the technical expertise and staffing is limited) working on permanent repairs.

14.7.4 Replace Damaged Equipment

In the event of a "smoking hole" scenario in which network equipment is damaged and must be replaced, temporary recovery equipment can be an extremely valuable solution to restore the network and its services temporarily until permanent replacements can be acquired and installed. Since restoration time is often extremely critical, here are some steps to shorten the time it takes to deploy and configure this equipment:

- *Procure the equipment in advance.* This eliminates any time lost in the purchase, manufacture, and shipping of the equipment.
- *Mount the equipment in mobile deployable units.* Large network carriers can deem it worthwhile to invest in equipment built to be transportable and dedicated to the purpose of disaster recovery. Network equipment can be mounted into mobile units that are designed to operate like "data centers on wheels," complete with self-contained power, cooling, and racks. These can be tractor-trailers that can be transported by truck, or fly-away containers that fit into airplanes.
- *Ensure the recovery equipment is in a constant state of readiness.* Check the equipment regularly and perform preventive maintenance on it. If the production network is being upgraded, for example to new software releases, then upgrade the recovery equipment along with the production network equipment, so that it matches the equipment it would be replacing as closely as possible.

Restoration equipment can be connected into monitoring systems for ongoing alarm management, so that any problems in the equipment can be detected and remediated, to ensure that all of the equipment is known to be active and operable at all times. All this work ensures that readiness saves valuable time when a disaster strikes.

- *Maintain current, complete, and accurate backup files for all equipment configurations.* These backups downloaded into temporary restoration equipment, enabling it to take on the identity of the equipment it is replacing without spending additional time configuring the equipment from scratch.
- *Preplan network designs.* Even if replacement equipment is readily available, precious time can be lost designing the architecture of the replacement solution. Preplanned designs, or software support for ad hoc designs, can reduce this time and shorten the overall recovery.

14.7.5   Open a Customer Service Command Center

Whether or not a disaster impacts a network customer's service, very often customers will have special needs that must be channeled and prioritized. Sometimes, customers need to report network outages. Other times, even without a network outage, customers have new demands on the network, such as additional bandwidth requirements to handle increased communication needs, or the provisioning of new services to deal with relocation of customer data centers or administrative offices. A customer service command center can accept all the customer needs, funnel them into appropriate channels, prioritizing as needed, for example to ensure that national security, emergency management, and critical infrastructure needs are handled first. This command center can also service as a bidirectional communication interface between customer service or sales teams and the network managers, so that customers can obtain timely and accurate information about restoration and recovery activities taking place.

14.8   Technologies

A wide variety of technologies play an important part in disaster preparedness and management for networks.

14.8.1   Restoring Connectivity

Whether network cabling can be terrestrial (i.e., buried underground), aerial (i.e., strung along utility poles), or undersea, all cabling is exposed to many environmental threats. One of the most common types of damage to networks is the loss of physical connectivity due to cable damage. A number of technologies are available to restore connectivity while the cable is undergoing physical repair. These include:

- Cell Sites on Wheels (COWs) and Cell Sites on Light Trucks (COLTs) are often deployed in disaster areas to bolster a wireless network's capacity. These operate exactly like a permanent cell tower, except that they are mobile.
- Point-to-point radio technologies: A variety of technologies using licensed and unlicensed spectrum, which can be chosen based on distance and speed requirements. Typically, these systems are used to establish a connection to a hop-on point onto the network backbone. An advantage of these technologies is that they can be portable units, easily moved, and quickly installed. However, they frequently require line-of-sight, and can be impacted by the same kinds of conditions that impact visibility (i.e., severe fog, foliage). Also, they typically do not provide connectivity over long distances, though in some cases multiple radio connections can be connected end-to-end to achieve somewhat longer connections.
- Satellite communications: Portable satellite base stations, for example mounted into vans or trucks, can be deployed to establish network connectivity. Because satellite communications can be widely used across any geographic area and can be quickly configured, they are frequently used in the earliest stages of a disaster. However, delay conditions can make satellite communications infeasible for applications that are subject to latency.
- Free-space optics: This emerging technology involves laser-based optical connectivity. But unlike traditional fiber-optic solutions, the laser travels across air instead of glass fiber. Free-space optics offers similar benefits of point-to-point radio solutions, with the additional advantage that the optical connection can support much higher data rates. However, connectivity can be interrupted if anything disrupts line-of-sight between the laser transmitter and the receiver.

14.8.2 Restoring Operational Support System

Essential to the recovery of operational support systems is the ability to access the data used by these systems. Databases are absolutely critical to network management, used for functions such as recording tickets, maintaining the network inventory, and storing usage statistics for billing purposes. Remote data storage enables the recovery of any data despite the loss of primary data storage mechanisms. A number of technologies are available for remote data storage, ranging from mature technologies such as tape backup through more recent technologies such as disk mirroring and replication for more continuous, real-time remote data storage.

Another dimension of OSS recovery is the recovery of the servers and software applications. This can be accomplished through failover on alternate equipment, ideally installed in data centers that are geographically separated from the primary servers. Failover can either be triggered manually or automatically, with automatic failover typically involving less downtime because of the speed of response. Emerging capabilities such as virtualization support more dynamic allocation of computing resources to apply toward applications needing additional computing power, whether it be due to a surge in extraordinary demand or physical loss of primary computing power.

14.8.3 Restoring Power

Another very frequent form of damage to networks is the loss of power. Some technologies available to restore power include:

- Portable generators: These can range from small units like homeowners might purchase for personal use, to large units with higher power capability and hauled by truck.
- Permanently installed generators: These are especially suitable when power demands are very high, and the generators themselves are very large. Some permanently installed generators can operate off natural gas, eliminating the need for refueling as long as the natural gas supply is not interrupted. This is an appealing option because movement of people and supplies can be very difficult in a disaster situation.
- Batteries: Since batteries can only provide power until they are discharged, they are normally used to support network equipment only temporarily until generators are able to meet the power requirements. When generators are installed permanently and with autostart capability, batteries are expected to support the equipment for only a few minutes, until the generators are activated. At this point, specialized control equipment can transfer the load from the batteries to the generators without interruption to the equipment.

14.8.4 Enabling a Safe Work Environment

When chemical, biological, or radiological agents are involved in a disaster, a network provider might need to have people working on the network itself, repairing or rebuilding network electronics and cabling, while also cleaning up these dangerous agents. Often, a subset of the network operations team is established as a "Hazmat Team," trained on how to operate in the presence of hazardous materials, using special gear.

- Decontamination units focus on protecting people by removing dangerous agents from them. They are dispatched to the "warm zone," which is defined as the area between the "hot zone" where the agents are prevalent and the "cool zone," which is safe for people to operate. People enter the unit from the hot zone,

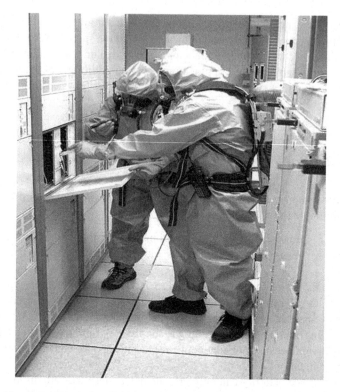

Fig. 14.6 Chemical, biological, radiological, or nuclear response

go through various stages of being "hosed down," and leave to the cool zone with replacement clothing.

- A wide variety of protective gear can be used by people who need to operate within an area with environmental hazards. These can range from simple paper air filtering masks to fully protective suits and self-sustaining breathing equipment, such as those shown in Fig. 14.6.

14.9 Open Questions/Future Research

14.9.1 Improving Predictability

Looking ahead, the most exciting opportunity in the area of disaster preparedness and resiliency is technology to improve the *predictability* of disasters. It is always easier to manage a disaster when you know it is coming. A surprise is always harder to manage than a predicted event. Technological advances can take what is a surprise today and make it a predicted event tomorrow.

To see how important predictability can be, one need only look back in history at the evolution of hurricane prediction. Weather forecasting was almost nonexistent, a 100 years ago, so hurricanes could not be predicted or tracked. This is largely what caused the extreme deadliness of the famous Galveston hurricane of 1900, in which 6,000 people died. Earlier that day, life seemed normal on this small Texas island, and the weather deteriorated so quickly that it was impossible to evacuate or make any preparations before the storm hit.

Now, with advancements in weather-forecasting technologies, we can watch hurricanes form from their earliest stages as tropical depressions thousands of miles away from land. We can track their path and predict the location and severity at landfall. This provides precious time to take precautionary action.

Our opportunity space for future research is to consider "surprise" disasters that can happen today, determine leading indicators and signatures of those events, and provide the measurement and alerting capabilities so that we can get warning in advance. The possibilities are practically endless, and can include software bugs, cyber attacks, earthquakes, or health pandemics. In almost all cases, the essence of prediction is complex data mining and correlation to detect underlying patterns, trends, and anomalies in the earliest stages of the incubation of a potential disaster. In the case of cyber attacks, the data sources can include network traffic patterns. Earthquake prediction could involve analysis of seismological data. Health pandemic prediction could involve analysis and correlation of leading medical indicators, such as medication purchases, emergency room visits, and test results.

14.9.2 Managing Traffic

Another exciting research opportunity is in the area of management of Internet Protocol traffic flows to help manage extreme traffic volumes and congestion conditions that arise during disasters. We have learned that when a network is used for lifeline and safety communications as well as flow of critical information, it is impossible to engineer a network to handle the extraordinary volumes and patterns that occur at the time of a major disaster. This is exacerbated even more when the same network experiences any loss or damage to capacity. Network managers need the ability to prioritize traffic and control the flow to avoid congestion conditions. These capabilities are largely "brute forced" in today's IP network. Technological advancements to provide intelligent traffic routing and congestion management capabilities can dramatically improve network resiliency moving forward.

14.9.3 Other Opportunities

Technology advancements will also continue in areas that shorten the time to design and implement a disaster recovery solution. Software to provide specific engineering designs to address unique scenarios at the time of a disaster can shorten the design time. Configuration management software can improve the ability to maintain real-time configurations offline, which reduces the time it takes to recover service on backup equipment and minimizes any loss of data. Even improvements on cabling and physical connections can reduce recovery time, by providing quick-connect mechanisms that reduce slow manual processes such as splicing and wiring.

14.10 Conclusion

Disaster recovery starts with disaster preparedness. To achieve and sustain network resiliency requires significant investment of effort and financial resources, starting way before an identified disaster is imminent. It starts with the earliest phases of technology selection and network design, and continues through installation and on-going operation. It means understanding risks and vulnerabilities and making sound business choices. It also involves disciplined execution of disaster recovery plans, once a disaster strikes.

Because of the significant investment of effort and financial resources involved, the message about importance of business continuity and disaster preparedness needs to start from the very top of the company. Formalizing a governance process, instituting standards and policies, and establishing a dedicated and empowered planning function of business continuity professionals are all important steps toward achieving a resilient network.

14.11 Best Practices

Below are the key messages of this chapter, captured into a brief summary of best practices to keep in mind as you develop your approach to disaster preparedness and resiliency.

Disaster Management and Resiliency "Best Practice" Principles

- Understand which assets are truly mission critical, and focus planning efforts accordingly
- Prioritize investments using a risk-assessment methodology which quantifies probability, impact, and ability to control outcomes
- Institute disciplined command-and-control capabilities
- Practice disaster management plans and use the drills to identify improvement opportunities
- Provide ongoing life-cycle management attention to disaster-management plans
- Strive toward anticipating and predicting disasters wherever possible

References[2]

1. Caralli, R. A., Stevens, J. F., Wallen, C. M., White, D. W., Wilson, W. R., & Young, L. R. (2007). Introducing the CERT Resiliency Engineering Framework: Improving the Security and Sustainability Processes, from http://www.sei.cmu.edu.
2. Coates, J. (2006). Anticipating disaster from research, or putting the fear of God into top management. *Research-Technology Management, 49*(1), 6–9.
3. Coutu, D. (2002). How resilience works. *Harvard Business Review. 80*(3), 46–55.
4. Elliott, D., Swartz, E., Herbane, B. (2001). *Business continuity management: A crisis management approach*. Boca Raton, FL: Taylor & Francis.
5. Financial Industry Regulatory Authority. (2008). FINRA Manual, from www.finra.org.
6. Flin, R. (1996). *Sitting in the hot seat: Leaders and teams for critical incident management*. Chichester/England: Wiley.
7. Hiles, A. (2007). *The definitive handbook of business continuity*. New York: Wiley.
8. Hollnagel, E., Woods, D., & Leveson, N. (2006). *Resilience engineering: Concepts and precepts*. Aldershot/England: Ashgate.
9. Keanini, T. (2003). Vulnerability management technology: A powerful alternative to attack management for networks. *Computer Technology Review, 23*(5), 18–19.
10. McEntire, D. (2001). Triggering agents, vulnerabilities and disaster reduction: Towards a holistic paradigm. *Disaster Prevention and Management, 10*(3), 189–196.
11. Reinmoeller, P., & van Baardwijk, N. (2005). The link between diversity and resilience. *MIT-Sloan Management Review, 46*(4), 61–65.
12. Sheffi, Y. (2005). *The resilient enterprise: Overcoming vulnerability for competitive advantage*. Boston, MA: MIT Press.
13. Snedaker, S. (2007). *Business continuity and disaster recovery planning for IT professionals*. Amsterdam: Elsevier Science & Technology Books.
14. U.S. Department of Homeland Security. (2006). National Infrastructure Protection Plan, from http://www.dhs.gov.
15. van Opstal, D. (2007). Transform: The resilient economy: Integrating competitiveness and security, from http://www.compete.org.
16. Wallace, M., & Webber, L. (2004). *The disaster recovery handbook: A step-by-step plan to ensure business continuity and protect vital operations, facilities, and assets*. New York: AMACOM.
17. Weichselgartner, J. (2001). Disaster mitigation: The concept of vulnerability revisited. *Disaster Prevention and Management, 10*(2), 85–94.

---

[2] The following references are offered for those who would like to learn more about the subjects of business continuity, disaster management and recovery, and resiliency. They include descriptions of techniques and technologies, summaries of national policy challenges, and insights into the role of leadership before and during a disaster.

Part VII
Reliable Application Services

Chapter 15
Building Large-Scale, Reliable Network Services

Alan L. Glasser

15.1 Introduction

This chapter is concerned with a particular class of software: large-scale network services, such as email systems providing service to millions of subscribers or web servers supporting e-commerce services to many customers simultaneously. To set the context of network service software, it may be helpful to understand how such software is similar to or different from a few other classes of software. Network services are generally expected to be "highly available;" that is, they are expected to be available at any time, 365 days of the year. This is in contrast with many Information Technology (or IT) systems that are designed to support a specific business function, and may be allowed significant periods of scheduled downtime, e.g., they may be down for "maintenance" on weekends. It is also informative to contrast network services software with end-user (or "shrink wrapped") software. While end-user software often gets deployed in far higher quantity than network services, such software gets upgraded in a manner that is often known to and under the control of the end-user. Microsoft, Apple, and other vendors have conditioned their end-user communities to expect and tolerate upgrades. Such conditioning of end-users has not been the case for network services, and expectations are generally much higher for network service availability. Finally, while we present techniques for producing reliable software for large-scale network services, this chapter will not cover "carrier-class" software (the quintessential example being the software running the public switched telephone network). We define carrier-class software as software that, if it fails at all, is typically down for at most 5 minutes per year, or stated alternatively, software that has an availability of at least 99.999%. While there are many other characteristics of carrier-class software, another key one that contrasts somewhat with network services is that carrier-class software rarely requires operator intervention.

A.L. Glasser (✉)
Distinguished Member of Technical Staff, AT&T Labs Research, Middletown, NJ, USA
e-mail: aglasser@att.com

C.R. Kalmanek et al. (eds.), *Guide to Reliable Internet Services and Applications*,
Computer Communications and Networks, DOI 10.1007/978-1-84882-828-5_15,
© Springer-Verlag London Limited 2010

The class of software covered in this chapter is not expected to run without any human intervention; in other words, the software need not be completely non-stop and self-healing (as is often the case in "carrier-class" software). It is far more expensive to develop software that needs no (or minimal) human intervention. However, it is important to recognize that with human (or operator) intervention come failures [1] that have their own costs; it is often reported that for highly reliable systems, one-third of the failures are due to hardware failures, another third are due to software failures, and the remaining third are due to human, i.e., operator, error.

Within this scope, we will identify the key concepts and techniques that have proven to be valuable in the production of reliable network service software. The overall approach may be characterized as "documentation heavy," since reliable software requires a very clear, well-understood view of the system. Many of these concepts and techniques are also applicable to the production of other classes of software.

Network services need to be reliable, because the businesses that they support cannot afford the impact of frequent software failures. Reliable software is not defined to be bug-free software; it is the software with a particular probability of running without failure in a given environment for a specified period of time. Availability is a measure of the percentage of time that the service is available for end-users to use over a period of time, typically one year. For example, a software system may be designed to be available 99.99% of the time over a year. Alternatively, the design requirements may allow the system to be unavailable for 0.01% of a year over a year or approximately 53 minutes per year. Many network services are sold with a Service-Level Agreement that includes, among other terms, a stated mechanism for measuring availability, a contracted level of availability, and a set of financial penalties (including early contract termination) for failure to meet the contracted level of availability. Cost is a key factor in producing reliable software. The fundamental engineering problem to be solved is to make an appropriate trade-off between the costs of producing reliable software against the cost of any business-impacting service failures. In the remainder of this chapter, we discuss techniques for producing reliable software.

Section 15.2 presents an overview of the system development process, Section 15.3 presents the generation of requirements, Section 15.4 presents the architecture deliverables, Section 15.5 presents the design and implementation process, Section 15.6 presents testing, and Section 15.7 presents the support processes.

15.2 System Development Process

In many parts of the software industry, process is considered as a panacea. Unfortunately, many IT groups are burdened with rigid formal software development processes that add overhead without contributing much to software reliability. The perspective presented in this chapter is that process is a way of thinking, not a substitute for thinking. This chapter does not cover process definition or process improvement (this material is covered amply elsewhere; see, for example, [2]). Instead, we describe the activities necessary to produce reliable, robust large-scale network service software.

While some software is built by a single individual, working alone, this chapter addresses the more common production of software developed by a group of people [3]. Development of large-scale network services requires execution of distinct functions: requirements, architecture, design, implementation, test, and support. While a large organization may be able to assign each staff member to perform only a single function, most organizations will not have that luxury. Care should be taken when assigning staff to carry out more than one function. Requirements are best produced by staff with no other job function; when this is impossible due to resource constraints, an effective second task for the requirements staff is the test function. Architecture is best performed by a single, designated architect. This individual should be accountable for the service and is often supported by a number of subject matter experts and/or experienced designers (more on this in the Architecture section, below). Design and implementation are functions that should be treated effectively as a single function; they should not be assigned to separate staff groups. Test is ideally a dedicated team, but may be combined with requirements. Testing should never be combined with design and implementation, as this defeats the notion of an independent system test. Finally, deployment and support, while ideally staffed as an independent team, may be combined with design and implementation (it should be pointed out that software with a history of production-discovered problems warrants an independent deployment and support team, as this will allow the design and implementation team to better adhere to a project schedule and deliver on development commitments).

The most important element for the successful development of production software by a group of people is a common understanding of the project and its details. Groups that lack a common understanding of the project cannot avoid failures which, at best, result in project delays as they are remedied, and at worst, result in project cancellation. The goal of any network service development project is to produce reliable software that satisfies its customers. The best way to ensure that all the people involved in a project have a common understanding is for the project to produce and use high-quality documents. Some key document categories include requirements, design, test plans, test cases, and project plans. Drafts of these documents are produced first and reviewed by the project team for completeness, clarity, and accuracy; the goal of the review process is to produce higher quality documents than would otherwise be realized. When a document is deemed complete, it is placed under a formal change control process, which simply means that any future changes to the document require a careful review and approval process that assesses all the impacts on the project that such changes would engender. For example, a significant new feature might be deferred to a future release due to the rework it might require on the current release and the concomitant schedule extension necessary to accommodate the rework.

The author of a piece of software makes certain assumptions in its development. Wherever assumptions are made, either in requirements or architecture documents or anywhere else, they should be clearly documented, and as design, implementation, test, and deployment occur, they should all be continually tested and confirmed. If assumptions made are no longer valid, a re-evaluation may be necessary.

15.3 Requirements

Requirements typically start at a relatively high level, describing the primary business functions of the software. The most important questions that the initial, high-level requirements document should answer are:

- What is the problem you are trying to solve?
- Who is the customer of the system?
- Who are the users of the system?

An initial high-level requirements document would, when complete, be followed by a software architecture document (described in the next section). After the architecture is produced, lower-level requirements are produced for each of the major components of the architecture.

The key consumers of the high-level requirements document are the customer (or sponsor) of the system and the system architect. The customer or sponsor reviews the document to confirm that their needs are accurately captured therein[1]. The high-level requirements document governs and guides the architecture.

Two key consumers of lower-level requirements documents are the design and implementation team and the test team. The design and implementation team builds software that implements the requirements, and the test team develops test cases that confirm that the requirements are implemented properly. It is important that requirements be written in a form that allows for the implementation of both code and test cases. The requirements should be written in a manner that avoids, as much as is feasible, specifying how the software should be built, and instead should focus on specifying what it is that the software should do. How the software should be built is a design, and not a requirements activity, and designers resent having design choices dictated as requirements as they usually place unnecessary constraints on possible solutions. Also, mixing design and requirements will usually reduce the clarity of the requirements and may confuse testers. In addition, the requirements must be testable (e.g., a requirement that includes non-quantitative, vague language, such as "the system must gradually shift connections" is not testable). Writing good requirements is as difficult as, if not more difficult than, writing good code.

Requirements fall into two broad categories: functional and non-functional. For example, an Internet Service Provider (ISP) email platform would include the functions of accepting email from subscribers for forwarding to recipients, accepting

---

[1] Gaining concurrence from the customer or sponsor may require more than the production of a high-level requirements document, such as the development of demonstration software.

email for subscribers from other email systems, allowing subscribers to access their mailbox, and minimization of unwanted/undesired messages. The functional requirements will address what the software must do to provide those functions and specify all the features made available to the service's end-users. Use cases [4] should be used to document each of the key features.

Additionally, the email platform will have non-functional (also known as operational) requirements – for example, a requirement that the email platform must log data about every SMTP session and that each log entry must include various parameters that describe that session, such as the start time, end time, and IP addresses involved. The non-functional requirements address all the capabilities necessary for operating and supporting the service.

The high-level non-functional requirements for network services must spell out the expectations for reliability and availability clearly and specifically, because meeting these expectations will drive architecture and design decisions. For example, the requirements must define the hours of operation of the service. If it is 24 hours per day, 7 days per week, it needs to be stated. If something else,that needs to be stated. The requirements for network services typically include a time for upgrades and other maintenance activities that will impact the end-user availability[2]. Such periods are called "maintenance windows". The expected duration, maximum allowed duration, expected frequency, and maximum allowed frequency of maintenance windows are important requirements that will drive the architecture. These requirements may be as simple as "at most one maintenance window per week of no more than 2 hours duration beginning at 08:00 UTC." All the reliability and availability requirements will be driven by the service's sponsor as well as the organizations supporting and operating the service.

For network services, the non-functional requirements are typically as numerous and complex as the functional requirements. These requirements address manageability, operability, availability, reliability, system capacity, throughput, latency, and other non-functional areas[3]. The high-level requirements document defines these requirements for the overall system. The lower-level requirements documents define these requirements for each individual component. Other important non-functional requirements cover behavior under overload, upgrades, and compatibility. Additionally, four areas of non-functional requirements that must be addressed are:

1. Provisioning: describes features that the software must provide to allow objects (e.g., subscribers, accounts, mailboxes, etc.) that need to be known to the system to be added to, changed, or removed from the system.

2. Operations: describes features that the software must provide to the operations staff to allow them to operate the service. For example, what software commands must be provided to allow an operator to determine if the software is operating

---

[2] Overall system availability (e.g., 99.99% availability) excludes such maintenance activities; i.e., availability is measured against all time other than scheduled maintenance activities.

[3] The sponsor or customer should provide a load forecast to aid in the formulation of the performance requirements.

normally and, if it is not, what software commands must be provided to allow an operator to restore correct operation.

3. Administration: describes capabilities that the software must provide to allow the system to be configured (or administered) to support the various range of configurations needed to support the business. These requirements also typically address the configuration and administration of the underlying operating system and the security requirements for the system.

4. Maintenance: describes the requirements on software needed to support periodic or on-demand maintenance tasks, such as periodic backups or on-demand connectivity tests.

The non-functional requirements tend to distinguish network services (as well as "carrier-class" software) from other classes of software.

Careful, thoughtful generation and review of requirements is expensive in terms of staff effort and calendar time. However, since poorly specified, vague requirements rarely, if ever, result in the desired service behavior, and the alternative is even more expensive rework and calendar time or cancellation of the effort.

15.4 Architecture

Large-scale network services are best developed by first developing a well-thought architecture in response to the high-level requirements.

A successful architecture must have conceptual integrity. Ideally, the architecture should be produced by a single individual, or, if not feasible, by a small team led by "the architect" [3]. The architect can delegate the architecture of each subsystem in the logical architecture (see below) to different team members. Also, in large organizations, where individuals can specialize in relatively narrow technologies, it is advantageous for the architect to consult with these subject experts (e.g., server and storage experts) in producing the physical architecture.

There are three components of architecture: the logical architecture, the physical architecture, and the performance and reliability model.

The performance and reliability model is covered in greater detail in Chapter 16 of this book. Here, we simply note that this portion of the system architecture is driven by the logical and physical architecture and needs to include usage and traffic assumptions, demand forecasts, transaction flows (through the physical architecture), capacity and usage forecasts, component resource budgets, analysis of reliability, and establishment of component downtime budgets. Additionally, this component of the architecture needs to provide "back-of-the-envelope" estimates as to how the architecture meets the throughput and latency requirements.

The performance of the production system needs to be measured and reported to ascertain whether it is meeting the architectural and design expectations, and, often more importantly, whether it is meeting any performance criteria set forth in any service-level agreement. The architecture must address how these needs will be met.

As stated earlier, the expected system capacity is an important non-functional requirement of the system. This and related performance requirements (e.g., throughput and latency) drives the architecture to a specific design point that will support those requirements. It is rare indeed that a system architected for a given design point functions cost effectively (or, for that manner, in any way effectively) beyond an order of magnitude above or below the design point. For example, in architecting a system capable of supporting 1,000 transactions per second, it would be rare to find this same architecture effective at less than 100 or more than 10,000 transactions per second. Thus, the architecture should be completely re-thought if the design point needs to change by an order of magnitude or more.

Another crucial aspect of architecture is designing how the system will behave under overload. The system should be engineered to process requests up to a given offered load level within the latencies specified in the requirements. When the offered load exceeds that specified in the requirements, the system should behave as gracefully as possible. When the protocols used to provide service are TCP-based, a simple technique is to set a maximum on the number of connections supported. Additional offered load above the connection limit will consume some network and CPU resources, but existing connections should be serviced reasonably, possibly with longer latencies (due to resource contention). Services that utilize UDP (or other, non-connection protocols) present more challenges for handling excessive load. Load-shedding techniques, like simply dropping some fraction of requests, may be warranted. It is clearly desirable to minimize the processing of any work that will ultimately be dropped; in other words, requests should be dropped early, before the system consumes or commits resources. Load-shedding mechanisms should not themselves increase the amount of processing that the system must perform. However, for protocols like SIP (utilizing UDP transport), a more intelligent approach to load-shedding may be applied, such as refusing to establish any new sessions while continuing to service requests for established sessions (i.e., dropping all requests to establish new sessions and dropping no requests related to existing sessions). Stress testing (see Section 15.6, below) should be used to measure the system behavior under overload.

After production of the architecture deliverables, the project should undergo an Architecture Assessment (see Section 16.3).

Following Architecture Assessment, the production of lower-level requirements documents occurs, each corresponding to one of the major functional components identified in the architecture.

The remainder of this section describes key items that the logical and physical architecture deliverables must address.

15.4.1 Logical System Architecture

The logical system architecture document provides a high-level logical solution to the initial high-level requirements.

The scope of the document needs to be clearly stated; in particular, it is essential to clearly enumerate what is not covered by this document, stating why those items are not being covered and where (in what other documents) those items will be addressed.

The constraints placed on the system need to be covered. These can be constraints placed on component selection (e.g., only software from a particular vendor may be used for database needs). Alternatively, they can be constraints related to integration with other systems (e.g., billing information will need to be in a particular format due to this system's integration with an existing billing system) or the relationship that this service might have with other services (e.g., network access controls constraints on this service due to its bundling with an access service). Finally, the most important set of constraints provided are those that are related to the service's performance and reliability. Performance constraints are typically per-transaction latency requirements (e.g., 99% of the time, a transaction of type $XYZZY$ must be completed within 100 ms) or scalability requirements (the system must be able to support 10,000 concurrent $XYZZY$ transactions). The reliability constraints are typically specified in terms of the service's availability (e.g., the system must be available 99.99% of the time).

The architect should distill and clearly document the principles followed in producing the architecture, so that all of the subsequent design efforts can adhere to these principles. Two examples of such principles are where the state is maintained (or where the state is *not* maintained), and how data is replicated (and the strategy employed for replicating a database master). A key role for the architect following the production of the architecture deliverables is monitoring adherence to the architecture, a key aspect of which is adherence to the architecture principles. This "policing" role is key to maintaining the conceptual integrity of the architecture as it is implemented.

The design portion of the architecture document should begin with a high-level block diagram (e.g., see Fig. 15.1, which is a high-level block diagram of a service to provide wholesale web or phone access to email and calendar capabilities) and text to describe each of the blocks, their function, and the interfaces that each block presents to the other blocks. Each of the blocks in the high-level block diagram typically represents the subsystems of the system being architected. For each of the subsystems deemed core to the project (or that otherwise warrant this level of detail), the single block in the high-level block diagram should be exploded to show the next level of detail, similar to what was done for the high-level block diagram: text to describe each of the blocks, their function, and the interfaces that each block presents to the other blocks.

Following the subsystem discussion, the document must identify all the existing external systems that the architecture relies on and the details of the exact interfaces used. The various block diagrams should graphically indicate the interfaces to these external systems.

The discussion within the document to this point has been primarily block diagram and interface-related, and the next area to cover is the data architecture used. This would include identification of all databases used in the architecture, and for

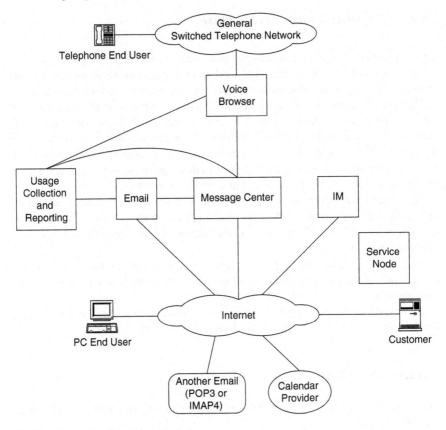

Fig. 15.1 Example of high-level block diagram

each database, identification of key data elements, as well as expected queries and updates, with usage profiles (e.g., each *XYZZY* transaction results in *Q* queries and *U* updates).

Following data architecture, the document should address security by identifying the security mechanisms to be employed in the architecture (e.g., use of Access Control Lists, secure transport, or password encryption algorithms) as well as an analysis to ensure that the identified mechanisms are sufficient for this service.

The document should close with a discussion of issues and risks. The architect, having produced this detail about the service, will undoubtedly be aware of a number of issues that have not been addressed in the document, but need to be tracked and resolved to assure the success of the project. Finally, the architect will also be aware of the quantifiable and non-quantifiable risks remaining in the project. These should be documented and the project should be managed with an eye towards mitigating those risks.

15.4.2 Physical System Architecture

This subsection describes the material that needs to be included in the physical system architecture: server, network[4], and storage engineering as well as system and server management. The subsequent subsections address each of these areas.

The functional blocks of the logical architecture need to be realized on physical servers running in a specified operational environment, and the physical system architecture provides that realization. The physical and logical architectures are often developed together, typically with the physical somewhat lagging behind the logical. While constraints may limit certain choices in developing the physical architecture, the physical architecture should not limit the logical architecture.

Hardware alternatives considered and discarded should be documented, clearly indicating the analysis that led to the discard. This analysis will undoubtedly be of value when the chosen hardware is discontinued by the manufacturer and new hardware must be chosen.

The physical architecture needs to result in a series of engineering drawings that provide sufficient detail to allow all the hardware to be ordered, deployed, and interconnected.

Finally, an important output of the physical architecture should be the expected capital and operations costs, normalized per end-user or subscriber.

15.4.2.1 Server Engineering

The primary consideration in server engineering is to design in redundancy to provide reliability.

The assignment of logical functions to individual servers is a key part of server engineering. The key considerations in such assignment are the data needed by each logical function. When two logical functions always (or almost always) act on the same data, or when one logical function is the producer of a huge volume of data consumed by a second logical function, those functions are excellent candidates to reside on the same server. Another key consideration is the impact of a server failure on each logical function and what strategies might be employed to minimize the impact of such failures. Logical functions that are effectively or inherently stateless (e.g., a proxy for the POP3 protocol) can fail with minimal impact, while those that are inherently state-full (e.g., an LDAP directory) need a server design that minimizes the impact of a hardware failure. Stateless servers are also easily scalable (often referred to as *horizontally scalable*), while state-full servers are not easily scalable.

---

[4] Network engineering is covered elsewhere in this book and is not covered here, except for a few recommendations that aid overall service availability.

Stateless servers are typically accessed[5] via a virtual IP (VIP) address that represents a pool of real, physical servers (for details on the network engineering needed to support this, see [5]). The logical functions to be performed on such servers will be accessed via an IP protocol (e.g., HTTP). At any point in time, some number of those physical servers will be operational, performing the logical functions required of them. Should one fail, all functions "in flight" will fail. Typically, clients of this VIP will need to determine whether the function failed (e.g., via an exception like a TCP reset or a timeout) and take appropriate recovery action. A simple, useful technique that is worth attempting prior to more drastic measures is to simply re-try the original request again. With appropriate network engineering, the new request will simply be routed to another server that is operational and will succeed.

State-full servers typically require a sparing strategy. The simplest such strategy is to deploy two physical servers for every state-full server needed. To the extent that the software can support it, this could provide very fast recovery from a server failure. This will require that the internal state of the software be replicated to the spare in a manner that would allow the spare to assume the function of the primary, should the primary fail at any point. Such an arrangement is generally referred to as active-active. The performance cost of state replication can become prohibitive and various optimizations are usually taken to replicate at particular junctures. The replication points are chosen so as not to leave the spare in an unusable state if the primary fails between the points. While the spare will be able to quickly take on the role of the primary, some in-flight client functions, at the time of primary failure, will fail and need to be re-tried. A simpler strategy is known as active-standby. In an active-standby approach, the standby server will assume the function of the just failed active server. All in-memory state will be lost and all in-flight client functions will fail. This approach is useful when the key state of the functions is stored on external storage that can be shared with a spare. Depending on the external storage chosen, a spare might automatically assume the active role; on the other hand, it may require human intervention to configure equipment to give the spare the necessary identity and access to assume the active role. Another key consideration in an active-standby arrangement is the cost of providing pairs of servers. Again, depending on the external storage chosen, another alternative is to allocate one spare for every N active servers, or more generally, allocate K spare servers for every M active servers.

It is wise to be pessimistic on performance when engineering servers, and thus, have a designed-in safety margin on latency and capacity.

Another important networking consideration is the assignment of at least two public IP (or VIP) addresses to be allocated for each externally visible TCP/IP service (e.g., for an email service, inbound SMTP to subscribers' mailboxes would be a service, and outbound SMTP from subscribers would be another service) to avoid disruption in the event of routing configuration errors. Also, the authoritative DNS for the domain needs to return two separate address records, each containing one of

---

[5] Such access may be from an end-user of the service (e.g., via a browser or email client) or from another system, either internal to the service or from a customer or third-party server.

the two addresses. These two IP addresses should be allocated from two blocks of addresses that contain a lot of space between them (the two blocks are not "near" each other). In other words, it should not be possible to combine the two blocks into a single routing prefix that might be accidentally hijacked, which would prevent customers from accessing the service. Assuming that all clients will make the proper use of the two DNS address records (and not simply rely on the first record), this technique should prevent accidental hijacking of an address block from impacting this service [6, 7].

15.4.2.2 Storage Engineering

This section presents storage reliability considerations and tradeoffs, and the need to practice recovery operations to minimize downtime when a failure occurs.

Data stored on disk presents a number of engineering issues to be worked through as a part of the system architecture. The required performance and capacity of the disk subsystem for particular sets of data as well as the required availability of that data must be identified. Data that has similar performance and availability requirements, whose combined capacity requirements can be satisfied by a given single-storage solution, are candidates for sharing that solution. Some services, like a Content Distribution Network cache, may have very low availability requirements for data that is cached (i.e., the stored data is simply a copy of the authoritative data source that is stored elsewhere). The physical system architecture must specify the storage to be employed in the system. Reliability of disk drives and redundancy in storage engineering are beyond the scope of this chapter; interested readers are referred to [8, 9].

In spite of carefully designed disk subsystems, there could be a catastrophic disk subsystem failure, or with similar effect, a software failure that causes data corruption of all redundant copies of data in the disk subsystem. Such a failure always results in unplanned system downtime; the duration of such an outage needs to be minimized. Recovery from such a failure requires having a recent backup of the data (i.e., a copy of the data on separate secondary storage, typically tape media). In order to achieve recency of the backup data, backups need to be performed regularly at frequent intervals. While backup is a well-known, commonly instituted practice, what is equally important and rarely done is periodic data restoral to spare disk drives. Backup media that is unreadable at the time a restoral is required will become a major system catastrophe that may not have any viable recovery. One possible result is to restore service without the lost data. For an ISP email platform, this might mean restoring service to end-users with new, empty mailboxes. Another possible result is that the lost data can be extracted from other systems, each containing a portion of the needed data, but this will typically be a long duration process and service cannot be restored until it completes. Backups and regular periodic restoral to spare disk drives need to be specified in the requirements and supported by operations training and documentation, in addition to being covered by the architecture.

Another important consideration in providing reliable storage is the use of multiple data centers for mitigating the effect of a disaster in a single data center (disaster recovery is covered more fully in Chapter 14 of this book). In this section, we are concerned with spreading equipment among multiple data centers so that a failure in a single data center will only cause a partial service outage. An example is an email service supporting millions of end-user mailboxes, where a fraction of the mailboxes are hosted in each data center so that a site failure only impacts a fraction of the end-users. This approach does not achieve true disaster recovery (which can be very expensive), but it will result in higher availability of the service than placing all equipment in a single data center. If multiple data centers are used to host the equipment required by the service being architected and there is a key database or directory that is a critical resource required for the service to operate, it is advisable to maintain a replica in at least one (or more) of the other data centers. A simplified case is a SQL database master with one replica. In this case, the replication would occur over the WAN (possibly via a tunnel). Such an arrangement should allow the service to continue running if the master data center site experienced a major failure or disaster. In some cases, manual procedures may be necessary to promote the replica to the status of master, and insert, update, and delete transactions will fail until that promotion occurs. The key to achieving success with this "master-slave" approach is to regularly exercise "fail-over", meaning that the operations organization will, on a regular basis (say once a week at a low traffic point), deliberately stop the master and promote the replica to master. Typically, when the prior master is restored to service, it will run as a replica to the new master until the next regular "fail-over" or true failure. This approach of regular "fail-over" should also be employed for any state-full server schemes. When the operations organization is familiar with the "fail-over" process, a true failure is dealt with as a relatively minor inconvenience (at least as far as the familiarity of the steps required to restore service are concerned). Whenever these processes become exceptions that only get executed rarely, they rarely get carried out correctly or well. As with backups and restorals, this fail-over behavior needs to be specified in the requirements and be supported by operations training and documentation, in addition to being covered by the architecture.

15.4.2.3   System and Service Management

This section describes support systems, instrumentation and logging, secure access, and considerations for software installation and upgrade.

The System and Service Management section of the architecture document needs to describe the monitoring and operations principles and mechanisms to be employed to manage the service, which needs to be addressed both from an end-to-end service perspective and for each component.

A key goal of this portion of the architecture is to establish a foolproof and reliable mechanism for monitoring the health of the service by the operations staff. For an enterprise that has an established operations organization, the architect will probably need to find a solution that will fit into existing monitoring mechanisms and tools used by that organization. For example, there may already be an SNMP trap monitoring infrastructure.

Software systems that monitor the health of the network service should never fail in a manner that allows a network service failure to go unnoticed. This places a more stringent reliability requirement on the monitoring systems than on the network service. Some techniques to achieve this are to avoid sharing code between the network service and the health monitoring software, use of a separate staff to build the health monitoring system, and using off-the-shelf, proven reliable software either from a vendor or from open source (e.g., OpenNMS and Nagios). There is a cost associated with this approach, and for a business developing a single network service, this cost may prove prohibitive.

For an organization that can afford it and needs to support multiple network services, having support systems that are independent of and separate from the network service also presents a cost-savings opportunity: the support systems can be shared across multiple services. Examples of such systems are SNMP management systems for monitoring SNMP traps and trouble ticketing systems for managing and tracking problems (and their resolution) in the network (services as well as other components like routers, switches, etc.). These support systems need to be very reliable as their failure can mask a network service failure; they also need to be managed well (e.g., backed-up regularly).

The monitoring system must proactively poll the service to determine that it is working correctly and not simply rely on the service reporting faults.

To provide data for monitoring, one must first address the approach taken to logging key events. Such events may simply be informational (e.g., a typical web server access log), but must also cover faults discovered by the software. Faults are assigned a severity, typically minor, major, and critical. A minor fault is one that needs attention today or within 24 hours, and if ignored, will result in end-users being able to detect service degradation. Some examples of minor faults are various resources such as disk file system capacity or average CPU consumption being above some threshold, say 80%. Other thresholds such as the rate of retries exceeding some threshold may also be a possible minor fault. A major fault is one that requires attention within a prescribed amount of time, typically 2–4 hours. Thresholds are an example of major faults, perhaps set at a higher utilization level than a minor fault, such as 90%. A critical alarm is an indication that a component or a major subsystem of the service has failed and requires immediate attention. Examples of critical faults are loss of connectivity to key resources and missing key configuration data needed to provide the service (for which there are no reasonable defaults). An SMTP email Message Transfer Agent (MTA) that has lost all connections to the system's directory and cannot re-connect after repeated retries and thus cannot ascertain whether an addressed user, named in a RECIPIENT command, is a subscriber, is an example of a "loss of connectivity" critical fault. All these events must get logged to disk storage in a reliable manner, as this data is indispensible in troubleshooting in-service problems. One choice for achieving reliable trap processing is to utilize multiple SNMP receivers, requiring all the originators to send to multiple receivers, and to filter-out redundant traps downstream, within the management infrastructure.

While the architect must provide guidelines to the developers on when to generate a trap, it is often the case that further processing on the received traps is necessary prior to raising an alarm to the operations staff. The system receiving the traps should be configurable to some level so that every trap does not, in general, result in an operations alarm. It is often the case that multiple traps can be combined, especially when they occur at roughly the same time, into a single alarm event. Correlation of traps across components of the service as well as across services is also desirable. A typical behavior for which operator intervention is undesirable is when the software attempts a TCP connection to another system that initially fails (this should generate a trap and log entry, but not cause an immediate alarm), but is re-tried and subsequently succeeds on the second attempt. If the second attempt failed, it too would generate a trap and log entry, and the combination of the two traps within a specified time period would be configured to raise an alarm. Another behavior that should be detected by monitoring is continual, repeated failure and restart, as this is often not easily detected by the network service itself.

While seemingly mundane, standardization of log format within the team simplifies specification of alarm correlation rules[6] and aids training of all staff: design and implementation, test, support, and operations. The architecture should define the standard log format. A single line of text per entry is recommended. It should always include a date and time in a prescribed format for both elements, a specified resolution for the time (e.g., seconds or milli-seconds), and a well-known time zone (Coordinated Universal Time or UTC is an excellent choice). Various other fields that might be a part of the standard are process-id, user-id, client-IP-address, end-user-id, etc. Typically, some fields will be particular to the functionality of the service; e.g., an SMTP MTA will have some unique fields to log compared to a POP process, such as the domain provided on an SMTP command. The architecture sets the principles and standards to be followed. The format of each log needs to be documented as a part of the design process.

An important set of architectural principles to be established in this area is how much or how little should be logged as "informational" entries, and whether the amount of data logged should be fixed or determined by a configurable parameter (e.g., the "log level"). Such a configurable parameter necessitates further principles associating different classes of information with particular values of the parameter, so that there is consistency across the system in how such logging is controlled and occurs. Such "informational" entries are not actionable events, but, at one extreme, provide data about every transaction (e.g., each SMTP session and each message within that session processed by an MTA), and, at the other extreme, provide no data for the "expected" activities (like a successful SMTP session). For maximum flexibility, each subsystem, component, or program should be independently configurable. Also, while it simplifies the operations training and documentation to have common values for such configurable parameters across the subsystems, components, or programs, there are often good arguments to be made for a particular piece of the service to utilize a unique set of values (e.g., bit masks) to control different informational entries.

---

[6] To simplify the specification of alarm correlation rules, the system and/or tools used to perform alarm correlation will drive commonality requirements on logging (e.g., common date and time formats, allowing rules to determine multiple failures within a given time interval).

When troubleshooting problems, it is often helpful to have as much information as possible about the system behavior. Also, there may be value to service planners, particularly, capacity planners, in capturing a large number of informational entries. On the other hand, such an approach will require careful attention to the performance impact of such logging as well as attention to rolling logs and preserving log data, while avoiding any impact to the service. An occasionally successful alternative to logging for troubleshooting is to utilize a packet sniffer (e.g., tcpdump, wireshark, or snoop) when the logging would contain a subset of the sniffed data.

Another important consideration is the ability to provide secure access to developers to gather data or otherwise observe the service to help troubleshoot a problem. One proven technique is to provide an entirely separate LAN infrastructure for all operations, administration, and maintenance (OA&M) activities (including developer access), and providing a secure tunnel or VPN access for the developers to access the OA&M LAN. This general approach also keeps logging and trap traffic separate from service traffic, which is generally a good idea to aid overload troubleshooting (e.g., diagnosing a DDoS attack).

Finally, the architectural principles for software installation should be established. At one extreme, software installation may need to occur on a server that is completely out-of-service and from which any prior version has been first removed. At the other extreme, software installation occurs while the prior version is running and providing service, and only a minimal duration outage is required to stop the old version, likely perform some administrative tasks (e.g., adjust some symbolic links) and start the new version. The former is simpler to implement, and the latter results in minimal down time. In Section 15.7.2, operational concerns related to software installation, upgrades, and deployment are discussed.

15.5   Design and Implementation

15.5.1   Design

There are many texts dedicated exclusively to software design. This section will focus on the aspects of design that are essential to producing reliable software. The design of a software component has two primary classifications: external design and internal design. The external design describes how others can use this component and the internal design describes how the component is constructed.

From an external perspective, each significant functional component of the architecture should have a corresponding design document, which, at a minimum, describes all of the interfaces presented by the component to other components in the system. Thus, the application programming interfaces (or APIs) exposed by each architectural subsystem to the rest of the system must be documented (using, for example, javadoc or doxygen). Expected sequences of API calls, along with sample code that implements a demonstration of that portion of the design, should be documented. Data, in the form of database tables, flat files, or anything else, represents a key external interface. Data that this component produces or consumes, for or from other components, should be documented as a part of the external design. The data local to the component would be described in the internal design.

Another important interface that must be documented is the operations interface. This would describe how the component is installed, updated, removed, configured, started, checked (for current operational status), re-started (if applicable), and stopped. While the details of internal-to-the-component data remain in the internal design, the operations staff needs to know all the files, databases and tables, directories, and any other data that the component needs, uses, consumes, and produces. All this can aid troubleshooting (e.g., when an operator is mistaken about the location of the current directory and inadvertently removes all the files therein). Descriptions of each and every event that the component might log, including sufficient detail to enable troubleshooting, represents an important portion of the operations interface. Additionally, various key performance indicators (KPIs, typically counters) should be included in the design, along with simple mechanisms for operations staff to observe those indicators. Expected value ranges of each KPI should be documented for the operations staff. It is very often the case that such indicators are predictors of problematic trends. Each user interface should be documented; this is typically done by providing prototype user interface code or "wireframe" figures and text describing navigation. User interface design is beyond the scope of this book (see [10, 11]).

The internal design typically focuses on key algorithms chosen, trade-offs made, and performance considerations.

15.5.2 Organization

An effective way to organize the design and implementation staff, given that the system has been decomposed into components, is to assign components to individual staff members. An individual component should never be assigned to multiple staff members. If a single large component is identified, which is undeniably too large to be the responsibility of a single staff member, it should be decomposed, if at all possible, into multiple smaller components. General purpose or utility components should be avoided; items that would be added to such utility library should instead constitute new, albeit small, specific functional components. This design approach requires identifying a bottoms-up component structure for the integration of components. At the bottom layer, each component should, in general, be functionally independent of all other components. Such components might be generally useful in future projects and should be built in a general fashion to foster reuse. At some point, a component must be built that depends on bottom layer components and so on, up the dependency hierarchy. The bottom-up dependencies drive the project schedule: the bottom layer should be built first and so on, up the hierarchy. Each component will be made available for integration with the other components when it has been fully unit-tested by its developer. It is typically the case that problems that arise are attributable to the most recent components added to the integration area.

This approach results in increased accountability, as there is never a question as to who is responsible for a particular function. It also fosters increased ownership of the software by the staff members, as each staff member knows that they alone have complete responsibility for their components. More than one person needs to be familiar with the software or else there is a potential, software single-point-of-failure (e.g., the one person is unavailable when a bug is discovered). A "buddy system" that clearly identifies a specific backup person for each component works well. This results in an individual being the primary on a number of components and the backup on a different set of components.

Managing a project of many small components, though somewhat tedious, allows for quite accurate estimation of effort. This results in increased predictability as well as visibility of the overall development process, affording earlier identification of problems than might otherwise be the case. Finally, given the availability of good API documentation for each component, this approach decreases developer inter-dependence, as it reduces the need for extensive inter-developer communication and results in fewer and smaller integration delays (but with typically more integration points). This approach fosters a "test early, test often" environment[7], as each integration culminates in integration testing to certify that the integration was successful. It avoids "big bang" integration efforts that, when they do not go smoothly, result in long delays in sorting out which (often many) components have problems.

15.5.3 Configurability

The configurability of network services deserves careful design attention. Any parameter that might change over time should be designed to be a configuration parameter and not a constant in the code. The use of a constant in the code would require a new code delivery and certification prior to achieving the change, while the former, with appropriate operations documentation, could be achieved by the operations staff acting alone. It is sometimes not clear why a particular parameter might change in the future; when in doubt, it is best to make it a configuration parameter. Default values, whenever they make sense, should be provided for each parameter. Examples of parameters are directory names for various data (e.g., the directory in which log data should be written), and fully qualified domain names or IP addresses and corresponding ports (and, if relevant, protocol or protocol version) for other systems that this component must communicate with (e.g., SNMP

---

[7] "Test early, test often" should be followed in any case; it fosters easier and faster bug detection than waiting.

receivers). The design needs to recognize the environmental differences present in different test environments (e.g., unit test and system test) as well as in the production environment, and support these different environments via simple configuration changes. Clearly, changing code to support these different environments is not desirable. In addition to allowing for the exact same source code to support various test environments as well as (potentially multiple) production environments, this design for configurability allows for recovery from a class of failures (e.g., failure of an SNMP receiver) via a simple change to the configuration data. Another important consideration is whether a configuration change requires a network service stop and start, or a trigger from an operator instructing the service to re-read its configuration data, or if the service automatically detects and implements configuration changes (e.g., having a thread detect that a configuration file changed, and ingest and process that file). While the simplest implementation is a service stop and start, automatic detection provides the least service impact.

15.5.4   Maintainability and Modularity

An important consideration in producing reliable network service software is the maintainability of the source code. It is almost always the case that modularity and maintainability are positively correlated. Fewer lines of code are preferable to more lines of code, since it is less expensive to completely test and certify fewer lines of code, and less code simplifies enhancement and bug repair because there are fewer places to look for the place in the code to change. While an approach that emphasizes a high level of modularity should drive the internal design of the code, it is often the case that implementers replicate code in multiple methods or functions, failing to notice a lack of modularity. An approach to design that does not emphasize modularity often results in "yank and put" or "copy and paste" replication of code fragments. Such replication throughout a subsystem will clearly suffer from reliability issues when a bug is discovered in such a fragment, and it is only repaired in the section that first exhibits the bug. Also, as code replication is typically only apparent upon reading the code, it is detected, if at all, during code review. Designing a single common method usable by all callers may be challenging due to a need for similar, but not identical behavior in all cases. In such a case, the designer must include additional parameters whose function is to modify the behavior of the common method to achieve the necessary variations in behavior. In the extreme, there may be good cases to be made for multiple methods. These are important internal design choices. It can be very helpful to future code maintainers to capture these choices in an appropriate document (which can be comments in the code).

To establish that code is being written for human rather than just machine consumption, a process of code reviews (also known as walk-throughs, inspections, or peer reviews) must be instituted. Code inspections are valuable in finding bugs, but the focus deemed most important here is the production of understandable, readable source code. Such inspections can improve code via suggestions to improve modularity, and more generally, to refactor [12] the code. At least one staff member, other than the author, must be adequately familiar with the code to be able to fix a problem should one arise when the author is unavailable. When a "buddy system," like the one described earlier, is instituted, a buddy code review, where the primary code owner leads the backup person through the component's code, is a lightweight but effective way to introduce a component to a backup person. Learning the code after a problem arises is often painful and expensive. Again, this represents yet another engineering trade-off: incur the cost of code reviews and establish them as a regular activity to minimize the time to repair a bug versus waiting for a fault to occur and doing "whatever it takes" at the time of the bug to repair it. When a "whatever it takes" approach is used without the author, it is often the case that an imperfect repair results. In such a repair, the bug is repaired, but other functionality, not exercised in the bug scenario, may no longer work correctly. While it is difficult to compare costs, the availability of a large-scale network service is always higher when problems are fixed correctly without introducing new problems.

Sometimes the demanding performance requirements of network services tempt the designers and implementers to sacrifice modularity and maintainability to obtain high performance. This is rarely necessary: careful design can usually achieve the required performance with modular and maintainable code. The emphasis on performance can also lead to unnecessary, premature optimizations. If the code meets its performance requirements, then further improvements are not needed, and to the extent that such improvements impact the code's maintainability, they are undesirable. Also, when a performance problem is discovered as a result of measurements of the code via testing, such a problem is often best solved by algorithmic or architectural changes, rather than ad-hoc code changes. When a sophisticated algorithm is the solution, the resulting code may be difficult for the casual reader to follow. Comments in the code referring the reader to a detailed description of the algorithm employed, or if no such description is available, providing that description in the code's comments, will improve the maintainability of the code.

15.5.5 Implementation

Reliable network service software is software that is commented, tested, and written in a language with ongoing support, using libraries and other resources that are themselves of production quality and well-supported, under source control, with a bug-tracking system.

The amount of effort required to produce reliable network service software for production use is typically much higher than that required to produce prototype or personal-use software. A prototype (or proof-of-concept) of a network service is often used to demonstrate a few key functions to show the value of the service to potential customers or funders. The things that distinguish the source code of production software from that of non-production software are typically around dealing with unexpected errors. Non-production software may ignore errors, as they can "never happen" (e.g., an existing TCP connection to a well-known server goes stale owing to a fail-over behind the well-known server's load balancer). In production, everything that can "never happen" always does. Retry and other recovery strategies need to be carefully designed and implemented. Building in various "fall-backs" to handle some amount of external system unavailability (e.g., queuing requests to unreachable TCP/IP services, using previous query results for an established period of time) is necessary. In terms of easing the effort required to produce a reliable, production quality service, having a working prototype is rarely more than an aid in clarifying requirements; converting prototype code into reliable, production quality code is often more expensive than just re-coding the service with clear production requirements.

15.5.5.1   Commenting

Comments in code should be supportive and accurate; out of date, inaccurate comments are more harmful than no comments at all. Comments such as the infamous "RIP LVB" next to a constant of 1827 [13] do not help an individual unfamiliar with the code to debug a problem. Code needs to be written to be read and understood by other humans; compiling or interpreting with no errors is necessary, but not sufficient. Many development teams establish coding guidelines (or standards) to be followed to aid the production of code meant to be read and understood by other team members.

15.5.5.2   Unit Testing

Developers need to unit-test their code. A set of unit tests need to be developed in addition to the code. That test code represents a regression test suite that can be re-run whenever a change is made to the code. Besides straightforward tests of the external APIs, one of the most valuable approaches to unit test code is coverage testing [14]. In coverage testing, one determines which lines of code have been executed by a set of tests, and more importantly, which lines of code are yet to be exercised. There are many tools available to assist in measuring code coverage. Since these tools almost always instrument the code to measure coverage, it is always a good idea to re-run the test cases used to determine coverage with a normal (non-coverage test) build, to make certain that the coverage tool does not hide any latent bugs. Tools are available for managing, developing, and maintaining unit test suites (e.g., J unit).

15.5.5.3   Development Tools

Reliable software cannot be produced by unreliable tools. New languages with possibly buggy compilers and/or support libraries should be avoided. Debugging one's own code is challenging enough; determining that the root cause of one's bug is because of a compiler bug is adding insult to injury.

Good debugging tools aid the production of reliable software. Tools that detect memory leaks are invaluable in producing software that needs to run continuously[8]. Enabling and heeding compiler warning messages, or using other code analysis tools, can help to eliminate bugs prior to execution. Strong type-checking helps avoid many errors.

15.5.5.4 Change Management

Change management is a key aspect of producing reliable network service software. It manifests itself to developers in the form of a source code control system (current popular tools are CVS and subversion; older tools are the venerable SCCS and RCS). All the source code and project documents must be managed by a source code control system (also known as revision control system or version control system). These tools allow the source code used to create a particular build of a component at a particular point in time to be exactly reconstituted. This is necessary because when a bug is reported on a particular version of the system running in a particular installation, the desired solution is to just fix the cause of the bug and not change any other aspect of the software whatsoever. This allows for high-quality fixes to be deployed. An important aspect of repairing production problems is recreating the production problem in a test environment. This can be difficult if the problem requires environmental conditions and/or loads that are difficult to recreate outside of the production environment. However, not being able to reconstitute the exact source code and rebuild it (with the same tools that built the production instance) is a solvable problem. Introduction of new "features" while fixing an old bug often introduces new bugs; the new "features" are typically far from being thoroughly unit tested, and the interactions of the new "features" with the bug fix will not be carefully considered due to time pressure. Further, as we would see in the next section, independent system test will always focus on certifying the fix to the production problem; any additional testing (e.g., of new features) should not be forced upon the system test organization in the form of a high-priority production bug fix.

A bug-tracking system (e.g., bugzilla, trac, or many other such systems) is a necessary tool in the production of reliable network service software. It is used to record problems and track repairs. Integration with a source code control system may be an attractive feature, but loosely coupled tools can often be coerced to produce any necessary project reports with some simple additional script writing.

15.5.5.5 Support Needs

In addition to producing high-quality source code, another development deliverable as important as source code is a document for each alarm that might be raised to the

---

[8] In cases where continuous operation is not a hard requirement, automatic or scheduled process restart (sometimes called process rejuvenation) can be used to get "clean" memory. That said, software that exhibits no leaks is probably always more reliable than software that leaks.

operations organization[9]. The document describes the steps that the operations staff must follow to remedy the situation that caused the alarm to be raised (it might be the case that the action to take is to call the developer, regardless of the hour, but a better approach is to enable the operations staff alone to remedy the situation[10]). The elements of an alarm document should include: the level (e.g., critical, major, or minor), sample text of such alarms, the software component(s) reporting the alarm, the cause, the effect on the service, and a procedure to remedy the situation. If no such document exists, or, more importantly, if there is no procedure to remedy the situation, then the alarm should not be raised. The test organization needs to be able to cause each alarm and test each procedure. The network service should never cause an alarm to auto-clear from the network monitoring system[11]; all alarm clearing should require operations intervention (they may be provided with tools to clear multiple alarms at once). These documents as well as training material for the support staff (see Section 15.7, below) are all additional development deliverables, and should utilize the same change-management tools as those used for source code (e.g., CVS).

In addition to the obvious software components to be built, support staff often identify the need for various support tools that should be built (e.g., producing a report from the logs that helps identify a particular class of problem).

While perhaps stating the obvious, the service has a great dependency on all of the project's documents and source code. This data should be backed-up regularly, and periodically stored remotely from the development environment, to provide some level of insurance against a disaster impacting the development environment.

15.6   System Test

System test attempts to identify the remaining defects in the software following unit testing. Testing cannot improve the quality of poorly designed or implemented software; this is often stated as "you cannot test in quality; it has to be designed in."

System test staff should be distinct from the software development staff to allow for an independent quality assessment of the software.

The software that system test installs is ideally built by a support organization, and should never be built by the software developers. This guarantees that someone

---

[9] This is in addition to the event log documentation described earlier in the chapter.

[10] A special class of alarms falls into the category of events that "should almost never happen." For such alarms, directing operations staff to call the developer is acceptable. However, if what "should almost never happen" begins to occur frequently, then the developer should provide more detail on the action to be taken by the operations staff.

[11] It is a good idea to simply provide an informational log entry when a problem that had been previously reported has been cleared.

other than the software's author can successfully build the software; something that might prove crucial in troubleshooting and repairing a production problem when the author is unavailable.

The function of system test is primarily to measure the software's adherence to the requirements. To this end, the first activity typically undertaken is to assure that all functional requirements are met. Failure to meet a requirement will result in the tester creating an entry in the project's bug-tracking system. All the non-functional requirements must also be certified, although this will often be more difficult than certifying functional requirements. Installation, upgrade, removal, start, restart, and stop of the service must be tested. Each possible alarm should be generated and the developer-documented procedure to alleviate the alarm condition should be tested. The system test organization typically requires a rather expensive hardware environment to accomplish the testing of all latency, throughput, and performance requirements. In addition to mimicking the production environment, this testing requires equipment and tools to simulate the production loads. System test organizations may have a set of developers who concentrate on developing custom test tools.

In addition to certifying that the software meets the requirements, it is also important to design tests of adverse conditions (so called "fault injection", "failure injection", or "rainy day" testing), where anything and everything that can go wrong does go wrong (this may include, as an extreme case, cutting cables, such as an Ethernet cable, connected to a system under test: "the technician thought the cable wasn't being used"). This also extends to entering invalid data in any way in which the service accepts data, which includes the special case of misconfiguring the service, to the extent possible, and for all these cases, observing its behavior.

Another set of important tests is stability or endurance tests, which will typically take place at a prescribed load, not exceeding the engineered load, for an extended period of time (e.g., many days). These stability or endurance tests will often uncover latent bugs, such as memory leaks in the software. It is often helpful, if possible, to have the system test team stress-test the system by overloading it or driving the system past its engineered load for a relatively short period of time (minutes or hours), and then reducing the load back to the engineered load. The system should recover, without operator intervention, when the load is reduced. On the other hand, it might be the case that the system fails entirely at some overload (it is important to test at an overload level that is gradually reached, as well as at an overload level that is reached suddenly, because the system might behave differently to the two approaches to the same overload). It is helpful to establish whether or not it is possible for a value of overload (i.e., larger than the engineered load) to consume all available resources such that no useful work gets done, and if so, to document that value for the project team.

While we may hope that the service's business sponsors accurately forecast demand, it would not be good for the service to be overly popular only to have it crash owing to overload. Also, network services might very well be the target of denial-of-service or distributed denial-of-service attacks; overload testing is one

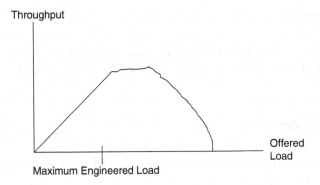

Fig. 15.2 Throughput versus offered load

way to determine how the service will react to such attacks. An important output of overload or stress testing is a graph indicating throughput versus offered load (see Fig. 15.2).

Any bug found in the production environment following system test should be considered a defect against the system test team. It is not reasonable to hold the developers responsible for all the defects when the function of the system test team is to identify defects following developer turnover. Whenever a bug is detected in the production environment and a fix is developed, that fix must be tested. This first implies that the production bug can be reproduced in the system test environment, so that the fix for the bug can be certified as fixing the bug. It is often a good idea to re-run a number of functional tests to ascertain that the software has not deteriorated as a result of the fix. One valuable technique is to be able to automate much of this regression testing and easily determine that the fixed code produces the same results as the previously released code. The standard UNIX command *diff* can be used to compare results of multiple regression test runs when the relevant outputs can be captured in files. When this data contains date or time stamps, various techniques[12] can be used to eliminate them as differences that require attention.

There are a number of key metrics that the system test team should track, such as number of bugs found over time and the overall fault density. Sufficient testing with appropriate software reliability engineering [15] should predict the number of faults remaining. Criteria for exiting system test should be established prior to beginning test and should target a specific fault level not to be exceeded, as well as zero critical or major outstanding bugs being found over some period of just completed testing[13].

---

[12] One technique is to encapsulate all the date and time stamp string generation in a single project module. That module needs to be configurable (e.g., via a configuration parameter) to always return the same value.

[13] A critical bug is one that prevents the service or system from functioning; it is sometimes referred to as a "severity 1 problem." A major bug is one that prevents a portion of the service or system from functioning; it is sometimes referred to as a "severity 2 problem."

15.7 Support

In this section, we address how operations and support staff may be organized, deployment of hardware and software, and managing service outages.

15.7.1 Organization

The operations and support staff are often organized into four (or more or less) distinct "tiers" of support.

"Tier 1" comprises individuals in the operations organization who first notice that a service has failed. They typically have very little service-specific knowledge, but they know how to distinguish a hardware failure from a software failure, and can follow procedures to contact hardware suppliers to perform hardware repair or maintenance. There is a need to identify and assign staff to Tier 1 within the defined hours of operation. Tier 1 staff may be trained to follow some developer-produced operations documents, e.g., documents that describe some classes of problems that might be cleared by a restart of the service or a system reboot.

"Tier 2" staff are the individuals in the operations organization who have a combination of hardware, operating system, and service-specific software knowledge, and can typically diagnose which of those three elements are at fault in an otherwise questionable failure scenario. They have developer-produced documentation for specific faults (i.e., "alarms") as to what procedure should be followed to restore service.

"Tier 3" staff are the individuals, often within the development organization, who have extensive service knowledge and can reconfigure the service to get it up and running without a software change.

"Tier 4" staff are the individuals who can diagnose and repair software faults in the service. They are the developers.

Training is required for Tiers 1 and 2, and may be required for Tier 3. Training promotes a common, correct understanding of the network service. Training needs to inform the staff of all the anticipated failures, how they could occur, and how they can be resolved. The amount of training depends on the support staff's level of service awareness and ability, and the completeness of the documentation targeted at the Tier.

At a minimum, Tier 1 and Tier 4 are required. Tier 1 can always escalate all but hardware/reboot failures to Tier 4. The system and service management health monitoring must generate Tier 1 observable "alarms" for failure conditions. Many alarms will be owing to the service being down or difficulty communicating with subtending services; alarm documentation and Tier 1 staff should suffice to get the service restored most of the time. However, continual failures will result in escalation.

A poor substitute for Tier 1 staff, which may be acceptable when the Service-Level Agreement allows for significant down time, is automatic alarming (via email) to Tier 4 staff. Alternatively, another low-cost approach is to eliminate Tiers 2 and 3 with Tier 1 monitoring, and escalating any and all events requiring attention to a prioritized list of Tier 4 staff, possibly going up the management chain if no one can be reached. A "group cell phone" can be used, which is passed (following a weekly "on call" list) from one Tier 4 member to another, allowing the instructions to the Tier 1 staff to simply call one phone number to gain support.

When equipment is remote from Tier support staff, arrangements must be made for some staff at the equipment site to support hardware supplier access for repair and possibly for service reboot attempts.

15.7.2   Deployment

Whenever a new service is deployed on new hardware or when new hardware is added to support an existing service, two classes of certification, operational readiness testing and network validation testing, need to be carried out, typically by Tier 2 or 3 staff. This certification testing is done to certify that the hardware, operating system, application software, network connectivity, and the overall operation is functional prior to providing service to the customers. These tests have been proven valuable in identifying where a problem exists prior to customer service, thus improving service availability (the alternative is to simply enable the service, hope for no problems, and then perform general troubleshooting if a problem arises). Operational readiness testing typically consists of the following steps: verify that each element has a valid maintenance contract; perform a hardware stress test/burn-in to verify that there are no hardware problems and that nothing was damaged in shipping; where applicable, verify and, if necessary, configure backup functionality; verify that the crash dump capability is configured and functional; install logins for the production service; and verify the service functionality. Service functionality tests include starting, checking (for current operational status), and stopping the service, as well as rebooting the system and checking that everything that is supposed to start automatically does, and that anything that is not supposed to start automatically does not. Network validation testing certifies that all network connectivity to or from each new piece of hardware functions correctly (this is often and best carried out using software other than the actual service application software, e.g., telnet or nc as a client for testing TCP connectivity to a server). Another category, network management validation test (sometimes incorporated into operational readiness), tests whether the service can be properly monitored and whether the service can communicate (e.g., via SNMP) with the monitoring systems.

Changes to the software may be minor simple configuration value changes or major upgrades. Since, following any new problem, the most frequently asked question is always "What changed?" it is mandatory to have a process whereby every change made by the support staff is recorded (e.g., in a simple file, but on a system quite distinct and separate from the servers supporting the service, since they may be down when questions about "what changed" need to be answered). The items that should be recorded include who, what, where, when, and why for every change.

Deployment of a new version of the software needs to be carefully planned and supported. A flash-cut from one version to the next presents a number of problems. It will require the service to be entirely down during the time it takes to get the new version up and running. If the new version cannot be installed while the previous version is running, the amount of out-of-service time increases. As the reliability of a piece of software is established by having the software operate reliably for an extended period of time in a full production (i.e., not test) environment, a new version is, by definition, not reliable[14]. A flash-cut, then, presents the operations organization with the problem of supporting a new, unknown, unreliable implementation rather than the previous, known, reliable implementation[15]. As a result, following a flash-cut, an entirely new version of the software will not have the confidence of the operations organization and they will suspect the software prior to suspecting an operator mis-step.

An alternative to a flash-cut, though more expensive, is to maintain compatibility between versions, allowing a new version to be deployed on a single machine at a time. An effective confidence building approach is to first deploy a new version for a period of time (e.g., a week) on a single machine, and if no critical or major problems arise, deploy on a few more machines and continue this process every few days until the new version is entirely deployed. When major new features are being introduced, it is important to control them via configuration options, which, initially, are set to disable those features so that end-users see consistent behavior (e.g., it is undesirable to have two web servers behind a load balancer presenting different user interfaces, one with the old version and one with the new, as this will confuse the end-users and will almost certainly result in a spike in customer complaints). Once the new version is fully deployed, the new features can be enabled via configuration changes (see the discussion on configurability in the next section). This approach requires that each new version, via configuration, maintains backward compatibility with the previous version.

Deployment of a new release of software needs to be carefully planned. Given the desire to gradually phase in new software, all the steps required need to be documented in a deployment plan and reviewed with the developers, testers, and operations staff. Whenever possible, the cut-over should be tested in a non-production environment to work out any problems prior to the actual deployment. It is mandatory that a tested back-out plan accompany the upgrade plan. Objective criteria to determine readiness to begin the deployment as well as continue at major steps within the plan must be established (these are often referred to as

---

[14] Software is like wine – it improves with time.

[15] This is not to say that the known version is perfect. Operations staff will always prefer the devil that they know to the one that they do not know.

"entrance criteria"). The planning for the deployment needs to estimate the durations of each activity. The planning must also determine the worst case scenario – the set of circumstances that leads to the longest period of service unavailability. This worst case duration must not violate any service-level or other agreements. This activity must occur in a "maintenance window." During a maintenance window, client access to the service is normally disabled in some fashion; e.g., for an end-user web page oriented service, the service is configured (perhaps via DNS) to return a special web page indicating that the service is temporarily unavailable owing to maintenance. To determine that the deployment was a success, objective "exit" criteria must be established. Such exit criteria typically take the form of successful test results as a result of testing the production system to ascertain that it is functionally performing as expected. Such testing needs to be similar, but not identical, to normal client access, as such client activity during a maintenance window should never access the running system. Thus, this "in-window" testing might use specific IP addresses or special domain names supporting the testing rather than the normal domain names. When configuring a single server behind a load balancer, exposing that server directly, via its IP address, is a good way to test it while still in the maintenance window. The worst case scenario often arrives following the upgrade when the last of this "sanity" testing seriously fails and the back-out plan needs to be executed.

15.7.3   Managing Outages

In an enterprise with multiple lines of business, each with multiple large-scale network services, operations coordination across related services is highly desirable. It may very well be the case that planned maintenance on one service that is called by a second service will cause a high alarm level on the second service.

Unfortunately, in spite of best intentions, there may be occasions when the support staff cannot quickly identify the cause of a service failure. When such a situation arises, it is best to maintain coordination across the different tier support staffs while providing information to all as new items are discovered. A proven technique to aid this is a conference call (sometimes called an "outage bridge" when used to identify a failure cause), on which all active support staff participate. A helpful addition is an instant messaging tool to allow pairs or larger groups to share data. Managers of the support staff will also need to follow the activity and join the conference call. There is often a separate conference call running in parallel, on which mangers participate where the lower (or lowest) level managers either sequentially or simultaneously (two phones with appropriate mute and volume controls) participate on both calls.

Finally, it may be suspected that the service outage is due to third-party, vendor supplied software (e.g., the operating system or the database management system). When this is the case, it is often necessary to add the vendor's support staff to the outage bridge and provide the vendor (or vendors) with the requested data (forced dumps being common) or, in extreme cases, direct access to the failing systems.

15.8   Service Reports

Various data gathered by the service should be combined and reported on a periodic basis to aid in the management of the service. Some data might best be gathered and reported daily, such as a performance summary of activity on the service[16]. Other data might best be gathered and reported less frequently, weekly, monthly, or quarterly. Figure 15.3 shows a quarterly availability report for a service; it shows the goals (or targets) as well as the actual achieved levels for availability and a number of related service measurements. Figure 15.4 shows a portion of a daily report for an email service (for a single server); it provides various statistics about messages, recipients, and bytes processed, including an hourly histogram, busy hour and busy minute statistics, and message distribution statistics. Figure 15.5 shows a daily report of account subscriptions for an ISP email service; it shows the distribution of accounts against the number of subscribers.

2009 Goals	2009 Year End Target	Jan 09 Actual	Feb 09 Actual	Mar 09 Actual	Q1 09 Target	Q1 09 Actual
Availability	99.99%	99.98%	99.98%	99.99%	99.99%	99.98%
Reduce MTTR	160	137	270	132	160	179
Reduce Incidents	1830	139	153	169	456	461
Reduce Incidents > 60 Mins	1005	74	95	84	249	253
Reduce Caused by Change Outages	257	12	20	26	63	58
Reduce Procedure Caused Outages	330	22	33	26	81	81

Fig. 15.3   Quarterly availability report

---

[16] For web-server reporting, webalizer is a useful tool.

```
----------  Messages Sent----------
Transmitted Messages:        3,015,994
Transmitted Recipients:      3,016,044
Total Bytes:           305,851,785,029
Rejected Recipients:            10,159
Deferred Recipients:            12,268


------------  Message Distribution by Hour    -----------
00:00    125,101   08:00    61,027   16:00    213,672
01:00    104,898   09:00    65,705   17:00    201,212
02:00     93,829   10:00    83,778   18:00    205,569
03:00     77,064   11:00    97,707   19:00    190,757
04:00     75,120   12:00   126,519   20:00    177,327
05:00     55,289   13:00   149,461   21:00    161,212
06:00     48,108   14:00   169,670   22:00    150,355
07:00     55,568   15:00   198,273   23:00    128,773
-----------------------------------------------------------

Busy Hour: 15:39-16:38   Max:  223,715  Messages/Hour
Busy Min:  19:06         Max:    4,776  Messages/Minute

Message Distribution by Size in bytes
    38% are 9,999 or less
    70% are 22,999 or less
    80% are 34,999 or less
    90% are 57,999 or less
    95% are 115,999 or less
    98% are 358,999 or less
    Average is 101,409
    Maxim um is 15,725,197

Message Distribution by Recipients per message
    99% are 1 or less
    Average is 1.000017
    Maximum is 2
```

Fig. 15.4 Sample of an email service report

```
                         Active Subscriptions          742951
                         Suspended Subscriptions          7107
                         Number of accounts with...
                         2 active subscribers : 119465
                         3 active subscribers : 48932
                         4 active subscribers : 26120
                         5 active subscribers : 13573
                         6 active subscribers : 9035
                         7 - 10 active subscribers : 2728
                         11 - 25 active subscribers : 299
                         26 - 50 active subscribers : 0
                         51 or more active subscribers : 0
**Fig. 15.5** Sample of an     Total Active Secondary Email Ids = 416596
account report
```

15.9 Summary

In this chapter, we presented an approach to building large-scale network services. Other approaches undoubtedly exist, and this approach is certainly not the only possible path to success. However, for us, this approach has proven successful in providing many reliable network services. We conclude this chapter with a summary of the "best practice" principles.

- Provide accurate, clear, and understandable requirements to ensure that the resultant software behaves as expected.
- The architecture of a software system must have conceptual integrity. This is best achieved by designating a single individual as the architect.
- Clearly document all interfaces.
- Avoid any single-point-of-failure by designing in sufficient redundancy.
- Practice recovery operations regularly.
- Establish a reliable mechanism to monitor the health of the service.
- Establish a standard log format.
- Assign exactly one person as the primary developer of each module; each module should have an assigned backup person (to avoid a human single-point-of-failure).
- Test early, test often.
- Modularity helps to reduce source code size, which improves maintainability.
- Write code for human (and machine) consumption.
- Production software is considerably more difficult to implement than a prototype: plan accordingly.
- Change management allows for deployment of fixes that do not introduce new, unrelated problems.
- Software should be built by someone other than the software's author. This guarantees that the software can be built when the author is unavailable.
- Successful deployment of a new version of software requires careful planning.
- Plan for service outages. It is rare that such planning will go unused.
- Care should be taken when assigning staff to carry out more than one function.

References

1. Oppenheimer, D., Ganapathi, A., Patterson, D.A. (2003). Why do Internet services fail, and what can be done about it? 4th Usenix Symposium on Internet Technologies and Systems.
2. Persse, J. (2006). Process improvement essentials: CMMI, Six Sigma, and ISO 9001. O'Reilly Media, Inc.

3. Brooks, F.P (1995). *The mythical man-month: Essays on software engineering.* Reading, MA: Addison-Wesley.
4. Schneider, G., Winters, J.P. (2001). *Applying use cases: A practical guide.* Reading, MA: Addison-Wesley.
5. Bourke, T. (2001). Server load balancing. O'Reilly Media, Inc.
6. Bono, V.J. (1997). 7007 Explanation and apology. NANOG email of Apr 26, 1997.
7. Zhang, Z., Zhang, Y., Hu, Y.C., Mao, Z.M. (2007). Practical defenses against BGP prefix hijacking. Proceedings of the 2007 ACM CoNEXT conference.
8. Patterson, D.A., Gibson, G., Katz, R. H. (1988). A case for redundant arrays of inexpensive disks (RAID). Proceedings of the 1988 ACM SIGMOD international conference on Management of Data.
9. Schroeder, B., Gibson, G.A. (2007). Disk failures in the real world: What does an MTTF of 1,000,000 hours mean to you? Proceedings of the 5th USENIX conference on File and Storage Technologies.
10. Tognazzini, B. (1992). *Tog on interface.* Reading, MA: Addison-Wesley.
11. Spolsky, J. (2001). *User interface design for programmers.* Berkeley, CA: Apress.
12. Fowler, M. (1999). *Refactoring.* Reading, MA: Addison-Wesley.
13. Bosworth, E. (2008). The IBM 370 programming environment. Lecture Notes. Department of Computer Science, Columbus State University.
14. Cornett, S. (2009). Code coverage analysis. http://www.bullseye.com/coverage.html. Accessed May 17, 2009.
15. Musa, J.D. (2004). Software reliability engineering: More reliable software faster and cheaper, 2nd edn. Indiana: AuthorHouse.

Chapter 16
Capacity and Performance Engineering for Networked Application Servers: A Case Study in E-mail Platform Planning

Paul Reeser

16.1 Introduction

Proper capacity and performance engineering (C/PE)[1] is critical for the success of developing and deploying any complex networked application. All too often, systems and services are rushed to market without proper capacity/performance planning, resulting in myriad problems including costly hardware upgrades and software rework, loss of revenue due to poor quality and late delivery, customer dissatisfaction, and missed market opportunities. In contrast, by planning for performance and scalability from the earliest stages of product architecture and design, the chances of "doing it right" the first time are greatly improved. Industry studies have proven the positive business case for building C/PE into software development: upfront costs are usually only 1–3% of total project budget, while long-term savings are typically ten times the upfront investment [1]. All mature software development organizations have a well-defined process in place to systematically plan for capacity, performance, and reliability throughout the software development and service deployment life cycle [2].

In this chapter, we discuss the typical capacity, performance, availability, reliability, and scalability engineering activities required to deploy a networked service platform. These activities should begin at the earliest stages, and span the entire platform life cycle: from architecture, design, and development, through service test and deployment, to the ongoing capacity management of a mature service. During the service development life cycle, an iterative, "layered" approach to addressing C/PE is often necessary to meet schedule constraints, wherein more detailed passes are successively made over each assessment area, rather than completing each task before moving to the next. In general, successful C/PE requires staying "one step

P. Reeser (✉)
Lead Member of Technical Staff, AT&T Labs Research, 200 S. Laurel Avenue, D5-3D26, Middletown, NJ 07748, USA
e-mail: preeser@att.com

[1] The term "capacity/performance engineering" in the chapter title and throughout this chapter broadly refers to the expansive set of activities required to assess and manage platform capacity, performance, availability, reliability, and scalability.

C.R. Kalmanek et al. (eds.), *Guide to Reliable Internet Services and Applications*, Computer Communications and Networks, DOI 10.1007/978-1-84882-828-5_16, © Springer-Verlag London Limited 2010 ahead" of the product life cycle. In the architecture phase, for example, we try to identify improvements that lead to a better design. In the design phase, we try to identify improvements that lead to the development of more efficient software. In the development phase, we try to create an environment that leads to more effective testing, and so on.

The aim of this chapter is not to present an exhaustive C/PE "how to" manual, as there are many books devoted to the topic (cf. [1, 3, 4]). Rather, our goal is to highlight the areas where proper C/PE is especially critical to the successful deployment of a networked service platform. At the highest level, the goal is to ensure that the service meets all performance and reliability requirements in the most cost-effective manner, wherein "cost" encompasses such areas as hardware/software resources, delivery schedule, and scalability. With this goal in mind, the process (shown in Fig. 16.1a) begins with an understanding of what functionality the platform provides and how users interact with the system (*Architecture Assessment*), including the flow of critical transactions, the workload placed on the platform elements, and the service-level performance/reliability metrics that the platform must meet (*Workload/Metrics Assessment*). Next, we develop analytic models and collect measurements to predict how the proposed platform will handle the workload while meeting the requirements (*Reliability/Availability Assessment* and *Capacity/Performance Assessment*). Finally, we develop engineering guidelines to size the platform initially (*Scalability Assessment*) and to maintain service capacity, performance, and reliability post-deployment (*Capacity/Performance Management*).

These C/PE assessment activities are depicted relative to the typical software development and delivery life cycle phases in Fig. 16.1b.

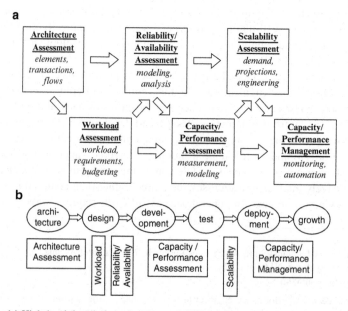

Fig. 16.1 (a) High-level description of end-to-end C/PE process and (b) timing of C/PE activities relative to platform delivery phases

16.2   Basic Probability and Queuing Concepts

Prior to introducing the case study, we briefly review some straightforward concepts from elementary probability analysis and queuing theory. These simple concepts and their associated results will be leveraged at various points throughout the C/PE process described in the remainder of this chapter. Readers who are already familiar with such concepts as *birth and death* models, state transition balance equations, Markovian queuing systems, and Little's Law may skip this section and proceed to Section 16.3. Readers who desire a more thorough treatment of these concepts may explore any of the countless probability and queuing texts (cf. [5–8]).

From [5], a discrete random variable X is said to be *Poisson distributed* with parameter $\lambda > 0$ if its probability mass function $p(n)$ is given by

$$p(n) = P\{X = n\} = e^{-\lambda}\frac{\lambda^n}{n!}, \quad n = 0, 1, 2, \ldots.$$

A continuous random variable X is said to be *exponentially distributed* with parameter $\lambda > 0$ if its probability density function $f(x)$ and its cumulative distribution function $F(x)$ are, respectively, given by

$$f(x) = \begin{cases} \lambda e^{-\lambda x}, & x \geq 0 \\ 0, & x < 0 \end{cases} \text{ and } F(x) = P\{X \leq x\} = \begin{cases} 1 - e^{-\lambda x}, & x \geq 0. \\ 0, & x < 0. \end{cases}$$

The mean and variance of X are, respectively, given by λ^{-1} and λ^{-2}. The 95th percentile of X is the value of x such that $F(x) = 0.95$. Solving the above equation for x yields $x = -ln(0.05)\lambda^{-1} = 3.00\lambda^{-1}$. That is, the 95th percentile of an exponentially distributed random variable is three times the mean. Exponentially distributed random variables are said to be *memoryless* in that

$$P\{X > s + t | X > t\} = P\{X > s\} \text{ for all } s, t \geq 0.$$

A stochastic process $N(t), t \geq 0$ is said to be a *counting process* if $N(t)$ represents the number of "events" up to time t. Furthermore, $N(t)$ is said to be a *Poisson process* if (among other conditions) the number of events in an interval t is Poisson distributed with mean λt. That is, for all $t \geq 0$

$$P\{N(t) = n\} = e^{-\lambda t}\frac{(\lambda t)^n}{n!}, \quad n = 0, 1, 2, \ldots.$$

For a Poisson process $N(t)$, let T_1 denote the time of the 1st event, and let T_n for $n > 1$ denote the time between the $(n - 1)$st and the nth events. The sequence T_n of inter-event times are independent and identically distributed (i.i.d.) exponential random variables with mean λ^{-1}.

The Poisson process is one example of the general class of exponential models known as *continuous-time Markov chains*. These models are completely characterized at any time by their state at that time (memoryless), and the time between transitions from one state to another is exponentially distributed. Markov chains that always transition from state n to state $n + 1$ are called *pure birth* processes, whereas those that always transition from state n to state $n - 1$ are called *pure death* processes. More generally, a Markov chain that can transition from state n to either states $n + 1$ or $n - 1$ (such as the number of jobs in queue) is called a *birth and death* process.

One example of a birth and death process is the *Markovian* queuing system. Suppose that jobs arrive at the single server according to a Poisson process with rate $\lambda > 0$ (i.e., inter-arrival times are i.i.d. exponentially distributed with mean λ^{-1}), and suppose that service times are i.i.d. exponentially distributed with rate $\mu > 0$ (mean μ^{-1}). Such an exponential queuing system is typically denoted by $M(\lambda)/M(\mu)/1$, or M/M/1 for short. More generally, the notation $M(\lambda)/M(\mu)/C/K$ (or M/M/C/K for short) commonly denotes a Markovian queuing system with Poisson arrivals, exponential service times, $1 \le C \le \infty$ servers, and $0 \le K \le \infty$ buffers.

The service discipline (i.e., the order in which waiting jobs are served) can vary from the implicit *first-in-first-out* (FIFO), to *last-in-first-out* (LIFO), or *processor-sharing* (PS) wherein each job in the system receives an equal "slice" of service, or random order, or priority order, and so on. Fortunately, most metrics of interest (such as average queue length, or average time in system, or average server utilization) are insensitive to the particular service discipline due to work conservation laws. However, service order does impact variances as well as metrics for individual jobs.

Let $X(t)$ denote the number of jobs in an M/M/1 queuing system at time t, and let

$$P_n = \lim_{t \to \infty} P\{X(t) = n\}, n = 0, 1, 2, \ldots$$

denote the *steady-state* probability that there are n jobs in the system. For each $n \ge 0$, the rate at which the system enters state n equals the rate at which it leaves state n (flow in = flow out). This principle is known as *equilibrium*, and the resulting set of equations is known as *state transition balance equations*. For the M/M/1 system, solving these "flow in = flow out" balance equations in terms of P_0 yields $P_n = \rho^n P_0$, where $\rho = \lambda/\mu$ is the utilization. Note that there are $n - 1$ unique equations and n unknowns. The nth equation comes from the fact that the probabilities must sum to 1; hence,

$$1 = \sum_{n=0}^{\infty} P_n = P_0 \sum_{n=0}^{\infty} \rho^n = \frac{P_0}{1 - \rho}.$$

Thus, $P_0 = 1 - \rho$ and $P_n = \rho^n(1 - \rho), n \ge 1$.

Next, let L denote the average number of jobs in the system, and let W denote the average time spent in the system (delay). L and W are given by

$$L = \sum_{n=0}^{\infty} n P_n = (1-\rho) \sum_{n=0}^{\infty} n\rho^n = \frac{\rho}{1 - \rho} \text{ and } W = \sum_{n=0}^{\infty} \frac{n + 1}{\mu} P_n = \ldots = \frac{\tau}{1 - \rho},$$

where $\tau = \mu^{-1}$ is the average service time. The expression for W is derived by noting that a job arriving to find n jobs already in the system expects to wait for $n + 1$ service times (the n jobs ahead of it, plus its own service).[2]

Comparing the expressions for L and W, we see that $L = \lambda W$. This relationship is referred to as Little's Law [9], which states that the average number of jobs in the system equals the average arrival rate times the average delay in the system, *independent* of the arrival or service distributions. Although this formula seems deceptively simple, it applies under general (non-Markovian) conditions, and is an extremely powerful "back-of-the-envelope" (BoE) result that we employ often throughout the C/PE process.

Other common BoE results that we often rely on include the expression for W, which states that the average delay equals the average service time divided by (1 – utilization), as well as the expression for L, which states that the average number of jobs in the system equals the utilization divided by (1 – utilization). Although these expressions are derived assuming Markovian arrival and service distributions, they are generally applicable as a rough estimation for most common queuing situations in stable steady state. (For transient scenarios, such as the rate of queue growth following server failure, comparable fluid-flow approximations can be used.)

As a final note, the M/M/C Markovian queuing system has been studied widely, and has many applications in computer engineering [10]. Other non-Markovian queues that have wide applications include the M/D/C system, wherein service times are deterministic (D), and the B/M/C system, wherein jobs arrive in batches (B). Generally speaking, any variations on the M/M/C exponential system that "smooth" either the arrival process or the service process (such as the M/D/C queue) tend to reduce the coefficient of variation (CV),[3] while those where either process is more "bursty" (such as the B/M/C system) tend to increase the CV. As a result, the 95th percentile will be less than three times the mean for smoother (than exponential) distributions, and more than three times the mean for burstier distributions. For example, in computer systems in which the CPU executes virtually identical code for each job (e.g., a server that specializes in one function), the service process may appear more deterministic. In this case, the 95th percentile delay will be less than three times the mean. Practical experience suggests that the 95th percentile delay for common systems is typically two to three times the average delay.

16.3   Case Study

Throughout this chapter, we use an Internet Service Provider (ISP) e-mail platform as a unifying case study to illustrate many of the C/PE tasks. Most likely, we all have one or more Internet accounts through which we can send and receive e-mails,

---

[2] This Markovian property results from the memoryless nature of the exponential distribution, and is referred to as *Poisson Arrivals See Time Averages* (PASTA).

[3] The coefficient of variation (CV) is a normalized measure of dispersion of a distribution, defined as the ratio of the standard deviation σ to the mean μ (CV $= \sigma/\mu$).

maintain a personal web page, access newsgroups and web logs, and participate in a variety of online activities such as chat rooms and gaming. In most cases, we pay an ISP to provide basic Internet access ranging from narrowband dial-up, through broadband DSL and cable, up to wideband FTTH. Features such as e-mail, web page hosting, and news then come "free" with our Internet access subscription.

But have you ever wondered what goes on "behind the scenes" to provide a "free" feature such as e-mail? In reality, the cost and complexity of providing a fast, reliable ISP e-mail platform for millions of subscriber mailboxes is a real C/PE challenge. With many large ISPs offering 1 GB mailboxes, these providers potentially need to provision and maintain many terabytes of online storage, and meet stringent delay requirements while processing many millions of e-mail messages daily.

Figure 16.2 illustrates an example functional architecture for a large ISP e-mail platform. Such a platform typically consists of numerous functional components, each performing specialized tasks and conforming to multiple protocols for sending, receiving, and retrieving e-mails. These software components could all run on the same physical server, and many e-mail platform vendors offer an "all-on-one" configuration. From a performance, reliability, security, and scalability standpoint, however, such a solution has severe limitations. For example, the server capacity of an "all-on-one" configuration is limited by the most stringent performance metric (e.g., message retrieval), resulting in costly over-engineering relative to other metrics (e.g., message delivery). By partitioning functionality across servers, each component can be optimized relative to its own unique metrics. Or, sizing an "all-on-one" solution to meet storage needs may require more disk than one physical server can manage. Or, putting the inbound and outbound mail delivery processes on the same physical server may result in security vulnerabilities such as "mail relay", where spammers attempt to mask their identity to relay mail through your server (by spoofing the sender as an on-net user so that the server passes the mail through to an off-net recipient). Thus, architects and C/PE planners must determine

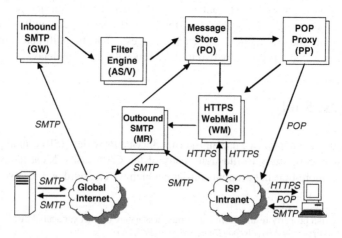

Fig. 16.2 Example ISP e-mail platform functional architecture

the expected market segment that their solution targets, and plan accordingly. Unless the target market is very small, partitioning of software components onto dedicated hardware sized for the component is more cost-effective.

With this understanding in mind, we assume throughout the remainder of this chapter that we are delivering an e-mail platform to serve a large ISP. Accordingly, there are typically numerous identical replicas of the functional components in Fig. 16.2, each running on its own physical hardware. Thus, the physical architecture for a large ISP e-mail platform can consist of many hardware servers, and will typically look very much like the functional architecture illustrated in Fig. 16.2. As a result, we will henceforth use the word *server* interchangeably to refer to either the specialized functional (software) component or the dedicated physical (hardware) element on which it resides.[4]

Referring again to Fig. 16.2, a typical large e-mail platform includes inbound Gateway (GW) servers to receive incoming e-mail from the Internet, running the industry-standard Simple Mail Transfer Protocol (SMTP) on the Internet-facing side. These GWs typically perform a variety of filtering functions to screen out unwanted and threatening e-mails (e.g., spam, viruses, and worms), often employing specialized anti-spam/virus (AS/V) filtering software on outboard servers. Messages that pass filtering are then forwarded to Post Office (PO) servers, where messages are stored in user mailboxes until they are retrieved or deleted. Unlike the other mail platform components, the POs are usually "stateful" in that a user's mailbox typically resides on only one PO, and messages destined to a particular user must be routed to a particular PO. (As we will discuss later, this fact is particularly relevant to ongoing C/PE.) Collectively, the GWs and POs constitute the message delivery and storage platform.

Next, users can typically access their e-mail over the ISP Intranet through a number of interfaces. The oldest such access mechanism is the industry-standard Post Office Protocol (POP), where a POP software client residing on the user's PC connects to a POP proxy (PP) server to retrieve e-mails. The PP server in turn connects to the appropriate PO and typically "drains" all messages in one transaction, downloading them to the user PC and removing them from the PO. The user can then read the messages from their local storage. In addition to POP, another widely used access mechanism is the industry-standard Secure HyperText Transfer Protocol (HTTPS), wherein an HTTP browser residing on the user's PC connects to a WebMail (WM) server to retrieve the e-mails. The WM server in turn connects to the appropriate PO (possibly via the PP), and typically provides a list of all stored messages. The user can then choose to retrieve and/or delete the messages (usually one at a time) from the PO, resulting in a series of transactions. Typically, messages

---

[4] In reality, ISPs typically support multiple applications in addition to e-mail (e.g., newsgroups and web hosting). These applications typically share physical resources, either through virtualization, common transactions (e.g., authentication), or shared infrastructure (e.g., LANs). For the purpose of illustrating the C/PE tasks, we assume that all physical resources are dedicated to the single e-mail application. In the case of resource sharing/virtualization, the C/PE analysis must account for the impact of additional workload, reduced resource availability, and contention.

remain on the PO server until the user explicitly deletes them, or the PO eventually deletes them as a result of optional mail aging policies. (Again, this fact is particularly relevant to ongoing C/PE.) Although POP and HTTPS are the most prevalent consumer access protocols, other options are common, including Internet Message Access Protocol (IMAP) and proprietary mail clients (e.g., MS Outlook). Collectively, the PPs, WMs, and POs constitute the message retrieval platform.

Finally, users can typically send e-mails through a number of interfaces. The oldest egress mechanism is again SMTP, wherein an SMTP client residing on the user's PC connects to an outbound mail relay (MR) server to send e-mails. These MRs typically perform the same filtering functions as the GWs, again often employing specialized filtering software on outboard AS/V servers. Messages that pass filtering are then forwarded to the recipient ISP's GW over the Internet, or to the appropriate PO server if the recipient is "on-net" (hosted by the same ISP as the sender). In addition to SMTP, another widely used egress mechanism is again HTTPS, wherein the browser connects to a WM server, which forwards the message to an MR. Collectively, the MRs and WMs constitute the message egress platform.

16.4 Architecture Assessment

Section 16.4 describes the *Architecture Assessment* activities. These tasks are usually performed during the architecture and design phases of the platform life cycle. The goals at this stage are to

1. Identify critical functional (software) and physical (hardware) elements
2. Identify critical user transactions and develop a descriptive model of the flow of transactions through the platform elements
3. Identify critical element resource limits and potential performance- and scalability-limiting platform bottlenecks ("choke points")

For example, the critical software elements in this e-mail platform are

(a) Inbound SMTP GW and AS/V filtering processes
(b) PO message delivery, storage, retrieval, and deletion processes
(c) POP and HTTPS message retrieval processes
(d) Outbound SMTP GW, HTTPS, and AS/V filtering processes

Similarly, the critical hardware elements in this e-mail platform are

(a) Inbound SMTP GWs, outbound SMTP MRs, and AS/V servers
(b) PP and WM message retrieval servers
(c) PO message storage servers

Examples of software/hardware elements that may not be considered critical (at least in the first iteration) include databases to store user identities, credentials, and e-mail preferences, secure servers to authenticate HTTPS users against their credentials, directories to map user identities to physical mailbox locations, servers to manage access control lists (ACLs) and spammer "blacklists," log servers to record transaction access and summarize daily usage volumes, scripts to migrate mailboxes from one PO to another PO for load-balancing, and probe servers to measure transaction reliability and performance. Such noncritical elements can be explicitly considered in successive iterations if their associated transaction volumes or resource consumptions turn out to warrant it.

Once the critical software/hardware platform elements are identified, we next identify the critical user/system transactions. First, these critical "use case" transactions must include all those that will have associated service-level metrics. If we do not explicitly model transactions for which a requirement will be specified, then we will not know in a timely manner if the requirement can be met. For example, any common user-initiated transactions, such as retrieving a message, must be considered as critical. In addition, critical transactions must include those that may be particularly usage- or resource-intensive. If we do not explicitly model transactions that may consume significant resources, then we will not know in a timely manner if the system will have adequate capacity. For example, if the e-mail service implements a message aging policy, traversing the storage directory to find messages older than N days can be extremely CPU-intensive, even though there is no associated performance metric.

For the e-mail platform, some of the critical transactions are

(a) Receive and filter an inbound or outbound SPAM/virus message
(b) Receive, filter, and deliver a safe inbound message
(c) Receive, filter, and deliver a safe outbound message locally
(d) Receive, filter, and deliver a safe outbound message to the Internet
(e) Retrieve a mailbox contents via POP (including moving the contents to a trash bin for subsequent deletion)
(f) Retrieve a mailbox list via HTTPS
(g) Retrieve a single message via HTTPS
(h) Delete a list of messages via HTTPS
(i) Traverse the storage directory to find messages older than N days

Examples of transactions that may not be considered critical (at least in the first iteration) include interactions with a database server to identify a user or update user e-mail preferences, sending a non-delivery notice (NDN) back to the originating ISP when a message recipient is not found, writing transactions to a logging server, updating the AS/V rule set when new spam signatures are identified, migrating mailboxes from one PO to another PO to load-balance the storage levels, running daily scripts to summarize transaction volumes, and so on. Such non-critical transactions can be explicitly evaluated in successive iterations if their transaction volumes or resource consumptions turn out to be higher than anticipated, or if the involved elements turn out to be bottlenecks.

These critical platform elements, and many of these critical transaction flows, are captured in Fig. 16.2. Given this characterization, we can begin to identify possible resource limits and potential capacity- and performance-limiting platform bottlenecks. Listed below are a number of typical e-mail platform choke points. This list is by no means intended to be exhaustive. Rather, these are a few of the numerous bottlenecks that can be identified early in the platform delivery process:

- The ISP does not have direct control over the incoming message arrival process. The source ISP could deliver messages as they are received (one at a time, one SMTP connection per message), or store messages destined for a particular ISP and deliver a batch of many messages at once (in one SMTP connection). As a result, the inbound SMTP process running on the GWs needs to be able to handle a highly variable input stream with highly variable connection times. This in turn suggests that the GWs need to have a large amount of RAM, and a mechanism to commit messages to disk prior to closing the SMTP connection (to ensure message delivery reliability).
- The rules governing AS/V filtering are highly dynamic and ever-expanding. Spam is growing exponentially, with volumes doubling every few years. And as a new spam, virus, or worm signature is identified, the filtering rule set must be updated with this new signature. Thus, the GW must be able to keep pace with the ever-growing processing demands of this CPU-intensive function. For this reason, the AS/V function is often moved to an outboard filtering engine such as a high-density, rack-mounted, disk-less blade server, where processing power can be grown in a cost-effective manner. This in turn allows the GW server to be specialized to its more memory-intensive task.
- Mailbox management is of particular concern for any e-mail platform. Without proper policies to control message retention (e.g., an aging policy that deletes unread messages older than 60 days), PO storage needs will grow exponentially. Even so, the POs need to be able to handle huge volumes of data and support large disk subsystems. As a result, PO storage is often moved to expandable NFS-based network attached storage (NAS), or even to a storage area network (SAN).
- Finally, the user experience is typically dominated by message retrieval, where stringent performance and reliability metrics are often defined. Hence, the user-facing PP and WM servers must be sized to provide adequate capacity to meet the delay requirements even under failure conditions (e.g., two of N servers are down, or, in the case of redundant sites, half of all servers are unavailable due to, say, site router failure).

16.5 Workload/Metrics Assessment

This section describes the *Workload/Metrics Assessment* activities. These tasks are usually performed during the design phase of the platform life cycle. The goals at this stage are to

1. Characterize the anticipated critical (usage- or resource-intensive) transaction workload and develop representative workload models (transaction mix)

to describe platform usage during typical and extreme scenarios (e.g., under element failure or during peak holiday periods)
2. Characterize the anticipated transaction performance and reliability requirements/metrics
3. Develop software component resource estimation and budgeting models for the representative transaction workload scenarios
4. Identify needs to optimize the platform architecture (e.g., splitting software components across multiple servers) based on budget constraints

16.5.1   Workload Models and Requirements

For an e-mail platform, many of the critical transactions were listed in the previous section. Table 16.1 provides an example transaction mix for the normal and peak scenarios. These workload parameters can be estimated through a variety of channels, including past platform experience, competitive assessments, industry benchmarks, and market research. In addition, sensitivity analyses can be performed to understand the C/PE ramifications of significant changes in the expected workload profile.

Next, we must specify performance and reliability requirements for a subset of the critical transactions. Often, these requirements are driven by what customers are demanding, or by what competitors are offering, or by what the product planning organization thinks will be required to differentiate this product from those offered by competitors. Frequently, these requirements are built into a contractual service-level agreement (SLA) with the customer, including specific penalties (such as a specified credit on the monthly service cost) when an SLA metric is violated.

Performance and reliability metrics can take many forms. Traditionally, these metrics have been specified in terms such as "average delay less than X seconds" or "availability greater than $Y\%$". More recently, many service providers have adopted approaches such as the 6 Sigma methodology [11] to specify these metrics in terms

Table 16.1 Representative transaction workload models

Critical transaction	Normal rate (tps)	Peak rate (tps)
Receive/filter inbound (IB) spam message	2,000	3,000
Receive/filter outbound (OB) spam message	1,000	1,500
Receive/filter/deliver safe IB message	500	750
Receive/filter/deliver safe OB message locally	100	150
Receive/filter/deliver safe OB message to Internet	400	600
Retrieve mailbox contents via POP	100	150
Retrieve mailbox list via HTTPS	100	150
Retrieve single message via HTTPS	200	300
Delete list of messages via HTTPS	150	200
Traverse storage directory to find old messages	0.001	0.001

of a unified Defects per Million (DPMs) rate. In a nutshell, a transaction defect can occur in any one of three areas:

1. *Accessibility* (simply speaking, the availability of the operation)
2. *Continuity* (the reliability of the operation)
3. *Fulfillment* (the performance quality of the operation, e.g., latency)

For example, an e-mail transaction can be considered defective if

(a) The transaction fails to complete (i.e., no response is received)
(b) The transaction completes, but an incorrect response is received
(c) The transaction completes, and the correct response is received, but the response time (or other appropriate metric) violates its target

The overall DPM is defined as 10^6 * {the fraction of defective transactions in excess of target}. Specifically, the number of defects (raw count) is the actual number of transactions violating their targets minus the allowable number of transactions violating their targets. For example, for the "deliver a safe inbound message" transaction, a typical target might be "95% of measured delivery times <10 min". In this case, the DPMs would be max {[(observed fraction >10 min) − (1 − 0.95)]*10^6, 0}.

Regardless of how the metrics are defined, a number of characteristics must be addressed. First, they must be *specific*. Consider, for example, a response time requirement for a "retrieve message" transaction. We must specify any characteristics that impact delay, such as message size, the point at which the stopwatch begins (user clicks on link) and ends (first packet is received), access link speed, and so on. Second, they must be *measurable*. A service-level metric is useless to you and your customers if it cannot be accurately measured and verified. As a result, you need to consider how you plan to measure the requirement. Will you need a software client add-on to capture and report measurements? Will you deploy a hardware sniffer at select user end points? Will you subscribe to an outside vendor's performance verification service? Will you develop a separate measurement platform to launch synthetic transactions into your platform? Third, they must be *controllable*. You may have difficulty meeting contractual SLAs if you do not control all components in the critical path of the metric. For instance, defining a response time metric to include rendering by the user's browser makes you vulnerable to the user's PC. Or defining a metric to include network transport is dangerous if you do not control the access/egress networks. For example, we may define a metric for "deliver message locally" rather than "deliver message to Internet" because the ISP does not have control over the Internet, or the recipient ISP's platform.

Using this approach, we can define the DPM components for each critical transaction. For example, the direct measures of quality (DMoQs) associated with the "retrieve message via HTTPS" transaction are shown in Table 16.2. Given these DMoQs, we can tolerate up to 10^6*0.05 = 50,000 DPMs associated with the "retrieve message via HTTPS" transaction: up to 10^6*0.005 = 5,000 *accessibility* DPMs and up to $(10^6 − 5,000)$*0.002 = 1,990 additional *continuity* DPMs, with the balance as *fulfillment* DPMs.

Table 16.2 Example metrics for "retrieve message via HTTPS" transaction

DMoQ	Target	Definition
1. HTTPS read availability	99.5%	Proportion of attempts that complete prior to time out
2. Read reliability (given 1.)	99.8%	Proportion of attempts that complete successfully
3. 95th Percentile response time (given 1. and 2.)	20 s	Time from clicking on link until contents fully displayed

16.5.2 Resource Estimation and Budgeting Models

Performance modeling must begin as early as possible in the platform development process. Many platform planners assume that useful models cannot be constructed until after the software is developed and tested. Unfortunately, if we wait until performance/scalability problems are uncovered during testing, it is often too late to make architectural changes without costly rework. Early-stage performance models need not be overly complex. In fact, simple "back-of-the-envelope" (BoE) models often provide valuable insights into performance issues. Resource estimation and budgeting is one such modeling effort that can bear significant fruit early in the platform life cycle [12].

Throughout the remainder of this chapter, we attempt to maintain a consistent set of symbolic notation in mathematic formulas wherever possible. We consolidate much of this notation here so that the reader can refer back to one place to refresh their memory. Let

R_i denote the rate of transaction i (in transactions per second, or tps)
N_j denote the number of instances of component j (parallel servers)
C_{ij} denote CPU consumption of transaction i on component j (s)
$\rho_j = \sum_i R_i C_{ij}/N_j$ = CPU utilization per replica of component j
$T_{ij} = C_{ij}/(1 - \rho_j)$ = delay of transaction i on component j (s)[5]
$T_i = \sum_j T_{ij}$ = end-to-end delay of transaction i (s)
$\overline{T}_i$ denote the end-to-end delay requirement of transaction i (s)
$\overline{T}_{ij}$ denote the delay budget of transaction i on component j (s)

The process of resource estimation and budgeting is iterative, and varies depending on the stage of platform life cycle. Prior to development, when resource consumptions cannot yet be measured, designers must estimate resource costs based on the detailed component design. Resource *estimation* is a "bottom-up" approach in that we first estimate the hardware/software component resource consumptions C_{ij} and determine the number of servers N_j required to meet the delay requirements $\overline{T}_i$. Thus, the goal of software component resource estimation is essentially to minimize N_j such that $T_i \leq \overline{T}_i$. Resource *budgeting* is a "top-down" approach

---

[5] This expression results from a BoE model for delay W reviewed in Section 16.2.

in that we first specify delay allocations $\overline{T}_{ij}$ for each component and determine the maximum resource consumptions C_{ij} allowable while still meeting the budgets. Thus, the goal of software component resource budgeting is essentially to maximize C_{ij} given N_j such that $T_{ij} \leq \overline{T}_{ij}$. By performing both estimation and budgeting, we can identify gaps in the design and focus development resources on the most critical components. As development proceeds, the results of the estimation and budgeting eventually align.

With this process in mind, consider again the "retrieve message via HTTPS" transaction. The critical path flow of this transaction is

$$\text{Client} \leftrightarrow \text{Access network} \leftrightarrow \text{WM server} \leftrightarrow \text{PO server.}$$

Thus, delay objectives must be budgeted to each component in the critical path. Assume that to meet a 95th percentile delay requirement of 20 s, you must target an average response time of 10 s.[6] Assuming that the performance metric is specified to be from the moment the user clicks on the browser link until the first packet of a 100 kB message is received, the client is essentially removed from the critical path. Assuming that the ISP provides an access network capable of sustaining 1 Mbps, the transmission of a 100 kB message should take no more than 1 s including protocol delays. Of the remaining 9 s, assume that our rough sizing of the workload indicates an initial allocation of 3 s to the WM server and 5 s to the PO as a starting point. We keep the final 1 s in reserve (a "kitty") to allocate later in the process in the event of minor overruns. This initial allocation is somewhat arbitrary, since we can perform sensitivity analyses around the allocation of time among components to optimize the configuration.

Consider the WM server (the PO server budgeting is similar). The WM server is in the critical path of three critical transactions: "retrieve single message via HTTPS" (transaction 1), "retrieve mailbox list via HTTPS" (transaction 2), and "delete list of messages via HTTPS" (transaction 3). From Table 16.1, the peak transaction rates are $R_1 = 300$ tps, $R_2 = 150$ tps, and $R_3 = 200$ tps. Assume that development has not yet completed, but the designers estimate that the WM CPU consumptions per transaction are $C_1 = 20$ ms, $C_2 = 40$ ms, and $C_3 = 30$ ms. (For simplicity, we drop the subscript j as we only consider a single component.) Then the WM server CPU utilization per replica is $\rho = \Sigma R_i C_i / N = 18/N$, and the average delay of transaction 1 (in seconds) is $T_1 = C_1/(1 - \rho) = 0.02N/(N - 18)$. Finally, solving the expression $T_1 \leq 3$ s for N yields $N \geq 18.1$ WM servers. Thus, given the peak workload and resource consumption estimates, the current projection is that at least 19 WM servers are required to meet the average delay objective for transaction 1. (This number could increase further once a similar analysis is performed for transactions 2 and 3.) This approach is "best case" in that it ignores contributions to end-to-end delay other than CPU contention. For instance, disk

---

[6] As discussed in Section 16.2, both analytic modeling and practical experience suggest that the average delay for user-initiated jobs with common code execution is typically one-third to half of 95th percentile delay. As part of the budgeting exercise, we can perform sensitivity analyses around this 95th percentile-to-mean assumption.

and network I/O time and protocol delays will "eat into" the delay budget, leaving less time for CPU processing. These factors are usually illuminated during the testing phase, and can be captured during the performance modeling. This approach is also "worst case" in that the underlying BoE model $T = C/(1 - \rho)$ assumes a high-degree variability that is frequently not observed when computer systems deterministically execute identical code for each job.

This budgeting exercise often sheds light on opportunities to optimize the platform architecture based on the resource constraints. For example, we may find that too many critical transactions are competing for the same resource, resulting in the need to over-engineer that component to meet the most restrictive requirement. By splitting the functionality across specialized servers (say one pool of WM servers to handle transactions 1 and 3, and another pool to handle transaction 2), we may be able to meet all requirements with fewer total servers. Or we may find that one particular design estimate for component CPU consumption leads to an inefficient use of the resources. By budgeting a smaller target for that component, we may be able to better focus development resources on the most critical components, thus leading to a more efficient product.

16.6 Availability/Reliability Assessment

This section describes the *Availability/Reliability Assessment* activities. These tasks are usually performed between the design and software development phases of the platform life cycle. The goals at this stage are to

1. Develop reliability block diagram models to quantify long-term (steady-state) service availability, and birth and death models to quantify short-term (transient) platform reliability, and identify reliability-impacting platform bottlenecks (such as single points of failure)
2. Perform reliability sensitivity and failure-mode analyses to identify and quantify the reliability impact of required platform enhancements
3. Propose additional reliability requirements and engineering rules

16.6.1 Availability Modeling

Prior to software development, we can begin to assess platform availability and reliability. To determine the availability of the platform for various activities, we first estimate the availability of all components and identify which components are required to perform the activity. The data required for each component in estimating transaction availability are

- The mean-time-to-failure (MTTF)
- The mean-time-to-repair or restore (MTTR)

- The "K of N" sparing policy (discussed below)
- The software + procedural "scaling factor" (discussed below)

The availability A of each element is given by $A = \text{MTTF}/(\text{MTTF} + \text{MTTR})$, and the downtime DT (in minutes per year) is given by $DT = 525{,}600(1 - A)$.

The sparing policy depends on whether or not persistent state information is retained. For stateless components such as the GW server, the notation "K of N" denotes that the component is available if at least K of the N replicas are operational. For stateful components such as the PO, the notation "1 of $K + N$" (typically 1 of 1 + 1) denotes that there are K primary servers and N warm standbys. For 1 of 1 + 1 sparing, if the primary component fails, the state is re-created on the warm standby, and the subsystem is down for the duration of this failover procedure (given by the MTTR).

The availability for a block of elements is given by

$$A_{k \, \text{of} \, n} = \sum_{i=0}^{n-k} \binom{n}{i} A^{n-i} (1 - A)^i.$$

For example, $A_{N-1 \, \text{of} \, N} = N A^{N-1} - (N - 1) A^N$, $A_{N-2 \, \text{of} \, N} = \frac{1}{2}(N - 1)$ $(N - 2) A^N - N(N - 2) A^{N-1} + \frac{1}{2} N(N - 1) A^{N-2}$, and so on. Note that this general model includes as limiting cases the "series" (N of N) and "parallel" (1 of N) systems, given by $A_{\text{series}} = A^n$ and $A_{\text{parallel}} = 1 - (1 - A)^n$.

Two approaches are commonly employed to account for the effects of software faults and procedural errors on the platform availability:

- Perform rigorous software reliability analysis to measure and estimate the mean time between faults/errors and MTTR, and explicitly include these components in the reliability critical path
- Scale the hardware availability estimates based on common "rules of thumb" to account for software/procedural impacts

Clearly, the first approach is more accurate and application-specific, provided data can be obtained at the current stage of platform delivery. There are numerous approaches to this analysis, such as software reliability engineering (SRE), fault insertion testing (FIT), and modification request (MR) analysis (cf. [13, 14]). More often than not, however, direct measurements of software/procedure failures are not available until the platform has been through system test and/or deployed for some time. As a result, the second approach is more common at this early stage. One common methodology is to scale the hardware downtime to reflect software/procedural faults. Based on experience [15], the recommended factors are listed in Table 16.3.

Let S denote the scaling factor, and let the subscripts H and T denote the hardware (only) and total (hardware + software + procedural) availability measures. Then $S \equiv DT_T/DT_H = (1 - A_T)/(1 - A_H)$. Thus, once we compute the hardware downtime DT_H and availability A_H, the total downtime DT_T is given by $S(DT_H)$, and the total availability A_T is given by $A_T = 1 - S(1 - A_H)$.

Table 16.3 Recommended hardware-to-total DT scaling factors

Platform life-cycle stage	Level of component complexity		
	Simple, simplex	Moderate, average	Complex, redundant
New	15	20	25
Evolving	9	12	15
Mature	3	4	5

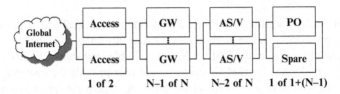

Fig. 16.3   Example reliability block diagram

The process usually begins with the construction of reliability block diagram (RBD) models. These models define "blocks" of platform elements along the critical path of transaction flows, where each block has an associated probability of failure. For example, Fig. 16.3 shows a typical RBD model for the "receive/filter/deliver safe IB message" transaction.

As can be seen, there are two access links from the Internet to the GWs. In this example, assume that this portion of the path is available if at least one is operational (1 of 2). There are multiple stateless GW servers, any one of which could receive the next connection. Assume that this portion of the path is available (i.e., has sufficient capacity to handle the workload without performance degradation) if no more than one GW is down (hence $N - 1$ of N must be up). There are multiple stateless AS/V servers, any one of which could receive the next filtering request. Assume that this portion of the path is available if no more than two AS/V servers are down (hence, $N - 2$ of N must be up). Finally, there are multiple stateful PO servers, only one of which normally contains the destination mailbox. Assume that there is one spare PO available in the event that any primary PO fails. Then, this portion of the path is available if either the primary PO for this mailbox is operational, or the spare PO is available to serve this mailbox. The spare PO in turn is available if all other $N - 1$ POs are operational. Hence, 1 of $1 + (N - 1)$ must be up. Further explanation of how failover to the spare PO actually works is given later in Section 16.6.2 when we discuss detailed reliability modeling. (For simplicity, we ignore other components in the critical path, such as access routers, load-balancing switches, and LAN hubs.)

Next, we estimate the MTTF and MTTR parameters for each element in the RBD model. The MTTF estimates are typically based on industry-standard assumptions or vendor analyses of server hardware availability, whereas the MTTR estimates are typically based on knowledge of your data center operations and staffing (e.g., 15 min to detect and reboot a server, 4 h to diagnose and replace a

Table 16.4 Example availability analysis

Element	MTTF (h)	MTTR (h)	S	K	N	A_H	DT_H (min/year)	DT_T (min/year)	A_T
Access	40K	24	5	1	2	1.00000	0.2	1	1.00000
GW	5K	8	25	9	10	0.99989	59.8	1496	0.99715
AS/V	10K	4	15	18	20	1.00000	0.0	1	1.00000
PO	5K	4	25	4	5	1.00000	132.7	3319	0.99369
Critical path	–	–	–	–	–	0.99988	192.8	4807	0.99085

LAN card, and 24 h to ship and replace a component not available on-site). Once the model is constructed, we can easily perform sensitivity analysis of these parameters.

For example, consider the RBD in Fig. 16.3. Table 16.4 shows the results of this availability modeling exercise. Columns two to four provide the assumed MTTFs, MTTRs, and scaling factors for the elements along the critical path. Columns seven to ten show the resulting downtimes and availabilities. The PO server requires special treatment. The availability A_H given in Table 16.4 only reflects the availability of the primary PO or spare PO (in parallel). We must also reflect the failover time in the PO downtime DT_H. Assume that this procedure requires 1 h to migrate the file system from the failed PO to the spare, and another 15 min to reboot the server. Thus, every 5,000 h (the PO MTTF), we incur a 75-min downtime to restore service, or 131.4 min/year added to DT_H.

As can be seen, the estimated total availability A_T for the "deliver safe IB message" transaction is 99.1%. If A_T is less than the target requirement proposed in Section 16.5.1, then we must consider enhancements to the architecture and/or data center operations. For example, the biggest contributors to the downtime are the GW and PO servers. By planning for additional GW servers, we can provide enough capacity to handle two failures ($N - 2$ of N). If this change does not provide sufficient benefit to meet the requirement, then we can consider alternative storage architectures that could reduce the PO failover time below the 1-h assumption. These and other sensitivity analyses are easily facilitated by this modeling approach.

We must also be careful not to over-simplify the analysis. Otherwise, we may overlook potential single points of failure (SPoFs). For example, this analysis assumes that element failures are independent. In the case of the access links, this assumption implies that the physical links are diversely routed (i.e., each link takes a separate physical path between the data center and the Internet). If this assumption is not true (e.g., the links terminate on the same edge router, or the logical links "ride" on the same higher-capacity physical fiber), then failures are not independent (e.g., a fiber cut can take out both links). As another example, if the AS/V servers are blade servers, then they reside in a blade center chassis. If there are SPoFs in the chassis (e.g., power supply or cooling fan), then we could lose all AS/V servers in the chassis if the chassis fails. Or, if the data center does not have battery or diesel power backup, then the loss of commercial power could result in the catastrophic failure of all servers at once.

16.6.2 Reliability Modeling

Once RBDs are constructed for the critical transactions, we can begin to look at element reliability in more detail where warranted. For example, consider again the PO server failover behavior described in the previous section. Assume that the procedure for handling PO outages is as follows: If the primary PO serving a given mailbox goes down, the data center staff first tries to reboot the PO. With probability c (referred to as the "coverage" factor to denote that the remedial action – in this case, a reboot – "covers" the failure event), the PO successfully comes back up. Otherwise, the PO is considered failed. If the spare PO is available, then state is migrated onto the spare PO (failover), which becomes the new primary PO for the given mailbox. Once the failed PO is repaired, it becomes the new spare. Otherwise, if the spare PO is unavailable (i.e., another PO failure occurred and that PO is not yet repaired), then the given mailbox is unavailable.

The PO availability state space can then be described as follows. Let

A denote the state "primary PO is active"
D denote the state "primary PO is down"
F denote the state "primary PO is failed"
S denote the state "spare PO is available"
U denote the state "spare PO is unavailable"

Furthermore, let

N denote the total number of PO servers
λ denote the PO failure rate $= \text{MTTF}^{-1}$
μ_R denote the PO repair rate $= \text{MTTR}^{-1}$
μ_B denote the PO reboot rate $= (\text{time to reboot})^{-1}$
μ_F denote the PO failover rate $= (\text{time to failover to spare})^{-1}$
c denote the reboot coverage factor

As with most modeling efforts, we take a layered approach to this reliability modeling (starting with the simplest model first, and adding successively more detail until the benefits diminish). With this approach in mind, the simplest model results from assuming that the spare PO is always available. The state transition model for this case is shown in Fig. 16.4.

Hopefully, "A/S" is the predominant state. Transitions from state "A/S" to "D/S" occur at rate λ if the primary PO goes down. Transitions from "D/S" back to "A/S" occur at rate $c\mu_B$ if the reboot succeeds, whereas transitions from "D/S" to "F/S" occur at rate $(1-c)\mu_B$ if the reboot fails. Finally, transitions from "F/S" to "A/S" occur at rate μ_F if the primary PO fails over to the spare. Service is available if the PO is in state "A/S". As discussed in Section 16.2, this state transition diagram

Fig. 16.4 Simple PO server state transition diagram

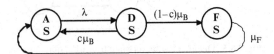

describes a *birth and death* model. Solving the resulting equilibrium balance equations yields

$$P(A/S) = \frac{\mu_B \mu_F}{\mu_F(\lambda + \mu_B) + (1 - c)\lambda \mu_B}.$$

For $N = 5$, $\lambda = 1/5,000$, $\mu_B = 4$, $\mu_F = 1$, and $c = 0.5$, the probability that the mailbox is available $P(A/S) = 99.985\%$, resulting in a PO hardware downtime DT_H of 78.8 min/year. Thus, reflecting the detailed data center operations procedure (attempting a reboot before failing over to the spare PO) results in a reduction in our PO hardware downtime estimate from 131.4 to 78.8 min/year.

In fact, we can see now that the original estimate of 131.4 min/year is an upper bound, since it essentially assumes that $c = 0$ (i.e., every failure results in failover). In contrast, the new estimate of 78.8 min/year is a lower bound, as it assumes that we only ever have one concurrent PO failure. This observation illustrates the point that much of the early C/PE analysis involves developing simple models to provide upper and lower bounds on the true answer. If the bounds are tight, then we can often move on to the next problem without the need to develop a more detailed model.

In this case, the bounds are not tight. So adding the next layer of detail, we assume that the spare PO is sometimes unavailable due to the failure of another PO. Furthermore, we assume that at most one other PO has failed at any moment in time. This state transition model is shown in Fig. 16.5.

Again, "A/S" (shown in the upper left corner) is hopefully the predominant state. Transitions from "A/S" to "A/U", or from "D/S" to "D/U", occur at rate $(1 - c)$ $(N - 1)\lambda$ in the event that one of the other $N - 1$ POs fails (thus making the spare PO unavailable), whereas transitions from the bottom row state "*/U" to the top row state "*/S" occur at rate μ_R in the event that the failed PO is repaired. Transitions from "A/*" to "D/*" occur at rate λ if the primary PO goes down. Transitions from "D/*" back to "A/*" occur at rate $c\mu_B$ if the reboot succeeds, whereas transitions from "D/*" to "F/*" occur at rate $(1 - c)\mu_B$ if the reboot fails. Finally, transitions from "F/S" to "A/U" occur at rate μ_F if the primary PO fails over to the spare PO. Service is available if the platform is in either of states "A/S" or "A/U".

Solving the (much more complicated) equilibrium balance equations for $N = 5$, $\lambda = 1/5,000$, $\mu_R = 1/4$, $\mu_B = 4$, $\mu_F = 1$, and $c = 0.5$ suggests that the probability that the mailbox is available $P(A/S) + P(A/U) = 99.9849\%$, resulting

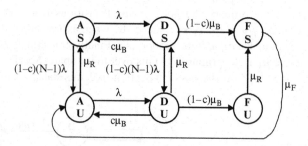

Fig. 16.5 Detailed PO server state transition diagram

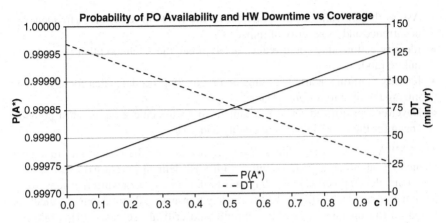

Fig. 16.6   Sensitivity of PO availability to coverage

in a PO hardware downtime DT_H of 79.3 min/year. Thus, adding this next layer of detail results in a further refinement in our PO hardware downtime estimate from 78.8 to 79.3 min/year. As with the RBD modeling, sensitivity analyses are easily facilitated by this modeling approach. For example, Fig. 16.6 shows the probability that the PO is available $P(A/^*)$ and the PO hardware downtime as a function of the coverage factor c. From this type of analysis, we can then set development targets for recovery times and coverage factors.

Additional layers of detail are possible. For example, we can model the totality of failure possibilities for all N POs. Here, the states can be represented by (i, j), where $i = 0, \ldots, N$ is the number of active POs, and $j = 0, 1$ is the number of available spares. However, given the minimal change achieved by the last refinement, further detail is not warranted in this case.

16.6.3   Failure Modes and Effects Analysis

Failure modes and effects analysis (FMEA) is a proactive, systematic software quality assurance methodology, utilized during the design phase to help identify and correct weak points in the platform design, thereby addressing potential reliability problems prior to deployment. FMEA identifies both remedies to avoid outages, and mitigations (e.g., alarming and recovery procedures) to reduce recovery time. FMEA is powerful yet easy-to-use (one brainstorming session can yield significant improvements), and it typically pays for itself if just one failure is averted in the field. More specifically, FMEA is a disciplined design review technique intended to

- Recognize and evaluate potential failure modes of a system and their effects on user-perceived performance and reliability

- Assess the criticality of the potential failure mode in terms of its frequency of occurrence and its severity of impact
- Identify actions that could reduce or eliminate the likelihood that the potential failure mode occurs
- Identify alarming, alarm handling, and recovery procedures that focus on minimizing the time to restore service
- Develop a prioritized set of recommendations to achieve the greatest potential "bang for the buck" in terms of quality and TTR

The FMEA process is as follows: First, we decompose the system into functional elements (autonomous code modules with well-defined interfaces) and construct functional decomposition block diagrams to illustrate how the different subsystems are interconnected. Next, we identify the key transaction flows among the elements based on the operational workload profile and critical use cases. (This information is readily available from the Architecture and Workload assessments described previously.)

Now, for each element/interface, we identify the possible failure modes and their likely effects. This step is typically accomplished during a brainstorming session with the platform architects, system engineers, lead developers, and lead testers, where the team addresses such questions as:

- What happens if interface X is slow, or hangs, or times out?
- What happens if external system Y is down for an extended period?
- What happens if the response is malformed, or inappropriate?

Next, for each failure mode, we populate an FMEA spreadsheet with the following information:

- Failure mode (what can go wrong?)
- Failure effects (what are the impacts?)
- Frequency (how often does it occur?)
- Severity (how critical is it?)
- Detection (how is it recognized?)
- Root cause (what is the underlying event?)
- Remedies (what can be done to avoid the failure mode?)
- Mitigations (what can be done to alarm/recover quickly?)
- Effort (how costly – staff, capital – is it to do?)

Remedies are proactive approaches that result in outage avoidance by eliminating the underlying root cause (e.g., fix the software design, or add redundancy to remove SPoFs). *Mitigations* are proactive approaches that result in outage minimization by reducing their impact (e.g., alarming to provide early warning/detection, alarm handling procedures to facilitate detection, or recovery procedures to expedite short-term restoral/repair).

Once a robust list of failure modes has been compiled, we review the spreadsheet to identify "low-hanging fruit," such as

- Failure modes for which the remedy is trivial to implement (even if the criticality is low, eliminating these failure incidents is beneficial)

- Failure modes for which the effects are catastrophic (even if the effort is high, these failures must be eliminated through design improvements or minimized through alarming/recovery procedures)
- Failure modes for which the frequency is high

Finally, we prioritize the identified failure modes, and develop recommended action plans to address them. The priority of each failure mode is based on three factors: *frequency* of failure, *severity* of impact, and *effort* to remedy. One approach to prioritization is simply to assign numerical values to each factor, and use the product (or sum) of the values to determine priorities. The lower the product (or sum), the higher the priority (e.g., a product of 1 is number 1 priority). Example assignments are shown below:

- Frequency

  - Level 1 (100/year): error response code, time out, core dump
  - Level 2 (10/year): CPU board failure, database corruption
  - Level 3 (1/year): hard disk crash, commercial power outage
  - Level 4 (rarely): lightning strike, flood, locust, alien attack

- Severity

  - Sev 1 (catastrophic): complete loss of system or major function
  - Sev 2 (critical): severe reduction in functionality or performance
  - Sev 3 (major): significant functionality/performance degradation
  - Sev 4 (minor): slight degradation affecting limited population

- Effort

  - Level 1 (trivial): no change to code base, no regression testing
  - Level 2 (minor): one staff-day of rework, little retesting
  - Level 3 (moderate): one staff-week of rework, some retesting
  - Level 4 (major): complete redesign of critical module

As an illustration of applying the FMEA methodology, a few sample FMEA scenarios for the e-mail platform are listed below:

1. Failure mode: Communication disrupted between the GWs and AS/Vs

   - Effects: Messages back up in GW memory, queues overflow, further SMTP connections denied, message integrity possibly compromised
   - Detection: Alarms monitoring GW memory usage, queue volumes
   - Root Causes: OB GW and/or IB AS/V process died? LAN failure?
   - Remedies: Redundant LANs, multiple virtual IP addresses (VIPs)
   - Mitigations: Alarm on queue thresholds, throttle SMTP connections, write IB messages to GW disk to guarantee integrity/avoid loss
   - Frequency: 2 (e.g., once per month)
   - Severity: 3 (i.e., significant functionality/performance degradation)
   - Effort: 3 (e.g., 2 weeks to design/code/test write-to-disk capability)
   - Priority: 18 (i.e., 2*3*3)

2. Failure mode: PO physical disk storage exhaust

   - Effects: Inability to store/send messages, message corruption/loss
   - Detection: Alarms monitoring PO disk usage, GW queue volumes
   - Root causes: Disruption in PP/WM message deletion or PO garbage collection/disk clean-up? Unusual spike in volume or SPAM attack?
   - Remedies: Rate-limit message ingestion, adequate spare PO storage
   - Mitigations: Throttle message ingestion, off-load messages to tape
   - Frequency: 4 (e.g., rarely with proper C/PE planning)
   - Severity: 1–2 (i.e., possible loss of service to many users)
   - Effort: 1–2 (e.g., small effort to proactively monitor storage levels)
   - Priority: 9 (4*1.5*1.5)

3. Failure mode: User authentication services disrupted

   - Effects: Inability to access mailbox, retrieve/send messages
   - Detection: User complaints to customer care, DMoQ probe failures
   - Root causes: Authentication process failure or database corruption? Intranet connectivity disruption? Denial-of-service attack?
   - Remedies: Dual active–active authentication DBs, process monitors
   - Mitigations: Auto-restart process, roll back DB, or restore from tape
   - Frequency: 3 (e.g., once per year)
   - Severity: 1 (i.e., possible loss of service to all users)
   - Effort: 4 (e.g., major redesign of DB integrity/backup architecture)
   - Priority: 12 (3*1*4)

Among these failure modes, "PO physical disk storage exhaust" is the highest priority at 9, followed by "user authentication services disrupted" at 12, then "communication disrupted between GWs and AS/Vs" at 18.

16.7 Capacity/Performance Assessment

This section describes the *Capacity/Performance Assessment* activities. These tasks are usually performed during the software development and testing phases of the platform life cycle. The goals at this stage are to

1. Identify ongoing transaction usage measurement/monitoring requirements and develop a unified measurement architecture for performance data collection, storage, distribution, reporting, and visualization
2. Measure per-transaction server resource consumptions (e.g., CPU, memory, disk, and I/O) and performance, under normal and overload conditions, and quantify maximum system throughput and system capacity
3. Develop element/platform performance models to identify performance-limiting bottlenecks, and perform sensitivity analyses to identify and quantify the performance impact of required enhancements
4. Identify necessary overload controls to prevent performance degradation at high load and propose engineering rules to avoid overload

16.7.1   Performance Data Measurement Architecture

Once software development has begun, we next turn our attention to planning for an effective capacity/performance measurement environment that will facilitate upcoming software testing as well as post-deployment ongoing scalability planning. As discussed previously, the ability to accurately measure transaction performance is critical for offering and supporting customer SLAs. A reliable performance measurement architecture is often one of the most overlooked aspects of software development, resulting in costly rework to build it back into the platform "after the fact." Yet, it is one of the most important components of any successful platform. The foundation for this measurement architecture is often laid during this phase, as we prepare to measure performance in the laboratory.

C/PE is responsible for thoroughly identifying all relevant application traffic/workload and resource consumption/usage measurements. Each platform element must be instrumented to measure its own application workload and resource utilization. Each software component is responsible for "application-aware" measurements, while the server OS is responsible for basic, hardware-level measurements. For example, the GW application must be instrumented to track such application-level workload metrics as the number of SMTP connections, the number of received messages, the number of AS/V filtered messages, the number of messages transmitted to the POs, and so on. Each such measurement should be reported at various levels of aggregation (e.g., total per day, during each hour, and during the busiest 5 min (B5M) or the busiest 1 min). The GW server (OS) must track resource utilizations, such as 5-min samples of CPU and memory utilization, disk and network I/O operations, and so on. (Fortunately, most OSs routinely track these system activity metrics, so special measurement code development is typically not required.)

This measurement architecture is discussed in more detail in Section 16.9.

16.7.2   Performance Testing

Software testing typically consists of three parts. First, during "unit" testing, individual software components are tested in isolation to ensure that they function as designed. Second, during "system" testing, components are collectively tested in an end-to-end manner to ensure that interfaces are operating properly and transactions are processed as expected. Third, during "load/soak" testing, collective components are stressed by generating multiple concurrent transactions to assess system behavior under expected load and under overload [16]. C/PE plays a role in all three parts.

During the unit test phase, the actual transaction CPU consumptions C_{ij} and "no-load" transaction delays T_{ij} are collected. This allows us to iteratively update the software estimation/budgeting analysis performed earlier, and to begin to gather the parameters and insights required to build element performance models. For instance, the budgeting formula reduces to $T_{ij} = C_{ij}$ at no-load ($\rho \approx 0$). If T_{ij} is significantly larger than C_{ij} at no-load, then we know that other contributions to end-to-end delay (e.g., disk I/O time) must be explicitly captured during upcoming performance modeling. In the mean time, the budgeting analysis can be updated to reflect these additional delays. For example, if the unit testing reveals that the additional delay is associated with an operation that is not highly dependent on the load on this component (such as waiting for a timer to expire, looking up a record in a database dominated by other transactions, or session protocol handshake delay), then this additional delay can be treated as a fixed cost added to the transaction delays T_{ij} during the budgeting calculation.

On the other hand, if the unit testing reveals that the additional delay is associated with another server resource such as disk I/O, then the expression for the delay T_{ij} of transaction i on component j must be expanded to include another load-dependent component, the disk controller. Thus, we now have $T_{ij} = C_{ij}/(1-\rho_{Cj}) + D_{ij}/(1-\rho_{Dj})$, where ρ_{Cj} and ρ_{Dj}, respectively, denote the CPU and disk utilizations per replica of component j, and D_{ij} denotes the disk consumption of transaction i on component j (which must be measured along with C_{ij} during unit testing). Continuing the earlier analysis in Section 16.5.2, assume for simplicity that the actual measured C_i's match the design estimates for transactions 1–3, and assume that the disk consumptions per-transaction are measured at $D_1 = 40$ ms, $D_2 = 100$ ms, and $D_3 = 50$ ms. Then, the WM server disk utilization per replica $\rho_D = \Sigma R_i D_i / N = 37/N$, and the average delay of transaction 1 (in seconds) is $T_1 = C_1/(1 - \rho_C) + D_1/(1 - \rho_D) = 0.02N/(N - 18) + 0.04N/(N - 37)$. Now, solving the (quadratic) expression $T_1 \le 3$ s for N yields $N \ge 37.5$ WM servers. Thus, at least 38 WM servers are now required to meet the average delay objective for transaction 1 due to the disk I/O bottleneck.

At this stage, we can also begin to identify automated workload generation tools capable of generating a production-level workload in the system and stress test environments. Depending on the application protocols in use, a commercial load testing tool may be available that emulates multiple users generating common transactions (e.g., delivering SMTP messages and retrieving/deleting messages via POP or HTTP). Otherwise, custom tools must be specified and developed to generate load. In either case, the load generation platform must be designed with scalability in mind, since a stress test environment that cannot drive the application servers into overload is of limited value. This often requires numerous user-emulation servers, together with a collection server capable of integrating the separate performance measurements. (Again, this stress testing infrastructure is itself a service platform, requiring its own C/PE effort.)

During the system test phase, components are tested in a pair-wise manner to ensure that interfaces are operating properly, and eventually "strung" together to ensure that transactions are processed as expected end-to-end. At this point, we begin to get a clear picture of server resource consumptions along the entire critical path, and can evaluate the best-case (no-load) transaction performance. The first step is to verify that the sum of the delays observed during unit testing match the end-to-end delay observed during system testing. If not, then we must break down the end-to-end delay to determine the source of the discrepancy. Are there unexpected interactions between platform components impacting performance? For example, to unit test the WM server processing a "retrieve message via HTTPS" transaction, we likely had to "hairpin" the request across the PO server interface and immediately return the response to the WM server (the requested message). During system testing, the WM server has to wait for the PO to return the message. Does the act of putting the WM process to "sleep" waiting for the response cause additional resource consumption, adversely impacting performance? Any learning from this exercise contributes valuable insights required to build element performance models.

During the load/soak test phase, end-to-end components are stressed to assess system behavior under expected load and under overload. Unlike in the unit and system test phases, where the C/PE role is more passive (gleaning data and insights as a by-product of the test effort), we take an active role in driving the stress testing. The first step is to develop a comprehensive load/soak test plan specifying how load will be generated and performance will be measured, the characteristics of the workload to be generated (transaction mix and volumes, message sizes and mix, mailbox sizes, and so on), and the specific performance metrics to be captured (usr, sys, and wio CPU consumption, and disk and network I/O rates).

There are numerous goals of this stress testing. One goal is to produce a so-called "load–service curve" characterizing the service performance (e.g., transaction delay) as a function of offered load (tps). A typical load–service curve is shown in Fig. 16.7. As can be seen, the delay starts at the best-case (no-load) value and remains relatively flat at low loads. Eventually, the transaction delay begins to rise rapidly as the bottleneck resource begins to saturate, approaching a vertical asymptote corresponding to a bottleneck resource utilization of 100%. This load level is often referred to as the "maximum throughput," the highest level of load that the

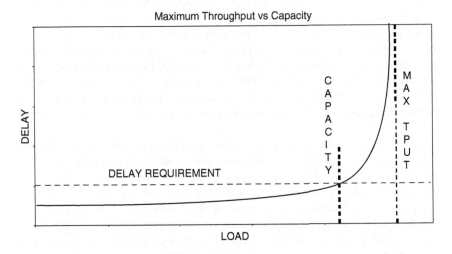

Fig. 16.7   Maximum throughput versus system capacity

system can handle without replication of the bottleneck component. Also shown in Fig. 16.7 is an example delay requirement for this transaction. The point at which the delay curve hits the requirement is often referred to as the "system capacity," the highest level of load that the system can handle without violating the requirement. Note that system capacity < maximum throughput (always), and often system capacity << maximum throughput.

Although the load–service curve depicted in Fig. 16.7 is typical of a well-behaving system, other abnormal behavior is frequently observed. It is critical to pay attention to any observed abnormalities, as these are opportunities for performance improvement. For example, we sometimes see a load–service curve that increases linearly with load (i.e., delay at 2 tps = delay at 1 tps + X, delay at 3 tps = delay at 1 tps + $2X$, and so on). This behavior is indicative of serialization within a process, where each request is single-threaded through a portion of the code (e.g., a synchronization lock). Other times, we see the maximum throughput asymptote occur at a point where resource utilizations are <<100%. This behavior is indicative of a software bottleneck (e.g., connection table entries and file descriptors). Frequently, we see a load–service curve that approaches the maximum throughput asymptote and then bends backward. This behavior is indicative of a "concurrency penalty" that occurs at high bottleneck utilizations (e.g., excessive memory paging and context switching). In all cases, these abnormalities are indications of performance problems that must be addressed.

Note that for platforms such as our e-mail system, in which most components are stateless and multiple replicas can exist, stress testing is iterative. For example, say that in the first round of testing we found that the WM server was the throughput-limiting bottleneck for the HTTPS transactions, while the PO server's highest-utilization resource only reached 40%. Then in the second round of testing, we should deploy two WM servers and verify that maximum throughput doubles. If so, then in the third round of testing, we should deploy three WM servers. At this point, the bottleneck resource should shift to the PO, and maximum throughput should increase to no more than 2.5 times the original throughput. In this manner, we can begin to determine the appropriate balance of machines required in our deployment configuration (e.g., 2.5 WM servers for each PO server). Furthermore, if the system capacity achieved during this third round of testing is, say, one-tenth of the expected peak workload, then we can also begin to determine the appropriate number of machines required in our deployment configuration (e.g., 25 WM servers and 10 PO servers).

Another goal of stress testing is to identify engineering rules for the platform components. As discussed above, the capacity of a component is the level of utilization above which one or more transaction delay requirements are violated. Many planners bypass the "load–service" analysis and assume that system capacity is tied to a particular utilization level, say 80% or 90% utilization of the bottleneck resource. In reality, system capacity is dictated by the requirements, as depicted in Fig. 16.7, and not by the utilization level. Through stress testing, we can determine the component utilization levels above which performance is adversely impacted. Based on these levels, we can then define engineering rules required for ongoing capacity/performance planning. For example, we may discover that to meet transaction requirements, user-facing components such as the WM or PP servers must be engineered to, say, 50% utilization, while system-facing components such as the GW or AS/V servers can be engineered to, say, 80% utilization. Once the platform is deployed, we can then monitor service-level metrics and adjust these engineering rules based on actual field performance under actual field workloads (discussed later). Other factors, such as observed historical volatility, or the impact of server/site failures, may also affect these engineering rules.

16.7.3   Performance Modeling

Frequently, the ability to adequately measure component behavior during stress testing is limited by a number of factors, such as schedule constraints (time and personnel), equipment availability, workload generator capabilities, and so on. One of the most common factors is that the laboratory environment is not equipped with machines of the same caliber as those planned for deployment in the field. As a result, performance models may be required to estimate field performance. These models can range from simple BoE formulas, to detailed queuing models and simulations.

As reviewed in Section 16.2, one common BoE model results from Little's Law [9], which states that the average number N of jobs in the system equals the average arrival rate λ times the average delay D, or $N = \lambda D$. Given the expected transaction rates, message sizes, and estimated or measured service times, we can easily predict the average number of concurrent inbound SMTP connections, the average number of messages in process in the GW memory, the average throughput of messages over the egress network, and so on. Through this simple analysis, we can identify potential required platform enhancements such as faster processors or more memory in the servers, bigger links between the data center and the Internet, and so on.

Another common BoE formula from Section 16.2 states that average delay D equals the average service time T divided by $(1 - \rho)$, or $D = T/(1 - \rho)$, where utilization $\rho = \lambda T$. (This model was employed in the estimation and budgeting analysis in Section 16.5.2.) Also from Section 16.2, the average number of jobs in the system $N = \rho/(1 - \rho)$. These simple formulae can be used to deduce numerous powerful observations about our platform. For example, suppose that we expect each GW to handle 80 tps, and we measure CPU consumption per-transaction to be 10 ms. Then the expected GW CPU utilization $\rho = \lambda T$ is 80%, the expected number of SMTP connections in progress $N = \rho/(1-\rho)$ is 4, and the expected transaction delay for an arriving request $D = T/(1-\rho)$ is 50 ms (i.e., the service times for the four connections in progress plus that of the arriving request).

One reason to develop detailed queuing models is to explain unexpected behavior observed during testing. As mentioned previously, abnormal behavior is frequently observed during stress testing, and performance models can often help the development team to know where to look during detailed code examination, by providing possible explanations for the observed behavior. Another reason to develop performance models is to perform parametric sensitivity analyses around the usage assumptions (transaction workload mix and message/mailbox size) to quantify the performance impact of deviations from the assumptions, and to identify required platform enhancements. Yet another reason is to further evaluate system behavior under overload, and recommend overload controls to prevent performance degradation at high load. For example, we can identify appropriate limits on the number of simultaneous SMTP connections to the GW servers, thereby deferring load to nonpeak periods and avoiding GW overload. Finally, another reason is to evaluate the impact of proposed features and enhancements that have not been developed (and hence cannot be measured), allowing the development team to prioritize future features based on which gives the biggest performance "bang for the buck."

As an illustration, consider the following actual stress test results [16]. (The remainder of this section is extracted from Ref. [16] with express permission. In particular, we reuse Figs. 16.4 through 16.8 and associated text from Sections 16.3.2 through 16.3.7 on pp. 291–298.) Figure 16.8 shows the measured delay D and CPU utilization as a function of the number of concurrent simulated users N. Each user submits a transaction, waits for the response, submits another transaction, waits, and so on. As can be seen, the delay increases as more "load" (in the form of concurrent users) is offered to the server, but is not yet exhibiting the classic "hockey stick" behavior that is observed when the bottleneck resource saturates. Yet, the CPU utilization curve has leveled off at 65–70%, well below expectation if the CPU were the bottleneck.

Although this CPU behavior seemed odd, it was not sufficient to get the attention of the development team. (After all, the system is handling more and more concurrent "load," right?) So to better understand and explain what is happening, we can

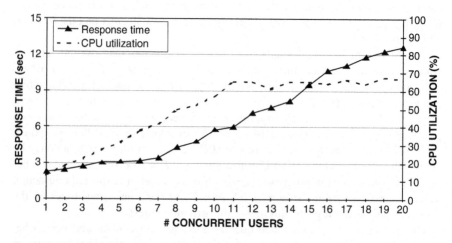

Fig. 16.8 Concurrency–service curve for a closed system

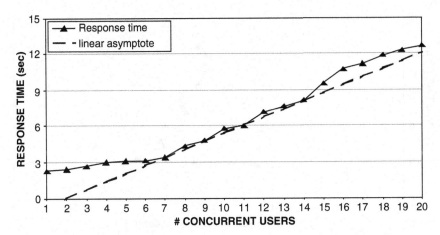

Fig. 16.9   System saturation in a closed system

turn to queuing theory and modeling. First, we note that stress testing open systems by emulating users submitting transactions serially in a loop creates a *closed* system. That is, there are a fixed number of transactions in the system, corresponding to the number of concurrent users. Contrary to expectation for open systems, increasing the concurrency level does not necessarily result in increasing the load level. Thus, this delay curve is not a traditional load–service curve. In fact, for closed systems, it can be shown that as the bottleneck resource saturates, the relationship between N and D approaches a *linear* asymptote with a slope equal to the bottleneck resource holding time (rather than a vertical asymptote, as expected in open systems), and the transaction arrival rate $\lambda = N/D$ stops increasing and levels off.

As can be seen in Fig. 16.9, we have already hit the asymptote at a concurrency level of seven simulated users. In other words, the (unknown) bottleneck resource has already saturated, the arrival rate has leveled off, and the "concurrency–delay" curve is riding along its asymptote. In fact, it appears that the curve actually starts to diverge from the asymptote at higher levels of concurrency. By plotting delay D as a function of load $\lambda = N/D$, we can translate these stress test results into equivalent load test results. As shown in Fig. 16.10, maximum throughput peaks at $\sim$2 tps, then decreases. That is, as N increases beyond seven simulated concurrent users, there is actually a drop in capacity ("concurrency penalty"), likely due to context switching, object/thread management, garbage collection, and so on.

With this knowledge in hand, the developers finally began to believe that there could be a problem. As Fig. 16.8 shows, the CPU was not the bottleneck (nor were any other hardware resources), so some unknown "soft" resource bottleneck was preventing full utilization of CPU resources. Candidate "soft" resources include OS/application threads, file descriptors, TCP transaction control blocks, I/O buffers, virtual memory, object/code locks, and so on. After discussions with the development team, we theorized that transactions were being serialized through a lock on one or more significant synchronized code regions (e.g., some Java-related kernel

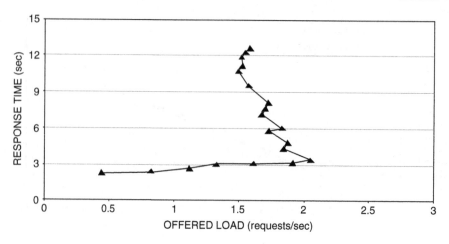

Fig. 16.10 Equivalent load–service curve for a closed system

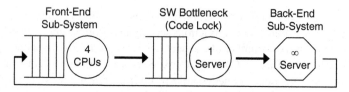

Fig. 16.11 Model of a closed system with software bottleneck

system call). To test this theory, we developed a simple queuing model (shown in Fig. 16.11) consisting of three serial queues: a CPU node (modeled as a four-server queue to represent the four CPUs in our test machine), a software bottleneck node (modeled as a single-server queue to represent the theorized code lock), and a fixed delay node (modeled as an infinite-server queue to reflect any load-independent components in the measured delays).

The modeling results are shown in Fig. 16.12. As can be seen, this simple model produces a good fit to the test results, providing significant insights into the performance of the system. In particular, the approach characterized the system performance limitations, identified a significant software bottleneck in the code that prevented the system from fully utilizing the CPU resources, and exposed the system's behavior under overload. The development team then ran a number of profiling tools to uncover the source of the code serialization. Two culprits became evident: first (at the application level), writes to the log file were synchronized, and second (at the kernel level), the *createObject* method was single-threaded. To address the first source, the logging method was rewritten to allow concurrent writes to the transaction log. To resolve the second source, many objects were moved from transaction (request) scope to application scope to avoid much of the object

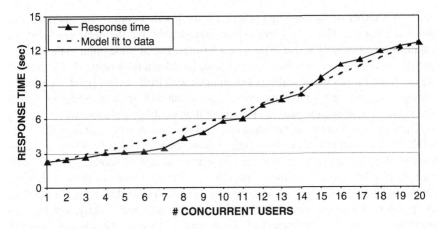

Fig. 16.12 Model fit to test results

creation, de-referencing, and garbage collection activity. Collectively, these changes eliminated the software bottleneck and resulted in a dramatic improvement in the software performance.

16.8   Scalability Assessment

This section describes the *Scalability Assessment* activities. These tasks are usually performed between the development and deployment phases of the platform life cycle. The goals at this stage are to

1. Develop platform-wide scalability models that reflect aggregate resource consumption (e.g., storage)
2. Identify scalability-limiting bottlenecks that impact the platform's ability to scale linearly with usage, and quantify the scalability impact of proposed architectural enhancements
3. Provide capacity–deployment ("facility–demand") projections comparing platform capacity to forecasted usage growth over time
4. Provide additional scalability requirements and engineering rules

Once we have a handle on the predicted "current" performance (i.e., the behavior expected at service launch), we next take a look at the likely long-term platform performance/scalability as the workload grows beyond the near-term engineering limits. Simply speaking, a service platform can be called *scalable* if a 2× increase in load requires no more than a 2× increase in resources. For new deployments, we can expect that doubling the load requires much less than twice as much equipment, since we can hope to achieve some economies of scale as resources are utilized more efficiently. In addition, as the load grows, the peak:average ratio tends to drop due to a number of factors (e.g., source ISP or Internet congestion smoothes out the traffic bursts). Thus, the average load may double, but the peak load (that we engineer for) may only increase by, say, 1.5 times. But at some point in the service growth, all economies and efficiencies of scale have been fully realized, and the best we can hope for is a linear scaling of equipment with load. At that point, we need to consider whether or not there are any resources that will begin to exhibit nonlinear scaling (i.e., doubling the load requires more than double the resources).

There are many common but often overlooked examples. For instance, data center floor space and power are frequently limited, especially if you choose to locate your platform in a mature data center, if you are hosted in another entity's facilities, or if you require contiguous space for growth. Solutions to these scalability limitations (e.g., relocating to another data center, or establishing a second site, or upgrading the power distribution plant) are often extremely costly, so advanced planning is critical if you expect platform demand to grow rapidly. And even if the data center itself is not a scalability bottleneck, connectivity to the Internet can be. Access links and edge router ports can eventually exhaust, requiring costly and time-consuming link/router upgrades. Advance planning for scale (e.g., budgeting for one 10 GigE link rather than hoping to add multiple 1 GigE links "on the fly") can save cost and headaches in the long run. And some components may scale in "blocks," requiring infrequent but costly upgrades to grow. For example, blade servers reside in blade centers, so adding another blade may require adding a new blade center chassis. Or adding storage to a NAS or SAN may require upgrading the storage appliance.

One approach to planning for scalability is to determine the number of components required per unit of "demand." In the case of our e-mail platform, the most effective unit of demand is a mailbox. Thus, we want to determine the number of GWs or POs required per (say) one million mailboxes. This is a two-stage process: first, we determine the measure of usage to which each component's capacity is most sensitive, and measure/estimate the component capacity in terms of that metric, then we determine what a typical mailbox generates in terms of each of these measures of usage (often referred to as a *usage profile*). Integrating these results yields the example set of scalability engineering rules, illustrated in Table 16.5.

Table 16.5 Example e-mail platform scalability engineering rules

Server component	Usage metric	Server capacity @100%	Engineering limit	Peak usage per mailbox	Servers per one million mailboxes
GW	IB messages	100 m/s	70%	2/h	7.9
MR	OB messages	80 m/s	60%	1/h	5.8
AS/V	I/O messages	60 m/s	80%	3/h	17.4
PO	Storage	5 TBs	80%	10 MBs	2.5
PP	Retrieved messages	100 m/s	60%	1/h	4.6
WM	Retrieved messages	50 m/s	60%	2/h	18.5

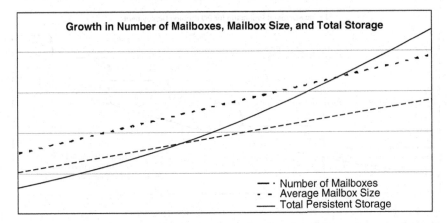

Fig. 16.13   Example mailbox number, size, and storage growth

Consider again our ISP e-mail platform. As mentioned earlier, storage of messages is stateful (i.e., persistent messages for a particular mailbox reside on a particular PO). As a result, persistent storage is of critical concern from a scalability standpoint. Total storage growth has two distinct components: growth in the *number* of mailboxes, and growth in the *size* of mailboxes. So even if the number N of mailboxes and the size S of mailboxes both growth linearly over time, the total storage NS increases super-linearly with time (as illustrated in Fig. 16.13). An added wrinkle results from the fact that different mailboxes grow at different rates. Thus, the particular mailboxes on one (stateful) PO may collectively grow at a different aggregate rate than those on another PO. This in turn leads to C/PE issues associated with load-balancing (discussed in detail in Section 16.9).

The result of this compounded growth means that PO storage does not scale linearly. Over time, our PO scalability engineering rule in Table 16.5 will decrease due to growth in the average mailbox size. (In fact, this result is true for most other components, as changes in such factors as message sizes or filtering rules or usage profile will impact the engineering rules.) In the case of storage, however, this concern is particularly relevant, as many service-level metrics are sensitive to mailbox size. So even if we de-load a PO to account for increasing per-mailbox size, at some point the size of a mailbox can become too large to meet delay requirements. For example, consider the "retrieve mailbox list via HTTPS" transaction from Section 16.5. Eventually, mailboxes may become so large that we cannot process the "list" command in the allotted time. By considering these scalability bottlenecks early in the process, we can identify required architectural changes. For instance, in the case of mailbox size, we can consider tiered storage, where messages that have not been accessed in N months are moved to slower secondary storage. A static list of such messages can be compiled only every time the contents of secondary storage change (thus avoiding the delay of real-time compilation every time the user performs a "list" command). Or we can consider implementing an e-mail aging policy (discussed previously) to manage mailbox growth.

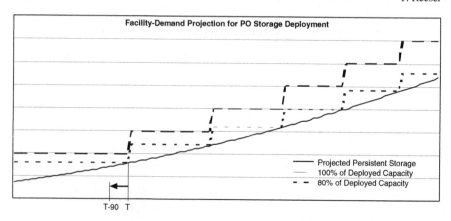

Fig. 16.14 Example PO storage "facility–demand" projection

Another component of the scalability assessment is the development of so-called "facility–demand" projections. (The term originated in teletraffic engineering, where there is a need to forecast the provisioning timeline for new "facilities" – voice and data trunks – as a function of projected growth in demand.) Consider again the growth in PO storage, and assume that the persistent storage curve in Fig. 16.13 represents a forecast of storage growth over time. Figure 16.14 shows the resulting facility–demand projection for PO storage. The dashed line represents 100% of the total deployed storage, whereas the dotted line represents 80% of deployed storage (the desired engineering limit). As can be seen, each time the projected persistent storage level hits the engineering limit of currently deployed storage, a new PO must be deployed. Thus, if the PO provisioning lead time is, say, 90 days (including a cushion to absorb variability in demand), then this facility–demand projection provides a forecast for when in the future new PO servers must be ordered. These capacity–deployment projections play an essential role in the ongoing capacity/performance management once the platform is deployed (discussed in Section 16.9).

16.9 Capacity/Performance Management

This section describes the *Capacity/Performance Management* activities. These tasks are performed during the deployment and growth phases of the platform life cycle. The goals at this stage are to

1. Implement a measurement architecture capable of collecting, warehousing, and reporting/visualizing all performance (usage and resource consumption) and reliability (failure and outage) data

2. Implement a monitoring architecture capable of measuring, tracking, and reporting all platform quality metrics (DMoQs) and transaction/service-level objectives (SLAs/SLOs)
3. Implement capabilities required to analyze usage trends against service metrics to project platform usage growth and predict platform capacity augments required to maintain acceptable service levels
4. Identify/reflect unique characteristics of the service environment that impact C/PE (e.g., seasonality, shifts in traffic mix, and cyber attacks)
5. Automate performance management and capacity-deployment planning activities where appropriate

16.9.1 Measurement/Monitoring Infrastructure

Congratulations! Your service platform has been deployed. But your C/PE work is far from over. As discussed previously, a reliable measurement and monitoring architecture is one of the most important components of any successful platform, and it is critical to any post-deployment C/PE activity. Hopefully, the foundation was laid during the testing phase. Now we need to ensure that the measurement platform is robust and scalable. It must be capable of collecting, storing, processing, and reporting all relevant performance (usage and resource consumption) and reliability (failure and outage) data across all platform elements.

In particular, C/PE is responsible for specifying consistent, reliable mechanisms for performance data collection, storage, processing, distribution, reporting, and visualization. Data collection mechanisms may include native OS utilities, Simple Network Management Protocol (SNMP)-based MIBs, off-the-shelf "measureware" agents, and custom-developed code (often required for application-level data). The data storage architecture must be designed with extreme scalability and longevity in mind, typically consisting of a number of polling servers, flat-file and relational database servers, and reporting servers. It is all too common to see a poorly designed data storage architecture that "runs out of steam" soon after platform introduction. (This data storage infrastructure is itself a service platform, often requiring its own C/PE effort.) In addition to performance data, this warehouse should also include a comprehensive database of platform topology and server configuration data, including hardware profiles, software versions, and connectivity maps. The data distribution, reporting, and visualization architecture must be carefully designed to ensure that data is readily available in the appropriate formats. For example, "canned" reports and graphics may be required for executive dashboards, whereas raw data feeds may be required for capacity planning tools and ad hoc analyses. Finally, the data push (or pull) from platform elements to data warehouse to capacity management tools/users should be fully automated where possible, taking into consideration such security issues as firewalls between production sites and back-office systems. (For example, will FTP or e-mail work between a GW server on a secure production LAN and a collection server on a management LAN?)

Like the measurement architecture, the monitoring architecture must be designed for extreme scalability and robustness. C/PE is responsible for specifying consistent, reliable mechanisms for collection of any performance and availability data that are required to monitor and validate all service-level metrics. As discussed previously, these metrics should be specific, measurable, and controllable. A contractual service-level metric is useless if it cannot be accurately measured and verified. As a result, you need to consider how you plan to monitor the requirement. A number of approaches are possible, including client software add-ons, end-point hardware sniffers, outside vendor services, and parallel monitoring platforms.

For example, consider the last approach of a separate measurement and monitoring platform. First, such a monitoring architecture typically consists of a number of probe servers to launch synthetic transactions. These probe servers emulate an end-user performing typical transactions, such as sending, listing, retrieving, and deleting messages. It is important to locate these servers so that the entire *controllable* transaction path is exercised. For instance, placing these servers in the same data center as the e-mail platform unnecessarily bypasses much of the ISP Intranet infrastructure, while placing them in an off-net data center introduces Internet and possibly peering connectivity issues that are out of the ISP's control. Second, the monitoring platform typically consists of a number of probe mailboxes, distributed evenly across all POs in the data center. Third, the monitoring architecture typically consists of a well-defined set of synthetic user transactions that comprehensively cover all service-level metrics. For instance, if SLAs are defined for receive safe message, send safe message via SMTP, retrieve message via HTTPS, and retrieve message via POP, then the synthetic transactions must mimic these operations. As an example, assume that one such service-level metric is "receive safe 100 kB message within 15 min of sending 95% of the time." The probe server thread can send a safe 100 kB e-mail message to a probe mailbox, sleep 15 min, and attempt to retrieve the message via HTTPS then via POP (thus removing the message). The probe server can keep track of successes and failures, and compute the 95th percentile over time. This single synthetic transaction allows us to monitor all SLAs defined above (send, receive, and retrieve) simultaneously. Finally, the monitoring platform typically consists of database and reporting servers, capable of providing "canned" reports and supporting ad hoc analyses. And of course, the SLA monitoring and verification process should be fully automated.

16.9.2   Resource Growth Projections

One of the primary post-deployment capacity/performance management roles is to monitor the growth in consumption of critical platform resources, project when resources are likely to exhaust, and determine when resource augments must be scheduled based on deployment lead times. As introduced in Section 16.8 and illustrated for the PO storage resource, this task is facilitated by development and maintenance of "facility–demand" projections. Besides PO storage, another key e-mail platform resource is server CPU utilization. A typical process for developing "facility–demand" projections of server CPU utilization consists of the following (performed separately for each element type – GW, MR, AS/V, PP, WM, and PO):

1. First, collect 5-min samples of CPU utilization of all active servers
2. Compute the time-consistent 5-min average across all active servers
3. Compute the daily average busy hour (BH) server CPU utilization

   (a) This is the maximum rolling 1-h average of 5-min averages.
   (b) Other measures of peak utilization are possible, including busiest 5 min (B5M) and 95th percentile of 5-min samples (for typical daily traffic profiles, BH and 95th percentile values are similar).

4. Compute the weekly peak BH (or B5M or 95%) server CPU utilization

   (a) This is the maximum rolling 7-day peak of BH values.

5. Compute the linear trend through the series of weekly peak values
6. Compute the headroom threshold (HT) based on engineering limits

   (a) The HT $=$ (engineering limit)$^{-1}$. For example, if the GW engineering limit is 60%, then the GW HT is $1/0.6 = 1.67$.
   (b) This headroom is intended to provide sufficient spare capacity to absorb historic volatility without suffering degraded performance.

7. Compute the CPU "consumption" trend $=$ HT*{CPU utilization trend}

   (a) When utilization hits the engineering limit, consumption hits 100%.

8. Finally, project the CPU consumption trend into the future (say 1 year)

   (a) Server augment is required when the consumption trend hits 100%.
   (b) With each augment, the utilization and consumption trends "step down" by $N/(N + 1)$, where N is the number of active servers prior to augment. For example, if $N = 3$ then the consumption trend will be reduced from 100% to 75% when the fourth server is deployed.

A typical set of server engineering limits and resulting HTs are given in Table 16.6 (including other platform infrastructure elements as well).

   As an illustration of the "facility–demand" projection process, consider the GW CPU utilization curves shown in Fig. 16.15. (This chart represents an actual GW component for a large cable ISP.) The thin solid curve shows the daily BH CPU utilization (the results of steps 1–3 above). The bold solid curve shows the weekly

Table 16.6 Typical engineering limits and headroom thresholds

Engineering limit (weekly peak BH CPU)			
33%	50%	60%	75%
DNS, databases	Network infrastructure	GW, MR, PP, WM	AS/V, PO
3× HT	2× HT	1.67× HT	1.33× HT

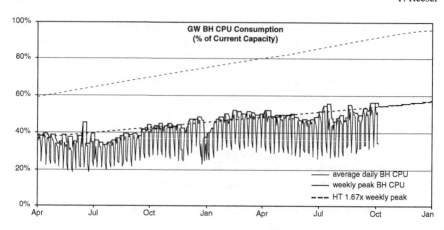

Fig. 16.15 Example GW CPU "facility–demand" curve

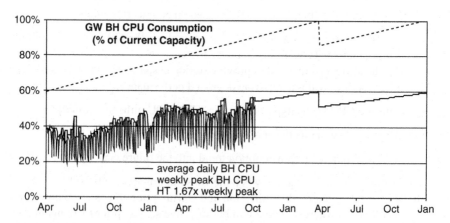

Fig. 16.16 Example GW CPU "facility–demand" projection

peak BH CPU utilization trend (steps 4 and 5). The dotted line shows the CPU consumption trend based on a 60% engineering limit, and thus a 1.67× HT (steps 6 and 7). As can be seen, the daily BH curve exhibits weekday peaks as well as weekend troughs. As such, any trend through this daily data would be unduly skewed by the weekend data. In contrast, the linear regression through the weekly peak data (shown as a dashed line) captures only the weekday behavior, thus providing a more realistic basis for a trend of peak CPU utilization.

Finally, Fig. 16.16 shows a projection of the CPU consumption trend five quarters into the future (step 8). As can be seen, CPU consumption is projected to hit 100% in March, signaling the need to deploy a new GW. (Equivalently, the CPU utilization is projected to hit the 60% engineering limit of currently deployed capacity.) Thus, if the GW provisioning lead time is 60 days, then a new GW server must be ordered in January.

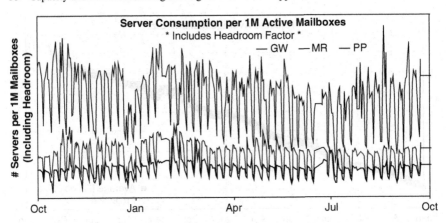

Fig. 16.17 Example "server consumption per mailbox" trends

Another value to tracking CPU consumptions is the ability to project resource needs per unit of "demand." In the case of an e-mail platform, it is valuable to project CPU consumption per mailbox for each platform element. With this knowledge in hand, the capacity/performance planner can then readily assess the impact of service growth. For example, assume that the ISP is planning to acquire a new market area (through the acquisition of another ISP, or the common swap of markets between ISPs to consolidate geographic footprints). Given the number of mailboxes to be added to the platform, you can quickly determine how many new servers must be deployed to accommodate those mailboxes. As an illustration, Fig. 16.17 shows example trends for the number of GW, MR, and PP servers required per one million new mailboxes, including associated headroom levels. (This chart represents actual server components for a large DSL ISP.)

16.9.3 Traffic Growth Projections

Another primary post-deployment capacity/performance management role is to monitor the growth in traffic/usage (demand) of critical platform transactions, and reflect any unique characteristics of the service environment that impact capacity/performance engineering. These unique characteristics include seasonality, session/state management, load-balancing, off-site backups, shifts in traffic mix, and cyber attacks. Of particular interest in e-mail platform C/PE (or any end-user-driven service platform) is the impact of seasonality. As discussed previously, capacity planning must reflect daily periodicity (by engineering based on BH or 95th percentile) as well as weekly periodicity (by engineering based on weekday peaks). In addition, capacity planning must reflect yearly periodicity (seasonality).

Consider the seasonal growth in e-mail storage. Figure 16.18 shows an example of growth in average mailbox size over a 3-year period. (This chart represents

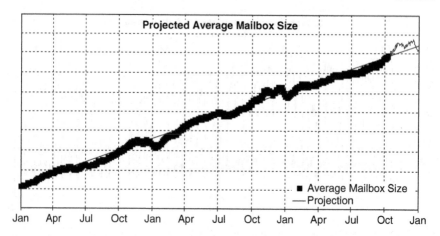

Fig. 16.18 Example mailbox storage growth and seasonality

actual mailbox growth for a very large cable ISP.) As can be seen, storage utilization exhibits strong seasonality. Storage levels surge around holidays (specifically,
Valentine's Day, Halloween, and the December religious celebrations). In the case
of consumer e-mail, these surges are due largely to the popularity of digital greet-
ing cards, digital holiday photos, and holiday-themed animated executables. Peak
utilization exceeds the trend (shown as a solid straight line) by as much as 10%
during holidays. Thus, if we planned PO storage capacity based on average storage growth, then we could experience a serious capacity shortfall (and significant
negative publicity) during holiday periods of peak demand.

   Also shown in Fig. 16.18 is a projection of mailbox size during the upcoming
holiday period (shown as a thinner solid curve during the final quarter). As can
be seen, this projection is not simply a linear trend, but rather mimics the year-
end behavior observed during the previous year. There are a number of possible
approaches to developing such a fluid-flow model of storage growth, most of which
essentially involve "replaying" the previous year's traffic behavior scaled by year-
over-year volume changes.

   To illustrate at a high level, let S_t denote the stored volume at the beginning of
day t, let I_t and D_t, respectively, denote the incoming and deleted volumes during
day t, and let F_x denote the year-over-year scaling factor in volume x (where $x =$
storage s, incoming i, and deleted d). One approach is to replay the scaled daily storage change: $S_{t+1} = S_t + F_s(S_{t-364} - S_{t-365})$. Another approach (utilized for the
projection in Fig. 16.18) is to replay the scaled daily incoming and deleted volumes:
$S_{t+1} = S_t + F_i I_{t-364} - F_d D_{t-364}$. Regardless of the approach used, developing such a seasonality-based projection allows for more accurate capacity planning
during peak periods.

   As another example of seasonality, consider the seasonal variability in data center
access link utilization. Figure 16.19 shows a real example of daily IB traffic variability over the course of a year (normalized by June volume). As can be seen,

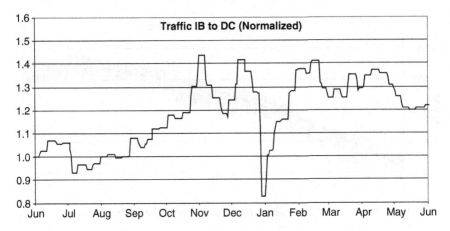

Fig. 16.19 Example seasonal variability in link utilization

bandwidth utilization also exhibits strong seasonality, with traffic levels surging around Halloween, Christmas, and Valentine's Day. Overall, the traffic volume is increased by 20% over the year. Even more striking is the 1.7× difference in traffic volumes between the year-end lull (83% of June volume) and the Halloween surge (144% of June volume). Again, the lesson is that such seasonality must be reflected in any capacity planning projections to avoid serious capacity shortfalls during holiday periods of peak traffic.

Next, load-balancing is of particular concern for stateful components such as the PO server. As mentioned previously, different mailboxes grow at different rates. Thus, the particular mailboxes on one (stateful) PO may collectively grow at a different aggregate rate than those on another PO. Thus, operational procedures must be developed to monitor and balance the storage growth on individual POs (in addition to aggregate storage growth) to ensure that particular POs do not prematurely exhaust.

Finally, as an example of shifting user behavior and traffic mix, consider the mix of message retrieval between HTTPS and POP. Figure 16.20 shows a real example of the percentage of users accessing their mailbox via HTTPS (WebMail) instead of POP over a 3-year period. As can be seen, HTTPS penetration increased steadily from 35% to 50% over the first two years and then leveled off. From an e-mail platform C/PE perspective, this HTTPS saturation is good news, since WM users are far more expensive to support than POP users (due to increased PO storage and server CPU consumption). Note also that the HTTPS:POP mix exhibits strong weekly periodicity, with higher WM penetration during weekdays (indicating that many users of this consumer ISP service retrieve their personal e-mail via HTTPS from their workplace computer during the week, and then use POP from their home computer over the weekend).

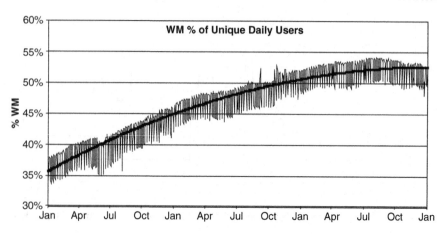

Fig. 16.20 Example shift in message retrieval behavior

16.10 C/PE "Best Practice" Principles

We conclude this chapter with a summary of C/PE "best practice" principles to guide you in your next effort.

- Develop and maintain a business-relevant transaction workload profile for use during initial platform sizing and ongoing new feature testing
- Define realistic, measurable service-level objectives tied to workload
- Specify comprehensive engineering rules for relevant service elements based on sound capacity/performance/reliability modeling and analysis
- Implement a single, consistent, comprehensive, authoritative database for platform topology and configuration data
- Thoroughly identify relevant usage/resource consumption metrics
  - BH server resource utilizations and 95th percentile traffic metrics
- Implement a consistent, reliable, scalable architecture for performance data collection, storage, and distribution (leveraging SNMP MIBs on switches and lightweight resource "measureware" agents on servers)
- Develop a highly-scalable warehouse for performance data, providing automated push/pull from elements to data warehouse to tools/users
- Implement a consistent, reliable mechanism for usage/performance data reporting and visualization, minimizing the required number of capacity/performance management tools/interfaces to be maintained
- Develop tools to provide historical and projected views of data, with
  - Flexible aggregation capabilities (by server type, technology, and so on)
  - Trending on peak (e.g., 95th percentile) values, not averages
  - Ability to reflect anticipated future events in trending/projections

- Provide automated triggers to determine required capacity augments based on defined engineering rules/metrics
- Implement a well-defined deployment process with known lead times

Acronyms

ACL	access control list
AS/V	anti-spam/virus filtering server
BH	busy hour
B5M	busy 5 min.
BoE	back-of-the-envelope
C/PE	capacity/performance engineering
DMoQ	direct measure of quality
DPM	defect per million
DSL	digital subscriber line
DT	downtime
FIFO	first-in-first-out
FIT	fault insertion testing
FMEA	failure modes and effects analysis
FTP	File Transfer Protocol
FTTH	fiber-to-the-home
GW	IB SMTP Gateway server
HT	headroom threshold
HTTP	Hyper-Text Transfer Protocol
HTTPS	Secure HTTP
HW	hardware
IMAP	Internet Message Access Protocol
IB	inbound
i.i.d.	independent identically distributed
I/O	input/output
ISP	Internet service provider
LAN	local area network
LIFO	last-in-first-out
MIB	management information base
MR	OB Mail Relay server
MRA	modification request analysis

MTTF   mean-time-to-failure
MTTR   mean-time-to-restore
NAS   network attached storage
NFS   network file system
OB   outbound
PO   Post Office server
POP   Post Office Protocol
PP   POP Proxy server
PS   processor-sharing
RBD   reliability block diagram
SAN   storage area network
SLA   service-level agreement
SLO   service-level objective
SNMP   Simple Network Management Protocol
SPoF   single point of failure
SRE   software reliability engineering
SMTP   Simple Mail Transfer Protocol
tps   transactions per second
VIP   virtual IP address (aka VLAN)
WM   WebMail server

References

1. Smith, C., & Williams, L. (2002). *Performance solutions – a practical guide to creating responsive, scalable software*. Reading, MA: Addison-Wesley.
2. Chrissis, M., Konrad, M., & Shrum, S. (2003). *CMMI: Guidelines for process integration and product improvement*. Reading, MA: Addison-Wesley.
3. Jain, R. (1991). *The art of computer systems performance analysis: Techniques for experimental design, measurement, simulation, and modeling*. New York: Wiley-Interactive.
4. Menasce, D., Almeida, V., & Dowdy, L. (2004). *Performance by design – computer capacity planning by example*. Upper Saddle River, NJ: Prentice Hall PTR.
5. Ross, S. (1972). *Introduction to probability models*. New York: Academic.
6. Cooper, R. (1981). *Introduction to queueing theory* (2nd ed.). New York: North Holland.
7. Lazowska, E., Zahorjan, J., Graham, G., & Sevcik, K. (1984). *Quantitative system performance – computer system analysis using queueing network models*. Upper Saddle River, NJ: Prentice-Hall.
8. Kleinrock, L. (1975). *Queueing systems, volume 1: theory*. New York: Wiley-Interscience.
9. Little, J. (1961). A proof of the queueing formula $L = \lambda W$. *Operations Research 9*, 383–387.
10. Hennessy, J., & Patterson, D. (2007). *Computer architecture: a quantitative approach* (4th ed.). Boston, MA: Elsevier-Morgan Kaufman.
11. Snee, R. (1990). Statistical thinking and its contribution to total quality. *American Statistician, 44*(2), 116–121.
12. Smith, C. (1990). *Performance engineering of software systems*. Reading, MA: Addison-Wesley.
13. Musa, J. (1999). *Software reliability engineering*. New York: McGraw-Hill.

14. Billington, R., & Allan, R. (1992). *Reliability evaluation of engineering systems* (2nd ed.). New York: Plenum.
15. Reeser, P. (1996). Predicting system reliability in a client/server application hosting environment. *Proceedings, Joint AT&T/Lucent Reliability Info Forum.*
16. Huebner, F., Meier-Hellstern, K., & Reeser, P. (2001). Performance testing for IP services and systems. In Dumke, R, Rautenstrauch, C., Schmietendorf, A., & Scholz, A. (Eds.), *Performance engineering – state of the art and current trends.* Heidelberg: Springer-Verlag.

Index